BRUNELLO TO ZIBIBBO
The Wines of Tuscany, Central and Southern Italy

Nicolas Belfrage was born in Los Angeles, raised in New York and England. He studied in Paris, Siena and London, taking a degree at University College London in French and Italian. A Master of Wine since 1980, he has been working in, and writing on, Italian wines since the early 1970s. His books include the double award-winning *Life Beyond Lambrusco*, published by Sidgwick & Jackson in 1985, and the companion to the present volume, *Barolo to Valpolicella – The Wines of Northern Italy*, published by Faber and Faber in 1999. He contributes regularly to various publications, including *Decanter*, *Wein Gourmet* and Winepros.com. In 1994 he sold his specialist Italian wine-importing business and moved to Tuscany. Today he spends his working life between Florence and London, writing and acting as a wine broker.

Brunello to Zibibbo

The Wines of Tuscany, Central and Southern Italy

Nicolas Belfrage

MITCHELL BEAZLEY

Brunello to Zibibbo
The Wines of Tuscany, Central and Southern Italy
by Nicolas Belfrage

First published in Great Britain in 2001 by Faber and Faber Limited.
This edition published in 2003 by Mitchell Beazley, an imprint of
Octopus Publishing Group Limited, 2–4 Heron Quays, London E14 4JP.

Copyright © Octopus Publishing Group Ltd 2001, 2003
Text copyright © Nicolas Belfrage 2001, 2003
Maps © John Flower 2001

A CIP catalogue record for this book is available from the British Library.

ISBN: 1 84000 790 7

The author and publishers will be grateful for any information
which will assist them in keeping future editions up-to-date.
Although all reasonable care has been taken in the preparation
of this book, neither the publishers nor the author can accept any
liability for any consequences arising from the use thereof, or the
information contained therein.

Phototypeset by Intype London Ltd

Printed and bound in the UK

This second of two I dedicate to my second of two,
Ixta

Contents

===

Acknowledgements	xiii
List of profiled producers	xiv
List of maps	xx
About this book	xxi
The Italian wine label	xxvi
Introduction	1
1 VINE AND WINE	4
Viticulture: getting it right from the ground up	4
Oenology: typicity versus internationalism	15
2 CENTRAL ITALY WEST	24
Production areas	30
Grapes, wines and producers – red	38
Sangiovese	38
The wines in Tuscany: Chianti Classico	41
Other Chianti sub-zones	94
Montalcino	111
Montepulciano	136
Carmignano	146
Montecarlo and Colline Lucchesi	151
Maremma	152
Other Sangioveses of Tuscany	159
The wines in Umbria	160
The wines in Latium	163
The wines in Romagna	163
The wines in le Marche	168
Montepulciano	169

Sagrantino 169
Other red grape varieties 174
  Canaiolo Nero 175
  Cesanese 176
  Ciliegiolo 177
  Colorino 177
  Malvasia Nera 179
  Mammolo 179
  Aleatico 179
  Moscato rosa 180
Grapes, wines and producers – white 180
  Trebbiano 180
    The wines in Tuscany 185
    The wines in Umbria 186
    The wines in Latium 190
    The wines in le Marche and Abruzzo 191
    Vin Santo 193
    The wines of Trebbiano Romagnolo 195
  Malvasia Bianca 196
    The wines in Latium: Frascati et al 198
    Vernaccia di San Gimignano 202
Other white grape varieties 205
  Vermentino 205
  Moscadello 206
  Ansonica 207
  Grechetto 208
  Drupeggio 209
  Verdello 209
  Bellone 210

3 CENTRAL ITALY EAST 211
Production areas 214
Grapes, wines and producers – red 216
  Montepulciano 216
    The wines in Abruzzo 219
    The wines in le Marche and other regions 224
Other red grapes 228
  Sangiovese 228
  Barbarossa 228
  Cagnina 229

Lacrima di Moro d'Alba 229
Vernaccia di Serrapetrona 230
Aglianico 231
Grapes, wines and producers – white 231
Verdicchio 231
Albana 237
Other white grapes 238
Pagadebit/Bombino Bianco 238
Biancame, Bianchello, Passerina 239
Maceratino 239
Pecorino 239
Falaghina, Greco 240

4 THE SOUTH AND ISLANDS 241
Campania and Basilicata 247
Grapes, wines and producers – red 252
Aglianico 252
The wines in Campania 254
The wines in Basilicata 258
Other red grapes 264
Sangiovese 264
Barbera 264
Sciascinoso (a.k.a. Olivella) 264
Guarnaccia 265
Primitivo 265
Grapes, wines and producers – white 265
Fiano 265
Greco di Tufo 269
Falanghina 270
Coda di Volpe 272
Biancolella and Forastera 272
Asprinio 273
Puglia 274
Grapes, wines and producers – red 279
Negromaro 279
Primitivo 291
Uva di Troia 296
Montepulciano 298
Malvasia Nera (M.N.) 299
Aglianico 299

CONTENTS

Sangiovese 300
Bombino Nero 301
Grapes, wines and producers – white 302
Verdeca 302
Bianco d'Alessano 303
Pampanuto 303
Bombino Bianco 303
Greco di Tufo 304
Impigno and Francavilla 304
Trebbiano Toscano and Malvasia Toscana 304
Moscato Bianco 305
Calabria 305
Grapes, wines and producers – red 308
Gaglioppo 308
Other red varieties 310
Grapes, wines and producers – white 314
Greco di Cirò and Greco di Bianco 314
Other white varieties 315
Sardinia 317
Grapes, wines and producers – red 322
Cannonau 322
Carignano 326
Monica 329
Bovale 330
Cagnulari 331
Pascale di Cagliari 331
Nieddera, Nieddumannu 331
Girò 332
Nebbiolo 332
Sangiovese 333
Grapes, wines and producers – white 333
Vermentino 333
Nuragus 336
Vernaccia di Oristano 337
Malvasia di Sardegna 340
Moscato Bianco 341
Nasco 341
Torbato 342
Semidano 345
Trebbiano 345

Sicily   345
Grapes, wines and producers – red   350
  Nero d'Avola   350
  Nerello Mascalese and Nerello Cappucio   358
  Frappato di Vittoria   363
  Perricone or Pignatello   365
  Other red varieties   365
Grapes, wines and producers – white   366
  Cataratto   366
  Inzolia/Ansonica   368
  Grillo   371
  Marsala   371
  Grecanico Dorato   378
  Carricante   378
  Damaschino   379
  Trebbiano Toscano   379
  Malvasia   379
  Moscato Bianco   380
  Zibibbo   381

5 INTERNATIONAL VARIETIES IN CENTRAL
  AND SOUTHERN ITALY   389
Bordeaux grapes – red   391
  The wines in Tuscany   392
    Bolgheri   392
    Suvereto – Val di Cornia   398
  The wines in Central Italy excluding Tuscany   409
  The South and Islands   410
Burgundy grapes – red   412
Rhône grapes – red   414
Burgundy grapes – white   416
Bordeaux grapes – white   420
Rhône and the rest – white   421

6 BLENDS   424
Red blends   425
  Tuscany   425
  Central Italy excluding Tuscany   428
  Southern Italy   428
White blends   430

Tuscany and the centre 430
The South and the islands 433
Sweet white blends 434

7 ITALIAN WINE LAW 436
  IGT (Indicazione Geografica Tipica) 437
  DOC (Denominazione di Origine Controllata) 440
  DOCG (Denominazione di Origine Controllata
    e Garantita) 441

Appendix A – Suggested revision of IGT system, by region,
    in alphabetical order 445
Appendix B – Suggested revision of DOCs 449
Appendix C – A critique of the DOCGs, in alphabetical
    order 456

Glossary 460
Key to Italian pronunciation 468
Bibliography 470
Index 472

Acknowledgements

I would like to thank the following for their generosity in terms of time and effort in helping me to prepare this book:

Gilberto Arru, journalist, Sardinia; Marco de Bartoli, Marsala and Pantelleria, Sicily; Gigi Calzetta, La Vite, le Marche; Stefano Campatelli, Consorzio Montalcino, Tuscany; Raffaele Cani and Antonello Pilloni, C.S. Santadi, Sardinia; Silvia Fiorentini, Consorzio Chianti Classico, Tuscany; Salvatore Foti, oenologist, Sicily; Severino Garofano, oenologist, Puglia; Nicodemo Librandi, Cirò, Calabria; Professor Piero Mastroberardino, Campania; Professor Luigi Moio, oenologist, Campania; Franco Pasetti, oenologist, Abruzzo; Paolo Solini, Consorzio Montepulciano.

Special thanks to Vita de Vita who revived my faith in Sicilians and organised a trip to Sicily via the good offices of various individual producers after Dino Agueci, President of Sicily's Istituto della Vite e del Vino, an organisation whose purpose is supposed to be the promotion of the wines of Sicily, had rejected my request for help with the curt message, left on my answerphone not by him but by his secretary: 'La risposta è negativa' ('The answer is no').

As in the previous volume, I would also like to thank my wife Candida and my business colleague Colin Loxley for their continuing support.

List of profiled producers

Accademia dei Racemi; Manduria, Puglia (tel. 099 9711660; fax 9711530)
Adanti; Bevagna, Romagna (tel. 0742 360295; fax 361270)
Altesino; Montalcino, Tuscany (tel. 0577 806208; fax 806131)
Ama, Castello di; Gaiole in Chianti, Tuscany (tel. 0577 746031; fax 746117)
Antinori; Florence, Tuscany (tel. 055 23595; fax 2359877)
Antonelli; Montefalco, Umbria (tel. 0742 378802)
Argiano, Tenuta di; Montalcino, Tuscany (tel. 0577 864037; fax 864210)
Argiolas; Serdiana, Sardinia (tel. 070 740606; fax 743264)
Avignonesi; Montepulciano, Tuscany (tel. 0578 757872; fax 757847)
Badia a Coltibuono; Gaiole in Chianti, Tuscany (tel. 0577 749498; fax 749235)
Banfi; Montalcino, Tuscany (tel. 0577 840111; fax 840444)
Barberani; Baschi, Umbria (tel. 0744 950113; fax 0763 340773)
Barbi; Montalcino, Tuscany (tel. 0577 848277; fax 849356)
Basciano; Rufina, Tuscany (tel. 055 8397034; fax 8399250)
Basilisco; Rionero in Vulture, Basilicata (tel. 0972 720032; fax 715960)
Benanti; Viagrande, Sicily (tel. 095 7893438; fax 7893436)
Bigi; Orvieto, Umbria (tel. 0763 316224; fax 316226)
Biondi-Santi; Montalcino, Tuscany (tel. 0577 848087; fax 849396)
Borgo di Colloredo; Campomarino, Molise (tel. 0875 57453; fax 57110)
Boscarelli; Montepulciano, Tuscany (tel./fax 0578 767277)
Botromagno; Gravina, Puglia (tel. 080 6965865; fax 3269026)
Brolio, Castello di; Gaiole in Chianti, Tuscany (tel. 0577 7301; fax 730225)
Bucci; Ostra Vetere, Marche (tel. 071 964170; fax 02 6554470)
Bukkuram; Pantelleria, Sicily (tel./fax 0923 918344)
Cà Marcanda; Bolgheri, Tuscany (tel. 0565 763809)
Cacchiano, Castello di; Gaiole in Chianti, Tuscany (tel. 0577 747018; fax 747157)

LIST OF PROFILED PRODUCERS

Cafaggio, Villa; Panzano, Tuscany (tel. 055 8549094; fax 8549096)
Calatrasi; San Cipirello, Sicily (tel. 091 8576767; fax 8576041)
Calò, Michele; Tuglie, Puglia (tel./fax 0833 596242)
Camigliano; Montalcino, Tuscany (tel. 0577 844068; fax 816040)
Candido; Sandonaci, Puglia (tel. 0831 635674; fax 634695)
Capannelle; Gaiole in Chianti, Tuscany (tel. 0577 749691; fax 749121)
Caparzo; Montalcino, Tuscany (tel. 0577 848390; fax 849377)
Capezzana; Seano, Tuscany (tel. 055 8706005; fax 8706673)
Capichera; Arzachena, Sardinia (tel./fax 0789 80612)
Caprai; Montefalco, Umbria (tel. 0742 378802; fax 378422)
Carpineto; Greve in Chianti, Tuscany (tel. 055 8549062; fax 8549001)
Casa Emma; Barberino Val d'Elsa, Tuscany (tel. 055 8072859; fax 0571 667707)
Casa Sola; Barberino Val d'Elsa, Tuscany (tel. 055 8075028; fax 8059194)
Casano, Misette; Pantelleria, Sicily (tel./fax 0923 918155)
Casanova di Neri; Montalcino, Tuscany (tel./fax 0577 834455)
Casato, Fattoria del; Montalcino, Tuscany (tel. 0577 849421; fax 849353)
Casavecchia; Castellina in Chianti, Tuscany (tel. 0577 741167; fax 0577 740424
Case Basse; Montalcino, Tuscany (tel. 02 461544; fax 48195341)
Castel de Paolis; Grottaferrata, Latium (tel. 06 9413648; fax 94316025)
Castelgiocondo; Montalcino, Tuscany (tel. 0577 848492; fax 849138)
Castellare; Castellina in Chianti, Tuscany (tel. 0577 740490)
Castelluccio; Modigliana, Romagna (tel./fax 0546 942486)
Cerro, Fattoria del; Montepulciano, Tuscany (tel. 0578 767722; fax 768040)
Chigi Saracini; Castelnuovo Berardenga, Tuscany (tel. 0577 355113; fax 355628)
Ciacci Piccolomini; Montalcino, Tuscany (tel. 0577 835616; fax 835785)
Col d'Orcia; Montalcino, Tuscany (tel. 0577 808001; fax 844018)
Colli di Catone; Monteporzio Catone, Latium (tel. 06 9449113; fax 9448695)
Colonnara; Cupramontana, Marche (tel. 0731 780273)
Colosi; Messina, Sicily (tel. 090 53852; fax 47553)
Colpetrone; Gualdo Cattaneo, Umbria (tel. 0578 767722; fax 768040)
Contini; Cabras, Sardinia (tel. 0783 290806; fax 290182)
Contucci; Montepulciano, Tuscany (tel. 0578 757006; fax 752891)
Copertino, C.S.; Copertino, Puglia (tel. 0832 947031; fax 930860)
Coroncino; Staffolo, Marche (tel. 0731 779494; fax 770205)
COS; Vittoria, Sicily (tel. 0932 864042; fax 869700)

Costanti; Montalcino, Tuscany (tel. 0577 848195; fax 849349)
D'Ambra; Foro d'Ischia, Campania (tel. 081 907246; fax 908190)
D'Angelo; Rionero, Basilicata (tel. 0972 721517; fax 723495)
De Bartoli; Marsala, Sicily (tel. 0923 962093; fax 962910)
De Castris; Salice Salentino, Puglia (tel. 0832 733608; fax 731114)
Decugnano dei Barbi; Orvieto, Umbria (tel. 0763 308255; fax 308118)
Di Majo Norante; Campomarino, Molise (tel. 0875 57208; fax 57379)
Donnafugata; Marsala, Sicily (tel. 0923 999555; fax 721130)
Drei Donà; Forlì, Romagna (tel. 0543 769371; fax 765049)
Duca di Salaparuta; Casteldaccia, Sicily (tel. 091 945111; fax 953227)
Falesco; Montefiascone, Latium (tel. 0761 825669; fax 825803)
Farnatella; Sinalunga, Tuscany (tel. 0577 355117; fax 355651)
Farneta; Sinalunga, Tuscany (tel. 0577 631025; fax 631027)
Fazi Battaglia; Castelplanio, Marche (tel. 0731 813444; fax 814149)
Felsina; Castelnuovo Berardenga, Tuscany (tel. 0577 355117;
  fax 355651)
Feudi di San Gregorio; Sorbo Serpico, Campania (tel. 0825 986266;
  fax 986230)
Fontana Candida; Monteporzio Catone, Latium (tel. 06 9420066;
  fax 9448591)
Fonterutoli, Castello di; Castellina in Chianti, Tuscany (tel. 0577 740476)
Fontodi; Panzano, Tuscany (tel. 055 852005; fax 852637)
Frescobaldi; Rufina, Tuscany (tel. 055 27141; fax 2802050
Garofoli; Loreto, Marche (tel. 071 7820162; fax 7821437)
Ghizzano; Peccioli, Tuscany (tel. 0587 630096; fax 630162)
Grattamacco; Bolgheri, Tuscany (tel. 0565 763840; fax 763217)
Hauner; Salina, Sicily (tel. 090 9843141; fax 9222665)
Il Palazzino; Gaiole in Chianti, Tuscany (tel. 0577 747008)
Il Poggione; Montalcino, Tuscany (tel. 0577 844029; fax 844165)
Illuminati; Controguerra, Abruzzo (tel. 0861 808008; fax 810004)
Isole e Olena; Barberino Val d'Elsa, Tuscany (tel. 055 8072763;
  fax 8072236)
Jerzu, C.S.; Jerzu, Sardinia (tel. 0782 70028; fax 71105)
La Elorina, C.S.; Rosolini, Sicily (tel. 0931 857068; fax 857333)
La Fiorita; Montalcino, Tuscany (tel. 0577 835511; fax 835521)
La Madonnina; Greve in Chianti, Tuscany (tel. 055 858003;
  fax 8588972)
La Massa; Panzano, Tuscany (tel./fax 055 852722)
La Parrina; Orbetello, Tuscany (tel./fax 0564 862636)
La Vite; Maiolati Spontini, Marche (tel. 0731 700385; fax 703359)
Le Boncie; Castelnuovo Berardenga, Tuscany (tel. 0577 359116;
  fax 359383)
Le Casalte; Montepulciano, Tuscany (tel. 0578 798246; fax 799714)

LIST OF PROFILED PRODUCERS

Le Chiuse di Sotto/Brunelli; Montalcino, Tuscany (tel. 0577 849342; fax 224797)
Le Macchiole; Bolgheri, Tuscany (tel. 0565 766092; fax 763240)
Le Pupille; Magliano, Tuscany (tel./fax 0564 505129)
Le Terrazze; Numana, Marche (tel. 071 7390352; fax 7391285)
Librandi; Cirò Marina, Calabria (tel. 0962 31518; fax 370542)
Locorotondo, C.S.; Locorotondo, Puglia (tel. 080 4311644; fax 4311213)
Lungarotti; Torgiano, Umbria (tel. 075 9880348; fax 9880294)
Mancinelli; Morro d'Alba, Marche (tel. 0731 63021; fax 63251)
Marchetti; Ancona, Marche (tel. 071 897386; fax 897376)
Masciarelli; San Martino sulla Marrucina, Abruzzo (tel. 0871 85241; fax 85330)
Masseria Monaci; Copertino, Puglia (tel./fax 0832 947512)
Mastroberardino; Atripalda, Campania (tel. 0825 614111; fax 614231)
Mastrojanni; Montalcino, Tuscany (tel. 0577 835681; fax 835505)
Melia; Alcamo, Sicily (tel./fax 0924 507860)
Melini; Poggibonsi, Tuscany (tel. 0577 989001; fax 989002)
Merlini; Montescudaio, Tuscany (tel./fax 0586 681694)
Moncaro; Montecarotto, Marche (tel. 0731 89245; fax 89237)
Monte Bernardi; Panzano, Tuscany (tel. 055 852400; fax 852355)
Montepeloso; Suvereto, Tuscany (tel./fax 0565 828180)
Montepò, Castello di; Scansano, Tuscany (tel./fax 0564 580231)
Montevertine; Radda in Chianti, Tuscany (tel. 0577 738009; fax 738265)
Montevetrano; San Cipriano Picentino, Campania (tel./fax 089 882285)
Moris Farms; Massa Marittima, Tuscany (tel. 0565 919135; fax 919380
Moroder; Varano, Marche (tel./fax 071 898232)
Murana; Pantelleria, Sicily (tel. 0923 915231)
Nottola; Montepulciano, Tuscany (tel. 0578 684711; fax 687623)
Nuova Agricoltura; Pantelleria, Sicily (tel./fax 0923 915712)
Odoardi; Nocera Terinese, Calabria (tel. 0984 29961; fax 28503)
Ornellaia; Bolgheri, Tuscany (tel. 0565 762140; fax 762144)
Palari; Messina, Sicily (tel. 090 694281; fax 637247)
Pancrazi, Marchesi; Montemurlo, Tuscany (tel. 0574 652439; fax 652157)
Paternoster; Barile, Basilicata (tel. 0972 770224; fax 770658)
Pertimali; Montalcino, Tuscany (tel./fax 0577 848721)
Piaggia; Poggio a Caiano, Tuscany (tel. 055 8705363; fax 8705833)
Pieri Agostina; Montalcino, Tuscany (tel. 0577 375785; fax 844163)
Pieve Santa Restituta; Montalcino, Tuscany (tel. 0577 848610; fax 849309)
Planeta; Sambuca di Sicilia, Sicily (tel./fax 0925 80009)
Poggio Antico; Montalcino, Tuscany (tel. 0577 848044; fax 846563)

Poggio Scalette; Greve in Chianti, Tuscany (tel. 055 8546108; fax 8547960)
Poggiopiano; San Casciano, Tuscany (tel. 055 8229629; fax 8228256)
Poliziano; Montepulciano, Tuscany (tel./fax 0578 738171)
Ponte a Rondolino; San Gimignano, Tuscany (tel. 0577 955077; fax 955012)
Querciabella; Greve in Chianti, Tuscany (tel. 055 853834; fax 8544657)
Rallo; Marsala, Sicily (tel. 0923 721633; fax 721632)
Rampolla, Castello dei; Panzano, Tuscany (tel. 055 852001; fax 852533)
Regaleali/Tasca d'Almerita; Vallelunga Pratameno, Sicily (tel. 0921 544011; fax 542783)
Riecine; Gaiole in Chianti, Tuscany (tel. 0577 749098; fax 744935)
Rivera; Andria, Puglia (tel. 0883 569501; fax 569575)
Rocca delle Macie; Castellina in Chianti, Tuscany (tel. 0577 7321; fax 743151)
Rocca di Montegrossi; Gaiole in Chianti, Tuscany (tel. 0577 747267; fax 747836)
Rodano; Castellina in Chianti, Tuscany (tel./fax 0577 743107)
Rosa del Golfo/Calò Giuseppe; Alezio, Puglia (tel. 0833 281045; fax 992365)
Roxan; Rosciano, Abruzzo (tel./fax 085 8505767)
Rubino; Brindisi, Puglia (tel. 0831 571955; fax 571655)
Ruffino; Pontassieve, Tuscany (tel. 055 83605; fax 8313677)
Salcheto; Montepulciano, Tuscany (tel. 0578 799031; fax 799749)
San Felice; Castelnuovo Berardenga, Tuscany (tel. 0577 359087; fax 359223)
San Giusto a Rentennano; Gaiole in Chianti, Tuscany (tel. 0577 747121; fax 747109)
San Guido; Bolgheri, Tuscany (tel. 0565 762003; fax 762017)
San Patrignano; Ospedaletto, Romagna (tel. 0541 362362; fax 756718)
Sangervasio; Palaia, Tuscany (tel. 0587 483360; fax 484361)
Santa Anastasia, Abbazia; Castelbuono, Sicily (tel. 0921 671959; fax 091 220199)
Santadi, C.S.; Santadi, Sardinia (tel. 0781 950127; fax 950012)
Satta, Michele; Castagneto Carducci, Tuscany (tel./fax 0565 773041)
Sella & Mosca; Alghero, Sardinia (tel. 079 997700; fax 951279)
Selvapiana; Rufina, Tuscany (tel. 055 8369848; fax 8316840)
Taburno, Cantina del; Foglianise, Campania (tel. 0824 871338; fax 50084)
Talenti; Montalcino, Tuscany (tel./fax 0577 844043)
Taurino; Guagnano, Puglia (tel. 0832 706490; fax 706242)
Terrabianca; Radda in Chianti, Tuscany (tel. 0577 738544; fax 738623)

Terre Dora di Paolo; Montefusco, Campania (tel. 0825 968215; fax 963022)

Terriccio, Castello del; Castellina Marittima, Tuscany (tel. 050 699709; fax 699789)

Trinoro, Tenuta di; Sarteano, Tuscany (tel. 0578 267110; fax 267303)

Tua Rita; Suvereto, Tuscany (tel. 0565 829237; fax 827891)

Umani Ronchi; Osimo, Marche (tel. 071 7108019; fax 7108859)

Val di Suga; Montalcino, Tuscany (tel. 0577 80411; fax 849316)

Valdicava; Montalcino, Tuscany (tel. 0577 848261; fax 848008)

Valdipiatta; Montepulciano, Tuscany (tel. 0578 757930; fax 717037)

Valentini; Loreto Aprutino, Abruzzo (tel./fax 085 8291138)

Valgiano; Valgiano, Tuscany (tel./fax 0583 402271)

Vallone; Lecce, Puglia (tel. 0832 308041; fax 243108)

Vecchie Terre di Montefili; Greve in Chianti, Tuscany (tel. 055 853739; fax 8544684)

Vermentino, C.S.; Monti, Sardinia (tel. 0789 44012; fax 449128)

Vetrice, Villa di; Rufina, Tuscany (tel. 055 8397008; fax 8399041)

Vicchiomaggio, Castello di; Greve in Chianti, Tuscany (tel. 055 854079; fax 853911)

Volpaia, Castello di; Radda in Chianti, Tuscany (tel. 0577 738066; fax 738619)

Zecca; Leverano, Puglia (tel. 0832 925613; fax 922606)

Zerbina; Marzeno di Faenza, Romagna (tel. 0546 40022; fax 40275)

List of maps

Key map	xxviii
Central Italy West	26
Chianti Classico	42
Montepulciano and Montalcino	110
Northern Maremma	153
Central Italy East	212
Southern mainland	242
Sardinia	316
Sicily	344

About this book

Brunello to Zibibbo – The Wines of Tuscany, Central and Southern Italy is the second of two books on the wines of Italy, the first being Barolo to Valpolicella – The Wines of Northern Italy. As I explained in the companion volume, the original idea was to cover all Italy in a single work, but it soon became apparent that in view of the enormous development of Italian wines in the past few years this was not going to be possible in a sensible space.

The idea behind the titles is to suggest a quasi alpha-to-omega approach to the subject, as well as a geographical spread. Admittedly, B to Z does not quite cover the alphabet, though B to V is worse, nor do Brunello – the grape of Montalcino, and Zibibbo – the grape of the island of Pantelleria, off the coast of Tunisia, quite represent the extremes of the north–south span from Romagna to Sicily. But the idea is there, and it was necessary also to use familiar or at least colourful names.

Apart from the principal matter of the book, the organisation of which is explained below, I have once again provided, at the beginning of the book, a list of profiled producers with telephone and, where possible, fax numbers to enable readers to carry their own researches a bit further. By 'profiled producers' I mean those about whom I have written a paragraph or more as distinct from merely mentioning; although, as I have said later, this selection does not necessarily imply any value judgement.

Readers will also find, at the end, a Glossary which should explain any obscure wine terms; a Key to Italian Pronunciation, which I stoutly maintain is an important tool for understanding Italian wines – once you get the sound, somehow the flavours too fall into sharper focus; and a Bibliography. What they won't find, I fear, is an analytical list of the wines of Italy according to grape variety, something I promised in Barolo to Valpolicella but which I am unable for Byzantine reasons to deliver. I hope that readers will find the Rapid Guide to Italian Wines provided in the companion volume as useful. It is certainly far more compact.

And now, a few words on how the book works.

In both of my previous books on Italian wine I have been accused of getting off to a slow start, by speaking at length of the general aspects of viticulture, oenology and law relating to the subject. I thought this time of consigning these chapters to the end of the book, after discussion of the wine zones themselves. In this way casual readers would be able to plunge right into the nitty gritty, while students requiring more background would find it available at whatever point they might want it. On second thoughts, however, I have decided to leave the introductory notes on viticulture and oenology where they are, with the recommendation that those who *want* to get going immediately with the wine zones should skip this section initially, leaving it until afterwards. I do feel, however, that these general reflections on the realities facing the Italian wine scene provide a useful foundation on which to build a better understanding of the rest of the book, even in retrospect.

As for the chapter on law, since it is mainly devoted to a proposal for changing the law rather than to explaining the law as it stands, I think it is proper to leave it to the end. A simple explanation may be found in *Barolo to Valpolicella*, pp. 23–25. The bare bones may also be found in the brief section on the wine label at the end of this preface.

The meat of the book is in the chapters on the three regions: Central Italy West; Central Italy East; and the South and Islands. Each has a a general introduction, followed by a rapid tour of the principal wine-producing zones, communes or areas, region by region. The names of these areas will be <u>underlined</u> on first mention.

This is followed – and here I am largely repeating what I said in the earlier volume – by a consideration of the major indigenous grape varieties of each zone, from three points of view: the grape itself, discussed under section headings in SMALL CAPITALS, the wines principally associated with that grape (headings in **Bold**), and the producers which best represent those wines (headings in ***Bold italic***).

In dealing with producers I have used the following conventions in an attempt to make clear to the reader what's what. It is worth spending a few seconds memorising these conventions as confusion may otherwise ensue.

On **first mention only,** in any given chapter, the name of the producer in a list of producers will be printed in **bold**. Thereafter in that chapter that producer's name will be printed normally except where he/she is subsequently profiled. Readers may consult the index to check for previous mentions. For profiled producers I have provided, in a separate section, telephone and fax numbers, where available, to enable travellers to contact them should they so wish.

Following the producer's name I give the name of his/her principal wine or wines, relevant to that section, in brackets; this may be a DOC name, but it is more often a *cru* name. Following this, on first mention, with few exceptions, I give the name of the town or commune in which the winery is situated.

Where the system used is not in conformity with the above I hope the nature of the information given is clear from the context.

I should also mention that the location, be it commune or village, which may be a *frazione* (see Glossary), is generally given in conformity with one or both of the major guides to Italian wines, *Vini d'Italia* and *I Vini di Veronelli* (see Bibliography); this in order that those interested may be able to seek further information in those guides.

So if you want to know more about a producer whose name is not in bold, check the index for other mentions; or check the profiled producers' list for phone or fax numbers and contact them. Producers are generally profiled in the section which relates to their best-known or most prestigious wines, but to avoid repetition and loss of focus, the profile often includes details of all his or her wines of note, not just those of the grape in question.

Here is a schematic presentation of the layout:

Region	*Production areas*
CENTRAL ITALY WEST	TUSCANY <u>Chianti Classico</u>

Grapes, wines and producers

Major indigenous grapes		*Associated wines*
SANGIOVESE		**Chianti Classico**

Producers	*Wines*	*Town/commune*
Castello di **Volpaia** (bold on first mention)	Coltassala	Radda (not given after first mention)

MAPS

We have taken a somewhat idiosyncratic approach to maps in this book, as in its predecessor. We have indicated most of the relevant wine zones either by showing the borders or by a system of arrows, though it seems to me a bit pointless to show every single wine zone of Italy for two reasons. First, because there are far too many of them, a very significant proportion of which are of little or no real interest to an international audience; second, because it is usually sufficient simply to indicate the town which has given its name to a given DOC – readers will understand that the zone is to be found grouped around that town. Thus we have distinguished between 'Main wine towns', amalgamating what in the previous volume we called 'Towns giving their name to wine zones' – and readers should understand that this may be an indirect use, as for example 'Colli Aretini' which is derived from the town of Arezzo – and 'Main wine towns', i.e. towns which are important but may not have given their name to any wine; and 'Other wine towns', meaning, generally, a town in which one or more producer has his winery. This latter in order to give readers the possibility of roughly tracing a given producer's whereabouts should he/she wish to visit.

A final word, on commercial links. Following publication of *Barolo to Valpolicella* certain persons took me to task for not declaring to the reader that I make my living more from trading in wine than from writing about wine; it is a rare creature who makes a reasonable living out of wine-writing alone. So let me make the situation clear.

I have been involved in the wine trade for over 30 years. Prior to that I tried to make it for a while as a writer, an ambition which at the time came to nothing, as it does for countless young aspirants. However, I found after a few years working in wine that I could combine the two professions, the one enriching the other. On the one hand, in my travels with a journalist's hat on I met numerous wine producers whom I later represented on a commercial basis, as a wine retailer and importer/distributor, with my company Wine-cellars, and subsequently as a broker with my present company Vinexus. On the other hand, my commercial dealings presented countless opportunities to travel, taste wines and meet people, opportunities which I would never otherwise have had if only because I could not have afforded the expense from the meagre return as a wine writer. I am certain that I would never have been able to write any of the three books I have produced on Italian wine, certainly not this one and its companion, without that commercial backup.

Italian wine, for some obscure reason known only to the gods, has been my life, and numerous are the producers in these pages whom I have represented commercially at some level – retail, wholesale, as a broker – at some time past or present, and possibly future. I have been keenly aware in presenting these producers that objectivity is of the essence, and I have made an earnest if perhaps not always successful attempt to divorce journalism from commercial interest. I cannot deny that I tend to know more about the producers with whom I have worked, but I can be quite sure that if I have chosen to work with them it is because I believe in the qualities which have subsequently found their way into print. On a conscious level, at least, I am not guilty of any distortion aimed at commercial advantage. On the other hand, I *have* written positively and at length about producers with whom I have never had, and am never likely to have, or have long since ceased to have, any commercial dealings; an example of the former being Angelo Gaja, who was kind enough to declare my previous book *Barolo to Valpolicella* 'excellent' (*ottimo*).

Readers are probably aware that some of the most distinguished wine writers of the past and present have been involved in some way in the wine trade. It is 'an honourable tradition', as one well-known contemporary specialist writer referred to it. I hope that the reader of this book will trust me to have been honourable and even-handed in the presentation of producers, and I am happy to discuss with any individual what connections there may be or may have been with any given producer. I do not, however, consider it in the best interests of literature to indicate precisely in the text what my relations may be or may have been with them – such a procedure risks becoming tedious and would result, I believe, in greater distortion than otherwise.

In the circumstances I will just have to trust the reader to trust me when I say that my overriding interest in writing this book was to write a good book and not to push my petty interests.

The Italian wine label

As with any wine produced in the EU, the *principal* or *legal* label is obliged to carry certain mentions. I emphasise the words 'principal or legal' because there is a growing trend towards using a purely decorative label on the apparent front of the bottle, in which case the legally required information must be carried on what is to all intents and purposes the back label.

The basic requirements include the following:

1. An acknowledged denomination or appellation followed by the appropriate quality designation, e.g. 'Chianti Classico – Denominazione di Origine Controllata e Garantita'.
2. Name and address of the responsible bottler.
3. Country of origin.
4. Alcohol by volume.
5. Contents.

Given that these essential elements are in place and clearly visible, other information may also be added, e.g. name of the estate; name of a *cru* (brand name or vineyard); lot number (code for the date of bottling); description of the wine, or how it is made; the words (required only in Italy) 'Non disperdere il vetro nell'ambiente' ('Do not litter the environment with glass').

Things to watch out for on the label are as follows:

1. *The denomination*: tells you where the wine comes from as well as what type of wine it is, what grapes should have been used in its production, what its maximum production should have been in vineyard and winery, what the significance of extra wording like 'Riserva' or 'Superiore' is, etc.
2. *The quality designation*: possibilities are four, two in the category of Quality Wine, two in the category of Table Wine:

a. DOC – Denominazione di Origine Controllata: the standard quality designation, indicating that the wine's origin and characteristics have theoretically been controlled;
b. DOCG – the above plus 'e Garantita', meaning that the controls are more stringent and that the wine has been passed by a tasting commission (also the case for some, but not all, DOCs);
c. IGT – Indicazione Geografica Tipica, the higher Table Wine qualification, meaning that the origins of the wine are controlled but less stringently (even) than DOC and the quality criteria are (even) less severe;
d. Vino da Tavola – subject to few controls and not allowed to indicate on the label a vintage, a place of origin or a grape variety.

3. *Wording relating to the bottling*: some wines are bottled where the grapes are grown – estate-bottled – and some are bottled in another area, even in another country. The former tend to be better and, certainly, are more likely to be genuine. Forms of words indicating estate-bottling include: '*Imbottigliato all'origine . . .*', '*imbottigliato dal viticoltore . . .*'. The indication '*imbottigliato a . . .*' means that the wine was bottled away from the place of production or using wines or grapes bought in.

4. *Additional quality indications*: these are regulated and you can't just throw in any old superlative, like '*Stravecchio . . .*' (very old) or '*Superiore . . .*'. The latter, for example, is supposed to indicate a higher grade, but sometimes means merely a slightly higher level of alcohol. To be sure of the significance or these words it is necessary to consult the rules for the particular DOC(G).

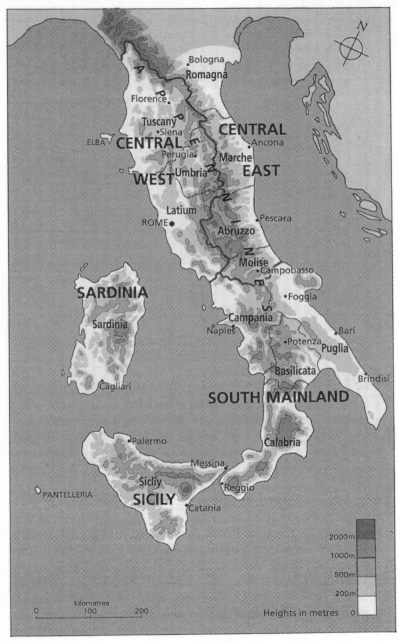

Key map

Introduction

Somewhere in Plato's *Republic*, I seem to recall, there is the image
of a circle of light surrounded by darkness. The light represents
knowledge, and the darkness, ignorance. As the circle of light
grows, so does the circumference of darkness.

It sometimes seems thus with the subject of this book, Italian
wine. As the knowledge grows, so does the area of ignorance. In my
first book on Italian wine, *Life Beyond Lambrusco* (1995), I had the
naïve idea that I could present Italian wines in a way that would
reduce the complexities of the subject to a point where it became
reasonably easy to understand. I even subtitled it *Understanding
Italian Fine Wine*. I now recant and humbly confess that this is a
hopelessly misguided ambition.

For the problem is not just with the knower, it is also with
the known, or at least the knowable. In the time between the
publication of *Life Beyond Lambrusco* and the present so much
has changed, improvements have taken place on such a vast scale,
and enthusiastic producers have mushroomed at such a rate that
it seems an impossible dream to wish to pin the thing down.
More negatively, the number of names that one has to deal with – of
zones (including IGTs), of producers, of individual wines DOC(G)
– has spiralled almost uncontrollably. In this latter respect, at least,
I have made what will no doubt prove a vain attempt, in the chapter on law and in the subsequent Appendices A, B and C, to propose
changes which might make more sense than does the present near-
chaos.

But perhaps I am exaggerating the complexities of the subject. As
in *Life Beyond Lambrusco*, as well as in the companion volume to
this one, *Barolo to Valpolicella*, I have tried to reduce the number
of categories to be dealt with by considering wines, after a brief

overview and geographical tour of the relevant wine zones of a given area, according to their dominant grape variety, further reducing the multiplicity by segregating varieties peculiar to Italy from those now generally referred to as 'international', dealing with the latter in a separate chapter.

This has presented its own problems, in that, in the part I call Central Italy West, one grape, Sangiovese, is so dominant not just in Tuscany but also in Romagna, Umbria, Latium and the Marche, that it consumes about a quarter of the total space available for the entire book. While in the south there is little in the way of inter-regional varieties, so that each region – or almost – has to be considered on its own.

As I have come to know Italy and Italians, however, I have learned that simplicity, clarity and rationality are not virtues to be expected here. Curious: the Romans were such a rational race, with their Latin conjugations and declensions, their social hierarchy and their military organisation, their ambitions of universality, their formalised and rather cold art forms: their masculinity. How, from those roots, did this modern Italy so full of contradiction and creativity and individualism, of anarchical inspiration, of feminine warmth evolve?

It is a rhetorical question – I do not offer an answer, nor do I intend to search for one in the kaleidoscopic maze of post-Roman history. That is not my brief or my function. Then what is? What is the purpose of this book, and what would be the purpose of buying it?

The best I can come up with is that I wanted to present a record of the state of Italian wine, in which vineyard I have laboured nearly 30 years, at the turn of the millennium. So that not only can contemporaries form a fairly total picture of how it is but also so that interested parties 50 or 100, or 200, years from now will be able to look back upon how it was 'then'. Of course, there are plenty of books and publications on Italian wine: but most of them are guides, which only look at the latest wines; or coffee-table items with more pictures than words (no one can accuse Messrs Faber of producing such a thing!); or are limited to a certain geographical region or topic. It is my purpose, in these pages, and in conjunction with *Barolo to Valpolicella*, to present the Italian wine scene as a whole, complete with background and foreground. As we are speaking of the wines of all Italy it cannot go into too much depth, but it can steer the reader in the direction of a general understanding of the situation. That, at any rate, is the theory.

No one is more acutely aware than I of the extent to which I have underperformed in this, in the sense that however much one may write, there is far more that one cannot write about for lack of time and space and, referring to my opening remarks, for sheer lack of knowledge. Some zones and many producers worthy of attention have received little or none, and I deeply regret this lack. But I hope that, at the end of the book, readers will feel that Italian wines, if not simplified, if not clarified, are at least less of a confusion in the mind; or, perhaps, that they will appreciate the extent to which confusion is an integral and necessary, sometimes even beautiful, part of the picture.

And, like Plato's seeker after knowledge, I hope that readers will then take it on themselves to push back the ever-increasing perimeter of darkness. For, as I have said elsewhere, there is no way ultimately that one is going to learn about objects of taste, smell and touch just by reading about them. They need to be tasted, smelled and touched. The corks, many of them, need to be drawn, and conviviality, not clinical 'tasting', must ensue. Only thus does one truly enter into the magical world that is Italian wine.

I

Vine and wine

──────

VITICULTURE: GETTING IT RIGHT FROM THE GROUND UP

When, in the mid-1970s, I first began looking carefully at the Italian wine scene, after several years specialising in the wines of France, I remember being somewhat shocked by the shabby, run-down condition of Italian vineyards. There were none of those neat rows of vines, like lines of soldiers, with perfectly weeded terrains, clean, orderly and well-tended, that were commonplace in Bordeaux, Burgundy, and Champagne. Italian vineyards, by contrast, were untidy, full of grass and weeds, and sparsely planted with low numbers of vines per hectare and, consequently, high yields per plant.

To a significant extent, and especially in central Italy, since northern Italy had been viticulturally specialised for longer, this was the legacy of *mezzadria* (share-cropping), that system, which had ruled agricultural production for centuries, whereby a proprietor divided his land into parcels tended by families who, paying their ground rent in kind, attempted to achieve self-sufficiency by raising animals and planting a variety of crops all mixed together. Thus vines, fruit and olive trees, corn and vegetables were all jumbled up in the same plot. Obviously the grapes that resulted were unlikely to be of an elevated quality level.

Those shabby vineyards that shocked me were not, of course, *mezzadria* ones, because by the time I came on the scene in the early 1970s they were mostly specialised, i.e. planted solely to vines, however shabbily, and not mixed crops. But they were what had arisen in the immediate aftermath of *mezzadria*, in the 1950s and 1960s, when farmers – landlords receiving their land back from

4

the sharecroppers, or tenants renting them or buying them in at low prices – had started planting proper vineyards. Having no experience of quality viticulture, for which there was in any event little demand, and having no inkling of concepts such as clones, production per hectare or production per plant, they had followed the crowd, accepted the vine material they were sold, and gone for volume.

This state of affairs persisted for some years. Wine makers and merchants felt it was more important, in the first instance, to get their *cantine* in good order rather than spend time sorting out vineyards which, often enough, didn't belong to them anyway. It wasn't really until the 1980s that the idea began to take root that, whatever you did in the winery, good wine ultimately could only come from good grapes. It was as recently as then that the era of the quality vineyard in Italy really began.

Of course, as has often been observed, experiments in viticulture differ radically from those in *cantina* in that they take a lot longer to reach a conclusion. In the winery it is sufficient to have the money and the will, and the desired changes may take place more or less immediately – or at least between one vintage and another. If the changes haven't worked you can scrap them and try again next year. If they have, all you need to do is tweak them from time to time.

Not so in the vineyard. The only final test as to whether an experiment – say with a new clone, or a different rootstock, or combinations of the above, combinations which could also include planting density, training height and shape, seeding between rows – has worked is the taste of the resulting wine. And before you get to that stage you have to prepare the ground, plant the young vines, wait for them to produce (minimum 3 to 4 years), then wait again for them to reach various levels of maturity (8 years, 12 years, 20 years; some producers, like Franco Biondi-Santi, maintain that a vine does not reach the apex of its quality potential until it is 25 years old). Not to mention having to wait till the resulting wine has matured sufficiently to be properly judged. If an experiment hasn't worked in these time-scales it can be a long, long way back to the drawing board.

Probably the highest profile project to address the problems of viticultural quality at the turn of the century is Chianti Classico 2000, undertaken by the Consorzio Vino Chianti Classico, the technical arm of the Consortium, as distinct from the promotional side or Consorzio del Marchio Storico, in conjunction with the agricultural departments of the Universities of Florence and Pisa. I am not saying that this has been the most successful vineyard experiment undertaken in Italy since trials began in earnest somewhere around the mid-1980s, with a few exceptions which go back as far as the 1950s and 1960s. But it has been the most publicised and documented, and is a good theoretical as well as practical paradigm for purposes of giving readers an idea of the kind of activity that is going on in various parts of central and southern Italy in our time.

The background runs something like this – the following being based on an article originally written for *Decanter*, with certain additions, subtractions and corrections:

It was 1982 and I had been invited by the Consorzio Gallo Nero, as it was then called, to tour Chianti Classico. As we drove round the historic vine-land I was struck afresh by the beauty of the Tuscan hinterland and even mildly impressed by the quality of some of the wines, which was indeed quite an improvement on what I had encountered several years earlier.

In those days my Italian wasn't so good, and at first I thought I was mishearing what the director of the Consortium was saying to his colleague in the back seat. I thought I heard him say that in the boom years of the 1950s and 1960s, a large area of the Chianti zone had been planted to an inferior clone, or clones, of Sangiovese, ones designed for high quantity production, and not quality.

It was like hearing someone say that a major part of the Côte d'Or had been replanted with volume vine-stock, or that Lafite after several centuries was introducing plants from Entre Deux Mers. No, it couldn't be true, my Italian was just playing tricks.

'People in a hurry always make mistakes', the director continued. At which point I turned round and asked him what he meant. I threw back at him all that I thought he'd been imparting and waited for him to refute it. Instead, he grudgingly admitted it was true.

Those had been heady days, back in the 1950s and 1960s, following the abolition of *mezzadria* and the commencement of the DOC system for Chianti in 1967. Chianti – with its distinctive wicker flask or its Bordeaux bottle with the black rooster insignium – was enjoying healthy sales internationally, even at lowish prices, as honest if uninspired Italian cuisine of the second- or third-grade, pasta–pizza–saltimbocca style, caught on round the world. Superbly sited run-down properties, *case coloniche* belonging to impecunious landowners whose tenants had left the land after *mezzadria*'s demise, were going for a song. And moneyed fools rushed in from Florence, Milan, Turin, Rome, Genoa and points abroad to realise their dream of a country estate in the land of the *Rinascimento*, a countryside covered by vineyards and olive groves and decorated by stately cypresses.

The newcomers, or their advisers, who along with their ignorant future employers were also sucked into this low-pressure area, knew little about clones of *vitis vinifera* and cared less. They knew only that they had to get rid of the promiscuous fields of the share-cropping era, with their fruit and olive trees, their tomatoes and runner-beans between plants or in alternate rows, and create specialised vineyards. Where to obtain the material? Everyone told them to go to Rauscedo in the north, Italy's biggest wine-grape nursery. So off to Rauscedo. You want Sangiovese? Here you go – Sangiovese. Plenty of volume and not too much fuss. Thank you very much.

The scene shifts to Greve, the year is 1987. The occasion, the annual Festa del Chianti in the famous triangular *piazza*. The then director of the Consorzio Chianti Classico, Dr Tonveronachi, is chatting with the Consorzio's chief agronomist, Carlo Ferrini, now an independent consultant. They are discussing the problems arising from a vine-land planted to quantity clones in a production and market environment increasingly directed towards quality. More to the point, they are deliberating on the inescapable fact that from around the turn of the century it will be necessary to replant the majority of the vineyards of Chianti Classico, which will then be 30 or more years old. Obviously the mistakes of the previous planting boom will need to be corrected, but more than that, there will need to be a maximisation of Chianti's potential from all points of view. That is cost of production, possibilities for mechanisation, especially in view of the vanishing species of field-worker, and in

7

terms of both absolute quality and quality in relation to quantity – the producer's eye view of what consumers perceive as value for money.

In short, they are discussing how they will be able to give guidance to producers concerned about what to plant in the refurbishing phase of the early years of the twenty-first century, and how to plant it.

Thus 'Chianti Classico 2000' was born, although it wasn't until the following year that it was officially launched with the collaboration of the universities, finance from the Ministry of Agriculture and the Tuscan regional authorities, subsequently also from the EU, and, most important of all, with the first experimental planting. During the period 1989 to 1991 plantings continued, until there were 14 experimental vineyards in areas scattered throughout the Chianti Classico zone, covering a total area of just under 24 hectares; one further hectare was added in 1995–6. Each vineyard was devoted to one of the six themes of the programme (see below). In addition, five micro-vinification laboratories were set up from 1993 in separate communes of the zone, the purpose of which obviously was to produce the liquid which would ultimately determine the success or otherwise of the experimental plantings via laboratory analysis and sensory evaluation; each laboratory contained a number of units, each unit being devoted to one of the six themes. A network of field meteorological stations was further established to gather data concerning local microclimates and in respect of humidity, dew formation, temperature (air and soil), wind (velocity and direction), solar radiation and rainfall. Finally, a computer database was established to enable researchers to organise and analyse the information deriving from all these sources.

At the beginning of the project, as mentioned, six themes were identified for analysis. The first two had to do with clonal selection, on the one hand of existing Tuscan clones, mainly of Sangiovese but also of Canaiolo and Colorino, on the other of newly developed ones. Clonal selection was considered the heart of the project, since it was by observation of the vigour and health, i.e. freedom from virus and resistance to cryptogams, of these clones, and by subsequently testing their resultant wines that the answer would be found to the essential question that growers would ask: what to plant?

The next question, thus the next theme, was: on what to graft? So, experimentation with rootstocks. The main criterion here was to find rootstocks that limit production while adapting themselves reasonably to the soil-types in which they are planted as well as to the principal vine.

Next question: what should be the density of planting? The existing average was low – between one and two thousand plants per hectare – implying a relatively high yield per plant at a time when most experts agreed that low production per plant favours quality.

Next: what training system to employ? Eight systems were experimented with, including the traditional *capovolto toscano* or Tuscan arched cane, cordon spur at different heights and in different styles, *alberello* (bush) and lyre.

Finally: what, if any, seeds to cultivate between rows – natural or artificial grass, clover, fescue, brome.

Establishing the parameters for evaluation and seeing the vines through their early years occupied the primary phase of the programme. The first year in which a significant amount of fruit, from existing Tuscan clones, was produced was 1993, but it was felt best to give the vines a further couple of years to establish their character and adapt to the *terroir*. The wines then had to complete their oenological processes before becoming available for sensory evaluation.

It was not until 1995 that the Consorzio's analytical and organoleptic tests began in earnest, and not therefore until the late 1990s that it was felt that there was sufficient evidence in wine form to begin drawing conclusions.

Such conclusions as have more or less tentatively been reached are as follows:

Existing clones

The principal clone planted between the late 1950s and the early 1970s, R10, does turn out to be defective in various ways, namely in displaying lower grape sugar and significantly lower acidity with less phenological substances compared with other already approved Sangiovese clones – nine in all. This indicates that R10 inclines to give wine of relatively simple structure and inadequate ageing potential. Which explains a lot, even if we already knew it.

The three clones yielding the 'most interesting results from both the agronomic and the oenological standpoints' are F (for Florence) 9–48, R (for Rauscedo) 24 and 19T (for Tebano, a zone of Romagna). Over a period of years these have shown a tendency to ripen earlier than others and display especially high levels of phenological substances, deep colour, especially R24 and 19T, and good alcohol levels. R24 and 19T are also the least productive of the clones tested.

It should be noted that these clones are being used not only in Chianti Classico but also in other classic zones of Tuscany where replanting is going on. The Tenimenti Angelini group, for instance, uses these three plus R5 and R23 not just in their vineyards in Castellina in Chianti (San Leonino) but also at Montepulciano (Trerose) and Montalcino (Val di Suga), putting paid somewhat to the marketing spin that these zones only use their own peculiar sub-varieties like Prugnolo Gentile in Montepulciano or Brunello in Montalcino.

Newly developed clones

At the time of writing there are no oenological results from the newly developed clones since the processes of selection, screening for viruses and productivity and propagation to the point where there are sufficient plants with which to carry out field experiments obviously took a few years longer than in the case of the existing clones. For the record, a complete list of the criteria looked for in deciding which of the many experimental clones to propagate, after establishment of essential health properties, is as follows: 'limited shoot growth and early cessation of vegetation, modest productivity, medium or low bud fertility, loose bunches of reduced dimensions, small berries, thick skins, intense colours, early and uniform ripening in the context of the plant and the bunch, high sugar content, constant production, resistance to the principal pests and diseases.'

From an initial base of 239 'presumed clones' 31, of which 21 were Sangiovese, 8 Canaiolo and 2 Colorino, were passed as virus-free, and from this number 4 Sangioveses were approved by the Ministry of Agriculture in 1999, namely the less-than-poetically titled CHCl-2000/1, CHCl-2000/2, CHCl-2000/3 and CHCl-2000/4. It is from this material that most Chianti Classico vineyards will presumably be planted in the future, although for the moment growers are using the existing clones pending further field trials and propagation by nurseries.

Rootstocks

The rootstocks used in the above-mentioned experiments were two: 420A and 1103P. 'No particularly significant difference between the two types emerged in the studies'. However, in the two experimental vineyards selected for the study of rootstocks many other types have been tried, and it is too early to say what effects these would have combined with the selected clones. The main points of consideration regarding rootstocks are adaptability to soil conditions and effect on limiting production.

Density

The two vineyards chosen for this experiment were planted to clone R10 on the above rootstocks at densities ranging from 2,500 and 10,000 plants per hectare, via 5,000 and 7,500. Those who have replanted in recent years seem to have gone mostly for something between 5,000 and 6,000, partly because this is approximately the number for which a conventional tractor can be used, partly because, as stated, it is generally agreed, independently of the present tests, that higher density and lower production per plant is positive in quality terms. A few, like Tenimenti Angelini, who have what the French call *tracteurs enjambeurs* – vine-straddling tractors – have gone up to 7,000, and some have gone significantly higher. Whether the CC2000 tests have proved anything definitive is a moot point, especially as only the existing defective clone (R10) was used.

Training

The two vineyards selected were planted, again, to R10 on two separate rootstocks and to seven (in one case) and eight (in the other) formations. The formation which seems to have been considered the most successful, particularly judging by its almost universal application today, is *cordone speronato* (cordon spur), where a permanent lateral arm is led off at a right angle to the vertical trunk, generally fairly low down, with a varying number of fruiting buds whose canes are attached to horizontal wires. A system which has been found to produce excellent quality fruit but which is less easily mechanisable is the ancient *alberello* (little tree), with say four arms gathered together at the top and attached to a vertical cane. Producers who have opted for this style tend to be small and highly quality-oriented such as Fattoria le Boncie at Castelnuovo Berardenga. Larger growers who have tried the system do so in limited sections of their properties, e.g. Castello di Cacchiano. Another system found considered successful by a few quality producers is the lyre; Castello di Ama has planted a part of its vineyard to this system.

Seeding between rows

The two vineyards selected were fortunate in having the R24 clone planted. Of the five types of cultivation attempted in each, Stefano Porcinai has hazarded that the best results are attained not with traditional methods or natural seeding, but by seeding with a plant which rejoices in the Latin name of *festuca rubra* and in the even more melodious English one of 'red or creeping fescue', which apparently has the effect of reducing vegetation, producing loose bunches and delivering a more balanced and concentrated product.

The Chianti Classico 2000 project has its critics, including some from within its own ranks, but such information as it has so far been able to provide has been useful to the growers who have already planted or field-grafted their vineyards afresh. It is estimated that some 30% of the Chianti Classico vine-field had undergone renovation by the dawn of the new century, and it is hoped that by the year 2010 the figure will be near enough 100%.

By the year 2025, therefore, a very different picture of Chianti Classico will present itself, both visually and, especially, organoleptically. Vineyards planted to the new clones with new systems will be largely mature, and ready like they have never been – not in history, certainly not in the twentieth century – to put forth the best wine of which they are capable. It is only then that we will see just *how* good Chianti Classico can be.

As I have said, CC2000 represents only one of many experiments being undertaken throughout the centre and south. Elsewhere in Tuscany large independents such as Antinori, Ruffino, Banfi and Il Poggione are doing their own research, sometimes along similar lines to the above, sometimes homing in on different aspects. Agricola San Felice, at Castelnuovo Berardenga, has for example, with the help of the universities of Pisa and Florence, set 2.5 hectares aside under the name Vitiarium for the study of alternative native varieties of Tuscany. Among these is the extraordinary Pugnitello grape which just may become an important blending variety in future, perhaps taking over from the more aggressive Bordeaux grapes – having teetered on the edge of extinction only a few years ago. San Felice is also carrying out studies on Italian varieties from other zones, such as Aglianico (Campania), Cannonau (Sardinia), Montepulciano (Abruzzo) and Nebbiolo (Piemonte).

Indeed, San Felice's ex-director, the late Enzo Morganti, was perhaps the earliest pioneer of clonal selection of Sangiovese in the 1950s and 1960s when he was *fattore* at Lilliano – work which he continued when he transferred to San Felice in 1967 until his death in 1994, and which is being continued by his colleagues to this day. Enzo Morganti's own daughter, Giovanna, at her tiny property called Le Boncie at San Felice, has followed in her father's experimental footsteps by returning to the traditional *alberello* or bush method of planting – considerably more work in the vineyard but, she claims, giving a better balanced plant and ultimately higher quality fruit. The other major Tuscan champion of *alberello* is the house of Avignonesi, which has introduced in its vineyards both at Montepulciano and in Puglia the ancient *settonce* method recommended by the Roman writer Columella. This is based on a hexagonal pattern of vines with one in the middle, making seven (*sette*), modelled after the design on the Roman *settonce* coin. According to owner Ettore Falvo, Avignonesi at the time of writing have 30 hectares planted to this system, at between 7,000 and 7,500 vines per hectare, and are planting another six hectares every year.

Tuscan growers of lesser dimensions but no less passion for perfection have been carrying out their own researches as well. A leading light in this respect is Paolo de Marchi of Isole e Olena.

At Montefalco in Umbria, Marco Caprai and his consultant Attilio Pagli, in conjunction with Professors Valenti of the University of Milan and Nicolini of the Cantina Sperimentale of the Institute of San Michele all'Adige, have been carrying out a remarkable series of experiments since the early 1990s on the clones of Sagrantino, a variety which, like most Italian varieties, indeed, had never previously undergone any form of study. They started by taking cuttings from all the Sagrantino plants in the area, generally the odd plant here and there growing in courtyards or gardens, and gathered together 100 different biotypes. These were planted out and after a period 60 were selected for further planting in four different situations in two different sites in the area, giving a total of 240 subjects for observation concerning vigour, resistance to disease, productivity etc. After three years they sent the grapes for micro-fermentation to San Michele, and studies are presently taking place as to the quantity and type of polyphenols, ability to age, aroma.

Caprai and co. also undertook several of the tests mentioned in connection with Chianti Classico 2000, specifically concerning density – they tried up to 13,000 plants per hectare, but found that 8,000 was the highest practical number; training formation – they established that a variation of *alberello* was best; rootstock – as in many other places 420A has been found to provide the best combination of hardiness and low productivity; and seeding between rows. Using the early results of their tests, and putting their money where their mouth is, Caprai have planted 23 hectares to the best clones using *alberello* training at 8,000 plants per hectare, purchasing new small tractors to fit the scheme.

They have also amused themselves experimenting with various well-known and less well-known varieties from abroad, such as Syrah, Tannat and Grenache from France, Tempranillo from Spain and Xinomavro from Greece as well as Pinot Noir, Merlot and Cabernet Sauvignon. Their recently introduced Poggio Belvedere is a wine made from 90% Sangiovese and 10% a blend of all the rest.

Even southerners are waking up to the needs of getting the vineyard right for the challenge of the twenty-first century – or northerners and outsiders are doing it for them. An excellent example of south–north collaboration is the work being carried out by the dominant force on the Calabrian wine scene, Librandi, with the help of one of Italy's premier oenological consultants, Donato Lanati of Piemonte, and with the indirect counsel of the biggest name in Italian viticultural research today, Professor Attilio Scienza of the Agricultural Institute of the University of Milan.

The work here is not just restricted to cloning and related factors as per the Chianti Classico trials but also involves a fundamental study of the soil-types available to the producer with the aim of matching them as closely as possible to the right varieties. This because Librandi's project is to create a centre for the propagation of the most promising varieties of Calabrian origin, cultivars of which Librandi have spent several years collecting in various parts of the region.

Other aspects of the work of researchers like Scienza are highlighted by this quote from a paper given by the Professor on the subject of the propagation in various parts of Italy of Merlot:

> Merlot, in order to express its quality potential requires, more than other varieties, greater attention to the characteristics of the soil and to the ratio of fruit production to leaf-area, reducing fruit-set on the one hand and vegetative vigour on the other, improving the ratio between the surface area of the berry and its volume and, in warmer climates, retarding the tendency to precocious ripening.

As can be seen, the subject can get quite complex and technical, and I don't propose here to get into all the ins and outs of viticultural research – merely to indicate the nature and the intensity of the work that, in truth, is only beginning in the field of Italian viticulture. This work promises to bring forth, quite literally, fine fruit and the next couple of decades will indeed be an exciting time for the wines of central and southern Italy.

OENOLOGY: TYPICITY VERSUS INTERNATIONALISM

The word 'tipicità' is quintessentially Italian. Its apparent translation, 'typicity', does not actually exist in English. On the other hand, the English 'typicality' does not quite convey the flavour of 'tipicità'. To say that something is 'typical' in English is to put it in a subtly mediocre context, but the Italian word conveys nothing of mediocrity. In wine-speak, tipicità is generally something that is either distinctly negative or distinctly positive, depending on your point of view. One tends to be either for it or against it.

There is a tendency to link typicity with tradition, but this is not an entirely satisfactory association in an Italian wine context. Tradition can be an irrational, hide-bound thing, and adherence to *la tradizione* has a lot to answer for in the context of Italian wines and their struggle to gain acceptance in the world. It was in the name of tradition that people in the 1960s and 1970s, and beyond, wanted to hang on to their clapped-out old barrels, to the old, partially oxidised styles of wines, to methods of vine-growing and winemaking which had seen their day. It was in the name of tradition that new wines, for example 100% Sangiovese wines like Monte Vertine's Le Pergole Torte, than which nothing could have greater *tipicità* in a Tuscan context, were refused the DOC – for *mancanza di tipicità*, lack of typicity, an example of the confusion I am referring to – when they were probably the best wines of the year.

Typicity in its proper context is probably best defined by reference to what the French call *terroir* (Italian equivalent: *territorio*). This is an amalgam of considerations linking soil, climate and micro-climate, grape variety and customary practices. It is the role of the human, at least in the area of fine wines, to ensure that all of these come together to create a liquid which is unique, generally by following in the footsteps of one's fathers, whilst introducing such improvements as do not radically alter the nature of the product. This is the special gift of wine – its ability to transport the consumer to a small patch of the earth's surface which is alone able to bring forth such and such a combination of smells, tastes and sensations.

Italy has one of longest winemaking histories in the world. Indeed, the more ancient wine-zones of Asia Minor, Greece and Northern Africa either are or have been, for a period of centuries, under Muslim rule, which at best discourages and at worst prohibits wine production, so that Italy, with some 3,000 years of more or less enthusiastic winemaking behind her, stands as the most important repository of ancient wine lore. It was from Italy, via the Romans, that wine production spread to other countries of the ancient world – Gaul, Iberia, even the Teutonic lands. And over these millennia, the multifaceted Italian civilisation has built up hundreds of individual wine cultures, each a *territorio* unto itself.

In the past 30 years, undoubtedly, Italy has made giant strides in improving the quality of her wines, so that today they are capable of standing alongside the planet's best – and, as we have seen above, they are likely to get considerably better. At the same time, there has been a widening of the wine market to include the entire world, and the market itself has made certain demands upon production, which in turn has raised certain questions about how wine should be made.

Put most simply, the questions in the modern producer's mind is: Do I make my wine to please the market, or do I make it to please myself and my fathers? Do I aim for universality, or for individuality, for *tipicità*? If universality, will not my wine get lost in a sea of others of similar style, coming from various parts of the world, some of which can achieve a similar result at considerably lower cost? If *tipicità*, will not the market turn away, saying: this wine is too peculiar; I recognise nothing familiar in it; give me something I can feel comfortable with?

Italian winemakers and wine organisations have attempted to answer these questions in a broad gamut of ways. The extremists are those who say 'to hell with *tipicità*', the important thing is that my wines should give pleasure and satisfaction to people and not raise more questions than they are capable of answering'; or, on the other hand, those who, without really weighing up the ramifications of their actions take a rigidly conservative if not reactionary stance, saying 'I'll make my wine to please myself, and if they don't like it, let them drink something else'. The majority has sought refuge at one point or another in the middle ground.

One of the principal battles of the war centres on grape variety. As I have said elsewhere, more than once, perhaps Italy's greatest contribution to the wealth of the wine world consists in her patrimony of individual grapes, of which there remain literally hundreds, although still more hundreds, if not thousands, have drastically declined or, sadly, become extinct over the past couple of centuries. Many of these latter failed to survive the nineteenth-century onslaughts of oidium, peronospera and phylloxera, or were low-volume or in other ways problematic varieties – problems that could perhaps have been ironed out by modern methods of selection and cloning – and so were sacrificed to the gods of high-turnover during the mid-twentieth century when quantity was the name of the game.

In a land which, over the centuries, underwent a series of political, social and linguistic upheavals which effectively divided it into hundreds of fractions – and unification, we should recall, took place less than 150 years ago – each of these varieties or sub-varieties found a home a greater or lesser time ago in a particular zone or zones. In some places they have by tradition been vinified varietally. In others they have been used for specific purposes in blends, to give more colour, more perfume, greater softness or roundness, although there was, and certainly is today, a certain flexibility respecting such usages.

The essential point is that they were/are varieties which, separately or together, had stood the test of time – occasionally a very long time – in a given zone, with its particular customs and cuisine.

Now, if you introduce into a varietal wine like, say, Brunello di Montalcino, an element of Cabernet Sauvignon, or even of the less aggressive Syrah – not saying that anyone does, mind – are you not distorting Brunello's '*tipicità*' (never mind the fact that you are breaking the law)? The answer surely is yes.

On the other hand, should you introduce into your Chianti Classico an element of Cabernet or Merlot, as many do, are you really distorting the type, given that the wine is by tradition a blend? Here the answer is not so clear. Some would say you are distorting it because, although Chianti is generally a blend, the Bordeaux grapes are so characterful that the true aromatic character of Chianti becomes progressively lost the more you add. Others take the view that the Bordeaux grapes 'improve' the blend and that quality must precede authenticity. These people might maintain that it is a matter of degree – as long as you only add X% it should be all right.

The situation in Chianti Classico at the time of writing is that you may add 15% – the producers are currently requesting that this figure be increased to 20% – of grapes like Cabernet or Merlot to your Chianti and the official line is presumably that this does not denature the wine. It was 10% until 1996 and there were plenty of cries against that. It might have been 25 or even 40% – as some producers were agitating for. There is no way that Chianti Classico with 40%, or even 20%, let's be honest, of Cabernet Sauvignon can be called '*tipico*' in any traditional sense, good or bad.

My personal view, as stated elsewhere, is that the international grapes are fine in the Chianti Classico zone, for example, as long as the resulting wine does not call itself Chianti Classico. There are some splendid Cabernet or Merlot affected blends in the zone and long may they continue – as Toscana IGT.

Obviously the above arguments apply to many different grape varieties and wines in central and southern Italy; I have simply used two of the most famous as examples.

Another of the major issues on which disputes are pursued after the Italian fashion revolves around the use of oak. There is no doubt that France has influenced Italian fine wine in a much bigger way via the products of the Massif Central and Vosges than via grape varieties. Thirty years ago there was virtually no French oak in Italy, and very little in the way of small barrels of *barrique* or *tonneau* size (2.25–5 hectolitres). At that time the best producers used oak from Slavonia in ex-Yugoslavia, in sizes between 7 and 100-plus hectolitres. Others used chestnut, or acacia, or other locally available woods.

Today a major winery of a major wine zone in Italy will be full of small French oak barrels with perhaps a few from the USA, Hungary, Russia, Austria or elsewhere. Where space exists there are large, sometimes tastefully vaulted barrel rooms such as one finds in the Médoc. Where it's tight, the *barriques* can be found in twos and threes on top of or underneath *botti* (large barrels), in the fermentation or bottling areas or the tasting/hospitality room. Even the traditional *botti* are increasingly made from French oak, though the main trend in respect of large barrels is to get rid of them – of course there are exceptions.

The point about wood is that it is an ideal medium not only for maturation of wine, as it is organic, like wine itself, and slightly porous, as distinct from stainless steel – our age's other favourite winemaking material, which is inert and airtight – but also in certain circumstances for the alcoholic or malolactic fermentation of wine. A wine fermented and stored in stainless steel can develop aromas, particularly hydrogen sulphide or 'bad eggs'/'drains', via an electrochemical reaction of the sulphur in the wine with the inert container, whereas that danger does not exist in oak. A wine which has undergone one or both of its biochemical changes – from grape sugar to alcohol, from malic acid to lactic acid – is likely to have more stable tannins and pigments than a wine which never sees wood, or one which is only placed in wood after both fermentation processes are over. A wine which has been aged in oak – and here, the smaller the barrel, the greater the effect, there being a lower ratio of wine to wood-surface – will tend to be more rounded and more complete in the mouth, not to mention the extra potential for ageing accorded to the wine by the wood tannins.

It is true – and this used to be widespread, though no longer – that a wine aged in an unhygienic, poorly tended barrel can develop dirty, 'stavey' aromas. This is unlikely today, now that such dangers are understood, and it is much more probable that the aromas the wine will pick up from the wood are the vanilla of the oak itself or the toast (coffee-grounds, dark chocolate) from the char applied to the insides of the staves.

The problem, which has arisen in Italy, is that far too many wines are being made where the wood aromas dominate those of the wine. It is true that there is a certain predilection on the part of the market for wines which have a toasty vanilla smell to them, the reason being that consumers associate these smells with high quality as coming from Bordeaux or Burgundy. But at the end of the day, as they say in football-speak, it's not wood aromas that wine is supposed to be about.

In this respect one finds an amazing naivety current among Italian winemakers. Many of them seem to think that it is enough to age a wine X months in an expensive new barrel to justify a fancy packaging, an effete name and a high price. They have not cottoned on to the fact, known to the most canny winemakers, that wood should be regarded 'as a mechanism and not as a condiment'. Where a wine has a big structure and plenty of flavour it can survive an extended period in new small oak barrels, which have the greatest porosity but which yield the most aromas, without being overwhelmed. But where these features are present only to a moderate extent, in a less robust wine or a weak vintage, the smaller and the newer the barrel the more the wine is going to be taken over and lose *tipicità*.

Another aspect of modern Italian oenology that threatens *tipicità* is the increasing influence of itinerant oenological consultants. These are superstars brought in by generally wealthy proprietors keen to make their mark on the wine world. They zoom up and down the *autostrade* of Italy in high-powered cars or dash from north to south and back again by plane or helicopter, dispensing counsel as if from Olympus on high. The mobile telephone and the computer are indispensable tools of their trade. I am not suggesting that their advice is not necessary – indeed their work has done much to improve the overall standard, and certainly standing, of Italian wines, and has saved many an ignoramus with more dollars than sense from making an ass of himself in the marketplace. The risk, however, is that consciously or unconsciously they tend to stamp their mark on the wines they produce. It takes a lot of introspection and humility for such a person to put himself in the background and try and bring out in the wine only the characteristics inherent in the *territorio* and the proprietor – especially as the latter often doesn't himself quite know what he is looking for. And introspection and humility is not on the whole what the consultant oenologist is most noted for, although as in everything there are exceptions.

Yet another problem for *tipicità* is the influence of the journalists, both Italian and foreign. One well-known and well-established producer, who makes wines of delicacy rather than power – wines, that is, which generally do not do well in blind tastings or therefore score well with journalists – complained that 'if you don't get at least 90 points you can't sell your wine'; this in the context, it should be said, of wine at a fairly elevated price level. So the temptation is clearly there to make wines which will please the pundits who dish out the points, which obviously must affect the will to make it how it comes. To reverse a catchphrase: 'if it isn't working (selling), fix it'.

There is no need to specify which publications have this influence, they are well enough known. Nor, I am sure, is it in any way their intention to have this effect upon the psychology of producers. I myself dispense points in a certain context, although with no visible effect on anybody's thinking, and I am certain that I have no such intention. One highly influential Italian publication, indeed, holds as its basic creed the principle that artisanally produced products are to be encouraged; yet it is observable that all too often the best marks go to wines affected by oak and the 'international style' of winemaking – deep colour, concentration of extract, accent on primary fruit, smooth tannins from youth.

Wine criticism is a highly subjective pursuit and all the power lies in very few hands – this in itself is dangerous. No doubt, judging by the following the main pundits have, it is a necessary activity. Yet there are aspects of it which, it seems to me, do themselves invite criticism; and these are not my criticisms, but those of numerous producers with whom I have spoken, and who would of course not dare to voice them to the pundits themselves.

The policy of judging wines by pre-bottling sample is obviously open to abuse: the producer can select his barrel or tank – it would be surprising if he did not – and this is likely to be better than the most recently bottled sample. This is sometimes called the 'cuvée du journaliste'. It is even a little dodgy to ask the producer to send a bottled sample – he will send the best bottling, or even do a special bottling. The most satisfactory method, used by some, is to order the bottle from a shop or, these days, from an on-line distributor.

The practice of lining up scores of wines in a blind tasting and zooming through them at breakneck speed would seem to give short shrift to a product over which people may have sweated for months or years. Sixty wines at three minutes each, which isn't very long, will still take three hours to taste, by which time the most practised taster's palate and indeed mind – for however much you spit, some goes down – will be in no fit state to make objective judgements concerning somebody else's life work. Naturally the wines with the most obvious characteristics – of fruit aroma, of oak – are the ones most likely to grab the taster's attention and get pulled forward for a second taste, while the subtle ones are left behind. But obviousness is not necessarily a feature of tipicità, nor even of quality.

As a wine journalist who has done and continues to do all of these things from time to time, if increasingly reluctantly, I am not trying to apportion blame or to take a holier-than-thou stance. I am merely commenting on the dangers of the profession. I would take the view that the wine is more important than any judgement about it. The producer is more important than the critic, since we can still drink wine without critics, but not without producers; and the critic needs to bear that in mind.

It would be impertinent to suggest that Italy is the only country to have problems relating to tipicità; other old world producing nations certainly have them, as indeed do new world nations, along many of the same lines. It's just that Italy, having more points of difference, is more impaled on the horns of the dilemma than most.

My own view is that it is important to differentiate fine wines the one from the other as much as possible, not by deliberately going out of one's way to produce quirky smells and tastes but simply by the constant effort to bring forth from one's small patch of earth a product which reflects that patch's unique character. This means not blending classic wines with foreign grapes, be they international or from other zones, should said grapes be of a dominating type; using oak as a means of vinification and ageing and not as a seasoning; retaining such ageing characteristics as the wine traditionally possessed (firm acids and tannins), allowing them if necessary to be harsh in youth in the interests of greater glories farther down the road, despite the urgings of press and pundits calling for wine to taste like breakfast: coffee, chocolate, fruit-juice, jam, vanilla and toast.

This should **not** be read as a plea to Italians to kick out all their *barriques* and international grapes. There is a place for them too – indeed some of the Italian Cabernet–Merlot wines and Italo–Gallic blends that have developed over the past 30 years are among the country's finest and most creative wines today – just don't confuse them with the classics. In this context I fully agree with Angelo Gaja when he rants about the injustice of people saying that Italy should not produce the sort of wines that the whole of the rest of the world is producing merely because she is capable, unlike them, of something else.

Nor should what I say be interpreted as a rejection of modern technology – like the barrel, technology can be a highly positive force, used correctly, that is to say, subordinately. But technology alone, or technology supreme, can produce 'technological' wines, wines which may be analytically flawless but in some undefinable way lack what can only be described as soul. The world is going too technological in too many directions already. Surely wine's special role is to resist this trend towards homogeneity and to hold out for individuality. To carry the point into the philosophical realm, such individuality need not be taken as an indicator of ontological multiplicity: in this context, uniformity and unity are, paradoxically, a pole apart.

Remembering and applying these principles will, I feel, prove beneficial for Italian viniculture in the long run, not just spiritually but commercially. Wine people will always in the end come looking for something different, and Italy in her own long-term interests should take care to maintain her differences, not, certainly, to the exclusion of international styles, but as the golden arrow in her quiver.

2

Central Italy West

If the northwest, especially Piemonte, is the most exciting wine-producing zone of Italy, and if the northeast is the most 'international', the centre west, in particular Tuscany, is undoubtedly the most dynamic. This is the engine-room of the sometimes-called Italian wine *rinascimento* (the French word *renaissance* is usually used, but the Italian *rinascimento* would seem more appropriate), just as it was the epicentre of the cultural and spiritual earthquake that shook the world in the fifteenth century.

The Apennine ridge runs right through central Italy like a backbone, creating a definite geographical split between east and west. With one or two exceptions, however, the main one being the Gran Sasso at just over 2,900 metres, the Apennines are a modest range of mountains compared with the Alps. Driving across them between, say, Bologna and Florence, or Forlì and Pontassieve, or Fano and Arezzo, or Ancona and Perugia, or Pescara and Rome may be an exhilarating up-and-over motoring experience, but it does not have the breathtaking quality of a crossing of the Alps.

This does not, of course, prevent the Apennines from being an important influence on climate and microclimate, and hence on viticulture, in the zone. Conditions south and west of the ridge are a mix of the mountainous and the Mediterranean, but with more contrast than east of the ridge, there being much more distance between the two, especially in Tuscany and Umbria; the latter, in fact, is the only landlocked region south of the Po. In the north of Tuscany, on the southern foothills of the Apennines east of Florence, the climate is relatively continental, with cold winters and hot dry summers, the mountains being important for their protection against the *tramontana* – the north wind. Heading south of the mountains – that's to say in Chianti Classico, Siena, western Umbria and northern Latium – the ubiquitous hills offer their own protection, while rivers like the upper Arno and upper Tiber, and lakes like Trasimeno, Corbara and Bolseno are more important as temperature moderators than the somewhat distant Tyrrhenian Sea. In this sector altitude plays a significant role in wine quality. The hills of the landlocked wine-growing areas may be anything up to 600 metres plus, but with important exceptions, the best red wines generally come from grapes grown at between 250 and 500 metres. White wine-grapes may succeed at altitudes up to 700 metres.

As one heads west towards the Tyrrhenian Sea the hills get lower and the wine-styles change, becoming according to some less elegant, according to others more generous due to riper tannins and lower acid levels. There is, indeed, a developing success story at or near sea-level from south of Livorno down to around Suvereto, then again from Grosseto south to the Latium border: a reclaimed marshland called the Maremma (*mare* = sea). Mean temperatures here are significantly higher than towards the mountains. Native varieties tend to come fleshier and juicier, a style which the world today seems to appreciate, calling it 'fruit-driven'; while French varieties, especially those associated with Bordeaux, have thrived. In recent years there has been a steady flow, bordering on a gush, of inland producers purchasing land here, either to be able to use the riper grapes for blending or for purposes of making wine under one of the up-and-coming DOCs – Bolgheri, Val di Cornia-Suvereto, Morellino di Scansano, Massa Marittima.

Parenthetically, to put a different light on it, the whole of central Italy, as well as being wine country, is olive country. Farther north than the Tuscan and Romagnan Apennines one cannot succeed with olive trees in Italy, except in the vicinity of Italy's largest lake, Garda, near Verona. This juxtaposition of the vine and the olive tree is quintessential to this land of the Etruscans, and while such a meeting exists elsewhere in Italy, especially in the south, in no other area is oil of such personality matched by red wine of such grandeur.

In such a large zone it is impossible to generalise about soils. Of course, drainage is important always, and this is provided in a number of ways. In Tuscany there is the famous *galestro*, a crumbly, schistous rock which provides the perfect structure for adequate but not excessive retention of water. Soil of a similar argillo–calcareous chemical make-up in more solid or more granular form is called

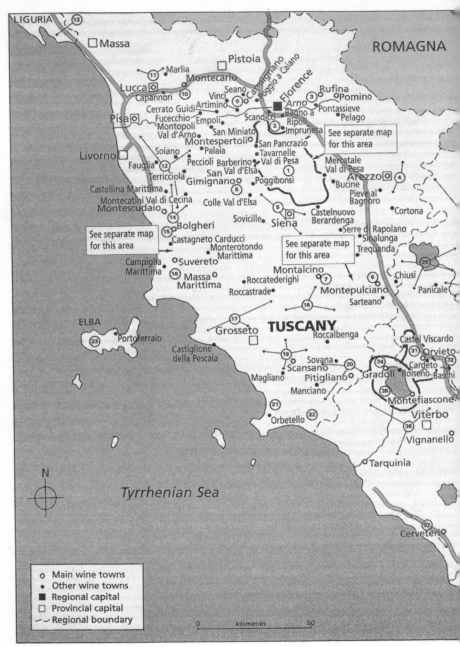

kilometres   50

Central Italy West

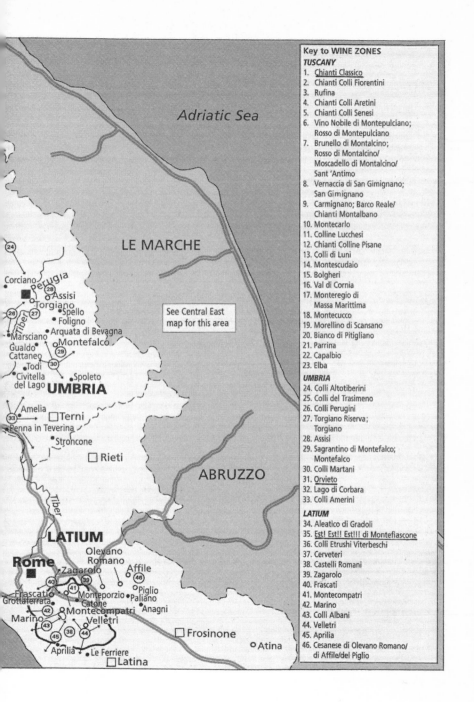

Adriatic Sea

LE MARCHE

Corciano
Perugia
Assisi
Torgiano
Spello
Foligno
Arquata di Bevagna
Marsciano
Montefalco
Gualdo
Cattaneo
Todi
Civitella del Lago
UMBRIA
Spoleto
Amelia
Terni
Penna in Teverina
Stroncone
Rieti

ABRUZZO

See Central East map for this area

Tiber

LATIUM
Rome
Olevano Romano
Zagarolo
Affile
Frascati
Grottaferrata
Monteporzio
Piglio
Paliano
Catone
Anagni
Montecompatri
Marino
Velletri
Aprilia
Le Ferriere
Latina
Frosinone
Atina

Key to WINE ZONES

TUSCANY
1. Chianti Classico
2. Chianti Colli Fiorentini
3. Rufina
4. Chianti Colli Aretini
5. Chianti Colli Senesi
6. Vino Nobile di Montepulciano; Rosso di Montepulciano
7. Brunello di Montalcino; Rosso di Montalcino/ Moscadello di Montalcino/ Sant 'Antimo
8. Vernaccia di San Gimignano; San Gimignano
9. Carmignano; Barco Reale/ Chianti Montalbano
10. Montecarlo
11. Colline Lucchesi
12. Chianti Colline Pisane
13. Colli di Luni
14. Montescudaio
15. Bolgheri
16. Val di Cornia
17. Monteregio di Massa Marittima
18. Montecucco
19. Morellino di Scansano
20. Bianco di Pitigliano
21. Parrina
22. Capalbio
23. Elba

UMBRIA
24. Colli Altotiberini
25. Colli del Trasimeno
26. Colli Perugini
27. Torgiano Riserva; Torgiano
28. Assisi
29. Sagrantino di Montefalco; Montefalco
30. Colli Martani
31. Orvieto
32. Lago di Corbara
33. Colli Amerini

LATIUM
34. Aleatico di Gradoli
35. Est! Est!! Est!!! di Montefiascone
36. Colli Etrushi Viterbeschi
37. Cerveteri
38. Castelli Romani
39. Zagarolo
40. Frascati
41. Montecompatri
42. Marino
43. Colli Albani
44. Velletri
45. Aprilia
46. Cesanese di Olevano Romano/ di Affile/del Piglio

27

albarese. In parts of the Maremma, interestingly, there is a lot of gravel, as in Bordeaux. In white wine areas such as Orvieto and Frascati there is *tufo*, very similar to that of classic French white wine areas such as Vouvray.

As for exposure, with so many hills to choose from, it is not difficult to find a good south, southeast or southwest slope. Less common are flatland sites, which is fine where quality wine is concerned, less desirable when one is trying to compete in the low-price category, as producers, or at least industrialists, were here until the 1970s. This is a crucial factor in the need to work a reperception of these wines in world eyes, because with labour costs as high, yields as limited, and blending with cheaper liquids from outside the area as controlled as they have become it is no longer possible to achieve the 'cheap and cheerful' plonks that earned Italy in general, and Tuscany and the Veneto in particular, their industrial reputation in the years following World War II.

The natives of these parts, descendants of the Etruscans, the Umbri and the imperial Romans, are a self-assured lot, impressed neither by the sabre-rattling secessionists of the north nor by the corrupt and idle – as they see them – of the south whom, however, they despise considerably less actively than do their northern brethren. These are people who have learned, through centuries of political chaos and upheaval, just to get on with life, if necessary, almost preferably, without an effective government. They are the quintessential Italians, theirs being the dialect which became the national language, theirs being the heritage of perhaps the greatest empire and some of the greatest paintings, sculpture, architecture and poetry the world has ever known. Theirs, indeed, being a land to which the world is irresistibly drawn, as the hordes of tourists flooding Florence or Siena or Rome for most of the year will confirm.

No doubt the beauty of the countryside is a major factor in bringing the moneyed classes here from other parts of Italy and the world. Not for nothing are the hills of central Tuscany nicknamed 'Chiantishire', although Germans and Americans, not to say Swiss and Japanese, seem thicker on the ground these days than the Brits from whose presence the nickname is obviously derived. The superb – and superbly preserved – medieval cities, with their almost overwhelming wealth of culture and history, are another irresistible draw: think of Tuscany's Florence and Siena, Lucca and Pisa,

Livorno, Arezzo, San Gimignano and Volterra, Montepulciano and Montalcino; think of Umbria's Perugia and Assisi, Orvieto and Todi. Latium, for its part, may not have a number of historic cities, but it does have the big one: Rome.

For nearly 3,000 years wine has been an integral part of the culture of central Italy. Artefacts attesting to the fact that the Etruscans, who first came to the area, probably from the east, around the ninth century BC, were winemakers and bibbers have been traced back to the seventh century BC. Even today there are names associated with wine production in central Italy that were on the scene six, seven, or more centuries ago: Antinori, Firidolfi, Frescobaldi, Gherardesca, Guicciardini, Ricasoli, Strozzi. All of these, Antinori above the rest, have been involved in one way or another in the return of the wines of central Italy to respectability. But there are plenty of new names on the wine scene too, especially in Tuscany, and more and more every year.

One of the features of this migration of the rich to Tuscany and Umbria has been the need for professional viticultural and oenological advice. The people who have purchased abandoned or, more recently, restored properties at ever-soaring prices from the 1960s through to and beyond the present, are on the whole wine ignoramuses, quite unlike the hands-on growers and producers of the northwest. They are people who often have more money than they know what to do with, who may even be looking for a handy little loss-maker – which the vast majority of Tuscan wine operations succeed to a greater or lesser extent in being – for tax purposes, who fancy the idea of being the lord of a great wine-estate but who haven't the first idea how to go about it.

Step forward the Oenological consultant, a demi-god descending from the heights of Conegliano or San Michele all'Adige or Alba, the nation's top three specialist wine academies, or from the oenological or agrarian faculty of one of the universities to offer the bewildered proprietor the chance of making Italy's 'greatest wine'. I was told by one of these superstars that whenever he interviews a prospective client he asks them: 'What do you want?'. Invariably they answer: 'I want to make great wine'. He replies: 'If you will make every investment I ask you to, and ensure that every instruction that I give you is followed, then I can make you great wine'. This, he said, tends to have something of a dampening effect on those whose capital is not of the inexhaustible variety.

The brightest lights in the established consultancy constellation today are: Nicolò d'Afflitto, Franco Bernabei, Maurizio Castelli, Stefano Chioccioli, Riccardo Cotarella, Carlo Ferrini, Vittorio Fiore, Attilio Pagli and Paolo Vaggagini, the last named tending to specialise in the wines of Montalcino and Montepulciano, as does Pietro Rivella; also Donato Lanati who, though based in Piemonte, handles some of the hottest accounts in Tuscany. Among the doyens of the genre are Giulio Gambelli and the master of them all, Giacomo Tachis; emerging names include Alberto Antonini, Luca d'Attoma, Roberto Cipresso, Giorgio Marone, Gabriella Tani.

As for wine styles, you can get just about anything you want from somewhere in central Italy, although the emphasis is very much on red table wine. Within this category there is everything from light everyday quaffing red to the big and full and, at least according to the hype, very long lasting. And, of course, there is the amazing phenomenon of the SuperTuscan.

There is, however, an increasing amount of good dry white table wine amid the rivers of Trebbiano and Malvasia-based mediocrity. Some of this derives from native grape varieties, which have returned to favour after a longish period in the doldrums of the industrial era. But most of the running is being made by whites based on varieties of Gallic origin and featuring some blends which would make a French classicist's hair stand on end, for example: Sauvignon Blanc together with Chardonnay and Gewürztraminer – i.e. Bordeaux with Burgundy and Alsace.

Passito wines play a small but significant role in the centre. Best known is Vin Santo, which comes both in unfortified and fortified form, though the latter is rarely of much interest. There is also a tiny but increasingly important production of late-harvest sweet whites, including botrytised or 'noble rot' styles, mainly in the Orvieto area. Among sweet reds there are scattered examples of such oddities as Moscato Rosa, Aleatico and Montefalco's *recioto*-like Sagrantino Passito.

PRODUCTION AREAS

The best-known wine area in Tuscany, if not in all Italy, historically and actually, has got to be <u>Chianti</u>, a name first recorded in connection with wine, white in this instance, in the year 1398.

The name actually refers to a geographical area, originally Ager Clantius, later Kiantis, delineated by the Pesa and Arbia streams and including the central Tuscan communes of Radda, Castellina and Gaiole in what is today the province of Siena. To these had been added, by 1716 when Grand Duke Cosimo III of Tuscany issued his famous *Bando* or decree delineating four Tuscan quality wine areas, naming Chianti as one of the four, the commune of Greve (in whose charming triangular *piazza* the wines were historically marketed) with its important *frazione* Panzano as well as fractions of other communes – the 1716 version being, in fact, very similar to the Chianti Classico zone of today.

These communes, together with sections of San Casciano Val di Pesa, Tavarnelle Val di Pesa, Barberino Val d'Elsa and Poggibonsi to the north or west, and Castelnuovo Berardenga to the south and east, have combined since 1932 to form the classic Chianti area known, appropriately, as Chianti Classico. The chief production remains, of course, the Sangiovese-based Chianti Classico DOCG, although as every year goes by there is more and more experimentation having little to do with traditional practices (more in the section on Chianti Classico, under Sangiovese, and in the chapter on International Varieties). Currently, Chianti Classico may be made from Sangiovese at 75–100%, Canaiolo at up to 10%, Malvasia Bianca and Trebbiano at up to 6% and other grapes 'recommended or authorised' (read mainly Bordeaux varieties and Syrah, but increasingly lesser Tuscan natives like Colorino and Malvasia Nera) at up to 15% – soon to become 20%.

It was also in 1932 that six other zones peripheral to Chianti Classico, which, having noted the success of the name Chianti on the market and having adopted similar practices in their vineyards as well as the use of the historic name for their wines, were granted the right to sell their product as 'Chianti' with their own geographical name attached. At the same time provision was made to allow the use of the name Chianti, with no attachment, to be used in other areas of central Tuscany. All the original Chianti producers got out of it was the right to append the epithet 'Classico' to their name. This act of piracy (which should be reversed) is considered elsewhere.

The most important of these subsidiary areas, Rufina, is a small zone in the Apennine foothills on either side of the Sieve River, which flows into the Arno east of Florence and into the hills beyond.

It is centred on the commune of Rufina (pronounced ROO-fee-na and not to be confused with the producer Ruffino – roof-FEE-no – which it invariably is) but extends into Pontassieve and one or two others communes.

On the high slopes above Rufina is the village of Pomino, another of Grand Duke Cosimo III's four nominees for demarcation in 1716, with DOCs Rosso and Bianco of somewhat Frenchified style. The DOC Rosso includes both Cabernets as well as Merlot, and Pinot Nero, on a Sangiovese base; the Bianco is based on Pinot Bianco and Chardonnay.

The other sub-zones of so-called Chianti are all, like Rufina, peripheral to Classico and surround it like a circle. Moving clockwise from Rufina at around one o'clock is Colli Aretini, centred on Arezzo, at approximately 3 o'clock. Between 5 and 7 o'clock is the sizeable area known as Colli Senesi, which takes in important production zones in their own right such as Montepulciano, Montalcino and San Gimignano.

Montespertoli, a relatively recent addition not included among the original six, lies at around 9 o'clock in the near west, while farther out towards the west, between 9 and 10 o'clock, is the sub-zone Colline Pisane. At around 11 o'clock is the area known as Montalbano, which also takes in Carmignano, and at around 12 o'clock, is that called Colli Fiorentini, situated, as the name suggests, of the hills around the city of Florence.

Internationally the most famous Tuscan wine-area after Chianti is Montalcino, which centres on a striking medieval hilltop commune about 40 kilometres south of Siena. The name derives from the Latin *Mons Ilcinus*, mountain of the Holm oak, the town's symbol, and appears in three DOC(G)s, Brunello, Rosso and Moscadello di Montalcino. For purposes of bringing within the system all those 'experimental' wines happening here, as in so many places, the multi-DOC Sant'Antimo, named after a superb Benedictine abbey 15 or so kilometres south of the town, has been established, covering Chardonnay, Sauvignon, Pinot Grigio, Pinot Nero, Sauvignon, Merlot, as well as a Rosso (including Novello), a Bianco, a Vin Santo and an Occhio di Pernice (see Glossary).

Half an hour's drive east of Montalcino is another marvellous medieval hilltop town, Montepulciano (from Latin *Mons Politianus*), which has a Sangiovese-based DOCG (Vino Nobile) and DOC (Rosso) to its name. Here Sangiovese is called Prugnolo

Gentile, not because it is gentle – far from it, some of the hardest Sangioveses in Tuscany come from here – but because it is said to be of lofty breeding, genteel. Much of its production in the past – it was a papal favourite as far back as the fourteenth century – was in fact in the hands of the local nobility. Hence the denomination Vino Nobile di Montepulciano DOCG. Indeed, in 1680 Francesco Redi went one further hailing it as 'of every wine the king', a claim with which other producing zones of Tuscany, let alone Italy, might justifiably take issue today.

A new DOC, Orcia, between Montalcino and Montepulciano, featuring wines based on Sangiovese and Trebbiano, came on stream in 2000.

West of Florence, also half an hour's drive, in the Montalbano area, is the hilltop town of <u>Carmignano</u>, which gives its name to yet another of Grand Duke Cosimo III's four quality areas, produced on the surrounding slopes. Grapes grown here are mainly Sangiovese, but the denomination – re-established in 1975 after a long period in the doldrums, mainly by the efforts of the premier producer, Count Ugo Contini Bonacossi of Tenuta di Capezzana – saved the producers the heartache of having to pretend otherwise by specifically including Bordeaux varieties in the blend. DOCs Barco Reale and Rosato are basically cascades (see Glossary) from the DOCG. The DOC also covers Vin Santo and Occhio di Pernice, and Chardonnay has a certain presence in this tiny area.

Also from the west side of Florence, but south, slightly nearer to Siena, comes the only white member of Tuscany's DOCG set, Vernaccia di <u>San Gimignano</u>, from a grape which by the way bears no resemblance whatsoever to any other of that name (the word derives from the Latin *vernaculus* = home-born; cf. 'vernacular'). San Gimignano, yet another picturesque medieval hilltop town, is known to tourists worldwide for its several very tall towers which, apparently, were much more numerous in the Middle Ages. These days, together with improving white wines, an increasing number of reds – Sangiovese-based, of course – are issuing from this zone, a few at quite elevated quality level, leading some to conclude that it is really a red-wine area *manqué* and that it only perseveres with its often boring and overpriced whites because of successful marketing. This movement has been officialised with the coming of the San Gimignano DOC which covers *Rosso* and *Rosato* as well as Vin Santo.

Driving west again from Carmignano one arrives in the province of Lucca, another superb historic city, its most distinctive feature being intact medieval walls and a *piazza* based on the shape of the ancient Roman arena. Wines associated with Lucca are <u>Montecarlo</u> and <u>Colline Lucchesi</u>, both allowing fairly complex blends for their Rosso and Bianco, Montecarlo's having more of a French nuance. Montecarlo Rosso DOC may include both types of Cabernet, Merlot and Syrah as well as Sangiovese, Canaiolo, Ciliegiolo, Colorino and Malvasia Nera. The Bianco allows for the inclusion of Sémillon, Sauvignon, Pinot Grigio, Pinot Bianco and Roussanne with the more typical Trebbiano and Vermentino.

The above are the principal wine-producing areas of inland, mainly upland, Tuscany. Closer to the Tyrrhenian Sea, along the coastal strip south of Livorno known as the northern Maremma or Costa degli Etruschi, there are various areas which have come from nowhere in the past few years – usually very few indeed – to the accompaniment of great international acclaim. If the spirit of experimentation is strong elsewhere in Tuscany and central Italy, here it is a major driving force, partly perhaps because these areas do not have a long tradition of fine-winemaking, having in low-lying places been malarial marshland until well into the twentieth century (Mussolini, apart from making the trains run on time, also finished off the work of draining these pestilential places); and partly because certain of the wines produced here have enjoyed amazing success in world markets in the past few years.

Principal among these is undoubtedly <u>Sassicaia</u>, from the 1994 vintage an officially recognised sub-zone of the DOC <u>Bolgheri</u>, named after a charmingly arty village near to, indeed part of the commune of, Castagneto Carducci, which latter, larger but scarcely less picturesque, sits on a height a few kilometres inland from the coast. The success of the Bordeaux-inspired wines of Bolgheri has encouraged producers in the immediate vicinity and beyond, in <u>Montescudaio</u> slightly to the north, for example, and <u>Val di Cornia/Suvereto</u> to the south, to aim for really high quality at the upper end of the price spectrum, and not just with Bordeaux grapes but with Tuscan varieties too, notably Sangiovese and the under-rated white Vermentino. This latter, associated today principally with Sardinia, is in fact a variety linking the entire Italian Riviera from Tuscany right round to the French border.

Farther south still, in the province of Grosseto in the <u>Maremma</u>

proper, while the Bordeaux grapes are a growing presence it is good old Sangiovese that makes the strongest showing in the DOC areas <u>Massa Marittima</u>, <u>Scansano</u> and <u>Parrina</u>, not to mention the recently established <u>Montecucco</u>, more or less linking Montalcino and Scansano. Not many producers have begun operating in this new area – Livio Sassetti of Montalcino's Pertimali is one – but now that Scansano land prices have risen sharply others can be expected to move in decisively.

Scansano, for its part, has experienced an extraordinary re-emergence in recent times, with various major producers, including Antinori, Barbi Colombini, Jacopo Biondi-Santi, Brancaia, Cecchi, Fonterutoli, Poliziano and Querciabella buying a stake in what they see as a bright future. Massa Marittima is now witnessing something of an awakening too, with the fame of Moris Farms spreading and with Ezio Rivella, ex of Banfi in Montalcino, and San Felice of Castelnuovo Berardenga in Chianti Classico establishing vineyards here as well. Sangiovese is also the principal variety on the island of *Elba* which lies off the Maremma coast, where the DOC discipline also features two grapes associated with the south: Aleatico, which makes sweet red wines in Puglia; and Ansonica, a characterful white grape native to Sicily where it is known as Inzolia.

Various attempts have been and are being made to bring the straggling *vini da tavola* of superior quality – sometimes known as SuperTuscans – within the system. One is the DOC <u>Colli dell'Etruria Centrale</u>, which coincides with the Chianti delimited area in the widest sense, and whose *disciplinare*, red wine-wise, is not so very different from that of Chianti (So why use it?, you ask. Answer: very few people do). The Bianco is slightly less pointless, giving producers the option of reducing Trebbiano to a minimum of 50% of the blend (the rest being made up, generally, of the French white varieties); most quality growers would reduce it to zero.

But Colli dell'Etruria Centrale is neither varietally nor geographically adequate to meet a situation in which quality red wines of less than 50% Sangiovese are rife. The battle has raged for some time between growers on the one hand (No!) and industrialists on the other (Yes!) as to whether there shall be a DOC Toscana covering the whole of the territory and allowing just about anything, or whether an eventual new DOC should cover only the recognised quality areas. Those who say no point to the fact that, already, there exists an IGT <u>Toscana</u> (or <u>Toscano</u>, used as a masculine adjective) which should keep everyone happy, and which indeed is being increasingly resorted to. The concern of the industrialists, they maintain, is more in the area of price than of quality. One can sympathise with both positions.

There are a number of Tuscan DOC/place names which I haven't mentioned for the reason that they are too obscure, or too new, or both, to have amounted to anything in the market-place. Some of them may be mentioned later.

Producers in <u>Umbria</u>, the region east of southern Tuscany and northern Latium, backed up by the Apennines and split east from west by the Tiber, often complain that they are considered by wine writers and others as nothing much more than an appendage of Tuscany. I myself have been taken to task for this, but I have to say at the risk of sounding unrepentant that there is some truth in the rumour, since the dominant red grape here is the Tuscan Sangiovese and some of the biggest names on the Umbrian wine scene either belong to or are controlled by Tuscans: e.g. Antinori at Castello della Sala, Orvieto. Adding insult to injury, even the Tiber rises in Tuscany – just.

It would be grossly unfair, however, to exaggerate this influence. For example the wines of <u>Torgiano</u> – tantamount to saying the wines of Lungarotti, the only significant producer and virtual inventor of the denomination – while grapewise mainly Tuscan or French, have a unique character of their own. This is mainly manifested by Torgiano Riserva, a DOCG blend based on Sangiovese which may be aged, or rather refined, up to 10 years before being released on the market – something very few Tuscans would willingly do. Permitted additional varieties include Montepulciano. Other varietals included in the Torgiano *disciplinare* – as DOC, not DOCG – are Cabernet Sauvignon, Pinot Nero, Pinot Grigio, Chardonnay and Riesling Italico. There is also a Bianco, a Rosso and a Spumante.

Another giant of Umbrian originality, in quality if not quantity, are the red wines of <u>Montefalco</u> based on the extraordinary Sagrantino grape, exclusive to this tiny area. The Secco and Passito are DOCG, while Montefalco Rosso, though including Sagrantino, is mainly Sangiovese. Montefalco Bianco is a blend of Grechetto, Trebbiano and other white grapes.

One of Italy's more interesting white wines comes from around

Orvieto, an ancient Etruscan stronghold superbly perched on a high outcrop of *tufo*, with its famous cathedral the facade of which is considered by many the finest in Italy. Orvieto, which may be Secco or Amabile, is a blend of several grapes, including Umbrians Grechetto and Drupeggio, as well as Trebbiano Toscano, here called Procanico, Verdello, Malvasia and others. Increasingly, good to excellent Grechetto is produced here under the denomination IGT Umbria. The same is true of Sangiovese-based, Cabernet-influenced red wines, which, as at San Gimignano, are being discovered to have considerable potential here.

Which concludes the list of Umbria's unique wine-areas. Others of a more or less minor nature (vinously) include Assisi; Colli Altotiberini from the Tiber valley north of Perugia; Colli Amerini from the southwest of the region on the Latium border; Colli Martani, from around the picturesque tourist-town of Todi; Colli Perugini, from around the regional capital Perugia; and Colli del Trasimeno, from the shores of the lake where Hannibal whipped the Romans in the third century BC. All of these are more or less of Tuscan typicity, the reds being based on Sangiovese and the whites on Trebbiano/Malvasia; although there is the odd non-Tuscan note struck in the form of Montepulciano and Ciliegiolo and even Barbera cropping up among the reds and Grechetto, Verdicchio and even Garganega among the whites. Colli Martani has a Grechetto *in purezza* on its books, and pure Grechetto is also produced in Montefalco.

There are several wine-producing areas in the region of Lazio or Latium, most of them having little significance in the context of the international wine market. The outstanding exception is the hilly zone called Castelli Romani stretching south and east from Rome's outskirts, embracing, principally, Frascati but also such other moderately well-known names as Marino, Velletri and Colli Albani. The vast majority of the production of these areas is white table wine based on Trebbiano and the equally boring Malvasia di Candia, almost all of it plonk – though a tiny handful of serious growers, using the superior Malvasia Puntinata as well as Viognier and other French varieties of either hue, are now making some exciting stuff, red table wines and dessert wines as well as dry whites.

The only other area with a name – apart from the bit of Orvieto that sticks into northern Lazio from Umbria – is Montefiascone whose Est! Est!! Est!!! is better known for the fanciful tale of its discovery in medieval times than for the latter-day quality of its Trebbiano-based white. Other moderately significant production areas include Cerveteri on the coast northwest of Rome, although the main claim to fame of Cerveteri is not wine but an extraordinary Etruscan necropolis which visitors to the town are strongly urged to visit; and Aprilia, south of Rome. The rest, whether recognised as DOCs 20 odd years ago or very recently, are of such an obscurity as almost to render the mention of their names a waste of space. It is a pity that this also applies to the wines of the Ciociaria Hills, east of Rome, where the native red grape called Cesanese – del Piglio, di Affile, di Olevano Romano – is capable of making wine of more interest than most of the existing stuff would suggest.

GRAPES, WINES AND PRODUCERS – RED

SANGIOVESE

Unlike the northwest, with its numerous indigenous grape varieties all jostling for position in this locality or that; or the northeast, with its arrays of mainly international but also local varieties; or indeed the south and islands, like the northwest a hotbed of ampelographical heterogeneity; the centre of Italy is dominated by just one grape, Sangiovese.

Almost certainly of Tuscan origin, the nation's most-planted variety – around 100,000 hectares, producing around one-tenth of all wine in the land – is totally dominant in Tuscany as in Romagna, with a major presence in the Marche and in Umbria, as well as having a lesser but significant presence in Latium, Campania, Puglia, Sardinia and Sicily. Indeed Sangiovese is planted in at least 16 of Italy's 20 regions, not to mention in several wine regions of the world, with increasingly impressive results in California and Australia. With Barbera, Sangiovese is undisputedly the nearest Italy gets to an 'international' variety.

It is suggested with no great conviction by Calò, Scienza and Costacurta in the recently published bible on Italian grape varieties, *Vitigni d'Italia* (Calderini, Bologna 2001), that the name may derive from the north Tuscan dialectal *sangiovannina*, indicating an early-budding grape. Others claim more poetically, if not necessarily more accurately, that the name comes from the Latin *Sanguis Jovis*, meaning 'blood of Jove', indicating that the wine was traditionally seen as a substantial brew; cf. Bull's Blood. Sub-varieties and clones abound, even within small areas, sometimes graced with exotic or parochial names like Sangiogheto (the first recorded name, by Soderini in his *La Coltivazione delle viti*, 1590), San Zoveto, Sangioveto (in central Tuscany and Elba), Brunello (in Montalcino, though for fear of Californian rip-offs the name no longer applies to a grape but only to a wine), Prugnolo Gentile (Montepulciano), Morellino (southern Maremma), and Romagnolo (Romagna), all of which have greater marketing than ampelographical significance. The fundamental distinction, it has been confirmed by Calò as well as Silvestroni and Intrieri, is between Sangiovese Grosso and Sangiovese Piccolo, the adjectives mainly referring to berry size. Contrary to what one might expect, the Grosso, corresponding to the principal biotypes cultivated in Romagna and Tuscany, is generally considered superior, and is more diffuse. But the reality is that over a period of time within a given area it becomes difficult if not impossible to distinguish between them, giving one to think that perhaps there is no fundamental distinction after all.

Certain it is, at any rate, that numerous sub-varieties and clones exist in today's vineyards, with very different behaviour patterns, especially in terms of production volume, although soils, exposure, altitude, availability of water and training systems all play their part. Perhaps the main point to remember in respect of Sangiovese is that it is, as one producer described it, an 'unstable' variety; or, as another put it, it is highly 'adaptable', capable of changing radically, even morphologically in terms of leaf shape, bunch character and berry size, according to its immediate environment. So that, whereas a Merlot or Cabernet Sauvignon will behave similarly from one commune to the next or from one part of the vineyard to another, confining its variations by and large to sugar and acid content, the same Sangiovese planted on two different parts of the same slope may develop the kind of dramatically diverse characteristics described. To put this in perspective, while in all of Italy there are only a handful of clones of Cabernet Sauvignon, in the commune of Montalcino alone the different types of Sangiovese number well into the 30s.

Currently, at a time of widespread replanting to replace the many vineyards laid down between the late 1950s and the early 1970s, numerous research programmes are taking place under the auspices of the major nurseries like Rauscedo as well as of various large private producers (Antinori, Banfi, San Felice) and growers' consortia (Chianti Classico, Montalcino, Montepulciano) in conjunction with university agricultural faculties (Firenze, Pisa, Bologna, Piacenza, Milano) to determine the best clones in terms of productivity and freedom from virus infection, most compatible root-stocks, best training systems and planting densities, as well as optimum viticultural systems – seeding between rows, between alternate rows, with what. This is dealt with in greater detail in the chapter on Vine and Wine.

Carefully tended, in a good year, Sangiovese will produce no more, and from a quality-conscious producer considerably less, than 8–10 tonnes of fruit per hectare,[1] will have a fairly extended growing season, being harvested from mid September well into October, and will yield grapes of medium colour, firm though balanced acidity and ripe tannins together with an aromatic scale in which morello cherry, or perhaps more precisely what Americans call 'sour cherry', and dried tea-leaf are features. Overproduced, in adverse conditions, a lesser Sangiovese will be sour in the negative sense, tough, weak in aroma and colour, desperately needing the kind of correction industrialists used to give it legally and occasionally continue to give it illegally with wines or musts from Abruzzo and points south.

As Giacomo Tachis puts it, the Sangiovese is a 'genius of difficult and bizarre character'. It is very susceptible not only to soil variations but also to the vagaries of the weather – again, much more so than the 'international' varieties. And this, he says, applies not so much to ripening in terms of sugar content as to the extract contained in the grape's skin. This polyphenolic content varies from year to year not only in quantity but also in quality. For this reason, savvy growers will not plant all their vineyards to a single clone, but will mix them in such a way as to maximise their chances of obtaining a reasonable crop every vintage.

As Vittorio Fiore, another of Tuscany's leading oenologists/consultants, says: 'It is undoubtedly a variety difficult to tame

---

1 Italians express production figures not in hectolitres of wine per hectare, as do the French, but in quintals (100 kilos) or tonnes (1,000 kilos) of grapes per hectare. To calculate approximate hectolitres per hectare it is necessary to multiply the tonnes by 7. Thus 10 tonnes of fruit will yield approximately 70 hectolitres of wine.

mainly due to the high level of polyphenols which make it, even when apparently ripe, hard and impenetrable'. Hence its nickname Ingannacane, 'fools the dogs', which, when they steal it off the vine, instead of sweet fruit get a mouthful of hard tannins. But in the end it 'gives great satisfaction, especially in the right conditions, as do exist in many parts of Tuscany, producing, if properly worked, wines of great power and marvellous quality'.

Another important feature of the Sangiovese is its ability to blend in well with other varieties, whether in majority or minority proportion. More on this in the following paragraphs and in the chapter on blends.

The wines in Tuscany: Chianti Classico

What is Chianti Classico?

Any debate centring on this world famous wine must begin with that question, the initial answer to which must be: We don't know, or, We're not sure. While Brunello di Montalcino has at least a clear ampelographical identity – 100% Sangiovese – Chianti Classico has gone from being a blend of Tuscan grapes, including whites, to a blend of Tuscan plus international grapes to a single varietal and back to a blend of Tuscan grapes, without the whites, all in the last quarter of the twentieth century. And all of these identities have persisted into the twentieth-first century.

Certainly, Chianti (Classico) is and always has been a Sangiovese-based wine, and as we have seen one of the principal problems the winemaker has, in respect of Sangiovese, is how to deal with the grape's polyphenols, inclined as they are to be deficient in colouring matter and sometimes overabundant in hard tannins. So in a sense, the history of Chianti is the history of the various attempts to deal with these substances.

The principal method used for softening tannins and achieving satisfactory colour levels has traditionally been mixing and blending. Mixing in the vineyard was, and to some extent still is, achieved by resort to the *uvaggio di vigneto*, proposed in the middle of the nineteenth century by Barone Bettino Ricasoli, of Sangiovese plus Canaiolo Nero and Malvasia Bianca, the latter for early-drinking wines, as distinct from Riservas. To this had been added, by the time of DOC recognition in 1967, the even more downgrading Trebbiano, together with such other local varieties, authorised for

Key to wineries/producers

1	Agricoltori del Chianti Geografico	63	Le Fonti
2	Aiola	64	Le Masse
3	Antinori (Cantina)	65	Le Pici
4	Badia a Colitbuono	66	Le Scalette
5	Badia a Passignano	67	Lilliano
6	Borgo Salcetino	68	Machiavelli
7	Borgo Scopeto	69	Marcellina
8	Brancaia	70	Melini
9	Capannelle	71	Montagliari
10	Carobbio	72	Monte Bernardi
11	Carpineto	73	Montecchio
12	Casa Emma	74	Montegiachi
13	Casale dello Sparviere	75	Montevertine
14	Casa Sola	76	Montiverdi
15	Castelgreve	77	Nittardi
16	Castellare	78	Nozzole
17	Castell' in Villa	79	Ormanni
18	Castello d'Albola	80	Querciabella
19	Castello dei Rampolla	81	Pagliarese
20	Castello della Paneretta	82	Peppoli Antinori
21	Castello di Ama	83	Pietrafitta
22	Castello di Bossi	84	Podere Capaccia
23	Castello di Brolio	85	Podere Il Palazzino
24	Castello di Cacchiano	86	Podere La Cappella
25	Castello di Cerreto	87	Podere Tramonti
26	Castello di Fonterutoli	88	Poggerino
27	Castello di Monsanto	89	Poggio al Sole
28	Castello di Querceto	90	Poggio Piano
29	Castello di San Polo in Rosso	91	Pruneto
30	Castello di Selvole	92	Riecine
31	Castello di Verrazzano	93	Rietine
32	Castello di Volpaia	94	Ripanera
33	Castello d'Uzzano	95	Riseccoli
34	Castello La Leccia	96	Rocca delle Macie
35	Castello Vicchiomaggio	97	Rocca di Castagnoli
36	Castel Ruggero	98	Rocca di Montegrossi
37	Cecchi	99	Rodano
38	Cellole	100	San Fabiano Calcinaia
39	Cennatoio	101	San Felice
40	Chigi Saracini	102	San Giusto a Rentennano
41	Cispiano	103	San Leonino
42	Colle Bereto	104	Santedame
43	Collelungo	105	San Vincenti
44	Colombaio di Cencio	106	Savignola Paolina
45	Concadoro	107	Selvole
46	Conti Serristori	108	Terrabianca
47	Dievole	109	Valtellina
48	Fattoria Casaloste	110	Vecchie Terre di Montefili
49	Fattoria di Petroio	111	Vignale
50	Fattoria Le Fonti	112	Vignamaggio
51	Felsina	113	Vignavecchia
52	Il Poggiolino	114	Vignole
53	Isole e Olena	115	Villa Antinori
54	La Madonnina	116	Villa Arceno
55	La Massa	117	Villa a Sesta
56	La Sala	118	Villa Cafaggio
57	La Selvanella	119	Villa Cerna
58	Le Bocce	120	Villa Calcinaia
59	Le Boncie	121	Villa La Pagliaia
60	Le Cinciole	122	Villa Rosa
61	Le Corti Corsini	123	Villa Vistarenni
62	Le Filigare	124	Vitiano
		125	Viticcio

Chianti Classico

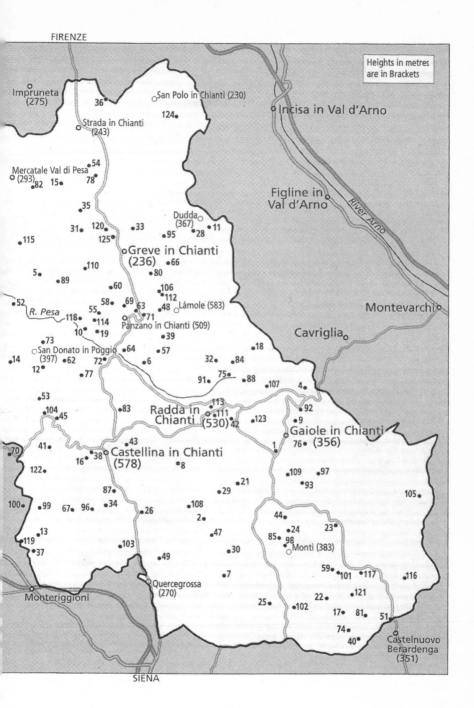

the area, as Colorino, Malvasia Nera and Mammolo. The grapes were planted together, seven rows out of ten, say, being planted to Sangiovese, one to Canaiolo, a half perhaps to Colorino or Malvasia Nera, the rest to whites. And, regardless of ripening times, which obviously vary from variety to variety, they would also be harvested together, and vinified together, the soft Canaiolo and juicy white grapes stretching and cutting those tough Sangiovese tannins.

The inclusion of the indigenous and aptly-named Colorino, obviously, was aimed at giving growers the opportunity of including something in the vineyard mix which would compensate for the loss of colour brought about by the inclusion of the lighter reds and whites. More and more, however, from the early 1970s on, quality producers were turning for this purpose to the richly hued, relatively trouble-free, early-ripening French varieties such as Cabernet, Merlot and Syrah, which would generally be planted and vinified separately. This state of affairs was recognised by the decree of 1984 which, while making Chianti a DOCG, admitted up to 10% of other recommended or authorised grapes, for which read mainly the above.

Largely to satisfy the commercial element, which in 1967 was dominant, deep-coloured wines or musts, such as Montepulciano from Abruzzo or Negroamaro from Puglia, were also allowed in the DOC blend – at up to 15%, no less. Although this has since been banned, it is amazing how much southern wine still finds its way by road-tanker to more northern parts of Italy, not excluding central Tuscany, there mysteriously to disappear.

In 1996, crowning a long campaign on the part of producers and their consortium, Chianti Classico was recognised as a DOCG separately from other Chianti sub-zones. Under the new rules the white grape and Canaiolo Nero components were reduced to an optional 0–10% role, while the presence of 'recommended or authorised complementary varieties' was increased to 15%. These, be they French or Italian, must of course be grown within the Classico zone.

In 2000 a further 5%, with Sangiovese at a minimum of 80%, was agreed upon by producers bringing the maximum of international grapes in the blend to a possible 20%. Too high, complain those who fear that Chianti's authenticity is being sacrificed on the altar of gold, since it is easier to sell one's wine at high prices when it contains an international element (Bordeaux grapes, new oak), the pundits who award points being apparently irresistibly attracted to such styles. Too low, say others who would like to internationalise the style even more – up to 25%, though murmurings of 40% have also been heard.

As in the cases of Madeira and Jerez, long sea-journeys were another method used in past centuries for accelerating the maturation of Sangiovese. The principal traditional method of ageing, however, has been in large barrels – 30 to 100 hectolitres' capacity, or more – of Slavonian oak, or local chestnut or acacia. This process could last years, resulting almost inevitably in a loss of colour and freshness, i.e. in oxidation. The tendency today is to age Sangiovese for a much shorter period in smaller barrels – preferably French oak *barriques*, where the price of the wine can justify the outlay.

Barriques can do an excellent job of rounding out the austerities of Sangiovese, but there is a downside, which is that Sangiovese, less robust and more subtle than the Bordeaux varieties, can fairly easily lose its identity under layers of vanilla or toast on the nose and palate, just as it can under layers of Merlot or Cabernet. For which reason, there are those who still stick to the larger barrels of the more neutral Slavonian oak for maturation purposes. A good compromise, which some producers are resorting to, is large barrels of French oak, obviously not turned over as quickly as *barriques*.

According to some modernists, the ideal method is to carry out one or both of the biological processes of alcoholic or malolactic fermentation in oak. This, they claim, has the effect of fixing what colour has been extracted from the skins, perhaps by resort to high initial temperatures using stainless-steel containers, or perhaps stainless-steel roto-fermentors, to draw out the more easily leeched anthocyanins, leaving behind the tougher tannins when the partially fermented liquid is racked off into wood to complete its processes. Carrying this to its logical conclusion, more and more producers are today introducing, or reintroducing, the vertical oak *tino* for primary fermentation purposes.

Length and method of maceration are live issues in Chianti Classico – some preferring shorter (but not ridiculously short, as practised by some ultra-modernists in Alba) maceration times with more breaking up of the cap, either by manual punching down or by using mechanical punchers which can be moved from vat to vat on overhead rails. Some use roto-fermentors, as we have seen, though the majority still resort to pumping over.

The *governo all'uso toscano* is another traditional method for softening Chianti. Here the finished wine is subjected to a minor refermentation by the addition, round about December following the vintage, of a small proportion (5 to 10%) of partially raisined grapes. The resulting increase of alcohol and glycerol give the wine a fatter feel, against which the tannins seem less tough. A less subtle way of achieving the same objective, increasingly used by industrialists these days, is by *governo* with unfermented grape must. Less subtle still would be the addition of glycerine, for instant viscosity and sweetness. This of course is illicit, but it is justified by its practitioners on the grounds that the resultant wine is often much improved without distortion of flavour or risk to health; glycerol, after all, being a natural byproduct of the fermentation process. It is not just Italians who do this, it should be noted: there is plenty of glycerine-adding in France and other producer nations.

The main point about Chianti is that, like Bordeaux, it is by tradition a blended wine, and for the most part remains so. However, producers in various parts of the extended Chianti region are edging towards pure Sangiovese, where vineyard practices are sufficiently rigorous to achieve a good result. It was in 1996 that Chianti Classico altered its qualifying requirements to enable a pure Sangiovese to qualify as DOCG.

There exist basically two types of Chianti Classico: the one destined for early drinking, unofficially referred to as *normale*, and the one best laid down for a few years, called Riserva.[2] Riserva, from 1996, has had to be aged two years from the 1 January following the vintage, plus three months in bottle, although the latter requirement is due to be subsumed in the former; so release date for Riserva will be 1 January two years on. Unlike other classic Tuscan reds, there is no mandatory wood-ageing period; however, Chianti Classico Riserva does normally receive a year or two's *affinamento* in barrel, these days more often than not in *barrique*. A *normale*, on the other hand, will receive relatively little

---

2 Being an unofficial, though commonly used, term, *normale* is printed in this text in italics, lower case. Riserva, like Passito and others, is an official term, and is printed normally, with a capital.

oak treatment, usually in the traditional *botte*, and may be available from 1 October of the year following the harvest, depending on the judgement of the producer. But even this is changing, with people like Castello di Ama proclaiming that their Chianti Classico *normale* is the equivalent of a Bordeaux *grand cru*.

People inclined to consider the Chianti Classico zone in the light of their knowledge of Bordeaux or Burgundy often ask the question: to what extent do Chianti Classicos vary according to the commune from which they derive?

We have already seen that altitude, in terms of climate, plays an important role in wine quality and character in Tuscany. The difference in mean temperature, and therefore in flowering, ripening and picking times, can be considerable between, say, 250 and 500 metres. As a general rule, the higher the altitude the greater the potential for elegance of aroma but also the sharper the acidity and the tougher the tannins, if only for being more exposed because of the lesser ripeness of fruit. By the same token, the lower the altitude the greater the potential for generosity and fleshiness of fruit character, but at the same time the lesser the subtlety of flavour and firmness of structure. Given that just about the whole of Chianti Classico, and most of greater Chianti, is hill-valley country, it may make more sense to consider the altitude of the vineyard within the commune, rather than the commune itself, when assessing this aspect of quality.

That said, as a general rule, the central sections of Chianti Classico, e.g. Panzano, the hills north of Greve, the upper slopes of Radda, Castellina and Gaiole, with its famous *frazione* Monti, bring forth wine of relatively greater perfume and elegance, while communes with lower average altitudes, like Castelnuovo Berardenga, Castellina Scalo and San Casciano produce wine of richer fruit and more depth.

In the same way, the soil of the higher communes is inclined to be less fertile than that of those lower down, nearer stream-beds, which would only add to the quality effects described in relation to altitude/temperature.

Other influences on quality not necessarily linked with particular communes would be choice of clone and rootstock and viticultural practices such as density of planting, bunch-thinning and production per plant as distinct from per hectare. The great ferment going on in the vineyard in respect of these various factors is discussed in the chapter on Vine and Wine. Vinification techniques obviously also have an important part to play, as we have seen to some extent.

Let's just say that, with all the intensity of activity and change going on in Tuscan vineyards nowadays, the question of the importance of the commune is not yet answered; but that it would appear that commune is much less important than it is, say, in the Haut Médoc or Côte d'Or.

So, to return to the original question: What is Chianti Classico? All right, it's different things to different people, but we can have an opinion.

Mine, as previously indicated, is that Chianti Classico, as such, should not include varieties which are foreign to the zone and to the style of the wine, varieties which distort the element of *terroir* in the wine. I have no problem at all about the blends which contain these grapes, which are sometimes, even most of the time – pending the full maturation of the vineyards recently planted to improved clones of Sangiovese and other Tuscan varieties – superior as wines to the 'real thing'. But I do not think they should be called Chianti Classico. Whether it consists of Sangiovese blended or unblended, Chianti Classico should, in my submission, be purely Tuscan. It is not as if Tuscany lacks the material with which to produce great red wine of unique personality. And the added bonus of such a policy would be that, at last, consumers will know where they stand.

Commercially, Chianti Classico production, hovering somewhere around a quarter of a million hectolitres, from over 7,000 hectares of vineyard, can be divided into two categories: that of the big players, and that of the small to medium-size growers. The most prominent of the former, like Antinori and Ruffino, opted out of the producers' consortium some years ago because they were expected to pay dues on a total production basis, and preferred to focus their expenditure on their own production and promotion rather than on that of a generic group. The others, constituting the large majority in total production terms (around 80%) – and including some serious-volume producers like the cooperatives Grevepesa and Chianti Geografico, as well as heavyweight privates like Rocca delle Macie and Cecchi – remain in part or in whole members of the Consorzio Chianti Classico. This organisation was founded in 1924 in order to defend the Chianti name, which they opined with considerable justification should apply only to wines of the historic area outlined earlier. They failed in their original aim, but the Consortium remains the oldest, one of the most important, and certainly the best known in Italy.

The Consortium has two principal functions to perform, promotional and technical, since 1987 divided between two bodies. The Consorzio Vino Chianti Classico is responsible for the control of quality and for overseeing the adherence or otherwise to production regulations which they are also instrumental in establishing. Members may seek advice on matters viticultural and oenological and long-term research projects, such as Chianti Classico 2000 (see chapter on Vine and Wine), are undertaken. Those who are members of the Consorzio del Marchio Storico may, in addition, use the familiar black rooster insignium on approved bottles of Chianti Classico (not on the rest of their production – Vin Santo, SuperTuscan, etc.). Those who feel they do not need such marketing support, or especially its cost, may still enjoy the benefits of membership on the technical side.

The Consorzio del Marchio Storico used to be known as the Consorzio del Gallo Nero (black rooster), but in the 1980s the American giant Gallo took them to court over the use of the name 'Gallo', and won! A more biased and ridiculous decision it would be difficult to find in legal annals, yet it stands in one of the Consorzio's best markets, so they were forced to change for all markets to avoid confusion of identity.

One further point on the commercial side. It is observable that various producers make wines that would technically, by the rules of today, qualify as Chianti Classico DOCG, yet their producers choose still not to call them so, preferring the more modest denomination of IGT Toscana just as they chose *vino da tavola* in years past. Why this snub? They will give you various reasons, but the underlying motive is financial. If it were not by now established tradition it would be strange to relate, but the fact remains even after the loosening up of the law that the name Chianti Classico – especially the first of the two names – is seen by these producers as a downward drag on image and on the price producers can expect to get away with on the market. There are producers, like Castello di Ama, Castello di Fonterutoli and La Massa with Giorgio Primo, who are making determined bids to pull away from this situation, but wines like Tignanello, Flaccianello, Fontalloro, Capannelle, Percarlo, Il Carbonaione, Le Pergole Torte all remain IGT and show little sign of going to DOCG if they can help it. This of course is an embarrassment for the authorities, but there is nothing they can do about it except wait until such time as the image of Chianti Classico loses its stigma and achieves the prestige of the likes of Brunello di Montalcino and Barolo. That day is still some way off and indeed there are even now high-profile producers who are preparing to pull their wines, even the lesser ones, out of the DOCG altogether.

The producers

There are some 600 members of the Consorzio Chianti Classico, of which 260 bottle their own wine, not to mention all those Chianti Classico producers who do not belong to the Consortium at all and who represent about 20% of production. Considering Chianti Classico producers, including their 'alternative' wines, to be among the most inventive and quality conscious of Italy, I have given them somewhat disproportionate coverage, but obviously, in a book dealing with all the myriad wines of central and southern Italy, I must be selective. I have therefore included most of those I have found to be at least capable of producing excellent Sangiovese, plus some who are important for other reasons: size, tradition, image. Exclusions unjustifiable in absolute terms are inevitable, and I hope that readers will not interpret omissions, or mere mentions, as evidence of any negative judgement. I am only too well aware of the toil and love that goes into making a wine operation successful, and of the injustice of journalists dismissing someone else's life's work out of ignorance or on the basis of a hurried tasting. This statement applies all the more to zones condemned to receive in this book considerably shorter shrift.

The producer profiles below are arranged alphabetically according to the commune in which wineries, or principal wineries, are situated, and the communes, Florence apart, are presented alphabetically since there is no obvious geographical order, while an order of merit would be invidious. Generally, a given winery's range will often go beyond Chianti Classico, indeed beyond Sangiovese, in terms of grape varieties, wine styles or even zones. Their entire production is nonetheless discussed here because they are principally associated with Sangiovese in (for the most part) a Chianti Classico context. This may lead to some minor repetition in relation to later chapters (on international varieties and on blends) but it is done in the interest of giving as complete a picture as possible of a given profiled producer's production.

In the lists of 'Other Producers', however, only pure Sangiovese or Sangiovese-based wines, DOC(G) or not, will be mentioned. Other wines of these producers, where relevant, will appear in the relevant chapters.

Communes of Chianti Classico

Florence

Antinori. Antinori, the *azienda-leader* of Chianti Classico, have no *cantina* in Florence, only a *cantinetta*: a wine-bar/restaurant occupying a small part of the impressive fourteenth-century Palazzo Antinori in Piazza Antinori. But then, Antinori have *cantine* in various places, so it is apt that their centre of operations should be considered this Palazzo, where the company has its offices and the family its principal residence. As Piero Antinori says: 'It was normal, in the Middle Ages, for merchants to live in and work from the same building. We are simply carrying on the tradition.'

While Antinori have been in the wine business since 1385, it is doubtful that the company ever saw so much progress in so short a time as in the final quarter of the twentieth century. Led by Marchese Piero, Antinori have, as is universally recognised, been the standard-bearers of the Tuscan and, ultimately, Italian wine *rinascimento* with wines like Tignanello, the first SuperTuscan to blend Cabernet Sauvignon with Sangiovese; Solaia, first to attempt the mirror-image blend of Cabernet with some 20% of Sangiovese, and still, perhaps, the greatest of its type – indeed, placed first by the *Wine Spectator* (31 December 2000) in a list of the 100 best wines of the world!; Cervaro della Sala, a Chardonnay plus Grechetto blend from Umbria; and others. All kinds of vineyard experiments have been carried out at the company's various estates along similar lines to those of Chianti Classico 2000 (there is an interchange of information with the Consorzio and others), including trials with clones, the planting of new varieties, varying planting densities and techniques. But most of all Antinori, especially in the last 15 years of the century, have engaged in what, were they not so aristocratic in their presentation, might almost be construed as a

TIGNANELLO

Vino prodotto con uve sangiovese e, in piccola parte, cabernet in un antico podere di proprietà Antinori sito nella frazione di Mercatale Val di Pesa, e imbottigliato nelle proprie Cantine dai Marchesi

TE DUCE PROFICIO

Antinori di Firenze viticultori dal 1385 e fornitori brevettati delle case Reali d'Italia e di Svezia, di S.A. il Duca d'Aosta e della Santa Sede.

1997

ANTINORI

IMBOTTIGLIATO IN SAN CASCIANO V.P. DA
MARCHESI ANTINORI S.r.l. - FIRENZE - ITALIA

750 ml ℮

TOSCANA
INDICAZIONE GEOGRAFICA TIPICA

ITALIA
13,5% vol

frenzy of property development and acquisition, attaching wineries and wine-farms by purchase or leasehold from Piemonte to Puglia, from California to Hungary, with most of the activity taking place, naturally, in Tuscany.

The expansion began in 1985 from a necessity – the need to be able to rely on their own-grown grapes in a market situation where merchants, as they had traditionally been, were finding it increasingly difficult to source quality fruit, as growers increasingly took to vinifying their own fruit and selling the higher-value wine rather than grapes; and from an already healthy base consisting of four core properties. These included San Casciano, now their principal *cantina* for white wines; Santa Cristina (140 hectares of vineyard), home of the vineyards of Tignanello (47 hectares) and Solaia (10 hectares) and centre of production for other Tuscan reds such as the ex-Chianti Classico now Sangiovese-plus-a-bit-of-Merlot blend Santa Cristina IGT (3 million plus bottles) and Chianti Classico Riserva Tenute Marchese Antinori, representing a selection of grapes from the various Chianti estates; the magnificent Castello della Sala (140 hectares) near Orvieto in Umbria, purchased by Piero's father Niccolò in 1940, where whites of categories great to good are produced including two Orvieto DOCs, Cervaro della Sala – one of Italy's few world-class whites, and an unusual noble rot wine called Muffato della Sala plus varietal Pinot Nero, Chardonnay and Sauvignon – the latter in two versions, under the Antinori label and another, posher one under the Conte della Vipera label, this being a collaborative effort with Ladoucette of France's Loire; and what used to be called Tenuta Belvedere, now Tenuta Guado al Tasso, the family summer retreat on the coast at Bolgheri, traditionally a *rosato*-producing zone (theirs, Sangiovese plus 15% Cabernet Sauvignon, is called Scalabrone), today the home of their increasingly refined Bolgheri SuperTuscan, 80% Cabernet Sauvignon plus 20% Merlot and others, called, *appunto*, Guado al Tasso, as well as of a white Vermentino.

To these have been added the following – and here we will speak only of central and southern Italy, leaving aside Prunotto in Alba (see *Barolo to Valpolicella*), Bataapati in Hungary and Atlas Peak in California:

- 1985 – Peppoli: 55 hectares under vine, purchased on the occasion of the family's 600th anniversary as Chianti producers. This is where they make their single-estate Chianti Classico, the idea being freshness of fruit with little wood character; made from Sangiovese plus a little Merlot as well as Canaiolo and Malvasia.
- 1987 – Badia a Passignano: a potential of 140 hectares under vine, with a replanting process with the best massal-selected clones from Santa Cristina going full steam ahead. The grapes

today are all Sangiovese (until recently there were also some international varieties), and the wine is Antinori's estate Chianti Classico Riserva.

Between this period and the next purchase Antinori went through something of a crisis, selling a large chunk of their shares to Whitbread, then buying them back in 1991. So capital was being employed in other directions. Even so, expansion didn't stop.

- 1990 – La Braccesca, Montepulciano: acquired on leasehold, this is today the centre of production of the firm's Vino Nobile, sold under the estate name, plus a Rosso di Montepulciano called Abazio and an improving varietal Merlot.
- 1990 – Monteloro: 95 hectares northeast of Florence for the production of white wines. 80 hectares of old-style vineyard were t-budded to Chardonnay for use in the firm's big-selling white, Galestro, and Villa Antinori Bianco.
- 1993 – Le Maestrelle, Montepulciano/Cortona area: the property had 150 hectares under vine when purchased, much of them planted to inferior whites. It is currently undergoing a massive replanting programme for the production of Sangiovese and Merlot.
- 1995 – Pian delle Vigne, Montalcino: 60 hectares planted to a mix of old Sangiovese vines and new, the latter including five different clones of the Brunello grape, Sangiovese Grosso.
- 1995 – Fattoria Aldobrandesca, in the up-and-coming southern Maremma: 45 hectares of white and red varieties, the former being displaced for the latter, plus 6 hectares of Aleatico for making a sweet red wine.

Following these acquisitions Antinori have purchased a new property, called Le Mortelle, at Castiglione della Pescaia in the province of Grosseto, where planting is about to begin. They then turned their expansionist attentions to the south, in particular to Puglia, where they have acquired two new properties, one in Castel del Monte (100 hectares at Tenuta di Tormaresca) and one in the province of Brindisi (500 hectares at San Pietro Vernotico near Brindisi). Grapes planted include Aglianico, Cabernet, Merlot and Chardonnay, and wines so far introduced on the market are called Tormaresca Rosso, Tormaresca Bianco and Castel del Monte Chardonnay.

What's next? A lot will be determined by the younger generation, Piero's three daughters Albiera, Allegra and Alessia, backed by the powerful technical director Renzo Cotarella. Albiera has already taken over at Prunotto, in Alba, while Allegra is taking on increasing responsibility for public relations and Alessia, now a qualified oenologist, seems destined to play a major role on the technical side. Beyond them – well, Albiera Rimbotti, *née* Antinori, has already produced the son that eluded Piero, and Allegra has had one too, as back-up. But putative future *capo* Vittorio Rimbotti's grand-dad, in his early 60s and looking 10 years younger, while discreetly stepping back, is still very much the boss.

Other producers based in Florence

Frescobaldi
See under Rufina

Barberino Val d'Elsa
Casa Emma. This is a fairly typical success story of a medium–small wine-farm in the annals of Chianti Classico during the last third of the twentieth century. Purchased by the Lepri Bucalossi family in the early 1970s as a country retreat, the estate's olive groves and vineyards were transformed from promiscuous to specialised culture during the rest of that decade, while the *cantina* was created and the *casa colonica* lovingly restored. In the 1980s the wine was sold to merchants like Antinori and Ruffino, but from the 1990s as Chianti Classico began to attract more prestige and a better price the family decided to bottle their own product and turned to a professional consultant, in this instance Nicolò d'Afflitto. The result has been national (occasionally in the *tre bicchieri* class) and international recognition and distribution based on some delicious wines of modern yet Tuscan concept. An addition to the ranks of outstanding varietal Merlots of middle Italy, called Soloìo (*solo io* = I alone), is also offered – a wine of great charm and concentration, aged 15 months in French *barrique*. The lead product, Chianti Classico (90% Sangiovese, 10% Malvasia Nera/Canaiolo/Colorino, aged 1 year partially in 30 hectolitre Slavonian oak *botti*, partially (30%) in *barrique*), is of generally bright, perky fruitiness and great drinkability, while the Riserva (95% Sangiovese, 5%

Malvasia Nera), aged 2 years in 7 hectolitre barrels of French oak, is more structured and capable of development in bottle, whilst retaining an archetypal Tuscan fruit character with, thankfully, no excess of wood aromas.

Casa Sola. This 120-hectare farm adjacent to Isole e Olena, of which over 22 are under vine, was purchased in the 1960s by the Genovese family of the Counts Gambaro, but it was only in the late 1980s that the current proprietor, Giuseppe Gambaro, began taking wine production seriously. The fact that Maurizio Castelli and Giacomo Tachis' understudy, Giorgio Marone, are consultants past and present underlines his determination to turn what is undoubtedly a golden potential into reality. I have been following the wines for several years and can testify that, with every vintage, they get better and better, shedding another layer of rusticity and that leathery toughness associated with this area of Chianti Classico and focusing that bit more on fruit and complexity.

This is an estate where Bordeaux grapes and *barrique*-ageing play a part in all wines, that part being quite minor in the *normale*, increasing in the Riserva to arrive at the SuperTuscan Montarsiccio, one-third Sangiovese plus two-thirds Cabernet/Merlot, aged 24 months in French *barrique*. Oak aromas, however, rarely if ever prevail over those of wine.

Isole e Olena. In *Life Beyond Lambrusco* I said Isole was 'one to keep an eye on'. Observers who took this advice might almost have been blinded by the meteoric rise since that time of this estate of 45+ hectares of vineyard. It has become almost an emblem of modern-style, high quality Chianti Classico, nay Tuscan wine – indeed Isole would probably be included in most people's top 10 in Italy. Paolo de Marchi, whose Piemontese family bought the estate in the 1960s and who, being the only one of six children to take an interest in agriculture, took charge in the mid-1970s, is an original. There are several reasons for maintaining this, the principal one being that he is one of the very few proprietors in this zone, certainly from outside, who also commands operations in the vineyard and the winery – with a bit of help, but not much, from Donato Lanati, as well as from his experienced and well-travelled resident *cantiniere* Giampaolo Chiatini. In the matter of PR, having a good if charmingly Italianesque command of English as he does from a stint in the California wine industry, Paolo is highly popular as a speaker internationally, yet manages to maintain his innate modesty and no-bullshit approach which is probably why he is in such demand. Or could it be for his wines that they seek him? The Chianti Classico, always so approachable while maintaining a serious side and an uncompromising individuality; the varietal, *barrique*-aged Sangiovese Cepparello, one of the first of its type and still one of the best, capable of maintaining a youthful freshness well into its second decade – an outstanding creation by any reckoning which would have been Paolo's Riserva had varietal Sangiovese been allowed as Chianti Classico at the time he initiated it in the early 1980s; the quasi Rhône-like Syrah 'Eremo' from the Collezione De Marchi, Paolo having been probably the first to recognise Syrah's potential in modern Tuscany – he usually uses a bit of Syrah to improve the *normale*; the world-class Collezione De Marchi Cabernet Sauvignon, surely one of the top five in Italy in that genre; the Chardonnay Collezione De Marchi, capable of Burgundy Premier Cru heights when Paolo can be persuaded not to filter,

which was only once, alas, on which occasion it threw a tartrate deposit; and not forgetting the scrumptious Vin Santo, one of the finest of the modern fruit-driven style.

Paolo is one of those for whom the best is never good enough, and he is constantly looking for new ways to improve in *cantina*, in terms not just of methodology but also of structure – he recently completed a large and impressive barrel hall and winery. His greatest efforts in past years, however, have been reserved for the vineyard – it says a lot that two of the four new clones recently developed for the Chianti Classico 2000 project come from Isole e Olena – and in particular for the creation of new vineyards out of the stony slopes of his terrain. The sight of massive boulders forming walls for broad new terraces is symbolic of the Sisyphean lengths to which he will go to achieve that perfection which will always, for him, hover tantalisingly just beyond his grasp.

Other producers of Barberino Val d'Elsa capable of good to excellent Sangiovese wines include the following (names of producers in bold, at first mention, followed by best wines, in brackets, where the wine-name is other than, or more than, simple generic Chianti Classico (CC) or Chianti Classico Riserva (CCR)): **Castello della Paneretta** (CCR Torre a Destra; Quattrocentenario – 100% Sangiovese; **Le Filigare** (CC; CCR; Podere le Rocce – Sangiovese + Cabernet Sauvignon); **Monsanto** (CCR Il Poggio; Fabrizio Bianchi – 100% Sangiovese; Tinscvil – Sangiovese + Cabernet Sauvignon).

Castellina in Chianti

Fattoria **Casavecchia**. 'Save a tree, drink Puiatti' is the motto at this estate where oak-ageing is taboo, as in Collio from whence the owners of this medium-sized vineyard hail. Vittorio Puiatti, one of Italy's earliest pacemaker oenologists of the wine *rinascimento*, may be built like a tree (actually, more like a very large bush; his son Giovanni is the tree), but the vinous gems he's been turning out in his native Friuli for 30-odd years have all been achieved without a splinter of assistance from the Massif Central, nor from Slavonia, nor from any other forest. Pure fruit flavours, unadulterated by wood aromas, are what Vittorio believes in, and having extracted them for decades in the Collio from grapes like Chardonnay, Pinot Bianco, Sauvignon and the like, he decided in 1991 to apply his methods to red wines in a zone with a red wine vocation, Tuscany.

His portfolio includes five wines: two pure Sangioveses, a Merlot, a Cabernet and a blend of all three. Il Sogno (the dream) is the Chianti Classico, a wine of elegant perfume and fruity intensity, the tannins so smooth that you can close your eyes and believe it's white. Nerisso, a Sangiovese of selected bunches, is the Chianti Classico Riserva, having a tad more tannin but sporting still that creamy texture which is Puiatti's trademark and a lovely fruit-acid balance reminiscent of his whites. The Merlot, called Capetino, and the Cabernet, Carfino, both boast waftings of brambly fruit on the nose and more of a red wine tannin structure, with, still, that white wine acidity. The blend, Seriolo – 60% Sangiovese, 20% Merlot and 20% Cabernet Sauvignon – sums up the roundness and sweet fruitiness, the clean lines, the purity and finesse of the Puiatti style.

All wines, indeed, are more typically Puiatti than typically Tuscan. And think of the contribution to the fight against global warming!

Castellare. This property, with 25 hectares of vineyard in a beautifully sited southeast facing *conca* below the town of Castellina, on soils of calcareous marne and *galestro* with little clay, tends to give wines typical of the best of its commune, characterised by bright, racy, red-berry fruit with a firm backbone of acidity and ripe tannin, capable of medium-term ageing. Yields are low, viticulture tends towards the organic – hence the birds, always different, on the labels – the *cantina* is a model of modernity and efficiency and all ageing takes place in small French oak (2.25–5 hectolitres), even in respect of Chianti Classico *normale*. Thankfully, the wines are rarely taxed by an excess of wood aromas – something of which consultant oenologist Maurizio Castelli is not generally guilty. The vineyards are mature, having for the most part been planted around the time owner Paolo Panerai, a noted Milanese journalist/ publisher, purchased the property in 1979. Tuscan and French varieties – Sangioveto (do not dare to call it Sangiovese around here), Canaiolo, Ciliegiolo, Colorino and Malvasia Nera in the former instance, Cabernet Sauvignon, Chardonnay and Sauvignon in the latter – are kept strictly apart, the former accounting for Chianti Classico, Riserva and Riserva Vigna Il Poggiale as well as the house SuperTuscan I Sodi di S. Niccolò, whose particular personality derives from the inclusion at up to 15% of Malvasia Nera, giving warmth, spice and perfume. Everything is perfect, not least the publicity machine, not surprisingly given the calling of the proprietor.

Castello di Fonterutoli. The Mazzei family, father Lapo, sons Filippo and Francesco, supported by one of Tuscany's outstanding oenological consultants Carlo Ferrini, wanted to celebrated the 600th anniversary of the original Ser Lapo Mazzei's earliest inscription of the word 'Chianti', in 1398, with a bang. In the process two well-established wines which had reaped the highest points and praises from Italian and international pundits were scrapped and a new one, combining the best of them and called Castello di Fonterutoli Chianti Classico, was introduced. (Note: This wine is sometimes classed as a Riserva, sometimes not, but is always called Castello di Fonterutoli as distinct from plain Fonterutoli, under which name the Chianti Classico *normale* is marketed.) A bold move, intended to show the world that a top producer had sufficient faith in the revival of the historic denomination that it was prepared to make considerable sacrifices to prove it. And, indeed, the early versions of the new wine are excellent:

from Concerto, the SuperTuscan it replaced, it brought the support of high quality Cabernet Sauvignon grapes, but reduced from 20 to 10% so as to retain more Tuscan typicity without losing power. From the defunct Riserva Ser Lapo it brought the refining effect of French *barrique* on Sangiovese of good concentration. From both it brought high quality grapes from the Siepi vineyard at 260 metres altitude and the Fonterutoli vineyard at 450 metres – over 60 hectares under vine in total. Deep of colour, with a wealth of berry fruit, dark-chocolate and coffee aromas, plus, despite the ripeness of the tannins, a hefty structure which will insure considerable longevity, well into the twenty-first century, Castello di Fonterutoli is a wine to sit with the best in the world.

But the Mazzei have not taken idealism so far as to abandon the SuperTuscan. Their internationally acclaimed Siepi, because of its 50–50 blend of Sangiovese and Merlot, remains necessarily an IGT – indeed one of the finest SuperTuscans in existence. Even the 90% Sangiovese Poggio alla Badiola (also includes a bit of Cabernet Sauvignon and a modicum of Merlot), a wine which could strictly speaking qualify for the DOCG, remains as an IGT, the justification being that it is their third wine – after Castello di Fonterutoli and plain Fonterutoli; and for the Mazzei DOCG must mean the best.

Rocca delle Macie. It is not perhaps for wines of outstanding quality and personality that one looks to Rocca delle Macie – although they may not agree – rather for value for money. And one gets it – one reason, perhaps, why the production of this large estate, founded by movie-mogul the late Italo Zingarelli in 1973, with 250 hectares of vineyard (from four estates in Chianti Classico, not including the recently acquired 80+ hectare estate in the Scansano area) producing 4.5 million bottles annually distributed in 88 provinces in Italy and 45 countries abroad, has achieved in a relatively short period the status of second most-sold brand in Tuscany with a wine-list presence in fully 25% of Tuscan restaurants. As they say of the ethnic eatery, if the natives are in there it must be good.

But one mustn't forget that price is only one of the factors in the formula 'value-for-money' – nor indeed are Rocca by any means the cheapest around; just reasonable, a virtue which appears to be going out of fashion. The Chianti Classico *normale* never fails to deliver drinkability combined with typicity; the Riserva gives that bit extra, as it should. Chianti Classico Tenuta Sant'Alfonso takes concentration and complexity on another step, and the Riserva di Fizzano represents the peak of the DOCG Chiantis. In a recent tasting the varietal Sangiovese Supertuscan Ser Gioveto showed at the top of the pile: a wine neither cheap nor expensive but, with its coffee and spice and fruit that's real nice, delivering a lot of quality per price. Roccato too, a blend of Sangiovese and Cabernet, can achieve respectable heights.

With consultant Giorgio Marone overseeing the oenological aspect the already good quality level may be expected to rise.

Rodano. The wines of Rodano – owned by Vittorio Pozzesi, President of the Chianti Classico Consortium, though it is his son, Enrico, who runs the estate – are not easy to evaluate, but that they have a very definite personality is undeniable. 'Chewy', 'potent' 'porty', 'fiery' are words that occur in my notes, together with 'notes of tobacco', 'leather', 'plum'. Not typical descriptives of Chianti Classico, but then the conditions of the estate are not typical – at below 300 metres altitude one of the lowest in the zone, with soils much less stony, having little galestro. Pitting the single-vineyard Chianti Classico Riserva Viacosta against the SuperTuscan Monna Claudia (50% Sangiovese, 50% Cabernet Sauvignon), the latter *barrique*-aged of course, I found the house style worked better in the traditional format. Here is a Chianti to put in a Rhône line-up (as it happens, Rodano is Italian for Rhône), lacking the elegance of Bordeaux and the aromaticity of Burgundy, perhaps, but having rather the power of a Châteauneuf-du-Pape.

Like a growing number of Tuscan producers, Rodano have recently introduced a varietal Merlot called Lazzicante which, while having the aromas of the grape – berry, blackcurrant – reflects the kind of structure typical of the *azienda*. The traditional approach, however, is assured as long as master-taster Giulio Gambelli is still in charge of the oenological side.

Other producers of Castellina capable of good to excellent Chianti Classico are: **Borgo Scopeto** (now owned by Tenuta Caparzo of Montalcino); **Casale dello Sparviere** (CC; CCR; this recent arrival is one to watch); **Cecchi** (CC Messer Pietro di Teuzzo; CCR Villa Cerna; Spargolo – 100% Sangiovese these are the showcase wines of a producer formerly noted for volume production); **Collelungo** (CC Roveto); **Concadoro** (CC Vigna di Gaversa; note an organic grower); **La Brancaia** (CC; Brancaia – Sangiovese + Merlot); Castello **La Leccia** (CC; CCR; Bruciagna – 100% Sangiovese); **Lilliano** (CCR; Anagallis – Sangiovese + Colorino); **Nittardi** (CC Casanuova di Nittardi; CCR); **San Fabiano Calcinaia** (CCR Cellole; Cerviolo Rosso – Sangiovese plus Cabernet and Merlot); **San Leonino** (see profile on Tenimenti Angelini under Val di Suga, Brunello di Montalcino); **Tramonti** (CC).

Castelnuovo Berardenga
Fattoria di **Felsina**. The best thing Giuseppe Mazzocolin ever did was to fall in love with Gloria Poggiali, not only because she is a lady of exceptional quality but also because her father just happened to have acquired, in the mid 1960s, this large and wonderfully endowed wine estate, presently with 57 of the several hundred hectares under vine, in the extreme southeast corner of the Chianti Classico zone. Schoolteacher Giuseppe fell in love all over again, this time with wine, departed the classroom in Veneto in 1982 and has devoted himself heart and soul ever since, with the expert guidance of consultant and master-taster Franco Bernabei (since 1983), to making this one of the greatest estates in the land. While producing one of Italy's finest Cabernet Sauvignons in Maestro Raro, as well as one of the better Chardonnays in I Sistri, it is into his various pure Sangiovese wines that Giuseppe pours the lion's share of his boundless enthusiasm.

Most important from a volume point of view is Chianti Classico *normale* (production around 150,000 bottles, though Giuseppe aims comfortably to exceed 200,000 when all new plantings have been carried out), which displays the firmness yet fruitiness conferred by the various sub-zones at his disposal, and which is often better than many people's Riserva. During the late 1990s, Giuseppe was able almost entirely to replant Felsina's Chianti Classico vineyards, with massal-selected vines from the estate itself plus a bit of R24, thanks to the purchase in 1995 of the neighbouring Pagliarese property, with its 25 hectares of 40-year-old low-yielding vines (note: the Pagliarese brand has now ceased to exist). When Felsina's vineyards are back up and running, it will be Pagliarese's turn for replanting. The work never stops.

Felsina do produce a Riserva *normale* (non-*cru*), which they sell entirely on the American market. More important, however, is Riserva Rancia, surely one of the greatest Sangioveses in absolute,

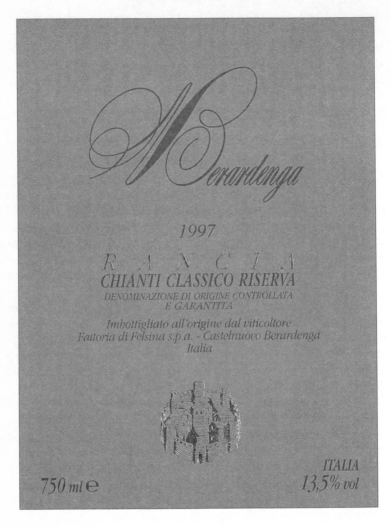

having a personality and equilibrium all its own, earthy yet elegant, complex yet fine. And it's a Chianti Classico! – one of the very first to match Montalcino in expressing the full potential of Tuscany's very own grape variety.

The soil at Rancia's three sites, totalling around 6 hectares for a production of some 30,000 bottles, is all of the Chianti type – *galestro* with *albarese*, stony, plenty of *scheletro*. The soil at the three sites of IGT Toscana Fontalloro, totalling a little over 6 hectares, which some consider Felsina's finest product, is, however, split between the Chianti type – from the one site within the zone – and the heavier, richer more clay-based soils of the two sites outside the Chianti Classico delineated zone, giving a fascinating combination of power, body and aristocratic breeding, which even long ageing in new oak *barriques* cannot overcome.

Agricola **San Felice**. In certain ways this property of 750 hectares, including a village of ancient origin, a Relais & Châteaux hotel, an 18-hectare site devoted to experimental viticulture and, oh yes, some 160 hectares of commercial vineyard is emblematic of what is best in Chianti Classico, past, present and future.

The architect of success was Enzo Morganti, among Tuscany's most original pioneers, who was brought in to run the property in 1967, when it was purchased by the insurance company RAS. Today it also controls a major vineyard in Montalcino, Campogiovanni, and a relatively newly acquired one at Massa Marittima in the Maremma. Morganti had spent 20 years at Tenuta di Lilliano as *fattore*, where he had developed various improved clones of Sangiovese by massal selection. He brought with him not just the clones but also a passion for viticultural and oenological research, which culminated in the establishment, in 1987/8, of San Felice's famous Vitiarium (see Chapter 1), and which has characterised the estate through the ensuing years.

Morganti it was who, first of all, developed the 100% Sangiovese style way back in 1968 when he brought out the first edition of Vigorello, still one of the most sought-after of the SuperTuscans, although today the wine contains 40% Cabernet Sauvignon – which he was also one of the first to plant, in 1974. It was he, also, who, foreseeing the time when Chianti would be split by the international–indigenous argument, began experimenting with the alternative native varieties that might one day be needed to support or even replace the great grape. The first wine to emerge from these experiments was the outstanding Poggio Rosso, a single-vineyard Sangiovese with 10% of the native Colorino which had been used sporadically in Tuscan blends for centuries but never at such high quality level. True, Colorino is today being recognised as an excellent grape for blending with Sangiovese, giving all the colour and grit of Cabernet without the opposing and dominating perfumes (cf. Rosso di Sera from Poggiopiano); but one has to bear in mind that Poggio Rosso was first introduced in 1978. To my mind, Poggio Rosso is one of the best, and certainly best-value, wines that Tuscany has to offer in absolute, one which I would far rather drink than any of the Sangiovese–Cabernet or Sangiovese–Merlot blends which so captivate the international audiences.

An extra treat: from the 1999 vintage, Poggio Rosso has also contained a small (5%) proportion of a grape developed through San Felice's researches into native Tuscan vines, called Pugnitello. A non-commercial sample of this wine (San Felice also have extensive facilities for micro-vinification of the experimental grapes) proved to have an impressively opaque colour, distinctive wildfruit aromas and tremendous mouth-feel, terrifically tannic but with a sufficient concentration of fruit to cover the astringency. It will certainly make a great blender!

Hats off to current winemaker, Leonardo Bellaccini, and his team for keeping the Morganti spirit alive, for continuing with the experimentation while maintaining the excellent quality and value of wines like Il Grigio Chianti Classico Riserva (400,000 bottles produced) and the straight Chianti Classico (600,000 bottles).

Podere **Le Boncie**. This is the private estate of Giovanna Morganti, daughter of the late Enzo Morganti (see San Felice). In fact, Giovanna's few hectares, bequeathed by her father after he had seen to it that she had a proper training in wine production, are adjacent to the many of San Felice, though hers have quite a different aspect, being relatively densely planted in the ancient *alberello* (bush) formation where all operations must be carried out by hand. This may sound traditionalist – and Giovanna is a traditionalist in certain other ways too, allowing Tuscan varieties only in her vineyards (Canaiolo and Mammolo, as well as the rare Foglia Tonda, in support of Sangiovese), using oak *tini* for fermentation; indeed, Giovanna was one of the initiators, in Tuscany, of this now spreading back-to-the-future trend. But it would probably be more accurate to describe her as a perfectionist, a lady with a clear idea of what kind of wine she wants to achieve and how to achieve it. Yields are very low – around 35 hectolitres per hectare – and the use of chemicals is minimised. For maturation purposes she uses neither the traditional *botte* nor the modernist *barrique* but *tonneaux* of between 5 and 7 hectolitres.

Giovanna Morganti's sole wine is her 'Le Trame' Chianti Classico, not called Riserva (though it virtually is one), whose fine, almost delicate – dare I say feminine? – style would not go down especially well with the prevailing punditry, which requires great depth and concentration, but which should be pleasing to those who remain in favour of subtlety and *delicatesse* in wine. Finely tuned, with well-stated berry fruit, it is of those which, while not eliciting initial gasps of delight, become more convincing as the liquid level descends, so that one is always reluctant to see the last drop disappear – unless there's another bottle, of course.

Other producers of Castelnuovo Berardenga capable of good to excellent Sangiovese include: Castello di **Bossi** (CC; CCR Berardo; Corbaia – Sangiovese + Cabernet Sauvignon); **Castell'in Villa** (CC; CCR; Santacroce – Sangiovese + Cabernet Sauvignon); Fattoria di **Dievole** (CC Novecento; Broccato – 100% Sangiovese); Fattoria di **Petroio** (CC; CCR); **Poggio Bonelli** (CCR; Tramonto d'Oca – 100% Sangiovese).

Gaiole
Castello di **Ama**. This sizeable estate was purchased in 1977 by a group of Romans and is managed today by the daughter of one of them, Laura Sebasti, and her viticulturist-winemaker husband Marco Pallanti. Since the mid-1980s the estate has been associated with the highest quality that Tuscany has to offer, in respect both of Chianti Classico and of SuperTuscan. Pallanti was responsible, since the early 1980s, for identifying the merits of particular sections, or *vigneti*, of the estate – some 90 hectares under vine, over a quarter of the total planted to the lyre formation – and for regrafting or replanting them according to his concept of their optimum potential. Until the early 1990s Ama were best known, indeed, for their four high-quality, high-priced Chianti Classico Riservas, each one featuring Sangiovese, naturally, with some other variety – for example, Bellavista (with Malvasia Nera), a wine of rich, spicy aromas and warm but elegant fruit; and Casuccia (with Merlot), deeper, rounder and no doubt more international in style, though less typically Tuscan.

Today the *crus* have been reduced to the two mentioned above and the estate has become better known, in an international context at any rate, for the SuperTuscan Vigna l'Apparita, from Merlot

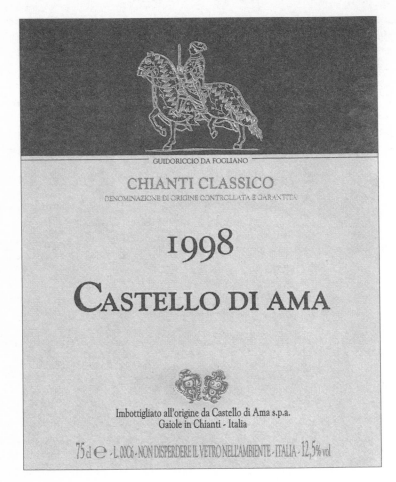

GUIDORICCIO DA FOGLIANO

CHIANTI CLASSICO
DENOMINAZIONE DI ORIGINE CONTROLLATA E GARANTITA

1998

CASTELLO DI AMA

Imbottigliato all'origine da Castello di Ama s.p.a.
Gaiole in Chianti - Italia

75 cl ℮ · L. 0006 · NON DISPERDERE IL VETRO NELL'AMBIENTE · ITALIA · 12,5% vol

plants grafted in the early 1980s onto Canaiolo and Malvasia Bianca in a clay-rich four-hectare section of the Bellavista vineyard and trained, unusually, on the open lyre formation. L'Apparita, indeed, has become almost as famous in its genre as Sassicaia did among Cabernets Sauvignon of the world in the 1970s, and its tremendous depth of fruit, its power combined with elegance, has brought it glory in numerous tastings and competitions. Other SuperTuscans include a Pinot Nero (Il Chiuso), convincing enough by Italian standards but certainly not world class like l'Apparita;

and a Chardonnay (Al Poggio) of which, again, the most that can be said is that it is good in a Tuscan context.

Today, however, Sebasti and Pallanti are shifting the emphasis somewhat away from the *crus* and the SuperTuscans and towards the not-so-humble Chianti Classico (they would have a fit if you referred to their Chianti Classico as *normale)*, considering as they do that the most representative wine of their estate is not that of which they produce tiny quantities in top vintages but that of which they make 200,000 bottles every year. The idea, now that the vineyards are mature and things are running smoothly, is to pour maximum resources and effort into making outstanding Chianti Classico which can be sold at the sort of price that would make a Bordeaux *châtelaine* happy. Certainly, the Chianti Classico, 100% *barrique*-aged (25% new) is several cuts above your run-of-the mill stuff, having very sleek tannins, subtle fruit and a finely balanced elegance that few under that denomination can rival; but as yet it has not achieved the class or, to be fair, quite the price of a top *cru classé*; although the latter is certainly not for want of trying.

Badia a Coltibuono. This is one of the most historic estates of Chianti Classico, from the point of view of both the past millennium and the past half-century.

The breathtaking monastery which is the administrative centre of the estate – the 50-plus hectares of vineyard are at a distance of some 15 kilometres, in the high-quality sector of Gaiole called Monti – was first established by Benedictine monks in the mid-eleventh century. It remains to this day a haven of beauty and peace somehow despite the hordes of tourists arriving daily to eat in the excellent *osteria* or to do a tour of the cellars and a tasting or to study at the feet of culinary guru Lorenza de' Medici, mother of the present generation of owners.

In 1846 the Abbey, which had been secularised in Napoleonic times, was purchased by Michele Giuntini, whose great-great grandson, Piero Stucchi Prinetti, husband of Lorenza, took over after World War II. Piero was one of the first Chiantigiani to try and reinvigorate the wine whose reputation had fallen so low as to be identified worldwide by the wicker flask. He had gone a long way towards achieving his goal when, in 1985, he passed the estate's management to his son Roberto, a qualified agronomist and ex-student at the famous Californian oenology school, Davis.

Roberto, later joined by his elder sister Emanuela, current present president of the Consorzio del Marchio Classico, set about rationalising production, dividing it between brands made from bought-in grapes and wines (currently 900,000 bottles: the 'Coltibuono' range) and wines of the estate vineyards (around 300,000 bottles: the 'Badia a Coltibuono' range). A horizontal tasting of the six Sangiovese-based wines – three of each range – confirms that he has found a way of differentiating each wine in a crescendo of quality, rising from the light, fresh-fruity 100% Sangiovese di Toscana 'Cancelli', from grapes acquired anywhere in the region; through the Chianti 'Cetamura', from grapes bought anywhere in Chianti, similarly fresh and unwooded, but more intense, with a distinct aroma of blueberries; then the Chianti Classico 'RS', again from bought-in grapes and a wine of whose depth of aroma and medium-level tannins combined with sheer drinkability he is sufficiently proud to market under his own initials; to the first wine of the Badia a Coltibuono range, Chianti Classico, with an extra degree of elegance and depth playing with well-stated berry-cherry fruit and good tannins; to the second, Chianti Classico Riserva, aged in 15–20 hectolitre French oak casks – a wine of warmth, richness of bitter-cherry fruit, fine tannins and a long, sweet, elegant aftertaste; to the crowning glory, Sangioveto, a 100% Sangiovese aged in French *barriques* of four ages for about a year, this being a wine of great generosity and complexity of bouquet, a wealth of very fine fruit in the mouth and ripe but plentiful tannins – a wine, in a word, capable from a good vintage of ageing for years if not decades.

Roberto Stucchi is a believer in fruit over oak, and of Tuscan varieties over international ones, feeling that it is vital to follow the traditions of his forebears, improving on them within their territorial context while keeping all processes as natural and stress-free as possible. To this end he has brought the vineyards to the point of being officially organic, while he and his family have built a superb state-of-the-art fermentation winery in Monti, in the heart of the vineyards, a multi-levelled construction allowing the grapes/musts/wines to be moved entirely by gravity rather than the harsher pumping, and which incorporates a variety of devices, such as a punching-down mechanism movable from tank to tank by rail, for working the grapes as gently as possible to extract only the positive elements.

The latest development at Badia is the amicable parting, after 20 years, of wine consultant Maurizio Castelli and the hiring of oenologist Luca d'Attoma. The combination of Roberto's cautious new-traditionalist approach and d'Attoma's exuberant perfectionism should prove a powerful force in the future.

Castello di **Brolio/Barone Ricasoli.** The Barons Ricasoli have been proprietors of this most impressive of castles, one of a number built in the middle ages to defend the territory of Florence against that of Siena, or vice versa, since 1141.

Ever a political clan, its most famous scion was Baron Bettino, Italy's Prime Minister for a while after unification in the mid-nineteenth century and the 'father of modern Chianti'. He defined Chianti as a blended wine, saying that: 'The San Gioveto grape gives the wine most of its aroma and a certain sensory vigour', while 'Canaiuolo (sic) adds a sweetness that tempers its austerity without mitigating its aroma' (probably the nicest words said about Canaiolo in the last 150 years). The erroneous idea that he advocated white grapes for all wines is something for which he has been unjustly maligned, since he specifically stated that while 'Malvasia . . . softens the first two grapes', it 'could be eliminated in wines destined for ageing'. Ignorant lawmakers in the mid-twentieth century managed to miss this caveat and made Trebbiano and/or Malvasia a necessary part of the blend, from which *faux pas* Chianti suffered grievously for most of the latter half of the twentieth century.

At the dawn of the twenty-first century the Ricasoli, under Baron Francesco, great-great-great-grandson of the 'Iron Baron', is still in control, though there was a period between the 1960s and the early 1990s when the estate almost got away. Chianti's sad decline in the post-World War II period had forced Francesco's father, also called Bettino, to sell the Brolio name together with the winery, though he maintained ownership of the castle and the vineyards. First under Seagram, then under United Wine Producers and lastly under the Australian firm Hardys the Brolio/Ricasoli reputation sank to shameful depths. It was only in the early 1990s, when Francesco realised that drastic action would be required to preserve not just his family's reputation but the very viability of the business, that things began to improve.

In 1993 Francesco, at the time operating as a photographer in Florence, succeeded with some difficulty in prising the brand and the winery away from Hardys. Knowing little about wine production or estate management, he was wise enough to surround himself with experts in both, bringing in one of Tuscany's finest viticultural and oenological consultants, Carlo Ferrini, to oversee production and Marchese Filippo Mazzei of nearby Fonterutoli to mastermind operations. Between them they oversaw the cleaning and restoration of the dilapidated winery with its ancient barrels, installing the latest oenological equipment, purchasing hundreds of new small and medium-sized barrels to replace the dead wood. In the vineyards a major replanting programme was undertaken, introducing the clones, planting densities and training systems which projects like Chianti 2000, of which Ferrini had been the originator, were indicating as suitable for the zone, and reducing yields to levels consonant with quality wine production. A task of crucial importance has been the identification of particular vineyards for particular wines – for the estate's 225 + hectares of vineyard are divided into various sectors or 'paddocks', as Aussies would call them.

The quality of the new estate wines now, with a series of good to excellent vintages behind them, is beginning to reflect the quality of the work put in over the past six or seven years. Pride of place is given to the recently introduced Castello di Brolio, a Chianti Classico made from a selection of the best Sangiovese grapes of the estate and aged in *barrique* for 18 months – a long time for Sangiovese, so the fruit has to be outstanding in order to stand up to it. The influence of Filippo Mazzei here is clear – also at Fonterutoli he has placed a Chianti Classico at the top of the image-tree, even if, as at Brolio, the market, still wary of the name Chianti, has not quite caught up with the concept.

Other winner wines from Brolio include the appealingly drink-able Brolio Chianti Classico, as distinct from Castello di Brolio – even this gets 10 months in small oak; Chianti Classico Riserva Rocca Guicciarda, later picked (usually in October) and aged in *tonneaux* for 20 months – a wine for laying down; the SuperTuscan Casalferro, based on Sangiovese but blended with Cabernet and Merlot, macerated up to 18 days and *barrique*-aged for a similar number of months – a wine dense of extract but nicely harmonious; Formulae, partially aged in American oak – an unashamedly 'international' style of wine, made to please the American market; the *barrique*-fermented Chardonnay Torricella; and Brolio Vin Santo.

Buyer beware: wines branded 'Barone Ricasoli' without mention of Brolio are likely to be made from bought-in rather than from estate-grown grapes.

Castello di **Cacchiano**, *frazione* Monti. The Barons Ricasoli-Firidolfi, one of Tuscany's oldest families and closely related to the Ricasolis of Brolio, have been owners of the Castello di Cacchiano since the eleventh century, but it was only in 1974, under Elisabetta Balbi Valier, widow of the recently demised Alberto Ricasoli-Firidolfi, younger brother of the above-mentioned Baron Bettino, that they began bottling wine from the vines of the property. Baronessa Elisabetta retired in the mid-1990s, dividing the estate between her elder son Giovanni, who has taken Cacchiano, and the younger Marco (see Rocca di Montegrossi). Today, Cacchiano has some 30 hectares under vine at around 400 metres altitude on the lower slopes of Monti, the castle being at 500 metres.

Baron Giovanni has some very clear ideas as to how to proceed in future. Most particularly, he has made the decision to discontinue production of the estate's 'SuperTuscan' RF, the last vintage of which was 1995, and to concentrate all his efforts on Chianti Classico. In good but not great vintages the wine will be labelled, simply, Chianti Classico Castello di Cacchiano. In exceptional vintages it will be called Chianti Classico Millennio – this latter being virtually a Riserva, but not so labelled. He will not make both wines in the same vintage. To underline his determination that Millennio should be from top vintages only, between 1996 and 1999 he has made the wine only once – in 1997 – despite the fact that 1998 and particularly 1999 were both distinctly better years than the average. The only red wine that will be made in every vintage is Rosso Toscano IGT, basically the best of the rest.

This would seem a conservative step, yet Giovanni is by no means conservative when it comes to vineyard improvements, particularly in respect of the inclusion of a foreign element, in this case Merlot, in the Chianti Classico blend. The aim is to arrive at a blend of 85% Sangiovese and 15% Merlot, in which variety he has a strong belief, although the proportions of recent vintages are not yet at this level. Meanwhile, the policy is to improve quality in the vineyard both by gradual replanting using the best of today's clones and rootstocks, and by increasing densities and experimenting with training systems. Indeed, Cacchiano is associated with the Chianti Classico 2000 programme for this purpose and has recently planted a vineyard with 9,300 plants per hectare trained to *alberello*.

These improvements, inevitably, will take a little time to come through fully in the bottle, but what's the hurry? When you've been around for a thousand years – the *millennio* in question referring to the past thousand, not the next – a mere 10 or 20 years here or there isn't much. And if proof be needed that Cacchiano are already turning out wine of outstanding character, it is only necessary to taste the Millennio 1997.

Capannelle. This hilltop estate, above the town of Gaiole, was the creation of Roman industrialist Raffaele Rossetti who between 1975 and 1989 planted five hectares with Sangiovese plus token amounts of Cabernet, Merlot, Malvasia Nera and Colorino, a further eight hectares having now been planted. Rossetti, a fanatic for hygiene who insists on stainless steel for every pipe or bracket that comes into contact with the wine and has a fit every time he sees a speck of dust or a worker not wearing rubber gloves and boots and a white smock, never had any time for officialdom. So it wasn't long after his arrival on the Tuscan scene that he joined the exodus from the DOC(G) and declared his very expensive and exclusive wine '*vino da tavola*'. Most of it remains so today, although following the takeover in 1997 by the American James Sherwood – Rossetti retains a presence and a small interest – they have re-introduced a Chianti Classico of the basic sort, if anything from Capannelle can indeed be called basic; certainly not the prices.

The principal wines, made by resident oenologist Simone Monciatti with help from one of the best and least self-promoting itinerant consultants, Andrea Mazzoni, remain, however, IGT. They include the lead wine, simply called 'Barrique' (it gets two years in them), Sangiovese plus 10% of Cabernet Sauvignon and 5% Colorino, a wine of deep colour and spicy, cherry-fruit aromas mixed with spice and roast coffee coming from the oak-char; and '50 & 50' (sic), a blend in more ways than one, consisting of 50% Merlot from Avignonesi of Montepulciano and 50% Sangiovese from Capannelle – this being distinctly more Bordelais in character, having almost a jammy fruit with ripe, fine-grained tannins and notes of coffee and dark chocolate; also a barrique-fermented Chardonnay aiming fairly successfully at Burgundian complexity and restraint despite the Bordeaux bottle. Exceptionally, in honour of the millennium, they put together a Sangiovese–Cabernet (10%) blend of three vintages of the 1990s which they called '2000', with a spaceship bedecked hologram for a label. Despite an astronomic price it failed to achieve lift-off with the pundits, though its structure suggests it might be looking a lot better around 2010.

Il Palazzino, *frazione* Monti. The growers of Monti all seem very pleased with themselves in a quiet sort of way, as if entertaining no doubt that this sub-zone, some 400 metres above sea-level, with the clayey-calcareous soil called *albarese*, loose and moderately fertile, with good southern exposures, is the finest in all Chianti. Brothers Alessandro and Andrea Sderci, of a family whose roots in Monti go back generations, are making wines which give substance to the smugness, wines whose tantalising juiciness belie the relative meagreness of the soil and which, though *barrique* does enter the equation – in part for the Chianti Classico, wholly for the Riserva – put fruit firmly first, the vanilla and gentle wood-smoke of the oak merely adding interest and complexity while rounding out the mature tannins to provide a necessary backdrop for all that ripe Sangiovese. If the Chianti Classico is one of the sexiest of its type, the Riserva, Grosso Sanese, is more so, having greater concentration and almost a succubus-like power to pull you right inside its womb. It should be noted, too, that Grosso Sanese began as a *vino da tavola*, and was brought into the DOCG as an act of faith in the regeneration of that once and future prestigious denomination.

Riecine. This small estate on the outskirts of Gaiole town – 5 hectares under vine, practically all to the high-quality R24 clone of Sangiovese – has always maintained an Anglo-Saxon interest. Owned for many years by a Londoner, the late John Dunkley, it was taken over in the mid-1990s by Gary and Lindsay Baumann, while winemaker Sean O'Callaghan, English despite the name, stayed on as director and part-owner. Given their size, Riecine have concentrated on top quality, wines of dense fruit and plenty of backbone, for the long haul, a goal which they achieve with admirable consistency. Even the Chianti Classico tends to be more structured and less early drinking than most, though it comes round nicely after three to five years. So you can imagine what the Riserva is like. As for the 100% Sangiovese SuperTuscan, La Gioia, at its best it is a highly concentrated, firm and richly textured wine capable of improving over at least a decade in bottle, indeed unlikely to give maximum *gioia* until about its fifteenth year.

Rocca di Montegrossi, *frazione* Monti. Marco Ricasoli is the younger son of the younger son. His father, Alberto Ricasoli-Firidolfi, was the younger brother of Baron Bettino Ricasoli who inherited Castello di Brolio, Alberto getting the lesser Castello di Cacchiano. In Marco's case his elder brother Giovanni has inherited Cacchiano and he is left with a property which used to be part of that domain. Nevertheless, Marco is sanguine, optimistic and determined to succeed with his 17 hectares of vineyard, with the invaluable help of consultant agronomist-oenologist Attilio Pagli.

The main theme of Marco's future production, which he has been developing from 1994 with the first fully independent vintage coming in 1998, is to be total separation of the indigenous and the international in respect of grape varieties. Current vintages have not achieved this ideal, as the Chianti Classico Riserva Vigneto San Marcellino has in the past had a modicum of Merlot in the blend and the SuperTuscan Geremia will, until 2002, be pure Sangiovese. From that time, however, Geremia will be entirely composed of Merlot and Cabernet Sauvignon, and the Chianti Classicos, *normale* and Riserva, will consist exclusively of Sangiovese and Canaiolo – in which latter Marco, unusually, is a great believer, to the extent that he has recently planted a hectare to the grape when everyone else is busily grubbing it up.

On the subject of dividing the varieties Marco is clear. 'It is a pity', he says, 'to produce Chianti Classico which may be good wine but which isn't Chianti Classico. Merlot and Cabernet do very well in our soils and can make great wine, but in blend they drown the finesse of Sangiovese. I think that instead of using so-called "ameliorative" blending varieties we should and can get a lot more from our own grapes. That is why we have been working on our Sangioveses and that is why I have placed my faith in Canaiolo.'

A taste of his 1999 Chianti Classico, deep-coloured, full, fruity and structured, is ample illustration that he is moving in the right direction.

San Giusto a Rentennano, *frazione* Monti. Once part of the Brolio estate of the Ricasoli, this property came into the Martini di

Cigala family in 1956, since when it has remained very much an affair of that clan, the current proprietors being Luca, Francesco and Elisabetta. They were among the first in Chianti Classico, back in the mid-1980s, to perceive the shifting world taste towards primary rather than tertiary aromas, the mark of their wines being depth of fruit, which is not by any means to say that they lack structure – indeed the top wines are quasi-Brunello-like in their underlying build. Percarlo, a 100% Sangiovese SuperTuscan, is the one that has won them their lofty reputation abroad, particularly in the USA – a wine of rich berry, rather than cherry, fruitiness overlying a firm tannicity which promises, from the best vintages, years of drinking ahead. The power is such, indeed, as to overcome any awareness of the fact that the wine has spent up to two years in *barrique*, which many would say is excessive for Sangiovese – and indeed, very often, it is. A characteristic earthiness runs through the red wines of the estate, and it shows in both the Chianti Classico Riserva and especially the *normale*, the latter having that touch less fruit to jazz it up, the former, however, like Percarlo, displaying the fruit cum backbone of a wine capable of considerable ageing.

The latest addition to the range is a Merlot called La Ricolma, which has received wildly enthusiastic reviews from tasters.

Other producers of Gaiole capable of good to excellent Sangiovese include: **Agricoltori del Chianti Geografico** (CC Contessa di Radda; CCR Montegiachi; I Vigneti del Geografico – Sangiovese + Cabernet Sauvignon); **Colombaio di Cencio** (CC; CCR; Il Futuro – Sangiovese + Cabernet Sauvignon); **Lamole e Vistarenni** (CC & CCR Lamole di Lamole; CCR Villa Vistarenni; CCR Campolungo); Castello di **Meleto** (CC Pieve di Spaltenna; CCR; Rainero – 100% Sangiovese); **Montiverdi** (CC Cru Villa Maisano Questo; CC Vigneto Cipressone; Calesco – Sangiovese + Cabernet Sauvignon and Merlot); **Rocca di Castagnoli** (CCR Capraia; CCR Poggio a' Frati; Stielle – Sangiovese + Cabernet Sauvignon); Castello di **San Polo in Rosso** (CC, CCR, Cetinaia – 100% Sangiovese); **San Vincenti** (CC; CCR; Stignano – 100% Sangiovese); Fattoria **Valtellina** (CC; CCR; Convivio – Sangiovese + Cabernet Sauvignon).

Greve

Carpineto. Antonio Zaccheo and Giovanni Sacchet began this operation in 1967 in the days when grapes were plentiful and cheap and people skilled at selecting fruit and turning it into quality wine were thin on the ground. About Sacchet's skill in this latter regard there was never a shadow of doubt – he was once voted 'International Winemaker of the Year' by the International Wine & Spirit Competition in the UK. While the going was good he was able to create from bought-in grapes an impressive range of wines, covering the red classics of Tuscany – Chianti Classico, Vino Nobile di Montepulciano and Montalcino – and the major whites of central Italy, as well as a couple of excellent SuperTuscans called Farnito (Cabernet Sauvignon, Chardonnay) and a marvellously original, inexpensive, youthful, Sangiovese-based, oaked *vino da tavola* called Dogajolo – fondly known in Australia as 'the Dog'. Meanwhile, the buyer's market of yesteryear was turning into a nightmare of a seller's market, good grapes were becoming like gold dust and growers were welshing on agreements left, right and centre, so in the 1990s Carpineto were forced to buy land to consolidate their position – in the same way as much larger negociants like Antinori and Ruffino. Today, between Chianti Classico, Montepulciano and Gaville, outside the DOCG area, they control some 120 hectares of land planted to Sangiovese, Cabernet Sauvignon, Chardonnay and Sauvignon Blanc.

Though their range is wide, Carpineto, being situated winery-wise in Greve, have always been Chianti Classico specialists. Over the years their *normale* and Riserva wines have stood out time and again in blind tastings for their fruit, vibrancy, aroma, life, where so many were dead or dying. Montepulciano, however, is a second speciality – they have 30 hectares under vine there today, and they were making soft and succulent Vino Nobile when so many others tasted like liquid stone. And while others have progressed, Carpineto's wines continue to shine with seriousness, typicity and – most important – sheer drinkability.

La Madonnina. Controlled since 1970 by the Casa Vinicola Triacca, who originated in Lombardy's Valtellina where they remain one of the most avant-garde producers, this is an estate of unusually large proportions for Chianti Classico, with over 100 hectares of vineyard if you count those in preparation. Oenologist Luca Triacca, with the assistance of consultant Vittorio Fiore, is putting together some serious Tuscan wines in serious numbers (too often serious numbers means lightweight wine). The Chianti

Classico Bello Stento, Sangiovese plus 10% Canaiolo, is aged exclusively in stainless steel for 24 months before release, and its youthfulness and dark cherry aroma together with very soft tannins and bright fruity acidity make for a glass of wine of good typicity that's a pleasure to drink. The Riserva, 100% Sangiovese aged partially in *barrique*, partially in *botte*, has plenty of sweet cherry fruit though it is outshone by the single-vineyard Riserva Vigneto La Palaia, with 10% Cabernet Sauvignon in the mix, aged entirely in new *barrique*, an international-style wine with a richer, more brooding feel and deep, almost chocolately aromas on the finish. The *vino da tavola* Il Mandorlo, 80% Cabernet Sauvignon/20% Sangiovese, *barrique*-aged for 18 months, is a well-made wine, still youthful yet relatively soft even after four to five years ageing, though it somehow lacks the typicity of the other two wines.

Poggio Scalette. Readers who may be surprised to find an IGT, or SuperTuscan if you prefer, in a section on Chianti Classico are reminded that the overall subject here is not Chianti Classico but Sangiovese. This small estate, purchased in two sections in 1991 and 1995 by celebrated oenological consultant Vittorio Fiore and his wife Adriana, is situated in the heart of Chianti Classico and produces some of the best Sangiovese in absolute terms. It had for years been Vittorio's dream to have his own vineyard, and when he got the chance to acquire 4.5 hectares in this highly favoured spot, just above Querciabella (q.v.), he jumped at it. At first view the vineyards appeared in poor shape, still in mixed or 'promiscuous' cultivation and long neglected; but an ancient farm-hand, a throw-back to *mezzadria*, informed him that the vines were planted in the 1920s. He realised that this was the original Sangiovese di Lamole, the Chianti clone *par excellence*, and some of the plants were still producing high quality, if low yield, grapes. He intermingled them with clones he had had some part in developing in Romagna, at the Zerbina estate (q.v.), and came up with the SuperTuscan Il Carbonaione, a 100% Sangiovese wine of the highest quality, as Parker, *Wine Spectator* and various pundits have all agreed.

Fiore was able in the mid-1990s to add another 7 hectares to the estate, of which 1.5 hectares are on impressive old dry-stone-walled terraces. But he will stick to making just the one wine, using only grapes of excellence, selling the rest off, as wine, in bulk. Of his four sons, Jurij has remained to oversee operations while Vittorio continues to rush in 17 directions as seems to be the fate of famous wine-consultants in Tuscany.

Anyone looking for liquid evidence that Sangiovese *in purezza* is capable of making wine that is not just good, but great, need look no further than Il Carbonaione.

Why is Il Carbonaione classified as an IGT (Alta Valle della Greve) when it could be Chianti Classico? Is this not a snub to the great denomination by one of Sangiovese's most influential exponents? Vittorio Fiore answers that in 1992, when the wine was born, the rules did not permit a 100% Sangiovese to call itself Chianti Classico. Since then the rule has changed, now it could be Chianti Classico, but his customers, he says, are used to the wine as IGT, and anyway Alta Valle della Greve is a more specific denomination. The only way Vittorio is going to change now, he says, is when and if Alta Valle della Greve becomes a recognised sub-zone of Chianti Classico. What he probably means, as alluded to earlier, is that he won't change until he thinks he can get the price he wants under the Chianti Classico DOCG.

Querciabella. In the unlikely event of there ever being a Bordeaux-like classification of the great estates of Tuscany, Querciabella would surely be in the running for *Premier Cru* status. Founded in the early 1970s by wealthy industrialist Giuseppe Castiglioni, whose wine-enthusiast son Sebastiano has taken over the direction of the estate, Querciabella has arrived at a point where one expects at least near perfection from every bottle that comes from the line. They even achieved *tre bicchieri* status with a Chianti Classico *normale* in 1995 – something few indeed have been able to emulate. Said wine is not pure Sangiovese – there's a small percentage of Cabernet Sauvignon and Merlot in it; it is also to some extent *affinato* in *barrique* – but of second passage. What else can it, and the finer, more concentrated Riserva ascribe their success to, then, except for great care in the vineyard, low yields, expert wine-making? This latter responsibility falls to resident oenologist Guido de Santi, a man soft of speech and a million miles removed from the type of self-promoting loud-mouth that seems to be springing up in Tuscany as the wines attract more international acclaim.

The top red, IGT Camartina, is the one that gets the new *barriques*, as well as at least 25% Cabernet Sauvignon. Launched in 2002 was another SuperTuscan, Palafreno (Sangiovese-Merlot).

Perhaps the most surprising wine, however, is the white Batàr (was Bâtard, but they had to change it under pressure from you know who). This is a 50% Pinot Bianco/50% Chardonnay, *barrique*-aged job of astonishing complexity and concentration, at times just a bit o.t.t. in terms of richness and oak, but one nonetheless which would not be put to shame in a line-up of the world's top dry whites.

Vecchie Terre di Montefili. Hailing from Prato, the textile town west of Florence that has accounted for the wealth of so many Florentines over the past thousand years, Roccaldo Acuti knew plenty about cloth but precious little about making wine. Unlike some, he was willing to recognise this fact, so when in 1979 he acquired this charming estate way up in the hills west of Greve he was canny enough to place his vinous fortunes in the hands of master winemaker Vittorio Fiore. Step one accomplished, but there's another. Fiore always makes his position as a consultant clear to prospective employers who want him to make them 'great wine': If you give me all the equipment I need and follow my instructions to the letter, then I will make you great wine. Sounds simple, but it's amazing how difficult wealthy egotists find this prescription. Acuti was the exception, and the result is two of the finest SuperTuscans in the business, Bruno di Rocca, and Anfiteatro. The former, a Cabernet Sauvignon/Sangiovese blend, is a wine of great concentration, packed with fruit, the tannins ripe and not aggressive and capable of carrying the wine forward for many years. If I had to choose just one, however, I would go for Anfiteatro, supposedly a pure Sangiovese – though rivals swear it's got a significant French influence – which can stand up comfortably to the top Montalcino Brunellos. The fruit is concentrated and rich, the oak is beautifully judged so that hints of woodsmoke and coffee add contour instead of getting in the way; but the best thing about it is the texture, fine-grained and substantial yet smooth, like quality silk. Well, he is a textile man.

Castello **Vicchiomaggio.** Standing high on a hill slightly north of the town of Greve, one of the most impressive of the *Rinascimento* castles whose original purpose was to protect the Florentine territory from Sienese and other raiders, Castello Vicchiomaggio has been the property since 1966 of the Matta family, then wine merchants of London. Today the estate is controlled by oenologist John Matta, backed by consultant Giorgio Marone, and things have moved a long way from those early days. The original 6 hectares of promiscuous culture have given way to 30 of specialised vineyard, all, since the law changed in 1984, planted to red varieties of mainly Tuscan origin – Sangiovese, Canaiolo, Colorino – but to an increasing extent also from France. Indeed, the second generation of specialised vineyard has arrived, with John's father's earliest plantings now giving way a couple of hectares a year to the sort of denser configuration of selected clones which characterises the Tuscan scene today. The work, slow and expensive though it be, is necessary to the steady improvement of quality to which John is committed. Yet he comments: 'The single most frustrating thing in agriculture is that when you decide to do something you don't see the fruits for seven or eight years.' And the rest.

Progress in the *cantina* has parallelled that in the vineyard, though here all that is required is investment, so it can be quicker. All vinification equipment has recently been modernised, and almost all the large old Slavonian oak barrels have given way to French oak ones of between 2.25 and 25 hectolitres capacity.

The wines are all individualised according to the vineyard of their derivation. Grapes for the basic Chianti Classico San Jacopo (90% Sangiovese, plus Canaiolo and Colorino) are from vineyards replanted during the first ten years; designed as an early drinking, fresh Chianti, San Jacopo comes on sale as soon as the law permits, in October following the vintage. Chianti Classico Riserva Petri comes from Vigna Petri, planted in 1966 – so, all old vines except for the 5% Cabernet element, which tends to enhance the wine's colour and structure. Chianti Classico Riserva La Prima comes from the oldest vines, planted between 1925 and 1968: an excellent example of a traditional style Chianti, made entirely from Tuscan varieties according to modern precepts, e.g. 12–15 months in French *barrique*, La Prima is Vicchiomaggio's most individualistic and best product, even though Ripa delle More, 100% Sangiovese aged a similar time in small French oak, has attracted more journalistic attention. To conclude, Ripa delle Mandorle is a sort of modestly priced SuperTuscan, a *barriqued* blend of Sangiovese (85%) and Cabernet Sauvignon.

Other producers capable of good to excellent Sangiovese in Greve include: **Montecalvi** (Montecalvi – Sangiovese + Cabernet Sauvignon); Castello di **Querceto** (CCR Il Picchio; La Corte –

Sangiovese; Querciolaia – Sangiovese + Cabernet Sauvignon); **Riseccoli** (CC, CCR, Saeculum – Sangiovese, Merlot + Cabernet Sauvignon); Castel **Ruggero** (CCR); Castello di **Verrazzano** (CCR; Sassello – Sangiovese); Fattoria di **Vignamaggio** (CC Vitigliano; CCR Monna Lisa); **Viticcio** (CC; CCR Beatrice; Prunaio – Sangiovese).

Impruneta
A very few Chianti Classico producers are here, including: **Lanciola II** (CCR Le Masse di Greve; Terricci – Sangiovese + Cabernet Sauvignon).

Panzano
(A *frazione* of Greve, but sufficiently important to be considered in its own right.)

Villa **Cafaggio**. Stefano Farkas is one of the few Chianti Classico proprietors who has built a reputation for high quality with minimal recourse to external consultancy – although recently he has engaged the services of Stefano Chioccioli, thus enabling him to see to the wider requirements of the estate. Taking over from his Hungarian-exile father in the mid-1970s, Stefano maintained quality in this felicitously sited wine-farm, boasting today over 30 hectares of vineyard, plus a few rented, in Panzano's famous *conca d'oro*, in an era when few others were getting it right, and continues strongly to this day. Along the way he, with many others, picked up on the international trail, but judiciously, adding carefully selected Cabernet Sauvignon, and later Merlot, clones to his vineyard repertoire. He was also among the first in Chianti to plant the Sangiovese Grosso sub-variety from Montalcino, and in the late 1990s was one of the earliest to put into practice the Consorzio's Chianti Classico 2000 findings in respect of Sangiovese clones, planting a substantial proportion of the vineyard to F9 A5 48 as well as R24, T19 and VCR5.

Farkas produces two *barrique*-matured SuperTuscans – today IGT Toscana: San Martino, Sangiovese-based, a wine of considerable depth and individuality, made from very ripe grapes harvested around the middle of October; and Cabernet-based Cortaccio, whose blackcurranty-berry fruit gives it a marked *bordelais* style. Both are substantial, almost chewy wines, with a particular undercurrent of vanilla coming from the average 18 months in new French *barriques*, but with fruit predominating. A certain oakiness occurs too in the Chianti Classico Riserva Solatio Basilica, from old Sangiovese vines, although this wine tends to have less power and more perfume, greater intensity of fruit character, and in terms of authenticity is perhaps the estate's most successful wine. The Chianti Classico and normal Riserva are well made, too, particularly the former, being, as it should be, a relatively light, early-drinking Tuscan red for all occasions. Through all the wines there runs a very definite house style, reflecting the philosophy and personality of one of Chianti Classico's genuine individualists.

Fontodi. Indisputably among the high flyers of all Italy, this stunningly situated estate, whose 60-odd hectares of vineyard cover the slopes south of Panzano in what is virtually the centre of Chianti Classico, began its modern era in 1968 when the Manetti family, *terracotta* manufacturers of Florence, took control. The young Giovanni Manetti, who runs the estate today, began to play an active role in the *azienda* in 1979, taking on as oenologist Franco Bernabei, who had been an agronomist with Ruffino and had only shortly before started up as an independent consultant at Selvapiana. The two of them, together with Giovanni's brother, travelled to various countries – France, California – to pick up ideas on how to improve quality, and they brought them back with a determination to succeed.

Fontodi's two renowned *crus*, Flaccianello (10 hectares) and Vigna del Sorbo (8 hectares), had been planted up to a decade earlier, but it was the new team that really brought out the quality in them. Flaccianello was one of the first of the 100% Sangiovese SuperTuscans, while Vigna del Sorbo, once the Cabernet Sauvignon vines had been grafted onto the old Canaiolo and Trebbiano stock, was to become one of the first Sangiovese–Cabernet blends. There is a certain irony in this, as the pure-Tuscan Flaccianello, a wine of great breeding, finesse and durability, reflecting the uppish altitude and stony soil of the site, remains an IGT while the international blend Vigna del Sorbo, with that touch more roundness and fruitiness, is classified as Chianti Classico.

Many things have happened since those days. Pinot Nero and Syrah have been planted, and today Fontodi are among the most accomplished producers of those varietals in Tuscany, under the

Case Vie label. The *cru* vineyards have been left with their old vines, except where holes have been created by the passing of individual plants, but they have been the source of valuable material for the replanting of other vineyards – the present total being 67 hectares under vine. Indeed, Fontodi have been for over 20 years in the forefront of producers experimenting to improve vineyard conditions in the zone, and have played an active part role in the Chianti Classico Consortium and in its viticultural programmes.

An important step was taken in the mid-1990s when a new *cantina* was built working entirely on the gravity principle (no pumps) and was fitted out with all the latest vinification equipment. For maturation purposes Fontodi rely for the most part on French

oak, Flaccianello and Vigna del Sorbo receiving up to 16 months in *barriques* (a part of Flaccianello also does the malo-lactic in small wood), while even the Chianti Classico is given a year in barrels of which 80%, mainly used, are French *barriques*. In fact, one of the principal efforts of the estate in recent times has been to upgrade the quality of the basic Chianti Classico, to which end the Riserva has been discontinued so that the better grapes can go into that wine.

It may not seem a particularly exceptional tale. But anyone looking for a model operation on which to base a study of all that's dynamic and forward-looking, whilst remaining natural, in Chianti Classico today need look no further than Fontodi.

La Massa. Giampaolo Motta's 27 hectares of vineyard are situated in Panzano's *conca d'oro*, referred to above as one of the finest viticultural sub-zones of Chianti Classico. Giampaolo, now in his late 30s, came to Tuscan wine from a Neapolitan tanning family, and to this superb estate, purchased in 1992, via apprenticeships at John Dunkley's Riecine, Zonin's Pian d'Albola and the di Napoli's Castello dei Rampolla. With the help of oenologist Carlo Ferrini, Giampaolo, determined from the start to achieve excellence, has guided his estate to the position of being one of the most highly regarded in Tuscany today.

Motta makes only two wines, which in Bordelais fashion he likes to think of as his *grand cru* and his 'second wine'. The *grand cru*, recognised as such by pundits and consumers in the know, is Giorgio Primo, an upmarket Chianti Classico made up of 90% Sangiovese with 10% Cabernet Sauvignon and Merlot, not just aged in *barrique* but vinified there in the sense that, after the alcoholic fermentation, he leaves the wine in small wood for 6 months with *bâtonnage*, a regular stirring-up of the lees more normally associated with white wine production. The result is a wine combining succulent fruit and firm structure, attractive in youth but capable of extended ageing. Giorgio Primo is rightly regarded today as one of Tuscany's new aristocrats.

The 'second wine' is also a Chianti Classico, with 90% Sangiovese plus Canaiolo, Cabernet and Merlot. Giampaolo is at present considering removing this from the Chianti Classico register since, he says, it is getting 'too near to Giorgio Primo' and anyway 'the price of Chianti Classico is too restricted'. If he does change the chances are that the percentage of French grapes will increase considerably since, he says, their results are 'so much better' than those of Sangiovese, even the recently planted Sangiovese whose results are 'so much better' than the old.

Monte Bernardi. Stak Aivaliotis is a London photographer of Greek-Cypriot parentage with a lifelong passion for, not just wine, but great wine. He made a lot of money shooting adverts through the 1970s and 1980s and spent most of it on the best that Bordeaux, Burgundy and the rest had to offer. Slowly, the conviction grew that he, too, had to make wine – not just good wine, as I say, but great wine, at the level of Château Le Pin, or higher. He considered various wine-producing areas, and in 1988, with his painter wife, Sharon, bought Monte Bernardi.

It took a few years to get going but by 1992, with Giorgio Marone as consultant oenologist, Stak from his 6 hectares of vineyard, mostly planted in the late 1960s, was making 'the best wine in Chianti' (whatever his other vices or virtues may be, Stak does not suffer the pangs of modesty). The range grew and developed until – to cut a fairly short story even shorter – he had worked out his wines and his methods.

Wines: there are three – Paris (this being Stak's middle name, given to the Chianti Classico), 100% Sangiovese; Sa'etta, again 100% Sangiovese, a selection from his best vineyard, Vigna Grande; and Tzingana, a Bordeaux-style blend consisting of Merlot, the two Cabernets and Petit Verdot – these having been grafted onto existing unwanted varieties like Canaiolo, Trebbiano and Malvasia.

Methods: Extreme selection in the vineyard, pressing by old-fashioned (but new) basket press, 4 days pre-fermentation maceration, fermentation in stainless steel, malo-lactic completed in *barrique*, then 10–12 months – no more, he feels this is the exact right period – in small French oak, some new, some used; finally, bottling without filtration. No buying in of grapes or wine, no additives (apart from SO_2), no cultured yeasts, in short, pure wine. This is one of his hobbyhorses: 'Maybe the world wants homogenised wines', he laughs, 'but I want the real thing. And my wines, today, are not just pure, not just real, they are among the best in the world. The Bordelais aren't doing it any more', he claims, 'too many tricks. Maybe there are still a few Burgundians who can give me a run for my money; that's it.'

The wine world has responded positively, both press-wise and sales-wise, and Stak today is able to sell all his very high-priced production without trouble to Brits, Americans, Japanese and, increasingly, Italians. Trouble has arisen on the domestic front, however, with Stak and Sharon having split up and at loggerheads as to what to do with the estate. But Stak swears he's not leaving. 'I love what I'm doing, and I think I have a contribution to make. I'll be here till they carry me away in a wooden box.' No doubt the wood will be best quality oak from Nevers and Allier.

Castello dei **Rampolla**. See chapter on international varieties.

Other producers capable of good to excellent Sangiovese in Panzano include: **Carobbio** (CCR; Leone del Carobbio – Sangiovese); **Casaloste** (CC; CCR; CCR Don Vincenzo); **Cennatoio** (CC O'Leandro; Etrusco – Sangiovese); **Il Vescovino** (CC Vigna Piccola; Merlotto – Sangiovese + Cabernet Sauvignon); Podere **Le Cinciole** (CC; CCR Valle del Pozzo; CCR Petresco); **Le Fonti** (CCR; Fontissimo – Sangiovese + Cabernet Sauvignon); **Vignole** (CC; CCR).

Poggibonsi
Melini/GIV. GIV (Gruppo Italiano Vini), 'the largest wine company in Italy and one of the leading companies in the world' (it says in their brochure) is much more than Melini, but if one had to pick one flagship winery among the ten they operate in north–central Italy it is fair, I think, to nominate Melini.

Melini, founded in 1705, is not the oldest of GIV's properties – that honour falls to the Antica Fattoria Macchiavelli estate, founded 1639. However, it is arguably the most prestigious and certainly the best known internationally, Melini having been a by-word for Chianti for well over a century. With 163 hectares of vineyard in several sub-zones of central Tuscany and a winery at Gaggiano di Poggibonsi with a capacity of 10 million litres, not counting the cellar at San Gimignano for the ageing of their *cru* Le Grillaie, Melini are a major force in Chianti Classico even without the supporting presence of GIV's Macchiavelli and Conti Serristori in Sant'Andrea in Percussina, all directed by oenologist Nunzio Capurso. Feathers in their cap include the fact that their Riserva La Selvanella, from an estate in the commune of Radda, was from 1969 the first single-estate wine in Tuscany, and one of the first in

Italy; going back a bit, the fact, too, that they were among the first to export Chianti internationally successfully following the development of the now despised but then revolutionary wicker flask in the mid-nineteenth century; and, coming forward to the present, the fact that they have been among the most active proponents of revitalising the Chianti vineyard with newly developed clones and planting methods.

Melini's lead wine is, in fact, la Selvanella, a wine which has always had class but has recently been made more 'international' (Cabernet, *barrique*). But their Chianti Classico I Sassi and Riservas Laborel and Granaio, the latter single-vineyard *cru* being today reserved for Germany and England, are all finely crafted if slightly over-modern wines as are the inevitable Merlot, the 70% Sangiovese 30% Cabernet Sauvignon Coltri Uno and its mirror-image Coltri Due.

As to Macchiavelli/Serristori, which it is fair to consider in the same profile since the wines are made by the same people, they – and particularly Macchiavelli – have excelled with Riserva Vigna Fontalle Riserva and the SuperTuscan Cabernet Solatio del Tani Ser Niccolò, although their most surprising success has been the Pinot Nero Il Principe, surprising because it actually is an excellent wine from a variety one would not expect to, and which rarely does, excel in Tuscany.

Briefly, GIV's other estates in central Italy include Bigi in Orvieto and Fontana Candida in Latium, both internationally acclaimed in their own right. The wineries of the north have been touched upon, or more, in *Barolo to Valpolicella*.

In the past few years GIV have also joined the bandwagon heading south with the holding company GIV Sud, whose objective is to invest in existing wineries in the regions of Sicily, Puglia, Campania and Basilicata. First acquisition was a controlling interest in Sicily's Rapitalà. Next came a 60% interest in Terre del Vulture in Basilicata. The latest deal involves a 60-hectare vineyard in Puglia's Salento peninsula, with the possibility of expanding to 100 hectares.

The following excerpt from a GIV press release, relating only to wholly owned properties and not to GIV Sud, will give readers an idea of the actual and growing power of this group. 'With 800 hectares of vineyard, 10 production cellars in the most acclaimed wine regions and a wide selection of famous brands, GIV achieved a consolidated turnover of 372 billion lire in 1998 (over 400 billion in 1999, 6.4 million cases), including the associated businesses of Carniato Europe of Paris and Frederick Wildman of New York. 61.4 million litres of quality wines were sold in total, 25% in the domestic market and 75% in the export market in more than 60 countries.' The most important markets are, in order, Germany, USA, UK, Canada, Japan.

So it's not only the Yankees that play hardball.

One other producer of Poggibonsi capable of good to excellent Sangiovese is **Ormanni** (CCR; Julius – Sangiovese + Merlot).

Radda

Montevertine. The late Sergio Manetti was one of the founders of modern Chianti Classico, even though he himself left the Consortium, and waved bye-bye to the DOC, as Chianti was then, in 1981. He was as ahead of his time then as he was behind it, in the best possible way, at the time of his death in November 2000.

It was in 1967 that Manetti, then an industrialist (no relation to the Manettis of Fontodi), bought this small property between the village of Volpaia and the town of Radda. The first year he made wine, 1971, happened to be a great vintage, and his Chianti went down well at the annual Vinitaly wine fair. He became enthusiastic, caught the bug to the point of giving up his main work a few years later and turning entirely to the production of wine with the intention of reaching the highest possible quality standards. He asked the 'master taster' Giulio Gambelli to help him with the blends, looked after his vines like children, although he had three fine ones of his own – twin daughters Anna and Marta, son Martino – who take over from him now that he's passed on.

Today the estate has nearly 12 hectares of vineyard, all planted to traditional Tuscan varieties: Sangiovese – almost 85% of the total, Canaiolo, Colorino, Trebbiano and Malvasia.

Sergio was ahead of his time because his wines were too good to be '*tipico*', for which reason they were on occasion refused the DOC Chianti Classico. His especial crime was to make what was then a novelty and a blasphemy, a pure Sangiovese called Le Pergole Torte, which had no chance with a tasting commission unable to accept the innovations of a varietal wine aged in *barrique*. So he decided to have nothing further to do with officialdom and for 20 years he marketed his wines by their brand names: Montevertine and Montevertine Riserva (equivalent of Chianti Classico *normale* and Riserva), Il Sodaccio (all three of these blends of Sangiovese and Canaiolo) as well as Le Pergole Torte.

Sergio was behind the times, too, because he refused to introduce international grapes into the equation. He did not want his wines, he declared, to 'follow a fashion spreading all over the world. What happens', he asked, 'if they become boring to people? It would take years to retrace our steps. Is it not possible, we ask ourselves, to make great wines with Sangiovese?'

The answer is yes and Sergio Manetti's wines, unfashionably angular and un-fruit-driven as they are, yet as pure as anything you'll find from this ampelographically confused corner of the wine world, and capable of ageing wonderfully as the dispensers of points would find if they were to judge wines not when they're young but a few years down the road, are the proof of the pudding.

Fattoria **Terrabianca**. How many wine-lovers have dreamt of throwing it all in and starting a new life as a producer? So when, in 1987, at the age of 44, Roberto Guldener gave up a lucrative fashion business in his native Zurich to set up Terrabianca in Radda he was taking the dream one giant step further. With true Swiss thoroughness he approached the matter systematically, making sure he had the right consultant (Vittorio Fiore) and the right site before launching himself into the semi-unknown. His preparations paid off, and today Guldener's wines shine among the best examples of their respective types in Tuscany. With 23 hectares of grapes at Radda, plus another 20 or so at the rented property of Castello di Cerreto nearby, he created wines of Tuscan yet modern, international character.

The accent is indeed on the word 'Tuscan', Guldener being a strong believer in blending from different zones to achieve excellence, to which end, in 1996, he purchased a property near Massa Marittima in the Maremma called Il Tesoro, where the aim is to arrive at 30 hectares under vine. The Chardonnay, plus a touch of Sauvignon, of the *barrique*d white Piano della Cappella has benefited from the input of a bit of the rich, characterful Vermentino, while the IGT Toscana reds – that's all of them bar Vigna della Croce Chianti Classico Riserva – now enjoy the riper

Sangiovese and Cabernet of the Maremma to offset the elegance but astringency of the same varieties from Radda.

The outstanding wine of the estate, for me, is the pure Sangiovese Piano del Cipresso, an irresistible and – if ever there was one – archetypal expression of the 'sour cherry' style of Sangiovese. Campaccio 'speciale' – effectively a Riserva, though the word may not be used for a non DOC wine – is a Sangiovese/Cabernet Sauvignon blend of great depth and penetrating flavour in the now widespread 'Tignanello' style; there is also a very well made Campaccio *normale*. Vigna della Croce Riserva, the sole DOCG Chianti Classico, enjoys the ripe tannin/smooth fruit style common to the wines of the property, while Scassino, formerly Chianti Classico, is a tasty, forward and fruity red of Tuscan type.

Castello di **Volpaia**. In *Life Beyond Lambrusco* I featured just one Chianti Classico producer and Volpaia was it. At that time, in the early 1980s, they were ahead of the game, having achieved in their wines an elegance and distinction which few could emulate, thereby making an early and crucial contribution to the raising of the image of Chianti Classico generally. Since then numerous Chianti Classico wineries have taken the road towards excellence, creating wines of every style, but Carlo Mascheroni and Giovanella Stianti, with the help of Maurizio Castelli, and in more recent years of the acclaimed consultant Riccardo Cotarella, have stuck to the road of elegance and perfume rather than power and opulence. It is to some extent a way consistent with the position of their vineyards – at between 450 and 600 metres some of the highest in Chianti – and with the nature of their soil, which has a marked sandy component. But it is also totally consistent with their personalities, gentle and refined, yet quietly determined to pursue beauty, whether it be in the discreet manner in which the stainless steel tanks and multiple barrels of the winery have been tucked away in various buildings of the delicious eyrie that is the *borgo* of Volpaia, whether it be in respect of the annual art exhibition during which the town becomes host to large numbers of lovers of fine wine and painting.

As far as the wines are concerned, the twin turrets of the castle are the SuperTuscans Coltassala and Balifico. The former is pre-dominantly Sangiovese with a small percentage of Mammolo, *barricato* of course, its intense cherry-fruit and floral aromas being joined by hints of vanilla to create an olfactorally delightful and organoleptically satisfying experience. The latter is a blend of Sangiovese, at two-thirds, and Cabernet Sauvignon and Franc, combining gentle soft-fruit aromas (strawberry, loganberry) with the same fine-grained tannins that grace the Coltassala. The Chianti Classicos, *normale* and Riserva, have less of the concentration and intensity of the SuperTuscans but they share the tendency towards gracefulness. The *normale* is a wine of relatively early drinkability, while the Riserva is deceptively structured and capable of considerable longevity. Sangiovese is the bedrock, of course, but the back-up varieties include an eclectic selection in Syrah, Pinot Nero and Merlot as well as the two Cabernets, plus that Tuscan Mammolo which gives to Coltassala in particular its distinctive floral bouquet.

Other producers of Radda capable of good to excellent Sangiovese include: **Castello d'Albola** (CCR; Acciaolo – Sangiovese + Cabernet); **Borgo Salcetino** (CC; CCR Lucarello; Rossole – Sangiovese + Merlot); Podere **Capaccia** (CC; CCR; Querciagrande – Sangiovese); **Colle Bereto** (CCR; Il Cenno and Il Tocco – Sangiovese + Canaiolo and Malvasia Nera); **Livernano** (Puro Sangue – Sangiovese); **Poggerino** (CC; CCR; CCR Bugialla); **Pruneto** (CC); **Vignavecchia** (CCR; Raddese – Sangiovese).

San Casciano Val di Pesa

Poggiopiano. What went right here is still an open question, but something did, because from nowhere suddenly everyone in the late 1990s was talking about Poggiopiano, especially about their extraordinary SuperTuscan Rosso di Sera – from the rhyme: *Rosso di sera, bel tempo si spera* (Red sky at night, shepherd's delight); the label displays a large, blood-coloured setting-sun. The Bartoli family, father Beppe, brothers Stefano and Alessandro, run this 7-hectare vineyard just up the road from the Antinori winery in San Casciano, to which have been added the vineyards of another property of a slightly larger size recently acquired on a long-term rental basis. Just ordinary Tuscans they are, not nobles, not wealthy industrialists, the sort of people you might expect to meet in Burgundy or Piemonte – although, like a number of producers in Tuscany, their roots are not in wine; they only got into it in the early 1990s – but rarely in ultra-chic Chianti Classico, the kind of people who invite you into their functional non-designer kitchen for a glass and a chat or perhaps a meal of delicious Tuscan *casalinga* cooking.

The original *cantina*, still small and a little cramped, has been modernised now, and will be supplemented by the one at the new vineyard. But it was little more than a blueprint in the late 1990s when, to their astonishment, the world's wine press was besieging them and buyers were begging for wine they'd already over-allocated. A major secret of their success, no doubt, is the oenological attentions of one of the rising stars in the ranks of Tuscan consultants, Luca d'Attoma, a magician with Sangiovese and *barrique*. I was there when Luca first presented Rosso di Sera to a group of distinguished young winemaking colleagues, before its release, and not one of them would believe it didn't have any Merlot in it. It's true, though, this deeply fruity, fine-textured wine is Sangiovese with about 15% Colorino, not a drop of anything 'international'. Even the Chianti Classico, containing a modicum of Canaiolo instead of Colorino, has a deceptively deep, berry-fruit style which makes it attractive to modern wine-lovers; only the aromas announce that, no, these wines are Tuscan, Tuscan all the way, like their makers.

Other producers of the Chianti Classico section of San Casciano capable of good to excellent Sangiovese include: **Castelli del Grevepesa** (CC; CC Montefiridolfi; CC Clemente VII; CC Lamole; Coltifredi – Sangiovese); **Corti-Corsini** (CC Don Tommaso; CC Le Corti; CCR Cortevecchia); **La Sala** (CCR; Campo all'Albero – Sangiovese + Cabernet); **Ripanera** (CC, Terra di Ripanera – Sangiovese, Cabernet, Merlot).

Tavarnelle Val di Pesa
Good producers include: Podere **La Cappella** (CC Querciolo; Corbezzolo – Sangiovese + Merlot); **Montecchio** (CC; CCR; Pietracupa – Sangiovese + Cabernet); **Poggio al Sole** (CC; CCR Casasilia).

Other Chianti sub-zones

Similar regulations apply for the other seven Chianti DOCG sub-zones, plus plain Chianti DOCG, in relation to which, at least in respect of the traditional Sangiovese-based style, Chianti Classico is considered by most – 80% correctly – and certainly considers itself to be very superior. To the denizens of the Classico zone these others are opportunistic exploiters of a famous denomination to which they have no geographic right. As I have said elsewhere I am on their side, not just for the benefit of Classico but for that, too, of the others, as well as for the name of Chianti itself, and of the DOCG qualification in general.

Taking the last point first, it is absurd that wines considered by experts as being of least value in their respective zones should qualify as DOCG while being dwarfed by other DOCGs or DOCs or even IGTs. Such anomalies mock the system itself. Examples would include Chianti Montalbano DOCG, which in the case of Tenuta di Capezzana is third in order of quality, after Carmignano DOCG and Barco Reale DOC – indeed it's fourth if you include IGT SuperTuscans like Ghiaie della Furba. Or Chianti Colli Senesi, which producers in Montalcino could make but generally don't, considering both Brunello DOCG and Rosso di Montalcino DOC, indeed Sant'Antimo Rosso DOC, not to mention certain IGTs, to be of considerably greater prestige. As for just plain Chianti DOCG, which may be produced in various areas where the sub-zonal denominations do not apply, the wine rarely rises above the mediocre (there are exceptions), and is more likely to be cheap and, if not nasty, certainly far from being a worthy representative of Italy's highest quality designation.

Note to lawmakers, therefore: if you want us to believe in the integrity of your system, do not allow low-grade wines to be included in the highest bracket. The obvious corollary is that, if you continue to do so, we will hesitate to give credence even where it is due, and the prejudice that Italians are not to be trusted will continue to have food on which to thrive.

So why does it happen, you ask? Because the industrialists fear that, without the world-famous name Chianti, they would lose too much, and the industrialists have money and power with which to fight their corner. Short-sighted, certainly, and narrow-minded, because there are perfectly acceptable alternatives. In place of Chianti DOCG you could quite easily have Toscana IGT, Toscana being as recognisable and as attractive a name to the world at large as Chianti. You could even, I suppose, have Chianti DOC (dropping the G), but for God's sake spare us from Toscana DOC, because that again would degrade the system, Tuscany being far too vast and varied an area to able to claim 'typicity' on a region-wide basis. Even Toscana IGT is pushing it, but at least it's not making any grand claims.

As for the sub-zones, would not plain Rufina be better than Chianti Rufina? It gives a clear and unique identity, without fudging. Similarly, Montalbano for Chianti Montalbano, or Colli Senesi for Chianti Colli Senesi.

However that may be, for the foreseeable future these remain Chianti sub-zones, and as we are on the subject of Chianti we must clear that hurdle before moving to what are for the most part considerably more important things.

Rufina and Pomino

Rufina is probably the only 'Chianti' zone, apart from Classico, which can justify qualification as a DOCG. One reason is that there is no denomination of greater prestige within its boundaries, as for example Brunello di Montalcino within Colli Senesi. The best wines made from Sangiovese grapes, at least at 75% minimum, are generally categorised as Chianti Rufina DOCG, and only non-conformist SuperTuscans, of which there are far fewer than in Classico, break ranks. Production is in any event small – about one-tenth that of Classico, about one-fortieth of all 'Chianti'.

No doubt because they are grown in a zone of relatively low mean temperature, being hard up against the Apennine mountain ridge, with a soil similar to that of Chianti Classico – galestro with limestone, and clay – but a ripening time generally several days later, Rufina wines are known for their acidity and their longevity. A well-made version is capable of lasting 50 years or more, as has been demonstrated convincingly by a 50-year-old Selvapiana Riserva tasted recently against a number of considerably less aged yet less well-preserved wines from the most illustrious producers of Tuscany. Another major grower, Fratelli Grati, still stores thousands of hectolitres of wine up to 10 or more years old in cask and tank.

As for Pomino, after the village of the same name, geographically it is virtually an enclave within Rufina, the vineyards being on slopes high above the left bank of the Sieve River faced by, indeed surrounded by, the DOCG Rufina zone. The tiny amount of red produced as Pomino, around 1,500 hectolitres, comes almost entirely from the vineyards of Frescobaldi, who own 96 of the 100 hectares of the Pomino zone. Pomino Rosso, however, while

Sangiovese-based (60% minimum) is a blend of grapes which one does not and could not find in Rufina (minimum 15% Cabernet and 10% Merlot). The thinking behind this is presumably that the internationals will have less trouble ripening at altitude than Sangiovese.

The producers

Fattoria di **Basciano/Masi.** One must distinguish between the *azienda agricola* Basciano, an estate in the hills above Rufina opposite Pomino, and 'Renzo Masi', a *négociant* house making wines from bought-in grapes. Both were founded in 1930 by Paolo Masi, father of Renzo and grandfather of the present manager and winemaker of the same name (Paolo). This latter, one of the rare ones in Tuscany who succeeds with no help at all from the brigade of famous consultants, took over the reins of Basciano in particular around 1990 and since then has been upgrading the vineyard as well as the techniques in *cantina* with conspicuous success. I personally have marvelled at the steady increase of vineyard area planted on the slopes across from our house in Tuscany and at the unwavering professionality and personality of the wines, made from grapes which Paolo believes in handling with the greatest care because, he says, 'Soft tannins only come from whole, unharmed grapes pressed gently'.

Fattoria di Basciano today consists of 30 hectares of vineyard, of which 20 are presently in production, the grape mix being approximately 80% Sangiovese and 3% Colorino with Cabernet Sauvignon, Merlot and Syrah making up the balance, the latter two planted recently. The lead wine in terms of volume is Chianti Rufina (100,000 bottles), which like the Riserva contains only Tuscan grapes. There are two more upmarket IGTs, Vigna il Corto – 90% Sangiovese, 10% Cabernet Sauvignon, and I Pini – same grapes but 50–50 (the Merlot and Syrah will go into these when ready). The winemaking process is the same for both of the latter and the Chianti Riserva: long maceration, up to 30 days, then straight into *barriques* of first, second and third passage for the malo-lactic, where they remain for over one year. And the results? Reliably good, sometimes exciting. Indeed, a recently elaborated wine of the Renzo Masi range, called Erta e China, was included in the *Wine Spectator* Y2K list of the 100 best wines of the world – so you can imagine the level Paolo and his team are capable of with their own material.

Marchesi **Frescobaldi**. Although Frescobaldi have their offices in Florence and have vineyards in various Tuscan zones, their main cellars and their most historic and prestigious properties are in the zone or commune of Rufina; hence their inclusion here.

Frescobaldi rest their reputation on two impressive pillars: their 700-year, 30-generation experience as growers and winemakers, the present hierarchy consisting of brothers Vittorio (President), Ferdinando and Leonardo (Vice-Presidents), with several younger Frescobaldis already involved in the business; and the fact that, with some 800 hectares planted to the vine in various parts of Tuscany, they are probably the largest family-owned producers of quality wines in Europe. Their strengths do not end there, however, having in Lamberto Frescobaldi, son of Vittorio, and Nicolò d'Afflitto, one of the star consultants of the age, a pair of highly talented oenologo-agronomists of Tuscan origin but with wide international experience.

Perhaps their most representative property is Castello di Nipozzano, in the DOCG zone of Rufina, where some 180 hectares are planted principally to the Tuscan varieties Sangiovese, Malvasia Nera, Canaiolo and Colorino; and to Cabernets Sauvignon and Franc, with a bit of Merlot. From this property the principal wines are Castello di Nipozzano, a traditional-style Chianti Rufina Riserva of some considerable ageing ability updated to include an element of *affinamento in barrique*; Mormoreto, 100% Cabernet Sauvignon, *barrique*-aged (50% new) for 18 months, a wine whose complexity and harmony have come on apace since d'Afflitto took over in 1995 (here; he has been with Frescobaldi since 1991 in Montalcino); and what is in my view the greatest of all Frescobaldi wines, despite the chi-chi surrounding others, Montesodi, a Sangiovese-based wine of exceptional refinement and *razza* from a splendid 22-hectare vineyard at the crown of a high hill which, as I have observed many times from my office window at the other end of the valley, is always the last spot on which the sun still shines of a summer's evening. Montesodi was probably the first of the top Tuscans to take the now increasingly fashionable DOCG route, having been classified since its first appearance as Chianti Rufina rather than as Vino da Tavola.

The wines of Castello di Pomino are of an entirely different ilk, being grown at between 500 and 700 metres and consisting in whites at two-thirds of production, even though Pomino, histori-cally, is famous for its reds, having been mentioned in Grand Duke Cosimo III's 'Bando' of 1716 as one of Tuscany's four high-quality zones. It was an ancestor of the present Frescobaldis, Vittorio degli Albizzi who, in the mid-nineteenth century, brought to this zone the

French varieties which today predominate. Best-known wines are Pomino Bianco (Chardonnay with hints of Pinots Grigio and Bianco), vastly improved since d'Afflitto arrived, and today one of the best-value Tuscan whites around; and Pomino Benefizio, the latter a single-vineyard wine benefiting, to a larger extent than the Bianco, from discreet small-oak ageing; and, unusually, a Tuscan white of some bottle-ageing potential. Pomino Rosso, based on Sangiovese with a good dollop of Pinot Nero and a little Merlot, is, it has to be said, rather less interesting than either of the whites.

In 1989 the Frescobaldis purchased a large property in Montalcino called Castel Giocondo, from which they have been producing, ever since, a classic, well-structured but *barrique*-influenced Brunello (Castelgiocondo) and a relatively insubstantial, but early-drinking, Rosso (Campo ai Sassi), plus one of the first of the now spreading breed of pure Merlots from Tuscany, Lamaione. In 1995 the Frescobaldis formed a joint venture with the Mondavis of Napa called Luce della Vite, and since 1993 (from existing wines) and more significantly since 1995 (from grapes of both Castel Giocondo and the joint-venture vineyards) a seriously high-image, high-priced blend, 50–50 Sangiovese–Merlot, called Luce. The style is unashamedly 'international', rich of flavour and texture with tannins smoothed down and fruit interweaving with fine oak; personally, as I have indicated, I prefer the pure Tuscan-ness of Montesodi. A second wine of this venture is Lucente, 85% Sangiovese/15% Merlot from various parts of the Frescobaldi marquisate, *barrique*-refined (of course), which from its second vintage, 1996, has shown increasing promise. The same partnership completed, in 2002, the purchase of Lodovico Antinori's prestigious Ornellaia estate in Bolgheri.

From the other Frescobaldi properties, in the Colli Fiorentini and Scansano zones principally, come various other wines, the most important of which from the turnover point of view is Chianti (was Chianti Rufina) Remole, of which annual production easily exceeds a million bottles. There must, after all, be some bread upon which to spread the butter and the jam.

Tenimenti **Ruffino**, Pontassieve. It is hard to decide on a central 'home' for this ubiquitous firm, since their estates and vineyards, owned or rented, are scattered throughout Tuscany. However, the rule I've been following is that a firm's seat is where their principal *cantina* finds itself, and this for Ruffino, since inception over 100 years ago, has meant Pontassieve, a town in the Rufina growing zone east of Florence where the Arno meets the Sieve as they flow down from their respective Apennine sources.

Actually, since the Folonari brothers, Brescian owners of Ruffino since 1913, split asunder in June 2000, the title Tenimenti Ruffino has been deprived of some of its finest estates and wines, though some excellent ones, together with the *cantina* at Pontassieve, remain. Brothers Marco and Paolo, with next-generation Adolfo, Luigi and Carlo, still oversee production here of the firm's lead wine, the world-renowned Chianti Ruffino, in its millions of bottles; a wine which, as a quasi-industrial product, retains a very respectable level of drinkability. As, indeed, do Chianti Classicos Santedame and Aziano as well as the IGT Toscana Fonte al Sole – all 100% Sangiovese wines of easy, almost jammy fruit and low-level structure: crowd-pleasers.

But the Folonaris – or what's left of them in this branch – are fond of saying that Sangiovese is a grape capable of every style of wine from the light, easy and early-drinking to the big, concentrated and long-maturing. They demonstrate the latter with what has proved one of the most reliable of quality restaurant Chiantis over the years, Riserva Ducale, produced from selected grapes from various of their Chianti Classico estates, and its superior version, made only in better vintages from top selection fruit, Riserva Ducale Oro (gold label). On a level similar to that of Riserva Ducale is the Vino Nobile di Montepulciano Lodola Nuova, while Brunello di Montalcino Greppone Mazzi can be put on a par with 'Oro', retaining, however, a structure and a character typical of good Brunello.

Ruffino's big guns in the top quality department, however, are in no case varietal Sangiovese, not even if you allow for 15% of other grapes within a 'varietal'. Nearest to it comes Romitorio di Santedame, IGT Toscana and what you might call a 'SuperTuscan', 40% Sangiovese but with the balance made up of the cognate Colorino, one of Tuscany's more obscure but, when vinified right, most exciting grapes. This is a wine chock full of the wild cherry and blackberry aromas of the Tuscan hills with firm acidity and ripe tannins at a level capable of allowing improvement and conservation for years, a wine of real indigenous character, only marginally attuned to the 'international' taste by ageing in French *barrique* – but deftly, so that the primary aromas predominate. Before the family split I wrote the following:

> That Romitorio is my personal favourite is certain, though some would take issue with this judgement and vote Il Pareto as Ruffino's top wine. While I agree that this 100% Cabernet Sauvignon SuperTuscan, produced not under the Ruffino label but under that of the Nozzole estate, is tremendously impressive in terms of its fullness and complexity (berry fruit, raisin, dark choc and coffee, toast and spice, long sweet finish) I am always inclined to prefer originality, a virtue which Romitorio with its archetypal Tuscan-ness holds in trumps.
>
> But perhaps the most famous of Ruffino's top wines is Cabreo Il Borgo, 70% Sangiovese with 30% Cabernet Sauvignon, much hailed and festooned with laurels since its first appearance in 1983: a wine, in good years, of tremendous concentration and richness of fruit, perhaps more muscular than subtle, but very modern, and endowed with considerable ageing potential. The twin white, Cabreo la Pietra, a *barriqued* Chardonnay complete with *bâtonnage*, is equally impressive for concentration and wealth of fruit, although it suffers a little from one-dimensionality. Its non-oaked partner, Libaio – 85% Chardonnay with a drop of Pinot Grigio – perhaps works a little better making as it does less claim to complexity.

Pareto and Cabreo have gone now to the other branch of the family, consisting of brothers Italo, Ambrogio and Alberto Folonari of the newly formed Tenute A&A Folonari, who have taken control of Nozzole, Cabreo and other major estates, including relatively recently acquired ones in Bolgheri and Friuli. They have received what I am told is an 'enormous sum' of money (well in excess of 100 billion lire), which they say they will use to improve existing estates and purchase new ones apart from those in Friuli. However, the Tenimenti Ruffino branch, now with 10 estates including 400 hectares of vineyard, are also intending to expand, and are promising to replace the missing lead wines with products of similar style.

The first one off the bottling line is Modus, an IGT Toscana made up of Sangiovese at 50%, Cabernet Sauvignon at 30% and Merlot at 20%. This is by way of replacement of Cabreo Il Borgo, while standing in for Cabreo La Pietra is the *barrique*-fermented and aged 100% Chardonnay La Solatia. In place of Il Pareto will come a varietal Merlot on which they are working at the moment. And now – having fairly gushed with praise of the Colorino–Sangiovese blend Romitorio di Santedame – I learn that the 40% Sangiovese is being replaced, from the 1997 vintage on, by Merlot. I am not at all convinced this is a step in the right direction, since whatever is gained in depth will be lost, and more (in my view), in indigenous character. Still, I haven't tasted it yet, so I'd better reserve judgement.

Fattoria di **Selvapiana**. This property has been in the Giuntini family since 1830, the present incumbent – since 1957 – being

Francesco Giuntini Antinori (he never uses the last name, from his mother, to avoid any accusation of passing off). Nor, today, does he need to, the name Selvapiana commanding in its small way as much respect in Italy and abroad as that of Antinori. Francesco, one of Tuscany's great gentlemen, a man of wit and charm, of profound literacy and spirituality not to mention of immense courage, considering the tenacity and humour with which he has fought against the potentially severe disabilities caused by a recent motor accident, took over the estate in 1957 and has presided over its transformation from purveyor of bulk wines to maker of some of Tuscany's finest and most individual bottles. The 25-plus hectares of vineyard are today looked after by his adopted son and heir, Federico Masseti who also makes the wine under the guidance of consultant Franco Bernabei.

Selvapiana's star is the single-vineyard Chianti Rufina Riserva Bucerchiale, a Sangiovese *in purezza* since long before the days when such a thing became theoretically possible – Francesco Giuntini being no respecter of legal niceties when they make no sense. Bucerchiale is a wine of tremendous purity and gracefulness – truly a noble wine – whose austerity will often prevent it from showing at its best for several years, and which therefore doesn't necessarily shine in comparative tastings of young wines against the richer more obvious products of the new oenology, but which is capable, in great years, of outlasting almost any other wine Tuscany can put up. The non-*cru* Riserva used to be almost as good, developing wonderful tertiary aromas to go with the primaries after a few years; however they discontinued production after 1997. The straight Rufina could sometimes, in lesser years, seem a bit lean and sharp, but that Selvapiana purity always runs right through it as it does through all wines of this estate and now that what used to serve as the grapes for Riserva are going this should no longer be a problem. Indeed the *normale* in good years may in future be expected to be among the great Chiantis. Chianti Rufina Riserva Fornace, with a small percentage of Cabernet and some ageing in *barrique*, is less 'Giuntini' than 'Bernabei-Masseti' in conception (Francesco is no lover of wood aromas in wine), a wine combining Selvapiana's austerity with a touch of the fleshiness of the new wave. Worthy of mention too is their Pomino Rosso Petrognano – virtually the only Pomino to stand against the hegemony of Frescobaldi.

The good folk at Selvapiana also used to keep the loveliest little *bastardino* dog called Giacomino for the Belfrage family when the latter arrived for protracted stays nearby, but sadly Giacomino was killed by Tuscan hunters with the delightful habit of putting out poisoned meat for foxes (and dogs) which might disturb pheasant nests. R.I.P.

Villa di Vetrice/Fratelli Grati. The Grati family, whom I have known for 20 odd years and who are, in fact, landlords of my 'office' in Tuscany, are an institution in Rufina, where they are the largest producers and landowners after Frescobaldi. Grandfather Grato Grati, himself of the third generation at this estate, is the doyen of the family, which resides at the splendid sixteenth-century Villa di Vetrice in the Apennine foothills – foot-mountains more like – overlooking the town of Rufina from its perch in the midst of over 100 hectares of some of the best-exposed vineyard in Tuscany. He married Alice Paoli who brought into the family another sizeable estate called Monte, halfway up that 1,000 metre height called Monte Giovi, said by some to have given its name to the Sangiovese grape.

While Grato reigns in the vineyard, the wines are made by his son Gianfranco, whose marriage to Nicoletta Bati brought yet another sizeable estate – called Prunatelli – into the fold. The fifth generation, Cristiana and Gualberto, look after sales, promotion and administration.

The Grati operation is solidly traditional, although they have in recent years made some efforts at modernisation. Their clones are all original to the zone, being derived from cuttings from their own best vines identified as such over a five-year period. Although the vast majority of their vineyards are specialised, i.e. planted to vines only, some, at Monte and at Prunatelli, are cultivated according to the 'promiscuous' method – mixed in with fruit and/or olive trees – and far from yielding the least impressive fruit the grapes from these are sometimes the best, due to the great age and very low production of the vines. Riserva wines are matured, sometimes for several years, in large old Slavonian-oak *botti* – they have recently installed some newer, smaller French and American oak barrels – and the kind of glass-lined cement tanks that practically everyone was cheerfully tearing out of their cellars to make way for stainless-steel tanks until they were informed by no less a figure than Giacomo

Tachis that they were making a big mistake. (Glass-lined concrete may not look as shiny as stainless steel; however, acting like a large bottle, it is now belatedly considered superior for purposes of storage.)

For years Grati have specialised in value-for-money wines and as such have been hugely successful in Italy and on numerous export markets, notably in Britain where their wines can be found up and down the land in supermarkets, wine shops, wine bars and restaurants. Indeed Villa di Vetrice Chianti Rufina remains, in this era of ever-intensifying competition, the best-priced authentic/traditional Chianti on the market. Recently, with the help of oenologist Carlo Corino, they have begun moving upwards in terms of absolute quality, particularly with their Chianti Rufina Riserva Campo al Sorbo, as well as with their old reserve wines under the Grato Grati label – 1982, 1990 and 'Quindici Anni', this last being a blend of three vintages with an average age of over 15 years, put together by yours truly.

Like Selvapiana, Grati excel quality-wise in Vin Santo and Extra Virgin Olive Oil, the former sometimes being up to 15 years old at the time of release, the latter being produced and bottled according to the estate of provenance: i.e. Vetrice, Monte or Prunatelli. Green and peppery in youth, smoother and more buttery with time, a typical Grati oil will be redolent of artichokes and asparagus with various spicy notes on the palate. Unlike many, they may be kept for several years without losing their savour. The 1999 harvest oil from Vetrice won the Ercole d'Oro for olive oil of intense fruit, the most prestigious award for oil in Italy.

Other producers of Chianti Rufina (CR) and Chianti Rufina Riserva (CRR) of a good standard include: Tenuta di **Bossi/Marchesi Gondi** (CR San Giuliano; CRR Marchese Gondi; CRR Villa Bossi), Pontassieve; **Colognole/Contessa Spalletti** (CR; CRR del Don), Rufina; **Lavacchio** (CRR; Cortigiano – Sangiovese + Cabernet), Pontassieve; **Travignoli** (CRR; Tegolaia – Sangiovese + Cabernet), Pelago; Castello del **Trebbio** (CR Lastricato), Pontassieve.

In the other Chianti sub-zones the wines that go by that name are either overshadowed by more famous denominations, or their producers choose to call their best wines by some other name, downgrading them to the status of IGT – or elevating them, depending on how you look at it. This is not to say that one cannot find good and even excellent Sangiovese-based wines in these zones. We shall consider the significant producers according to denomination and/or province, beginning in that same province of Florence in which Rufina is situated.

Montalbano and Colli Fiorentini/Province of Florence
For the record, as far as I am aware, there is no important producer of the Montalbano sub-zone who does not also make the much more prestigious Carmignano (q.v.).

There are, however, a number of good Sangiovese producers in the hills of the province of Florence who find themselves excluded from the major Florentine denominations of Carmignano, Chianti Classico and Rufina, and have to put up with Colli Fiorentini or Montespertoli or IGT (or even Vino da Tavola). They include: Fattoria **Baggiolino** (Chianti Colli Fiorentini Titolato; Poggio Brandi – + Ciliegiolo), Scandicci; Fratelli **Bini** (Gheppio – + Nebbiolo), Empoli; **Cerro del Masso**, the property of Alberto Antonini, for a time chief winemaker at Antinori, now one of the latest additions to the roving consultant brigade (Chianti Cerro del Masso), Cerreto Guidi; Fattoria **Corzano e Paterno** (Chianti Terre di Corzano; Il Corzano – Sangiovese + Cabernet), San Casciano; **La Casetta** (I Balzini Rosso – Sangiovese + Cabernet), Barberino Val d'Elsa; Castello **Il Corno** (Chianti Colli Fiorentini San Camillo), San Casciano; Fattoria **La Querce** (La Querce – Sangiovese + Canaiolo/Colorino; La Querce Selezione Speciale), Impruneta; Majnoni **Guicciardini** (Chianti Riserva), Barberino Val d'Elsa; Fattoria **Montellori** (Castelrapiti Rosso – + Cabernet Sauvignon), Fucecchio; **Petreto** (Chianti Colli Fiorentini; Podere Bocciolé – Sangiovese), Bagno a Ripoli; Castello di **Poppiano**, Montespertoli; **Villa Spoiano** (Solatio – Cabernet + Canaiolo; Sotto la Villa – Sangiovese), Tavarnelle Val di Pesa.

Colli Aretini/Province of Arezzo (south and east of Florence)
Probably the most interesting estate in this sub-zone is the centuries-old, archetypally Tuscan Fattoria **Petrolo** of Lucia Bazzocchi Sanjust at Mercatale Valdarno. Their Chianti Colli Aretini, *normale* and Riserva, are good, but the star – at least until the Merlot Galatrona came along – is the *barrique*d SuperTuscan Torrione;

Giulio Gambelli is consultant. Tenimenti Luigi **d'Alessandro/**
Fattoria di Manzano of Cortona, while better known for their
wines of French grapes – notably the Syrah Podere Il Bosco –
make an excellent varietal Sangiovese by the name of Podere
Migliara.

Other good producers include **Villa Cilnia** (Chianti Colli Aretini &
Riserva; Vocato – Sangiovese + Cabernet), at Pieve al Bagnoro; and
Villa la Selva (Chianti Riserva; Felciaia – Sangiovese 100%) at
Bucine.

Colline Pisane/Province of Pisa

This is not a zone traditionally noted for fine wine, but a small
number of producers stand out. One, at Peccioli, is the ancient
Tenuta di **Ghizzano**, which estate, owned and farmed continuously
since the fourteenth century by the noble Venerosi Pesciolini family,
began turning its mind towards serious quality only in the mid-
1980s. Their Chianti Colline Pisane is remarkably characterful for
its modest price, so much so that it tends to sell out shortly after
release – something you couldn't say for many simple Chiantis.
Their top wine, Veneroso, is Sangiovese-based at 50%, plus
Cabernet and a bit of Merlot; very stylish and aristocratic. Recently
they have brought out an outstanding pure Merlot, called Nambrot.
Carlo Ferrini is the consultant oenologist.

Another, at Palaia, is **Sangervasio**, an estate recently completely
overhauled thanks to the dynamism of owner Luca Tommasini.
Although a few years will be needed before all the improvements in
vineyard and *cantina* make themselves fully felt, Sangervasio have
shown both with their Chianti Le Stoppie and, especially, with the
SuperTuscan A Sirio (Sangiovese with a bit of Cabernet) that they
can produce fleshy, charming Sangiovese at interesting prices. Luca
d'Attoma is consultant oenologist.

Other Pisans worthy of mention in a Sangiovese context are **Badia
di Morrone** at Terricciola (VignAlta – Sangiovese; N'Antia –
Sangiovese + Cabernet); Bruno **Moos** (proprietor Peter Mock) at
Soiana (Soianello; Fontestina); Fattoria di **Sassolo** at San Miniato
(Chianti delle Colline Pisane; Acquabona); and Fattoria **Uccelliera**
at Fauglia (Castellaccio Rosso). The highest-profile Pisan property
of our time, Tenuta del Terriccio, gives short shrift to Sangiovese
and will be considered under International Varieties.

Colli Senesi/Province of Siena

Two properties situated in the commune of Sinalunga stand out in the hinterlands of the province of Siena, dominated otherwise by the giants Montalcino and Montepulciano not to mention San Gimignano and indeed Chianti Classico, all considered individually. One is **Castello di Farnetella**, where Giuseppe Mazzocolin finds time, when not dealing with matters of Felsina Berardenga or indeed making Sauvignon or Pinot Nero (Nero di Nubi) at Farnetella, to make a very good – and excellent value-for-money – Chianti Colli Senesi (Sangiovese + 8% Merlot), plus an IGT alternative to Chianti, for those markets which consider the Colli Senesi DOC to be *squalificato*, called Lucilla (Sangiovese + 15% each of Merlot and Cabernet). Sangiovese is also at the base of their upmarket *cru*, produced in magnum only at the rate of 1,000 magnums per year, called Poggio Granoni (+10% each of Cabernet Sauvignon, Merlot and Syrah).

The other is Tenuta **Farneta**, whose ordinary Chiantis are ordinary indeed but whose two supposedly pure-Sangiovese SuperTuscans, Bongoverno and Bentivoglio, can be excellent (owner Albino Bianchi is a 'friend' of Giacomo Tachis, wink wink). In value-for-money terms, Bentivoglio is a considerably better buy than Bongoverno.

At Castelnuovo Berardenga the large and ancient estate of the noble family **Chigi Saracini** (900 hectares, of which 70 are planted to vines), the principal vineyards of which are situated just outside Chianti Classico denominationally but in a totally different zone geologically – Siena's *creta senese* as distinct from Chianti Classico's *albarese* and *galestro* – has modernised its considerable production under the present ownership of the bank Monte dei Paschi di Siena. Chianti Colli Senesi, Chianti Superiore (Sangiovese with Ciliegiolo and Colorino) and Poggiassai (Sangiovese + Cabernet) are forward, fruit-driven wines of exceptional drinkability for their genre and price.

Other good Sienese producers who have managed to find properties not situated in one of the four big-league zones cited above are: **Colle Santa Mustiola** (Poggio ai Chiari), Chiusi; **Ficomontanino** (CCS Tutulus), Chiusi; **Il Colle** (Chianti), Trequanda; **Il Podere San Luigi** (CCS San Luigi; San Luigi – Sangiovese + Colorino), Colle Val d'Elsa; and **Poggio Salvi** (Vigna del Bosco – Sangiovese), Sovicille – not to be confused with the property of the same name in Montalcino.

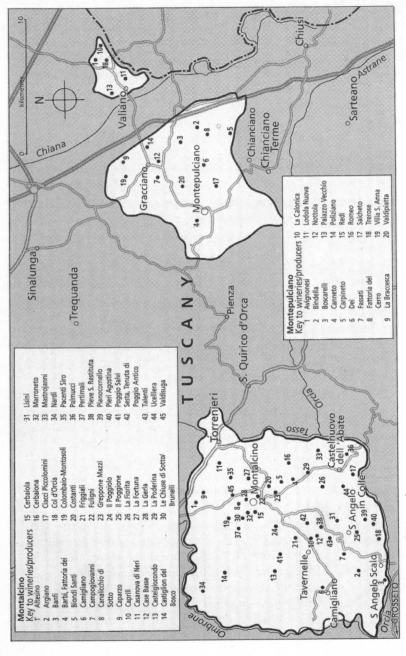

Montepulciano
Key to wineries/producers
1 Avignonesi
2 Bindella
3 Boscarelli
4 Canneto
5 Carpineto
6 Dei
7 Fassati
8 Fattoria del Cerro
9 La Braccesca
10 La Calonica
11 Lodola Nuova
12 Nottola
13 Palazzo Vecchio
14 Poliziano
15 Redi
16 Romeo
17 Salcheto
18 Trerose
19 Villa S. Anna
20 Valdipiatta

Montalcino
Key to wineries/producers
1 Altesino
2 Argiano
3 Banfi
4 Barbi, Fattoria dei
5 Biondi Santi
6 Camigliano
7 Campogiovanni
8 Canalicchio di Sotto
9 Caparzo
10 Caprili
11 Casanova di Neri
12 Case Basse
13 Castelgiocondo
14 Castiglion del Bosco
15 Cerbaiola
16 Cerbaiona
17 Ciacci Piccolomini
18 Col d'Orcia
19 Colombaio-Montosoli
20 Costanti
21 Friggiali
22 Fuligni
23 Greppone Mazzi
24 Il Poggiolo
25 Il Poggione
26 La Fiorita
27 La Fortuna
28 La Gerla
29 La Poderina
30 Le Chiuse di Sotto/Brunelli
31 Lisini
32 Marroneto
33 Mastrojanni
34 Nardi
35 Pacenti Siro
36 Palmucci
37 Pertimali
38 Pieve S. Restituta
39 Pianocornello
40 Pieri Agostina
41 Poggio Salvi
42 Sesta, Tenuta di
   Poggio Antico
43 Talenti
44 Uccelliera
45 Valdisuga

Montepulciano and Montalcino

There wouldn't be much point in producing high-grade Chianti or non-DOCG Sangiovese in Montalcino or Montepulciano, but there's plenty of point in the white wine zone of San Gimignano, and growing activity too. Best of the bunch of Sangiovese producers, that I've found, is the Luenzo of Vincenzo **Cesani**, a wine made from late-picked Sangiovese plus Colorino; Cesani also turns out a full-bodied, value-for-money Chianti Colli Senesi. Other good Sangiovese producers based in San Gimignano include: **Casa alle Vacche** (CCS Cinabro); **Casale-Falchini** (CCS Titolato Colombaia; Paretaio – Sangiovese + other Tuscan grapes); Fattoria di **Guicciardini Strozzi** (Sodole – 100% Sangiovese; Selvascura – + 5–10% Colorino; Millanni – + Cabernet Sauvignon and Merlot); **Il Paradiso** (Paterno II – 100% Sangiovese); **La Rampa di Fugnano** (CCS Via dei Franchi; Bombereto – Sangiovese); **Montenidoli** (Sono Montenidoli – Sangiovese + Malvasia Nera); **Mormoraia** (Neitea – Sangiovese + Cabernet Sauvignon); **Palagetto** (Sottobosco – Sangiovese + Cabernet Sauvignon); **Panizzi** (Ceraso – Sangiovese + Canaiolo); Fattoria **Paradiso** (CCS; Bottaccio – Sangiovese); Fattoria **Ponte a Rondolino** (Peperino – Sangiovese); **Signano** (CCS Poggiarelli); Vagnoni (CCS; I Sodi Lunghi – Sangiovese + Cabernet).

Leaving the denomination of Chianti, but remaining in the Province of Siena, we come now to what is today one of Italy's two or three most prestigious wines, namely:

Montalcino

If you are looking for high quality Sangiovese *in purezza* the place to go is Montalcino. Though its story has been brief by Tuscan standards – going back at most 150 years – the recent history of Brunello di Montalcino (the wine; it is no longer considered a grape variety for reasons explained) has been one of rise and rise, in terms of quality, prestige at home and internationally, volume of production, number of producers and price. Apart from Barolo and Barbaresco, this is the only red table wine VQPRD in the land which regularly fetches over 25,000 lire per bottle ex cellars – and frequently you can double that, or more – the handsome return enabling producers to invest ever more in time as well as in quality-enhancing equipment. Whether the wine is always worth the price is perhaps debatable. Let's just say that, from a good year, it should be; from a poor year, it isn't; and from a mediocre year, it's pot luck; or rather I should say: it depends on the producer.

Few today would dispute that, as a generic denomination, Brunello di Montalcino reaches the highest levels of elegance combined with power, concentration and sheer personality, of any of the Sangiovese family of wines. Chianti Classico Riserva cannot yet challenge it, too many of the potential DOCGs of that zone choosing to remain in the IGT bracket. Nor can Vino Nobile di Montepulciano yet mount a credible claim to superiority, though it is making noble efforts (see below).

Credit for Montalcino's success must go firstly to the Biondi-Santi family, beginning with Ferruccio Biondi-Santi, the 'inventor' in the late nineteenth century of Brunello di Montalcino. It was Ferruccio who, precisely because of the preserving properties of those unalleviated hard tannins of the Sangiovese Grosso clone he called Brunello, conceived of Brunello (the wine) as a *vino da invecchiamento*, a wine for long ageing, backing his judgement by laying down substantial quantities of the still extant 1888 and 1891. The image was further nurtured by his son Tancredi and polished to a high shine by Tancredi's son, Franco who, now semi-retired, has ceded much of the control on the business side – but not on the winemaking side – to his son, Jacopo.

Indeed it was the Biondi-Santi approach, which, when the original DOC *disciplinare* was drawn up in the mid-1960s, ensured that Brunello di Montalcino was required to be aged a minimum of four years from the 1 January following the vintage, a stipulation which still holds. Three and a half of these years were originally supposed to be spent in wood, but there has been such a fuss, over the decades, on the part of producers who maintain that too long a period in wood risks killing the fruit especially in lesser years (even Biondi-Santi agrees), that barrel-ageing was reduced to three and, now, two of the mandatory four years for the *normale* and two of the mandatory five years for Riserva. The *normale* must spend four months and the Riserva six months by way of *affinamento* in bottle. By the way, *affinamento*, refinement, is the word we are now supposed to be using instead of *invecchiamento*, ageing, whether it be in glass or wood; like the wine isn't getting 'older', but rather 'finer'. But I think I'll avoid the English translation – makes it sound like petroleum.

In the mid-1980s the problems of excessive wood-maturation

and waiting for a return on capital were partially addressed with the introduction of the DOC <u>Rosso di Montalcino</u>, using the same grapes (100% Sangiovese) but lowering the alcohol limit to 12% – compared with Brunello's 12.5% – and specifying as an ageing period a mere year from 1 September of the vintage, with no specification as to method. A vineyard which is recorded in the official album as suitable for Brunello may use its grapes also to make Rosso, provided the production maxima for Brunello, 8 tonnes per hectare, are enforced. On the other hand, a vineyard inscribed as suitable for Rosso, and therefore entitled to 10 tonnes per hectare, may not use its grapes for Brunello. This gives the producer certain room for manoeuvre, the idea being that only the best should be reserved for Brunello. Styles of Rosso vary widely from producer to producer, some being fresh, light and easy drinking, some being more sturdy and heading in the direction of Brunello, some swerving off towards the 'international' with the use of a limited period in French *barrique*.

In the mid-1990s, again, the possibilities were extended still further with the introduction of the DOC <u>Sant'Antimo</u>, among whose multiple sub-DOCs there exists a Rosso which may be Sangiovese, or any of, or combination of, the other 'recommended and authorised' grapes for the province of Siena, at any level from 0% to 100%, aged as long or as short a period as the producer chooses in whatever material he wants. Much more open than that you couldn't get.

A feature worth noting in relation to Montalcino is that the growers here have formed a consortium which is today probably the most effective in Italy, its circa 200 members representing around 98% of the total number of producers. In a land that is given to local dissension and infighting, this is a remarkable demonstration of unity, and it shows in the way that standards are maintained, goals are vigorously pursued, information is disseminated and tastings are organised. One might say that it is a pity more areas cannot seem to gather themselves into such a fighting force; but it is a fact that there are few areas where producers have such a community of interest. There are, for example, no 'industrial' producers in Montalcino, and the local cooperative is relatively weak.

As in Chianti, so in Montalcino altitude is a crucial factor in wine character. The highest point is the town itself, which sits slightly north and east of the centre of the area, at almost 600 metres. The vineyards around the town and along the ridges heading south towards Sant'Antimo or Sant'Angelo in Colle or Tavarnelle are the ones with greatest structure. Biondi-Santi's Greppo vineyard is in this district, as is Costanti, Poggio Antico, Fattoria dei Barbi, Case Basse, la Pieve di Santa Restituta (Gaja), Il Poggione, Talenti-Pian di Conte – some of the most illustrious and longest-lived of the Brunellos.

North of the town at lower altitude are the famous *crus* of Montosoli, Val di Cava and Canalicchio – here structure meets ripeness of fruit to produce what many consider the finest Brunello in the medium term, even if it lacks the power to run for decades. Highly rated producers like Altesino, Caparzo (La Casa), Baricci, Valdicava, Val di Suga (in part), Pertimali, Canalicchio di Sopra and Canalicchio di Sotto have vineyards here.

The most forward of the Brunellos are from the lower slopes of the area, often near the perimeter. The American-owned giant Banfi, near Sant'Angelo Scalo, is so situated, as are Argiano, Castelgiocondo, Castiglion del Bosco, Caparzo and Altesino (the non-Montosoli vineyards), Casanova di Neri (in part), Col d'Orcia (in part), Nardi.

The producers

Altesino. Owned since 1970 by Giulio Consonno of Prenatal, run by Director Claudio Basla with help on the oenological side from Pietro Rivella, brother of Ezio, this 20-odd hectare estate has for a quarter of a century been at the forefront of quality production in Montalcino. They are also among the most adventurous innovators, having, for example, planted Cabernet Sauvignon in the early days – even if it was by virtue of a mistaken consignment of cuttings for grafting – when virtually no one else in Montalcino was thinking of it. Cabernet plays a minor (30%) role in blend with Sangiovese in one of three red SuperTuscans, the somewhat variable Alte d'Altesi, and a major role (100%) in another, Borgo d'Altesi, considerably more convincing with its richly concentrated fruit interwoven with the barrel aromas of coffee and vanilla.

Sangiovese, obviously, dominates production. Of the two Brunellos, that labelled Montosoli, one of Montalcino's finest vineyard areas, consistently shows greater depth on the palate, more elegance and more length, with firm but ripe tannins and good balancing acidity; though built to last, it shares the house characteristic of being fairly forward. The other Montosoli wine is yet another SuperTuscan called Palazzo Altesi (this being the name of Consonno's impressive fifteenth-century palace, although it is not at Montosoli). Like Brunello, Palazzo is 100% Sangiovese and could be Brunello except that the producer deliberately wanted to show what could be done with top quality Brunello grapes vinified in French *barrique* rather than Slavonian *botti* and for a much shorter period than the law then required. The result is a wine of earlier drinkability than Brunello with, however, considerably greater structure than Rosso di Montalcino, and with quite a different aromatic profile.

Argiano. Until the early 1990s this large estate, with its massive sixteenth-century villa and its 100 hectares of land, about one-third of which are under vine, on a high plateau about 300 metres above sea level in the southern section of Montalcino, just above Banfi's territory, was owned by the vermouth producers Cinzano. In 1991 it was bought by Countess Noemi Marone Cinzano and in 1992 Giacomo Tachis took over as consultant, with Sebastiano Rosa, nephew to Sassicaia's Marchese Incisa della Rocchetta, as supervisor. Since that time the property has been going from strength to strength, quality-wise, turning out some of the fruitiest, most modern-style and best-balanced Rossos and Brunellos Montalcino has to offer, as well as outstanding Riservas in those exceptional years when they are produced.

In the mid-1990s they introduced Solengo, a new, radical blend of Sangiovese, Cabernet Sauvignon, Merlot and Syrah in roughly equal portions, a wine which combines seriousness with relatively soft fruit and sheer drinkability. Indeed, anyone looking for Montalcino wines with these characteristics overall will find Argiano's creations hard to beat.

Note that the property Argiano, owned by Cinzano, should be distinguished from its neighbour **Castello di Argiano,** owned by Giuseppe Sesti, who since 1995 has been producing excellent Brunello as well as a 40% Merlot/60% Cabernet Sauvignon IGT called Terra di Siena.

Banfi. When contemplating this gigantic American-owned, Italian run operation, 'the largest continuous wine estate in Europe', runs the blurb, one is constantly being bombarded with mind-boggling figures. There are 2,850 hectares, of which about a third are planted to vines. One hundred-plus million dollars have been invested in the estate since the purchase, beginning in 1977, of the properties at Sant'Angelo Scalo and at the eleventh-century Castello Poggio alle Mura, in the clearing and reshaping of the land and the planting of all those vineyards, and in the equipping of the enormous space-age winery with computers, stainless steel and countless barrels of various oaks and sizes and toasts.

The principal moving force behind this gigantic undertaking was Ezio Rivella, one of the key figures in the development of Italian quality wine post-World War II (for more on Rivella refer to *Life Beyond Lambrusco*, pp. 272–277). Ezio finally retired, however, in 2000 to do his own thing at his properties in the Maremma, in Chianti Classico and in Piemonte. The owners, American tycoon brothers John and Harry Mariani, who made their early millions selling Lambrusco in the millions of bottles and who, in the late 1970s, decided it was time for a move dramatically upmarket, bringing in Rivella to oversee the operation, have personally taken control of the 40 million dollar turnover business with John Mariani as President and Enrico Viglierchio, one of three Vice-Presidents, as Director General. Rudi Buratti, a long-time employee of the company, has taken over as winemaker from Pablo Harri who worked alongside Rivella for many years until his departure for Col d'Orcia.

Plans for the future include the continued upgrading of the vineyards and updating of winery technology, together with further restoration of the castle, a project begun in 1998 and scheduled to last until 2002 at a cost of some 20 million dollars.

As for the wines, they are not all works of art, to be sure, but there are two or three that get pretty close and another few which are impressive considering – if you'll pardon me – the numbers. For my money the ones that do not work – and this has been noted over periodic tastings – are the French varietals, and the more their natural habitat is towards the north, the less well they seem to do in the hot dry conditions of Montalcino. Thus the heavy Sauvignon Blanc Serena, the flat Pinot Grigio San Angelo and the fat, low-acid Chardonnay Fontanelle are the least successful, with the straight Merlot Mandrielle and the varietal Cabernet Sauvignon Tavarnelle also wanting an element of fruit-acid and elegance despite having some considerable concentration. Only Colvecchio, from a grape

(Syrah) used to hotter climes, shines as a good example – indeed one of the best I've come across in Italy.

The going starts getting good when you come to the home varieties. Considering they have 155 hectares planted to Brunello – at 600,000 bottles they are by far the market leaders – and 23 to Rosso di Montalcino it is impressive how much fruit they manage to get into the corresponding wines without losing seriousness. The use of oak, too, is finely judged – something one can only say when the vanilla or woodsmoke add a dimension rather than knocking out the essential fruit; they manage this in both the Brunello and, perhaps somewhat more surprisingly, in the Rosso. Another home variety, historically the variety of Montalcino, is Moscadello, a local version of Moscato Bianco; Banfi make a very tasty, nicely balanced, muscatty-perfumed sweet wine from late-harvested grapes, one that displays the grape well in a slightly oaked context, with good acidity so that the effect avoids being cloying.

But the two masterworks are blends. The best is called Summus, an unlikely mix of Brunello, Cabernet and Syrah, whose rich coal-tar and black-fruit aromas, sweet complex fruit on the palate and creamy texture, balanced by bright acidity, form a tapestry of taste-touch-smell which weaves in and out of the awareness almost entrancingly. Almost as good is the Bordeaux-style blend Excelsus, which manages concentration-cum-elegance in a surprising way, considering what Cabernet and Merlot do individually.

Fattoria dei **Barbi**. This estate constitutes one of the pillars upon which, historically, Brunello di Montalcino stands. The Colombini have been in possession of the Fattoria dei Barbi, apparently, since 1790, although the family has owned land in the Montalcino area since way back in the fourteenth century. In 1892 they were one of the first two bottlers of Sangiovese from Montalcino, and though the wines of the area went through a bit of a lapsus in the middle of the twentieth century it was Giovanni Colombini who in 1962, almost alone at the time, helped to re-launch the wines. After his death the running of the farm – indeed it remains a complete farm, producing typical Tuscan meats and cheeses as well as wine – was taken over by the formidable Francesca Cinelli Colombini, who has now ceded control to her son Stefano, while her daughter, Donatella, has moved sideways to form her own network of production called Le Fattorie di Donatella Cinelli Colombini, based on the Fattoria del Casato property previously linked to the Barbi estate (see below). Stefano is aided by resident oenologist Luigino Casagrande, with viticultural consultancy from Carlo Ferrini.

There is, today, in Barbi wines – Rosso, Brunello, the single-vineyard Riserva Vigna del Fiore and the recently developed Sangiovese/Merlot blend Brigante dei Barbi – an element of fresh-ness and fruitiness together with a ripeness of the phenolic content that never used to be there, except perhaps in their most individual wine, Brusco dei Barbi, a sort of lesser-aged Brunello. Not that Barbi wines have lost any of their old power, just a large part of that element of rusticity which used to make drinking them seem like rather hard work. Today they represent one of the best bridges between the traditional and the modern styles.

Biondi-Santi. One of the features of the Italian wine *rinascimento* has been the frequency of dire struggles between fathers and sons where the latter have wished none too ceremoniously to throw out old ideas and their manifestations and replace them with newer concepts and their fruits. Perhaps the most epic, and best publicised, of these battles took place in the mid-1990s between Franco Biondi-Santi and his son Jacopo. Great stuff for a novel.

In the blue corner, Franco, upholder of tradition, grandson of Ferruccio B-S the 'inventor' of modern Brunello as a 100% Sangiovese wine – so conceived nearly a century before Baron Ricasoli's cocktail of Sangiovese–Canaiolo–Malvasia–Trebbiano began to be challenged and discarded.[3] In the red corner, Jacopo, suffering the age-old embarrassment of the son whose father's convervatism is becoming sclerotic (as he sees it) to the extent that people are beginning to knock, or to mock. Jacopo wanted to change the methods of winemaking at Biondi-Santi, to introduce new grapes like Sauvignon Blanc or Merlot, to bring in *barriques* and trendy consultant oenologists and other exotica unthinkable to Franco.

Unable to convince his father of the superiority of his approach, in 1991 Jacopo took his family off to a nearby estate, Poggio Salvi, the property of his wife's family, the Tagliabue. For several years the feud raged and despite geographical proximity there was little or no

3 The Biondi-Santi story is given briefly in *Life Beyond Lambrusco*, pp. 220–224.

contact, a painful time for parents and especially grandparents aching to see their progeny. In this period Jacopo, with the help of Vittorio Fiore and Stefano Chioccioli, and using fruit from a variety of sources in Chianti Classico as well as in Montalcino, successfully established his new range including a Sangiovese aged a little over a year in non-toasted *barrique* (short, by Brunello standards), called Sassoalloro; an oaked SuperTuscan blend of Sangiovese and Merlot called Schidione and a surprisingly herbaceous and characterful Sauvignon Blanc called Rívolo. Both reds combine Biondi-Santi elegance and restraint with a certain primary-fruit and oak character lacking in classic Biondi-Santi Brunellos. But though relatively forward in style, Jacopo is hopeful that, from a top vintage, these wines will be able to weather the ravages of time in the grand family tradition – Sassoalloro (of which are produced the not inconsiderable quantity of 200,000 bottles) up to 40 years, Schidione (15,000 bottles) perhaps as much as the magic 100 years.

Meanwhile, back at the paternal Tenuta Greppo, a 20-or-so hectare vineyard just outside of the town of Montalcino at an altitude of nearly 500 metres, Franco was and is serenely continuing to make Brunello Riserva to last, or supposedly so, in the best vintages like 1997 and 1998, 100 years or more, as he demonstrated in a tasting in 1994 the 1891 had been able to do.[4] This entails using fruit from vines of a minimum of 25 years; the oldest vines on the estate, incidentally, are around 80 years and all are original Sangiovese Grosso developed from own cuttings, so none of Biondi-Santi's vines are from the bad old days of the 1960s and 70s. It also entails non-interventionist techniques which tend to produce wines not particularly suitable for early drinking – and which therefore rarely shine in comparative tastings but which can be deeply impressive in a vertical line-up (see www.winepros.com, December 2000).

Franco's other wines – the Brunello 'Annata', from vines over 10 years old, and the two Rossos from relatively young vines – are also of the austere rather than the ripe, plummy school favoured by modernists who feel the paramount need to impress Messrs. Parker et al. But at last, he says with his customary patrician tranquillity, the row with Jacopo has been ended by an agreement that Franco

---

4 For details of the tasting, which included the great vintages 1975, 1964, 1955, 1945, 1925, 1891 and 1888, see my article in *Decanter* dated March 1995.

does get to do his thing while he's in charge at Greppo while Jacopo takes responsibility for all wine distribution, uniting the paternal with the filial in a single marketing package.

I suppose I would class myself more as an admirer than as an enthusiastic drinker of Franco Biondi-Santi's wines: you've got to take your hat off to a 25+-year-old wine, such as the 1975, the 1964 or the 1955 – although the latter pair are really his father's wines – which comes across as positively youthful, bursting with life. I am not inclined to lay wines down for that length of time, as indeed few are today, but I would defend to the death – well, to the last glass if not the last gasp – the right of those who wish to continue working that diminishing vein in the name of the greatness and diversity of wine. And it does seem that much has been learnt in the course of the family hostilities and that the firm has emerged with a new strength and depth.

Camigliano. This estate seems, on arrival, almost to be caught in some medieval time-warp, isolated as it is in the back of beyond a few kilometres south of the town of Montalcino. It is in reality an entire medieval village complete with walls and castle, which, centuries ago, was a place of some importance, but which by the middle of the twentieth century had become the sort of self-sufficient agricultural commune based on the share-cropping system typical of that time. In 1954 the estate including the town and surrounding agricultural area was purchased by the present proprietors, Ghezzi, of Milan. Considerable investment and replanting, especially of late, plus the recently secured oenological attentions of Lorenzo Landi, have raised the level of quality steadily to the point where the Brunello stands today among the better wines of the traditional style from Montalcino. Brunello and Brunello Riserva receive prolonged maceration and are aged for over three years in Slavonian oak *botti*, and the unusually sturdy Rosso too gets a year in big oak. In the last few years, however, they have sought to go modern by planting some 14 hectares – an unusually high number for Montalcino – to Cabernet Sauvignon. The most important result of this is Poderuccio, a blend of Sangiovese and Cabernet with a splash of Merlot, aged up to one year in French *barriques* of which at least a part are new. A Super-Tuscan, therefore, but without the usual high SuperTuscan price tag, indeed arguably the best-value wine coming out of Montalcino today.

Caparzo. About one-third of the 120+ hectares belonging to this estate, founded in the late 1960s by a group of Milanese business-men, are planted to vines. Caparzo has never lacked for investment capital, so that Nuccio Turone, General Manager, and Vittorio Fiore, consultant, have from the beginning been able to make those experiments and purchases in vineyard and *cantina* that it is necessary for a great winery to make in the early years. Their aim in the vineyard has, in particular, been to find a 'blend' of Sangiovese clones that would complement each other in varying conditions. They have also since early days isolated sites of particular quality, as for example the La Casa vineyard for their top Brunello – indeed, La Casa has firmly established itself since the late 1970s as one of the great Brunellos – and the La Caduta vineyard for Rosso. These two wines, unlike the Rosso and Brunello *normali*, which are aged in traditional large Slavonian oak barrels, receive particular wood treatment: one year in small 7 hectolitre barrels for La Caduta; *barrique* treatment as well as *botte* for La Casa.

Caparzo's name, centuries ago, was apparently Cà del Pazzo – house of the madman – and this is the name which they have given to their 'crazy' (it was at the time of its conception, anyway; not any longer) blend of Sangiovese and Cabernet Sauvignon, one of the more convincing of its type in Tuscany, with plenty of fruit and discreet oak, sufficient tannin to allow it to age well but not so as to overly disturb when taken in youth.

Caparzo are also producers of one of the best white wines of Montalcino and indeed Tuscany: Le Grance, a Chardonnay – for body, plus Sauvignon – for 'nerve', plus Gewürztraminer – for aroma, aged 8 months in *barrique*.

Casanova di Neri. Giacomo Neri is one of the rising, or recently risen, stars of Brunello. With 22 hectares of vineyard in three prime sites distributed in various parts of the zone, and with the excellent Carlo Ferrini as consultant oenologist behind him, he has been able to put together one of the most representative of the modern-style Brunellos without going too far towards the modern. A typical Neri Brunello will be full yet vibrant of colour, complex and elegant of aroma with never an excess of vanilla or toast, sumptuous yet structured on the palate – a wine capable of that tricky balancing act of being drinkable early yet of ageing well. A Sangiovese specialist, with only token 'experimental' patches of other vines, Giacomo in a good year will make a preponderance of the zone's standard-bearer, Brunello, together with smaller amounts of the *crus* Brunellos Cerretalto and Tenuta Nuova, some Riserva and a restricted amount of Rosso. Rosso comes into its own, and Riserva goes out, only in lesser years. Maceration times and wood-ageing are fairly standard for today – the latter consisting in a judicious mix of traditional Slavonian-oak *botti* and 300 or 600 litre French-oak barrels.

Fattoria del Casato. This 50-hectare property with 13 hectares of vineyard, all planted to Sangiovese, was taken over in the late 1990s by Donatella Cinelli Colombini, daughter of Francesca Cinelli Colombini of Fattoria dei Barbi, continuing a family tradition going back over 400 years. Donatella, well known for her work in wine tourism – she was behind the introduction of the *Cantine Aperte* concept, whereby on a given day wineries throughout Italy open their doors to the public – wanted a feminine touch in her wines. So she recruited four ladies of wine, including Italy's sole permanent-resident Master of Wine Maureen Ashley, to put together between them, on an instinctual-organoleptic rather than the usual male intellectual-analytic basis, the final blend of the instantly famous Brunello Prime Donne (= first ladies). This is indeed a wine which, in its early manifestations, achieves feminine allure with its scented fruit and warm, spicy palate, while maintaining a firm, slightly tannic backbone. More classic and somewhat more austere, or perhaps simply less personalised, is the Brunello *normale*. A recent issue, the SuperTuscan Leone Rosso, is a blend of Sangiovese, Canaiolo and Merlot aged, of course, in French *barriques*. The grapes for this wine come, it should be said, not from Montalcino but from the 19 hectares of vineyard at Donatella's other property, Fattoria del Colle at Trequanda in the Colli Senesi.

Case Basse. Gianfranco Soldera is a Milanese insurance broker turned wine farmer, having bought this run-down property next door to la Chiesa di Santa Restituta, now Gaja's property, in 1972. The intention was nothing less than to make '*grande* Brunello', in which he and many others, but by no means all, are agreed that he generally succeeds (in lesser years he either doesn't make Brunello, or very little). Although Soldera qualifies the above statement by saying his wine is invariably 'great – at least for my nose; wine is after all a subjective business', nonetheless modesty, it is apparent, is not among his more salient qualities. Another instance: 'The rule in Case Basse', he says as we begin the tasting, 'is that one spits only bad wine. Therefore no one spits at Case Basse.' (One may find this amusing, or overbearing.) And another: 'Over there', and he points somewhat contemptuously to a point vaguely southward, 'is Banfi: best not to speak of them.'

The style of Soldera's wines – he makes only Brunello and Brunello Riserva from the Intistieti vineyard; his vines are 100% Sangiovese – is distinctly traditional, rather along Biondi-Santi lines. In the vineyard – of which he has around 8 hectares, with a couple more to come – he goes to extraordinary lengths to get perfect grapes; he is a fanatical ecologist, encouraging bats, birds and other insect-predators and using only well-matured compost for fertilizer.

In the winery he remains, against the trend, a firm believer in lengthy maceration and wood-ageing – in large *botte*, of course; 66 months is the longest he has achieved. Consequently the wines are somewhat evolved and never very deep in colour, rich in tertiary as well as dried fruit and floral aromas when they go on the market, which is always between one and three years later than most.

I was disappointed, I confess, when the great man failed to pull a single cork during our tasting, though I was driving and, of course, not spitting. But I had to agree that a couple of the wines tasted from barrel were *'grande'*. He nodded perfunctorily in acknowledgement. I was, after all, merely stating the obvious.

Ciacci Piccolomini. With some 35 hectares under vine – partly mature vineyard, partly recently planted – this estate, property of the Bianchini family, is not as small as its limited production and the sometime difficulty of acquiring its bottles might suggest. In fact, it is only since 1988 that the winds of quality-consciousness really started blowing, with the arrival of one of Italy's most promising and dynamic young winemakers, Roberto Cipresso. Roberto it was who insisted that the 1989, 1991 and 1992 vintages be downgraded, the resulting shortage of Brunello, after the tremendous success of the 1988 and 1990, causing the above-mentioned impression of incredibly short supply; always a good marketing ploy, to make people think you've sold out before you even begin; in this case, however, the shortage was genuine.

Subsequent vintages have brought Brunello Vigna di Pianrosso back into contention, and the richness of fruit and extract, combined with the smoothness of structure, make for as delicious a wine as it used to be when you couldn't get any. Almost more exciting, however, is the remarkable single vineyard Rosso di Montalcino Vigna di Pianrosso, a wine of great generosity of fruit with intense berry-cherry aromas and a sweet, almost porty finish thanks in part to a high alcohol content.

Ciacci Piccolomini, under Cipresso's guidance (Roberto has now been replaced by Paolo Vagaggini) were among the first in Montalcino to plant the noble French grapes, Cabernet, Merlot and Syrah. With the former they created – indeed, as far back as 1989 – a Sangiovese (at 60%) plus Merlot and Cabernet blend called Ateo, meaning atheist, i.e. one who does not believe in the gods of Montalcino who decree absolute subservience to Brunello.

With the latter they brought out the Syrah-based Fabius, a Sant'Antimo DOC which has attracted considerable praise in its early editions.

Col d'Orcia. Normally size and quality do not necessarily go together very well. Col d'Orcia, a 540-hectare estate stretching all the way from the river Orcia up to Sant'Angelo in Colle at 450 metres altitude, with 130 hectares under vine, is an exception. It was purchased from the Franceschi family of Il Poggione (q.v.) in 1973 by the father of current owner Francesco Marone Cinzano, who now lives in Chile. The estate, under the direction of Edoardo Virano backed by consultant Maurizio Castelli and winemaker Pablo Harri, head-hunted in the late 1990s from Banfi, has been turning out wines of ever riper and more modern style for a few years now, upgrading technologically as well, in collaboration with the University of Florence, as carrying out various vineyard trials on an eight-hectare site in respect of Brunello and Moscadello clones, planting density, suitability of rootstocks, bunch-thinning, grass-seeding and late-harvesting (with reference to the Moscadello);

in short, everything they're doing in Chianti Classico 2000 (see Chapter 1) and a little bit more.

If I had to pick out one word that describes the wines of Col d'Orcia as a group, I think I would plump for 'charming'. The word recurs throughout the notes on my tasting of their range of seven wines, starting with the simple, youthful and zesty Rosso degli Spezieri (Sangiovese + Malvasia Nera, Ciliegiolo, Mammolo and others), proceeding upwards through the Rosso di Montalcino (good fruit but with a bit more structure), through the more evolved yet still 'fruit-driven' Brunello (all, so far, aged in large barrels, though to some extent of French oak) and along to the Cabernet Olmaia, a Cabernet Sauvignon of Bordeaux origin which, despite being matured 16 months in French *barriques*, manages to maintain the accent on that ripe, soft, charming blackcurranty fruit (not many French Cabernets could get this much fruit in, I noted). And of course there's the sweet, and deliciously grapey Moscadello di Montalcino Pasceno, a dessert wine made from grapes both late-harvested – in late September, having ripened in August – and dried for a month off the plant.

There are, however, two wines that it would be difficult to describe as 'charming'. One is a *barrique*-fermented Chardonnay called Ghiaie Bianche, which doesn't, or didn't in the sample I tasted, manage to rise above its 13.5% of alcohol and left the palate feeling leaden. The other is a magnificent Brunello Riserva Poggio al Vento whose primary aromas have begun to be overtaken by tertiaries – an amazing mingling of fresh and dried fruit, leather and meat smells, coffee and spice, with almost a port-like sweetness at the back. A wine of great power and concentration, of uncompromising personality, with doubtless a long life ahead of it: 'charming' seems an inadequate epithet for what is surely one of Tuscany's outstanding vinous creations.

Costanti/Colle al Matrichese. Costanti is one of the historic names of Montalcino, and the Colle al Matrichese vineyard, just below the town is, despite its altitude, considered one of the finest sites. They also have a vineyard called Calbello lower down, at Montosoli, about half the size. Current owner Andrea Costanti's grandfather was one of the first in Montalcino to bottle his own product, beginning in 1964. Today Andrea, who as a very young man was obliged to take over the reins rather suddenly in 1983, enjoys the consultancy of Vittorio Fiore, and his classic wines are keenly sought after for elegance and breeding rather than for power, as is understandable considering the vineyard's altitude. The Rosso di Montalcino DOC from Colle al Matrichese is a wine of some structure for the denomination, and the Brunello has shed what toughness it used to have and now projects a more modern image with its juicy fruit and soft perfumes, underlain, however, by a subtle structure that will carry the wine forward for many years. Costanti also make a spicy, almost clovey 70% Merlot/30% Cabernet Sauvignon blend, called Ardingo, from the Calbello vineyard of which the first vintage in commerce was the 1998.

La Fiorita. This is the estate which Roberto Cipresso, mentioned above, bought in 1992 together with Lucio Gomieri, of Vignalta in Veneto's Colli Euganei. The first vintage, 1993, didn't come out until 1998, but then was bought in its entirety by Florence's most prestigious restaurant, Pinchiorri. The property is tiny – 4 hectares at the moment. Alongside Brunello is an IGT Toscana called Laurus, 100% Sangiovese, the first vintage being 1998. Given Pinchiorri's interest and the limited supply, not to mention the oenological skills of the proprietors, both wines will doubtless soon be among the most internationally sought after.

Il Poggione. Some years ago I was asked to tutor a vertical tasting of Il Poggione Brunellos up to 30 years old. Biondi-Santi aside it was the first time I had ever tasted a range of Brunellos going so far back – there are precious few producers who could manage it – and I was thoroughly impressed by the way the wines, as they matured, rather than lose youthfulness seemed to gain in personality and stature: a convincing demonstration that Brunello is a wine for long ageing, correctly made. And nobody made Brunello more lovingly, more passionately than Pierluigi Talenti, winemaker from 1958 until his death in 1999 at this large and historic estate – 90-plus hectares planted to vineyard, under the ownership of the Franceschis of Florence for some 200 years. Brunello Il Poggione is always correct, restrained maybe in youth, but capable of great development; the Riserva, from a vineyard planted in 1964, has all the grace and power that classic Brunello should have.

The much-lamented Talenti is gone now. But Fabrizio Bindocci, who worked alongside the great man for over 20 years and describes him as 'like a father', and who has taken over control of vinification as well as of the vineyards, is not short of new ideas. Bindocci and his team are building a new *cantina*, extending the already established use of home-grown clones of Sangiovese, developed with Rauscedo (R5 and R6), reducing the size of the *botti* for ageing the Brunello (though Bindocci doesn't want to introduce *barriques* for this purpose, for fear of distorting its natural character), working on new wines like the SuperTuscan IGT San Leopoldo – 50% Sangiovese, 50% Cabernets Sauvignon and Franc – which brings to the restrained and carefully balanced house style an exciting extra burst of berry fruit.

The legacy of Talenti lives on, and will continue to be respected, even if his heirs are wisely and discreetly moving with the times.

La Poderina/Saiagricola. See under Fattoria del Cerro, Montepulciano.

Le Chiuse di Sotto/Brunelli. With a name like his, Gianni Brunelli almost had to be a producer of Brunello, and indeed he is of an old Montalcino family. His father, however, had sold the estate, and Gianni had moved into the restaurant business with his famous

Osteria Le Logge just off the Piazza del Campo at Siena. In 1988 Gianni bought back the 2.5 hectare estate at Le Chiuse di Sotto, just below Montalcino town, purchasing in 1996/7 another 4.5 hectares south of the town which were planted to Sangiovese and Merlot. His Brunello today, made with the help of oenologist/consultant Paolo Vagaggini, is long aged in traditional Slavonian oak *botti* but has the depth of colour and rich, ripe fruit of a thoroughly modern wine, while boasting sufficient backbone to carry it through a couple of decades. He only uses *barrique* for the 10% of Merlot which he adds to Sangiovese to make his Sant'Antimo Rosso, a wine still in the experimental stage but which promises excellent things.

Mastrojanni. Though situated down in the southeast corner of the Montalcino zone, Mastrojanni are far from peripheral quality wise. Whatever Antonio Mastrojanni, with the help of consultant Maurizio Castelli, is doing in his 20 hectares of vineyard, he certainly is doing it in style, and even if the fruit does not appear as opulent as in some of the wines of the competition, nonetheless it is noticeable that Mastrojanni wines are able to maintain freshness and liveliness years after the vintage. The range consists of a fine-boned Rosso, a more structured Brunello as well as a single vineyard Brunello, Schiena d'Asino, a Riserva, at its peak, to die for (the 1990 was one of the finest Brunellos I have ever tasted), and a Sangiovese (75%) plus Cabernet Sauvignon blend called San Pio which delivers a surprisingly integrated fruit for a blend which often has difficulty in hanging together.

Pertimali. The smiling, lively if ageing face of Livio Sassetti greets visitors welcomingly to this extremely well run if deceptively artisanal *cantina* in the Montosoli sub-zone on the lower northern slopes of Montalcino. Aided by his two sons, Sassetti brings forth from his 7 hectares of beautifully tended vineyard Rosso, Brunello and Brunello Riserva of rare intensity and complexity, perhaps a touch on the light side colour-wise, except for Riserva, but having soft strawberry-raspberry fruit, spice and gamey aromas of almost Burgundian style, while not losing Tuscan typicity. To carry the analogy a bit further, if the Brunello *normale* might remind one of a Côte de Beaune, with its delicate colour and penetrating flavours; the Riserva comes over more as a Côte de Nuits, more powerful, concentrated and complex, capable, one is aware, of evolving beautifully to a ripe age.

Pieri Agostina. This is a small, relatively recently established estate formed, like Piancornello, from one part of a larger property bequeathed by the father of present *titolare*, Agostina Pieri. The running of it, as well as the winemaking, is handled by Agostina's son, Francesco Monaci, a young man of determined ideas and a taste for quality. At the time of writing, due to the youth of the *azienda*, the wine that has most drawn the attention, indeed praise, of the wine world is Rosso di Montalcino. Francesco is a strong believer in *barriques* for the ageing of the wines of Montalcino, the Rosso getting the new *barriques* to avoid an excess of oak aromas in the Brunello which goes into barrels of second and third passage, although in good years a strapping Riserva will also go into new *barrique* for a period. Which no doubt accounts in part for the rave reviews received on occasion by the Rosso.

The estate is small – 7 hectares at present – and Francesco does not want it to exceed 10. Most of the vineyards were replanted in the 1990s, so there is time to go before they reach maturity, although there is a 1.5-hectare vineyard which is 20 years old. So for the time being the Rosso – deep of colour, richly fruity with a firm backbone when it's at its best – will remain the standard bearer of the house of Pieri Agostina.

Pieve Santa Restituta. This is where Angelo Gaja casts his magic on that *other* great grape variety of Italy: Sangiovese. The estate was purchased in 1974 by Roberto Bellini, who for reasons of his own sold 90% of it to Gaja in 1994, the remaining 10% stayed Bellini's until 1999. When he arrived, Gaja found, apart from the beautiful fourth-century church, 11 hectares of vineyard planted to Sangiovese, to which he has added five more at a density of 5,000 plants per hectare as against the previous 2,300. The new clones and rootstock he acquired from nurseries in Alto Adige, guided by the redoubtable Professor Attilio Scienza, his aim being not just to achieve greater balance and concentration but also to reduce vigour, steering more of the earth's energy into the fruit and coincidentally, according to him, helping to combat the advancing and as yet ill-understood enemy, esca. In the new vineyards cordon spur is being replaced with a slightly lower simple *guyot* and, of course, *diradamento* is a *sine qua non*.

Gaja admits that, as far as Sangiovese is concerned, he is on a learning curve, but it is a challenge which, not surprisingly, does not daunt him – one gets the impression that he is quietly confident he can eventually outstrip the competition here as he has in Piemonte. But there is no hurry, the key is to learn as you go and 'be flexible'. By the time this book is published he will be well on the way to his projected 35 hectares and will have completely rebuilt the winery so that all operations will happen underground at naturally controlled temperatures.

For the moment, and for the foreseeable future, he will concentrate on two Brunellos: Rennina, from the best vines in the bulk of the estate; and Sugarille, from a 3.5-hectare vineyard planted by Bellini in the mid 1980s whose soil is less fertile and naturally produces smaller, looser bunches of greater concentration. There is, also, a third wine, called Promis, made from the grapes remaining after the selection of the other two, mainly from young vines. The difference between the Brunello *crus* is primarily in the vineyard, vinification techniques being similar: 2 to 3 weeks maceration, depending on the vintage; ageing in *barrique* for 12 to 18 months and in *botte* for 18 to 12 months, for a total wood ageing period of 30 months; no filtration.

The quality? As ever, an excellent standard, wines of indisputable concentration and complexity but with that extra quality displayed by all Gaja wines: perfect harmony of the parts. Already, since the first difficult year in 1994, he has made great strides, but one senses there is a lot more to come. No hurry. Keep learning. Be flexible. As Angelo commented to the *fattore* of neighbouring Case Basse, who opined that 'we Montalcinesi are very fortunate to have such lands': 'Yes', he replied, 'but we must not sleep.'

Poggio Antico. Paola Gloder was thrown in at the deep end when, at 20, her parents, who had bought the estate of 200 hectares, 21 of which are under vine, with a maximum of 33, a couple of years earlier, asked her to take over the running of it. She had to leave Milan, which was home, and learn everything about making and selling wine from zero. With the support of winemaker Massimo Albanese, who has now given way to Carlo Ferrini, she has had some spectacular successes in the world's press, although, the vineyards being at between 450 and 500 metres altitude, the grapes, which can develop wonderful aromas and structure in good years, don't necessarily ripen that well in lesser vintages. Part of this is due to the fact that Poggio Antico has made a policy decision to devote all their energies to Sangiovese, eschewing the Cabernets and Merlots and Syrahs that others plant to give themselves some diversity. Another aspect of Poggio Antico's production is the strictly traditional approach, using only large Slavonian oak *botti* for the *affinamento* and sticking to the minimum wood-ageing periods – three years for *normale*, four for Riserva – laid down under a law now superseded. Even Altero, a wine long classified as Vino da Tavola and only recently elevated to DOCG status, is nothing but a Brunello taken out of wood after two years. The wines all reflect this purity of approach, being archetypally 'Brunello' in style, even the Rosso; just a matter of degree, that's all.

Talenti/Pian di Conte. The late Pierluigi Talenti, grand old man of Montalcino, referred to above under Il Poggione, was given his own estate at Sant'Angelo in Colle by the grateful Franceschi family 20 odd years ago. From around 12 hectares of vineyard he made – and the estate, under his grandson Riccardo Talenti, with the help of Carlo Ferrini, continues to make – predictably excellent wines, including a Rosso of deliciously penetrating cherry fruit and a Brunello typically, for him, a bit closed in youth but which opens out and transforms itself marvellously with age. In his last years he came up with an original blend of Sangiovese, Canaiolo, Colorino and Syrah aged just three months in large wood, then bottled, called, simply, Talenti.

A word on these grapes. The Sangiovese used here is a clone which Talenti has himself developed over the years with Il Poggione, one which he considers ideal for the conditions at altitude in Montalcino; others seem to agree, because it is in some demand from neighbours. Canaiolo may be traditional in Chianti, but it is rarely found in Montalcino: the purpose here is to contribute lightness and drinkability, for Talenti (the wine), unlike many SuperTuscans, is specifically made to be drunk when young and vibrant with fruit. Colorino is another Chianti grape, used there, as here, for the strength of its phenolic substances, especially colour. As for Syrah, this relative newcomer in Tuscany, which seems to be working well for Banfi down the hill at Sant'Angelo Scalo, has given this wine a ripe, sweet fruit which would be almost syrupy in character were it not for the fairly chewy tannins.

Valdicava/Abruzzese. Vincenzo Abruzzese's grandfather was a sharecropper who, in the early 1950s, bought the plot of land he was working. It was another third of a century before Vincenzo, who had been working with his grandfather, took over the reins and began modernising and specialising in quality wine production, helped by consultant oenologist Attilio Pagli. His 15 hectares of vineyard, constantly being improved under the supervision of ex-Antinori agronomist Andrea Paoletti, are planted solely to Sangiovese, the majority inscribed as Brunello although he does bring forth a strapping Rosso which would leave many Brunellos standing. The Brunello *normale* may not always have the charm and rich, heady fruit that the Rosso has, but it has a structure capable of carrying it well into the future; a 'massive' wine, as someone described it. Top *cru* is the Riserva Madonna del Piano, from the best of his seven distinct vineyards.

In terms of vinification, Valdicava is a mix of the modern and the traditional, with *barriques* being used only for the malo-lactic fermentation, the rest of the ageing taking place in 25- to 50-hectolitre *botti* of Slavonian and French oak. Most fermentation is still carried out in stainless steel and glass-lined concrete, but he does have some oak *tini* in which he practises *follatura* or punching down of the cap.

Val di Suga. One of three Tuscan properties bought from Lionello Marchesi in 1995 by Tenimenti Angelini, an investment group of northern Italy controlled by the Angelini family, Val di Suga consistently proves itself to be among Montalcino's finest producers. From their 38 hectares of vineyard actually in production (20 more have recently been purchased), part of which are north of the town Montalcino, in an area producing wines of fruit and perfume rather than of big structure, part on the south side, where the wines come bigger and riper, Val di Suga, under the astute guidance of oenologist-director Mario Calzolari with the aid of consultant Fabrizio Ciufoli, make three distinct styles of Brunello plus a Rosso. Two of the wines are single vineyard: Vigna del Lago, from north of the town, so named because of the proximity of the vineyard to a small lake which helps to moderate the micro-climate; the wine of this name is perhaps their most classic, with less wealth of fruit, more of the leather and dried fruit character of traditional Brunello; and Vigna Spuntali, on the southern side, a wine of modern

concept, of generous fruit plus great robustness, ageability and finesse. Both, aged in small French oak, mainly new, regularly receive the plaudits of the national and press for their success in combining typicity with an international twist, Spuntali being the greater star, especially as the Vigna del Lago vineyard is due for imminent replanting.

The Brunello *normale* is made from a blend of grapes from both parts, as is the Riserva, which latter, however, has been discontinued (1995 was the last vintage). The former is a wine of relatively modern concept, aged increasingly in mainly used *barriques* rather than *botti*, and having plenty of ripe, supple feminine fruit over a masculine structure in terms of tannins. It is the attractive but by no means insubstantial Rosso that gets the *botte* ageing these days, yielding a wine of considerable structure for the genre, offset by a mouthful of fruit.

While Val di Suga acts as headquarters for the wine group, Tenimenti Angelini own two other prestigious wine estates in Tuscany: San Leonino – 44 hectares of vineyard at Castellina in Chianti, with six more to come; and Trerose – 60 hectares (heading for 68) at Valiano di Montepulciano. At both Angelini have applied the mix of modern technology and technique (e.g. new plantings to superior clones at higher densities – 5,000–7,000 plants per hectare; high technology in the wineries, extensive use of various types of French oak barrel), and respect for tradition that characterise and have so well served Val di Suga.

At San Leonino they are working hard to realise the potential of a vineyard of great promise, and signs are, with recent very fine vintages of Chianti Classico *normale* and Riserva as well as a stunning *cru* called Monsenese, that they are getting there. They also produce here one of Tuscany's rare successful varietal Syrahs, called Salivolpe.

Trerose is one of the estates which is leading Montepulciano out of the wilderness of over-structured, under-fruited wines into the era of sexiness and sheer drinkability. All three of the Vino Nobiles – *normale*, the excellent single-vineyard La Villa and the bunch-selected Simposio (the first two containing a bit of Cabernet, the last being pure Sangiovese) – combine good to excellent wealth of fruit and serious but ripe tannins; at their best, the two *crus* rank among the best wines ever to emerge from Montepulciano. From the 1999 vintage they have introduced probably the best example so far of Rosso di Montepulciano (Sangiovese plus Canaiolo and a hint of Syrah and Gamay). They are also turning out some unusually interesting whites, for Tuscany. Salterio is a serious Chardonnay, with 12 months barrel fermentation. Flauto is a Sauvignon, a little less convincing, fermented and aged 9 months in *barrique*. While the most adventurous, Busillis, is a varietal Viognier, one of the first to be attempted in Tuscany, fermented in the same style as Flauto but achieving, to my mind, a higher level of quality, especially when it's got a bit of bottle age, when it turns a yellowish hue and gives off super-ripe aromas of pineapple and other tropical fruits.

Other producers capable of excellent Montalcino wines include: **Baricci; Canalicchio di Sotto/Lambardi; Caprili; Castelgiocondo;**

Castiglion del Bosco; Cerbaiona; Fanti; Fuligni; Il Poggiolo; La Cerbaiola/Salvioni; La Fortuna; La Gerla; Lisini; Silvio Nardi; Tenuta Oliveto; Pacenti Siro; Piancornello; Pian delle Vigne/ Antinori; Poggio Salvi; Poggio di Sotto/Palmucci; Poggio San Polo; Salicutti; Salvioni; Scopetone; Uccelliera.

Montepulciano

The historic wines of Montepulciano – once, in centuries past, so highly prized – find themselves today somewhere between Chianti and Montalcino in style – at their best combining the elegance of Chianti Classico and the firm structure of Brunello. Like Chianti, Vino Nobile di Montepulciano DOC was conceived (in 1966) as a blended wine, similar varieties being involved – that's to say, Sangiovese (here called Prugnolo Gentile), Canaiolo Nero, Trebbiano and Malvasia, and, optionally, Pulcinculo (Grechetto Bianco) and Mammolo.

Things have shifted significantly since then, and the *disciplinare* for Vino Nobile DOCG today no longer contains any mention of white grapes. Since 1999 the mix has been Sangiovese at 70–100%, Canaiolo and Mammolo 0–20% and the usual *raccomandati o autorizzati* (read Cabernet/Merlot/Syrah) 0–20%. You can bet that the second 0–20% is made significantly greater use of than the first. Until 1999 a major difference with Chianti was that no allowance was made for a pure Sangiovese, which of course did not deter certain producers intent upon that style from producing it. Which, in turn, led to the law finally allowing it.

Until a few years ago certain mean-minded people might be heard sneering at Vino Nobile as nothing but a glorified Chianti, and indeed despite its illustrious past Montepulciano producers from the early years of the twentieth century until about the 1970s tended to prefer the Chianti name. Much work, however, was undertaken in the 1980s and 1990s to upgrade the image so that the wine could command higher prices and therefore pay for continued research and improvement, and today at the outset of the new millennium Vino Nobile is beginning again to justify its aristocratic denomination.

The challenge for the producers of Montepulciano has been to overcome the tendency of Sangiovese in this zone to severe austerity in terms both of acidity and tannin. The name Prugnolo Gentile –

'gentle wild plum' – seems to be rather a misnomer, or perhaps it is a fruit of wishful thinking, since Sangiovese here has tended to be neither gentle nor 'plummy', certainly in the sense of soft and fruity. Newly developed clones and vinification methods have helped considerably, and while austerity is still a mark of Vino Nobile that attribute is beginning to be turned to a positive end in respect of Riserva wines of good ageing potential, while the *normali* seem to get fruitier, and plummier, by the vintage.

The law regarding ageing, too, has helped, being less rigid here than in Montalcino, requiring a sensible two years *affinamento* from 1 January following the vintage before being sold, including a minimum of one year in wood. The Riserva must age three years, of which at least one in wood and six months in bottle.

However, one problem the producers of Montepulciano – who, incidentally, are far fewer in number than those either of Montalcino or of Chianti Classico – are going to need to be aware of is the risk of going too far in the direction of making Vino Nobile accessible and thereby losing the firm underlying grip that has traditionally been the calling card of the genre; the risk, as it were, of throwing the baby out with the bathwater.

Rosso di Montepulciano bears various resemblances to Rosso di Montalcino, in that it is made from the same grapes as the superior version and may even be made from grapes of vineyards registered for Vino Nobile – although the reverse is not true, i.e. you can't make Nobile, like Brunello, from vineyards registered for Rosso. The DOC, which allows for release on 1 March following the vintage, was introduced in 1989, but has not enjoyed a Rosso di Montalcino level of success, and some producers still seem to be trying to figure out what Rosso, in general and in particular, ought to represent. The tendency is to make a relatively light wine for early consumption.

The producers

Avignonesi. When in the 1970s Ettore, second of four brothers Falvo of Cortona, married Adriana Avignonesi, scion of a family having long roots in the Montepulciano area, a link was formed not only between two human beings but between two different philosophies of wine: that of an ancient and noble tradition as represented by the Avignonesi and that of the completely new world into which Italy was only just beginning to emerge, as represented by the forward-looking Falvos.

The marriage of the humans failed, except that it brought forth progeny for the continuance of the work; but that of the philosophies has flourished ever since, the house of Avignonesi being not only in the forefront of the rebirth of ancient Montepulciano as a great viticultural zone but also in the vanguard of that experimentation and adventurousness that has characterised the Italian wine *rinascimento*.

From their 100-plus hectares of vineyard spread over four estates, two in the Montepulciano DOCG zone (Le Capezzine, where they carry out various vineyard experiments including the testing of 33 ancient varieties indigenous to Montepulciano and I Poggetti, from whose 18 hectares of vineyard most of their classic Vino Nobile grapes are derived), one near Cortona (La Selva, with 57 hectares planted to international varieties), and another not far from Le Capezzine called Lombarda, recently replanted, each having its peculiar soil structure and microcimate, Avignonesi bring forth a heterogeneous selection of high-quality wines. Parcel by parcel they are replanting their vineyards to superior clones and varieties using such back-to-the-future training systems as the ancient high-density settonce as recommended by the Roman author Columella with *alberello* training (see Chapter 1). On the side of innovation are the *crus* of La Selva: the *barrique*-fermented Chardonnay Il Marzocco and Sauvignon Il Vignola, two of the earliest and still most successful of their type from central Italy, as well as the varietally named Merlot and Pinot Nero. On the other hand, nobody produces the classic Tuscan *passito* wines – Vin Santo (from Tuscan white grapes dried up to six months and aged in *caratelli* as long as eight years), Occhio di Pernice (from Sangiovese, 10 years' ageing) – in a more traditional manner, and for nobody's Vin Santo is the market so desperate to obtain just a handful of very expensive half-bottles.

Not without their traditional side, but with modern characteristics like the realignment of aromas towards the primary and away from the tertiary, are the various Sangiovese-based wines, including a Rosso di Montepulciano, but featuring mainly the hierarchy of Vino Nobiles – *normale*, Riserva and Riserva Grandi Annate, the latter made only, as the name implies, in outstanding vintages like 1997. In respect of these Avignonesi's style can be surprisingly austere, eschewing easy options like the addition of French grapes and total immersion in small French *barriques* and sticking to the 80% Sangiovese/20% Canaiolo + Mammolo formula, with ageing in a mix of oak sizes from *barrique* to 50-hectolitre barrels. The result being wines of great typicity if not always fully satisfying to the modern requirement of fleshy fruitiness; for pursuing which path with courage, three cheers are in order.

Avignonesi used to produce a Sangiovese–Cabernet blend called Grifi, aged in *barrique*, but today, apart from their Avignonesi Rosso, a blend of Sangiovese, Cabernet and Merlot produced in fairly large numbers – over 10,000 cases – they appear to have decided on a total separation between indigenous and international grapes, discontinuing Grifi – though it was one of the most established of the Tuscan SuperTuscans, certainly from Montepulciano – and introducing Desiderio, a Merlot-based wine featuring on the label a bull of the Chianina race native to Tuscany. Indeed, the Falvos are quite into animals, mainly horses from Puglia's Murge. The interest in Puglia has now extended to the acquisition of a property in that southern region, about which available details at the time of writing are sketchy.

Poderi **Boscarelli**. This estate, situated in the Cervognano sub-zone of Montepulciano, which some consider the best, has proceeded by stages since its purchase in 1962 to its present position as challenger for pre-eminence among all Vino Nobile growers. Perhaps the most important stage grew out of the tragic loss by current owner Paola Corradi of her husband Ippolito De Ferrari in 1983, a loss which pushed her to take on consulting oenologist Maurizio Castelli and to instil in her sons Luca and Nicolò, who today share the responsibilities of the estate, her passion and commitment to high quality. Today the 13 hectares of vineyard, principally of Sangiovese, with small amounts of Cabernet Sauvignon, Merlot and Syrah among red varieties, are being gradually replanted to superior clones at higher densities and the *cantina* has been re-equipped to facilitate optimum extraction from the carefully cultivated fruit. As for the Sangiovese-based wines, they are all marked by a serious typicity for the genre, of which the negative aspects – the tendency of the reds of Montepulciano to a certain austerity, as remarked upon earlier – are overcome by concentration of flavour and charm of aroma allied to a great finesse. Indeed the higher *crus* – Vino

Nobile Vigna del Nocio and the SuperTuscan Boscarelli, a 100% Sangiovese matured for 12 months in *barriques* – are endowed with a structure which, while allowing for relatively early drinkability, will also enable lengthy ageing, a fact demonstrated by bottles of the 1980s which remain remarkably resilient while displaying a great richness and development of aromas.

Fattoria del **Cerro**, Acquaviva near Montepulciano. This is the principal of three wine-estates controlled by the Saiagricola group, the agricultural arm of the insurance giant SAI, of which the main shareholder is a certain Ing. Ligresti of Milan. The property has no fewer than 156 hectares under vine, of which 84 are registered for the denomination Vino Nobile di Montepulciano, making Cerro the biggest private producer of the zone. It is therefore important for the sake of the denomination overall that they should be seen to work well, which they do in trumps, winemaker Lorenzo Landi achieving with top quality fruit wines which manage impressively to bridge the gap between serious structure and vibrant moreishness. With regard to that fruit, they carry out intensive experiments relating to clonal selection, planting density and pest control in conjunction with the Universities of Pisa and Florence and the Montepulciano Consortium, translating their findings into reality each time they plant a new vineyard. Possibly more importantly, they are among the most important planters of Colorino in Tuscany with over 20 hectares, which grape winemaker Landi considers vital to the depth of colour and wealth of polyphenols they are able to pack into their wines. Like San Felice, Cerro are also working on Pugnitello as a valid native blending variety.

Fattoria del Cerro's basic wines, Montepulciano Rosso and Vino Nobile, display an easy plummy softness with more or less intense cherry aromas and lowish acid-tannin barriers for the denomination: user-friendly wines, therefore, in quantities sufficient to ensure user-friendly prices. The Vino Nobile Riserva and the selection Vigneto Antica Chiusina have the backbone one would expect of wines made only in special years, but with a liberal covering of that same soft, velvety, concentrated fruit which makes all these wines a pleasure to drink. Considering that the problem of Montepulciano has traditionally been towards the opposite end of the spectrum – too much structure for the amount of fruit on offer – the wines of Fattoria del Cerro should be tasted before any inclination to write the denomination off becomes definitive.

Fattoria del Cerro also make a 100% varietal Sangiovese, *barrique*-aged for 24 months, called Manero – usually an excellent expression of the grape in international mode; and two French varietals, Cerro Bianco (Chardonnay) and Poggio Golo (Merlot), the latter (also with 24 months' *barrique* ageing) being one of the better versions of this trendy Tuscan genre.

Since space considerations render repetition difficult, Saiagricola's other principal Sangiovese property should also be mentioned here. La Poderina, purchased by Saiagricola in 1988, is an estate of 20 hectares of vineyard in the Castelnuovo dell'Abate sector of Montalcino, the principal wines, needless to say, being Brunello, Brunello Riserva and Rosso di Montalcino. In common with all the wines of Saiagricola these are extremely well made by Lorenzo Landi, the company oenologist, combining a correctness of style with elegance and exceptional drinkability. La Poderina also makes a small amount of the latest-fad wine for Montalcino, Moscadello.

Saiagricola also grow Sangiovese at their estate in Montefalco called Colpetrone, but the principal grape there being Sagrantino we will consider it under that heading.

Contucci. History oozes from every pore of the Contucci winery. The cellars, dating from medieval times, are visited by thousands of tourists yearly; the ancestral Palazzo in Montepulciano's central Piazza Grande, designed by Antonio da Sangallo the Elder, was built in the sixteenth century (a later Contucci, Andrea, called Sansovino, was himself a famous architect); the family have been growing vines since the *Rinascimento*, making wine since at least the seventeenth century, and bottling since the nineteenth century – with a bottle of the 1887 'Vino Scelto Montepulciano' (as Vino Nobile was then known) to prove it.

Today production is carried forward by Alamanno Contucci, careful craftsman of the wines derived from their 20+ hectares of vineyard, in various sectors of the zone. There is a strong tradition-alist flavour to the various Sangiovese-based wines produced – Vino Nobile, Riserva, Pietra Rossa and Mulinvecchio from the *cru* vineyards of those names, Rosso di Montepulciano and the pure Sangiovese Sansovino. Because of their austerity they are not wines to be drunk without food, and I have found that they tend to open out after a day's breathe, like the best traditional Barolos. As Alamanno gradually replaces aged barrels with new ones of both French and Slavonian oak, so are the wines shedding some of the 'old style'. But when you've been in the business for centuries, you learn not to hurry things merely to cater to passing fashion.

La Braccesca. See Antinori under Chianti Classico, San Casciano.

Le Casalte. This small estate is one of those which could be described as 'boutique'. It was in 1975 that Guido Barioffi of Rome and his wife, Paola, rescued it from the neglect it had fallen into and for years Guido, who has the soul of a gardener in the body of a bank manager – he is now retired from the latter position, and devoting himself more to the former – poured his weekends and his heart into bringing the 10-or-so hectares of vineyard to a state of perfection. This having been achieved, he began concentrating on the *cantina*, which is now heading for state-of-the-art. Today the estate is managed by daughter Chiara and the wines are made under the consultancy of the grand old man of Tuscan wines, Giulio Gambelli, whose quality-first attitude exactly matches that of the Barioffi, who are quite capable of declassifying a vintage which everyone else is bottling because the wine does not meet their exacting standards. Production consists of a Rosso of eminent purity and drinkability and a Vino Nobile which brings together ripeness of fruit and harmony of balance, with a great typicity which makes it one of the standard-bearers of that 'nobility' for which the wines of Montepulciano are known.

Nottola. This estate, with 14 hectares under vine and 10 more in preparation, is a relatively recently discovered star in the Montepulciano firmament. Purchased by the Giomarelli family in 1990, Giuliano Giomarelli, with the oenological assistance of Riccardo Cotarella, has been busy transforming vineyards and *cantina* into a force for the production of modern-style wines – Rosso, Vino Nobile and a pure-Sangiovese *cru* called Vigna del Fattore – with the accent on fruit. 'These people', I noted while tasting, 'have got the message of the market.' I suspect we will be hearing a lot more of Nottola in years to come.

Poliziano. This large estate was purchased by the Carletti family in 1961, but it was not until the 1980s, when present proprietor

POLIZIANO

1997

~ Asinone ~

Vino Nobile di Montepulciano

DENOMINAZIONE DI ORIGINE CONTROLLATA E GARANTITA

IMBOT.GIULIATO
ALL'ORIGINE DA
AZIENDA AGRICOLA
POLIZIANO
DI FEDERICO CARLETTI
MONTEPULCIANO
ITALIA

ITALIA
13,5% vol
750 ml

Federico Carletti came aboard, that it began the journey which has taken it to the highest level in Montepulciano particularly and Tuscany generally. Carletti is a viticulturist by training, and more than most who give lip-service to the theory that 'great wine is born in the vineyard', he backs the idea in practice, supported by one of Tuscany's great consultant agronomist/oenologists, Carlo Ferrini. The estate engages tirelessly in experiments relating to clonal selection, and not satisfied with the development of their own clone, which comes from vineyards 600 metres above sea-level at Rufina and is currently being propagated at Rauscedo under the name R. Sangiovese Poliziano, have brought in vines from other experimentalists like Il Poggione and Banfi in Montalcino. Two or three of these latter are being worked with presently at Poliziano and, according to Carletti, are showing the greatest promise in respect of quality combined with early ripening; the Poliziano clone, conversely, is about a week late compared with other Montepulciano clones.

This is not to say that the greatest attention is not also being given to the work in *cantina*. In particular, Carletti believes that it is essential to effect the maximum of colour extraction in the very early stages, when alcohol is low and the tougher tannins – the blight of modern Montepulciano; 'tannoni', Carletti calls them, making a play on words[5] – are relatively fixed in the skins. He is also a strong believer in French oak, particularly in the tonneau, for the affinamento process for Sangiovese. 'For the time being', he says, he does not believe in blending Sangiovese with the French red varieties, which (Cabernet Sauvignon) he vinifies separately for the excellent SuperTuscan Le Stanze. He is also strict about not making the Vino Nobile cru Vigna Asinone, nor the Cabernet–Merlot blend Le Stanze, in years of medium quality, preferring rather to ensure the quality of his basic Vino Nobile. In respect of the latter, at least, he will in future be able to offset lesser years using fruit from his recently acquired property, Lohsa, in the Scansano zone of Tuscany's Maremma.

The style of the Vino Nobile wines of Poliziano is deep and vibrant of colour, rich and concentrated of fruit, firm of tannic backbone but with that soft cherry-berry fruit overlaying the tannins, seemingly powerful but more thanks to concentration than to alcohol (he tries to keep the wines around 13% alcohol, where from other producers it can easily climb to 14+ in good years), and ultimately quite elegant. If all wines under the name Vino Nobile were on or near this level Montepulciano would be mounting a much more convincing challenge to the hegemony of Montalcino than it presently is; and, thanks to Poliziano's enlightened pricing policy, at a much better value-for-money ratio.

Salcheto. Although they purchased it in 1984, the Salcheto property of Cecilia Naldoni and Fabrizio Piccin is really the new boy on the block as far as quality Vino Nobile is concerned. By the mid-late 1990s they were beginning to make waves, but it was only with the advent of the new millennium that all the pieces were in place to guarantee, weather permitting, regular production of outstanding wine. The formula is simple enough and becoming familiar enough in theory, though practitioners as expert as Salcheto are still not so easy to find: rigourous care in the vineyard

---

5 The suffix -ino in Italian is diminutive; thus a ragazzino is a little boy, ragazzo; the suffix -one is augmentative; so a ragazzone would be a big boy. The word tannino is not a diminutive, but it sounds like one.

– they currently have 12 hectares under vine, heading for 16 – to produce strictly limited quantities of high quality grapes; a brand new winery with plenty of new wood, some *botti* but mainly *barriques* and *tonneaux*, mainly French, some American; the services of an expert consultant oenologist in the person of Paolo Vagaggini; and above all a will to perfection. Practically all of the estate's grapes are Sangiovese, and both the Vino Nobile and the Vino Nobile Riserva are 100% varietal, with the Rosso di Montepulciano having a bit of Canaiolo, although there are a few French vines by way of 'experimentation'. It all adds up to authentic Montepulciano character without the stringy leanness and toughness that has so characterised that denomination in the past. In brief, these are *vini veramente nobili*.

Tenuta **Trerose**. See Tenimenti Angelini Val di Suga, Montalcino.

Valdipiatta. This medium-sized estate – about 25 hectares under vine – is one of those that have mounted the swelling wave of quality wine production in Montepulciano. Under the ownership, since 1990, of Giulio Caporali, with the assistance of consultant Paolo Vagaggini for the winemaking, there have been significant improvements with the drastic reduction of yields and the planting of new vineyards with clones selected by the local Consorzio. Underpinning production is the classic Montepulciano threesome: Rosso, Vino Nobile and Vino Nobile Riserva – wines of modern conception, with the accent on fruit, but retaining a typical Montepulciano firmness of structure. Caporali has also in recent years come out with a couple of innovative blends called Il Trincerone, Merlot with Canaiolo, and Trefonti, which brings together Sangiovese, Cabernet Sauvignon and Canaiolo in a wine of plentiful berry-fruit aroma and considerable concentration.

'This is the best', declared my young daughter, sniffing the range and picking out the Trefonti, 'because it smells more like juice. But it doesn't taste like juice', she concluded after a sip. *Meno male*.

Other producers capable of good to excellent wines from Montepulciano include: **Bindella; Canneto; Carpineto; Dei; Fassati; La Calonica; Lodola Nuova/Ruffino; Palazzo Vecchio; Redi; Romeo; Villa S. Anna.**

Carmignano

This is another of Tuscany's historic Sangiovese wines to have fallen on hard times prior to the 1970s, despite a past of some glory.

The first historic mention of the wines of 'Charmignano' goes way back to 1396, and it is clear that it was a much prized product at that time since the merchant Marco Datini was willing to pay a price some four times higher than for other wines of the age.

Francesco Redi, in his famous *Bacco in Toscana* poem of 1673, says that with a glass of 'brilliant Carmignano' in his hand he need not envy Jove himself his nectar and ambrosia. And if anyone should dare to put water in his Carmignano, why, he will have nothing further to do with the perpetrator of such a heinous act:

Che saria
Gran follia
E brutissimo peccato
Bevere il Carmignano quando è inacquato
Chi l'acqua beve
Mai non riceve
Grazie da me.

As has been noted earlier, Carmignano was one of the four wine zones cited in the 1716 decree of Grand Duke Cosimo III de' Medici, and as such one of the oldest wines of denominated origin in the world.

In the 1930s, however, Carmignano was subsumed in the Chianti Montalbano zone, and for several decades production was limited both in quantity and quality. Even from these dark years, however, there remain to this day a few bottles of old vintages (1931, 1937) of Capezzana Riserva which are still nicely drinkable, although they have lost much of their colour.

It was not, however, until 1975 that the name Carmignano, now a DOC, was restored, thanks mainly to the efforts of Capezzana's Conte Ugo Contini Bonacossi. This latter also ensured that Carmignano was the first DOC in Tuscany officially to require the presence (then at 10%) of Cabernet in the blend; and this blend of Tuscany and France has become, if you like, Carmignano's 'new *tipicità*'.

Today Carmignano DOCG, though still a small zone (around 150 hectares, but increasing), is recognised as one of Tuscany's major red wines.

The *disciplinare* for Carmignano and Carmignano Riserva calls for a minimum of 50% Sangiovese, which in practice is almost invariably exceeded; a minimum of 10% Cabernet (Sauvignon or Franc) with a maximum of 20%, which in practice is **sometimes** exceeded, even though it's not supposed to be; a maximum of 20% Canaiolo and 10% Trebbiano – hence no minimum, so none of the good producers use these grapes any more in Carmignano; and an option of 10% other 'recommended or authorised' red grapes which in practice means Merlot, a bit of Petit Verdot, and now some Syrah.

The same blend applies to the DOCs Barco Reale, effectively Carmignano's 'second wine', and Rosato di Carmignano 'Vinruspo', so named because the share-cropper peasants in the old days used to rob (*ruspare*) a few demijohns full of the recently pressed grape-must they were sending to the landlowner as his due, which they then vinified in the jars half-buried in the earth. The wine is still made by a 5 or 10% bleed from the recently pressed red wine, and, by the way, is one of the best *rosato*s of Italy.

The Sangioveses of Carmignano, far from having the hardness of Sangiovese-based reds of other parts of Tuscany, tend to be rather on the soft and elegant side ('underwhelming', as one taster put it), and a bit of beefing up with the more aggressive varieties of Bordeaux is positive if not necessary. Indeed certain growers of the zone have been heard to mutter that they far prefer to work with Cabernet and Merlot ('the French grapes are beautiful, you never go wrong with them') than with Sangiovese, which is a 'poorer grape, much more difficult to work with, even though it does give great results when things go right.' Much hope is placed on the new clones of Sangiovese planted to greater density and producing less and better per plant; however, as elsewhere, though these are being planted at a considerable rate today, it is going to be necessary to wait a number of years before these bring forth their best products.

According to Ugo Contini Bonacossi Carmignano as a generic wine is going in the right direction today – and no small thanks to him. Following years during which his was really the only estate worth talking about, today a number of fine smaller properties are coming to the fore. The younger generation, some of them helped by excellent consultants like Stefano Chioccioli and Alberto Antonini, are taking wing and producing wines, always of elegance, but of increasing depth.

The producers

Tenuta di **Capezzana**, Seano. Count Ugo Contini Bonacossi, now in his 70s, is undoubtedly one of the most significant figures in Tuscan and indeed Italian viniculture of the twentieth century. His family have been in ownership of their splendid *Rinascimento* villa for several generations. His father, Alessandro, was a noted poet and gentleman farmer, and Ugo has carried on the latter tradition, bringing the wines of his estate as well as those of Carmignano

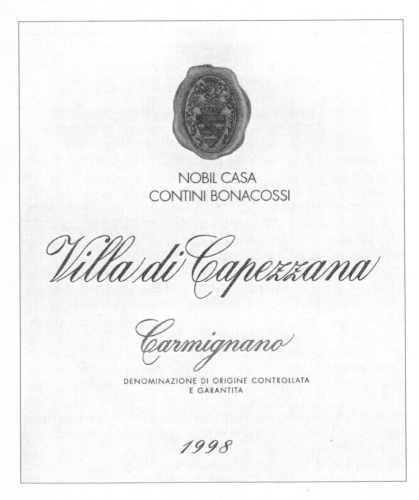

NOBIL CASA
CONTINI BONACOSSI

Villa di Capezzana

Carmignano

DENOMINAZIONE DI ORIGINE CONTROLLATA
E GARANTITA

1998

generally into international prominence. He has also persuaded over half of his seven children to join him in the family enterprise, no mean feat considering the diversity of their personalities, and even those who have not followed his lead are frequently to be seen around the ever-hospitable table, in the grounds, at the swimming pool with their no less numerous broods. A family portrait photographed years ago shows around 100 mostly smiling faces, and there are many more today. And if that's not enough people, there are always plenty of others tasting, eating or studying in the form of students at their cookery course, run by Ugo's charming wife Lisa, or of coach-loads come to see the wine or oil operation (they have their own oil press, and one of the finest olive oils in Tuscany), or of friends or friends of friends who have made appointments or just dropped by (the 'You don't know me but' syndrome). There is a permanent welcome in this house of controlled chaos.

There is nothing chaotic about the wine operation, however. They have been fine-tuning it for several decades now, since Ugo brought back cuttings of Cabernet Sauvignon from somewhere called Lafite in the 1960s, and reckon that today, as the new century dawns, they've got it about right. A major step occurred when, in the late 1990s, they took on Stefano Chioccioli as consultant in both vineyard and winery, Ugo's daughter Benedetta stepping in to act as resident winemaker. In the past they have produced both Carmignano and Carmignano Riserva DOCG – the latter being capable of amazing longevity considering its elegance in youth – with Barco Reale DOC in third place among Sangiovese-based reds and Chianti Montalbano in fourth. At present, however, they are phasing out the Riserva ('Since we are using *barriques* we don't need to wait three years', observed Ugo; the last vintage will be 1997) and upgrading Carmignano to position of top wine, with Barco Reale promoted to the position that Carmignano *normale* used to occupy. Chianti Montalbano will probably disappear when they replant the vineyards presently inscribed to that denomination. They also have an alternative Carmignano, Villa di Trefiano, which used to belong to Ugo's son Vittorio but which he sold back to the main estate and whose future is undecided (it will perhaps become an organic wine).

At present about 45% of their 100-plus hectares is inscribed in the *albo* as Carmignano DOCG, but there's a major replanting and new-planting programme in progress – using new clones and denser plantings, of course. They aim eventually to reach almost 100%, although they will keep a bit of Chardonnay for the white wine and some Trebbiano/Malvasia for their excellent Vin Santo. The vines they are concentrating on now, apart from Sangiovese, are Merlot and Syrah, which latter they have found to give excellent results in trials to date.

The blend for the above-mentioned wines is, of course, predominantly Sangiovese with as much Cabernet as they can get away with – the Cabernet being mainly Sauvignon rather than Franc, the latter tending generally to go in the lesser blends – and a modicum of Merlot. In future Syrah will also form a small part of the Carmignano blend.

Despite all the international influences – strong reliance on French blending-varieties, use of small French oak; and despite the fact that Carmignano wines are, as I have indicated, more noted for their elegance than for their strength, Carmignano as interpreted by Capezzana has a strong zonal character. It is not like Brunello or Vino Nobile, but it is not like claret or Bolgheri either; whatever the grapes or the method of vinification, the innate aristocratic breeding of the wines shines through, and it has to be said that with the coming of Chioccioli the wines have taken on a greater polish and an extra dimension of fruit, so that, always fine, they are becoming finer still.

Detached from the Sangiovese-based crowd stands another excellent wine, Ghiaie della Furba, until recently a strict Bordeaux blend – the two Cabernets plus Merlot – now something like a Bordeaux '*hermitage*', having as it does from the 1998 vintage a modicum of Syrah in its blend.

Piaggia, Poggio a Caiano. Mauro Vannucci is, so local rumour has it, an old rogue turned good. I can't tell you in what his roguery once consisted, but the goodness takes the form of a first-class Carmignano Riserva. He might agree that the power behind the goodness is knitwear, of which he is a manufacturer, and which doubtless paid for his fine purpose-built *cantina*, the new *barriques* it contains in plenty, and the services of one of Tuscany's up-and-coming wine consultants, Alberto Antonini. But try and tell him that wine, then, is just a hobby for him and he becomes quietly indignant. You understand that wine, for him, is in fact a passion when he preambles your tasting with: 'You are about to taste the best wine in the world. What? You don't believe me?' What do you say after that?

You can, in all honesty, agree that it is indeed a mighty fine vinous creation. But even if you were to disagree you know he would pay no attention to your opinion. Or would he?

Vannucci's Carmignano is made with what might be described as a 'new-classic' blend of Sangiovese (70%), Cabernet Sauvignon (20%) and Merlot (10%). Like the best clarets it is aged two years in *barrique*. If the year is below par, he declassifies to an IGT called Il Sasso, and if it isn't good enough for that he sells in bulk. He's got more orders than he can cope with from top Italian restaurants and various world markets. All very simple.

And, of course, the wine is the very best in the world. Well, you never know what old rogues might get up to if you rub them the wrong way.

Other good to excellent producers of Carmignano include: Fattoria **Ambra** (Riserva Le Vigne Alte Montalbiolo), Carmignano; Fattoria di **Artimino** (Riserva Medicea), Artimino; **Il Poggiolo** (Villa Riserva), Carmignano; Fattoria **Le Farnete** (Riserva), Carmignano; Podere **Lo Locco**/Pratesi, Seano.

Montecarlo and Colline Lucchesi

This Montecarlo is not a gambling mecca for decadent nobility and glitterati but a colourful hilltop commune of the province of Lucca in western Tuscany. The fact that some of the most talented young consultant oenologists are working in Montecarlo, examples being Luca d'Attoma at Fattoria La Torre and Stefano Chioccioli at Buonamico and Montechiari, is a sign that the zone has an interesting future. The DOC Rosso must be at least 50% Sangiovese, blended with various others of Italian and French origin. Until recently, the best Sangiovese-based reds were mostly at *vino da tavola*/IGT level, either due to an insufficiency of Sangiovese, as in the case of Fattoria del **Buonamico**'s Rosso di Cercatoia, or to an excess – cf. **Fuso Carmignani**'s 100% Sangiovese 'For Duke' (sic), the Duke in question being Duke Ellington. **Montechiari** Rosso is another pure Sangiovese IGT of class as, almost, is the Stringaio of Fattoria **La Torre,** which includes

10% Cabernet Sauvignon. Montecarlo Rosso DOC is now coming good in the hands of Carmignani (Sassonero) and Montechiari, as well as of **Wandanna** with their *cru* Terre dei Cascinieri. Other reds from the zone are mentioned under International Varieties.

Colline Lucchesi, the hills of Lucca, is one of those obscure DOCs which abound in Italy – that it has not been subsumed into Montecarlo, a name people recognise even if, in this instance, erroneously, is another example of Italian *campanilismo*, or inability to see beyond the local church-steeple. Given the insignificance of the DOC it is not surprising that producers tend to concentrate more on IGT wines, but there are a couple of respectable versions of Colline Lucchesi Rosso DOC from, respectively, **La Badiola** of San Pancrazio and Tenuta di **Valgiano** at Capannori. The latter's DOC Rosso di Palistorti adds Syrah and Canaiolo to a Sangiovese base. But Laura di Collobiano and Moreno Petrini, with winemaker Saverio Petrilli, are perhaps more proud of their IGT Scasso dei Cesari, a Sangiovese plus Merlot blend which undergoes its malo-lactic in cask and emerges with greater body and roundness of fruit.

Maremma

Costa degli Etruschi
The band of Tuscan coast stretching from Livorno in the north to Piombino in the south mainland, and on to the Isola d'Elba just off' the coast from Piombino – the northern section of the Maremma – is today being marketed as the Costa degli Etruschi: Coast of the Etruscans. The DOCs it takes in include Montescudaio, Bolgheri, Val di Cornia and Elba. Top wines from this area – and it has more than its share – tend to be heavily influenced by Bordeaux, so we will be looking at the various producers again in the chapter on International Varieties. However, there are some good to excellent Sangioveses coming from these parts as well.

Montescudaio
Until 1999, the *disciplinare* of this DOC harked back to the dark ages, requiring as it did a minimum of 15% white grape (Trebbiano or Malvasia Bianca) to be mixed into the *uvaggio di vigneto*, together with up to 85% Sangiovese – an archaism which other Tuscan denominations, in particular Chianti Classico, stopped

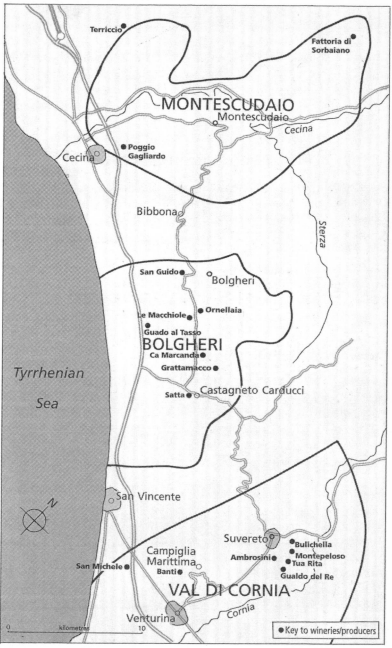

Northern Maremma

insisting upon in the early 1980s. Doubtless ignoring these precepts – anyway the requirement to include white grapes no longer holds – Fattoria **Sorbaiano** at Montecatini Val di Cecina make a reliably good DOC under the name Rosso delle Miniere; **Poggio Gagliardo** also score regularly with their Rosso Rovo. A winery which seemed to promise much, until they sold the estate recently to a consortium, was Merlini, making a pair of Montescudaio DOC wines called Le Colline (Sangiovese & Ciliegiolo) and the barrique-aged cru Guadipiani (Sangiovese & Cabernet Sauvignon). Whether the new proprietors will continue with the wines under these names seems unlikely, but there is a good chance the styles will be similar assuming the talented Luca d'Attoma continues as consultant oenologist.

Bolgheri

By far the most important aspect of Bolgheri as a DOC is in the Bordeaux-variety department, as previously indicated. The 1994-adjusted DOC does, indeed, provide for a Sangiovese at 70% maximum, but there is not much enthusiasm on the part of growers to avail themselves of the opportunity to produce a high quality DOC wine. The law's assiveness is demonstrated by its forcing a perfectly valid, indeed excellent, wine into IGT status for the crime of being pure Sangiovese. This is the Vigna al Cavaliere of Michele **Satta**, of Castagneto Carducci (of which commune Bolgheri is a *frazione*), which has been described as a 'minor masterpiece' and whose soft and graceful fruitiness does, indeed, demonstrate to perfection the potential of Sangiovese in an altogether more clement climate than that to which it is accustomed in the considerably higher altitudes of inland Tuscany. Another excellent Sangiovese-based wine (+ Cabernet, Merlot, Syrah) is Macchiole, from the estate of Le Macchiole.

Bolgheri Rosato DOC features the same *uvaggio* as the Rosso – indeed the Bolgheri DOC was originally set up to accommodate the *rosato* and the white wines of the area, being the traditional styles. In the past Sangiovese was dominant in *rosato*, but today the wine may well be obtained in part by a process of bleeding – known as *salasso* – from the main mass of the red in order to improve the latter's concentration; which means that Cabernet and Merlot will tend to be the dominant varieties.

Val di Cornia/Suvereto

Like Bolgheri, Val di Cornia, with its sub-zone Suvereto, a town some 20 odd miles down the coast from Bolgheri – indeed it has been hailed as the 'new Bolgheri' – is more into things Bordelais than things Tuscan. At least here the law graciously permits producers to make 100% Sangiovese if they so desire, and one who gets near with conspicuous success, with the help of consultant Fabrizio Moltard, is Fabio Chiarelotto, a Swiss Italian who in the late 1990s took over (from a Swiss German) at the excellent estate of **Montepeloso**. The wine called Nardo, which used to be the estate's top wine until the Bordeaux-style Gabbro took over, is from 1999 a blend of 90% Sangiovese and 10% Cabernet Sauvignon. It is a wine of great opulence of luxurious fruit beautifully mingled with the vanilla and coffee/dark chocolate of expensive *barriques*. Chiarelotto's Eneo, until recently pure Sangiovese, is now Sangiovese with a variable blend of Cabernet Sauvignon, Colorino and other local varieties. At the time of writing Chiarelotto is engaged in a major replanting programme, so quantities are very low, but he hopes to be back in full production, with a new wine or two to offer, by around 2005.

Also in the commune of Suvereto are **Ambrosini Lorella**, whose Subertum can be impressive; **Martelli e Busdraghi**, whose Incontri is made with the help of oenologist Attilio Pagli; and **Gualdo del Re** whose Val di Cornia Rosso Riserva DOC under the house name has been improving steadily over the past few years. Their neighbours **Tua Rita** concentrate mainly on Bordeaux grapes, as we shall see further on, but manage, with the help of oenologist Stefano Chioccioli, to turn out a more than respectable Sangiovese-based wine called Perlato Rosso. **Villa Monte Rico** also make a varietal Sangiovese, which reflects the ripeness and juiciness of which the grape is capable at these low altitudes.

The other significant commune of the Val di Cornia zone is Campiglia Marittima, where Jacopo **Banti**, **Graziani** and **Volpaiole** all turn out worthy versions of the DOC.

Massa Marittima

One of a series of hitherto obscurish but increasingly trendy wine-producing zones tucked away along or near the coast of Tuscany, Monteregio di Massa Marittima dates back as a DOC only to 1994 and has as yet to make much impact on markets, partly because production remains very small. Recently, interest has been shown by Ezio Rivella, ex chief of Banfi, and the giant Zonin, as well as the Chianti Classico producers San Felice and Castellare, the latter having established the first major Franco-Italian joint venture with Domaines Barons de Rothschild using Château Lafite's oenological consultant Christian le Sommer, so we can expect to be hearing a lot more of Monteregio in the near future.

The producer of this zone that has made the most impact on international markets is without doubt **Moris Farms**, owned by Adolfo Parentini and Caterina Moris, aided by oenologist Attilio Pagli. The estate is so called because the Moris family, of Spanish origin, have two farms – which for some reason they choose to refer to in English – one in the Scansano zone and the other, their principal address, at Massa Marittima. They produce a bit of DOC Monteregio, which they seem to play down in favour of their other wines, the main one being the by now famous Avvoltore, 75% Sangiovese, 20% Cabernet Sauvignon and 5% Syrah, macerated 25 days – long, for our time – and aged 12 months in new *barriques* in which they also do the malo-lactic fermentation. A longish (20 days) maceration is also resorted to for the Morellino di Scansano Riserva, of which 75% is aged in *barriques*, the rest remaining the same length of time (1 year) in large *botti*. Even the Morellino *normale* gets quite a long (15 days) maceration for a wine supposed to be forward and fruity, although here there is no wood ageing. Over 100,000 bottles of this wine are produced at a consistently high quality level, the wealth of extract being balanced by a vibrant fruit. Morellino Riserva, of course, is distinctly deeper and fuller, yet doesn't quite win the plaudits of the pundits to the extent that the IGT Avvoltore does – this latter being an intense and con-centrated, darkly attractive, international-style wine of a type that seems to be catching on in the Maremma (cf. Montepeloso's Nardo).

Probably the producer here of longest standing is Harald **Bremer**, a German wine shipper who purchased a property near Castiglione della Pescaia back in 1972 and who has been selling the constantly improving wine from it ever since, mainly in Germany; his DOC carries the sub-title Rosso Vetluna, Vetluna being also the name, on its own, of his more highly rated Cabernet Sauvignon.

Another small producer of worth is Fiorella Lenzi of **Serraiola** at Monterotondo Marittimo, who makes a smooth and characterful red called Lentisco from 85% Sangiovese and 15% Merlot. I **Campetti**, of Roccastrada, make a couple of characterful *crus* called Castruccio and Baccio, the latter aged in *barrique*. They are, however, perhaps better known for their whites, being among the first to venture into Viognier (Almabruna) and certainly among the best exponents of Malvasia Bianca (L'Accesa).

Scansano

This is the longest standing and highest ranking of the Tuscan coastal DOCs for Sangiovese, here called Morellino, although the relatively old zone has taken on quite a new look in recent years. Indeed nowadays when the relatively soft and fruity Sangiovese of these lower altitudes is being 'discovered' there is a veritable rush to invest in the glowing 'potential' – the word most used in connection with Scansano, since the 'actual' has yet to achieve excellence – of the Scansano DOC zone on the part of the boys with the bucks, so much so that land prices virtually quintupled in the last five years of the twentieth century. Those who have joined the inward rush include Antinori, Barbi Colombini, Cecchi, Coltibuono, the Mazzei of Fonterutoli (Belguardo) with the Widmers of Brancaia, Moris Farms, Poliziano (Lohsa), Rocca delle Macie and the Frescobaldi–Mondavi partnership.

One of the more spectacular arrivals of recent times is Jacopo Biondi-Santi (see under Montalcino), who in 1999 purchased the 360-hectare estate, including a fine tenth-century *castello*, of **Montepò**, from the family of Graham Greene – of the Beeb, not of the novels, though he was related. Jacopo's interest here is gradually to transfer grape production for his *crus* Sassoalloro, Schidione and Rívolo, plus the recently introduced 100% Cabernet Montepaone, to a site where grapes ripen more easily than in Montalcino or Chianti Classico. At the time of writing the percentage of producing vineyards is rather low but there is some fairly frantic planting as well as bulldozing going on to clear land for more – the ultimate goal being 90 to 100 hectares as the funds become available, 'without help from my father or father-in-law'. Grapes planted include new clones of Sangiovese, of course, as well as of Cabernet, Merlot, Ciliegiolo and Lancillotta, Sauvignon Blanc and Chardonnay.

Both in the vineyard and in the castle-winery there is 'everything to do', Jacopo says – but the enthusiasm is very much there to do it, as is the conviction that he will succeed. Jacopo trained as a viticulturist, but he takes a keen interest in oenology and has his own ideas about how wine should be vinified. Sassoalloro, for example, is fermented over a long period – up to 25 days – at a temperature which is never allowed to exceed 25 degrees Celsius, low for a red wine; and the *barriques* used for maturation are, unusually, non-toasted. It was while travelling widely in the wine world in the 1970s that he saw that the way his father was making wine was, in his words, limited and in danger of becoming 'fossilised' – hence the tension between father and son described above (see Biondi-Santi, Montalcino).

But now he has his own operation, and as long as he lets his father get on with his thing in Montalcino, Franco is happy for Jacopo to get on with his in Scansano. It is of such tensions and stresses, perhaps, that great ideas and great wines are born.

In recent years the running in Scansano has been made by two producers in particular: **Le Pupille**, of Magliano in Toscana, owned by the strikingly attractive Elisabetta Geppetti, where the wine-making for years was in the hands of the legendary Giacomo Tachis whose skills brought forth Morellinos of typically soft, velvety structure yet great intensity of Morello cherry fruit, though their main fame came not from Sangiovese but from their Bordeaux-style Saffredi. Tachis passed the bâton to Riccardo Cotarella, who then passed it briefly to Luca d'Attoma before it came into the hands of Bordelais consultant Christian le Sommer who advises such eminences as Châteaux Lafite and Latour. Meanwhile, Geppetti has lived through some fairly upsetting family ructions which have required the relocation of her winery. But the determination to achieve perfection remains through all the changes, and the wines remain as impressive as ever. Le Pupille's range includes a surprisingly soft, juicy Morellino di Scansano *normale*, a Riserva of greater structure and a *cru* called Poggio Valente which caused quite some excitement when the 1997 came out in 2000. The property's most famous wine, of course, the Cabernet/Merlot blend Saffredi, belongs in another section.

Perhaps the longest-serving quality Morellinista is Erik **Banti** of Scansano itself, whose DOC wine is overshadowed by two IGT *crus* called Aguilaia, blended with Aleatico, and Ciabatta. Others situated in the Scansano zone include **I Botri**, **La Carletta**,

Macereto, Mantellassi, Morellino di Scansano (the cooperative), Poggio Argentiera, Provveditore-Bargagli and Sellari Franceschini. A good if not inspired producer of Morellino whose winery is situated just outside the zone is **Villa Patrizia** at Roccalbenga, whose main wine is not actually Morellino but a very tasty Sangiovese/Merlot/Cabernet blend called Orto di Boccio.

Parrina

This is one of those DOCs which have grown up around, or rather has been created by, a sole producer, like Pomino around Frescobaldi in Rufina. The producer in this case is the aptly named **La Parrina**, an estate in the commune of Orbetello making a variety of products – oil, cheese, honey, fruits and vegetables, as well as wine – all· along very natural lines. The DOC calls for a minimum of 70% Sangiovese, but wisely allows the producer to choose Sangiovese for the rest, or any other recommended or authorised variety of the province of Grosseto. Franca Spinola, with the help of agronomist Federico Curtaz and oenologist Beppe Caviola, brings forth Parrina and Parrina Riserva for, respectively, early drinking or medium-term ageing. They, with the cru Muraccio, are remarkably pure and favourably priced, well suited to regular drinking from the point of view both of the pocket and the health. La Parrina's estate in the Scansano zone, is called Colle di Lupo and is managed by Franca Spinola's daughter, Costanza Malfatti.

Elba

Growers on the island of Elba have traditionally used Sangiovese for red wines, alongside their more distinctive Aleatico, which, however, tends to upstage it quality-wise. Two producers doing a reasonable job are **Acquabona** and Tenuta **La Chiusa**, both of Portoferraio.

Other Sangioveses of Tuscany

Apart from DOC(G) wines there are a number of one-off Sangiovese-based wines in Tuscany which do not fall under any particular category or under any recognised denomination except perhaps Toscana IGT, a classification devised specifically to catch all the renegades in some kind of official net. An example is the much-praised Pietrello d'Oro of **Meleta** at Roccatederighi in the province of Grosseto. Another is the *cru* Villa Patrizia of the producer of the same name, mentioned under Morellino di Scansano. There are doubtless numerous others springing up as I write.

Still that does not exhaust the range of Sangioveses in Tuscany, because there is a rare but potentially delicious dessert wine, usually though not invariably called <u>Occhio di Pernice</u>, based on Sangiovese at a minimum of 50% *uva passita* (that's to say, a *vin santo* from red grapes). This style is included in the DOC *disciplinari* of Bolgheri, Carmignano, Elba, Montecarlo, Monteregio di Massa Marittima, as well as in the three Vin Santo DOCs – VS del Chianti, VS del Chianti Classico and VS di Montepulciano. The outstanding practitioner of this Occhio di Pernice is universally recognised to be Avignonesi of Montepulciano, whose wine will finally achieve recognition as a DOC when the 1996 comes out in the middle of the first decade of the third millennium. This because minimum ageing requirements for VS di Montepulciano are twice those of the others – eight years as compared with three (*normale*) or four (Riserva). Avignonesi likes to carry it even further.

The wines in Umbria

While Sangiovese-based 'quality wine' in Umbria represents a mere fraction of that turned out in an average year in Tuscany, nevertheless Sangiovese is the ruling red variety in this landlocked but pivotal region situated in the very heart of Italy. For decades the style has been largely on the old-fashioned side, but the phenomenon that is Riccardo Cotarella, peripatetic oenological consultant, has been busily changing all that in the past few years, bringing to private producers and cooperatives alike, of Latium as well as of Umbria (indeed of Campania and elsewhere in central and southern Italy) French principles of fully ripe fruit, careful grape-handling with soft pressing and early polyphenolic extraction, and partial *barrique*-vinification and ageing, to bear upon the situation, transforming it here as well as in Latium out of sight.

Doubtless the best-known exponent of the traditional scene is Cantine Giorgio **Lungarotti**, one of the most illustrious names of Italian post-war viniculture. Among the first to reinstate the concept of quality in central Italy, way back in the 1960s, the late Giorgio Lungarotti achieved prominence not only with his wines, but also with the establishment of a yearly wine-tasting competition to establish the best wines of the land, called the Banco d'Assaggio, now alas rather past its sell-by date though they soldier on; also by the painstaking assembly, mainly by his wife, of one of the finest wine museums in the world, at Lungarotti headquarters in the village of Torgiano, near Perugia, near to the Lungarotti-owned 5-star hotel Le Tre Vaselle.

The lead wine of the establishment has always been Torgiano Riserva Vigna Monticchio, a Sangiovese-based blend of traditional central Italy style, including Canaiolo and, optionally, Ciliegiolo, Montepulciano and Trebbiano, which they voluntarily age for eight years or so, of which several in bottle, although the DOCG *disciplinare*, which only applies to the Riserva, calls for just three. Second to this is the Sangiovese–Cabernet–Canaiolo blend called San Giorgio, whose ageing is equally protracted. When the raw material is from a top vintage the policy works, the Torgiano Riserva emerging from its chrysalis with aromas evolved yet distinctive and complex, combining notes of leather, spice and dried fruits on top of a smooth, round and mellow structure; the San Giorgio differing mainly in terms of deeper colour and somewhat deeper fruit and fuller body, while displaying a mite less complexity and, well, authenticity. When, on the other hand, the vintage is not of the best (e.g. 1992) the wines can feel rather dried out and pruney, and one wonders whether eight years is not perhaps four too many. Nonetheless, Teresa Severini Lungarotti, Giorgio's step-daughter who took over from him as the head of production, is to be congratulated on getting the wines more often right than wrong and for sticking to her guns against the trend, which is for greater and greater 'fruitiness' (the way things are going we'll end up drinking alcoholic liquid jam with oak essence).

Other wines of the wide range tend to be well made rather than impressive or exciting. In the Sangiovese category the main one – indeed the bread-and-butter line of the *azienda* – is the famous Torgiano Rubesco, a reliable product made in very considerable volume (they control some 300 hectares of vineyard). Best of the rest is generally considered to be the varietal Cabernet Sauvignon and the Cabernet–Pinot Nero blend called Il Vessillo.

The mid-Umbrian commune of Montefalco is mainly known for Sagrantino. The wine known as Montefalco Rosso DOC, however, is based on Sangiovese, together with Sagrantino at 10–15%, plus others. The two principal grapes have a considerable affinity for one another and in my view Sagrantino is a more convincing blending partner with Sangiovese than are any of the Bordeaux, or indeed French, varieties, and some fine wines are produced as a result, none better than Caprai's Rosso di Montefalco Riserva. Another excellent example is Colpetrone's Rosso di Montefalco. Other good Rossos come from Adanti, Antonelli and Rocca di Fabbri. Since all these producers are, as indicated, more concentrated on Sagrantino production they will be considered again, and perhaps profiled, in the section on that variety.

There are plenty of Sangiovese-based wines in Umbria but, compared with Tuscany, and despite Cotarella's assiduous efforts, still relatively few which merit close attention. One of the better ones comes from C.S. dei **Colli Amerini** in Amelia in the province of Terni; their Rosso Superiore Carbio, a blend of Sangiovese and various other local and international varieties, tends to get good reviews, no doubt partially because their consultant is Riccardo Cotarella himself. Colli Altotiberini DOC and Colli Perugini DOC have similar *uvaggi*, a worthy producer in the latter zone being Gisberto **Goretti** of Perugia. The percentage of Sangiovese in Colli Martani must not fall below 85%, but I know of no notable producers. The percentage in Colli del Trasimeno, on the other hand, can be as low as 40%, with a fairly eclectic supporting cast. Good producers are **Lamborghini** (Trescone – Sangiovese plus Ciliegiolo and Merlot) at Panicale and **Pieve del Vescovo** (Lucciaio – a Sangiovese-based blend of several grapes) at Corciano, both of whose wines are made by – you guessed it – Riccardo Cotarella. Lamborghini also make a 50–50 Sangiovese–Merlot blend called Campoleone to the 1997 vintage of which Robert Parker awarded an astonishing 97 points; as you can imagine, the 4,000 bottles didn't hang around long after that. Cotarella, incidentally, is sometimes referred to as 'Parker's favourite Italian winemaker' – with what justification I am not sure.

Assisi's recently acquired DOC includes a good lashing of Merlot (10–30%) but is still predominantly Sangiovese; a decent producer is Fratelli **Sportoletti** (Villa Fidelia) of the picturesque tourist-town of Spello.

In true Italian style the best reds tend not to be DOC but IGT Umbria, and several of the best producers of Sangiovese-based wines are in fact white wine specialists centred on Orvieto. **Barberani** make a good blended wine called Foresco, as do **Bigi** and

La Carraia – in both cases called, simply, Sangiovese dell'Umbria. **Decugnano dei Barbi** score with the highly regarded 'IL', Tenuta Le Velette with Calanco, containing 35% Cabernet Sauvignon, and **Palazzone** with Rubbio.

The wines in Latium

Sangiovese figures in a number of wines – DOC or otherwise – of the Latium region, less noted anyway for red wine than for white of which there is a far greater production: approximately 90% against 10%. Despite a certain ubiquity, however, and despite a general reawakening of quality viniculture in this region, great in the political history of Italy but of hitherto relatively minor importance in vinous affairs, there are few examples of outstanding Sangiovese-based wine from Latium. Where Sangiovese is found it tends to be blended with Montepulciano, Ciliegiolo, the local Cesanese and/or something French. Among the reds it informs are Aprilia Sangiovese DOC, Cerveteri Rosso DOC, Circeo DOC, Colli della Sabina Rosso DOC, Colli Etruschi Viterbesi Rosso DOC, Genazzano Rosso DOC, Tarquinia Rosso DOC, Velletri Rosso DOC, Vignanello Rosso DOC. If you can find a top quality producer from any of those areas you are to be congratulated. Probably the denomination that comes nearest is Cerveteri Rosso, of which probably the best producer is C.S. **Cerveteri** (Vigna Grande; Fontana Morella) at Cerveteri itself – best because Riccardo Cotarella is director and oenologist at the *cantina*. Such Latian reds as are of real interest – and there are, as I say, an increasing number – have little or nothing to do with Sangiovese and will be reviewed in their place.

The wines in Romagna

Sangiovese not only prevails over all other black grape varieties put together on the western side of the Apennine ridge, it is of major importance on the eastern side too, in particular in Romagna and the Marche. Romagna, indeed, could almost be described as Sangiovese's second home, with a Sangiovese di Romagna DOC production, on average, well in excess of 100,000 hectolitres annually, spread over the provinces of Bologna, Forlì and Ravenna; and there's a whole lot more of non-DOC stuff behind that, made for selling *sfuso* to manufacturers of table wines in cardboard cartons and other supermarket-style containers. Even the vast majority of DOC production is of industrial quality, and would in a proper system not be considered 'quality wine' at all but at most *vino tipico.*

Unfortunately, the area's reputation as a whole has been tarnished by this cheap-and-cheerful image of the prevailing DOC, and it is hardly sufficient to stick on descriptives like Superiore or Riserva and expect consumers to accept that there is a substantial difference. Yet there is growing evidence from a handful of obstinate producers that the lower slopes of the massif, in the area south of the Via Emilia from Dozza east to Rimini and in particular behind Faenza and Forlì, are capable of bringing forth wines to challenge the best of Tuscany. One feels that this relatively unexploited country offers much potential for the budding Sangiovese freak, especially if he is willing to take on officialdom. Nor is the potential wanting for official recognition, the regional authorities doing as much as they can to make Romagna a centre for research and debate in relation to the Sangiovese variety.

Although we will be looking at the centre east as a separate sub-zone of central Italy, I feel that this is the place to consider Sangiovese for the sake of cohesion.

The producers

If, for reasons of space, one were obliged to choose one *azienda leader* from among the dozen-plus that are currently turning out Sangiovese di Romagna – or Sangiovese in Romagna, i.e. non-DOC – to a high standard, many might feel that the palm, historically, at least, should be awarded to **Castelluccio** of Modigliana in the province of Forlì. This estate, which in 1999 was purchased by the eminent oenologist Vittorio Fiore and his family (his son, qualified oenologist Claudio Fiore, is now resident in charge), has since the mid-1970s been pursuing a course in direct opposition to the norm. That is to say, a policy of planting high-quality, low-yielding clones on relatively high-altitude slopes (400 metres plus), dividing the production into *crus* according to site and, incidentally, charging what were considered outlandish prices for wines of a DOC that buyers were accustomed to purchasing by the truckload for a pittance. The original Sangiovese *crus*, planted in 1975 with Sangiovese clones specially selected to suit the terrain and to achieve high quality and limited production, were Ronco delle Ginestre and Ronco dei Ciliegi, a decade later supplemented by Ronco della Simia, now once again discontinued. Ronco delle Ginestre is generally the fullest and most complex of them, a worthy wine for game and full cheeses, Ronco dei Ciliegi is more notable for elegance than concentration while the *normale*, Le More, is being upgraded to take over Ronco della Simia's role as the one giving the most convincing expression of the pure, vibrant Sangiovese wild-cherry style. The two *crus*, depending on the vintage, are capable of a wealth of ripe fruit and quite a firm structure and are therefore capable of ageing well, while having marked individual differences – in a land where, until just a few years ago, the majority of wines seemed drawn from the same vat. Sangiovese di Romagna Le More represents a well-made, more accessible version both style-wise and price-wise. So it is fair, I think, to say that the place to come for high-quality Romagnan Sangiovese *in purezza* is Castelluccio. From their circa 16 hectares of vineyard they also bring forth, incidentally, a rather weighty *barrique*-fermented and aged Sauvignon called Ronco del Re of which they are proud but which would perhaps experience difficulties in a world Sauvignon tasting. A lighter version, called Lunaria, is also produced.

Perhaps the Romagnan estate most respected for overall quality today, however, is **Zerbina**. Cristina Geminiani, with help in the early stages, until around 1993, from her now-rival, Vittorio Fiore, has created, from the estate purchased by her grandfather in the 1960s, an oasis of high quality production. The principal grape, of course, is Sangiovese, from selected clones, mainly the native Romagnan RL Bosche, generally trained to *alberello*. She makes two versions of Sangiovese di Romagna Superiore, oaked and unoaked, called Torre di Ceparano and Ceregio respectively, and one single-vineyard – north-east facing, surprisingly – Riserva Pietramora. This latter, only produced in top years, is a magnificent brew on a level with the top Tuscans – deep and brooding, with plenty of melodious fruit on the palate and superb balance yet with an underlying power and structure which seems to grow with the years (I was fortunate enough to be invited to a vertical tasting covering the years 1986 to 1998) as she seeks riper and riper fruit in the vineyard. Indeed the magnificent 1998 is virtually 15% alcohol by volume. Both this and Ceperano are aged in French oak, but the latter, scarcely no less of a refined blockbuster and amazing value at half the price, shows it a touch more and is perhaps the more modern of the pair. Another distinctive difference between the two *crus* is that Pietramora is made from old vines planted by massal selection in the 1960s – with, today, a small percentage of *alberello*-trained vines – whereas Ceperano is entirely from *alberello*-trained vineyards which they started planting in the late 1980s. Ceregio, of course, is intended as the relatively light, fruity one and is made from the best of the rest.

Two other star wines emanate from this estate, one a Sangiovese/Cabernet Sauvignon IGT called Marzieno, the other a magnificent sweet wine from late-harvested Albana grapes called Scacco Matto (= check mate; hence the chessboard on the label). According to the *Vini di Veronelli* guide, this wine 'does not fear comparison with the best Sauternes'. While admiring the wine, which is certainly a lot more interesting and professionally made than the majority of Italian sweet wines, I think that is taking it a bit far. To be noted, however, that they have recently made a tiny quantity of a sweet wine of fantastic concentration reminiscent of top Sauternes or alternatively German Trockenbeerenauslese – which, indeed, is the nickname they are giving it pending a decision whether, in future, to put it on the market.

Zerbina, together with two other Romagnan estates, Drei Donà of Forì and San Patrignano of Ospedaletto di Coriano, have recently formed an association for the promotion of top quality Romagna wines under the name Convito di Romagna.

Drei Donà is an estate of 27 hectares under vine located in the central zone in the area behind the city of Forlì as the land rises up from the sea and the plain, gradually gaining height as it turns from hills into mountains. Current owner Claudio Drei Donà, with the help of his son Enrico and oenologist Franco Bernabei, has transformed an estate which has been in the family since the beginning of the last century from a country retreat to a serious wine-producing operation concentrating on high-quality Sangiovese.

Their principal wine is Pruno, a pure Sangiovese from massal-selected clones, made from the best fruit of a single well-sited vineyard of just under ten hectares and aged 15–18 months in small French oak before bottling. The first vintage of this wine was 1993, released in 1996, which I tasted in a vertical from 1993 to 1998. It was showing a bit of age but there was still plenty of succulence amid the leather, spice and dried fruit aromas. Of the other vintages the most recent, 1997 and 1998, were the stars, the latter, deep of colour with bags of fresh cherry character and good acid-fruit balance. Their second-string Sangiovese is called Notturno, 100% varietal, 60% oak-aged with the other 40% staying in stainless steel. Drei Donà also make a potentially good, if rather oaky for my taste, Cabernet Sauvignon *in purezza* modestly called Magnificat; and an interesting *barrique*-aged blend of Sangiovese (30%), Cabernet Sauvignon (30%), Cabernet Franc (20%) and Negretto Longanesi (20%). I had never heard of this latter before but it is an example of the plethora of near-extinct vine varieties, to be found all over Italy, which conscientious growers are trying to bring back from the brink.

The estate called **San Patrignano**, at Ospedaletto in the shadow of the San Marino rock over towards the Adriatic coast near Rimini, is surely one of the wine world's seven wonders. Essentially, this is a commune, founded in the late 1970s by the father of current director Andrea Muccioli, for people with drug-related problems determined, with the help of Muccioli and his staff, to re-establish their links with mainstream humanity. The community is 1800 strong, the average stay is over four years and they reckon, among other amazing facts, that by their programmes they have saved people from over 3000 years of penal detention.

Wine production is just one of the numerous activities by which the commune, together with private donations (NO government aid, Muccioli stressed; they do not want to be told by bureaucrats what they may and may not do), supports itself. At present they have 45 hectares under vine, the majority planted to Sangiovese, and they are aiming for 100 hectares. Of the many experts who donate their help to them in various fields (counselling and professional services), the one who advises on oenology is Riccardo Cotarella (see Umbria above).

The Muccioli–Cotarella team produces two wines from pure Sangiovese: Zarricante, from selected grapes of the entire property, aged one year in used barrique; and Avi, the single-vineyard top *cru*, 18 months in small new French oak. Both were shining from the 1999 vintage, the second year of Cotarella's reign, the Zarricante being perhaps more varietally typical with a beautifully stated cherry-berry fruit unobstructed by excessive oak, but the Avi being the more impressive, with massive fruit and a lot of barrel character which, I thought, was not excessive thanks to the concentration of the primary material.

Other good to excellent producers of Sangiovese di Romagna include: **Casetto dei Mandorli** (Vigna del Generale; Tre Rocche), Predappio Alta; **Celli** (Le Grillaie), Bertinoro; Umberto **Cesari** (Cà Granda), Castel San Pietro; Leone **Conti** (Conti Riserva), Faenza; Stefano **Ferrucci** (Bottale; Domus Caia), Castelbolognese; **La Berta** (Olmatello; Solano); Tenuta **La Palazza** (Pruno Riserva; Notturno – with Cabernet), Forlì; **Le Calbane** (Baricò; Le Calbane), Meldola; **Madonia Giovanna** (Fermavento; Ombroso), Bertinoro; Poderi dal **Nespoli** (Santodeno; Il Prugneto; Il Nespoli – from late-harvested grapes), Civitella dei Romagna; **Pandolfa** (Pandolfo; Godenza), Predappio; Fattoria **Paradiso** (Vigna delle Lepri), Bertinoro; **Tre Monti** (Riserva; Thea), Imola; **Trerè** (Amarcord d'un Ross Riserva), Faenza.

Others on a good level are **Casa Chiara** (Vir), Brisighella; **Colonna Giovanni** (Riserva Villa Rasponi; Rocca di Ribano), Savignano sul Rubicone; Tenuta **Uccellina** (Riserva), Russi. A reliable, relatively moderately sized cooperative (considering the giants that exist here, like Corovin and Ronco) is the **Brisighellese** (Brisigliè) at Brisighella.

The wines in le Marche

Moving southward along the Adriatic coast, at last we enter a region of central Italy in which Sangiovese's grip begins to show signs of weakening. True, the variety remains dominant, with some 8,000 hectares of vineyard planted to Sangiovese, approximately one-third of the total. The main Sangiovese zone is, in the north, the obscure Colli Pesaresi, with its sub-denomination Focara which would provide for a small blending-in of Pinot Nero were there any producers to take advantage of the provision; and, in the south, Rosso Piceno, with its sub-zone Rosso Piceno Superiore.

Yet despite the numbers it is here in the Marche that the influence if not the presence of Sangiovese is seen to start fading, since both of the region's most prestigious reds, including Rosso Piceno where it is in theory slightly less than an equal partner, and certainly Rosso Conero, the Marche's best and best-known red, are dominated by another grape variety. In both cases the usurping power is:

MONTEPULCIANO

This grape, second only in importance to Sangiovese among reds in central Italy, is grown to a limited extent west of the Apennines but is far more intimately associated with the eastern section, and will therefore be dealt with in the following chapter.

SAGRANTINO

To give second position of importance in an area as large and prestigious as west central Italy to a variety of such restricted production as Sagrantino may seem insulting to others grown in far greater volume such as Canaiolo, Cesanese and Ciliegiolo (recalling that the French varieties are treated elsewhere). The Sagrantino variety, in fact, is – or was until very recently – almost uniquely to be found in the environs of the villages of Montefalco and Bevagna and one or two others in the Umbrian province of Perugia, its total planted area being around 240 hectares, much of it being in *uvaggio di vigneto* with Sangiovese. The number of hectares planted purely to Sagrantino at the time of writing is not much more than 120, though that figure may be expected to multiply several times in coming years.

Sagrantino is said by some to have existed here at least since Roman times (is it the Itriola mentioned by Pliny the Elder?) by others to have been brought to the area in the Middle Ages by Franciscan monks, perhaps from the Middle East in the time of the crusades, perhaps from Spain. Either way, it has probably been around a long time, though there is little or no mention of it in ampelographical literature until the twentieth century. At no time in the past did it ever spread to neighbouring parts or even catch on big with local producers who have avoided it, in the same way as Piemontese growers have avoided Nebbiolo, because of its difficult character and low productivity, to some extent attenuated today by careful rootstock selection. It is thick-skinned, small-bunched and small berried, but big in every other way: colour, tannins, acids, extract, sugars – the latter especially when, like the Corvina of Valpolicella which it does not otherwise resemble, it is dried for purposes of making semi-sweet red. It does not resemble anything else, either: DNA tests have blown all theories of relationship with Sangiovese or Montepulciano apart.

So, really until the late twentieth century, Sagrantino kept a very low profile, being grown in very small patches in town and country gardens of the Montefalco area, giving rise to a large number of clones with slightly different characteristics, as has been discovered in studies carried out by Caprai and others in the past few years. Insofar as it was made into wine the process was a sort of artisanal *appassimento*, giving rise to a wine of between 30 and 100 grammes per litre residual sugar, a wine whose sweetness was cut on the finish by fierce tannins and an attendant bitterness, generally reserved for special occasions, such as the end of Lent; but not, as some myths have it, for use as communion wine – too strong.

Only three DOC(G) wines contain Sagrantino, all of which carry the name Montefalco. The nomenclature can be confusing, so it is well to get the significance of the names straight. Montefalco Sagrantino (or Sagrantino di Montefalco) is a DOCG, 100% varietal, made like any dry red table wine. It is a deep-coloured, tannic, potent wine of at least 13%, often more, suitable for game and other strong-flavoured dishes, dry – indeed sometimes called 'Secco', a word not often employed on red wine labels – but with a richness of extract and alcohol that gives it a quasi-sweet finish.

Montefalco Sagrantino Passito (DOCG) is, as we have seen, made from dried grapes in the *recioto* style. Montefalco Rosso DOCG, on the other hand, is a blend of Sangiovese, Sagrantino at a maximum of 15%, and other grapes, which these days often means Merlot, though Canaiolo is more traditional. It is medium-bodied, with a minimum of 12% alcohol, and suitable for a much wider range of dishes than the pure Sagrantino. The marriage of Sangiovese and Sagrantino is a particularly felicitous one, the former giving elegance and the latter a certain punch, which Sangiovese tends to lack. Why Sagrantino has not been tried as a blender by producers in Tuscany instead of the French grapes is something of a mystery. Rumour has it that a few brave souls elsewhere in central Italy are indeed trying out Sagrantino as a blending variety.

The producers

Despite its territorial limitations, Sagrantino has seen in recent times a considerable upsurge of interest on the part of the international community. Producers are few, outstanding producers are even fewer, but from those few are coming some Sagrantino wines of fabulous concentration, power and vigour, with the characteristically forceful tannin always present, even in the most 'modernist' examples.

The producer who best represents this modernist approach is undoubtedly Arnaldo **Caprai**, of Montefalco itself. The estate, whose *titolare* made his pile in textiles in the nearby town of Foligno, has been under present ownership since 1971, but it wasn't until Arnaldo's son Marco got interested in the late 1980s, bringing in Attilio Pagli as consultant (1991), that it began to develop as the *azienda leader* of these parts, though some competitors might deny that position, perhaps out of envy.

Arnaldo recounts the story about how he arrived at the winery one day in 1992 to find the four top branches of the six-branched '*palmetta*' formation, to which the plants in the main vineyard were shaped, cut away, only the bottom two remaining: at a stroke, two-thirds of production gone! If the father lost his rag with the son that day he has since had cause to rejoice at the national and international plaudits Caprai have won for their wines.

Pagli and Marco Caprai since that time have, in conjunction with various institutes, carried out some extraordinary experiments in the vineyard – on clones, foreign varieties, root-stocks, planting density and training formation – brief details of which are given in Chapter 1. They have also, at the end of the 1990s, entirely refurbished the winery – fermenting tanks with built-in systems for gently breaking the cap, a micro-oxygenation system for stabilisation of colours and other phenolic substances, central computer system, 1,200 new *barriques* of different provenances – for purposes of meeting higher quality specifications as well as a rapidly increasing capacity in coming years, as the more recently planted of the 90 hectares of vineyard presently planted, plus new vineyards, come into production.

The efforts, as indicated, have brought forth enviable rewards, their Sagrantino di Montefalco 25 Anni, introduced in the mid-1990s to celebrate their quarter of a century plus in the business, winning the coveted *tre bicchieri* with annual regularity. This is a wine of enormous concentration and power, displaying a broad spectrum of fresh and dried fruit, tar, coffee and dark chocolate aromas. The *normale* of the same denomination, if one can refer to wine of such trememdous character as 'normal', is scarcely left in the shade by the *cru*; while the Passito version, sold in 50 cl. bottles, is a blockbuster of a wine combining all the power and sumptuousness of the grape with a concentration and a refinement which make it a worthy *vino da meditazione*. Nor have they neglected Sangiovese in their search for perfection: Sagrantino aside, their Montefalco Rosso Riserva, principally Sangiovese plus Sagrantino and Merlot, being undoubtedly one of the finest red wines of Umbria, while the *normale* is always a reliable drink. An interesting recent addition to the portfolio is the previously mentioned Poggio Belvedere, 90% Sangiovese, the rest being made up of a mix of all the foreign grapes in the experimental vineyard.

For good measure, Caprai also make a couple of very respectable whites from Umbria's own Grechetto grape – Colli Martani Grecante and Colli Martani Grecante Vigna Belvedere, the latter being vinified in oak though the wine, nicely balanced with good fruit-flower aromas, does not suffer from an excess.

Caprai were also the first to sell a wine entirely 'on line', this being their 1998 Pinot Nero 'Nero Outsider', offered exclusively in a limited edition of 1,000 magnums in March 2000. This experiment is to be followed by others similar in years to come with other non-Italian varieties.

At the other end of the modernist–traditionalist spectrum is the firm of **Adanti** at Arquata di Bevagna, the longest-standing private producer in the area and one of the first to bottle Sagrantino Secco, in 1979, before which it was always vinified as a sweet *passito*. Today, under Donatella Adanti, aided by oenologist Mauro Monicchi, they are making valiant efforts to bring themselves up to date. The *azienda*, converted in the 1960s from an old convent built on Roman remains, has some 20 hectares of vineyard planted mainly to Sagrantino, Sangiovese and Grechetto, though with others – Cabernet, Merlot, Chardonnay and Piemonte's Barbera – included. The retired winemaker Alvaro Palini, one of the 'characters' of central Italian viniculture, is a man who always followed his own path, having little time for fashion, one manifestation of which being that the wines were never refined in *barrique* but in large traditional *botti*, followed by extended bottle ageing prior to release. Signor Palini, who still lives on the estate and undoubtedly still has an influence on production, is on record as stating that he doesn't give a jot for others' taste – 'The wines I produce must be pleasing to me!', he declares. A refreshing attitude.

The wines, all subtitled Arquata to indicate the subzone, are led by Montefalco Sagrantino and Montefalco Sagrantino Passito, the former being capable of considerable *invecchiamento* during which process it can change quite radically, losing aggressiveness and some of that old-fashioned style while gaining complexity, without tiring. The latter is a wonderful bitter-sweet reminder of what used to be considered great in Italian wine circles, though today it might be considered somewhat rustic. Arquata Montefalco Rosso – Sangiovese with a bit of Sagrantino and a touch too of Merlot – has a robustness most Chiantis can't match. A speciality is Arquata Rosso dell'Umbria, a blend of Cabernet Sauvignon, Barbera and Merlot, a wine – in a good year – of smooth, classy fruit and nice balance.

The whites – Grechetto Colli Martani DOC and Montefalco Bianco DOC, the former a pure varietal, the latter a blend of Grechetto, Chardonnay and Trebbiano – tend to be bigger and spicier, perhaps more evolved but with greater personality, than most 'modern' whites.

Between the modernist and the traditionalist styles lies that of **Antonelli** at Montefalco, with around 13 hectares of vineyard plus with another 12 planted but not yet in production. Filippo

Antonelli, whose family have owned this property since the late nineteenth century, brings forth, with the aid of winemaker Manlio Erba, Sagrantino di Montefalco *normale* and Passito, as well as Rosso di Montefalco, of power and authenticity highly expressive of his *terroir*. There are those who consider Antonelli the best of the bunch, faulting Caprai's style for being too international and Adanti's for an excess of the artisanal.

A relatively recent arrival on the scene is **Colpetrone** at Gualdo Cattaneo. Purchased in 1995 by the Saiagricola group, this embryonic operation promises to be a major contender for top awards from this small but jewel-like zone in years to come, judging by the quality level of the wines of Saiagricola's principal wine-estate, Fattoria del Cerro in Montepulciano (q.v.). First, however, it will be necessary for them to get their new vineyards into full production and their new *cantina* functioning. At present the wines, Sagrantino and Sagrantino Passito, while unsurprisingly reflecting excellent winemaking and good fruit, betray their lack of track record by a slight excess of oakiness and a general predominance of oenology over depth of fruit. For the moment the best wine is Montefalco Rosso, 70% Sangiovese, 15% Sagrantino, 15% Merlot, ripe and seductive with good balance and drinkability even in youth.

Other potentially good Sagrantino producers include, at Monte-falco: **Bea Paolo; Pambuffetti; Rocca di Fabbri;** Giuliano **Ruggeri;** and in other communes: Cantina **Terre de Trinci** (Foligno); **Colli Spoletini** (Spoleto); **Milziade Antano** (Bevagna). The Chianti Classico producer Cecchi have recently bought a property here and other big names are either in the process of purchasing or are 'interested'. But these are stories for the future.

OTHER RED GRAPE VARIETIES

As everywhere in Italy numerous local grape varieties exist in western central Italy. With the possible exception of Latium's Cesanese, however, none of them can be described at least qualitatively as being of major importance, so the following list is in alphabetical order.

CANAIOLO NERO

Formerly a highly rated variety (the grandiose alias *'vitis vinifera etrusca'*, cited in 1839 by Gallesi,[6] gives a hint as to its antiquity; a further clue being given by Pier dé Crescenzi's mention of 'Canajuola' in 1350 (*'bellissima uva'*, he calls it)), Canaiolo has been reduced in the last century to a blender for Chianti and other Sangiovese-based wines mainly of Tuscany, to a decreasing extent also of Umbria and Latium. Even in this capacity it has been much rejected, replanted or over-grafted in vineyards, even excluded from blends in which its presence is, or was, specifically prescribed. A number of disciplines, like that of Chianti Classico which calls for 'up to 10%' – i.e. no minimum, have now given growers the option of excluding it altogether, an option they are accepting in large numbers. One possible explanation for this is that ill-suited rootstocks reduced its vigour and quality following phylloxera, and some effort has been made in recent years to reinstate the once proud variety using improved rootstocks and clonal selection. Nevertheless it remains in our time in a state of widespread rejection.

Canaiolo ripens around the same time as Sangiovese, so they can be picked together as part of an *uvaggio di vigneto*; but its easy fruitiness and relative lack of backbone, which worked in its favour in the eighteenth century, are working against it in this era of the 'serious' red-wine maker. It dominates in no DOC *disciplinare*, though occasionally you do find Canaiolo in varietal or near-varietal form, generally as a *rosato* or a *novello*. An example of the former is the Canaiuolo (sic) of Montenidoli at San Gimignano. Two examples of normal red wine made mainly from Canaiolo are Poggio l'Aiole from Castello di Modanella in Serre di Rapolano, province of Siena; and Le Terrine from Castello della Paneretta in Barberino Val d'Elsa.

One recent convert to the cause of Canaiolo is Marco Ricasoli at Rocca di Montegrossi (q.v.) of Gaiole in Chianti, who has done away with international varieties in his Chianti blends in favour of the native Tuscan and, putting his money where his mouth is, has recently planted over a hectare to the grape. Marco claims that Canaiolo, where production in the vineyard is restricted and correct

6 Breviglieri and Casini, *Principali Vitigni ad Uve da Vino Coltivati in Italia*, Ministero dell'Agricoltura e delle Foreste.

vinification practices are followed, is capable of good depth of colour and elevated sugar levels, particularly because its thick skin enables it to be left for some time on the vine after ripening. It may lack depth, he maintains, and acidity – that's what Sangiovese is there for – but it can still age remarkably well.

CESANESE

Cesanese di Affile and Cesanese Comune are the two clones of this sturdy, *selvatico* variety, presumably native to Latium and produced since time immemorial in the Ciociaria Hills east of Rome. The former, a small-berried variety considered superior, is also the name of one of the three varietal DOCs, one of those mysterious denominations which seem to exist in a vacuum of nil production. Of the other two, Cesanese di Olevano Romano seems to be slightly on the increase, since the mid-1990s, from a nil base to a little over 1,000 hectolitres, while Cesanese del Piglio, the only one produced in any volume at all until recently, is heading in the other direction. In all three *disciplinari* the superior Cesanese di Affile may be substituted in entirety by Cesanese Comune, one reason perhaps why overall production is static. Or is it just that the benighted world has simply not yet woken up to the glories of Cesanese?

Today's Cesanese wines tend to be dry, still, alcoholic and full-bodied, though historically they tended to come medium-sweet with a bit of bubble, something like sparkling Recioto. Cesanese is also used as a blender in various DOCs of Lazio, for example Velletri Rosso in Rome's Castelli Romani, and Cerveteri, north and west of Rome, but perhaps its most glorious incarnation is in the Torre Ercolana of Colacicchi, of Anagni, where it blends with Cabernet Sauvignon and Merlot. Its most publicized recent convert is Tenuta di Trinoro's Andrea Franchetti, who swears he will achieve great things with it and who has already included in his second wine, Le Cupole.

Examples of Cesanese del Piglio may be tasted from the following producers: C.S. **Cesanese del Piglio**, at Piglio; **Coletti Conti** (Hernicus), Anagni; and **Massimi Berucci** (Casal Cervino), Piglio.

CILIEGIOLO

Ciliegia is Italian for 'cherry', and while numerous Italian wines are said to have aromas reminiscent of cherry, this is the only grape named after the fruit, rather, perhaps, for the cherry-like appearance of the ripe berries than for their perfume. However that may be, the variety, said by some to have been brought back from Spain by a pilgrim to Santiago de Compostela in the latter half of the nineteenth century, has descended from a state of some popularity in the early twentieth century to one of relative obscurity. Today it is mainly used as a blender, being fairly deep of colour, rich in grape sugar and low in acidity, and is specifically mentioned in a minor role in several Tuscan, Umbrian and Latian disciplines such as Montecarlo, Torgiano Riserva and Velletri. A varietal Ciliegiolo wine will tend to be fresh and fruity, for easy, early drinking, non-DOC and not easy to find. Perhaps the best producers of a pure Ciliegiolo in Tuscany are **Rascioni & Cecconello** with the appropriately named Poggio Ciliegio (*ciliegio* means cherry tree) at Orbetello in the Maremma, province of Grosseto. Also in the province of Grosseto is Villa Patrizia, whose Albatraia is light and fruity with little backbone – a luncheon wine for early drinking.

In the Marche Enzo **Mecella**, of Fabriano, makes a good Ciliegiolo/Merlot blend called Braccano.

COLORINO

This is a quasi-*selvatico* variety whose Tuscan roots go far back in time and which, it is said, can still be found growing wild in certain areas, especially in the Valdarno area upriver from Florence; there is in fact a sub-variety, considered superior, called Colorino del Valdarno. Colorino tends to small berries and small, *spargolo* bunches, and therefore should not be confused, as sometimes it has been, with Canaiolo (an example being what the eighteenth-century ampelographer Trinci called Canaiolo Colore[7]) whose berries are larger and bunches fuller and more compact. As the name suggests it is a grape whose skins pack plenty of anthocyanins, the phenolic substance responsible for colour in red wines. It is therefore useful in small proportions with Sangiovese, relatively light-hued at least

7 Cosimo Trinci, *L'Agricoltore Sperimentato*, Lucca 1738.

in its lesser clones. The colour is intensified when the grapes are semi-dried and employed in the *governo* process, imparting not just colour but also smoothness in the form of added alcohol and glycerol.

Some Tuscan producers are 'rediscovering' Colorino today after having flirted with the equally full-coloured but much more aggressively aromatic Cabernet. The aromas of Colorino, being Tuscan like Sangiovese, are much more cognate and complementary, resulting in a more convincing partnership, as can demonstrate the outstanding SuperTuscans Rosso di Sera from Poggiopiano in San Casciano, Anagallis from Lilliano in Castellina, Luenzo of Cesani, Polito of **Il Lebbio** in San Gimignano, all of which are made up principally of Sangiovese with a measure of Colorino. Other highly convincing examples of this blend include the earlier mentioned Poggio Rosso of San Felice; and the Vino Nobile di Montepulciano of Fattoria il Cerro, which estate indeed has planted over 20 hectares to this grape.

There are even those today who, despite the low production of the grape, are flirting with the idea of Colorino *in purezza*, one manifestation of which is the varietally named wine of Castello Il Corno at San Casciano. Probably the greatest single example of a

predominantly Colorino wine (60%) is Romitorio di Santedame, described above in the profile on Ruffino under the section on Rufina.

MALVASIA NERA

More prevalent in southern Puglia than in central Italy, though Piemonte also boasts a couple of DOCs based on black Malvasia, this soft, semi-aromatic variety, related, presumably, to the family of white Malvasias, is rarely used varietally but rather as a blender in various wines of Tuscany.

Well-known high-quality wines consisting approximately of 10% Malvasia Nera, with 90% Sangiovese, are the Chianti Classico Riserva Bellavista of Castello di Ama of Gaiole and the Super-Tuscan I Sodi di San Niccolò of Castellare at Castellina in Chianti.

MAMMOLO

Mammola means violet in Italian. This native Tuscan variety, first mentioned by Soderini in the early seventeenth century, is occasionally used in a very small proportion in certain Sangiovese-based blends in Tuscany, especially in the provinces of Lucca and Florence, to lift the wines' perfume – Sangiovese not being particularly noted for its primary aromas.

I know of no wine which features Mammolo in a major role, but one excellent wine to which Mammolo makes a small but significant contribution is the SuperTuscan Coltassala of Castello di Volpaia (q.v.).

ALEATICO

This grape, according to Breviglieri and Casini in the Ministry of Agriculture's *Commissione per lo Studio Ampelografico dei Principali Vitigni ad uve da Vino Coltivati in Italia* (hereafter referred to as '*Principali Vitigni*') is 'diffused more or less everywhere in Italy', but certainly in parts of Tuscany (read mainly coastal parts) and especially in the island of Elba. It is probably, according to the above, of Tuscan origin, evolved from seed in a zone where Muscat grapes were plentiful, thereafter developing its own peculiar characteristics. On the other hand, Calò, Scienza and Costacurta in *Vitigni d'Italia* suggest that it came directly from Greece 'in ancient times'.

Known for centuries under various names, including Livatica (from Latin), Liatica or Liatico, Aleatico is, according to the noted ampelographer di Rovasenda, 'a true Muscat, but the gentlest of all Muscat grapes'. It is a non-vigorous and low-yielding variety, which probably accounts for its being largely ignored by growers in the mid-twentieth century.

Despite its supposed ubiquity, there are precious few examples of Aleatico on the market today. **Acquabona** of Portoferraio on the Tuscan coast produce both Aleatico dell'Elba DOC and Aleatico di Portoferraio. **Cantina Sociale di Gradoli,** in Latium, makes Aleatico di Gradoli Riserva DOC. **Candido** of Sandonaci in the Salento Peninsula makes Aleatico di Puglia DOC – this latter, a wine of fairly light red colour, gentle muscatty aroma and soft almost jammy, yet not excessive, sweetness on the palate being the one you are most likely to encounter on wine shelves internationally.

MOSCATO ROSA

This grape, associated mostly with the north east zone of Italy, is reviewed on pages 193–195 of *Barolo to Valpolicella*. As I say there, it is a grape whose wine smells unmistakably of roses, which is lovely but – when do you drink it?

It probably hails from Greece or Dalmatia, via Venice. Certainly one exponent of it in central Italy, Giuseppe Mazzocolin of Castello di Farnetella in the Colli Senesi, got his shoots from Silvio Jermann of Collio. Giuseppe is rather unconvinced by its marketability, although two of the handful of central Italian estates that grow it, Avignonesi and Castel de Paolis, seem more committed. The latter's semi-sweet, perfumed wine is the most exotic and characterful example I have found south of the Po.

GRAPES, WINES AND PRODUCERS – WHITE

TREBBIANO

Just as Sangiovese reigns supreme in central Italy among red varieties in terms of volume production, so does Trebbiano among whites. There is, however, a major difference, in that, whereas Sangiovese can make wines of every sort from mediocre to brilliant, Trebbiano's products are much more tilted towards the mediocre and never get anywhere near brilliant.

Also like Sangiovese, and like Moscato and Malvasia too, the name Trebbiano refers to a broad family of interrelated sub-varieties springing, probably, from a common *selvatico* source, now defunct: cousins, you might say, as distinct from siblings. That source is said to be Etruscan, though I doubt anyone would stake their life on it. Calò, Scienza and Costacurta vaguely nod towards the 'eastern Mediterranean basin'. Trebbiano's first mention goes back as far as the early fourteenth-century work by Pier dé Crescenzi called *Ruralium Commodorum*, although the Roman author Pliny did refer, in his *Naturalis Historia*, to a '*Vinum trebulanum*' produced '*in agro Trebulanis*' near Capua in Campania, where today Trebbiano has minimal presence. We do not know if there is any connection.

Today, Trebbianos of various types are produced in various parts of Italy under various names and conditions and with varying levels of success – not to mention in parts of southern France, as Ugni Blanc or Clairette, and in Cognac, as Saint-Emilion. Its appearance in France is attributed to that period in the Middle Ages when there was considerable movement between central Italy and Provence in the form of popes and their retinues, poets and troubadors. It is, incidentally, fairly firmly established that the various French sub-varieties all spring from the one most commonly called today Trebbiano Toscano.

Trebbiano – the name without further qualification may generally be taken to refer to Trebbiano Toscano – has even established a presence in Eastern Europe, South Africa, Argentina and other lands. It owes its popularity not so much to any particular character it may have but rather to its dependable and generous productivity and its attractive visual aspect: the bunches are large, there are plenty of them, the grapes tending to turn a rather attractive light bronze on the sunny side when ripe. The berries are juicy and make good eating, as Soderini remarks in his early sixteenth-century treatise on Tuscan vines and trees – for those few, that is, who still tolerate pips in their fruit. Trebbiano furthermore is quite resistant to disease, has consistent sugar levels and good acidity.

That Trebbiano performs in different ways is due partly to the fact that it has been spreading itself around sufficiently long to have developed a wide variety of local attributes. To reduce the situation to one of reason and precision appears impossible. The noted ampelographer Marzotto summed it up neatly when he wrote in his *Uve da Vino* that the number of Trebbiani, due in part to their being planted in widely differing *terroirs*, and to a greater extent to their multiple names and synonyms, is such that 'chaos has been created of a complexity so great that growers and ampelographers found it difficult to find any solution'.

By far the most widespread sub-variety is the above-mentioned Trebbiano di Toscana, or Trebbiano Toscano, or Trebbiano Fiorentino Bianco, or Biancone (Cortona), or Procanico (Orvieto), or Trebbianone (Velletri), etc. etc., to which there were some 60,000 hectares planted nationally as of the mid-1990s, only about one-tenth of which were in Tuscany where growers are grafting it out faster than you can blink. Sicily, with nearly a quarter of the total, Puglia, Abruzzo and Umbria all have more, while Latium and the Marche have almost as much. DOC *disciplinari* which specifically or implicitly allow Trebbiano Toscano in the *uvaggio*, whether or not there exists a local sub-variety, include Soave, Valdadige, Trebbiano di Romagna, Vernaccia di San Gimignano, Verdicchio, Orvieto, Frascati, Trebbiano d'Abruzzo, San Severo and quite a few more as far south as Alcamo in Sicily and as far west as Arborea in western Sardinia; that is to say, most of the best-known names among dry whites of native Italian varieties. Almost invariably the effect is to neutralise and stretch, so you might think that it ought to have been a prime target of those Eurocrats who tried so assiduously if so ignorantly to reduce the level of the infamous wine lake of the 1980s in the direction of quality. On the contrary, Trebbiano Toscano plantings actually increased during that black period, because the farmers like it and politicians must take account of farmers' needs (read votes).

At least the use of Trebbiano Toscano in red wine *uvaggi di vigneto* such as Chianti, Vino Nobile di Montepulciano, Carmignano etc., written into the original DOC *disciplinari* of the 1960s and 1970s, has now largely disappeared, initially via growers' refusal to comply and, subsequently, by changes in the law forced by that widespread refusal. In the days when up to three rows in 10 of your vineyard had to be planted to white grapes, owing to the relatively high-volume performance of the Trebbiano vines, up to 50% of your red wine-must could be from white grapes. From the 1970s protests by serious producers against this absurdity grew so strident that even the bureaucrats had to shift their comfortable buttocks.

The second most-planted Trebbiano, with circa 20,000 hectares, is supposedly Trebbiano Romagnolo, although one is tempted to surmise that the vast majority of what passes for Trebbiano Romagnolo is in reality Toscano, masquerading as Romagnolo because the *disciplinare* does not allow any other type. But this is speculation, based on the fact that both have a general tendency to produce very large amounts of very similar, very boring, neutral wine. Indeed, the sub-variety called Trebbiano della Fiamma, for its burnished bronze hue when ripe, does bear a physical resemblance to Trebbiano Toscano, while the one called Trebbiano Montanaro from the hills of south of Modena, with which, according to Cosmo and Polsinelli,[8] Trebbiano della Fiamma 'has nothing in common', has a much greener hue when ripe, like Verdicchio.

There is in fact a theory to the effect that Trebbiano di Soave/Lugana is much less close to that of Toscana than it is to Verdicchio. Merely on a quality assessment of the wines of Lugana and the Castelli di Iesi as compared with those of Tuscany and Romagna (generally) this contention would seem to have some merit. Perhaps this Trebbiano 'Montanaro', grown in the Apennine foothills as distinct from the coastal plain, is the link between Verdicchio and the 'Trebbiano' of the provinces of Verona, Brescia and Vicenza. Many pundits today would include Verdicchio under the broad umbrella of the Trebbiano family, albeit mercifully far removed from the Tuscan model.

Trebbiano Giallo, yellow for the colour of its juice, otherwise known as Rossetto or Rossola, or Rosciola (Montefiascone) – these for the pinkish colour of the upper berries when ripe – or even Greco (at Velletri) to add to the confusion, is the sub-variety associated with the white wines of the Castelli Romani: Frascati, Marino, Velletri etc. Here it plays at most a supporting role to Malvasia, most plantings being at any rate of the Toscano strain.

As for Trebbiano d'Abruzzo, so many people have suggested that it is in fact Bombino Bianco that this has now become officially

8 Cosmo and Polsinelli, *Principali Vitigni*, op. cit.

accepted; the *Codice Denominazioni di Origine dei Vini* of the Unione Italiana Vini records them as being synonymous. The weight of opinion is so powerful in this direction that it is difficult to gainsay, and I certainly am not in a position to do so. However, certain Abruzzese growers are less than inclined to accept this thesis, saying that Bombino Bianco, while no doubt a cousin, is quite different from Trebbiano d'Abruzzo, which again is different from Trebbiano Toscano, Bombino being more productive and more acidic, as well as being more neutral of aroma. For whatever reason, it is today effectively overwhelmed in Abruzzese vineyards by the Toscano sub-variety, even though Bruni, Gaudio and de Girolamo were saying in the 1960s that 'in the Abruzzi and in Molise Bombino Bianco is the most diffused white variety in all provinces'. Contrast this with Fregoni and Schiavi's *I Primi Cento Nostri Vitigni* (1996), which records 'Trebbiano Toscano' as occupying nearly 8,000 hectares of vineyard space in Abruzzo, with 'Trebbiano d'Abruzzo' at nearly 3,000 hectares (therefore, presumably, different), and you have what is sometimes referred to as *un bel casino*. The question also arises as to whether Romagna's Pagadebit is in fact Bombino Bianco. The answer, apparently, is yes.

So are they all just variations on the Trebbiano theme? Very possibly, in origin at least, but for present purposes we will consider Bombino Bianco and Pagadebit, as well as Verdicchio, apart.

Two Umbrian sub-varieties identified by Dalmasso, Cosmo, Polsinelli et al. are Trebbiano Spoletino and Trebbiano Perugino, presumably cultivated in the vicinities of the cities of Spoleto and Perugia respectively. One doesn't hear much about them in relation to wines in bottle.

The principal wines nationwide in which Trebbiano Toscano serves as a major or minor blender, actually, potentially or theoretically, have been noted. There are many more, too numerous to mention. They may be DOCs or IGTs, invented increasingly, using a wide range of ingenious blends, for purposes of doing something with the excess Trebbiano grapes one is stuck with in the vineyard and which one has not yet got round to grubbing up or field-grafting. As for the main DOCs, which actually contain the name Trebbiano – Trebbiano di Romagna and Trebbiano d'Abruzzo – any implication in the above paragraphs to the effect that these vastly over-produced wines are for the most part utterly boring is entirely intentional. At least these days they are generally clean, not oxidised, not pasteurised, not over-sulphured. The only DOC based on 'Trebbiano', which is generally interesting or better is Lugana, whose grape, as has been indicated, may not be a Trebbiano at all.

The wines in Tuscany

There is a whole slew of dry whites from middle Italy in which Trebbiano Toscano is, or is supposed to be, or is even if it's not supposed to be, the dominant variety. A number of them are blends with inferior sub-varieties of Malvasia – Malvasia del Chianti or Malvasia di Candia – or indeed with other sub-varieties of Trebbiano, in which event they are likely to be profoundly unimpressive. The more the *disciplinare* calls for other grapes of interest, such as Vermentino or Grechetto or something French, the more the wine has chances of being reasonably good.

To describe every DOC of this type may risk sending readers off into slumber, especially as very few of them are ever likely to surface on your local wine emporium's shelf, and those that do are unlikely to stir much emotion; for the record, however, let them be listed. From Tuscany there are (in alphabetical order; producers mentioned where valid):

Bianco della Valdinievole, northwest Tuscany – minimum 70% plus Vermentino and others.
Bianco dell'Empolese, vicinity of Empoli – 80% minimum plus others.
Bianco di Pitigliano, southern Maremma, vicinity of Scansano – 50–80% plus Greco, Malvasia and Verdello and (optionally) Grechetto, Chardonnay, Sauvignon, Pinot Bianco. Producers: **La Stellata** (Lunaia), Manciano; **Sassotondo**, Sovana; Provveditore-Bargagli, Scansano.
Bianco Pisano di San Torpè, provinces of Pisa and Livorno – 75% minimum plus others.
Bianco Vergine Valdichiana, between Arezzo and Montepulciano – minimum 60% plus others.
Bolgheri Bianco, Bolgheri – 10–70% but Trebbiano in reality little used.
Colli dell'Etruria Centrale Bianco, central Tuscany – minimum 50% plus Vernaccia and internationals.

Colli di Luni Bianco, straddling Ligurian border – TT plays second fiddle to Vermentino, see under latter.

Colline Lucchesi Bianco, vicinity of Lucca – 45–70% plus Vermentino, internationals. Producers: La Badiola; Tenuta di Valgiano (Giallo dei Muri).

Elba Bianco, island of Elba – 80% minimum plus others. Producers: Acquabona and Tenuta la Chiusa.

Montecarlo Bianco, province of Lucca – 40–60% plus Sauvignon, Semillon, Roussanne, Vermentino and Pinots Bianco and Grigio). As can be seen, Montecarlo Bianco has one of the most imaginative *disciplinari* among Tuscan whites. Good producers of wines based on Trebbiano Toscano at Montecarlo (DOC or otherwise) include Fattoria del Buonamico (Bianco di Cercatoia), Fuso Carmignani (Pietrachiara), Fattoria La Torre, **Mazzini** (La Salita), **Michi** and Wandanna (Terre dei Cascinieri).

Monteregio di Massa Marittima Bianco, Maremma – 50% minimum plus others.

Montescudaio Bianco, vicinity of Cecina – 70% minimum plus others. Producers: Fattoria Sorbaiano (Lucestraia); Poggio Gagliardo (Vigna Lontana; Linaglia).

Parrina Bianco, southern Maremma – 30–50% plus Ansonica, Chardonnay and others. Producer: La Parrina (Podere Tinaro).

Val d'Arbia, province of Siena – 70–90% plus Chardonnay and others.

Val di Cornia Bianco, provinces of Livorno and Pisa – 60–70% plus Vermentino, Ansonica and the white Pinots. Good producers: Jacopo Banti (Poggio Angelica); Ambrosini Lorella (Armonia); Gualdo del Re (Val di Cornia Suvereto Bianco).

Probably the highest-profile generic wine among Tuscan Trebbianos today is called Galestro, a name taken from Tuscany's prevailing soil-type. The wine tends to be produced in industrial quantities by big boys like Antinori, whose Capsula Viola, aided by Chardonnay, Pinot Bianco and others up to 15%, actually displays some character and is a worthwhile summertime swig.

The wines in Umbria

Umbria has several DOC whites based on Trebbiano Toscano. The best known is <u>Orvieto,</u> in which Procanico (Orvieto's alias for the sub-variety), must presently form between 40 and 60% of the mix which – saving grace – also calls for more interesting local varieties including Verdello (probably the same as Verdicchio), Grechetto, Drupeggio (Canaiolo Bianco) and Malvasia Bianca di Toscana, as well as the odd 'international' at up to 15%. In the best Orvietos Procanico generally forms under 50% of the grape mix, and will form even less in the future, producers having requested that the percentage of Grechetto be increased at the expense of Procanico. Nevertheless, it is more appropriate to deal with Orvieto here than under Blends where the theme is more experimental, with international overtones, whereas Orvieto is very much a traditional Italian white.

Orvieto – the wine, as distinct from the magnificent cliff-top town of Etruscan origin with its superb cathedral – comes in various qualities: Orvieto, Orvieto Superiore, Orvieto Classico – from the traditional area – and Orvieto Classico Superiore; and in various sweetnesses: Secco, Abboccato, Amabile and Dolce. In the manner of Vouvray, the French wine it most resembles, while having completely different perfumes, Orvieto's level of residual sugar seems elastic, thanks in part to a tufaceous soil (like that of Vouvray), in part to a micro-climate, influenced by nearby Lago di Corbara, which moderates summer temperatures and offers the right amount of humidity in autumn to allow, several years every decade, the formation of noble rot. Indeed, this is one of the few zones of Italy able to produce *muffa nobile* wines on a regular basis.

Producers of Orvieto

Azienda Agricola **Barberani-Vallesanta**, Baschi. The Barberani family have been making the wines of Orvieto for the best part of a century, bottling since 1961. In 1965 they started planting specialised, as distinct from mixed culture, vineyards, the system then being to include all the grapes of the blend in an *uvaggio di vigneto* in the proportions called for by tradition (DOC for Orvieto did not come in until 1971). At that time they had around 20 hectares under vine. From 1985 they began planting their vineyards to single varieties, at the same time introducing the internationals Chardonnay, Sauvignon and Riesling. Today they have some 50 hectares and produce all wines from their own grapes, which are grown in a virtually organic mode in accordance with EC regulation 2078 which excludes the use of chemical fertilizers and systemic sprays.

Luigi Barberani, the current head of family, and his son Bernardo, backed by consultant Maurizio Castelli, produce Orvieto Classico DOC at various levels of style and quality. The basic wines, honest and excellent value for money, are Secco and Amabile, each having a 'Superiore' *cru* called, respectively, Castagnolo and Pulicchio – wines whose concentration and personality do indeed place them on a superior plane to the perfectly sound but relatively uninspiring; needless to say, the percentage of Procanico here is considerably lower. They also make a 'Superiore Dolce' from noble rot grapes called Calcaia. Another first-class sweet wine, Villa Monticelli, is made from late-harvested Moscato grapes.

One of Barberani's most characterful wines is the varietal Grechetto, which in a good year can combine the elements of richness, fatness, firm acidity and perfume to produce a wine of admirable balance and pace. They also make a red wine, Foresco, from Sangiovese, Cabernet Sauvignon and Cabernet Franc, which stands as a convincing example of the type of ripe, fruit-driven reds that are increasingly being produced in this historically white wine area.

Visitors to Orvieto can purchase Barberani wines at the Barberani shop, on a corner immediately facing the façade of the famous cathedral, probably Italy's most inspiring.

Bigi, Orvieto. This *azienda* was founded as far back as 1880, but for some years now has been part of the Gruppo Italian Vini empire (see Melini under Poggibonsi, section on Chianti Classico). Production is enormous – around half a million cases a year – many of which being destined for export, and while the Orvieto Classico *normale* can be rather industrially uneventful the Vigneto Torricella is and has been among the best of the genre, year after year, since the 1980s. Francesco Bardi, who also reigns at GIV's Frascati establishment Fontana Candida, is one winemaker who does not seem fazed by the need to turn out good wine in large volume.

Decugnano dei Barbi, Orvieto. The Barbi family took over this property, currently boasting 32 hectares of vineyard, in 1973, and for the past 20 years have been associated with Orvieto at the highest quality level. The blend of their wines – Procanico (40%), Grecchetto (25%), Verdello (20%), Drupeggio (10%) and Malvasia (5%) – is classic, as is the style: full-flavoured but with fine structure. Those who like unadorned fruit flavours will go for the Orvieto Classico Decugnano dei Barbi, as distinct from the straight Orvieto Classico, while those who prefer them decked with oak aromas will prefer the *barrique*-fermented Orvieto Classico Superiore 'IL'. *Barrique*, for fermentation and *affinamento*, is also a prominent factor in the late-harvest Orvieto Classico Pourriture Noble, picked with the maximum noble rot the season will allow towards the end of October/beginning of November: a creamy, vanilla-toasty, lightly honeyed wine with notes of ripe tropical fruit. They are particularly well known, too, for their Brut Metodo Classico, a blend of Chardonnay, Verdello and Procanico, considered one of the best sparklers in central Italy; also for their red wine 'IL', a convincing blend of Sangiovese, Montepulciano and Canaiolo.

One Orvieto Classico Superiore Secco which has caused quite a stir recently is called Opinioni, the fruit of a joint venture between three producers sharing one winemaker, the famous Riccardo Cotarella, previously mentioned. The producers are La Carraia of Orvieto, partially owned by Cotarella, whose Orvieto Poggio Calvelli is itself one of the best around; Cantina **Monrubio** at Castel Viscardo, a cooperative which offers Orvieto *crus* variously named Roio, Salceto, Fiorile and Soana; and **Cardeto**, another cooperative (at Orvieto, *frazione* Cardeto), whose Classico Superiore wines include two *crus* called Febeo and Colbadia.

Other good to very good producers of Orvieto in its various sweetnesses and quality levels include: Tenuta Le Velette (Lunato; Amabile), Orvieto; Palazzone (Terre Vineate; Campo del Guardiano), Orvieto; Tenuta di **Salviano**, Civitella del Lago.

Second in importance among Umbrian white DOCs is Torgiano Bianco, which must consist of between 50 and 70% Trebbiano Toscano. The only producer of any note at all is Lungarotti, who make a decent but rarely inspiring wine called Torgiano Torre di Giano. The *cru* Vigna il Pino has somewhat more to offer.

The list of other Umbrian white DOCs based on Trebbiano Toscano is even – indeed considerably – more obscure than for Tuscany. It includes:

Assisi Bianco (50–70% plus Grechetto and others); producer Sportoletti of Spello.

Colli Altotiberini Bianco (75–90% plus Malvasia Bianca and others).

Colli Amerini Bianco (70–85% plus Grechetto, Garganega and others); producer C.S. Colli Amerini of Amelia.

Colli Martani Trebbiano (85% minimum); producers Antonelli and Rocca di Fabbri, both of Montefalco.

Colli Perugini Bianco (65–85% plus Verdicchio, Grechetto, Garganega and others); producer **Umbria Viticoltori Associati** of Marsciano.

The wines in Latium

The highest-profile Trebbiano-dominated wine of Latium is Est!Est!!Est!!! di Montefiascone, theoretically 65% Trebbiano Toscano mixed with Malvasia Toscana and Trebbiano Giallo, whose fame, at least until recently, was greater than its reality. That said, one winery of Montefiascone has been eliciting excited praise from pundits in recent years. This is **Falesco**, a small property belonging to the Cotarella family one of whose brothers, Renzo, is technical director at Antinori, while the other, Riccardo, has become probably the most sought-after consultant of central and southern Italy. The DOC Montefiascone wines are the house-wine, simply named Falesco, and the *cru* Poggio dei Gelsi. Both are notable for aroma, body, fruit and elegance, in particular the Poggio dei Gelsi – so much so that one might even be tempted to think Cotarella had strayed just a little from the rigours of the *disciplinare* if one didn't know he wouldn't **dream** of such a thing. In suitable vintages there may also be a rather pedestrian late-harvest version.

While on the subject of Falesco I should mention their Roscetto, made from a sub-variety of Trebbiano more usually known as Trebbiano Giallo. Roscetto (aka Rossetto, Rosciola) is found almost entirely in the area of Montefiascone, where it forms part of the blend of Est! Est!! Est!!! Falesco's impressive *barrique*-fermented varietal is called Ferentano and though it tends to be a little over the top in oak aromas, it is predictably very well made as one would expect from the Cotarella brothers.

It is not for its whites, however, that Falesco is famous – good as they may be – but for its reds, Vitiano and Montiano, the former an extremely good-value blend of Merlot, Cabernet Sauvignon and Sangiovese, the latter a varietal Merlot, with its judicious mix of ripe berry, dark chocolate and coffee aromas, capable of eliciting some impressively high marks from Robert Parker.

Another good producer of Est! Est!! Est!!! is Italo **Mazziotti** of Bolsena, with a *normale* and the *cru* Canuleio.

The risk of encountering other really good Trebbiano Toscano-based wines among the obscurities of Latium is so small that it is safe, I think, simply to summarise the DOCs in list form: Aprilia Trebbiano (95% minimum); Cerveteri Bianco (50% minimum); Circeo Bianco (60% minimum) and Circeo Trebbiano (85% minimum); Colli Etruschi Viterbesi Bianco (80% maximum) and Procanico (85% minimum); Tarquinia Bianco (50% minimum); and Vignanello (60–70% Trebbiano Toscano and/or Trebbiano Giallo).

It is not widely known that Frascati, generally associated with the Malvasia grape, may be up to 100% Trebbiano, and down to 0%, without a drop of Malvasia in it – which is exactly what some of the cheapest blends are. Since quality Frascati is made predominantly from Malvasia, however, we will consider the wine under that variety.

The wines in le Marche and Abruzzo

Like crime in pre-Gorbachev Russia, Trebbiano Toscano does not officially exist in Romagna, so we pass on to the Marche where Trebbiano Toscano may have 20% of all plantings – well ahead of Verdicchio – but enjoys very little of the glory. The only DOC in which the variety is in the ascendancy is the not exactly scintillating Colli Pesaresi, with its sub-zone Roncaglia, located not surprisingly hard against the Romagnan border; Trebbiano Romagnolo thus performs a miraculous cross-border transformation of itself into Trebbiano Toscano. A decent Colli Pesaresi Roncaglia Bianco is turned out by Fattoria **Mancini** (Vigna Valserpe) of Pesaro.

The *disciplinare* for Falerio dei Colli Ascolani, produced in the south of the region, calls for 20 to 50% Trebbiano Toscano, together with Passerina and Pecorino plus up to 20% of other grapes. The better producers tend to hug the lower level for Trebbiano – nonetheless we will include it here as Trebbiano is, at least historically, the foundation. Falerio is a wine capable of rising somewhat above the plain of mediocrity that is Trebbiano-based wine generally, and there are several good producers including **Cocci Grifoni** (Vigneti S. Basso) at Ripatransone; **Ercole Velenosi** (Vigna Solaria) at Ascoli Piceno; **Le Caniette** (Lucrezia) at Ripatransone; **Saladini Pilastri** (Vigna Palazzi) at Spinetoli; **San Giovanni** (Leo Guelfus and Vigna Chiara – sur lie) at Offida; and **Villa Pigna** (Selezione) at Offida.

For every rule there is an exception, and for the rule that Trebbiano is a boring grape the exception is Esedra from **Oasi degli Angeli** of Cupra Marittima in the Falerio zone. This non-DOC wine is able to achieve a variety of perfumes one would never have believed possible from lowly Trebbiano. Is this some little-known, exotic clone of Trebbiano or is there some other secret? Perhaps it is simply that the answer to Trebbiano's neutrality is low yields and judicious oak ageing.

Crossing the border into Abruzzo we come across the denomination Trebbiano d'Abruzzo, whose *disciplinare* reads as follows: 'The wine "Trebbiano d'Abruzzo" must be obtained from grapes grown in vineyards composed of the varieties Trebbiano d'Abruzzo (Bombino Bianco) and/or Trebbiano Toscano' – plus up to 15% of other grapes. So the authorities seem content to accept that Bombino Bianco and Trebbiano d'Abruzzo are one and the same, despite the dissenting voices. In reality, however, the vast majority of vineyards are planted to the Tuscan type, so this is the place to consider the wine Trebbiano d'Abruzzo, rather than under Bombino Bianco.

The first point to note is that the growing zone covers practically all parts of the region where vines may be grown, with production averaging over 200,000 hectolitres per annum. Indeed, this is probably the area in Italy where Trebbiano, so called, does best in quality terms, producing wines which can be of good structure and balance, capable of some concentration and finesse in a moderately Burgundian mode from good sites where yields are restricted. Capable, indeed, even of very considerable feats of complexity and longevity in the hands of a master like Edoardo **Valentini** of Loreto Aprutino, whose Trebbiano d'Abruzzo has on occasion been rated among the finest white wines of Italy. This despite being trained on those high *tendone* trellises which generally favour quantity over quality. As far as producers are concerned, virtually everyone who makes good Trebbiano makes even better Montepulciano, so we will leave profiles for the most part to that section (under central Italy east). The best wines, however, may be noted. The best of all, indeed, has already been noted. But Valentini's Trebbiano d'Abruzzo, concentrated and complex and not a little evolved, is a one-off, the product of quasi-fanatical attention in the vineyard and fantastically severe grape selection at harvest-time, vinified with maximum naturalness then aged in *botte* and finally bottled by hand. Valentini's methods are artisanal, but he, the man, is a true artist – with an artist's temperament, mercurial and exacting.

Other good Trebbiano d'Abruzzos include: Dino **Illuminati** (Daniele), Controguerra; **Marramiero** (Altare), Rosciano; **Masciarelli** (Marina Cvetic), San Martino sulla Marrucina; Camillo **Montori** (Fonte Cupa), Controguerra; Bruno **Nicodemi** (Bacco), Notaresco; Casa Vinicola **Roxan** (Galelle), Rosciano.

In Molise – vinously not much more than an appendage of Abruzzo – the sole existing DOCs both have a Bianco based on Trebbiano Toscano. Biferno Bianco, which actually exists, requires a minimum of 65% of the sub-variety, together with Bombino Bianco (no mention of Trebbiano d'Abruzzo) and Malvasia Bianca; from which one understands why the DOC has set few producers' pulses to racing. The best example is undoubtedly the Molì Bianco of **Di Majo Norante** at Campomarino. Pentro, theoretically 60% minimum Trebbiano Toscano, seems to exist only on paper and/or in the minds of hopeful bureaucrats.

Vin Santo

That's about it for Trebbiano Toscano in central Italy although, as I say, it is to be found throughout the south and islands as well. It is not a tale of triumph and joy, but, by way of a happy ending, there is one wine in which the humble Tuscan Trebbiano shines: Vin Santo. Trebbiano Toscano is the preferred grape because of its excellent sugar/acid balance, although Malvasia, Sangiovese (in blend; on its own, Sangiovese's version of Vin Santo is called Occhio di Pernice, as we have seen), and other less traditional varieties such as Traminer or Sauvignon may also be employed. Styles vary widely – from dry or almost dry to medium-sweet to super-sweet, from oxidised and amontillado-like via the nutty lusciousness of old tawny port towards a quite candied-peel fruitiness, or even a quasi-tropical fruitiness.

Vin Santo, made from grapes hung up or laid on mats to dry for two to four months following the harvest, then long-fermented and aged in small barrels called *caratelli*, is at its best a magical combination of all the above features, traditonalist and modernist, enhanced increasingly frequently by a subtle hint of toasty vanilla from high quality oak. But the general trend is away from the oxidised in the direction of the fruity as producers aim to escape from the accusation that Vin Santo is too much like sherry to justify the price differential. It is true that Vin Santo tends to cost considerably more than sherry, but the process involved is very expensive and anyway **real** Vin Santo – as distinct from the fortified stuff, called *liquoroso* – is a totally natural, unfortified, unblended, untampered-with-in-any-way product, unique in the world of wines. And much better for you the morning after.

There are three DOCs specifically reserved for Vin Santo in Tuscany: Vin Santo del Chianti, Vin Santo del Chianti Classico, and Vin Santo di Montepulciano, all requiring three years ageing in *caratelli*, four years for Riserva, although some, notably Avignonesi,

leave it much longer. Outstanding producers include: in Monte-pulciano – Avignonesi (considered the king of Vin Santos – very long aged, extremely concentrated, tiny production), Trerose; in Chianti Classico – Castello di Cacchiano, Corzano e Paterno, Felsina (100% Malvasia), Isole e Olena, San Giusto a Rentennano; in Chianti (Rufina) – Tenuta di Bossi, Selvapiana, Villa di Vetrice.

Vin Santo has been included as a kind of footnote in the *disciplinari* of a number of central Italian multi-DOCs. These include: Bianco della Valdinievole; Bianco dell'Empolese; Bianco Pisano di San Torpè; Carmignano (best producer: Tenuta di Capezzana); Colli dell'Etruria Centrale; Elba; Montecarlo (best producer: Carmignani); Monteregio di Massa Marittima; Montescudaio; Pomino; San Gimignano; Sant'Antimo; Val d'Arbia.

Apart from Vin Santo, attempts have also been made to achieve sweet Trebbianos by giving the grapes a bit of surmaturation on the plant. One such, quite successful effort is La Faina of **Baroncini** in San Gimignano.

The wines of Trebbiano Romagnolo

Romagnans will fiercely maintain that this sub-variety is quite unique, and even though much of the actual product may be difficult to distinguish from the Toscano strain, in deference to their feelings and my kneecaps I think it best to give them reason. Claims by ampelographers that the Romagnolo strain is nearest among Trebbianos to Trebbiano di Soave/Lugana have already been commented on.

The vast majority of so-called Trebbiano di Romagna DOC is produced by massive cooperatives like Corovin or Ronco as adjuncts to their even vaster production of Sangiovese di Romagna. However, small to medium growers do exist, doing as good a job as is possible with what is essentially an uninspired variety. These include Celli (Poggio Ferlina); La Palazza (Rusla); San Patrignano (Terre del Cedro); Tre Monti (Imola); and Zerbina (Dalbiere).

Two other Romagnan multi-DOCs of recent devising feature Trebbiano Romagnolo as the principal component of the blend of their Bianco sub-DOC. These are Colli d'Imola and Colli di Rimini.

The wines of other sub-varieties of Trebbiano, barring those of Trebbiano di Soave/Lugana covered in *Barolo to Valpolicella*, are rarely if ever, to my knowledge, sufficiently interesting to cite individually, with the exception of Falesco's Roscetto cited above.

MALVASIA BIANCA

Malvasia is something of a catch-all name for a group of varieties whose scions perhaps originated in the same Greek locality but which with time and travel (not just all round Italy but all round the Mediterranean) have become almost as disparate as the sons of Adam, taking on quite different characteristics according to the different environments in which they find themselves. Or perhaps they started out with different characteristics, being from distinctly different parent varieties, since today's 'Malvasias' divide fairly sharply into the two fundamental types: the aromatic and the 'simple' or non-aromatic.

The Greek locality in question is the Peloponnesian port of Monemvasia, famous in the Middle Ages for its wines; marvellous place for a holiday, though I must say I saw no evidence of famous wines in the course of two fairly extended stays there, unless you include retsina out of crown-capped pop bottles. At the time of the Venetian occupation, around the thirteenth and fourteenth centuries, wines of various styles, sweet and dry, aromatic and non-aromatic, were transported to Italy under the name Malvasia, not only from Monemvasia but also from Crete, which the Venetians also controlled, and Chios. In time the vines behind the wines were also imported, some into northern Italy through Venice, some into southern Italy, through Sicily and Sardinia.

It is recorded that this very southern Mediterranean vine was present in northern Italian (Istrian) vineyards as long ago as 1300. Today Malvasia d'Istria has a certain presence in the northeast – especially in the Isonzo sub-zone of Friuli, but also in parts of the Veneto. Over towards the northwest, in Lombardy's Oltrepò Pavese, still more so in Emilia's Colli di Parma and especially in the Colli Piacentini, Malvasia di Candia is widely planted. This name, Malvasia di Candia, crops up again in Latium, in the Castelli Romani, where it is the volume producer together with Trebbiano Toscano, having usurped to some extent the role of the higher quality homespun sub-variety, Malvasia del Lazio, aka Malvasia Puntinata. Where Malvasia di Candia is concerned, however, the name applies to a grape that is not aromatic in any muscatty sense. Pundits try to explain the anomaly by saying it performs differently in different places – I seem to have said something of the sort myself, above – but if so it would be the only instance that I know of the same grape manifesting on both sides of the fundamental aromatic/non-aromatic dividing line.

Between Emilia and Latium there has existed, for several centuries at least according to commentators, the so-called Malvasia del Chianti or Malvasia Bianca, which acts or has acted as partner to Trebbiano Toscano in white table wine blends, or as one of the grapes of Vin Santo. Lacking body but lending a bit of perfume, though not exactly aromatic, and like Trebbiano a generous producer, Malvasia del Chianti is rarely made varietally but is to be found as a small part of the classic Tuscan *uvaggio di vigneto*.

In Sardinia the sub-variety Malvasia di Sardegna is used mainly for making sweet wines, which is probably what it does best and what it was doing originally back in the hot, dry, stony Peloponnese. This type probably came to Sardinia directly from Greece, rather than via Venice. The sub-variety used on the Eolian islands, called Malvasia delle Lipari the DOC from which bears the same name, is no doubt cognate.

So there is great confusion in relation to Malvasia generally – indeed Dalmasso et al. call the Malvasia question 'one of the most complicated tangles in ampelography'.[9] One thing that does seem clear about Malvasias generally, however, is that they only give good results when relatively low-cropped on stony, unfertile soil – and the sunnier the slope the better. In these conditions wines will achieve good alcohol and glycerol levels and a certain complexity of aroma, recalling – in the case of the aromatic sub-varieties – apricot or peach. Conversely, an over-cropped Malvasia grown on relatively rich soil will give low alcohol, thin wines without much if any bouquet, and with a tendency to oxidise easily.

Nowhere is this phenomenon more observable than in Latium, where Malvasia figures prominently, together with Trebbiano, in a host of wines of greater or lesser forgettability including Velletri, Marino, Montecompatri and Zagarolo of the Castelli Romani – including, indeed, the recently established DOC Castelli Romani Bianco itself – as well as in Circeo Bianco, Colli Albani, Colli

9 *Principali Vitigni*, op. cit.

Lanuvini, Colli Etruschi Viterbesi Bianco, Tarquinia Bianco, Colli Etruschi Viterbesi Bianco, and others more obscure still where Malvasia is in a minority proportion compared with Trebbiano. Rather than blend all these essentially similar brews together under one memorable and easily marketable name the lawmakers in their wisdom have recently extended the confusion by adding new names which haven't a snowball's chance in hell of catching on internationally.

The one name that consumers do recognise is Frascati, which, as mentioned in the section on Trebbiano, has a very plastic *disciplinare*, allowing it to be made from any combination of Trebbiano and Malvasia, which latter must be at least 70% Malvasia di Candia. Why the law should insist on the use of the inferior at the expense of the superior is perhaps not such a mystery when you consider the desire on the part of certain producers to keep on churning out the volumes of cheap mediocrity to which their market has grown accustomed. Fortunately certain growers are ignoring the law and making better wine using only low-cropped Malvasia del Lazio or even illicit quantities of Chardonnay, allowed at up to 10%, or Viognier, which latter has proved highly successful in this area, even if the law at the time of writing had not yet changed to allow it in officially. And since the cessation of bottling outside the Castelli Romani zone there has been a certain tendency for Frascati to revaluate itself in the public eye, even if the expectation that Frascati should be inexpensive has not yet died away. Fiddling continues, of course, but on a reduced scale, so that if at one time it was true to say that perhaps five times the volume of Frascati was sold in the world as there were vineyards registered to produce the grapes, the ratio today is probably nearer two to one.

The wines in Latium: Frascati et al

Latium, especially the area around Rome, and particularly the DOC of the commune of Frascati, is the region of Italy best known for its Malvasia-based wines, so it is appropriate to begin here. Frascati itself, as we have seen, can be anything from 0 to 100% Malvasia, but most of the commercial versions contain large dollops of Trebbiano. Indigenous character, however, only comes with appreciable amounts of Malvasia, and the greater the proportion in the blend of Malvasia del Lazio, allowed up to 30% but taken, as I have said, considerably higher than that by quality producers, the better the wine.

Internationally the best-known Frascati producer is undoubtedly **Fontana Candida** of Monteporzio Catone, a member of Gruppo Italiano Vini, conceived on industrial lines yet run by Franco Bardi (see Bigi, above, under Orvieto) and his team almost like a boutique winery. Their volume line, Frascati Superiore – the word 'Superiore' indicates a wine of 11.5% alcohol as against 11% – is surprisingly correct and characterful considering the millions of bottles produced. Even the *cru* Santa Teresa, from grapes in part grown by themselves, in part bought in, a wine of considerable substance, freshness and flavour, is produced at over 100,000 bottles. They also make a modest amount of a convincing Malvasia del Lazio, for those interested in tasting the grape *in purezza*.

One of the most successful Frascati producers over the years in the British market, also at Monteporzio Catone, is **Colli di Catone** of Antonio Pulcini. Antonio, whom I have known for years and who is certainly one of the most likeable fellows in the wine business, divides his production into two sections – that of the *commerciante* and that of the grower. In the first role, he turns out large numbers of genuine, good quality Frascati – at whatever level, you can rely on Colli di Catone for authenticity, which is saying a lot in the decidedly dodgy market for Frascati, a wine with a world-wide demand and an ever-dwindling supply as greater Rome eats its way architecturally into the vineyard area. Antonio is a great believer in the merits of Malvasia del Lazio, and the quality of his wines tends to rise as the percentage of this grape gets higher and that of Malvasia di Candia, and especially Trebbiano, diminish. His best-known product is that generally referred to as '*bottiglia satinata*' (frosted bottle), containing no Trebbiano and a prepon-derance of Malvasia del Lazio, which has been the introduction to real Frascati for millions of people all over the world.

Considerably higher up the scale, from Antonio Pulcini as grower, is Colle Gaio, a single vineyard wine of mainly Malvasia del Lazio where the quantity is reduced by bunch-thinning to around one-quarter of the permitted norm (Frascati is allowed 15 tonnes per hectare, no less, with 30 on top in certain years). Unlike most Italian wines Colle Gaio is made to last, and bottles of the 1987 and 1990 vintages are still showing well. To top this, Antonio has introduced in recent times a Malvasia del Lazio made entirely from free-run juice called Villa Ari.

But the wines that are particularly close to Antonio's heart are those of his own Casal Pilozzo, this being an estate with 10 hectares of vineyard and olive-grove surrounding a villa or Casale whose residents have included personalities from the Emperor Trajan's sister to Orson Welles, and whose foundations are pierced by hundreds of metres of subterranean tunnels which may have been used by persecuted Christians and which today are inhabited by large numbers of pampered bottles, white and red, awaiting their appearance in the arena of the international market.

The wines of Casal Pilozzo – all branded thus – include a Malvasia, a Grechello (Grechetto), a Cabernet/Merlot blend called Dedo and a Pinot Nero/Cabernet Sauvignon blend called San Cristiano, the reds being *barrique*-aged before bottling. All are aged at least two years before release on the market.

Very recent developments at Casal Pilozzo include a Malvasia del Lazio Passito, called Passione, which Antonio reckons is one of the most exciting wines he has ever made; and a Pinot Nero at 85% called Regina Vitae – not the sort of thing you'd expect on the outskirts of the Eternal City.

But then, Antonio Pulcini is not your ordinary man.

Also in Monteporzio Catone is another of the few important private players in a denomination dominated by cooperatives, this being **Villa Simone** of Piero Costantini, owner of one of Rome's most prestigious *enotecas*. From his 30 hectares of vineyard in the hills overlooking Rome Costantini brings forth two fine *crus* of Frascati Superiore, including Vigna dei Preti and Vigneto Filonardo, as well as perhaps the best of all Cannellinos, Cannellino being the sweet version of the genre.

Perhaps the one to burst with the most *éclat* upon the Frascati scene in the 1990s is **Castel de Paolis**, who backed the cheek of producing Frascati at twice the price anybody else was asking with a wine worth every lira. Ex-politician Giulio Santarelli, having fallen foul of the electorate together with everyone else in Craxi's Socialist Party during the *tangentopoli* scandals of the early 1990s (I hasten to add that Santarelli personally was not implicated in any shady misdoings), decided to shift his attentions to viticulture, and took the inspired decision of planting a grape which thitherto virtually did not exist in central Italy, namely Viognier. The experiment was an astonishing success, and Castel de Paolis's top Frascati *cru*, Vigna Adriana (after Giulio's wife), perhaps more richly suffused with peachy, creamy Viognier than the authors of the *disciplinare* had intended, has nonetheless revolutionised consumers' expectations from what was considered, with the few exceptions indicated above, largely an industrial product. Santarelli's Frascati Superiore and more modestly priced Frascati Superiore Campo Vecchio are also remarkably good in their bracket, the former showing Malvasia del Lazio in a particularly flattering light. To top it off he also makes a flavoury, balanced, not-too-sweet Cannellino. Not to mention various wines from other French grapes, Selve Vecchie (*barrique*d Chardonnay), Muffa Nobile (botrytised Sauvignon/Sémillon), Quattro Mori (Syrah and Merlot). And a rose-scented sweet one called Rosathea from a variety more associated with Alto Adige – Moscato Rosa. All, it should be said, at a distinctly high quality level, which will no doubt be maintained if not improved upon by Franco Bernabei who took over as oenologist from Lorenzo Peira in the late 1990s.

Other good producers of Frascati include **Casale Marchese** of Frascati and **Conte Zandotti** whose *cantina* is situated within the city limits of Rome itself. Perhaps the best of the numerous cooperatives is that of the commune of Marino called **Gotto d'Oro**, who indeed make a range of Malvasia-based wines including Frascati Superiore, Marino Superiore and Malvasia del Lazio.

In Marino also is one of the most respected private producers of the province of Rome, **Colle Picchioni** of Paola di Mauro and her son Armando. Not only is the Marino Oro – complex, spicily perfumed with a touch of vanilla to it from *barrique*-ageing – indisputably the finest of its denomination, it is one of the finest white wines of the Latium region. And their Marino Etichetta Verde – fresher, steelier, fruitier – is among the challengers.

Other Malvasia-based DOCs of the Castelli Romani have not thrown up notable heroes as yet, though it is worth noting the wines of Tenuta **Le Quinte** in Montecompatri, two *crus* called Virtù Romane and Casale dei Papi which rise well above the common level.

Heading north, while Malvasia of various types have a certain presence in Umbria, there is no single DOC which exhibits them in preponderance. The same is true in Tuscany, where, however, there do exist scattered examples of Malvasia *in purezza*, such for example as the *cru* L'Accesa of I Campetti at Roccastrada in the province of Grosseto. This is a delightfully light, aromatic wine supposedly from Malvasia di Candia – presumably the Emilian version thereof as distinct from the Latian.

Vernaccia di San Gimignano

The adjunct 'di San Gimignano' is necessary because the variety which informs the wine of that name is in no way related to any of the other Italian Vernaccias, of which there are several examples; the reason being that the name is probably derived from *vernaculus*, a late-Latin word meaning 'native' or 'local'. In the Middle Ages the praises of one particular version, 'Vernaccia di Corniglia', were sung by authors Boccaccio and Sacchetti – the grape involved, according to the early nineteenth-century ampelographer Gallesio, being a strain of Vermentino. Modern ampelographers, however, have eliminated the possibility of any relationship between Vermentino and Vernaccia.

Anyway, trading in a wine called Vernaccia was already being carried out in 1276 at San Gimignano according to the archives of that commune, the wine finding its way to the Roman Curia, the

House of Medici in Florence and other princes of Italy and England, apparently as some kind of offering. Pope Paul III's wine expert Sante Lancerio praised the Vernaccia of San Gimignano, as did poets of the stature of Redi. The wine, however, fell into a lengthy decline, and it was only in the latter half of the twentieth century that Vernaccia's reputation began making a serious comeback.

'In the land of the blind the one-eyed man is king', they say, and this is rather the case with Vernaccia di San Gimignano in Tuscany, where the competition among other native whites is limited to Trebbiano Toscano and Malvasia del Chianti; for which reason it is considered the premier white wine-grape of Tuscany; or at least of central Tuscany, the Vermentino of the coast being in my view at least potentially superior. Vernaccia di SG is a good yielder for which reason it is popular with growers, but it only delivers real quality when production is very restricted, bringing forth wines of a certain richness and importance of mouth-feel, sometimes almost an oiliness. Its aromas tend to the neutral, but it wears hints of wood-smoke, from vinification or ageing in gently charred French *barriques*, well. The other end of the spectrum is the unoaked fruit-driven style, which generally goes down well enough in a restaurant in San Gimignano even if it gets a little lost in competition with other high-profile white wines of the world, and even with other Tuscan whites from varieties like Chardonnay and Sauvignon, which today can be added to Vernaccia di San Gimignano at up to 10%; or like the previously mentioned Vermentino; or like Viognier, which is rapidly gaining popularity, though it has yet to achieve official recognition.

One skill in which the good burghers of San Gimignano have always excelled is marketing and publicity, and in this respect they have done some excellent work with the local brew. Thus Vernaccia di San Gimignano was the first wine ever to go on sale as a DOC, in 1967, and the second Italian white to achieve DOCG status. Vernaccia di San Gimignano DOCG must consist of a minimum of 90% Vernaccia and a maximum of 10% other grapes – non-aromatic, recommended or authorised for the province of Siena (read Chardonnay, in the main). Such official approval obviously does not guarantee prime quality, but there are producers whose dedication has brought forth wines of good quality, although not, I believe, at a level that will ever be describable as world class.

Perhaps the producer who has most caught the imagination of the wine world, while most influencing other producers in his zone, is Enrico Teruzzi of **Ponte a Rondolino**. This success probably owes as much to the striking packaging – he was the first to introduce the 'postage-stamp' label, for what is now called Terre di Tufi – as to the quality of the wines, which tend to be elegant and restrained with an unmistakable internationalist gloss. Teruzzi is one of the earliest and most enthusiastic of Italy's technophiles, presiding over a clockwork winery so replete with stainless steel, gadgets and computer-controls that it stands as one of the most advanced in Italy, though there is no shortage, either, of French *barriques*. He even restructured his vineyards to enable him to carry out mechanical harvesting where possible.

Teruzzi's top Vernaccia, the above-mentioned Terre di Tufi, of which, remarkably, over 200,000 bottles a year are produced, has graced restaurant tables the world over. Teruzzi reckons now that it is famous enough to stand on its own and does not need the DOCG – no doubt a ploy to introduce more of his preferred Chardonnay into the blend (Chardonnay is easy to pick mechanically, unlike Vernaccia). Meanwhile his Vernaccia di San Gimignano *normale*, having overcome technical problems of the late 1970s and early 1980s, in particular a tendency to oxidation, has become a model of technological correctness. Something of an innovator, Teruzzi has also invented a blend – for his IGT Carmen, named after his French ballerina wife Carmen Puthod – consisting in Vernaccia, Vermentino, Trebbiano and Sangiovese *in bianco* – this being

probably his most interesting wine. He was also one of the first in San Gimignano to recognise the vocation of the *terroir* for reds, introducing way back in the 1980s his characterful Peperino, a Sangiovese-based wine which started life as a relatively lightweight lunchtime quaffer but which has recently been beefed up considerably to suit the American market.

Other producers of Vernaccia di San Gimignano, or producers of Vernaccia at San Gimignano, capable of good to very good wines include: Baroncini (Poggio ai Cannicci); **Casa alle Vacche** (Crocus; I Macchioni); Casale-Falchini (Castel Selva; Vigna a Solatio); Vincenzo Cesani (V di SG; Sanice); Guicciardini Strozzi (Perlato; San Biagio); **Le Colonne** (Riserva); Montenidoli (Fiore; di Carato – *barrique*d); Mormoraia (V di SG; Ostrea – with Chardonnay); Panizzi (V di SG; Bianco di Gianni – with Chardonnay); Fattoria **Paradiso** (Biscondola); **Pietraserena** (Vigna del Sole); Fattoria **San Donato** (V di SG; Riserva); **Signano** (Riserva); **Vagnoni** (Mocali).

One producer making a good version of Vernaccia di San Gimignano whose *cantina* is outside the commune of San Gimignano is Melini (Le Grillaie) of Poggibonsi.

OTHER WHITE GRAPE VARIETIES

VERMENTINO

The origins of Vermentino are somewhat shrouded, and while some ampelographers maintain that it originated in Iberia, more specifically in southern Spain, there is no grape of that or any similar name extant in Spain today. It is thought that the Spanish name is Listan d'Andalusia, which I am told is an alternative name for Palomino. According to Raffaele Carlone[10] Vermentino arrived from Spain around 1300 in Corsica, where it was and is known both as Vermentino (in the south) and as Malvasia Grossa (in the north), and from which it subsequently travelled to Liguria. From Liguria it would have filtered westward into France, where it is variously known as Rolle (but Rolle is different, it seems, from Palomino) and Malvoisie à Gros Grains, and eastward into Tuscany, on whose

10 *Principali Vitigni*, op. cit.

Tyrrhenian coast, especially to the north towards Liguria, it enjoys today a notable and growing presence, although it is far more widespread in Sardinia.

A different scenario, recorded in the brochure of Sardinia's Cantina del Vermentino at Monti, has the vine leaving Spain in the Middle Ages direct for France where it took various names including Grosse Clarette, Malvois d'Espagne and Piccabon. From there it moved into Liguria where it was known as Pizzamosca, Corbessa and Vemettino. From Liguria it crossed to Corsica from whence, in the latter half of the nineteenth century, it moved to Sardinia, in particular to the corner of the island nearest to Corsica called Gallura.

Vermentino, then, is a grape which has historically been associated with warm coastal climates where temperatures tend to be more moderate than inland. In those conditions it produces wine of neutral aroma but good 'mouth-feel', having, when produced in reasonably modest quantity, a slightly oily texture which is nicely offset by a firm, lemony acidity. In the Alta Maremma it is increasingly used in blend with other grapes like Sauvignon or Chardonnay, but there are also some very good varietal Vermentinos.

Tuscan DOCs which feature Vermentino as the principal grape are Bolgheri Vermentino and Bolgheri Bianco, Candia dei Colli Apuiani, and Colli di Luni Bianco, which overlaps into Liguria. It is also specifically mentioned in the blends of Bianco della Valdinievole, Colline Lucchesi Bianco, Montecarlo Bianco, Monteregio di Massa Marittima Bianco, Montescudaio Bianco and Val di Cornia Bianco.

Good producers of Bolgheri Vermentino include Michele Satta (Costa di Giulia) and Tenuta **Guado al Tasso**. Vermentino also figures in the Bolgheri Bianco of **Grattamacco**. These are wines of good but rarely inspired level.

MOSCADELLO

For general comments on Moscato see *Barolo to Valpolicella*, pages 122–123.

This is a Tuscan, specifically Montalcino, version of Moscato Bianco, the sub-variety of Moscato used in Piemonte for Moscato d'Asti. A traditional wine for the area, more so indeed than

Brunello, Moscadello was dying out in Montalcino vineyards when Banfi decided to plant it in volume in the late 1970s. The wine is always sweet and aromatic, and may be made still or *frizzante*. A late harvest version is also provided for.

Banfi remain by far the biggest producers (see profile in section on Brunello di Montalcino) but others are beginning to warm to the idea of a sweet wine to widen their portfolio. The best and best known of these is Col d'Orcia with their late-harvest Pascena. Poggio Salvi's Aurico, distributed by Biondi-Santi, can also be good. Livio Sassetti's Pertimali produce two versions of sweet Moscadello, the 11% *normale* having the edge on the more expensive 14% Vendemmia Tardiva, to my mind, for freshness of flowery fruit on nose and palate.

In Orvieto, Barberani produce an aromatic and very tasty late-harvest sweet Moscato called Villa Monticelli.

ANSONICA

Ampelographers seem satisfied that Tuscany's Ansonica, of which the original name is Ansoria, shares a common origin with Sicily's Inzolia, the latter being by far its most important growing site. From Sicily it would have spread to Calabria and up to Sardinia, and it would have arrived in Tuscany, it is believed, from Sardinia.

The grape, then, while performing somewhat differently according to its surroundings, seems happiest in meridional Mediterranean climes and it is therefore highly unlikely that, as has been claimed, it was brought to Sicily by the Normans, who are not, it must be said, noted for their high quality grape varieties.

In its Tuscan manifestation it has settled in particular in the southern maritime areas, specifically on the island of Elba and in the zone of Monte Argentario/Isola del Giglio. These indeed are the two production areas recognised by the respective DOCs Elba and Ansonica Costa dell'Argentario. A good wine from this zone will typically be spicy and somewhat nutty on the nose, with a pleasantly juicy palate having balanced fruit and acidity; it can be slightly *amabile* or even, in its *passito* version, rich and redolent of dried fruits.

The Elba DOC recognises both a dry and a sweet style, good examples of the former coming from Acquabona and Tenuta La Chiusa of Portoferraio. La Chiusa also make a *passito* version.

The Costa dell'Argentario DOC recognises only a dry style, a representative producer being **Eredi Danei.**

GRECHETTO

Presumably of Greek origin, probably if somewhat distantly related to the Greco of Campania, having evolved differently over the millennia, Grechetto's area of influence today is almost exclusively confined to the region of Umbria. There's a bit in northern Lazio, another bit in southern Tuscany under the name of Greco, and several bits in the Marche under various names. But Umbria is where it has made its mark as a quality grape.

Grechetto may appear as a DOC under the umbrella of Assisi, or Colli del Trasimeno, in both of which cases it must form at least 85% of the total; and Colli Amerini Bianco, like Montefalco Bianco, must be at least 50% Grechetto. The Colli Martani denomination sports a Grechetto sub-DOC (85% minimum) as well as a separate one for the sub-zone Todi, a traditional and highly prized area for the variety. IGT Grechetto di Umbria has been a fairly common phenomenon, though it will die away as more and more of the wines come to be covered by DOCs.

Although today it is appearing varietally in a growing number of examples, Grechetto's traditional role has been as a blender for the spicing up of otherwise bland varieties such as Trebbiano Toscano and Malvasia Toscana. Bianco di Torgiano and Colli Perugini Bianco include significant amounts of Grechetto. But its most renowned incarnation is as an important though by no means exclusive element in the Orvieto blend, of which it may form up to a theoretical maximum of 45%, although that amount is due to increase at the expense mainly of Procanico (Trebbiano Toscano). As a blender, Grechetto was always planted together with the other varieties in an *uvaggio di vigneto*, but as it actually ripens later intelligent growers today plant it apart.

When Antinori started making Cervaro della Sala they boasted of the inclusion of Grechetto at 20%, against Chardonnay's 80%, to give it that certain Italian *je-ne-sais-quoi* – or to enable them, cynics have been heard to say, to claim there was something Italian in this otherwise very French creation. The fact that the percentages have now been altered to 90–10 may say something about how they assess the value of Grechetto's contribution.

Nonetheless some agreeable, characterful, if hardly world-beating wines are coming out under the varietal title. The best one I have come across is the version put out by Barberani of Baschi overlooking Lake Corbara, this being a wine of considerable richness of flavour and balance, demonstrating the grape's ability to achieve delicacy of aroma and a velvety mouth-feel at one and the same time. Less convincing to me is the more internationally renowned Marrano of Bigi of Orvieto, a *barrique*-fermented job of excellent primary material, which can demonstrate, it seems, the risks involved in oak-treatment of this grape, somewhat delicate of aroma and unstable of structure.

Other good Grechettos are produced by: Arnaldo Caprai (Grecante; Vigna Belvedere); C.S. Colli Amerini (Il Vignolo); Palazzone (L'Ultima Spiaggia), Orvieto; Pieve del Vescovo (Etesiaco); Rocca di Fabbri (Colli Martani Grechetto); Tili (Assisi Grechetto), Assisi; C.S. Tudernum (Colli Martani Grechetto di Todi), Todi. For what it's worth, Calò, Scienza and Costacurta maintain that DNA tests have shown that Grechetto di Todi is not the same as Grechetto di Orvieto.

In Lazio the multi-DOC Colli Etruschi Viterbesi includes a Grechetto sub-DOC, although production seems to verge on the non-existent. Under the same rubric there is a DOC 'Greghetto' which, be warned, is red; not that you're likely ever to see it.

DRUPEGGIO

Also known as Canaiolo Bianco, this minor variety has been in central Italian vineyards for as long as Canaiolo Nero than which, however, it is much less prevalent. Its purpose traditionally was to serve as a blender, often in *governo* form, for the bland Trebbiano, for purposes of adding perfume. Today it is best known as a component of the blend of Orvieto and other Umbrian whites. I know of no varietal version.

VERDELLO

According to some, Verdello is an off-shoot of Verdicchio; according to others it isn't, which seems the likelier proposition. Today it is mainly found in Umbria, notably in the Orvieto blend. A varietal version is produced by **La Palazzola** of Stroncone.

BELLONE

This is a grape native to Latium, quite possibly dating back to Roman times and beyond. Today it serves as a minor component of most of the wines of Castelli Romani, especially of Velletri.

3
Central Italy East

In *Life Beyond Lambrusco* this zone included Emilia, Romagna's political partner. In this book, however, I have taken the view that it is better to be oenologically than politically correct. Put simply, Romagna's principal wines and grape varieties, based on Sangiovese and Trebbiano with a few internationals and oddments, are indisputably of a central Italian style. Emilia's grape varieties, on the other hand, are either typical of the northwest (Barbera, Bonarda) or unique (Lambrusco, Ortrugo); even Malvasia di Candia, which Emilia shares with Lazio, at least in name, is more likely to have developed here and travelled there than the other way round. As for wines, the frothy style, which is dominant in Emilia and merely peripheral in Romagna, has much more in common with Lombardy's Oltrepo Pavese and Piemonte's Monferrato than it has with any area to the south or east.

Much of what has been said of the centre west is true here. The Apennine ridge runs right through from northwest to southeast and is a major influence on climate and land-lie. Here, however, the distance between peaks and sea – in this case the Adriatic – is much less than in the west. In the Marche and Abruzzo especially, the descent of the land via river valleys interspersed with rolling hills covered with vines and olive trees is sufficiently abrupt that often, if you can't see both Mediterranean and mountain-top, you won't have to turn many corners before you can. Thus winter cold and summer heat, exaggerated by the trapping effect of the mountains, are in turn moderated by the influence of the nearby large expanse of water.

The centre east seems more difficult to characterise than the other Italian wine zones. This may have something to do with politics – regional policy towards viticulture differing greatly between

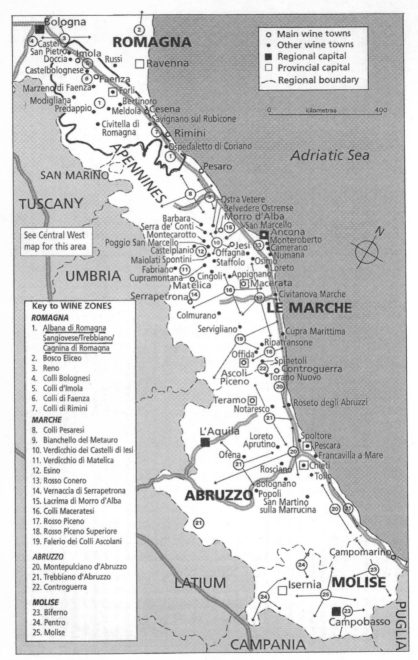

Central Italy East

Romagna and the Marche on the one hand, and between the Marche and Abruzzo on the other. As a generalisation, one could say that the farther south one goes the tighter the grip of the bureaucrats.

In particular, the authorities in Abruzzo, by manipulation of grants and subsidies, have imposed a region-wide concentration on just two varieties – Montepulciano and Trebbiano – for each of which the high-trellised *tendone* training system, now almost universally rejected by quality viticulturists in the rest of Italy, has been virtually *de rigueur*. Growers in Abruzzo are now voting with their secateurs and moving towards a greater breadth of vine material and more quality-oriented training systems, but the vast bulk of Abruzzo's viticulture remains old style. As for little Molise, they have traditionally tended to follow Abruzzo's lead, although that too is changing.

The biggest change, however, is noticed crossing the line northward from Abruzzo into the Marche: training systems become almost universally *spalliera*; grape varieties and wines become much more varied. The authorities responsible for the development of agriculture in the region adopt an altogether less hard-line approach to growers' desires and requirements, while striving to keep the flag of tradition flying. Thus while the Marche may share the Montepulciano and Trebbiano grapes with the neighbour to the south, they are inclined to blend the former, generally with Sangiovese, and downgrade the latter in favour of their very own, their pride and joy, Verdicchio.

Romagna is diverse again, having two distinct vinous identities. On the one hand it is an area of vast, industrial production. On the other it is a land of individualists. The main wine-growing area stretches from slightly east of the city of Bologna, which is virtually the dividing line between the two halves of the region, almost as far as the Adriatic coast at Rimini with its kilometres of tourist-infested sandy beach. Roughly speaking, the area north of the Via Emilia which runs from Bologna through Imola, Faenza and Forlì to Rimini is plainland, which of course is where most of the industrial output comes from. South of the road, where the land rises up towards the Apennines, there is an increasing number of enterprising growers trying to maximise the potential of the standard varieties while experimenting both with obscure native grapes and with the 'international' varieties. Associated with these is a series of delightful medieval villages such as Bertinoro and Dozza, in which latter the regional *enoteca* resides.

PRODUCTION AREAS

Officially designated quality wines from Romagna generally consist of the name of a traditional grape variety together with the suffix di Romagna as in Sangiovese di Romagna, Trebbiano di Romagna, Albana di Romagna, Pagadebit di Romagna, Cagnina di Romagna, all of which come in various styles. French varieties – Cabernet Sauvignon, Merlot, Chardonnay, Pinot Bianco, Sauvignon Blanc – are also much in favour these days with the trendy growers, who are increasing constantly in number and influence. I can see great developments in this area in years to come. New multi-DOCs – Colli di Faenza, Colli d'Imola and Colli di Rimini – have sprung up to cater for growers in the Apennine foothills who wish to use these grapes and others of Italian origin not necessarily native to these parts, such as Barbera.

Another growing zone of Romagna is along the coast, from Ravenna north to the border with Veneto. The zone as a whole is called Bosco Eliceo, which offers a Merlot and a Sauvignon as well as the indigenous Fortana and a Bianco based on Trebbiano. There is an outcrop of Trebbiano di Romagna here too, as well as plenty of high-yield Trebbiano grown on plains for use in blends or for industrial plonk.

Perhaps this is the opportunity to work in a recently established denomination called Reno, which straddles the Emilia–Romagna middle ground and which somehow got left out of *Barolo to Valpolicella*. Not that it's important in an international context, though quite a lot of wine seems to be made under the sub-DOC Montuni, made from the obscure Montù grape (a sub-variety of Trebbiano?). This in fact is one of the three sub-DOCs the others being Pignoletto and Bianco.

The Marche's principal DOC, from the point of view of inter-national renown, is Verdicchio dei Castelli di Iesi, the latter part of the name referring to a group of medieval fortified hilltop towns of which the main one, actually slightly outside the growing-zone, is Iesi, after the ancient, possibly pre-Roman, settlement of Aesis, which gives its name to the nearby Esino river (so nothing to do with Jesus – a common error). It is an area of rolling hills situated just west of the capital town of Ancona, which has specialised in white wine production for centuries; Ancona being, of course, one of Italy's principal fishing ports. Farther inland, in higher, sub-mountainous country, is the much smaller (from the point of view of production) zone of Verdicchio di Matelica, which some claim as the source of the finest Verdicchio; erroneously, on the latest evidence.

Literally on the southern outskirts of Ancona is Mount Conero, which gives its name to the region's best red, Rosso Conero, made from Montepulciano with the possible presence of Sangiovese. Producers of Rosso Conero often double as producers of Verdicchio dei Castelli di Iesi, and vice versa, although the areas do not overlap. More important from a volume, though not a quality, point of view is Rosso Piceno, a Sangiovese–Montepulciano blend which can be called Superiore only from a small area in the south on the Abruzzo border, though the non-Superiore, from a vast area covering most of the southeastern half of the Marche region, may be superior in quality.

Other DOCs are relatively insignificant, either because of very low production or because the general quality level rarely if ever qualifies them for wider attention. Among the former are Lacrima di Morro d'Alba, from just east of Ancona; and Vernaccia di Serrapetrona, from a tiny inland-upland enclave near Matelica; both of these are further discussed under grape varieties. The latter include Bianchello del Metauro, a normally uninspired white from the eponymous grape variety, from the north of the region; Falerio dei Colli Ascolani, an almost equally boring Trebbiano-based blend from a fairly large area in the southeast corner; and Colli Pesaresi Rosso, a Sangiovese-based red of little distinction from the north-east corner. From Colli Pesaresi come four other sub-DOCs, all too obscure to be worth mentioning. On the obscure side, too, are Esino DOC, designed to accommodate producers in the central area who would like to reduce the amount of Verdicchio in whites and Montepulciano/Sangiovese in reds while still keeping these native grapes as a base; and Colli Maceratesi, the base of which is the native Maceratino variety (80% minimum).

Abruzzo, bless it, presents less complications than any other Italian wine region, since until recently it recognised only two quality wines, Montepulciano d'Abruzzo and Trebbiano d'Abruzzo.

Both may come from any delimited wine area in the region, eliminating any differentials that might exist between sub-zones and leaving quality variations entirely up to individual producers, the vast majority of whom are co-operatives, or members thereof. Thus Abruzzo can claim credit for having introduced the questionable concept of regional typicity, a phenomenon which seems to be sweeping Italy at the moment, causing much heated debate.

It was only from the mid-1990s that other denominations began to creep in, starting with the multi-DOC Controguerra, which enables the classic grapes to be blended and the others – a mix of French and local grapes including Ciliegiolo and Passerina – to be made varietally. Controguerra's *disciplinare* is interesting in that it specifically forbids the *tendone* training formation, virtually ubiquitous until now in Abruzzo.

From a wine point of view, Molise is, as I have said, largely a clone of Abruzzo, although the DOC Biferno does provide for the addition of Aglianico in its red and *rosato*, and Bombino in its white, reflecting thus its more southern situation. The only other DOC until very recently was Pentro, which appears to exist on paper only. In 1998, however, a new regional DOC, Molise, was established following the Abruzzo principle, but expanding on it to include, at a minimum of 85%, the varietals Aglianico, Cabernet Sauvignon, Chardonnay, Falanghina, Greco Bianco, Moscato Bianco, Pinot Bianco, Sangiovese, Sauvignon and Tintilia (= Bovale Grande) in addition to Montepulciano and Trebbiano. The influence of nearby Campania as well as that of Abruzzo, and of course that of France, is reflected here.

GRAPES, WINES AND PRODUCERS – RED

MONTEPULCIANO

Let us be clear from the start that **this** Montepulciano is a grape variety having nothing to do with the town in Tuscany where Vino Nobile (from Sangiovese) is made – at least not today, although it may be that the Montepulciano grape branched off from Sangiovese in centuries past, a position stoutly maintained by several nineteenth-century ampelographers, though modern scholars tend to reject the possibility. Anyway, the two varieties' modern manifestations contain major differences of typology, and indeed Montepulciano is often used, usually illicitly, to correct Tuscan Sangiovese, which would be absurd if it were the same thing. Nor does Montepulciano ripen easily in the relatively cool climate conditions prevailing in, say, Chianti Classico. Indeed, west of the Apennines Montepulciano is much more at home in the warmer climes of Lazio, where it figures in a number of blends.

But Montepulciano's real home is along the east coast, centred on Abruzzo and extending north into Romagna and south as far as Puglia. In Abruzzo, where its presence is documented back to the early nineteenth century (no one really knows where it arrived from), it is practically unchallenged among red grapes, and can be found in every viticultural sub-zone in Abruzzo growing on the tall trellises called *tendone* (= big tent, because the raised carpet-like canopy completely covers the fruit). Detractors of this system may be interested to learn that the undisputed king of Montepulciano d'Abruzzo, Edoardo Valentini, maintains after many years of vineyard experiments that *tendone* is the best method for Montepulciano. Dr Richard Smart has also said that *tendone* can be a valid system provided that the canopy is thinned to let in the light. Some prominent growers, however, mainly in the northern, Marche end of the region, are moving towards French-style *spalliera* systems. While the vast majority of Abruzzo vineyards remain on *tendone*, however, *spalliera* is destined to take over gradually as vineyards are replanted.

Montepulciano is a relatively late-ripener, maturing generally in late September through to the end of October depending on site and weather. Its skins are rich in polyphenols, especially anthocyanins, so much so that its *rosato* wines, called Cerasuolo in Abruzzo, need no maceration at all in order to acquire a fully satisfying pinkness of hue, while red wines require no more than two or three days on the skins to finish up quite opaque, thus avoiding the tougher tannins where racking occurs early. Having the added bonus of moderate acidity, Montepulciano thus lends itself well to soft, full-coloured, fruity reds for early drinking, which is how the ubiquitous co-operatives of Abruzzo usually make them: chunky, fruity and easy. The same characteristics make Montepulciano an ideal blending grape (or wine), especially with wines high of acidity and low of colour content. That said, the tannins in the skins are such that with a longer maceration wines of great structure, complexity and ageing potential may also be achieved, as Valentini and a few others have shown.

Montepulciano d'Abruzzo is by far the most important DOC, with up to half a million hectolitres per annum or more being churned out, depending on the year. The current *disciplinare* allows for a thumping 14 tonnes per hectare production, with a 20% upward margin in 'exceptionally favourable years', making nearly 170 tonnes per hectare, of which Montepulciano on *tendone* on fertile, flattish terrain is eminently capable without the kind of drastic pruning and thinning applied by a Valentini. Such a system, then, leaves it up to the producer whether he wants to produce *grand vin* or cheap plonk. Montepulciano is capable of both.

Recently there has been established a new DOC which is Montepulciano d'Abruzzo *sottozona* Colline Teramane. Production here is limited to 11 tonnes per hectare, which is still excessive for the high quality of which Montepulciano is undoubtedly capable, and the only other grape allowed is Sangiovese at a maximum of 10%. Whereas in normal Montepulciano d'Abruzzo one has the right to add 'other non-aromatic red wine varieties up to a maximum of 15%' – which could mean the likes of Cabernet and Merlot as well as Sangiovese and other locals.

What is needed, now, is a move in law to improve the perception of the top wines of Montepulciano, currently constrained as I say to a share a DOC with rivers of respectable but unexceptional plonk. Already the Colline Teramane producers are preparing a DOCG, which will further reduce production maxima and make other improvements in a quality direction. The question is: what about the rest of Abruzzo? The Riserva version of Montepulciano d'Abruzzo introduced for the first time in 1992, requiring two years ageing from the 1st of January following the harvest, of which six months at least must be in barrel, is not going to convince the public that it is radically different, even if it were to be elevated to DOCG and restricted to a much lower yield.

In the Marche the main Montepulciano-dominated wine is Rosso Conero, although Rosso Piceno, including Superiore, usually contains more Montepulciano than Sangiovese. Biferno DOC of Molise is based on Montepulciano, with a bit of help from Aglianico, as is the virtually non-existent Pentro DOC.

In Puglia there are a couple of Montepulciano-based DOCs in the form of San Severo Rosso and Cacc'e Mmitte di Lucera, both predictably from the northern province of Foggia, although the variety is found throughout the region as a support grape for Negroamaro, Primitivo and Uva di Troia. One or two producers are trying it out varietally in the heat of southern Puglia, where it has traditionally been used as a blending grape, with highly encouraging results.

In Latium, too, it is widely employed as a blending variety, while having no DOC in which it is dominant except for the insignificant Cori Rosso.

The wines in Abruzzo

Production of Montepulciano d'Abruzzo being dominated in terms of hectolitres by the co-operatives, some of them quite massive, such as C.S. Tollo, C.S. Madonna dei Miracoli, the Citra group and others, private producers are fairly few and far between, though increasingly significant in terms of quality and image. They are hampered, however, by the enduring fact of a DOC situation which favours industrial production and low prices. Selling a Monte-pulciano d'Abruzzo at a medium, let alone a high, price can be hard work where the same denomination is on offer at much less. A pity, because middle-price Montepulciano d'Abruzzo represents probably the most affordable quality everyday red that Italy has to offer – the Italian equivalent of generic Côtes du Rhône – rivalled only by the Negroamaros of southern Puglia.

I have already indicated that one producer towers above the rest in terms of quality – this being Edoardo **Valentini** of Loreto Aprutino. Valentini is one of those geniuses who can be quite impossible as a person, though most forgive him because his wines are so wonderful. I once spent a good half-hour persuading him to sell a few cases of his Montepulciano d'Abruzzo to a client of mine, to which he finally agreed, adding: And how many cases does he want of the Trebbiano? None, I replied – he's only interested in the red. WHAAAAT!!! – he screamed. I have two sons, he ranted, and I cannot accept 'yes' for one and 'no' for the other. The dispute raged for some time, with his human son and heir trying to pacify him, alas to no avail. I never got the wine. Pity – it was fantastic.

Actually Valentini has three 'sons' (vinous ones), because he makes a Montepulciano d'Abruzzo Cerasuolo (pink) as well as the

Imbottigliato all'origine dalla
Azienda Agricola
VALENTINI s.s.
Loreto Aprutino - Italia
R.I. 251 PE
13,5% vol
e 75 cl

Vendemmia 1994

M ONTEPULCIANO
d'ABRUZZO
denominazione di origine controllata

NON DISPERDERE IL VETRO NELL'AMBIENTE

L 8.94

ETICHETTA E MARCHIO DEPOSITATI

Rosso and the excellent Trebbiano which my friend didn't want, although it sometimes attracts higher praise than the red. His methods are quite idiosyncratic, as you would expect. The root of all quality is the vineyard. From his approximately 70 hectares of grapes (he has a total of some 200 in two separate areas called Campo Sacro and Castelluccio, though these names do not appear on the labels; those that are not used for the vine are planted to olives and other crops) he selects a tiny percentage for making into wine, selling the rest as grapes to the nearby *cantina sociale* at Rosciano (Roxan; see below). Insisting that there is 'no rule' as to which particular part of the property this year's grapes should come from ('No rule, and no possibility of establishing one!', he instructs with wagging finger), he treats them all during the growing season with the care of a perfectionist, determining only at vintage time what is what, and this only after several passes. This cream is then pressed in old-fashioned presses and fermented in old-fashioned glass-lined concrete vats, ageing taking place (reds and whites, reds for several more years, though of course there is 'no rule') in old-fashioned Slavonian oak *botti* with, at all stages, minimal intervention. In other words, Valentini is of the school that believes great grapes will make great wine almost by themselves, you don't have to do anything except make sure nothing goes wrong.

Another major producer of the region is **Illuminati** of Controguerra in the north, near the Marche border. The *azienda* has been going since 1890, but the present owner, Dino Illuminati, has proved a dynamic force for improvement. Dynamic, indeed, is the word for this hyper-charged grower *commerciante* with the penetrating stare and the rat-tat-tat speech of a machine gun whose big idea, already in the early 1980s, was to 'refine the product in every possible way so that the consumer will cheerfully part with a proper price for a prestige bottle' (*Life Beyond Lambrusco*, p. 238). To this end he has invested time and money heavily to upgrade his operation, installing the latest technology, bringing in ex-Antinori technical director Giorgio Marone as consultant oenologist, experimenting in his 85 or so hectares (plus 15 rented) with diverse grape varieties, local and international, as well as with various original blends, even going so far as to train his new vines according to the relatively dense, relatively low-production-per-plant *spalliera* system rather than the *tendone* almost universally employed in Abruzzo until recently. Indeed the new Controguerra DOC, which Illuminati was partially instrumental in bringing about, specifically vetoes *tendone*, as mentioned above. Illuminati's wines today, then, incline away from the pure classicity of a Valentini, more towards internationality with a local base. His more classic, and longer established, styles include Montepulciano d'Abruzzo Riparosso, a hardy perennial, always a good drink with a serious backbone; and Montepulciano d'Abruzzo Zanna, though the latter gets a bit of refining in *barriques* as well as in the larger *botti*. More innovative have been the recently introduced Lumen (from the 1997 vintage, a Controguerra DOC), a *barrique*d blend of Montepulciano and Cabernet Sauvignon which has enjoyed considerable success in its early appearances on international markets; and Nicò, which adds Merlot to the above equation, the grapes receiving a slight period of *appassimento* for added power.

I was going to say that the range of Montepulcianos is completed by the Cerasuolo Campirosa, a wine of considerable depth of flavour and colour despite a minimum of maceration. However, Dino Illuminati informs me that he has developed a new wine (100% Montepulciano) at least as good as Lumen. At the time of writing this Controguerra DOC is provisionally named Pieluni, subject to approval.

Gianni **Masciarelli**, San Martino sulla Marrucina. The wines of Gianni Masciarelli, who took over this family estate in the 1980s, have for some years now attracted from mainly Italian pundits rave reviews of increasing intensity. This despite the fact that a significant percentage of his 60-odd hectares of vineyard are planted – as are the vast majority of vineyards in Abruzzo, at least where Abruzzo varieties are concerned – to the theoretically poor quality *tendone* system. But Masciarelli, backed by wife Marina Cvetic and oenologist Romeo Taraborrelli, compensates, as does Edoardo Valentini, for the system's shortcomings by drastically reducing production via severe green pruning, thereby achieving a depth of colour, a concentration of fruit and a breadth of aromas that are the more impressive for being contained in wines of such sheer drinkability. Masciarelli's masterpieces, Montepulciano d'Abruzzo Villa Gemma and Trebbiano d'Abruzzo Marina Cvetic, reflect his commitment to the indigenous varieties, even though he also produces some of the best Chardonnay and Cabernet Sauvignon – both also named after his wife – in central Italy. He nonetheless believes fervently that these varieties should be given international credibility with judicious oaking – indeed Masciarelli is a pioneer of oak-fermentation and maturation in this part of the world. His *normale* wines, straight Montepulciano d'Abruzzo and Trebbiano d'Abruzzo, as well as the white blend of Trebbiano and the local Cococciola, called Villa Gemma Bianco, don't see a lot of small oak, being produced in large numbers; about 20% of his total grape requirement is bought in for this purpose. But they remain among the best of their highly popular genre and are undoubtedly remarkable value for money.

Given their importance in the overall picture it is only right to consider the operations of a typical *cantina sociale* of Abruzzo. The one I know best – I go there frequently for business reasons, having learned that these are the lucky recipients of the majority of Valentini's grapes – is a relatively modest one in the heart of Abruzzo, at the village of Rosciano inland from Pescara, called

Casa Vinicola **Roxan**. Modest, I should say, by Abruzzo standards: Roxan actually represents some 700 growers, of which the largest is Edoardo Valentini, conferring grapes from around 1,000 hectares of vineyard.

Roxan began life in the mid-1970s and since inception has been run by a group of councillors who stick rigidly to the beaten path, but who make up for their lack of imagination by a firm resolve to deliver good quality and value for money at the levels in which they are involved: a policy they illustrate by giving wide responsibilities to consultant Rocco Pasetti, undoubtedly one of the best and most reliable oenologists in the region (Rocco also runs his own rapidly improving private family estate, aptly named Pasetti, at Francavilla a Mare) and probably the main reason why Valentini chooses to send his grapes here rather than to one of the several *cantine sociali* nearer to his property.

At vintage time, having basically only two varieties to work with, the task of the winemakers at Roxan is relatively straightforward. As the tractors with their loads of freshly picked grapes arrive at the winery, a refractometer on a robotic arm determines the first selection according to sugar level. The state of health of the grapes is also taken into account. Premium quality is separated off, and the rest goes into containers of various degrees of hugeness for fermentation and eventual sale in bulk, either in tanks to distant blenders, or in demijohns for the local populace. Subsequent selections will be made according to the evolution of the wine in the fermenting and ageing stages. In this way, they will end up with four or five different quality levels of wine from grapes of a single variety, single zone.

Of these levels, the top two are reserved for bottled wines. Roxan has two lines, each consisting of a Montepulciano, a Cerasuolo and a Trebbiano. The basic line, called, simply, Roxan, rejoices in deep colour and a balanced, eminently gluggable fruitiness, which many wines at higher prices would do well to emulate. The top line, called Galelle, has more structure and complexity and is given some wood ageing to bring out its finer qualities.

But the key to the success of the operation is reliability and simplicity at a price.

Other producers of Abruzzo currently coming forth with Montepulcianos of good to excellent standard include: **Barone Cornacchia**

(Poggio Varano; Vigna le Coste), Torano Nuovo; **Cataldi Madonna** (Tonì), Ofena; **Filomusi Guelfi**, Popoli; **La Valentina** (Binomio; Spelt), Spoltore; **Marramiero** (Inferi), Rosciano; C.S. **Miglianico** (Montupoli), Miglianico; Camillo **Montori** (Fonte Cupa), Controguerra; Bruno **Nicodemi** (Bacco), Notaresco; **Orlandi Contucci Ponno** (La Regia Specula), Roseto degli Abruzzi; **Pasetti** (Testarossa), Francavilla a Mare; C.S. **Tollo** (Cagiolo; Colle Secco), Tollo; Ciccio **Zaccagnini** (Abbazia San Clemente; Riserva), Bolognano.

The wines in le Marche and other regions

The only other Montepulciano-dominated denomination of real significance – in terms of prestige if not of volume – is the Marche's Rosso Conero. The growing area is a small one in the vicinity of Monte Conero on the southern outskirts of Ancona. Here too 14 tonnes per hectare production is allowed by the DOC, a provision that is bound to change since the zone is so small, the wines are currently under increasing demand and the only justification for the rapidly rising prices is high quality, which rarely if ever accompanies high volume. At present the only twist that justifies the high prices is Riserva, to qualify for which the wine must be aged for two and a quarter years from the January following vintage. But here, too, the yield maximum remains theoretically at 14 tonnes plus.

Rising demand, it must be said, is a recent phenomenon. Only a few years ago production was controlled almost entirely by *cantine sociali* and the big Verdicchio houses. Growers then mainly sold grapes at low prices or, all too often, accepted the ill-conceived bribes of the EU to extirpate their vineyards – often vineyards in prime positions which for bureaucratic reasons it is now difficult to replant. Credit must go to a large extent, it should be said, to merchant houses like Garofoli, Umani Ronchi and La Vite/ Monteschiavo for reviving interest in the DOC. But the real future of Rosso Conero as an important denomination is in the hands of the small specialists.

Foremost among these has been Alessandro **Moroder**, at Varano on the outskirts of Ancona. The Moroder family, indeed, has been growing grapes and other crops here since 1837, though Alessandro only began bottling in 1984, prior to which he sold his grapes to the local co-operative. In 1990 he made a decisive step by taking on peripatetic winemaker Franco Bernabei, which immediately paid dividends when the top line of the establishment, the Rosso Conero *cru* Dorico, was awarded *tre bicchieri* by the influential *Gambero Rosso Guide*. Since then this wine, which only appears in good years and goes into the *normale* in lesser vintages, has never had less than 2 *bicchieri*. It is a potent brew, never less than 13% with a deepish though not opaque colour, quite tannic on the palate – therefore, with the alcohol, capable of considerable medium-term ageing – though with an abundance of fruit to cover the tannicity, and with a certain woodsmoke or coffee-grounds undertone at the back of the palate coming from the *barriques* partially used, together with *botti*, in the maturation process; again, however, the fruit effectively covers the wood.

From their 20-odd hectares of vineyard Moroder make some 80,000 bottles of wine per annum, most of it Rosso Conero *normale*, always good because it benefits, in lesser years, from the input of the *cru*. Other wines include a respectable *rosato* called Rosa di Montacuto and an attractive sweet *passito* wine, from semi-dried Trebbiano, Moscato and Malvasia grapes, called L'Oro di Moroder.

The estate also grows various other crops, and the Moroder have recently initiated a business catering to tourists, wines and foods – some 80% of the products coming from their own farm. Pays to be covered. You never know what daft scheme the EU will think up next to 'save' European viticulture.

Another small estate, which has devoted its efforts to making fine Rosso Conero since the 1960s, is **Marchetti** of the intriguingly named Ancona suburb called Pinocchio. The younger generation, having prised the estate away from its previously idosyncratic and not always reliable ways, is now putting out wines of real depth and character, wines needing some time in bottle before achieving harmony. As in the case of Moroder there is the annual *normale*, plus a *cru*, produced in better years, called Villa Bonomi.

I have been impressed, too, by the wines of Fattoria **Le Terrazze** of Numana, where Attilio Pagli is winemaker. The *normale* is bright, brisk and highly quaffable, while the *barrique*-aged *cru* Sassi Neri has an extra depth and dimension – extraordinary depth of colour and a palate at once chewy and smooth, with flavours ranging from black cherry jam to leather and spice. Antonio and Georgina Terni also, in exceptional vintages, make a limited edition

Rosso Conero, Visions of J, which can outdo even Sassi Neri for power and complexity. There is also a highly attractive blend of Montepulciano, Syrah and Merlot called Chaos.

Other smaller growers who have impressed include: Luca e Beatrice **Lanari**, in the Ancona *frazione* of Varano – their *cru* is called Fibbio; Conte Leopardi **Dittajuti**, of Numana, who makes good Rosso Conero *normale* which is upstaged by his *crus* Pigmento and Vigneti del Coppo; **Malacari**, of Offagna, with the *cru* Grigiana; Enzo **Mecella**, of Fabriano, who makes a good cru called Rubelliano; **Poggio Montali** of Monteroberto, with their *cru* Poggio al Cerro and Poggio Montali; and Silvano **Strologo**, of Camerano, evidently a fan of Roman Emperors, whose *crus* Julius and Traiano, made with the help of oenologist Giancarlo Soverchia, have found favour with critics. The other good to excellent producers of Rosso Conero are biggish houses mainly concerned with Verdicchio. They include: **Fazi Battaglia** (Passo del Lupo), Castelplanio; **Garofoli** (Grosso Agontano Riserva; Vigna Piancarda), Loreto; **La Vite/Monte Schiavo** (Conti Cortesi; Bottaccio), Maiolati Spontini; **Umani Ronchi** (Cùmaro; San Lorenzo), Osimo. The biggest in volume terms is **Moncaro** (Terre Cortesi), a massive but highly streamlined and quality-conscious cooperative situated at Montecarotto, with control through their numerous members of over 50% of the total Rosso Conero vine-yard area.

The *disciplinare* for Rosso Piceno calls for a blend of Monte-pulciano at 35–70% and Sangiovese at 30–50%, plus up to 15% other red grapes, so in theory, at least, Rosso Piceno is a Monte-pulciano-dominated wine. The *normale* version can come from anywhere in the southernmost province of the Marche, Ascoli Piceno, as well as from large parts of the provinces of Macerata and Ancona; the Superiore, on the other hand, which is allowed a mere 12 tonnes per hectare production as compared with 13 for the *normale*, and whose minimum alcoholic degree must be half a degree higher, may only come from Ascoli Piceno. In practice, as a general rule, at least half of the total production of 50,000–60,000 hectolitres per annum is Superiore.

Among the best producers are **Boccadigabbia** (Villamagna) of Civitanova Marche; La **Cantina dei Colli Ripani** (Il Castellano; Leo Ripanus), Ripatransone; **Cocci Grifoni** (Il Grifone; Vigna Messieri), Ripatransone; Tenuta **De Angelis** (Superiore) at Castel di Lama;

Romolo e Remo **Dezi** (Regina del Bosco), Servigliano; La Vite/ Monteschiavo (Sassaiolo Riserva); Le **Caniette** (Rosso Bello), Ripatransone; **Saladini Pilastri** (Vigna Piediprato; Vigna Monteprandone) at Spinetoli; **San Giovanni** (Rosso del Nonno) at Offida; Ercole **Velenosi** (Poggio dei Filari; Il Brecciarolo) at Ascoli Piceno; **Villa Forano** (Villa Forano) at Appignano; and **Villa Pigna** (Superiore), Offida.

An estate producing outstanding Montepulciano without benefit – if indeed it is a benefit – of a DOC is **Oasi degli Angeli** at Cupra Marittima. The wine, made in tiny quantity from a minuscule vineyard, is called Kurni.

In Molise, the forgotten region sandwiched between Abruzzo and Puglia, you would need one hand to count the good producers on only if you had three fingers missing. The DOCs you could count with the missing fingers, there being three, Molise, Biferno and Pentro, of which only the former two function in reality.

The two producers who do make good and/or improving wine are **Di Majo Norante** and **Borgo di Colloredo**, both of Campomarino. Di Majo Norante, run by Alessio of that name, has been in the fine wine business for decades, his father Luigi having decided in the 1960s to pursue high quality exclusively with native southern Italian vine varieties – a difficult and courageous choice. Their range of wines, from some 50 to 60 hectares, is extensive and, apart from the slight dominance of Montepulciano among reds, strongly influenced by Campanian ampelography. It includes, among dry whites, expressive and well-typed varietal versions of Fiano, Falanghina and Greco, a worthy blend of Falanghina and Fiano called Ramitello and a delicious sweet Moscato called Apianae. The reds include an Aglianico and a Prugnolo (Sangiovese), again both nicely typed, and three Montepulciano/Aglianico blends – Molì Rosso (Biferno), Ramitello Rosso (Biferno) and Don Luigi (Molise), the last named, a wine of good structure overlain by generous fruit and a complex of fruit and spice aromas, being probably the best. The consultant oenologist used to be Giorgio Grai, of Alto Adige, but since 1999 the baton has passed to the formidable Riccardo Cotarella.

Borgo di Colloredo, on the other hand, is a rising star, one which may be expected to climb appreciably higher in the firmament given the enthusiasm of Enrico di Giulio and his brother and parents to bring forth something special from their 40-plus hectares of vineyard, which they are rapidly switching from *tendone* training to the lower *archetto* typical of classic Tuscany. Drip irrigation is being simultaneously introduced and the winery has been completely modernised. The di Giulios believe in a mix of grapes both indigenous and international, but Montepulciano remains the principal variety, dominating the Biferno Rosso blend. Their best product, indeed, is a varietal Montepulciano Molise – a wine of considerable depth of colour and a wealth of soft, succulent fruit.

In Puglia Montepulciano acts mainly as a back-up grape, as stated, and as such it is widely used, figuring in minority proportion in some of Puglia's best reds from Botromagno's Pier delle Vigne – with Aglianico – through Rivera's Il Falcone to the elegant Vigna Flaminio Rosso of Vallone and the full, finely balanced Duca d'Aragona of Candido.

The only part of Puglia in which Montepulciano dominates the DOC is in San Severo in the north, around Foggia. I know of no producer putting out a San Severo Rosso of anything beyond adequate quality. **D'Alfonso del Sordo** is perhaps the best name to go for, especially now that Severino Gorofano has taken over as consultant, though their better reds are both IGT (Casteldrione – Montepulciano plus Uva di Troia and Sangiovese; and Contrada del Santo – Uva di Troia and Montepulciano).

Montepulciano is occasionally produced successfully on the other side of the Apennines. An excellent example is Riccardo Cotarella's Montepulciano/Sangiovese blend Tertium out of C.S. **Cerveteri** in Latium.

A rare example of a good varietal Montepulciano from Tuscany is the Riflesso Antico of **Ambrosini Lorella** at Suvereto.

OTHER RED GRAPES

SANGIOVESE

See Central Italy West, pp. 38–41.

BARBAROSSA

This is a red variety found, as far as I am aware, only in the vineyards of Bertinoro, in the Province of Forlì, Romagna. Barbarossa was brought back from near-extinction by Mario Pezzi of Fattoria

Paradiso and named after the red-bearded Holy Roman Emperor in honour of his short stay in the area some centuries back. It makes a wine of impressive colour, extract and structure, capable of ageing over a considerable period. But it doesn't seem destined for widespread planting, given that it has gone nowhere in the 14 odd years since I first researched a book on Italian wine.

The fact that Barbarossa is nowhere mentioned in the recently appeared bible of Italian grape varieties, *Vitigni d'Italia*, by Calò, Scienza and Costacurta, gives me belatedly to think that Barbarossa is perhaps merely a synonym of some other variety. As far as I can see, however, the 'bible' gives no clue as to what that might be.

CAGNINA

A member of the Friulian Refosco family, related specifically to the Terrano, this grape may be found in restricted areas of the provinces of Forlì and Ravenna, in Romagna, where it produces some 3,000 hectolitres of wine annually. Cagnina di Romagna DOC tends to come fiercely purple of hue, strikingly *selvatico* of aroma and flavour, slightly sweet but with firm acid and tannin back-up. A no-nonsense individualist which I personally have fond recollections of applying successfully as a hangover cure one subjectively heavy morning in the objectively delightful wine-town of Bertinoro. I am sure there are others, but the only producer I know of is, once again, Fattoria **Paradiso** – of Bertinoro, of course.

According to Calò, Scienza and Costacurta, there is also a grape called Canina (sic) which is cultivated in Romagna and Tuscany. The authors make no mention of Canina or Cagnina in the entry for Refosco. On the other hand, they cite 'Cagnina' as a correct synonym of Canaiolo Nero and as an incorrect synonym of Canina. So the confusion is generously spread.

LACRIMA DI MORRO D'ALBA

Just pipping Montepulciano and Vernaccia – and, perhaps, Cagnina – at the post, this grape wins the all-Italy confusing-name stakes. 'Lacrima' might suggest the mythical Lacryma Cristi of Vesuvius (indeed Calò et al. say that it is the Lacryma Christi of Vesuvius, only problem being that there is no such grape mentioned in the modern *disciplinare* for the wine), while Morro d'Alba takes the imagination off towards La Morra in the zone of Alba, Piemonte. Add to this the alternative name of Gallioppa and you could be in Cirò in Calabria, with the Gaglioppo grape (q.v.), not to mention other erroneous synonyms cited in the 'bible'. Instead, say others, this is a one-off variety, ancient of lineage and exclusive to a very small area near Ancona around the commune of Morro d'Alba in the Marche. It may or may not be related to that Aleatico which is used in parts of Tuscany and Puglia for the making of sweet red wine. But Lacrima di Morro d'Alba – also the name of the wine – makes a dry, fairly light, fruity red, smooth, low in tannin, not dissimilar to Dolcetto. It achieved its greatest fame as a *novello* in 1995 when Luca Maroni, self-styled 'Taster of Wine', gave an example from the producer cited below an incredibly high rating in his annual guide, to general astonishment.

The best-known producer is Stefano **Mancinelli** of – you guessed it – Morro d'Alba. Mancinelli has made something of a speciality of his local grape and makes two *crus* – Santa Maria del Fiore and Sensazioni del Frutto, the former from old vines. The wines, purply-red of hue, have a medium depth of colour, red fruit and spice on the nose and an intensely fruity, smooth palate with good balancing acidity: wines to be drunk in the freshness of youth when at their most vibrant.

Other producers include: Mario e Giorgio **Brunori** of Jesi; Luciano **Landi** of Belvedere Ostrense; La Vite/Monteschiavo; Mario **Luchetti** of Morro d'Alba; and Maurizio **Marconi** of San Marcello.

VERNACCIA DI SERRAPETRONA

As previously indicated, this Vernaccia, being red, is not related to the white grapes of the same name from San Gimignano or from Oristano in Sardinia. There may, on the other hand, be a link with an obscure variety grown in the Solopaca area of Campania called Vernaccia di Vigna d'Arlo. Insofar as this one is produced at all (not much more than 1,000 hectolitres in total) it is as a sparkling wine, dry or sweet, or more often in-between – i.e. *amabile*. A minimum of 40% of the grapes for the wine must undergo *appassimento* before *spumantizzazione*. Another of Italy's endearing oddballs.

Massimo **Serboni** produces a dry and an *amabile*. Lanfranco **Quacquarini**'s version is *amabile*. Both producers, needless to say, are situated in Serrapetrona.

AGLIANICO

For general notes see the chapter on southern Italy/Campania.

Aglianico has a small presence in Molise, being officially written in to the DOC for Biferno Rosso. As we have seen, Di Majo Norante makes a good varietal Aglianico. It is doubtful whether the grape would perform acceptably north of this point.

GRAPES, WINES AND PRODUCERS – WHITE

VERDICCHIO

Verdicchio, the grape, has for hundreds if not thousands of years been grown in hills inland from Ancona as you head for the mountains and the Umbrian border. From thence it has spread to other parts of central Italy, although never with the success it is capable of achieving at home. Even in the Marche it nearly, in the middle of the twentieth century, succumbed to the all-conquering Trebbiano Toscano whose productivity was considered by growers in a volume-minded age to be preferable. Partly due to antiquated farming methods – training up trees, as part of a mixed crop typical of the *mezzadria* era and partly due to systems mistakenly adopted in the process of specialisation; Verdicchio vines in the 1950s and 1960s just weren't churning it out sufficiently to make growers a living. Fortunately, the development agency of the Marche got behind the local hero, developing, encouraging and to some extent financing pruning systems that counteracted the vine's tendency not to fruit on the first few buds of the cane. It worked. Trebbiano remains in the vineyards, but mercifully as a minority component.

A characteristic of Verdicchio, like other varieties whose name is based on the word *verde*, is that the grapes at harvest time are intensely green, though they may also display a tinge of copper. This may be accounted for by the existence, according to certain ampelographers, of two diverse sub-varieties, one greenish of hue, with a tight bunch, one having some golden tints and a loose bunch. Different sub-titles tend to support this contention, these including Verdicchio Bianco, Verdicchio Verde, Verdicchio Giallo, Verdicchio Vero – this last suggesting that at least one false one also exists.

Certainly, where picked early, there is an appley-greenness about Verdicchio's flavour, while when slightly late-harvested that green sharpness can turn to a honeyed butteriness, combined where production is limited with considerable richness of extract. Today Verdicchio is coming to be regarded as perhaps Italy's most characterful native white grape, with some very fine wines coming through lately to back the judgement. Verdicchio is also a wine capable of considerable ageing in the right circumstances, as the Riserva of Bucci and the Cuprese of Colonnara are able to demonstrate.

Parenthetically, it is not just the wine that ages well. Denizens of Ancona are fond of boasting that theirs is the province with the greatest human longevity in Italy. Ancona is also, they add with a wink, the province of greatest per capita wine consumption in Italy. And most of it is white! So much for the theory that red wine is best for the health.

The amphora-shaped bottle earned Verdicchio, the wine, a certain fame, or should I say notoriety, in the post-war period, although the gimmick was later seen to be more of a liability than a blessing because of its cheapening of the image. Serious producers have been distancing themselves from such marketing ploys for several years now, trying to refocus the attention on what's inside the container. They have succeeded up to a point, in that Verdicchio is no longer regarded as having to be desperately cheap, although the top stuff still hasn't managed to achieve such giddy prices as top Chardonnay is able to command. Whether it will establish itself as the superstar among whites that some seem to be suggesting it could remains to be seen. It has proved, at least, that it's got versatility, turning out good to excellent wines in a variety of styles – aperitif, dry late-harvest, sparkling (bottle- or tank-fermented), *passito*, and of course the traditional ideal-accompaniment-to-fish style as well as the modern oak-fermented version.

DOCs are limited to two, both of which call for a minimum of 85% Verdicchio: Verdicchio dei Castelli di Iesi and Verdicchio di Matelica, each recognising various versions, including Spumante, Passito and Riserva. Castelli di Jesi, by far the largest in volume terms, also includes a Classico zone, which accounts for some three-quarters of total production. Not surprisingly, Castelli di Jesi displays the greater range of styles, and with one possible exception distinctly the finer and better-balanced wines at the top, though most of the plonk comes from here as well.

Verdicchio plays a minor role in the *disciplinari* of other wines of the Marche, including the red Lacrima di Morro d'Alba, also popping up a couple of times as a supporting grape on the other side of the Apennines, for example in Colli del Trasimeno. Its principal other presence is in Lake Garda's Lugana, made entirely from Trebbiano di Lugana which DNA tests have recently proved, as indicated in a previous chapter, to be identical with Verdicchio, as indeed is Trebbiano di Soave.

The producers

Ten years ago Verdicchio production was largely in the hands of the 'big boys', either large *cantine sociali* like Moncaro and Colonnara or large privates like Fazi Battaglia and Garofoli. Since the mid-1980s there has, however, been significant upward movement by the little people and while some of the best wines are still coming from the larger wineries, it is the small grower who is proving most beautiful today.

One outstanding smallish producer of the Castelli di Jesi zone is Fratelli **Bucci** of Ostra Vetere. Ampelio Bucci, an economic consultant who spends weekdays in Milan, is the current owner of this beautifully sited agricultural estate of some 400 hectares – nearly 30 of which are vineyards dedicated to the production of high quality Verdicchio since the early 1980s – which has been in the Bucci family for over 200 years. Bucci makes just two white wines – a Verdicchio dei Castelli di Jesi *normale* which comes out every year, and a *cru* called Villa Bucci which appears only in the best years and which is a selection of the best *cuvées*, always kept apart until the selector, Giorgio Grai of Bolzano, reputed to have one of the finest palates in Italy, has determined the blend. For both wines production in the vineyard is restricted to 8 tonnes per hectare, and harvesting is always around two or more weeks later than others in the zone. Bucci almost boasts of his lack of hi-tech in the immaculate winery: 'We have no industrial equipment', he says; 'only cleanliness'. Both whites are aged in traditional *botti* of Slavonian and Italian oak – nothing French in vineyard or *cantina*. Yet the wines have something quasi-Burgundian about them, being at once taut and multi-dimensional, rich and racy – especially the Villa Bucci, an intellectual wine which asks more questions of the taster than it immediately answers; and which, given correct storage conditions, can last as long and develop as intricately as a fine Burgundy.

Another *maestro* of Verdicchio is Lucio Canestrari of Fattoria **Coroncino** at Staffolo. Canestrari and his wife began in 1981 with a smallholding including just under 3 hectares of vineyard. They began bottling in 1985 but aimed low in the market, and it wasn't until 1988, after they purchased their finest vineyard at Spescia, that they hit on the idea of sampling Michelin-rosetted restaurants with their wines. Before they knew it orders were coming in from all over Italy and the world and they were completely out of stock. They have never looked back.

Today, between vineyards owned and rented, they have 7 hectares in various locations. The top *cru* is Gaiospino, from Spescia, about one-quarter of which is fermented in new and second-passage French oak *tonneaux*, where it remains on the fine lees for about a year. It is a wine of tantalising aromas and silky mouth-feel, with almost a honeyed sweetness about it despite being technically dry. Uppish in alcohol, with a good acidity, it has the structure as well as the class to develop well in bottle over a period of years.

Il Coroncino is the *cru* of the original vineyard, where the small but well-equipped winery is situated. A wine of less *spessore* (weight: literally thickness), designed for earlier drinking, it nonetheless has much of the charm and complexity of Gaiospino. The straight Bacco is the house's *normale* – still tastier than the common run of Verdicchios by a margin.

Other small to medium-sized growers of the Castelli di Jesi zone capable of good to excellent Verdicchio include: Mario e Giorgio Brunori (San Nicolò), Jesi; **Casalfarneto** (Grancasale; Fontevecchia), Serra dé Conti; Mancinelli (Podere S. Maria del Fiore), Morro d'Alba; **Santa Barbara** (Le Vaglie; Stefano Antonucci), Barbara; **Sartarelli** – considered the best by some (Contrada Balciana; Tralivio), Poggio San Marcello; **Tavignano** (Selezione Misco; Vigneti di Tavignano), Cingoli; **Vallerosa Bonci** (San Michele; Riserva Barré; Le Case; also Passito Rojano), Cupramontana; Fratelli **Zaccagnini** (Salmàgina; Pier delle Vigne), Staffolo.

Among the large producers there are several which deserve honourable mention for having poured resources into the quality path of production: C.S. **Colonnara** of Cupramontana was founded in 1959 and today groups around 200 growers; their *cru* Cuprese is highly regarded both for its concentration and balance in youth and for its staying power, being capable of enduring and indeed of gaining complexity over an 8 to 10-year period.

Fazi Battaglia, of Castelplanio, originators of the amphora bottle and owners of no less than 340 hectares of vineyard, have worked hard to turn around their industrial image with wines like the highly esteemed Le Moie as well as the recently introduced botrytis-affected Arkezia Muffa di San Sisto (heavily oaked and untypical, but an interesting bottle), although the old amphora Titulus still sells too well for them to contemplate changing the packaging at present.

Cantine Gioacchino **Garofoli**, of Loreto, is one of the few long-running success stories of the Marche, its history stretching back 100 years and more. Present directors, brothers Gianfranco and Carlo Garofoli, have maintained the family tradition of pristine hygiene and high technology combined with the policy of grape-growing at a high level of quality in their extensive vineyards in the Castello di Jesi (Verdicchio) and Rosso Conero zones, backed by large amounts of bought-in grapes from growers with whom they have worked for decades. Top Verdicchio these days is their *cru* Podium, the grapes for which are slightly late-harvested: a wine of full colour and opulent fruit-and-spice aromas, a line of nicely balancing acidity running through its heart. The Riserva Serra Fiorese is a successful attempt at oaked Verdicchio, successful because the wine aromas predominate over those of wood. The *cru* Macrina, for which they have long been known, has had to make way for these two stars, but is still one of the best of the traditional Verdicchios. 'A marker', I described it in *Life Beyond Lambrusco*; I have not changed my mind.

Monte Schiavo, recently renamed, or surnamed **La Vite**, have been Verdicchio specialists since the late 1970s. Owned today by the powerful Pieralisi group, the world's largest olive oil processing equipment manufacturer, they control over 100 hectares of prime-site vineyard in the Castelli di Jesi zone from which, in their high-tech winery, under the surveillance of oenologist Pierluigi Lorenzetti, they make a range of Verdicchios from the modest amphora through to a high-class single-vineyard Riserva called Le Giuncare, recently introduced and aiming at the highest honours. *En route* are the single-vineyard Colle del Sole, nicely balanced and of good concentration considering the very considerable production; another single-vineyard *cru* called Coste del Molino, steely, racy and fine with plenty of flavour and an excellent structure, the ideal wine to accompany the many fish dishes of the

area; Pallio di San Floriano, single-vineyard and late-picked, about three weeks after the others, having a noticeably creamier texture and intensity of aroma – a wine which, incidentally, consistently comes top in blind tastings of the Verdicchio producers among themselves; and Bando di San Settimio, yet another vineyard *cru* whose opulence of flavour and considerable potential longevity comes from both late-picked grapes and a three-month sojourn in large oak barrels. Gigi Calzetta, the amiable director of the firm, is also rather proud of the sparkling Verdicchio of the establishment, Vigna Tassanare.

C.S. **Moncaro/Terre Cortesi** of Montecarotto have some 800 grower-members controlling over 900 hectares of vineyard, of which 500-plus are in the Verdicchio Castelli di Jesi alone, representing fully one-quarter of the total. Their *crus* Cà Ruptae and Vigna Novali are among the better ones of the traditional style, while Le Vele is made using New World oxidation-avoidance techniques.

Umani Ronchi, of Osimo, is a fairly large-scale establishment which has been improving year on year since being acquired in 1970 by the Bernetti family from Gino Umani Ronchi, becoming in the process one of the two or three most conspicuously successful Marchigiano producers of the latter part of the twentieth century. Their most successful wine over the years has been the Verdicchio *cru* Casal di Serra, although the more recent Riserva Plenio has stolen some of its thunder, as has the IGT Verdicchio/Chardonnay blend Le Busche. With Giacomo Tachis helping behind the scenes it is perhaps not surprising that Umani Ronchi also have international varieties like Sauvignon Blanc, Chardonnay and Cabernet Sauvignon to help out with the blends.

It is to be noted that all the above larger quality producers make red wines – Rosso Conero, Rosso Piceno and various IGTs – of good to excellent quality, these being mentioned or reviewed in their relevant sections.

ALBANA

An ancient variety dating back perhaps to Roman times, possibly even of Roman origin (from the Colli Albani), Albana's first mention in literature is to be found in the works of Pier d' Crescenzi of Bologna (1230–1310). Grown almost exclusively in the Apennine foothills between Bologna and Rimini, its main quality centres have always been in the provinces of Faenza and Forlì, especially round the town of Bertinoro which may have taken its name from the wine ('*vorrei berti in oro*' – 'I'd like to drink you in (a) gold (cup)'; or, alternatively, the wine is so good that it '*verte in oro*' – 'turns into gold'). The local subvariety here is called Albana Gentile or Albana di Bertinoro, less productive and having smaller bunches and berries than other members of the fairly numerous family, but bringing forth, it is said, the finest wines.

Albana's reputed golden qualities were good enough, at any rate, to win it the gold medal in the stakes to become Italy's first 'guaranteed' white wine, way back in 1986, to the accompaniment of widespread complaints that the existing wines didn't merit the honour, although since that time the wines have improved noticeably. Albana di Romagna DOCG comes in four styles: Secco, Amabile, Dolce and Passito. The sweeter it gets, the more likely it is to be worthy of its controversially lofty denominational status, even if the best of them, from semi-dried grapes, exist only in tiny volume. Traditionally, drying has been off the vine, but one or two producers are now resorting to late-harvest with noble rot to get the best from the variety. Zerbina have recently experimented with a super-late harvest berry-selected *trockenbeerenauslese* style which is stunning – but which is not for the time being present on the market.

Good producers, all of whom have been mentioned already under Sangiovese in the section on the centre west, include: Celli (I Croppi – Secco; Le Querce – Dolce; Solara – Passito); Umberto Cesari (Colle del Re – Secco dand Passito); Leone Conti (Vignapozzo – Secco; Vignacupa – Dolce; Non Ti Scordar di Me – Passito); Stefano Ferrucci (Secco; Dolce; Passito); Fattoria Paradiso (Gradisca – Passito); Tre Monti (Secco; Dolce; Passito); Tenuta Uccellina (Passito); Zerbina (Arrocco – Dolce; Scacco Matto – Passito).

OTHER WHITE GRAPES

PAGADEBIT/BOMBINO BIANCO

The name Pagadebit, which means 'pays the debts', referring to a vine-type capable of sizeable production, seems to have been applied at one time or another to a variety of grapes, not necessarily connected. The particular strain under consideration here is mostly to be found in the province of Forlì in eastern Romagna. Grown in Bertinoro it may add the name of the commune to the head-DOC Pagadebit di Romagna. Either way its wines may be Secco or Amabile, even *frizzante*; rarely memorable.

According to the official *Codice Denominazione di Origine dei Vini* Pagadebit is none other than Bombino Bianco, whose origins may, or may not, be Spanish. As the same august opus also specifically equates Bombino Bianco with Trebbiano d'Abruzzo, one is led to understand that Pagadebit is, therefore, the same as Trebbiano d'Abruzzo. 'However', intone Salvatore Del Gaudio and Domenico Giusto in *Principali Vitigni*, 'the descriptions of "Trebbiano abruzzese", of "Cacciò" and of "Pagadebito", studied by us in the province of Brindisi, differentiate themselves from one another in several respects, so that in the last analysis it seems possible definitely to state that the three are different varieties.'

One could ask whether the 'Pagadebito' studied in deepest Puglia is the same as the one found in Romagna. Anyway, not for the first time in the field of Italian ampelography, the situation is far from clear.

BIANCAME, BIANCHELLO, PASSERINA

These, according to some authorities, are synonyms for a variety grown in various parts of the Marche and figuring in such world-famous dry white DOCs as Bianchello del Metauro and Falerio dei Colli Ascolani, as well as in the red Rosso Piceno. Calò et al. seem to deny the identity of Biancame and Bianchello with Passerina, giving no reference to the first two, only to Passerina.

A good producer of Bianchello di Metauro is Claudio **Morelli** (La Vigna delle Terrazze; Borgo Torre; San Cesareo) of Fano in the province of Pesaro in northern Marche. Umani Ronchi's version is also very acceptable. Tenuta Cocci Grifoni, of Ripatransone in the province of Ascoli Piceno in the south, uses the name Passerina for their sparkling Brut. Passerina is also the name preferred in Abruzzo, where it forms the base of a sub-DOC under the recently established multi-DOC Controguerra; and in Latium, in the province of Frosinone. Passerina del Frusinate IGT is produced at a respectable level by **Massimi Berucci** at Piglio, **Coletti Conti** (Hernicus) at Anagni and **La Selva** at Paliano.

MACERATINO

Colli Maceratesi Bianco, an insignificant dry white from the province of Macerata in the Marche, is based on this variety whose already considerable obscurity is deepening progressively. It has been suggested that Maceratino is a sub-variety of Verdicchio, though the fact that the latter is specifically mentioned as a minority component of the DOC suggests that the relationship, if any, is tenuous. More probably, Maceratino is a member of the rather large and diffuse group of Grecos.

The excellent Boccadigabbia is the most prominent producer of Colli Maceratesi Bianco (Villamagna). Fattoria di **Forano** (Villa Forano), of Appignano, and **Saputi** (Castru Vecchio) of Colmurano, are two others.

PECORINO

Not a ewe's milk cheese, but another variety of eastern central origin which, perhaps because of a tendency to strident acidity, was heading in the direction of extinction when it was taken in hand by

Guido Cocci Grifoni of the eponymous *azienda* at Ripatransone. Cocci Grifoni's varietal Podere Colle Vecchio, while sharp, has almost enough fruit and interest to bring it into balance, and certainly it is a wine one should drink at least once, for the experience. There is an element of Pecorino, too, in the blend of Falerio dei Colli Ascolani Vigneti San Basso, this latter, however, having a roundness and a balance that the varietal can lack except in exceptional years.

FALANGHINA, GRECO

There is a very limited production of these grapes, together with Aglianico, in Molise (di Majo Norante). For general comments see Chapter 4, South and Islands, Campania.

4

The South and Islands

In these early years of the twenty-first century, as denizens of the wine world wax ever more feverish about the prospects for vineyard southern Italy, it is worth remembering that this has been wine country since at least the early centuries of the millennium before Christ. Greeks trading with and colonising parts of what they called Magna Grecia brought with them an already sophisticated wine culture, aspects of which survive and indeed thrive to this day. These include a system of training, which modern viticulturists are 're-discovering' as being one of the best in existence in terms of plant self-regulation, the *alberello* or bush; a unique style of wine-making using semi-dried grapes for the making of strong, time- and oxidation-resistant wines, today called *passiti*; and a number of excellent grape varieties some of whose names bespeak their ancient origin – Aglianico (hellenicum), Greco, Grecanico to mention three.

Like the Midi in France, Italy's Mezzogiorno – an exact translation of Midi – is a land of enormous promise; a fact that is today attracting serious wine people to it from other parts of Italy and the world. Indeed, given the number of unique grape varieties the Mezzogiorno disposes of, her promise is considerably greater.

But if the promise is great, the production is enormous. As a rough average, these six regions between them grow enough wine-grapes to rival the world's third largest producer, Spain. Just two regions, Puglia and Sicily, were they a single nation, which is quite unthinkable, would be the world's fourth or fifth biggest producer.

For despite its noble if distant past, the south in the twentieth century came to be treated as a source of concentrated grape must or high-octane blending wines for use – no longer permitted – in products like Chianti or Valpolicella, or by the vermouth industry

ABRUZZO

See Central East map for this area

MOLISE

LATIUM

Frosinone

See Central West map for this area

Isernia

Campobasso

San Severo

19

Lucera

Troia

Foggia

Orta Nuova

Cerignola

Canosa

20

Galluccio

Volturno

Solopaca

Castelvenere

Ponte

Cervaro

Cellole

1

Guardia Sanframondi

6

Benevento

7

Torrecuso

Foglianise

8

Caserta

Teverola

Sant'Agata de Goti

9

Taurasi

Barile

18

Aversa

2

Tufo

10

Salza Irpinia

11

Rionero

Quarto

Avellino

Atripalda

12

Montemarano

Naples

3

4

Sorbo Serpico

CAMPANIA

Potenza

Forio d'Ischia

5

Tramontio

Ravello

Salerno

BASI

ISCHIA

Sorrento

13

14

Amalfi

Furore

16

CAPRI

Castel San Lorenzo

16

Tyrrhenian Sea

Prignano Cilento

San Marco di Castellabate

17

Inset Map

continued from main map

37

Nocera Terinese

Catanzaro

Lamezia

38

Isola di Capo Rizzuto

35

CALABRIA

Bivongi

Verbicaro

Messina

SICILY

Bianco

Reggio di Calabria

Key to WINE ZONES
CALABRIA
35. Pollino
36. Donnici
37. Savuto
38. Scavigna
39. Lamezia
40. Ciro
41. Melissa
42. Greco di Bianco

Southern mainland

Key to WINE ZONES

CAMPANIA
1. Falerno del Massico
2. Aversa
3. Campi Flegrei
4. Vesuvio/Lacryma Christi
5. Ischia
6. Solopaca
7. Sannio
8. Taburno
9. Sant' Agata dei Goti
10. Greco di Tufo
11. Taurasi
12. Fiano di Avellino
13. Penisola Sorrentina
14. Costa d'Amalfi
15. Capri
16. Castel San Lorenzo
17. Cilento

BASILICATA
18. Aglianico del Vulture

PUGLIA
19. San Severo
20. Moscato di Trani
21. Castel del Monte
22. Gravina
23. Gioia del Colle
24. Locorolondo
25. Martina Franca
26. Ostuni
27. Primitivo di Manduria
28. Brindisi
29. Salice Salentino
30. Squinzano
31. Copertino
32. Leverano
33. Alezia
34. Nardo

Adriatic Sea

Barletta
Trani
Andria
Corato
PUGLIA
Bari

21 20

Fasano

Gravina 22

Gioia del Colle 23

Locorotondo 24

Ostuni 26

Martina Franca 25

Brindisi

28

San Pietro Vernotico

Latiano
Cellino
San Marco
Sandonaci 29
Manduria
Sava
Avetrana
Guagnano

Squinzano 30

Taranto
Lizzano
27 Salice Salentino
Maruggio

Leverano 32
Lecce
Copertino 31

Nardo 34

Galatina

Alezia
33
Matino

Ugento

Matera
Basento
Gravina 22

ICATA

Agri

N

Ionian Sea

Pollino 35

CALABRIA

San Vito di Luzzi
Cosenza
Donnici 36

Ciro 40 Ciro Marina
Melissa

Neto 41

Crotone

avuto
Nocera Terinese

continued on inset map

o Main wine towns
• Other wine towns
■ Regional capital
□ Provincial capital
˜ Regional boundary

0   kilometres   50

243

of the north or, ironically, by the French for purposes of giving body to the low alcohol *pinard* produced, or rather vastly over-produced, in the Midi. The percentage of total wine produced which finds its way into bottle, giving producers that bit of added value, is even in the early years of the present century quite derisory.

So while sharing the potential of the Midi, the Mezzogiorno has a long way to go before it emulates its rival's success. What those old Greeks knew had, by the middle of the twentieth century, been largely forgotten: that plenty of sun, limited rainfall with an element of stress, a lean, stony–rocky soil of good structure but lacking organic richness all add up to good wine provided you don't force the crops, you pick at the right time and you follow correct procedures in the winery. This is now being recognised in so many of the world's newer quality producing zones – Chile, Argentina, Australia to name a few; and even in the Midi, and parts of France. Why so late in Enotria itself?

The answer, of course, is that while the number of those who have woken up, or are waking up, to the potential is growing visibly, and beginning to receive quite a lot of journalistic hype, they are still a tiny minority in terms of numbers of growers/producers and even of total hectolitres produced. Every region can name a few good-to-excellent independent producers of medium to large size who have been around for a long time: Mastroberardino in Campania, Rivera in Puglia, Librandi in Calabria, Regaleali and Duca di Salaparuta/Corvo in Sicily, Sella & Mosca in Sardinia, for example, to each of whom special credit must be given for having pursued the quality line for decades before others contemplated following them. More recently there have been carpetbaggers from the north, indeed from abroad, who have seen what rich pickings the south might offer and who have begun investing there: these include Antinori, Kendall Jackson, Gruppo Italiano Vini, Zonin, Pasqua, Santa Margherita and, very recently, Ilva of Saronno (Amaretto) who have taken over the giant Corvo. Even successful southerners, like Feudi di San Gregorio of Campania and Calatrasi of Sicily, are spreading to other zones and, where Calatrasi is concerned, to other countries (Tunisia).

Likewise, every region can name the odd switched-on *cantina sociale* – Taburno in Campania, Copertino in Puglia, Settesoli in Sicily, Dolianova in Sardinia to name a few. But the south, still dominated in terms of volume by co-operatives even though their power has diminished much of late, seems on the whole content to trundle on in its 'traditional' way, using that much abused word to justify their resistance to change. And the small grape-farmers, who are legion, continue to regard viticulture as a sideline or a more-or-less enjoyable hobby rather than as an actual or potential business in its own right.

Members of the Lega del Nord denigrate southerners as *arabi*, people whose attitude to work and responsibility resembles that of the archetypal Mexican according to Gringos. 'This is not just another part of Italy, it's another country', was one comment. I am bound to say that, in the course of considerable dealings with southern Italians, I have more than once come upon delay, denial and evasion, tortuous thinking and dealing, even when such behaviour seems patently to run against the subject's own interests. A southerner is likely to have an idea about this or that wedged firmly in his mind, and nothing you can say will dislodge it. After a while one is simply obliged to recognise that reason will get you nowhere and that you might as well stop banging your head against the wall.

A much more insidious and altogether less charming aspect of non-change is bureaucracy, a blight admittedly endemic to the entire Italian state, but one which seems particularly to paralyse the south. The southern Italian bureaucrat's special function in life is to make sure that he justifies his existence and covers himself, especially in relation to his superiors, in such a way that if anything goes wrong he is not to blame. The best way to ensure that nothing goes wrong is to arrange for nothing to happen at all. This helps no end to frustrate inward investment and maintain *status quo* in a situation where rationalists might consider change to be urgently needed.

The people who were doing well out of the situation as it was until about a decade ago (booming bulk wine market and lots of juicy EU subsidies), that's to say the industrial and bulk wine merchants and the Mafia under one or another of its several sobriquets, have contributed much to the non-progress of the south. Now that bulk sales are declining and the subsidies are phasing out we are beginning to see a bit of enterprise among the previously too timid or too smug. But there is still plenty of mileage for the industrial producer who wants to control production and distribution and who would consider a flowering of small and medium-sized producer-bottlers threatening, since if they make good money bottling their wines he no longer gets their grapes, or at least not the best ones, and not as cheaply as before.

Indeed the old-style Mafia is still in the old-style business even today. One producer from the north, who bought a 300-hectare estate in Puglia, told of having to pull out following a series of fires on the estate after he had declined to contribute to a group which had promised him freedom from fires.

Despite all this, however, there *is* an increasing interest in the south from without, and a growing sense within, that there is a world out there that wants certain types of products at certain prices and that the south can provide these if only it can get its act together before it's too late. Today, 'experts' are being called in to advise on viticultural practices, oenological procedures and marketing; universities are taking an interest in long-neglected grape varieties, all kinds of tests are being carried out in respect of root-stocks, non-traditional varieties, new clones of traditional varieties, planting densities, training systems, fermentation temperatures, enzymes, yeasts, bacteria, blends, ageing methods, different oaks, complete with multiple micro-fermentations – highly complex operations requiring years before any kind of conclusion can be drawn. And, of course, the high-flying consultant oenologists of the north and centre are being called in increasingly to help southern producers produce vinous miracles in the shortest possible time.

So this is not the time to draw conclusions as to what the south will become in the new millennium. It could go either way, becoming the 'New California' that certain journalists have prematurely hyped it as, with specific reference to Sicily; or that bubble could burst to reveal that it was all just another misconceived marketing exercise. What one can say is that, in view of the tremendous potential that undeniably exists, if it goes the wrong way the producers of the Mezzogiorno will have only themselves to blame – if only for not standing up to the forces, psychological and external, which would hold them back.

Until now the zones we have considered have hung together thematically as far as ampelographical factors are concerned. The north west revolves around Piemonte, which shares Nebbiolo with Valle d'Aosta and Lombardy and Barbera with Lombardy and Emilia, Dolcetto and Vermentino with Liguria; although Piemonte's version of Vermentino, Favorita, would have come from the south rather than the other way round (see Sardinia). In the north east, apart from important pockets of autochthonous varieties in the Veneto, international grapes dominate the scene. In the centre west Sangiovese rules supreme, with Trebbiano and Malvasia also being found throughout. The same minus Malvasia are also dominant in the centre east, with Montepulciano taking over from Sangiovese as you go south.

In the south of Italy there are few such inter-regional binding factors. Basilicata aside, where the sole significant grape, Aglianico, is at least equally Campanian, each region has, and in many cases has specialised in, for centuries if not millennia, its unique varieties.

In such a situation, I propose in this section to consider each region (with the exception of Basilicata, for reasons explained) as a separate entity, starting with . . .

CAMPANIA AND BASILICATA

Talk about potential, there is virtually no region in Italy which can beat Campania in that department, though there are one or two areas in the south that could rival it. This is based partly on the fact that Campania, once, was the vineyard of the Romans, home to the imperial *grand cru* Falernian. Rome in the form of the sixteenth-century Papacy seems to have shared the view that Campanian wines were the nearest thing to nectar. It wasn't until the twentieth century that they slipped to so low a pass that even as recently as 1990 Burton Anderson could describe the Campanian wine-scene, with the shining exception of the house of Mastroberardino, as one of 'mediocrity . . . that still shows only feeble signs of recovery'.

Another aspect of this 'potential' relates to Campania's topography. Inland Campania, where much of the best viticulture is practised today, in the provinces of Avellino and Benevento, is hilly-going-on-mountainous, the Apennine ridge running right through the heart of the region. Some of the best vineyards, for red grapes, are as high as 500 metres, and for white grapes considerably higher. Latitude is thus to a large extent mitigated by altitude, to the extent that some of the latest-picked vineyards in Italy – nay, Europe – are in Campania; and not for white dessert wines, but red table wines.

However, the essence of Campania's recent spirited attempt to rise from the ashes of its own self-immolation is ampelographical. In the 1930s according to one expert, Campania boasted no fewer than 400 different grape varieties, some of them certainly and many of them possibly of ancient Greek origin. Although there remain only about a tenth of that number in today's commercial vineyards it still leaves 40, including such stars as Aglianico and Piedirosso in the red category, Falanghina, Fiano, Greco di Tufo, Coda di Volpe, Biancolella, Forastera among the whites. Some of these are grown only in a very restricted area – like Fiano in Avellino or Forastera on the island of Ischia. But such has been the *rinascimento* of the Campanian wine scene in the 1990s that for every single one of the above-listed grapes there is today someone, somewhere in Campania, making wine from it that is exciting, or verging on the exciting, wine of real character at prices that are still on the whole, if not cheap, reasonable. And as I am fond of saying, if one person is achieving excellence with a grape variety it means that others can do it too.

The list of the significant place names of the Campanian wine scene must begin with Taurasi, actually a small village in the inland/upland Province of Avellino (historical name: Irpinia, after which the local IGT is named), which gives its name to the south's most famous red wine, based on Aglianico (with 15% of other recommended or authorised grapes also admitted). Taurasi achieved DOCG status in 1993, and few would dispute its credentials, which is more than you can say for some.

Not far from Taurasi, due north of Avellino, is the village of Tufo, which gives its name both to a DOC white wine and to the grape from which it is made: Greco di Tufo. Needless to say the soil is predominantly volcanic *tufa*, ideal for white wine production. As for Avellino itself, its name is associated with the wines of another fine white grape, named Fiano. Each of these may contain up to 15% Coda di Volpe, while Fiano di Avellino may also add Greco and/or that insidious Trebbiano Toscano provided that the total of Fiano is not less than 85%.

In the province of Benevento Solopaca is moderately well known. This is another village giving its name to a DOC – a multi-DOC this time, embracing varietals like Aglianico and Falanghina as well as including the more conventional Trebbiano Toscano and Malvasia (Solopaca Bianco) and Sangiovese (Solopaca Rosso; plus Aglianico).

Deserving greater recognition is <u>Taburno</u>, this being the name of a mountain or group of mountains as well as a multi-DOC, created in 1993, which includes Aglianico, Piedirosso, Falanghina, Greco di Tufo and Coda di Volpe as well as a Bianco (Trebbiano Toscano and Falanghina), a Rosso (Sangiovese and Aglianico), a Novello (Aglianico) and a Spumante (Coda di Volpe and Falanghina). Production is dominated by the Cantina Sociale del Taburno.

Another relatively new name on the Benevento DOC scene, though distinctly less utilised as yet than Taburno, is <u>Sant'Agata de' Goti</u>. A small multi-DOC, production is dominated by the Mustilli estate, which turns out DOC reds based on Aglianico and Piedirosso as well as whites from Falanghina and Greco. Recently established too, and at present rather obscure, is <u>Guardia Sanframondi</u> or <u>Guardiolo</u> DOC: Bianco (Malvasia plus Falanghina), Rosso (Sangiovese 80% plus others), Falanghina, Aglianico, Spumante (Falanghina plus others). More recent still is <u>Sannio</u>, home of the ancient Samnites, the authors of whose *disciplinare* could not be accused of revolutionary fervour in their choice of grape varieties for their Bianco (Trebbiano Toscano at minimum 50% plus others) and Rosso (Sangiovese at minimum 50% plus others). The multi-DOC does, however, cover the following varietals: Aglianico, Barbera, Piedirosso and Sciascinoso (red); Coda di Volpe, Falanghina, Fiano, Greco and Moscato (white). Several of these may be made as *passito* wines, *secco* or *amabile*.

In the Province of Caserta, in the vicinity of Mount Massico north of Naples near both the coast and the Latian border, <u>Falerno del Massico</u> made in 1989 a reappearance after nearly two millennia in the shade. The Roman Falernian was, apparently, a white wine, quite possibly made as today from Falanghina. Today the name Falerno is also used for a Rosso, based on Aglianico and Piedirosso. The DOC caters too for a varietal Primitivo, something of a one-off as practically all Primitivo is cultivated today in Puglia.

Caserta also boasts a newish DOC called <u>Galluccio</u>, whose Bianco is based on Falanghina and whose Rosso is mainly Aglianico.

In the province of Naples the most famous name, although for eruptions other than vinous, is <u>Vesuvio</u> (no prizes for guessing the soil type), whose Bianco is based on Coda di Volpe with possible inclusion of Verdeca, Falanghina and Greco di Tufo. The Rosso or Rosato are mainly Piedirosso with some Sciascinoso and Aglianico. No one quite knows what the historic Lacryma Christi consisted of, but today's Vesuvio, of any hue, may be preceded by the commercially valuable words 'Lacryma Christi del' provided it has a half-degree more alcohol than the *normale*. White Lacryma Christi del Vesuvio may also come in the sweet Liquoroso style, or as a Spumante.

The picturesque peninsula of Sorrento is glorified by the DOC Penisola Sorrentina, whose Bianco consists of Falanghina at 40% minimum and/or Biancolella and/or Greco and/or others up to 40%, and whose Rosso mirrors those higher mathematics with Piedirosso in the starring role supported by Sciascinoso and/or Aglianico plus others.

On the other side of Naples Bay is the curious zone of Campi Flegrei, where the land rises and falls by several feet when the spirits of the underworld decree, said spirits sending up in various places a constant flow of steam to accompany the heaving rhythm. The soil here is volcanic, needless to say, but also sandy, and the vines are for the most part ungrafted. There aren't many places in Europe of which that can be said; only the spirits know how long it will last. As for the wines, the Bianco consists of Falanghina aided by Biancolella and Coda di Volpe, the Rosso of Piedirosso with Aglianico and Sciascinoso, though both Falanghina and Piedirosso may be produced varietally.

Another curiosity partly of this province (though it's mostly in Caserta) is the DOC Aversa, a sparkling wine made from the ancient Asprinio variety traditionally trained up poplar trees to a great height (though in its modern form it is trained to *spalliera*). In tree-supported vineyards the bizarre *disciplinare* allows no more than 50 plants per hectare with a yield per plant of up to 200 kilos! – one can imagine, then, the height of some of these vines. The phenomenon is typically Etruscan as distinct from Greek, and the admittance of the two distinct styles of training testifies to the fact that it was in Campania that the two greatest influences on Italian viticulture came face to face in the days before Rome was a power.

The islands of Capri and Ischia are also in the province of Naples. The former is of little distinction either qualitatively or quantitatively, though the DOC Bianco and Rosso are based on local varieties (Falanghina/Greco and Piedirosso). From the steep slopes of Ischia, on the other hand, come some excellent whites, mainly made by the firm of d'Ambra from a cast of varieties which stars the homespun Forastera and Biancolella among whites, Piedirosso and Guarnaccia among reds. Other local grapes getting less and less of a look-in are San Lunardo and Uvarilla (white) and Cannamelù (red).

Least prominent among Campania's wine provinces is Salerno, where modest quantities of Castel San Lorenzo are made from Barbera and Sangiovese (red) and Trebbiano and Malvasia (white). Such wines are predictably boring, though a Moscato similar to Asti's, here called 'Lambiccato', may amuse. The glorious, precipitous Amalfi coast brings forth small quantities of Costa d'Amalfi Rosso and Bianco from local varieties – Piedirosso and Sciascinoso for the former, Falanghina and Biancolella for the latter. Sub-zones of the DOC may be specified according to village: Furore, Tramonti and the touristically challenged Ravello.

From the southernmost section of the region come the obscurish wines of Cilento, where Aglianico may be used on its own or in blend, in the Rosso, with Piedirosso, Barbera and Primitivo; the Bianco being a centre–south blend of Fiano, Trebbiano, Greco di Tufo and Malvasia.

Salerno province's most famous wine is, however, undoubtedly Montevetrano, the Cabernet–Merlot–Aglianico blend from San Cipriano Picentino that shot to fame and became a sell-out a few years ago when Robert Parker awarded it a staggering 96 points.

Driving east from Naples, across the Apennine ridge towards the Adriatic coast, one would miss the region of Basilicata altogether if one stuck to the *autostrada*, ending up in Puglia south of Foggia. Taking the exit at Candela, but turning south towards Potenza instead of north towards Foggia, one would, however, pass Melfi and Barile (once a thriving barrel-manufacturing centre, from which the container derived its name) before arriving at the rather ramshackle town of Rionero. We are, at 650 metres altitude, in the centre of Basilicata's sole significant wine-producing zone, on the slopes of the extinct volcano Mount Vulture.

Mount Vulture rises to a height of nearly 1,400 metres, and it is in its shadow and on its rich volcanic soil that the best viticulture takes place, mainly downhill from the town at between 400 and 600 metres. Despite its southern situation, this is one of the coolest red wine-producing areas of Italy, especially in respect of night-time temperatures which can descend dramatically, favouring acidity but also aromas.

Some non-native white varieties – Chardonnay, Pinot Bianco, Incrocio Manzoni from the Veneto – are beginning to enter here, the climate being considered suitable for white wine production; indeed Moscato and Malvasia, artisanal and non-DOC but nicely aromatic, are traditional. It is comforting to note, however, that growers retain sufficient confidence in the potential of their beloved Aglianico that the likes of Cabernet and Merlot have so far made little impression.

The Aglianico del Vulture DOC zone actually extends well beyond the slopes of the mountain, stretching in fact from the Ofanto river which defines the Campanian/Puglian border to west and north as far as Lago di Serra di Corvo on the Puglian border to the east; in other words, the northern tip of the region. Perhaps Aglianico from Vulture should be called 'Classico', as in other parts of Italy, to distinguish it from the rather less refined products of lower down, whether from the Venosa plateau within the DOC area or from the hotter plains around Matera heading for the Gulf of Taranto. In particular, none of these latter has the crucial quality factor, which is Vulture's lavic soil.

But playing politics has never been a forte of growers here. As one producer said, the vultures disappeared from the mountain long ago; the politicians have taken over.

GRAPES, WINES AND PRODUCERS – RED

AGLIANICO

There are those who would rank this variety in the top three of Italy, alongside Nebbiolo and Sangiovese. It has to be said that hard, or rather liquid, evidence for such an assertion was somewhat lacking until recently, though it is also true that such evidence is beginning now to accumulate. It is perhaps fair to qualify Aglianico as the Mezzogiorno's nearest thing to a great red grape variety, although producers of Sicily's Nero d'Avola, Puglia's Negroamaro, Sardinia's Carignano plus one or two others might reasonably object.

The name has traditionally been said to derive from the word 'Hellenicum', meaning Greek – reasonable enough, since it is generally agreed to be of Greek origin; but this version is challenged by some who say it derives from Gauranico or Guarano which was a type of Falernian, according to Pliny.

Two regions, Campania and Basilicata, dispute the honour of being Aglianico's real home. Historically, the most probable scenario is that it arrived from Greece, perhaps carried by Phoenicians, between two and a half and three thousand years ago at a port near Naples, from which it would have spread up the coast towards Monte Massico, where Falernian came from, as well as inland by way of river routes, establishing itself in parts of Basilicata and west central Puglia, where as in other areas it would have proceeded to develop local characteristics as well as local names.

In Campania the most high-profile cultivation zone in recent times has been the historic area called Irpinia in the province of Avellino, and more specifically in the argillaceous–volcanic soils of the commune of Taurasi, at altitudes between 300 and 500 metres – high indeed for a red fine wine grape. One reason for this requirement for altitude seems to be that the grape grows in a contained way only where there are sharp differences between daytime and night-time temperatures – otherwise, in the heat of coastal areas, it is liable to go wild with vegetation, to produce too much sugar and to lose balance.

The predominant sub-variety here, Aglianico del Taurasi, is said to be the richest and most structured, hence the ability of its wines to age well over a period of decades.

A Campanian zone less well known for Aglianico, but equally valid with a considerably higher production, is the province of Benevento, where the main sub-variety is called Aglianico Amaro (literally 'bitter', though I'm told it's really a reference to the acidity). Producers claim Amaro as the most elegant of Aglianicos, although exactly how that squares with high acidity, or indeed bitterness, I'm not too sure.

In the region of Basilicata by far the most important growing zone for Aglianico is on the steep slopes of Monte Vulture and the gentler ones of the Venosa plateau. Aglianico del Vulture is in fact the name of the sub-variety here, claimed by locals to be the most mellow and – would you believe – best of those extant.

The salient features of Aglianico generally are a medium-thick skin enabling it to resist botrytis far into the autumn and a very late ripening period for a hot-climate variety, being harvested usually in the later half of October and into November, although earlier-ripening clones are now being developed. This feature, which it shares with Nebbiolo, doubtless contributes to its very considerable potential for complexity of flavour and perfume. It also shares Nebbiolo's tendency to high tannin and acid levels, especially malic acid, making a full malo-lactic fermentation essential for achieving user-friendliness. On the other hand, the natural acids give Aglianico-based wines very considerable ageing potential.

A variety of training systems is employed depending on locality: *canneto*, the bamboo-supported teepee-type *alberello* adaptation traditional in Rionero; *raggiera*, the Etruscan-style four-branched high-training method employed in Benevento; and even, in some older promiscuous vineyards, training up trees in the ancient Etruscan mode. But for serious wines, and most new plantings nowadays, the low-trained *spalliera/cordone speronato* tends to be favoured.

Aglianico is also grown in other parts of Campania and Basilicata as well as in pockets of Molise, Puglia and Calabria.

The wines in Campania

Despite a limited production of just a few thousand hectolitres per annum, and despite virtually total domination until fairly recently by a single *azienda*, the greatest reputation of all Aglianico wines belongs to Taurasi, the south's first DOCG. Taurasi is allowed to be blended with up to 15% of 'other non-aromatic red grapes' recommended or authorised for the province of Avellino, but internationals are not included and the most serious producers do not accept the law's offer, preferring Aglianico *in purezza*. The uppish altitude of the vineyards, plus the long growing season, tend to favour aroma rather than power, so Taurasi is not at all potent or burnt as one might expect from the south, but rather tends towards the complex and austere. It can take a number of years fully to open out, but when it does it can be magnificent, as demonstrated by the classic 1968 Riserva of Mastroberardino, a wine of amazing elegance, intensity and length, despite a modest alcohol level for these latitudes. On this subject, Antonio Mastroberardino, the doyen of the wines of Irpinia (the historic name of this upland zone), comments: 'To get 13 degrees is difficult; 14 is exceptional; 15 doesn't exist'; and this in the context of the magnificent 2000 harvest, when they did get near to the mythical 15%.

Taurasi today must be aged for three years of which one is in barrel, while the Riserva must be aged four years of which 18 months are in barrel. Its typical aromas are claimed to include wild cherry, blackcurrant and *frutti di bosco*.

Surprisingly, for a wine of such calibre, a production of 10 tonnes per hectare is permitted. Yields for the best wines are, however, considerably lower than this.

As indicated, production of Taurasi has historically been dominated by one producer, namely **Mastroberardino** of Atripalda near Avellino. Mastroberardino, in fact, make a range of wines covering most of the native varietals of Campania, but since they are best known for Taurasi it is appropriate to consider them here, together with the other principal wines of their production.

Everything about Mastroberardino exudes a sense of history. The house was founded in the seventeenth century on the site where the present winery, built in the nineteenth century, stands, and the present generation running the operation, the children of Antonio Mastroberardino, Carlo and Piero – the latter a university professor in his spare time – are tenth generation. Antonio himself, who remains the chief winemaker, began in this role in the mid-1940s. They were exporting the majority of their production as long ago as the late nineteenth century, something which practically no other producer in Italy today could say. In the winery they have a library of old books going back in some cases to the early days of printing, some of them by Latin authors like Pliny, the name of whose magnum opus, *Naturalis Historia*, they have used for a new wine recently unveiled.

Yet there are no cobwebs here, either in the buildings or in the minds of the Mastroberardinos. While retaining the laudable policy of using only native Campanian grapes – they have **no** Cabernet, Merlot, Chardonnay etc. in the 300+ hectares of vineyard they own or control under contract; only Aglianico, Fiano and Greco in Irpinia, with Coda di Volpe and Piedirosso at Vesuvius – they have gone towards consumer tastes with the use, occasionally exaggerated, of *barriques* for whites as well as reds. Their winery, though housed in a nineteenth-century building, is super high-tech with, for example, different software for computer control of every grape variety. They are making a heavy investment in bottle ageing, with half a million bottles at any given time resting in their designer cellars, and they are constantly devising ways of upgrading both their range and their packaging.

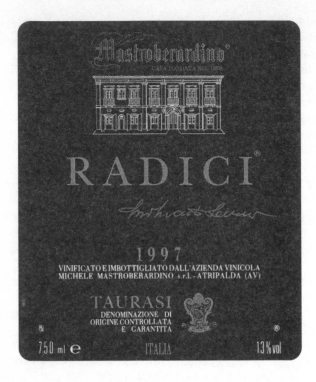

So Mastroberardino, despite their vast seniority in the context of the wines of Irpinia, should not be seen as either too old-hat – which they have been accused of – or too technical. Their aim is the marriage of the traditional and the contemporary. An example of this is their recently introduced *cru* Fiano, More Maiorum ('in the manner of the elders'), which they see as back-to-the-future because it reintroduces the concept of the aged white wine (6 months in *barrique*, then 2½ years, no less, in bottle). The process of cask ageing itself, Antonio argues, is neither new nor even a French idea but something the Romans were doing in these parts 2,000 years ago; and he will find a text in one of his old books to prove it. Their established *cru* Fiano, Radici, and the *cru* Greco di Tufo, Nova Serra, are since 1999 vinified but not aged in wood, which allows them contact with organic material during the stages of biochemical change without picking up noticeable oak aromas. The latest addition to the range, the previously mentioned Naturalis Historia, is a blend, not of Aglianico and Cabernet, but of Aglianico and Piedirosso, more associated with the Campanian coast, whose fleshy fruitiness and depth of colour do the same job as Cabernet without the intrusive aromas.

Perhaps the most exciting project they are working on, in conjunction with the Campanian government, is an experimental vineyard in the Vesuvian village of Pompey, planted in the Roman style to the traditional grapes of that zone, Coda di Volpe and Piedirosso. It is a perfect expression, not just of the tradition-inspired modernity of Mastroberardino, but of that of Italy as a whole.

As for their wines, Taurasi DOCG is obviously the flagship, and comes both as a *normale* and as the *cru* Radici (meaning 'roots'), from selected 'surmature' grapes of two different vineyards at an average of 500 metres altitude. This latter is a wine of some leanness in youth but which is capable of developing slowly in bottle to become (as for example in the 1988 that I tasted) very complete and harmonious, with clearly expressed red fruits and floral notes, a touch of tar and leather, capable of gracefully doubling its age at least. 'A shy person beginning to come out of its shell', I wrote. Not unlike its author.

Naturalis Historia could be a Taurasi, because the *disciplinare* does permit the 15% Piedirossi that it contains, but Mastroberardino don't want to confuse the public and have classed it as an Irpinia IGT. With its extra colour and degree it is a more modern wine, fleshier and fuller, with plenty of ripe red berry fruit, yet not without that touch of austerity which characterises classic Taurasi.

For the rest, Mastroberardino make a full range of wines from the grapes of Irpinia, including the Fiano More Maiorum already mentioned as well as a Fiano Radici to go with the Taurasi. They also make Lacryma Christi del Vesuvio red and white from Piedirosso and Coda di Volpe grapes.

Other good to excellent producers of Taurasi (T), or of Aglianico within the province of Avellino (IGT Irpinia), are: **Caggiano** (T. Vigna Macchia de' Goti; IGT Salae Domini), Taurasi; **Di Meo**, Salza Irpinia; **Feudi di San Gregorio** (T. Piano di Montevergine; IGT Rubrato; IGT Idem – with Piedirosso; IGT Serpico – with Merlot) Sorbo Serpico (see profile under Fiano); **Molettieri** (T. Vigna Cinque Querce; IGT Cinque Querce Rosso), Montemarano; **Struzziero**

(T. Campoceraso), Venticano; **Terre Dora** (T. Fatica Contadina; Il Principio) Montefusco (see profile under Greco).

In the province of Benevento, where conditions are similar to those in Avellino province, Aglianico appears under the multi-DOCs Sannio, Sant'Agata de' Goti, Solopaca and Taburno, the *disciplinari* of which allow between 10 and 15% addition of other red grapes of the zone. Good producers include: **Corte Normanna** (Sannio; Tre Pietre), Guardia Sanframondi; **De Lucia** (Sannio Adelchi; Solopaca Rosso Vassallo), Guardia Sanframondi; **Mustilli** (Sant'Agata de' Goti Aglianico Vigna Cesco di Nece), Sant'Agata de' Goti; **Ocone** (Aglianico del Taburno Pezza la Corte), Ponte; Orazio **Rillo**/Fontanavecchia (Aglianico del Taburno Vigna Cataratte), Torrecuso; Cantina del **Taburno** (Aglianico del Taburno Fidelio), Foglianise.

The other significant Campanian DOC featuring Aglianico is Falerno del Massico in Caserta province, up near the border with Latium, where Piedirossi, Primitivo and Barbera also come into the equation in the DOC. The ancient Falernian, apparently, was a white wine, so Aglianico is unlikely to have featured except possibly as *blanc de noirs*. Nevertheless some very fine not to say outstanding results are being obtained here, notably from two producers both followed oenologically by Riccardo Cotarella: **Villa Matilde** of Cellole (Falerno del Massico Rosso; Vigna Camarato; Aglianico di Roccamonfina); and **Galardi** of Sessa Aurunca (Terre di Lavoro – 80% Aglianico, 20% Piedirosso).

Two producers making good wine with Aglianico in the province of Salerno are **De Conciliis** (Naima – 100%; Zero – with other traditional varieties), at Prignano Cilento; and Luigi **Maffini** (Kleos – with Piedirosso), at San Marco di Castellabate.

The wines in Basilicata

The Aglianico wines of Monte Vulture in Basilicata have long been famed for their quality – the poet Horace was singing their praises a couple of thousand years ago. But in the mid to late twentieth century, as in so many other parts of Italy, quantity rather than quality became the prime criterion. Today more Aglianico del Vulture is bottled than there is DOC Aglianico in the whole of Campania, and there's a whole lot more still that gets sold in bulk to God knows whom for who knows what. The vast majority of the thousand or so vineyards are tiny plots worked by amateurs with other jobs or by farmers with other crops. Wine-production is controlled by co-operatives, and commercialisation is controlled by merchants, only a very few of whom, until very recently, have cared a damn about quality.

Those who do, however, can do an amazingly good job, and rightly claim parity with the best of Campania. As everywhere, *barrique* has begun to influence oenology here, and why not, one might consider, with the original barrel centre Barile itself on the slopes of the volcano which may be extinct today but whose legacy in the form of rich volcanic soil remains.

The producers

Casa Vinicola **D'Angelo**, Rionero in Vulture (pron. VOOL-too-ray). The grandfather of present owners, Donato and Lucio d'Angelo, began making wine in the early 1940s from grapes bought in from small growers. At first he worked only with bulk wine, but in the mid-1940s he started bottling. In the early 1960s his son Rocco built the present *cantina* in Rionero and from that time all wines were sold in bottle. Donato, having studied oenology at Conegliano, came into the winery in 1973, and from that time d'Angelo have been the major force in the wines of Vulture, and therefore in Basilicata.

In earlier days it was not necessary to own vineyards: there were hundreds of small growers from whom good grapes could be selected, especially if one paid a higher than average price for better quality. This remains true for the wines of Vulture more than for other regions. Nevertheless, it is always prudent to have one's own supply, which no one can take away. The phenomenon of growers using the best grapes for their own bottled product is beginning to happen here too, while at the same time small merchants are springing up to try and take advantage of the positive market situation built up by D'Angelo and a couple of others.

D'Angelo therefore purchased, in the mid-1980s, a 12-hectare site on the southern slopes of the mountain called Serra delle Querce, where he has planted mainly Aglianico with a bit of Merlot. Later he acquired the 5-hectare site of Caselle, from whose grapes he produces his Riserva. Today he estimates that around

two-thirds of his production under the d'Angelo label is covered by his own grapes. He also produces similar wines under the Tenuta del Portale label, for which all grapes are bought in.

It is worth noting that some of the more recent plantings of Aglianico at Serra delle Querce have been to a clone that d'Angelo have developed together with Professor Costacurta of the Istituto di Viticultura di Conegliano, called '*clone d'Angelo*'.

The d'Angelo wine *di base* is Aglianico del Vulture DOC, which according to the *disciplinare* must be 100% Aglianico. For a 'basic' wine it keeps up a high average standard, having good depth of fruit with hints of plum and bitter cherry, ripe tannins though some grip, and middling acidity; a wine of some elegance, aged in 50-hectolitre barrels for a year, no wood flavouring, thank God. The Riserva Vigna Caselle is made in a similar way, except that it gets two years in large barrel and displays extra concentration of fruit – red berry, *frutti di bosco* – and an extra finesse. Both of these have alcohol levels around 13%, not high for southern wine, as does the *cru* Canneto, an IGT Basilicata though it could be DOC. Canneto is made from from old vines with a yield of 4 tonnes per hectare (the DOC allows 10) and is aged 15 months in French *barrique*, one-third new, but the good news is that wood flavours do not impinge. The nose is of plums and tar and herbs, the palate is full but balanced with good acidity and firm but ripe tannins: a very serious wine, I noted.

Donato d'Angelo's new baby, of which he is very proud, is Serra delle Querce IGT, 70% Aglianico and 30% Merlot, aged in *barrique* separately, then blended. I agree that it is a well-made wine, but feel that the Canneto has more sheer personality.

Azienda Vinicola **Paternoster**, Barile. The Paternoster family have been involved in wine production in the town of the barrel, just round the mountain from Rionero, for generations, but it was Giuseppe, nicknamed Pino, the father of the present generation brothers Vito, Sergio and Anselmo and a graduate of Conegliano, who started bottling in the early 1950s. With d'Angelo they represent the old guard at Mount Vulture, though like them they continue to upgrade while respecting tradition, and their wines remain at an admirable level of quality even if they would perhaps not please the advocates of alcoholic fruit juice. Their circumstances are similar to those of d'Angelo too – they have some vineyards but still buy in a significant proportion of grapes from growers with whom they have long-standing agreements. Their *cantina*, like those of many smaller individual producers of the area – people who make wine for personal consumption – is excavated in the tufacous rock of the mountain.

Paternoster make about 100,000 bottles per annum of their basic Aglianico del Vulture DOC, a wine redolent of red berries and liquorice, having well-expressed varietal fruit on the palate and a structure which steers a judicious course between austerity and slackness.

Their top wine, about 12,000–15,000 bottles per annum, is an Aglianico del Vulture *cru* Don Anselmo, the grapes coming from old vineyards of very low production. This, which generally comes out some four to five years after the vintage, displays more spice and developed fruit on the nose and palate – they allow the grapes to surmature on the plant for 10–15 days in good years – with rounder tannins and a richer, more harmonious palate. An excellent example of a wine evolving to meet new market conditions without sacrificing identity.

Azienda Agricola **Basilisco**, Barile. Michele Cutolo is a gastro-enterologist with a mission to produce top wine from his seven hectares of vineyard on the slopes of Mount Vulture. As such he represents a breed that, though it be quite common in chi-chi places like Chianti Classico, is only beginning in remote Basilicata. The land here, he says, is 'excellent for vines but there are few decent winemakers'. He resolved this problem by hiring a consultant from Piemonte, Rossano Abbona, who oversees not only the vinification but also arranged for the wine to be bottled in Piemonte in the early years of production. Today Cutolo has his own small *cantina* dug into the tufa of the mountain and from the 1997 vintage he has been bottling *in situ*. He keeps things simple by producing just a few bottles – 20,000 at present, will rise to 30,000 and then stop – of a single wine, Basilisco Aglianico del Vulture DOC, which he ages in 20-hectolitre Slavonian oak *botti* with just a hint of *barrique*.

By harvesting late Cutolo is getting higher alcohol values than one would expect, or than are traditional, from these parts – 14.5% in 1999, nearly 14% in 2000. This hefty degree – also hefty colour and hefty concentration – no doubt will help to sell the wine in today's market, where big tends to mean beautiful. It remains to be seen how the wine ages in bottle, however, before investing it with the epithets 'elegant' and 'complex', as in the context of the classic style of wine from the zone.

Other producers of good Aglianico del Vulture are: **Basilium** (Valle del Trono), Acerenza; and Armando **Martino** (Oraziano), Rionero. Perhaps one should mention too the one called La Firma from **Cantina del Notaio**, of Gerardo Giuratrabocchetti, which was mentioned in an article in the influential magazine *Panorama* as being one of the 100 best wines of the world (no. 95, actually, but still). Needless to say the established producers were up in arms at this award to one who had only come out of the woodwork minutes before and who already was up there with Pétrus, Margaux and Sassicaia. Could there not, they wondered, have been a certain consideration involved in such an unlikely ranking? Surely not! Still, I haven't tasted it, so for all I know it deserves its meteoric rise to glory.

Outside the above areas the producers that I know of making reasonably good Aglianico are **di Majo Norante** in Molise (Terra degli Osci) and **Botromagno** in Gravina in Puglia (Pier delle Vigne – 60% Aglianico, 40 Montepulciano, *barrique*-aged). Aglianico is in fact a recommended variety in central Puglia's most famous DOC, Castel del Monte, as we will see under Puglia.

PIEDIROSSO

The name translates as 'red foot', and the grape is also known as Palombina or Per'e Palummo, meaning respectively little dove and dove's foot in dialect, the latter because of its red-coloured triple-branched stem like a three-taloned bird's foot. Calò et al. say that Piedirosso is very ancient and may be identical to the Colombina mentioned by Pliny.

I have heard it surmised in Campania that there is a resemblance to, not to say a kinship with, Friuli's Refosco which, you may recall, has a *peduncolo rosso*: a red stem. Both, it is said, are members of the Cot family of grapes, of which the best-known exemplar is Malbec.

The leaf-shapes of Piedirosso and Refosco, it should be said, are quite different. Nevertheless, the two do have points in common: intense colour, firm tannins, pointy acidity and wildfruit perfumes with a tendency to late ripening. The fact that sugar levels in Piedirosso easily surpass those of Refosco could be attributed to climatic factors.

Most wines which boast Piedirosso as a principal variety hail from the coastal area, which includes neighbouring islands; although the variety seems happy to oblige wherever it may find itself in Campania. Multi-DOCs which include Piedirosso as a named varietal include Taburno, Sant'Agata de' Goti, Campi Flegrei and Ischia, in which latter two it also makes a *passito*. Included in the DOC blend, either in majority or major-minority proportion, you will find Piedirosso in Flegrei Rosso, Capri Rosso, Cilento Rosso, Costa d'Amalfi Rosso, Falerno del Massico Rosso, Ischia Rosso, Penisola Sorrentino Rosso, Sant'Agata de' Goti Rosso (and Bianco!), Solopaca Rosso (optional) and Vesuvio Rosso, where it plays first fiddle to the world-famous Sciascinoso variety.

Producers include: Luigi Maffini (Cenito); **D'Ambra** (Ischia Per'e Palummo), Ischia; **Cuomo** (Costa d'Amalfi Furore Rosso Ris.; C. d'A. Ravello Rosso Ris.); Ocone; **Grotta del Sole** (Montegauro Riserva), Quarto.

OTHER RED GRAPES

SANGIOVESE

(For general remarks refer to section on centre west.)

Sangiovese is grown in all parts of Campania, generally being used as a blending grape, although it may be the principal presence in the following: Taburno Rosso; Sannio Rosso; Guardiolo (or Guardia Sanframondi) Rosso; Solopaca Rosso.

BARBERA

(For general remarks refer to section on the north west in *Barolo to Valpolicella*.)

Barbera has its own sub-DOC under the multi-DOCs of Castel San Lorenzo and Sannio, and dominates Sangiovese in the blend of Castel San Lorenzo Rosso and Rosato. It may have a presence in Falerno del Massico Rosso, also in Cilento Rosso, if you can find any. It is also found in the province of Benevento (Barbera del Beneventano – producer: Fattoria **Ciabrelli** at Castelvenere).

SCIASCINOSO (A.K.A. OLIVELLA)

Probably a Campanian native, though present also in parts of Latium, Sciascinoso may form part of the blend of the following

DOCs: Campi Flegrei Rosso; Costa d'Amalfi Rosso; Penisola Sorrentina Rosso; Solopaca Rosso; Vesuvio Rosso.

GUARNACCIA

Presumably Spain's Garnacha, or the Rhône's Grenache, perhaps via Sardinia's Cannonau, Guarnaccia informs the blend of Ischia Rosso together with Piedirosso.

PRIMITIVO

(For general remarks refer to the relevant section under Puglia.)

Brought to Campania from Puglia in 1910 by one Barone Falco, Primitivo has its own sub-DOC under the heading of Falerno del Massico. Michele **Moio** of Mondragone makes the best-known version. Primitivo may also form part of the blend of Falerno Rosso.

GRAPES, WINES AND PRODUCERS – WHITE

FIANO

Depending on what version you believe (if any), Fiano is either a native of Campania or a member of a family of grapes called Apianes brought to southern Italy from the Peloponnese, once called Apia. It is undoubtedly an ancient grape, mentioned specifically by Pliny in his *Naturalis Historia* ('*Apianis apes dedere cognomen, praecipue earum avidae*'; 'the bees gave Fiano its name, because of their desire (for it)'). Pliny's etymology has since been challenged on the grounds that it is not bees (*apes*), but wasps (*vespes*) that are attracted to the sweet grape, and it is claimed that the name really derives from either *appiano*, a type of apple, or Apia, once a place-name in the province of Avellino, now called Lapia, or *apium*, an aromatic plant of the celery family. It does in fact have an appley aroma, also herbal, but mercifully nothing reminiscent of celery.

Until recently it was cultivated almost exclusively in Irpinia, by Mastroberardino, whose veteran winemaker, Antonio Mastroberardino, claims to have rescued it from virtual extinction in the 1940s, his first vintage having been 1945, when, by gathering a bunch from here and bunch from there, he managed to produce 30 bottles. Yields need to be medium to low – not that difficult, considering its small berry and small bunch, limited amount of juice – to get real character from the grape, otherwise it slips all too easily into blandness. I noted in *Life Beyond Lambrusco* that Fiano needs to be sipped with considerable attention or its subtleties will pass you by and you will wonder what on earth you are paying so high a price for. Vinification techniques have improved, however, and several producers are making a much more luscious version than used to seem possible. 'Apple, pear and pineapple aromas, creamy texture, hints of toast and vanilla', I noted of a recently tasted version of Mastroberardino's More Maiorum.

In Campania, the only official mention of this grape outside of the Province of Avellino is in the blend of Cilento Bianco, which in any event exists more on paper than in real vineyards or bottles. Real bottles do come, however, from di Majo Norante in Molise. And Fiano is mentioned as a support grape in the *disciplinari* of Puglia's Locorotondo and Martina Franca. Today there are growers experimenting with Fiano in various parts of the south – Puglia, Basilicata and Sicily. Next thing you know it will be an international star, I don't think.

The producers

Feudi di San Gregorio, Sorbo Serpico. This trendy producer, making wines from most of the available range of Campanian varieties, might just as well have been reviewed under Aglianico in which they also specialise – indeed, slightly more. But it is with Fiano that they have made the greatest contribution, demonstrating the hitherto inadequately evidenced but regularly repeated assertion that Fiano is to be numbered among the great white grapes.

Feudi di San Gregorio are a relatively recent phenomenon on the Campanian wine scene – apart from Mastroberardino and d'Ambra who isn't? – but they have shot to the top in terms of international recognition, not just in a Campanian but in an all-Italian context. Owned by the brothers Ercolino – Mario the winemaker, Vincenzo the president, Luciano the administrator – and followed since 1999 by famous consultant oenologist Riccardo Cotarella, they started planting in the mid-1980s under the guidance of Professor Attilio Scienza and by the early 1990s were commercialising their wines.

They entered the new century heading for 100 hectares under vine at between 350 and 600 metres altitude and are aiming by 2004 to have 250, with operations under way in other parts of the south including Puglia and Molise. The philosophy is to produce wines from the historic indigenous vines of the south – although they do have some Merlot here and some Chardonnay in Puglia – using up-to-the minute research to identify the best soils/terroir, planting density, viticultural methods and of course clones for a given grape, as well as twenty-first-century technique and technology in making the wines; winemaking to take place, at least for Campanian wines, in a brand new state-or-the-art winery at Sorbo Serpico.

Feudi make four styles of pure Fiano. At the basic level, in the 'classico' range, is Fiano di Avellino DOC, from vineyards at between 400 and 500 metres above sea level. This is a wine of some fleshiness on the palate, having reasonable acidity for one which, like all Feudi's whites, has done the malo-lactic (they are looking for softness and roundness more than sharpness and brightness), with apple-pear and mineral notes, no oak. More interesting are the two late-harvest *crus*, the single-vineyard Pietracalda and the 'Selezione'

Campanaro, the latter picked at the end of October, fermented and aged six months in oak, a mix of large *botti* (Austrian oak) and French *barriques*. Campanaro is fermented out dry, achieving 13.5–14% alcohol with a certain degree of fatness and richness but nothing excessive, hints of honey and vanilla dominated by ripe apple and tropical fruit aromas – pineapple in particular. A wine of great personality.

Then there is Privilegio, made from surmature Fiano grapes which are then further dried on mats, with some botrytis occurring, to achieve a wine of opulent but not excessive sweetness which Mario Ercolino describes as '*come una spremuta di frutta*' ('like a freshly pressed fruit juice'). Mario is very proud of this wine. 'We should not make Sauternes – we need to make the most of our native fruit', he opines.

Fiano is also a principal component of another sweet wine in the 'Selezione' category, Idem Bianco – with, mainly, Moscato and Greco, Coda di Volpe and Falanghina – fresh, lively, fruity, medium-sweet with hints of orange peel and lemon.

Feudi's range is too broad to describe in detail, but their Grecos – DOC Greco di Tufo and the rich but dry, spicy/fruity late-harvest Cutizzi – and their Aglianicos – Taurasi *normale*, Taurasi *cru* Piano di Montevergine, the ripe but firm Rubrato and the *cru* Idem Rosso (with a bit of Piedirosso) – are all highly recommended at their level.

Probably their most high-profile wine is the IGT Serpico, made from 70% Aglianico plus Merlot (apparently Merlot has been cultivated in this area since before their relatively belated phylloxera outbreak; this is from 100-year-old ungrafted vines) and 'Sirica', which they think to be a type of Syrah (Mario also makes a pure 'Sirica' called Syriacus). This Serpico is a wine of full, rich colour, great extract, lots of ripe tannin, power and length – '*un vino che mi piace fare*', says Mario; '*un vino che risponde al mio gusto*' ('a wine I like making, a wine which responds to my taste'). And not only to his taste, but also to that of the most influential pundits and point-givers, Feudi being among the most feted of Italian producers today. Perhaps this, the combination of ancient grapes and modern techniques and concepts, is the way to glory for Italy generally.

Note, however, that Feudi will soon be bringing out a pure Merlot.

The only other significant producers of high quality Fiano are Antonio Caggiano (FiaGre – Fiano + Greco, dry, and Mel – same blend, sweet); Luigi Maffini (Kratos – with Greco); and of course Mastroberardino (Radici; Vignadora; More Maiorum).

GRECO DI TUFO

There are a number of grapes throughout Italy that bear the name Greco or something similar: Grechetto, Grecanico, Greco Bianco. Perhaps they are distantly linked, but it seems likely that the Greco of Campania, known more specifically as Greco di Tufo, is a variety on its own. It would in all likelihood have been imported from Greece during the first millennium BC, arriving at a port near present-day Naples and working its way inland until it arrived in the place now considered its classic domicile, in the environs of the village of Tufo in the province of Avellino. Like Fiano, it was heading for extinction in the middle of the twentieth century when rescued, according to him, by Antonio Mastroberardino.

There seems a reasonable chance that today's Greco di Tufo is none other than the Aminea Gemella mentioned by Pliny in his *Naturalis Historia* – Aminea because it belonged to a family of vines cultivated in the Aminea zone of 'Falernus Ager' in northern Campania; Gemella because it sprouts double or twin bunches about 50% of the time. Other ancient authors writing of the Aminea family include Cato, Varro, Virgil and Columella.

Greco di Tufo appreciates a tufaceous, volcanic soil, rich in sulphur, and a relatively dry micro-environment, in which case it can turn out a wine of good body and extract. Due to its colour at vintage time it is said to be the 'reddest of the whites', giving a must which without any maceration is distinctly pink in hue. The other Grecos of Campania, such as one finds in the provinces of Benevento (Taburno, Sant'Agata de' Goti) and Naples (Capri Bianco), are probably Greco di Tufo, as are those to be found in Basilicata, Puglia, in particular at Gravina, and Molise. The Grecos of Calabria are probably not related or, if so, distantly.

The producers

Terre Dora di Paolo, Montefusco. In 1994 there occurred between the brothers Mastroberardino, Antonio and Walter, and their respective offspring, a split of 'traumatic' proportions, whereupon Walter and his family, Paolo, Lucio and Daniela, went off to set up their own operation under the name Terre Dora, taking with them extensive vineyards planted about 50% to Greco di Tufo with the remainder split between Aglianico and Fiano. There are two sides to every story and certainly there are two very different sides to this one so perhaps it's better just to concentrate on the wines.

At the time of the split Terre Dora didn't have any reserves of wine, only the vineyards – some 120 hectares of them; now around 140 – so they began on the market with white wines rather than reds. Having more Greco than anything else they concentrated in that direction, so that today they are putting out a couple of *crus* Grecos, Terra degli Angeli and Loggia della Serra, as well as a generic. They are thus in a position to offer a cross-section of the styles of Greco one might expect to obtain from this area, from the easy-going, citric generic through the broad, generous Loggia della Serra to the tighter, more austere but finer, more aromatic Terra degli Angeli.

Other producers of good to very good Greco di Tufo are: Benito **Ferrara** (G. di T. and G di T. Vigna Cicogna), Tufo; Feudi di San Gregorio (Greco di Tufo and G. di T. Cutizzi); Mastroberardino (Vignadangelo).

FALANGHINA

This grape, which some have suggested may be of Greek origin, and which some have tentatively identified as the grape from which the Roman Falernian was made, has been known as Falanghina only since the nineteenth century. (A *falanga*, for the record, is a type of wooden stake used for supporting a vine; the suffix *-ina* makes it a small wooden stake.) It is a late-ripener which requires well-exposed, sunny slopes and not-too-excessive production to shine, but when it does so it shines brightly, making a wine of good extract and flavour, with a firm acid backbone enabling it to resist the passage of time in bottle. It is a grape of real interest deserving wider national and international attention.

It is produced as a varietal in Taburno, as well as in Sant'Agata de' Goti, where it also makes a *passito*. In Campi Flegrei, Solopaca and Guardiolo it may be made both in still and sparkling mode. In addition it is a principal variety in the following blends: Falerno del Massico Bianco, Taburno Bianco, Campi Flegrei Bianco, Capri

Bianco, Costa d'Amalfi Bianco, Guardiolo Bianco, Penisola Sorrentina Bianco, Solopaca Bianco.

THE PRODUCERS

Cantina del **Taburno**, Foglianise. Monte Taburno is a long, solid block of rock, which dominates the landscape west and slightly south of the city of Benevento in inland–upland Campania. In its shadow vineyards have been cultivated for thousands of years. Most of them, today, are in the hands of peasant-farmers or amateur viticulturists who confer their grapes to this large *cantina sociale*. The cooperative dates back only to the early 1970s, when it became apparent that the many small growers of the area needed a base where their produce could be transformed into a more valuable and durable item. Today there are around 310 members working about 700 hectares of vineyard. They started bottling in the mid-1980s and at present some two-thirds of production is sold in bottle. For a long time their winemaker was Angelo Pizzi, who spent years in the purgatory of the English wine industry. Pizzi has now gone to Orazio Rillo/Fontanavecchia, and since 1999, they have enjoyed the consultancy of Professor Luigi Moio of the University of Naples, who has been taking their wines in the direction of those of his previous employer, Feudi di San Gregorio.

Taburno specialise in white wines (though they also turn out some excellent Aglianico, including one from ancient layered pre-phylloxera vines called Cento Ottanta – some of the vines being estimated at 180 years of age), in particular from the Coda di Volpe, Greco and Falanghina varieties. Of these their main speciality is Falanghina, which since time immemorial has been producing on the soils of Taburno a particularly intense, well-structured brew. They make two varietals: Taburno DOC, made entirely in stainless steel; and the *cru* Folius, which their brochure describes as being: 'Fermented in *barrique* (Never)'. Actually it's always, the *barriques* being from Nevers. The former's perfumes are all apple and pear; those of the latter more custard apple and apricot with hints of pineapple, the texture being rich and almost creamy and the wood appearing only discreetly. Almost more Feudi than Feudi.

Other good to excellent producers of Falanghina include: De Lucia (Sannio Falanghina); Feudi di San Gregorio (Sannio Falanghina);

Cantine **Gran Furor** (Costa d'Amalfi Furore Bianco Fiorduva – with Biancolella), Furore; Michele Moio – being Professor Moio's family property (Falerno del Massico Falanghina); Orazio Rillo (Falanghina del Taburno); Villa Matilde (Falerno del Massico Bianco; F. del M. Vigna Caracci; Eleusi Passito).

Di Majo Norante, in Molise, use Falanghina in their Biblos (with Greco) and Ramitello (with Fiano).

CODA DI VOLPE

This is apparently the 'Alopecis' identified by Pliny a couple of thousand years ago, its present name deriving from the fact that the curve of its bunch is similar, it is said, to that of a fox's tail. Coda di Volpe is a grape of modest acidity and ripe, perfumed aromas, historically associated with the inland provinces of Benevento and Avellino although today its main use is as the base of modern white Vesuvio aka Lacryma Christi del Vesuvio. Apparently it thrives on volcanic soil. It is used as an anonymous softening agent in various blends, and is officially included in the blends of Solopaca Bianco and Campi Flegrei Bianco.

Good examples may be found from: Mastroberardino (Lacryma Cristi Bianco); Cantina del Taburno (Coda di Volpe Amineo).

BIANCOLELLA AND FORASTERA

Biancolella, also called Bianca Tenera because of its thin skin, is a maritime variety cultivated along the Campanian coast south of Naples, where it forms part of the blends of Costa d'Amalfi Bianco and Penisola Sorrentina Bianco. It is also found north of Naples in the Campi Flegrei, as well as on the island of Capri. But mostly it is associated with Ischia, where it is a component of Ischia Bianco as well as being recognised as a varietal under the Ischia multi-DOC. It is, apparently, the same as the Petite Blanche of Corsica.

Forastera is another of Ischia's specialities – indeed this one is not grown elsewhere in Campania, although the name suggests it is, or was, a 'foreigner', probably arriving from Sardinia during the nineteenth century. It has its own varietal under the multi-DOC, as well as being the principal variety of Ischia Bianco.

The main producer for both is **D'Ambra** of Forio d'Ischia. The d'Ambra family have been involved in wine production in this heavily touristified island an hour's boat-ride from Naples since the latter part of the nineteenth century, although it was the late Mario d'Ambra who brought the *azienda* back from the mediocrity it had fallen into in the middle of the twentieth century. Today the house of d'Ambra is run by Corrado and Andrea d'Ambra, the latter being the winemaker. They do not own much land themselves, but transform the grapes of some 200 growers on the island whose combined vineyards add up to around 100 hectares.

While making a couple of reds from Per'e Palummo (Piedirosso), d'Ambra specialise in whites, not least as 70% of the 600,000 bottles they produce are sold on the island, mainly to tourists during the summer months. Apart from a Biancolella *normale* they make a couple of *crus*, Vigne di Piellero and Tenuta Frassitelli, of which the latter is grown on a slope so steep, at up to 600 metres, that the grapes have to be brought down in a sort of funicular rail-cart. At their best these wines can combine admirable structure with a subtly fruity, sweet succulence which marries well with the seafood of the island's cuisine. The Forastera *normale* is somewhat less structured but the *cru* Vigna Cimentorosso, attractively fruity with a fine skein of acidity running through the heart, has reasonable ageing potential.

ASPRINIO

One of the most striking sights in the world of viticulture today is that of Asprinio vines in the DOC area of Aversa, north of Naples, climbing trees to heights of 20 metres or more in the ancient Etruscan training system referred to on today's labels as *alberata*. In the admittedly diminishing number of examples where this method, as distinct from the modern *spalliera*, is employed a single plant can produce a couple of hundred kilos of fruit – far indeed from the low-production-per-plant that is the ideal today.

The grape name is presumably derived from Latin *asper*, meaning harsh or tart, as the wine, Asprinio d'Aversa DOC, certainly has a very sharp, almost lemony character, no doubt in large part thanks to the volume of fruit per plant, and thus works better as a *spumante*, with a bit of residual sugar, than as a still dry white. Even then it would appear to have few prospects on the export market.

Caputo, of Teverola in the province of Caserta, produce a representative example of Asprinio d'Aversa, as well as a *metodo classico* with 6 g/l of residual sugar which spends three years on the lees.

Apparently Asprinio can be found in vineyards of southern Puglia, although there is no wine in whose *disciplinare* it is specifically mentioned.

Also present in Campanian vineyards in not inconsiderable quantities are various low-grade Trebbianos and Malvasias, as well as Puglia's underwhelming Verdeca; which seems absurd considering the number of characterful home-grown white varieties they have to choose from, until you remember that it is only extremely recently that quality, as distinct from quantity, has begun to re-assert itself as an economic priority in the minds of grape-farmers. A tiny bit of Moscato Bianco is also produced in Castel San Lorenzo for the making of the 'Lambiccato' mentioned above.

PUGLIA

The heel of the Italian boot is a long, narrow region, running 360 kilometres from northwest to southeast. Over such an extent you would expect considerable variations of environment, climate, soil, culture and agriculture. You would not be disappointed.

Modern Puglia, which some Anglophones still refer to by the Latin name of Apulia, divides both historically and actually into three distinct parts. First, the Capitanata, with Molise/Abruzzo to the north, Campania to the west, an area inhabited in ancient times by the tribe of the Dauni – indeed it is still known to some as Daunia. Today, on the fertile plains around Foggia, high-trellised wine and table grapes grow in great profusion, all too many of the latter being used for the purpose of the former.

The centre section, Peucezia, is dominated by the high plateau known as Le Murge, an outcrop of limestone hills 200–600+ metres high, with Basilicata to the west. In ancient times this area was inhabited by the tribe of the Peucezi, who together with the Dauni were subsequently known to the Romans as Apuli. They were great horse-breeders, and Murgia is still synonymous with a particular breed of equines. The soil here is lean and mean, stony not to say rocky, hence the ubiquitous dry stone walls and the curious inverted-cone constructions known as *trulli* in the southern part of the sector. The wines, with all that limestone, tend to be white – even the reds tend to be light, *rosato*s being more successful – and could perhaps be interesting if the grape varieties were any good, which with one or two exceptions they – the natives or quasi natives, at least – are not.

The southern tip of the region, running east and south from a line connecting Taranto in the south and Monopoli, a city on the Adriatic coast between Bari and Brindisi, is known today as the Salento peninsula, or Salentino. In ancient times this part was called Messapia, after the Messapi tribe which roamed through its forests of willow (*salice*). The woods have long been cleared for agricultural purposes, the nearest thing to forests today being ubiquitous groves of olive trees with ancient gnarled trunks metres round. It is from the iron-oxide-stained clay and limestone soils of this dry, sun-baked, low-lying country that come most of the best red wines of Puglia.

Puglia, especially the Salentino, has always been transit-country, mainly via the port of Brindisi, but also via those of Taranto and Gallipoli. In its time it has been trampled over by armies of Greeks, Romans, Byzantines, Normans, Spaniards, to name but a few, as well as by less aggressive cohorts of pilgrims, travellers, tourists, on their way from Italy to points east in the Mediterranean or vice versa. More recently it has been the point of entry for tens of thousands of indigent Albanians. It is a land that has been much exploited, not least viticulturally.

Although grapes have been grown here from time immemorial, and despite the fact that Puglia churns out something like twice as much wine as Australia, there has never before the present existed anything resembling a wine-culture, in the sense of fine bottled wine. The vast majority of the big reds of the south have been used in this century to bolster weaker wines of the north, either in the form of wine, or must, or concentrate. France, until recently Italy's number one export market – although to this day it is rare in the extreme to see a bottle of Italian wine on the shelf of a wine store in Italy's EU partner of 40 years standing – was also a major customer for bulk wine following Algerian independence, and remains so to this day.

As for the whites of the centre and north, they have been

important contributors to the production of vermouth, of which the northerners who blend and bottle remain the beneficiaries of the added value. Although Puglia boasts numerous DOCs on paper, less than 5% of actual production is officially blessed while not much more than 10% goes into bottle.

So little have Puglian wines been esteemed that even when good quality home-grown bottled wines did begin to emerge in the 1970s and 1980s the local wine-bibbing population refused to believe that a Puglian could ever possibly have finesse. Things are changing, but rather more slowly than one would think from the excited chattering of the press. There are several parts of the world today where Puglian wines are considerably more appreciated than in their own home. Indeed, in the very recent past, producers from the outside the region – from Italy's north and from Sicily, even from abroad – have been taking an increasing interest in Puglia. The most notable of these is Antinori with their acquisition of 100 hectares of vineyard in the Castel del Monte zone near Bari and 500 hectares at San Pietro Vernotico near Brindisi. Other invaders include the Avignonesi of Montepulciano in Tuscany, Californians Kendall Jackson, the Veronese house of Pasqua, Campanians Feudo di San Gregorio, and Sicilians Calatrasi.

Mind you, as far as the wines of the north of the region are concerned, apathy is largely an appropriate response. The most prolific producing zone, San Severo, is here, up-country from the city of Foggia. Its whites, some 40,000 hectolitres of DOC alone – never mind the bulk stuff – from Bombino Bianco, Trebbiano and Verdeca grapes, are at best inoffensive, more often plain boring. Reds and *rosatos* from Montepulciano and Sangiovese (10,000– 12,000 hectolitres) are scarcely more remarkable. The only other DOC of any significant production (around 4,000 hectolitres), the strangely named Cacc'e Mmitte di Lucera, based on Montepulciano and Sangiovese with a bit of Uva di Troia, is unlikely to be much of an improvement.

Central Puglia presents an appreciable jump up in quality. We are in what is today called the province of Bari, Bari being Puglia's major metropolis, where the DOCs Castel del Monte and Gravina shine with a certain lustre. Castel del Monte, named after the curious octagonal castle built by Emperor Frederick II of Swabia in the thirteenth century, is a multi-DOC featuring various varietals – including Aglianico for red and *rosato*, Chardonnay, Sauvignon,

Pinot Bianco and Pinot Nero. The wines of significant volume, however, are Rosso, a blend of Uva di Troia, Aglianico and Monte-pulciano – which is promising, and indeed delivers at least one wine of excellence, Rivera's 'Il Falcone'; Rosato, as Rosso but with a major component of Bombino Nero; and Bianco, from Pampanuto, Chardonnay and Bombino Bianco.

The DOC Gravina is limited to a white blend supposedly consisting of Malvasia del Chianti and Bianco d'Alessano or Greco di Tufo grapes, plus Bombino Bianco, Trebbiano Toscano and Verdeca. Other varieties may be authorised, but frankly Greco di Tufo is the only one that produces interesting quality; so, when you taste Gravina from the zone's sole significant producer, Cantina Botromagno, you may not be mistaken if you detect large amounts of Greco and not very much of anything else. The same producer makes a fine *barrique*-aged IGT Rosso delle <u>Murge</u> (called Pier delle Vigne) which is a blend of Aglianico and Montepulciano.

From central Puglia also come a couple of obscure reds, based on Uva di Troia, called Rosso <u>Barletta</u> and Rosso <u>Canosa</u>. There is, too, a modicum of sweet Muscat under the DOC name Moscato di <u>Trani</u> Dolce Naturale. Otherwise the only other area of note is <u>Gioia del Colle</u>, which is the point at which Puglian wines begin to get really interesting. For it is here, on the high plateau west and slightly north of the port of Taranto, that we first encounter one of Puglia's two most important grape varieties: Primitivo, although the multi-DOC also provides for a Trebbiano-based white, a Rosato and a blended Rosso as well as for a varietal Primitivo. There is also sweet Aleatico, both Naturale and Liquoroso, although these seem to exist more in some bureaucrat's head than on the ground. Aleatico di <u>Puglia</u> is a DOC from which at least one wine, to my knowledge, is actually produced, by Candido in the area of Salice Salentino.

The areas of <u>Locorotondo</u> and <u>Martina Franca</u>, on the border between Murgia and the Salentino peninsula, produce white wines made from the Verdeca and Bianco d'Alessano varieties with possible help (they need it) from Fiano, Bombino Bianco and, in the better examples, though it's not official, Chardonnay. This is *trulli* country, Martina Franca having the added distinction of being one of the most perfect baroque towns in Italy, nay, the world; that distinction being all the greater for the utter drabness and down-at-heel aspect of most southern Puglian towns.

In the Salentino proper, east of Taranto around the ancient towns of <u>Sava</u> and <u>Manduria</u>, which was once razed to the ground by the Romans in revenge for its harbouring of Hannibal's army, Primitivo has found its spiritual home. The *disciplinare* Primitivo di Manduria provides for a table wine version at minimum 14% alcohol as well as for sweet versions both Naturale and Liquoroso.

For the rest of the Salentino peninsula, which includes the provinces of Taranto, Brindisi and Lecce, the red wines are dominated by what is perhaps the major black grape of Puglia, Negroamaro. The DOCs containing Negroamaro as head of a blend consisting variously of Malvasia Nera, Montepulciano, Sangiovese and others are too numerous to do anything but list, which I will do in approximate order of commercial importance: <u>Salice Salentino</u>, <u>Brindisi</u>, <u>Copertino</u>, <u>Squinzano</u>, <u>Leverano</u>, <u>Matino</u>, <u>Alezio</u>, <u>Lizzano</u> and <u>Nardò</u>; all being names of small rather seedy towns with the exception of Brindisi which is a large rather seedy port.

These are all multi-DOCs covering between one and six other wines, including, invariably, a Rosato based on the same blend as the Rosso and, usually, a Bianco consisting of various grapes which may include Malvasia, Trebbiano, Bombino, Verdeca, Bianco d'Alessano, Chardonnay, Pinot Bianco, and Sauvignon, some of which may have their own varietal sub-denomination as in the case of Salice Salentino Pinot Bianco. Whether in the department of Rosso, Rosato or Bianco you may be sure that producers will do pretty well what they feel like, blend-wise, so it matters little what the law says. It has been argued fairly convincingly that, in a situation where the amount of wine produced to DOC is derisory in comparison with the total, and where the blends are all fairly similar and come from zones of similar conditions, it is absurd and indeed counter-productive in terms of consumer awareness to indulge so many names.

Finally, from <u>Ostuni</u>, northwest of Brindisi, there comes a dribble of Bianco made from the Impigno and Francavidda varieties, and of Rosso made from Ottavianello, which turns out to be nothing other than southern France's Cinsaut.

This gives an insight into the wealth of the ampelographical heritage of Puglia – a land where, prior to phylloxera, well in excess of a hundred grape types thrived. Though relatively few of the old ones have survived in healthy numbers, many new varieties, including most of the French 'internationals' as well as a few from northern Italy, e.g. Garganega and Incrocio Manzoni, have come in to fill the gap. This in itself is surely an indicator of great promise, even if the present reality is relatively modest.

The big three, as already suggested, are all red, and while none of them is world class, they are all capable of making excellent wines in their way. We will consider them in order of production of volumes of wine that can in some way be considered 'fine'.

GRAPES, WINES AND PRODUCERS – RED

NEGROAMARO

Negroamaro has been the big survivor in the southern Salento. Today there are something like 30,000 hectares planted to Negro-amaro, representing fully one-quarter of Puglian viticulture – this even after the EU's ill-conceived extirpation programme of the late 1980s/early 1990s robbed the land of some of the most valid, *alberello*-trained vineyards. Today *alberello* rubs shoulders with *spalliera* and even *tendone*, but the superiority of *alberello* and poverty of the *tendone* have belatedly persuaded quality-minded producers to retain, even occasionally replant with, *alberello*, albeit in some cases attached to wires for ease of mechanisation in what is called *alberello modificato*.

Very little is definitely known about where Negroamaro came from or when it arrived. No mention is made of the variety in documents on ampelography prior to this century, partly of course due to the fact that no one, including *Puglesi*, considered their wines in any way special.

It is reasonable to surmise that the modern name developed from the dialect *niuru maru*. Like the dialect, the probable source of the grape is Albania, via which it would presumably have arrived from Greece. There is every likelihood, although this has not to date been proved, that Negroamaro is closely related to the widely planted Greek variety Xinomavro.

Why did Negroamaro pull through when so many others didn't? According to Severino Garofano, probably the world's leading expert on the subject, it's because it was a darling of the growers. It is a stable variety, with a reliable production year after year, having good resistance to such diseases as peronospera and oidium, although it is somewhat vulnerable to *botrytis* brought by the kind of September rains that have plagued the region too often in recent years. It is resistant to drought, a necessary virtue in this region. Surprisingly, after all that, it is also capable of considerable quality.

The name suggests two of the reasons why. First, it gives grapes which have good depth of colour (*negro* = black) without at the same time being excessively tannic. Second, it has a slight but pleasantly *bitter* (*amaro, amarognolo*) taste at the back of the palate, to offset its almost jammy, Australian-style wealth of sweet fruit. The word *amaro* is sometimes confused with acid, and indeed Negroamaro retains reasonable acidity even in conditions of extreme heat and drought, enhancing balance. When grown on *alberello* it can achieve excellent concentration of flavour at highish sugar-levels without loss of volume, which makes it an interesting economic proposition.

Some of the best value-for-money wines from Italy today are based on Negroamaro. Most of the DOCs for Lecce and Brindisi provinces, mentioned above, allow production levels between 12 and 15 tonnes per hectare, although *alberello* vineyards will generally not achieve anything approaching such figures.

It is rare to find Negroamaro unblended, though it is usually dominant in the blend. Depending on the sub-zone from which it comes its wines will generally have between 10 and 20% of other grapes, including, usually, Malvasia Nera di Lecce or di Brindisi and Montepulciano, occasionally Primitivo.

Negroamaro is capable of making a variety of different styles of wine, and in this context the decision on picking time is crucial. For a big, butch wine, full of colour and high of alcohol, one might wait till the second half of October, even into November. In the absence of excessive rainfall the fairly thick skin will keep it healthy in these conditions. This style, of course, is primarily associated with blending wine, although some of the best-known quality wines are of the late-vintage style. Taurino's Patriglione is an outstanding example.

And if you want it even bigger and richer, you could try drying the grapes in the sun for two or three weeks to concentrate the substances and sugars still further. Drying in the sun has a similar effect on grapes in weeks to that produced by drying indoors has in months in the Veneto. The best example is Vallone's Graticciaia.

For a more refined, balanced table wine a grower will limit his production to about half the legal limit or less, pick in the second half of September, early October at the latest, and perhaps age in French *barrique* for a year or so. Excellent examples of this style are Candido's Duca d'Aragona and Leone de Castris' Riserva Donna Lisa.

Anachronistically, Negroamaro's greatest vocation has until recently been considered to be for the making of *rosato*. It can be a rather expensive process, in that, after about a day's controlled maceration in a glycol-cooled tank, perhaps 30% of the wine may be bled off for *rosato*, the rest being sold in bulk at low prices as what cynics call '*rosso per i francesi*'. The market for *rosato* wines being what it is, however, it is not possible to ask a premium price for a wine whose production costs would warrant such a request. Great value for money, therefore, for those who appreciate a refreshing yet intensely flavoured pink wine on a warm summer's evening.

There are today a number of good-to-excellent producers of Negroamaro-based wine in the Salentino. The best way to approach them is probably alphabetically.

Accademia dei Racemi, Manduria. This is a, nay the, major producer of Primitivo, hence the principal profile will be under that heading. Nevertheless they or their associates (see profile) are putting out some of the best Negroamaro-based blends in Puglia today, including (name of wine followed by associate producer, in brackets): Te Deum Laudamus, Salice Salentino (Casale Bevagna); Bizantino Rosso, Salento IGT (Perrini); Gorgolano, Salento IGT (Perrini), Alberello, Salento IGT (Felline); Armécolo, Salento IGT (Castel di Salve); Sole Leone, Salento IGT (Torre Mozza); Salice Salentino DOC (Torre Mozza).

Michele **Calò**, Tuglie. Around the middle of the last century Michele Calò, suffering like many southerners from lack of employment and income, took himself off to Metz in eastern France to work as a miner. He made enough to transfer to Milan, where he opened a small wine business. But he never forgot his native Puglia, and in the 1950s he returned to the family winery in his hometown Tuglie, the production from which he then began selling in Lombardy. From that base he and his sons were able to expand the business and in particular to upgrade, to the extent that today they are recognised, and particularly in northern Italy, as a producer of top quality Puglian wines.

The basis of their business is the Mjere selection of red, white and *rosato*, Mjere being the local dialect's version of Merum, Latin for good wine. The red and the *rosato*, both of which rejoice in the DOC Alezio, are of course Negroamaro based, the vines for the most part still being cultivated by the *alberello* method. Indeed, the *rosato*, in a good year, is one of the outstanding representatives of that delicious but ill-fated (market-wise) wine-style, while the red, having something of the purity and clean lines of a wine of the north, is among the most elegant of its type. It is topped, however, by the *cru* Vigna Spano, 90% Negroamaro and 10% Malvasia Nera, since 1986 an IGT Salento of superior concentration and structure made only in good years from a single six-hectare vineyard using the best selection of grapes.

Francesco **Candido**, Sandonaci. Brothers Alessandro – Sandro, to his friends – and Giacomo Candido are the proprietors of this sizeable estate of some 140 hectares of vineyard, plus another hundred or so planted to wheat, tomatoes and other crops. They took over from their father Francesco, who in 1957 was one of the first in Puglia to bottle quality wine – prior to which, from 1925, he had sold all his grapes. In the same year he brought in from the *Scuola di Enologia* at Avellino in Campania a young graduate who was to transform the approach to wine in the south of Puglia, Severino Garofano – a name we will be encountering on several occasions. Garofano left in 1962 but returned in 1978 to help the brothers build the house of Candido into one of the most experimental and quality-conscious members of what is now, in the light of recent developments, seen as the Salentino 'establishment'.

Candido's vineyards are mostly trained according to the *alberello* system, although more recently planted areas, especially for whites, are trained to *spalliera*. The proportion of reds to whites in this predominantly red-grape area is 90–10. Among the former are included, apart from Negroamaro, Montepulciano, Malvasia Nera, Primitivo, Aleatico and Cabernet Sauvignon. The whites include Chardonnay, Garganega and Sauvignon.

Candido's flagship wine has for many years been Duca d'Aragona, mentioned above, an excellent example of 'a modern style wine which nevertheless expresses its origins to the full'. This is a blend of rigorously selected Negroamaro at 80% with 20% Montepulciano, subjected to lengthy maceration and then aged in French oak *barriques*. A recent rival for top spot has been what is now called Immensum (originally 'L'Infinito', but there were problems registering the name), still 80% Negroamaro but with the remaining 20% made up this time by Cabernet Sauvignon. So far the sheer class of Duca d'Aragona, a wine of smooth, mature, beautifully balanced fruitiness keeps it ahead, not to mention its greater character of *terroir*. To be fair, the Duca is a hard act to follow.

One that does follow it well, in most vintages, is Cappello di Prete, traditionally Candido's 'second wine'. Like Duca d'Aragona an IGT Salento, Cappello's consistently smooth, plummy–pruney fruit (100% Negroamaro) and its modest price make it a frequent feature in journalistic lists of the best value wines in Italy.

At the more basic level, but always very well made, are the widely popular Salice Salentino Rosso DOC and its sidekick the fresh, medium-bodied Salice Salentino *rosato* called Le Pozzelle, both 95% Negroamaro with 5% Malvasia Nera.

C.S. Copertino, Copertino. Another of Garofano's babies, since 1962, this co-operative of 700 members and almost as many hectares, founded in 1935 in the heart of the rather uninspired town of Copertino in the middle of the Salentino plain, has an admirable track-record for consistently producing good wines of real character at the sort of competitive prices beloved of supermarket chains. Indeed one such colossus from Great Britain sent its buyer and quality control inspector to the cellar to check it out before sealing the deal for several thousand cases of Copertino DOC Riserva. They had been told, mistakenly, that the wine received extended maturation in large oak barrels, but by the time it transpired that this was not true and that there were in fact no barrels at all the supermarket group had already printed tens of thousands of back labels declaring months of wood-ageing. Fearful of the giant's wrath, the *cantina*'s representative kept the distinguished visitors busy tasting and visiting vineyards and aspects of the cellar until well into the afternoon, their requests to see barrel-ageing facility being met by 'Later, later'. Finally, just before they were due to depart, they insisted: 'And now we really must see the barrels before we leave'. 'Oh my God!', exclaimed their guide, 'the barrels, they are in another *cantina* several kilometres in the wrong direction. I'm afraid if we go there you will miss your plane.' The Brits were subsequently told that the barrels had been done away with as interfering with the pure fruitiness of the wine.

Which is just to demonstrate that the Puglians, for all the flatness of their land, have a lively sense of humour.

Conti **Leone de Castris**, Salice Salentino. This is the most historic of Puglia's wineries, tracing its roots back several centuries to the age of the Spanish occupation, the founder of the original winery, in 1665, having been a Spanish nobleman called Duke Oronzo Arcangelo Maria Francisco de Castris. At the beginning of the nineteenth century they were already shipping wine in bulk to the USA, and in 1925 they began bottling. By this time the inter-marriages of the de Castris and the Leone Plantera families had caused the fusion of names in its present form. After World War II the American market ordered their most renowned wine, *rosato* of course, under the Anglicised name of Five Roses, and this wine became almost the emblem of quality Puglian wine until well into the 1970s.

In their massive four-hectare winery in the town of Salice Salentino, Leone de Castris today turn out a range of wines, including several from international grapes, mainly white. The heart of their production, however, lies in their red wines, of which the star is Salice Salentino Riserva 'Donna Lisa', made entirely from Negroamaro grapes. This wine has on more than one occasion received the ultimate accolade of *tre bicchieri* in the *Gambero Rosso/Slow Food Guide to the Wines of Italy*, although not every-one is convinced that Donna Lisa is quite that exceptional. Perhaps it's the oak-component that the tasters find to their liking, Donna Lisa being aged in French *barrique* – this being an all-too-frequent and somewhat depressing response on the part of blind tasters to oaky wines: if the producer has deemed it necessary to spend a lot of money on wood the wine must be good. Which is not to denigrate it – Donna Lisa is certainly among the four or five best Negroamaro wines of Puglia, with opulent fruit and the ability to age well – but then why is it that the others don't get a similar recognition?

Other Negroamaro-based wines include the Salice Salentino Riserva non-*cru*; and of course the famous Five Roses Rosato del

Salento, a wine which has been completely revamped, freshened and modernised, since the days not so long ago when it was wood-aged and frankly, by today's standards, oxidised.

Masseria Monaci, Copertino. This is Severino Garofano's own property, acquired by him and the Calabrian house of Librandi – who are no longer connected – in the mid-1990s following the break-up of the business of the previous proprietor, Baron Bacile di Castiglione. The Baron had been one of the innovators of Puglian viniculture, and specifically that of Copertino, being the first, as far back as the 1970s, to introduce grapes like Montepulciano and Chardonnay. But none of the Baron's children were interested in carrying on with the wine business, so the winery and what was left of the vineyards – 30 out of what had been 180 hectares surrounding the premises on the outskirts of the town of Copertino – had to be sold.

The history of the *masseria*, or farm, goes way back, some 1,000 years, to when it was worked by Byzantine monks (*monaci*). Indeed, some of the original structures still survive, including various excavations below ground level which today are used as cellars or storage areas, but were originally intended as escape hatches against local and foreign persecutors, in the form of Catholics opposed to the Greek orthodox rites or Turkish pirates invading at harvest time to pillage and steal grain.

No one knows Copertino like Severino Garofano, and he has quickly built up an impressive array of wines. The base wine, Copertino 'Eloquenzia', is a pure Negroamaro, given an average of five days maceration on the skins, aged in glass-lined concrete without resort to wood, thus preserving its pure fruit character. Simposia, the *riserva*, though not so called, being an IGT Salento, is a blend of Negroamaro at 80% plus Montepulciano and Malvasia Nera and other secret ingredients that Severino will not reveal. Yields are more restricted, selection is more rigorous, maceration takes place over eight days and the wine undergoes some wood-ageing, which does not impinge on its deep fruit which, unlike the Copertino, is not meant to be drunk young but to gain in complexity with bottle age.

Masseria Monaci also produce a Primitivo IGT Salento called I Censi, less strapping and more refined than some of the block-busters of the Tarantino.

Rosa del Golfo, Alezio. Already in the late nineteenth century a certain Damiano Calò owned vineyards in the Salento peninsula, but the important leap came in 1939 when his son Giuseppe set up a distribution centre for the wine in the northern province of Lombardy. In 1958 a winery was purchased in Alezio, and in 1963 Giuseppe's son Mino launched the *rosato* Rosa del Golfo on the market, acquiring his fruit from quality-conscious growers using the traditional *alberello* method of training. Such was the success of this wine that the winery became known by the name of its most famous product from 1988.

Today the business is in the hands of another Damiano Calò, Mino's son. In this anti-*rosato* era their lead wine, still called Rosa del Golfo, an IGT Salento composed mainly of Negroamaro plus 10% of Malvasia Nera, is often held up as Puglia's, and probably therefore Italy's, finest *rosato*, fresh and flowery with great intensity of summer fruits on the palate. An IGT Salento Rosso, called Portulano, is also produced from the same blend – a wine of deep colour and good concentration of ripe brambly fruit with those hints of coffee and toast which come from a partial ageing in *barrique* (the remainder being aged either in *botte* or in stainless steel).

Tenute **Rubino/Piana del Sole**, Brindisi. This is an extremely new reality on the Puglian scene, but one that promises to be important in years to come. The Rubino family have 150 hectares of prime vineyard in the province of Brindisi (their *cantina* is actually within the city limits), 120 of which are dedicated to black grapes indigenous and otherwise – Negroamaro, Malvasia Nera, Montepulciano, Primitivo, Sangiovese and Cabernet Sauvignon – the remaining 30 being planted to whites – Chardonnay and Sauvignon. The vineyards were planted in the late 1980s and until the late 1990s the family sold grapes, their customers including some not unfamiliar names among Tuscany's oenological elite. Now, however, they have decided to go their own route and bottle their own wines with the help of Riccardo Cotarella who has taken over from Luca d'Attoma as consultant oenologist. There are two ranges – Piana del Sole being the more economical, Tenute Rubino being more upmarket. In the former is I Tamerici Rosso, IGT Puglia, a blend of mainly Negroamaro with some Malvasia Nera and Montepulciano, sporting lashings of soft, quasi jammy blackberry fruit, a delightful quaffing red; it is also extremely reasonably priced. In the latter is Gallico Rosso, a Brindisi DOC combining Negroamaro and Montepulciano, carrying the theme farther along the lines of concentration and intensity, its soft tannins giving easy accessibility to the wine until the back palate which features a certain grip. This is a property to watch.

Cosimo **Taurino**, Guagnano. Following the untimely death of the widely admired and loved, big, gruff *titolare* Cosimo 'Mimmo' Taurino at the beginning of the 1999 harvest, the ubiquitous Severino Garofano continues to ensure that all goes well winewise at this, probably the most renowned of Puglian estates in the latter part of the twentieth century. Cosimo it was who introduced to Puglia the now spreading concepts of delayed harvesting – for Patriglione, Puglia's most successful wine to date, at least in terms of image – and single-vineyard production – for Notarpanaro, another Negroamaro-based *cru* – not to mention that of the drastic reduction of yields in the vineyard to obtain maximum extract and balance in the fruit, something that Cosimo believed in so passionately that he withdrew his top wines from the local DOC in protest at the high level of permitted yields, labelling them, as do others today, Salento IGT.

Patriglione, an iron-fist-in-velvet-glove wine if ever there was one – tremendous power, yet nothing loud or brash about it, finishing on a surprisingly elegant note – is made from 90% Negroamaro and 10% Malvasia Nera from nearly 50-year-old *alberello*-trained vines, picked in mid-October, almost a month later than normal for Negroamaro, to benefit from the refining on the vine afforded by the considerable differences between day and night temperatures at this time of year. Yields average around five tonnes per hectare, about one-third of the permitted crop. The style, dry and very full-flavoured, with an alcoholic degree in excess of 14%, is not dissimilar to that of Verona's Amarone, except of course that the aromas are quite different, less cherry, more leather and spice, plus tobacco and coffee, no doubt more from the *barriques* than from the grapes.

Notarpanaro, from a 40-year-old vineyard at the heart of the 120-hectare estate, of which over 100 are planted to vines, is picked earlier, towards the end of September, though still on the late side for Negroamaro, which constitutes 80–85% of the blend, aided again by Malvasia Nera. The wine is aged about six months in *barriques*, considerably less than Patriglione, and indeed has a fruitier, less *impegnativo* style, very pure, loads of personality.

The Negroamaro range is completed by a highly popular (in international markets) Salice Salentino Riserva DOC (20% Malvasia Nera here too, briefly aged in *barriques*, and by a *rosato* typical of the area, indeed one of the best, called Scaloti, Negro-amaro at 100%.

Agricole **Vallone**, Lecce. This extended estate is owned by the Vallone family of Lecce of whom the surviving members are sisters Vittoria and Teresa and their nephew Francesco, son of one of the sisters' two prematurely deceased brothers. The property, consisting of several hundred hectares devoted to such crops as olives, artichokes, tomatoes and of course the vine, is divided into several parts, including a *cantina* at Copertino and offices in the city of Lecce as well as a superb fortified *masseria* north of Brindisi at Serranova. Vineyard-wise, however, the important sections are in San Pancrazio, a commune of the Salice Salentino DOC, where they have some 40 hectares of mainly Negroamaro, plus minority

percentage of Malvasia Nera, planted to *alberello* and *spalliera* –
they did experiment with *tendone* but found it too productive, so
they removed it; and in the commune of Brindisi, where a little
under one-third of their 300+ hectares is planted to vines – again,
mainly Negroamaro, plus Montepulciano and Malvasia Nera, five
hectares of Cabernet Sauvignon and three hectares between Merlot
and Cabernet Franc; plus a hefty 18 hectares of Sauvignon Blanc,
something of a surprise for a zone of such baking summertime
temperatures, until one learns that it's irrigated.

Vallone's Salice Salentino, Vereto, represents one of the better
versions of that now internationally recognised DOC, and demand
for it, particularly in northern Europe, is stretched to the limit
with Donato Lazzari, since 1963 Vallone's chief administrator and
agronomist (the consultant oenologist is, surprise surprise, Severino
Garofano), having to discourage new markets. It is put somewhat
in the shade, however, by the Brindisi Rosso from the Vigna
Flaminio estate, a deceptively easy-drinking, soft and alluring fruit-
packed red which actually has a lot more complexity than one
might at first suppose. It has been described in the *Slow Food Guide
to the Wines of Italy* as having various characteristics of the 'Grand
Vin' of Vallone, which I am about to describe.

The 'Grand Vin' goes by the name of Graticciaia, being a unique
southern Italian version of a dry, full-bodied red from dried grapes
– not, in the Amarone manner, for months under the eaves of the
winery, but for around three weeks on cane mats (*graticci*) in the
full glare of the autumn sun. The result is a wine of enormous
power and complexity, with a nose of ripe figs, spices, tar, hints
of chocolate and coffee from the *barrique* in which it is aged, and
a palate which is dense yet fine, rich and sweet but finishing dry,
with all those aromas and more playing tag in the mouth as the
liquid passes through to a fully satisfying, beautifully balanced
conclusion.

Vallone are, too, the authors of one of the best versions – in some
years the best – of Puglia's classic wine, *rosato*, under the rubric
Vigna Flaminio Brindisi Rosato, which completes their Negroamaro-based range. One should, however, make mention of a
delicious sweet white called Passo delle Viscarde which they make
from Sauvignon grapes dried in the manner of Graticciaia. This
wine has a creamy consistency and a rich, pineapple and custard
sweetness cut skilfully by Sauvignon's vein of lemony acidity.

Conti **Zecca**, Leverano. This is a large estate of some 800 hectares of which around 40% are planted to the vine. Zecca being one of the first to experiment with mechanical harvesting – also night-picking à la California, in order to avoid the aroma-burning heat of midday in August and September – most of the vineyards are trained to *spalliera*, although some of the really old plants are still free-standing. Conti Zecca, run by its oenologist-director Antonio Romano, have in the past been known for their keen prices and not-particularly-special quality, but in recent times they have made determined and largely successful efforts to upgrade while still maintaining their very competitive market stance. A key factor in the upgrading of the winery has been the drafting in of ex-Antinori consultant oenologist Giorgio Marone from Tuscany.

Negroamaro, as everywhere in these parts, forms the basis of their production, making the majority of the blend of their easy-drinking and inexpensive Donna Marzia Rosso del Salento IGT, together with Sangiovese and Malvasia Nera. In the more upmarket Leverano Rosso DOC and Leverano Rosso Riserva, both sourced in, and hence named, Vigna del Saraceno, wines of proportionately greater class and seriousness, Negroamaro accounts for 85% of the blend. There is also the inevitable *rosato* under the Leverano DOC Vigna del Sareceno, as there is indeed under the Donna Marzia label.

Recently, Zecca have come out with what, if this were Tuscany, would be called a 'SuperTuscan', called Nero. This blend of Negroamaro, Malvasia Nera and Cabernet has caught the admiration of Italian wine writers, who consider it one of the emblematic wines of the new Puglia. It is a wine of full fruity aroma mingling with spices and herbs and a touch of coffee from the wood, followed by a smooth, suave palate redolent of red berries, chocolate and vanilla.

Others making Negroamaro-based wines of a good standard include: **Cantele** (Salice Salentino Riserva), Lecce; **Fusione** (Promessa), Castellaneta; **La Mea/Maci** (Sire – 100% Negroamaro; Vita – with Cabernet Sauvignon; Dragonero – with Merlot; Bella Mojgan – with Malvasia Nera; Copertino Duca d'Atene; Salice Salentino Ribò), Cellino San Marco; **Libra** (Salice Salentino Albano Carrisi; Nostalgia Rosso – with Primitivo), Cellino San Marco; **Lomazzi & Sarli** (Brindisi Rosso Solise), Latiano; Cantine **Santa**

Barbara (Squinzano Rosso and Rosato, Brindisi Rosso and Rosato), San Pietro Vernotico; **Valle dell'Asso** (Copertino Rosso; Galatina Rosso and Rosato), Galatina.

PRIMITIVO

The name is said to derive from the Italian *primaticcio* meaning precocious, because with respect to other Puglian grapes Primitivo ripens up to a month previously – as early indeed, as the last third of August.

This does not, however, preclude Primitivo from packing in the grape sugar. From a low-lying *alberello*-trained vineyard near the coast in what has become its home territory, the DOC zone of Manduria in the province of Taranto, Primitivo has come to be the one favoured by growers precisely because of its high sugar content in a market situation based on degree-hectolitre. This is in part due to a thin skin which favours evaporation of the water content in the berries, but which conversely renders Primitivo vulnerable to botrytis in a rainy August/early September.

Elsewhere, in the province of Lecce in particular, Primitivo's hectarage has been more than halved by EU extirpation subsidies, mainly because the grape has a peculiar quirk that does not endear it to the growers there. This consists in Primitivo's ability to produce two, even three crops, from racemes opposite the main bud whose fruit ripens about 20 days later. One might think this an advantage, but until recently the growers of Lecce considered it more of a pain because the second crop's sugar-content is decidedly lower. The fact that this latter could in fact be an advantage – offering fruit characteristics more suitable to fine wine production: more perfume, higher acidity, generally better balance – was not seen as such in what, as I have said, is a situation of embryonic wine culture.

However, now that Primitivo has come into vogue, its price tripling in the last three years of the twentieth century, there is a certain move to replant it in the Salento peninsula using, of course, subsidies from the EU.

According to Severino Garofano, Primitivo would most probably have arrived in Puglia from the nearby Dalmatian coast, although its origin would have been farther inland in Croatia, where it is called Mali Plavac (little blue). DNA tests have satisfied Californian ampelographers that their Zinfandel is the same grape, doubtless sourced from the same place, probably at different times, probably indeed brought to the USA by Colonel Haraszthy in the mid-nineteenth century. Whether it arrived in Puglia from Dalmatia, or whether from France, is a moot point. France?! Apparently, in the seventeenth century an order of Benedictine monks arrived from southern France to set up a monastery at Gioia del Colle in the Murge, an area which as we have seen still boasts one of Puglia's Primitivo-based DOCs. Although there is no remaining trace of a Primitivo-type grape in France (there is, it seems, in Portugal's Douro, among the Port grapes), this theory has some believers, though the Dalmatian source, being more direct, seems more likely.

As we have seen, two growing areas specialise in Primitivo: Gioia del Colle, the original, in the Province of Bari, on the high plateau of the Murge where the DOC's minimum alcohol level is a mere 13% (Riserva – 14%); and Manduria, incorporating the town of Sava, where a table wine starts at 14% and a late-picked *dolce naturale* may easily have a *complessivo* – that's actual plus potential alcohol, in the form of residual grape-sugar – of 18%+. Manduria also provides for fortified or *liquoroso* versions, dry and sweet, although, unlike in California, little attempt has been made to produce quality port-style wines by the Pugliesi. Primitivo is also sometimes used in sweet wines based on Aleatico to give them a boost. Outside Puglia, Primitivo's only recognised presence is in Campania's Falerno.

Producers attempting to make a quality product from Primitivo prior to the 1990s were few and far between – perhaps there weren't any. The grape's role, in the latter half of the twentieth century, was to provide ship- or truck-loads of cutting wines of good colour and high octane for the table wine industry in northern Italy, France, Germany and elsewhere – even Spain, when there were shortages. But in the 1990s, no doubt partly because of the demonstrated connection with Zinfandel, the market for good Primitivo suddenly mushroomed, and the race was on to see who could get there first.

I followed the development of Primitivo from the early days of bottling to the present flowering of fine wine through one firm with which I had and have commercial connections, so I will tell it from their point of view although there are others, I am sure, who have an equally interesting tale to tell.

Accademia dei Racemi, Manduria. This firm grew out of a bulk business founded in the 1960s by Antonio Perrucci, father of the generation which controls the Accademia, elder brother and managing director Gregorio, whose wife Elisabetta is also involved, younger brother and winemaker Fabrizio, and sister Alessia. Antonio Perrucci's business, founded on intelligence gathered by his father over a long lifetime as a vine-grafter, during which he came to know all the best growers and vineyards and local characteristics of soil and micro-climate in the zone of Manduria and beyond, took off immediately thanks to the huge demand for cutting wines from a France divorced from Algeria. By 1994 he was prosperous enough to set his children up with a brand new winery and bottling line for the production and packaging of the cream of the grapes, this business being called Pervini.

The early Primitivos of Pervini showed promise, but there were faults: too much alcohol and extract, too little finesse, some off aromas which someone unkindly described as 'sick'. Fortunately the young Perruccis recognised themselves as being on a learning curve, and were willing to listen to advice from more experienced members of the national and international wine trade. They also saw themselves as being on something of a mission, to prove to the world that grapes from their land could produce not just good wines but wines of excellence.

In late 1995, partly through the good offices of yours truly, the consultant oenologist Roberto Cipresso visited Manduria and a relationship was established that has proved crucial to the development of the firm. To cut the story as short as possible, together with Fabrizio Perrucci, Cipresso developed the Felline line of wines, while Fabrizio carried on in full charge of the Pervini line, learning as he went from Cipresso.

The rain-soaked vintage of 1995 was a disaster for Primitivo, so they had to wait until 1996 before they had some prime fruit to work with. This meant they had time to prepare for the launch wine, buying in quality French oak of different sizes, but it also meant waiting a further 18 months before they were able to present their new wines. When they did, at Vinitaly 1998, they caused something of a sensation. The first Felline Primitivo had none of the old faults, but blended the strong alcohol and soft-fruit character of the variety with the finesse of oak-ageing, which Cipresso knew from experience how to manage so that fruit aromas prevailed.

The 1997 vintage was even better than 1996, and out of it came the wine which was to gain the company – at least the Felline branch of it – its first *tre bicchieri* award in the prestigious *Wines of Italy Guide* put out by Slow Food and Gambero Rosso. This was Vigna del Feudo, 60% Primitivo, 30% Montepulciano and the rest made up of Cabernet and Merlot. To challenge this, Fabrizio Perrucci working with Pervini had developed his own line of top quality Primitivo, launching the *tonneau*-aged Archidamo to loud international acclaim. He had also by this time purged the original Pervini Primitivo di Manduria of any off aromas, developed a tasty Primitivo del Tarantino called I Monili, more accessible both price-wise and alcohol-wise, and introduced a sweet unfortified Primitivo called Primo Amore to rival the sweet Zins of California, as well as perfecting the blend of Bizantino (mentioned above under Negroamaro).

Meanwhile brother Gregorio, or Gregory as he prefers to be called, was busying himself in other directions. Gregory, who is endowed with a rare combination of creative spirit and business acumen, was not just dreaming of but actively organising a network of small producers throughout the Salentino peninsula to raise Puglian viniculture to international standards. The idea was either to buy grapes or wine of which the growing and making would be controlled by one of his people or, where adequate facilities existed, to encourage growers to make their own wine according to precepts laid down by the group, such wines to be marketed by the group.

It was this group which became known as the Accademia dei Racemi – Academy of the Racemes – all members doing their own thing with their own grapes, their soil conditions and their microclimates, but attached to the main stem. The members do not even have to be small, but may include members of existing co-operatives willing to work along Accademia lines. Gregory calls this process 'creating a corner of quality'. And to help in the development of this project, or group of projects, Gregory began organising EU funds through Rome for capital expansion.

The Accademia dei Racemi was launched officially at Vinitaly in 1999 and by the following year had become a roaring success. A mark of this success consisted in the fact that, in the new century, it was not just the surviving old boys of Puglian viticulture who came to Vinitaly in the annually chartered coach but a sizeable group of youngsters, eager now for the first time to validate their land and their production.

The wines of the Accademia are many, and of diverse sorts. Most of those of Pervini and some of those of Felline and other associated producers are mentioned above, either in this section or in the previous section on Negroamaro. Perhaps it would be most helpful here to give the various producers' or estates' names with the principal wines featuring Primitivo in majority or minority proportion produced by each at the time of writing, mentioning varieties or blend components where they have not been previously given and are not obvious from the name of the wine.

Pervini, Manduria: Primitivo – P. del Tarantino IGT I Monili; P. di Manduria DOC Pervini; P. di Manduria DOC Archidamo; P. di Manduria Dolce Naturale DOC Primo Amore.

Others: Rosso Salento IGT Galante (Negroamaro plus Primitivo and Malvasia Nera); Rosso Bizantino; Gorgolano.

Felline, Manduria: Primitivo di Manduria Felline; Rosso Salento Alberello; Rosso Puglia IGT Vigna del Feudo; La Quadratura del Cerchio Vino da Tavola (Primitivo di Manduria 70%, Sangiovese Grosso di Montalcino 30% – this being an experimental wine of Roberto Cipresso).

Masseria Pepe, Maruggio: Primitivo del Tarantino IGT Portile; Primitivo di Manduria DOC Dunico (this latter a blockbuster of a wine – 14.5% – grown on *alberello* vines planted in sand).

Sinfarosa, Avetrana: Primitivo del Tarantino IGT; Primitivo di Manduria DOC Zinfandel. This latter was another early *tre bicchieri* winner.

Other producers associated with the Accademia, but who are not producing significant amounts of Primitivo, include: **Castel di Salve**, Ugento; **Casale Bevagna**, Guagnano; **Antica Masseria Torre Mozza**. This does not, however, by any means exhaust the list.

Other producers of Primitivo at a reasonable to good quality level include: **Antica Masseria del Sigillo** (Terre del Guiscardo – with Cabernet Sauvignon and Merlot), Guagnano; Cantele (Salento Primitivo); La Mea (Fra Diavolo); Fusione (A. Mano); C.S. **Locorotondo** (P. di Manduria Terre di Don Pepe), Locorotondo;

Lomazzi & Sarli (P. del Salento Latias); C.S. di **Lizzano** (P. del Tarantino; P. di Manduria Dolce Monte Manco), Lizzano; Masseria Monaci (P. del Salento I Censi); Rivera (Triusco); C.S. **Sava** (P. di Manduria Passione; P. di Manduria Mamma Teresa; P. del Tarantino Le Petrose; P. del Tarantino Terrarossa), Sava.

UVA DI TROIA

That this grape originated in Troy, in Asia Minor, is pure surmise, although why else would it have the name? Because it's named after the town east of Foggia named Troia, say some, not unreasonably. Either way it probably arrived from Greece in the millennium before Christ, and today has found its 'cultural epicentre' in the higher altitudes of Castel del Monte in the Murge, although it is cultivated, ever less it must be said, in various lower zones of the provinces of Bari and Foggia.

Uva di Troia likes warm climates, indeed one of its synonyms is Uva della Marina, such alcohol and body does it give near to sea level. It ripens rather late by Puglian standards, in middle to late October, is reasonably productive, reasonably consistent, reasonably resistant to disease, having the added advantage in modern times of accommodating itself quite docilely to mechanisation.

Then why does it appear to be vanishing from the vineyards of the earth at quite such a rate, one wonders? EU strikes again!

By far the most important Uva di Troia-based wine is Castel del Monte Rosso, although the *disciplinare* is a bizarre one, admitting Uva di Troia **and/or** Aglianico **and/or** Montepulciano with the 'possible addition of other non-aromatic red grapes at 35% maximum'. In other words, if you don't want to include Uva di Troia at all in your Castel del Monte Rosso, you needn't; or you can drown it out with something else. As it happens, the most important producer by far, Rivera, does major on Uva di Troia in their outstanding Riserva 'Il Falcone', so we have a chance to taste a quality version before it disappears completely.

The Rosato of the same DOC may also contain Uva di Troia, but doesn't to any extent. Other DOCs in which the grape features are either dwindling in production or have vanished out of sight. Rosso Barletta, a coastal red, does exist to some small extent. Rosso Canova and Ortanova Rosso seem more theoretical than actual. The nearest thing to a real wine outside of the above is the varietal made at the Cantele winery by New Zealand flying winemaker Kym Milne and on sale in British supermarkets at a surprisingly modest price.

As indicated, the most important producer of Uva di Troia is **Rivera**, Andria. This famous winery, which carries the name of the estate in which it is situated, as distinct from that of the DOC zone which, as indicated above, is Castel del Monte (named in turn after a striking octagonal castle with no apparent offensive or defensive capacity, built for mysterious reasons by Frederick II of Swabia at the beginning of the twelfth century), has been noted for quality bottled wines longer than practically any other in Puglia. The large property was purchased in the early twentieth century by Giuseppe de Corato, whose son Sebastiano founded the actual winery in the 1950s. Sebastiano was succeeded by his son Carlo, who in the past 20 or so years has made major changes in the vineyards, adding to the ampelographical patrimony, based on Uva di Troia (they also call it Nero di Troia), Montepulciano, Bombino Nero, Bombino Bianco and Moscato, by planting Aglianico, Primitivo, Sauvignon, Chardonnay and Pinot Bianco, several of which are made varietally under the Terre al Monte label. Carlo, one of the most respected of the establishment figures on the Puglian wine scene today, also installed a completely modern *cantina* in 1993 to keep the family firm abreast of market trends.

Rivera make a fairly wide gamut of wines using a number of different grape varieties, mentioned above. Their flagship wine, Castel del Monte Riserva Il Falcone, so named because Frederick II was apparently keen on hunting with falcons, is made principally of Uva di Troia – three different clones – and Montepulciano from old vines and aged 12 to 18 months in French oak *barriques*. It is a wine of around 13.5% alcohol, quite tight in youth with some firm tannins and a wild raspberry tinge to the aroma, capable of opening out with bottle age to reveal a complex of tertiary aromas, whilst the tannins gradually round out to reveal a very harmonious whole. A wine of elegance and moderate power, Il Falcone, as its name suggests, is best with game and roast meats.

The other wine from Rivera which features Uva di Troia, this time in minority proportion with Montepulciano, is Rupicolo di Rivera, a Castel del Monte Rosso of lesser concentration than Il Falcone, but capable of being drunk younger.

Rivera's other wines have been or will be mentioned under the appropriate grape varieties, though it is worth citing two recent introductions: the varietal Aglianico mentioned above called Cappellaccio; and the Primitivo IGT Puglia called Triusco, both *barrique*-aged to achieve the modern style.

Other producers of Uva di Troia, virtually all of them in the Castel del Monte DOC district, include: **Santa Lucia** (Castel del Monte Rosso and Rosso Riserva; Vigna del Pozzo), Corato; **Torrevento** (Castel del Monte Rosso and Rosso Riserva Vigna Pedale, Corato).

MONTEPULCIANO

(For general remarks on Montepulciano see chapter on Central Italy East.)

Montepulciano appears to have arrived in Puglia around the beginning of the twentieth century, and today forms the basis of the San Severo Rosso and Rosato wines produced in such volume in the Province of Foggia. A producer of good wine amid all the plonk is **D'Alfonso del Sordo**, at the town of San Severo.

Traditionally, Montepulciano has been less strong in the centre and south, but it has played a significant role in blends, with Negroamaro and Uva di Troia in particular, as we have seen. Today that role is extending, growers wisely preferring to use a blending agent which is at least semi-native to one which is completely foreign, like Cabernet Sauvignon. There are even blends in which Montepulciano is the dominant factor, like Priante (with Negroamaro at 30%, Malvasia Nera at 10%), from Castel di Salve, mentioned under Accademia dei Racemi; or Maestro (with Uva di Troia) from **Borgo Canale** at Fasano.

MALVASIA NERA (M.N.)

Two sub-varieties of black Malvasia, M.N. di Lecce and M.N. di Brindisi, are grown in Puglia, their differences less intrinsic than due to pedo-climatic conditions (Calò et al. regard them as synonymous). Like the white family, the blacks would have come from, or rather through, Monemvasia in the Peloponnese, probably in the early Middle Ages. They are medium-term ripeners giving good sugar levels with lowish tannin and total acidity, the aromas being slightly or not at all aromatic for which their direct connection with white members of the Malvasia family has been doubted. Malvasia di Lecce is mentioned at second or third fiddle in the *disciplinare* of every Negroamaro-based wine in the province of Lecce, although it has been losing ground in its supporting role, mainly to Montepulciano, due to its unimpressive ageing qualities. Malvasia di Brindisi is mentioned, also as a blender, in a number of other DOCs in the provinces of Brindisi, Taranto and even Foggia, although its principal use has been as a component of *filtrato dolce*, the concentrate that Italians are supposed to, but increasingly do not, use for purposes of boosting alcohol.

AGLIANICO

(For general remarks on Aglianico see the section on Campania and Basilicata above.)

As has been said, Aglianico is primarily a phenomenon of

Campania and Basilicata, but it has to some extent leaked across the border into Puglia, especially into the middle part of Le Murge. It needs relatively cool climes, and would doubtless find the low-lying flatlands of northern or southern Puglia too hot.

One producer that has made a good thing of Aglianico is Cantine **Botromagno** of Gravina di Puglia (see also under Greco). Their Pier delle Vigne Rosso Murge IGT is a blend of 60% Aglianico and 40% Montepulciano, *barrique*-aged and given quite a lot of bottle-ageing as well prior to release. This is a wine, perhaps typically for Aglianico, of elegance rather than power, not perhaps what one expects from Puglia but very tasty all the same. Severino Garofano is the consultant oenologist.

Rivera make Rosso and Rosato from Aglianico under the Terre al Monte label. The Rosso is a good example, medium full-bodied and elegant with typical aromas of cranberries and wild fruit. Ageing is in French oak *barriques* of second passage, so the wine receives the effect of oak without too much of the smell and taste. Recently, they have added to their range a more streamlined version of Aglianico Castel del Monte DOC called Cappellaccio, a wine which straddles the traditional–modern divide by achieving good varietal character – wild berry, with some intensity – and smooth tannins by dint of a year's ageing in new French *barrique*.

The latest producer to introduce Aglianico, along with Cabernet Sauvignon and Merlot, is Antinori at their estate called Tormaresca at Minervino Murge in the province of Bari. This property was purchased by the Tuscan giant from the Piemontese firm of Gancia towards the end of the 1990s. At the time of writing the only red to emerge, Tormaresca Rosso, is a relatively easy-quaffing, fruity/international-style unoaked blend of Aglianico with Cabernet Sauvignon and Merlot.

SANGIOVESE

(For general remarks on Sangiovese see chapter on Central Italy West.)

Italy's favourite red grape is used for blending purposes in a diversity of wines throughout Puglia, though only in Ortanova Rosso, which hardly exists, is it the principal variety.

Now that Puglia is an admitted focus of interest for Tuscan producers, who have always used Puglian grapes, musts or wines, but more or less clandestinely, Sangiovese is receiving ever more attention here. One of the itinerant oenological consultants from Tuscany, today heavily engaged in Puglian matters, has even opined that Puglia is a better place to grow Sangiovese than Tuscany. There is little evidence at the moment to support this heretical contention, but it is a fact that Sangiovese is turning up in more and more blends and even in the occasional varietal. An example is Castel di Salve's Il Volo di Alessandro. Rubino also produce a Sangiovese under the Terra dei Messapi label.

BOMBINO NERO

Noted for its abundant production of juicy if rather simplistic fruit, this grape's principal growing area in Puglia is in the area of Castel del Monte. The epithet *'nero'* (black) is something of a misnomer, as Bombino is light in polyphenols which, combined with its juiciness, makes for an ideal *rosato* grape.

The most famous version has for decades been that of Rivera, this being the wine that made them famous throughout Italy. To this day they describe it as their 'pride and joy'. Rivera Rosé (sic; they prefer the French word to the Italian *rosato*) is made from natural free-run juice without recourse to a press, which accounts for its freshness and delicacy of aroma and flavour. It tends to be a degree or two lighter in alcohol than the Negroamaro-based *rosato*s of the Salento.

Bombino Nero also enjoys a certain presence in Latium as Bonvino.

SUSUMANIELLO

One of the three principal components, together with Negroamaro and Malvasia Nera, of Brindisi's famous – or infamous – *filtrato dolce*, this native of Dalmatia is noted for its intense colour, firm acidity and generous productivity. With the decreasing demand for cutting wines Susumaniello is on the decline.

OTTAVIANELLO

This, apparently, is the same as southern France's Cinsaut. The name is said to derive from Ottaviano, a commune of the province of Naples whence it was brought to Puglia by the Marchese di Bugnano. An example of a varietal wine is produced by growers Michele Greco and Luciano Sardelli under the aegis of the Accademia dei Racemi.

ALEATICO

(For general remarks see chapter on Central Italy West.)

Aleatico is grown in many parts of Puglia, hence the principal DOC, Aleatico di Puglia. But its main presence is in the Salento and in the Province of Bari, having its own DOC, Naturale and Liquoroso, under the Gioia del Colle multi-DOC. Its wines are almost always vinified sweet, and although it may be blended with other grapes for body the best results are generally 100% varietal. It ripens in late September/early October but responds well to being left on the vine for a couple of weeks for a bit of surmaturation.

A typical sweet Aleatico from Puglia might have around 13% alcohol with 80 grams per litre residual sugar. Acidity inclines to be moderate, but sufficient to prevent the wine being cloying.

Two good, and good-value, examples are from Candido and Leone di Castris (Negrino).

GRAPES, WINES AND PRODUCERS – WHITE

None of the white varieties associated primarily with Puglia are of particular distinction. The interesting white wines, such as they are, are all being produced from French grapes, discussed in the chapter on international varieties, or from grapes associated with other Italian regions.

The Puglians include the following.

VERDECA

The origins of this grape are unknown, possibly because no one can be bothered to inquire. Certain it is that it is not related to Verdicchio, although that name figures among its synonyms. Verdeca is the mainstay, with Bianco d'Alessano, of what is probably Puglia's best-known white, Locorotondo, and its neighbour Martina Franca. Both wines, if you're lucky, will be fresh enough, if characterless. A lot of vermouth-base comes from this area.

Good Locorotondo – and Locorotondo DOC never really rises above that category – is available from the C.S. **Locorotondo** at the town of the same name in the heart of *trulli* country. This is the oldest cooperative in Puglia, founded in the early 1930s when the price of grapes was so low that growers were reduced to absolute misery. Today they boast over 1,200 members spread through the provinces of Bari, Taranto and Brindisi and turn out up to 15,000,000 litres of wine per annum, the cream of which is bottled. Having growers in three separate major zones their range is considerable and includes several versions of Locorotondo, most of them made from Verdeca plus Bianco d'Alessano. The top selection is called Tallinaio.

Other producers of decent Verdeca include: Michele Calò (Mjere Bianco); Leone de Castris (Messapia); Rivera (Locorotondo Still and 'Vivace' – slightly sparkling).

BIANCO D'ALESSANO

This grape is used extensively in blends throughout Puglia, often with Verdeca – at least on paper. The paper, however, does not accurately reflect the reality of our time, as this neutral variety giving straw-coloured wine yields more and more to the invading foreign hordes, as indeed to Verdeca, more productive and giving wine of a greener hue. If there is a varietal wine made from Bianco d'Alessano that is of any interest I do not know about it.

PAMPANUTO

A variety peculiar to the Castel del Monte zone, or perhaps rather a sub-variety of Bianco d'Alessano somewhat modified by the local *terroir*, Pampanuto is used at 65%, with 35% Bombino Bianco, in Rivera's respectable if uninspiring Bianca di Sveva.

BOMBINO BIANCO

See also Pagadebit, centre east.

Produced in massive quantities on *tendone*-trained vineyards in the flatlands of the Capitanata, for use in San Severo Bianco and a whole load of bulk stuff on top, Bombino Bianco can make as dull and tasteless a wine as you could hope to find. Where yields are reduced the wine can have a certain concentration and interest, though suitable more for the drinker than the thinker. D'Alfonso del Sordo does as good a job as any.

GRECO DI TUFO

For general remarks see section on Campania.

What little there is of this grape in Puglia tends to be in the centre west on the border with Campania from where it originates. Gravina, probably the region's most characterful white from non-French grapes, can be very tasty, with some fatness of texture and a pineappley, tropical fruit salady character to it. It is certainly amazing value for money coming from the one major producer, Cantina Botromagno, who despite the invitation of the *disciplinare* to use Bianco d'Alessano together with Malvasia prefer to dose their wine with Greco 'to the maximum extent'. This is a change introduced from 1991, when local lawyer Beniamino d'Agostino took the winery over from the local cooperative. Many of the growers – some 200 of them – who conferred their grapes previously to the *cantina sociale* previously do so now to Botromagno. Certainly quality is up, drastically, Beniamino and his colleagues having invested heavily in replanting the vineyards and re-equipping the winery.

IMPIGNO AND FRANCAVILLA

These are the main varieties in the famous Ostuni Bianco, backed up (oh joy!) by Verdeca and Bianco d'Alessano. I confess that I have never seen a bottle or tasted a drop of Ostuni Bianco.

TREBBIANO TOSCANO AND MALVASIA TOSCANA

For general comments see the section on central Italy west.

Mentioned in the blends of a number of Puglian whites, these neutral Tuscans seem to some extent to be taking over from the neutral Puglians, especially in the areas of bulk white production.

MOSCATO BIANCO

For general remarks see *Barolo to Valpolicella*, north west.

Sweet wines from super-ripe, slightly late-picked grapes are made from Moscato Bianco in central Puglia, especially round the town of Trani, on the coast northwest of Bari, where the style rates a DOC. The Dolce Naturale version is advised, the one called Liquoroso being somewhat clumsy. A typical Dolce Natural will have some 14–15% alcohol and a further four or more in residual sugar. The nose should have the usual floral-rosy-musky aromas of the ripe grape, and it should have a certain fat in mouth, while being harmonised by a firm acidity.

Good examples come from: C.S. Locorotondo (Moscato di Puglia IGT Olimpia); Rivera (Moscato di Trani Piani di Tufara); and Torrevento (Moscato di Trani Dulcis in Fundo).

CALABRIA

You might think there'd be a lot to say about Calabria, winewise. Big place. Ancient tradition, even though a goodly part of it is sheer myth, begun in imagination and perpetuated by 'the art of copying' – so we'll spare you it, except to say that it consists of variations on the theme that 'ancient Olympians imbibed here'. A great deal of uncultivatable mountain territory, true, but lots of suitable sites for quality viticulture on inland slopes or in foothills near coastlines, on which there are nearly 800 kilometres – certainly the arid, stony soil is not good for much else apart from the vine and associated crops – olives, tourists. And, with all those mountains, plenty of different combinations of altitude and exposure to choose from.

And, indeed, the production statistics are not unimpressive. Over 25,000 hectares of vineyard. Around a million hectolitres of wine produced annually. Not a lot by Puglian or Sicilian standards, admittedly, but not a cause for sneezing – near enough 130 million *pezzi*, if all of it were bottled.

Bottled? Aye, there's the rub. A mere 8% or less is suitable for bottling, or at least bottling and exporting – outside of Calabria, that is – and probably three-quarters of that comes from a single, quite restricted vineyard area, Cirò and surrounds. And even here production is controlled by a mere handful or less of merchant-producers, and within that handful one, Librandi, stands head and shoulders above the rest in terms of the international market.

So, out of this vast country with its illustrious vinous past, a land so prized by the Greeks that they named it Enotria; from this ancient territory with its undoubtedly outstanding vocation for fine wine production, we are reduced to a single producer? Well, not quite, there's Odoardi over on the west coast and there's, er . . .

'I feel very alone here', says Nicodemo Librandi. 'I long for the community of good winemakers that you find in Piemonte or Tuscany.'

The worrying thing is that almost nothing much has changed since the last time I went through the exercise of writing a book on Italian wines, a good 15 years ago. Whereas Puglia, or parts of it, has made significant strides towards hauling itself in the direction of the twenty-first century; while Campania has woken up to the hidden treasure of its native grape varieties after an age-long slumber; while Sicily struggles mightily to exorcise the evil spirits of the past and to realise its so-called 'quality revolution'; and while a growing number of producers join the quality bandwagon in Sardinia; Calabrian producers with very few exceptions have scarcely responded to the challenge of a new age dawning.

Perhaps it has something to do with the sense of isolation referred to above – there is a certain eerie, other-worldly feel about this mainland extremity compared with the rest of the south, even the islands. Perhaps it has to do with the political-economic situation after decades of oppression by such exploiters of ignorance as the 'Ndrangheta (the Calabrian mafia) and, worse still (shudder), the local government. 'They should all be massacred and thrown into a crematorium', said one kindly observer, commenting on the 'bassissimo livello' of local politicians who, he added, operate a 'politics of support' for the unsuccessful rather than one of encouragement for the ambitious.

At any rate, Calabrians cannot blame a shortage of interesting raw material to work with, since their region can boast a diversity of indigenous grape-types which most producing nations ought to offer their proverbial right arm for; they probably wouldn't, because they're so happy with Cabernet & Co; but they ought to.

Gaglioppo, Magliocco, Greco Nero, Nerello Cappuccio among reds, Mantonico and Greco di Bianco among whites – all of these either do or could produce interesting wines. And what's to stop the Calabresi, like everyone else, planting the international brigade? Indeed Librandi and Odoardi both have done so with conspicuous success.

As for the places of signficance, as I have said, the most important from the quantity/quality point of view is Cirò, as the DOC is called, with nearly 1,000 hectares of DOC vineyard. Indeed Cirò is the standard-bearer for all Calabrian viticulture. As one producer explained: 'You will find Calabrians in every part of the world. Since the only valid Calabrian wine is Cirò, from whatever part of the region they come, Cirò wine is their reference point.'

There are two Ciròs: the town on the hill has been there since Greek times and beyond, looking down over vineyards, olive groves and sea from a couple of kilometres inland; and Cirò Marina, on the coast as the name suggests, a relative newcomer thanks to the making good of the land which, until a few decades ago, was malarial swamp. The *disciplinare* for Cirò Rosso calls for the Gaglioppo grape with a possible 5% addition of whites, Greco or Trebbiano. Epithets like Superiore and Riserva, as usual, refer to higher alcohol level and longer ageing time, rather than to higher quality as such. The word Classico refers to wines from grapes grown within the communes of Cirò and Cirò Marina.

Cirò Rosato follows the same recipe as Rosso. Cirò Bianco is based on Greco Bianco, with a possible adjunct of Trebbiano. Neither is allowed the embellishing epithets.

Melissa, next door to Cirò, produces Rosso and Bianco along very similar lines. There's not much volume compared with what its neighbour churns out, but the total is probably around equal to the production of all the other DOCs combined in the rest of Calabria.

A tiny but excellent reality is that of the area of Bianco, not a colour in this instance but a village in the far south of the Ionian coast. Here delicious sweet wines are produced from Greco di Bianco, which is the name of the grape variety and of the DOC; and from Mantonico, which inexplicably is not recognised as DOC. Non-DOC Mantonico Passito is now being made also in Cirò from grapes left 15–20 days to dry in the sun.

The only other DOCs which are likely to be found on export markets today are Savuto and Scavigna, and this thanks to the other dynamic producer of Calabria, Odoardi. Odoardi is, indeed, the only significant producer of these DOCs, especially of the more recent Scavigna, which (the Rosso) differs from Savuto mainly in allowing a hefty dollop of international grapes into the blend (based on Gaglioppo, but Odoardi, not being an admirer of that grape, are trying to change that) by the 'recommended or authorised up to a maximum of 40%' route. Scavigna Bianco allows internationals by the same route. Savuto doesn't have a white.

All other DOCs are obscure not to say virtually non-existent. Heading south from just below the Basilicata border towards the centre of the region, more or less following the major *autostrada*, Pollino and Donnici both produce reds along lines similar to those of Cirò/Melissa Rosso, with Gaglioppo in the dominating role. Sant'Anna di Isola Capo Rizzuto, on the Ionian coast south of Pythagoras' Crotone, is similar. Bivongi, Lamezia, San Vito di Luzzi and Verbicaro are scattered multi-DOCs of little significance whose reds, whites and *rosato*s more or less follow the Cirò patterns.

GRAPES, WINES AND PRODUCERS – RED

GAGLIOPPO

Until recently mythologised as an ancient variety, dating back to when Calabria was a Greek colony, Gaglioppo's romantic image has been dented somewhat by research which has failed to find any confirmation of its existence in Calabria beyond about a century ago, when after phylloxera the vineyards were replanted; and indeed when the recently drained vineyards of present-day Cirò Marina, until then marshland, were first planted. Documents referring to the 100+ varieties existent in Calabria at that time fail to mention Gaglioppo. Calabrian producers still maintain that the grape is of Greek origin and has been in their vineyards *da sempre*; but they would, wouldn't they.

The fact that Gaglioppo became so popular after phylloxera no doubt owes much to the abundance and consistency of its production. It seems possible that Gaglioppo arrived in Calabria from Abruzzo/Marche, where, as in Basilicata and Campania, it can still be found. Indeed, it bears some resemblance to Aglianico, and a relationship has been suggested by a prominent Calabrian grower. Might there be something in this?

Well, like Aglianico, Gaglioppo is a vigorous variety, late ripening, high in tannin, and it has red flesh – unusual in quality red wine grapes. But it is distinctly lower in anthocyanins (colour substances), with a marked tendency for the wine to take on orange tints if not handled correctly. The aromas tend towards the floral and vegetal, unlike the cherry and spice of Aglianico.

In other words, more than to Aglianico Gaglioppo bears an uncanny resemblance to Nebbiolo – not that anyone is suggesting they are related. The resemblance has not in the past escaped the notice of certain large-scale producers of the Alba and Gattinara areas, where vintages are not so reliable as they are down south. Rumours of large road-tankers rumbling northward from Calabria in the dead of night have been heard in the past, although no one of course would dream of suggesting that such a thing could possibly happen today.

Some pundits, including Calò et al., have maintained instead that Gaglioppo and south-eastern Sicily's Frappato are genetically related, both being light in colour and vegetal-floral of bouquet. There may well be something in this. Until recently, Gaglioppo's tannins have constituted a major detractor from its ability to charm the wine-bibbing public at large. Attempts were made to resolve the problem by the most rational route, a shortening of maceration time on the skins. The result was less flavour, less colour – and no reduction in asperity. So Severino Garofano, consultant at large in Puglia who has also worked with producers in Cirò, hit on the idea of extending the maceration time, but at low temperatures and uppish sulphur doses in the early stages to inhibit fermentation, in order to give the tannins an opportunity to polymerise (cluster together) and so fall. The wines made in this way still have firm, but ripe tannins which seem, as in the case of Nebbiolo, to balance beautifully against the ripe, sweet, slightly decadent fruit.

Another method of reducing the problem of the oxidation of Gaglioppo's colouring matter is to introduce oxygen into the liquid at an early stage by the process of *delestage*, the transferring of must/wine from tank to tank and back again during the fermentation process. Micro-oxygenation (pumping air through the must) might be another solution for larger volumes.

OTHER RED VARIETIES

Mentioned as support grapes to Gaglioppo for the various DOCs are the Sicilian pair, Nerello Mascalese and Nerello Cappuccio; Nero d'Avola, also confusingly known as Calabrese, although it is almost certainly not of Calabrian but of Sicilian origin; Magliocco and Arvino, which are mentioned in the *Codice Denominazionei di Origine dei Vini* as synonyms for Gaglioppo, but which in tests carried out by Librandi behave quite differently (Magliocco[1] ripens later and gives a distinctly sturdier wine); Greco Nero, also known as Maglioccone – just to add to the confusion – and as Marsigliana, though some *disciplinari* list these as separate varieties; Nocera; and others including Sangiovese. None of these, apart from Sangiovese and the Sicilians, which are described in their place, seems of sufficient importance, or of sufficient clarity of identity, to be worth describing in detail, even were I capable of doing so. Though it is worth pointing the reader towards the entry on the house of Librandi at Cirò Marina, where plantings have been made of various Calabrian native grapes.

The producers

Azienda Vitivinicola **Librandi**, Cirò Marina. The Librandi family has been engaged in viticulture in the historic Cirò zone on Calabria's east coast for several generations. The father of present owners Antonio and Nicodemo, more enterprising than his forebears, established a winery in the middle of the twentieth century for the transformation of the raw material into wine, which he sold in bulk. He died, however, in the early 1950s, and elder brother Antonio was obliged to interrupt his studies and take over the business. It was he who raised the level another notch and started the process of bottling.

In 1971 younger brother Nicodemo finished his studies and entered the family business part time, switching to full time in 1975. While Antonio looked after production at home, Nicodemo hit the trail and started selling the wines at first in Calabria, then in

---

1 Magliocco Tondo is the sub-variety mentioned in 'Vitigni d'Italia' as being synonymous with Gaglioppo. The same work cites Magliocco Canino as an erroneous synonym of Gaglioppo.

northern Italy, followed, despite a total absence of linguistic skills, by northern Europe, especially Germany.

In 1975, wishing to improve production, the Librandi engaged the famous Puglian oenologist, Severino Garofano. In the early 1980s they expanded operations to a new vineyard area in the hills of Strongoli, several kilometres distant from their original near-sea-level vine-zone at Cirò Marina, where the Gaglioppo and Greco trained to *alberello,* from vineyards owned by them or whose fruit they purchase, provide the raw material for base wines Cirò Rosso, Rosato and Bianco, as well as for the Cirò *cru,* Duca San Felice.

Garofano it was who persuaded the Librandi brothers to plant, in their 40 hectares at Strongoli, among the first in Italy let alone in Calabria, grape varieties which today are spreading everywhere, namely Chardonnay and Sauvignon (for Critone), Cabernet Sauvignon (for Gravello, the *azienda*'s top wine, blended with Gaglioppo) and Cabernet Franc (for top-line *rosato* Terre Lontane) as well as the Calabrian Mantonico (for sweet wine Le Passule). These wines, excellent of conception and execution, have given Librandi an image – fully justified – as one of the most modern-thinking producers of southern Italy.

In 1997 Librandi and Garofano parted company and Piemontese consultant Donato Lanati stepped in, bringing with him the advice

of Italy's most prominent viticultural consultant, Professor Attilio Scienza of Milan University. It had been Nicodemo Librandi's dream for several years to bring together in a single vineyard the best indigenous varieties of Calabria, and he had undertaken numerous trips all round the region to source the material for his experiment. In the mid-1990s they had acquired a superb 160-hectare site at Rosaneti, beyond Strongoli, and in recent years with the guidance of Lanati and Scienza as to what variety would go best in which terrain they have been busily planting, at a rate of about 25 hectares per year, carefully propagated clones of Calabrian originals like Gaglioppo, Magliocco Canino, Arvino, Guarnaccia Nero, Castiglione Nero, Marsigliana, Greco Nero di Sibari, Mantonico Nero among reds, Greco di Bianco, Mantonico, Guarnaccino Bianco, Iuvarello Bianco among whites.

The first of the indigenous varietal wines, Magno Magonio, from Magliocco Canino vinified *in purezza*, appeared in the late 1990s and took critics and buyers by storm – the limited first edition was sold out not long after its appearance on the market. This is a wine of ruby colour – none of the premature orangeing of Gaglioppo – and distinct herbal-floral notes on the nose, having less sweet fruit on the palate than Gaglioppo but more spice, with an acidity and a tannin-base, ripe but present, capable of allowing it to refine 18 months in *barrique* and many years in bottle. Nicodemo is justifiably proud of it and considers it the new top of his range, even though the market would vote for his international style Gaglioppo–Cabernet blend Gravello, regularly included among the best four or five wines of the south, and I personally still prefer the unique Cirò Rosso Duca San Felice, a monument, in my opinion, to the Gaglioppo grape which has taken a lot of stick but which, on this evidence, is capable of great things. Duca San Felice, which is aged exclusively in steel and glass, has a nose of plums and prunes, dried fruits and herbs, something decadent but yet alluring. It is most attractive on the palate where the fruit is sweet, long and complex, almost a little porty on the finish like a good Nebbiolo.

'On our grapes, on our soils, on our wines no one has ever carried out any form of research', commented Nicodemo. 'We are doing it. We have certain advantages here in Calabria', he added: 'Plenty of sun and warmth, the tempering influence of the nearby sea, little disease, no hail. We Calabrians have always translated these advantages into high quantity and low prices. We are trying to change all that.

'I only wish there were more people doing similar work. The low image of Calabria hurts everyone. We try to promote the region by organising conferences where we invite all the most influential Italian and foreign wine consultants and press. Last time we did this, we invited scores of Calabrian producers to come and participate. Only Odoardi came.'

Azienda Agricola **Odoardi**, Nocera Terinese. Brothers Gregorio and Giovanbattista Odoardi, the former a radiologist, the latter full-time at the *cantina*, run this operation initiated in the 1970s by their late father who, though a medical man himself, had a passion for wine which he passed on to his sons; indeed the Odoardi family have been involved in viticulture since the sixteenth century. The winery, at some 600 metres altitude, is situated strategically between the DOCs of Savuto and Scavigna, between which they possess almost 60 hectares of vineyard – 40 in Scavigna – which they hope to make up to nearly 100 by the year 2004. To arrive at the winery it is necessary, starting virtually from sea-level, to drive up steep slopes via innumerable curves and past vineyards belonging in several instances to the Odoardi brothers, the lower ones being in the Savuto zone, the higher ones being Scavigna.

Considering only their *cru* wines, Odoardi make one single-vineyard Savuto, one single-vineyard Scavigna red and one white, plus a single-vineyard sweet wine. The Savuto – a red wine, because the DOC doesn't provide for a white – comes from Vigna Mortilla at 80–120 metres altitude, planted in the late 1970s to a mix of grapes including Gaglioppo (locally, for confusion's sake, called Magliocco or Arvino – 45%), Sangiovese (10%), Greco Nero (10%), Nerello Cappuccio (10%), Magliocco Canino (10%), Pecorello (here called Pecorino – 10%), Malvasia (5%). The vintage takes place normally in the second half of October and the wine is aged 12 months in French *barrique*. Recent versions of this wine, made with the help of their Tuscan consultant Stefano Chioccioli, have confirmed it as one of the best and most original of the Italian-style reds of the south.

Scavigna is a more recent DOC, dating back to 1994, and here not only are Odoardi the only significant producers but their uncle was virtually the author of the *disciplinare*. Scavigna Bianco allows Chardonnay, Pinot Bianco and Riesling Italico (their blend) on top of the Trebbiano and Greco Bianco which they ignore; their single-vineyard Pian della Corte is a soft, full-coloured, modern-style white with little or no resemblance to other Calabrian white wines. Scavigna Rosso boasts a very flexible DOC calling for Gaglioppo 'up to 60%' and Nerello Cappuccio at 'up to 40%', with 40% allowed for other grapes which could include Cabernet, Merlot and Aglianico (which, conveniently, is known locally as 'Gaglioffo'). Let's just say that, in their Scavigna Rosso Vigna Garrone Odoardi operate at the minimum end for the Calabrian grapes and the maximum end for the imported ones; an interesting blend, mix of the Italian and the international, structured yet intensely fruity, more individual than many of the international-style wines one sees on the market.

Future plantings will, I understand, involve Aglianico, Nero d'Avola, Syrah and Sangiovese, none of which, with the possible exception of Sangiovese, is traditional for the zone. Odoardi also make a dessert wine, Valeo, with Pantelleria's Zibibbo plus a type of Moscato whose identity is apparently a mystery and which they call, aptly enough, Valeo. It is a wine of marked grapey aroma, medium-sweet, with a marzipan and muscat palate, and they sell a lot of it to a wine-merchant in Paris, about which they are particularly proud.

Other good Calabrian red wine producers include: Caparra & Siciliani (Cirò Rosso Volvito), Cirò Marina; Lento (Lamezia Riserva), Lamezia Terme; San Francesco (Cirò Ronco dei Quatro Venti; Cirò Donna Madda; Martà – Gaglioppo/Merlot), Cirò; Statti (Cauro – Gaglioppo/Magliocco/Cabernet), Lamezia Terme.

GRAPES, WINES AND PRODUCERS – WHITE

GRECO DE CIRÒ AND GRECO DI BIANCO

It seems clear that these are varieties sufficiently different from the Greco di Tufo of Avellino to warrant separate attention; though it may well be that they are all ultimately related, and we may assume from the name that they were imported millennia ago by Greeks.

Ampelographers of the not so distant past have maintained that the Greco Bianco of Cirò and that of the town (confusingly) of Bianco 150 kilometres or so farther down the east coast are one and the same. Growers of Cirò like Librandi, who have plenty of the one and have recently planted some of the other, do not agree. Greco di Cirò is, they claim, a vigorous variety more given to high yields than to high quality. It performs best on the self-regulating *alberello*, giving a wine of fair body if rather low acidity. A good producer will capture its distinctive if subtle citric hints – orange peel, lime – but it's hard work to get good aromas at lower altitudes and the best producers are unhappy about it and intend to replace it with superior varieties, among others Greco di Bianco. Nor is there any legal reason why they should not do so, since as has been said they are officially considered the same thing.

For the time being, however, Greco di Cirò remains the mainstay of white wine production in Cirò thanks to its high productivity and despite its mediocre quality. Indeed Greco Bianco (as it is known in official writings) is the base grape of practically all the officially recognized dry white table wines of Calabria, and finds its way into the *disciplinare* of not a few reds too, including Cirò.

Greco di Bianco gives, according to Librandi, an altogether more concentrated, alcoholic and aromatic wine. In its home habitat it is mainly used to make sweet wine (which can be absolutely delicious) from grapes dried either on the plant or, briefly, in the sun.

The outstanding producer of Greco di Bianco at the town of Bianco is Ceratti.

OTHER WHITE VARIETIES

Mantonico, or Montonico, like Greco (probably) an ancient Greek import, can also give an outstanding *passito* wine, especially, again, from the area of Bianco, where it does not, however, enjoy DOC recognition. There is mention, too, of Mantonico in other DOCs, red and white, of Calabria, although there seems no certainty that it's the same thing. Librandi's delicious sweet wine, Le Passule, is made from Mantonico.

Trebbiano Toscano and Malvasia Bianca have made their way down here too, lending a further touch of the ordinary to wines which may already suffer from an excess of that commodity.

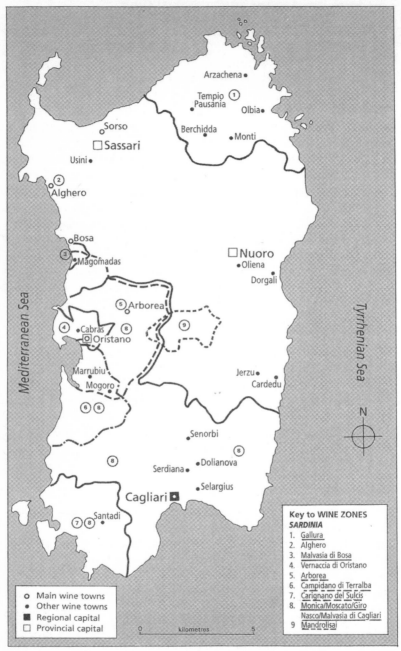

Key to WINE ZONES
SARDINIA
1. Gallura
2. Alghero
3. Malvasia di Bosa
4. Vernaccia di Oristano
5. Arborea
6. Campidano di Terralba
7. Carignano del Sulcis
8. Monica/Moscato/Giro Nasco/Malvasia di Cagliari
9. Mandrolisai

o Main wine towns
• Other wine towns
■ Regional capital
□ Provincial capital

kilometres

Sardinia

SARDINIA

Sardinia is a wine-land unto itself, with a range of grape varieties all its own, mostly of indigenous or Spanish origin, the region having been under Spanish rule for 400 years between the fourteenth and eighteenth centuries. Indeed Sardinia has been under foreign, including Italian, domination for most of its history, apart from a couple of centuries back in the Middle Ages. The list of overlords is like a who's who of Mediterranean powers: Phoenicians, Carthaginians, Etruscans, Greeks, Romans, Vandals, Arabs, Pisans, Genovese, Aragonese, Castilians, Piemontese, not to mention contemporary Italian Republicans. Italy is referred to by Sardinians not as our land but as the '*continente*', and wine sold there is regarded as an export. Somehow, through all of this, the island has managed to maintain a unique character, symbolised perhaps most poignantly by the ruins of the mysterious *nuraghi* – ubiquitous pre-historic pyramid-like structures about whose origins or purpose little or nothing is known – of the ancient inhabitants; and today by the still-thriving *dialetto*, with its polyglot origins.

It is a land of rugged topography, with plentiful craggy mountains and rocks and not a lot of arable soil – the exception being the Campidano plain in the south, which used to be regarded by the Romans as an essential source of grain. In other words, good for sheep and goats, olives and the vine, and not much else. The bark of the cork oak, of course – today big business in the northeast. And fish – Sardinia being famous for the clear, multi-coloured waters of its coastline, of which the absurdly over-touristified Costa Smeralda in the northeast is only one example. Strangely, though, the tourists never penetrate to the interior, where they would, were they to attempt it, find an atmosphere of mystery and peace, in many places almost timeless, nothing having changed it seems since forever. Good bandit country, too: maybe that's why non-Sardinians, especially rich ones of the Costa Smeralda ilk, steer clear.

Bandits are a logical outcome of the extreme poverty in which Sardinians have been held by their masters over the centuries. The Marxist cliché of the rich prospering on the backs of the poor has over the centuries been truer in Sardinia than in most places. Things were just beginning to look good for wine-farmers, at least, at the end of the nineteenth century when phylloxera struck, wiping out what had become a thriving wine industry with no less than 80,000 hectares of specialised vineyard – though 80% was in the province of Cagliari. An interesting light on those days is the fact that virtually all viticulture was on low-trained *alberello* with high density per hectare – around 12,000 plants – and with very low production per plant; all features to which quality viticulture is returning today. In the post-war period Sardinian viticulture became a matter of medium to high training – *spalliera* or *tendone* – low density, high production per plant and very high production per hectare; so lower alcohol, higher acidity, and much less character. To handle this glut of unwanted wine there grew up in the 1950s and 1960s a strong cooperative movement, heavily subsidised by politicians hungry for votes, to the enduring disgust of the private sector which has to finance itself, ampelographically and technologically.

The latest bandits, though well meaning, have been the EU with their subsidies for uprooting vineyards. In 1979 Sardinia produced 4 million hectolitres of wine; 20 years later the figure was around 750,000. From 40 *cantine sociali*, grouping some 25,000 producers responsible for 60% of Sardinian wine production, the number of cooperatives fell in the same period to 16, with several famous names, like Marmilla, going out of existence. The positive side of that coin, however, was that those which remained realised that they were no longer about production for the sake of production but that they had to compete on quality terms in the world market.

Today Sardinian viniculture seems to be finding its feet once again. Low-trained, low-producing vines planted 5 or 6,000 to the hectare are coming back into fashion, and those older-style vineyards that held out against the lure of the EU bribes – most extirpation happened in this high-quality area, rather than in that of the high-producing *tendone* – are being seen in a new, positive optic. There is no longer a fear of high alcohol wines, 13–15% and beyond, provided the extra octane entails a body and a depth that makes them stand out – Vermentino di Gallura Superiore DOCG being an excellent example. At the same time, the light, quaffing style championed by Sella & Mosca and others in the 1970s and 1980s has taken on more intensity and character, shedding some of that superclean neutrality that made them refreshing, yes, but boring, and today forms the other side of the base of a triangle of Sardinian style and quality.

The apex of the triangle consists in the 'meditation wines' of various types – this being a style for which Sardinia has tradition-ally been renowned. Magnificent wines of wonderful personality are being obtained today, from grapes like Nasco, Malvasia, Moscato, Vernaccia di Oristano and Cannonau, in the categories *dolce naturale, liquoroso dolce* and *secco*. Outstanding examples are Argiolas' Angialis, Sella & Mosca's Anghelu Ruju and, most unique of all, Contini's Vernaccia di Oristano Superiore, all of which we will encounter further on.

Taking the overnight car ferry from Livorno one arrives at Olbia bright and early and heads for the heart of the Gallura zone. This is Vermentino country *par excellence*, as is recognised by the fact that Vermentino di Gallura is Sardinia's only DOCG to date. The countryside is unspoiled (i.e. no tourists), rugged and rocky, with impressive outcrops like Monte Limbara dominating the skyline. The soil is granitic, both solid and decomposed, suitable for whites of structure. Cork oaks abound, stripped every nine years or more for their bark, the freshly stripped ones a deep glowing crimson to the top of the trunk, below where the branches form.

Production is dominated by cooperatives, in particular the Cantina del Vermentino at Monti, C.S. Giogantinu at Berchidda and C.S. Gallura at Tempio Pausania, on the opposite side of Limbara from the other two, these three having incidentally banded together to create a fourth brand for export purposes, Kàlike (Vermentino di Gallura). A bit of Vermentino di Sardegna DOC, allowed double the production of Gallura at 20 tonnes per hectare, is also produced – the DOCG must be at least 12%, Superiore denoting a minimum of 13%, while Vermentino di Sardegna may be as low as 10.5% – as is a certain amount of Moscato for the Asti-like Moscato di Sardegna. There is, too, a significant production of red wine, each *cantina* doing its own thing in this department and marketing the result usually as Colli del Limbara IGT, using a hodge-podge of local grapes like Nieddumannu, Pascale and Muristellu or Sardinian varieties like Monica and Cannonau; or international ones like Cabernet Sauvignon or Merlot; or varieties imported from the '*continente*', recently or decades back, like 'Nebbiolo' – most of which is apparently Dolcetto – and 'Brunello' (Sangiovese).

Apart from the cooperatives a sprinkling of private firms have managed to establish themselves also, notably Capichera at Arzachena, near the Costa Smeralda, who have succeeded in persuading buyers that their wine is worth three times the price of anyone else's – and they sell the lot.

From Gallura one may head down to the central-southeastern side of the island where Cannonau holds sway. The DOC here is plain Cannonau di Sardegna (Rosso or Rosato), since rival zones have never been able to agree on a common zonal denomination. The fact that around 90% of Cannonau is produced in this area, between Nuoro and Cagliari, without there being a specific zonal DOC rankles somewhat with major producers. There is, on the other hand, a provision to add the name Jerzu as a sub-zone, the same applying to Oliena to the north and Capo Ferrato farther south. The *cantine sociali* are even more dominant here, controlling the vast majority of production. Good private producers do exist, but they are few and far between.

The south of the island is where most vinous activity takes place, particularly in the area immediately to the north of the capital Cagliari, an area generally flat with some low rolling hills. Cagliari indeed is the umbrella name for a number of varietal sub-DOCs: the red Monica di Cagliari (there is also a Liquoroso version, as well as a DOC Monica di Sardegna at much heavier yield per hectare); the dry white Nuragus di Cagliari, allowed a whacking 20 tonnes per hectare production in the DOC; and the sweet-style Moscato di Cagliari, Malvasia di Cagliari, Nasco di Cagliari and Girò di Cagliari, although where the last three are concerned a dry wine, either natural or fortified, is also foreseen. Apart from these there is substantial production also of Vermentino di Sardegna – and here the 20 tonnes/hectare production allowed by the *disciplinare* is easily attainable, especially on *tendone*, unlike in Gallura – and a certain amount of Cannonau di Sardegna as well as of Carignano non-DOC.

The southwest corner of the island is the real stamping ground of Carignano, the DOC being Carignano del Sulcis (Rosso, Rosato, Novello, Passito). The country here is flat or at most gently rolling, the altitude is at or near sea-level and the summers are baking hot. Some of the best vineyards are grown on *alberello* in the coastal sands where phylloxera can't get at the roots, the resultant wines being big, warm and smooth.

The Campidano plain, running north and west of Cagliari, is primarily an area of grain production, but there is a certain amount of viticulture at the northern end. A limited amount of Sardegna

Semidano (dry, sparkling or Passito white) is produced here, sometimes under the name of the sub-zone Mogoro; a Passito version is also possible. There is also a modicum of the blended red Campidano di Terralba, a blend of Bovale, Pascale, Greco Nero, Monica and others. Here, also, is the zone of Arborea, where most of Sardinia's Sangiovese (Rosso and Rosato) and Trebbiano grapes are grown.

Slightly farther north is the zone of the unique Vernaccia di Oristano, described below under the grape variety. Another relatively unusual wine, Malvasia di Bosa, comes from a zone somewhat farther north again called Planargia – a name also used for the local IGT. This again is described in the section on grape varieties.

Towards the north of the western coast of the island is the picturesque and strongly Spanish-influenced port of Alghero, which gives its name to a number of sub-DOCs including, in the red department, Cabernet, Cagnulari, Sangiovese and a Rosso which may be from any of the authorised or recommended grapes for the province of Sassari, and which may manifest as a still wine, a Novello, a Spumante or a Liquoroso, the last named designed to cover Sella & Mosca's famous red dessert-wine, Anghelo Ruju Riserva. Alghero Rosato is from a similar grape mix. Alghero also covers a Bianco (still, Frizzante, Spumante or Passito), a Chardonnay, Sauvignon, Vermentino (Frizzante) and the area's very own grape variety, not found elsewhere on the island, Torbato. Apart from which, Sella & Mosca, the giants here – the giants of the private sector on the island, indeed – grow in their 500+ hectares of *tendone*-trained vineyard substantial amounts of Cannonau and Cabernet Sauvignon as well as bits of Nasco, Trebbiano, Carignano, Cabernet Franc, Merlot and Sangiovese. More on Sella & Mosca in the section on grape varieties, under Torbato.

To complete the quasi 360-degree tour of Sardinia's coastline we end up north and east of Sassari around the villages of Sorso and Sennori, whose names combine to form a DOC of little, almost non-existent production called Moscato di Sorso-Sennori. This wine, if you can find it, would be made of Moscato Bianco either late-harvested or *passito*, or it may be fortified in the Liquoroso Dolce form.

There is one wine that comes from the rocky-hilly Barbagia district at the heart of the island, almost equidistant between north and south and east and west. This is Mandrolisai, a Rosso (or

Rosato) from a blend of Bovale, Cannonau and Monica, with others allowed at a maximum of 10%.

GRAPES, WINES AND PRODUCERS – RED

CANNONAU

Sardinia's most-planted black grape – about 20% of total vineyard area – seems to have been brought by the Spanish during their lengthy occupation of the island between the fifteenth and eighteenth centuries. The precise date of introduction is lost in the mists of time, although the first mention of it, as 'Cannonadu', dates back to 1780. Ampelographers are satisfied that Cannonau is none other than what the French call Grenache, also of Spanish origin, and what in Seville is called Canonazo, in Aragon Granaxa originally, although Garnacha is the more common spelling in Spain today. Bruno Bruni, in *Principali Vitigni* (op. cit.) tells us that field studies comparing Cannonau and Grenache have led him to conclude that 'the first is a clone of the second'. Obviously, after several centuries in Sardinia the grape has taken on its own peculiar characteristics.

Cannonau is a vine of medium vigour, potentially very productive, thus requiring short pruning and a soil low in fertility. When grown on *alberello*, on slopes up to 700 metres, as was traditional until recently, it produces small amounts of wine of high sugar content, not particularly deep in colour, rich in tannin, or high in acidity. Lower down, on flatter land, production is greater but at the expense of elegance. The strong fruity-peppery character can be attractive but careful vinification is needed to highlight the soft-fruit aromas (strawberry, raspberry) and avoid a tendency to vulgarity. Picking usually takes place during the last third of September and the first half of October. Some say the wine is short-lived; some disagree. The fact that the latter are able to make excellent wine of medium duration suggests that they are right and the former simply haven't found the secret.

One producer whose aged Cannonaus are undoubtedly impressive is Alberto **Loi** of Cardedu in the province of Nuoro. Run by oenologist Sergio Loi, Alberto's son, with the help of his brother Alessandro, Alberto Loi have recently reconstituted themselves in terms of a new *cantina* and a new marketing strategy – basically taking the wines upmarket. With 50 hectares of their own, plus around another 50 whose grapes they buy, having an input in the viticultural side (and almost all planted to Cannonau; for other wines they bring grapes by truck from other zones), Loi have the capacity to establish a major presence for themselves and the Cannonau grape as a serious international proposition. Certainly the four-year-old and six-year-old Cannonau wines I tasted, of their top DOC *cru* called Riserva Alberto Loi were, despite some hefty alcoholic degrees finely balanced, showing some quite fresh strawberry/raspberry aromas on the nose and displaying a degree of opulence and elegance on the palate. I was not so convinced by some of the lesser wines, including the basic DOC Cardedu which had the right perfumes but a slightly clumsy structure, but I got the impression they were embarked on the right road, still experimenting but with quality in view. No doubt their most expensive wine, the IGT Tuvara, a *barrique*-aged blend of Cannonau at 75% and Carignano, Bovale and Muristellu, will refine as their newly purchased Carignano vineyards in the Sulcis come on stream.

The most important producer of Cannonau in terms of sheer volume is the Antichi Poderi di **Jerzu**, the *cantina sociale* at the town of Jerzu, perched picturesquely on a mountain slope below three spectacular rocky crags the main one of which rejoices in the name Porcu'e Ludu (mud-pig). The commercial director, Franco Usai, claimed that Jerzu's 45,000 hectolitres of Cannonau, from 900 hectares of vineyard owned by 500 *soci*, represents fully 80% of all production on the island. A large proportion of the vines are cultivated in a sort of *conca*, or shell, of which the town of Jerzu forms the focal point, at altitudes between 200 and 700 metres. The higher ones, mostly on *alberello* and a low-yielding rocky-schistous soil (as distinct from the more fertile decomposed granite of farther down), are obviously less productive and more difficult to work than those on the lower slopes or on the plain, and form the basis of the Cantina's best wines.

These consist of two fully varietal Cannonau di Sardegna wines. The first, called Marghia, is made from a selection of grapes coming from vineyards with a maximum yield of 5 tonnes per hectare; while the Riserva Chuerra comes from selected vineyards of a certain age, the wine being aged 18 months in oak barrels including some French oak *tonneaux*. Each displays the fiery 'peppery' character associated with Grenache, but there is not a great deal of complexity or *finesse* in the *normale*, somewhat more in the Riserva, as there should be where Franco Bernabei, the famous *enologo* of Tuscany, is involved. For the rest, one is tempted to say that the functional word in the phrase 'good raw material' – which the *cantina* definitely does enjoy, at least in potential – is 'raw', the wines showing little finesse or ability, as yet, to compete in the international marketplace.

Indeed, one feels generally of C.S. Jerzu that there is a lot more in the potential than in the reality.

The best by far of all Cannonau wines does not, however, come from the classic zone along the southern part of the eastern coast but from the centre–south, a few kilometres north of Cagliari. This is Turriga, an IGT from one of the two outstanding private producers of the island, **Argiolas** of Serdiana – the other being Sella & Mosca. Turriga, actually, is a Cannonau-based blend, with elements also of Carignano, Bovale Sardo and Malvasia Nera – no Cabernet or Merlot, I was assured by oenologist Mariano Murru. It is a single-vineyard wine from the Selegas sub-zone, the altitude being around 230 metres above sea-level, the soil being of medium chalky composition with numerous stones for structure. The brainchild of consultant Giacomo Tachis, this wine, aged 15 months in new French *barriques*, dates back only to 1988, but has established itself as one of Sardinia's, nay, one of Italy's greats. A breathtaking combination of concentrated fruit, fine ripe tannins and subtle oak, Turriga is above all, at a surprisingly modest 12.5%, an elegant wine, beautifully balanced. It demonstrates that great things may come from Cannonau and that Cannonau, like Grenache in the southern Rhône, needs judicious blending to bring out its best.

Argiolas have now introduced another winning Cannonau-based wine called Kore, the other grapes including Carignano, Bovale, Bovaleddu and a touch of Syrah and Merlot.

More on Argiolas under Bovale and Nasco.

Other significant producers of Cannonau di Sardegna include: C.S. **Dolianova** (Falconaro IGT, + other varieties), Dolianova; C.S. **Dorgali** (Filieri – Cannonau-based blend), Dorgali; Giuseppe **Gabbas** (Lillovè DOC; Dule – Cannonau-based blend; Arbeskia – Cannonau-based blend), Nuoro; Piero **Mancini**, Olbia; **Meloni Vini** (Le Ghiaie), Selargius; **Sella & Mosca** (Cannonau di Sardegna

Riserva; from a vineyard in the Oliena zone), Alghero; C.S.
Trexenta (Baione DOC; Conte Auda DOC; Tanca su Conti –
Cannonau-based blend), Senorbì.

We should not leave the subject of Cannonau, however, without
mentioning one of the most remarkable of Italy's *vini da meditazione*, Sella & Mosca's Anghelu Ruju, a *vino liquoroso* – meaning
alcohol is added port-style to retain a portion of the natural sugars
– made from grapes dried 15 to 20 days in the sun, the wine then
being aged at least five years in large casks. This delicious wine
has a dried-fruit cum *crème-brûlée* sweetness cut by a mildly

herby-spicy bitterness which keeps it in balance; very concentrated, very individual, very tasty and very recommended.

CARIGNANO

This vine is said to be of western Mediterranean origin, being known in Spain – as Cariñena, Mazuela – as long ago as the twelfth century. It has also long been present in southern, particularly southwestern, France – as Carignan, Carignane Noire, Bois Dur – and indeed in North Africa, specifically Algeria and Tunisia, from where it may even have originated. In Sardinia it has been grown 'for many centuries', as Biondo and Fazzi assure us in *Le Strade del Vino in Sardegna*; its main diffusion, however, would have been after phylloxera (Dalmasso, according to Breviglieri and Casini, *Principali Vitigni*). It apparently also exists in Tuscany and the Marche under the name Legno Duro (cf. Bois Dur), although I've never heard of it in any Tuscan or Marchigiano vineyard. On the contrary, continentals are rather inclined to buy Carignano from southern Sardinia to beef up and round out their SuperTuscans, some of the most famous not excluded. But we're not supposed to know that, and we certainly couldn't name names without getting into trouble.

Another conjectural history of Carignano's origins was tentatively advanced by the people at C.S. Santadi, whose vineyards lie in the heart of the Sulcis, in Carignano's stamping ground, the southwest. The grape may have originated in Asia Minor from whence it was carried by the Phoenicians to North Africa (Carthage), going from there into Sardinia and thence into Spain and France. Or perhaps it came to Sardinia first, before North Africa. According to this theory, then, the vine may have been in residence in Sardinia long before the Spanish arrived, although they may have brought their version to add to the local stock.

Carignano is a grape that thrives on heat and is quite resistant to pests and diseases, particularly in well-ventilated sites. Some of the best vineyards are in coastal areas, in soil so sandy that grafting onto American rootstock is not necessary. Sadly, the misguided EU-subsidised uprooting policy tore large gaps in a vineyard area which was until recently covered in wonderful old *alberello* vines, and where viable alternative crops are virtually non-existent. Alberello still reigns in the older vineyards, although single *guyot* training is taking over in recently planted vineyards for ease of mechanisation.

Carignano from a warm, low-lying *alberello*-trained vineyard gives a potent brew, full of colour and extract with no great tannicity, so it's very much a grape of our time. Some of the finest wines of Sardinia today (not to mention of Tuscany) are based on or assisted by Sardinian Carignano, including especially those of:

C.S. Santadi, Santadi. Situated in the heart of Carignano country, being the southwest corner of the island, the Sulcis, where temperatures are high, rainfall is scarce, and most quality viticulture takes place at low altitude, even along the sandy coastline where phylloxera cannot operate, the Santadi cooperative, Carignano king of Sardinia, surprises the observer in a variety of ways. First, by the sheer high quality of its wines, in a land where, 20 years ago, such levels, or anything near such levels, would have been considered unattainable, the role of the area previously – indeed to an extent presently – being to produce high octane cutting wines for purposes of anonymously rescuing the weedier products of continental producing zones. Second, by the combination of consistently high quality with serious volumes; for example, they make one of their principal wines, Rocca Rubia, upwards of 150,000 bottles a year; even of the flagship, *tre bicchieri*-winning Terre Brune they are capable of getting up to 100,000 bottles. Third, by the intelligence and market-awareness of the people who run the show – President Antonello Pilloni, Chief Executive Raffaele Cani and oenologist Piero Cella – in a land from which one might more readily expect the kind of neanderthal grunt which tends to emerge from the lips of your average meridional cooperative employee. And what greater proof of that intelligence than the fact that, in the mid-1980s, they recruited Italian wines' wisest sage, Giacomo Tachis, to act as their consultant.

The bare statistics of this impressive operation are around 250 *soci*, working some 500 hectares of vineyard, of which around 70% are planted to red grapes. 80% of this is Carignano, the best being trained to *alberello*; the rest is made up of Monica and bits of Sangiovese, Syrah and Cabernet Sauvignon. The whites are mainly Vermentino and Nuragus with a bit of Chardonnay and Nasco.

Speaking of surprises, one might also wonder at the number of different Carignano-based wines produced here – I confess it is not

entirely clear to me why it is deemed necessary to have quite so many. Top of the list, at least traditionally, is Terre Brune, from *alberello*-trained vineyards, which receives 15 to 18 months ageing in French *barrique*; a wine of great warmth and concentration, subtly powerful yet smooth and creamy of texture, with loads of ripe, dark-berry fruit, sophisticated and elegant despite its 13 degrees of alcohol. Another Carignano del Sulcis, now come to challenge Terre Brune, is Baie Rosso, made from grapes both of

Santadi and of another *cantina sociale* on the nearby island of Calasetta – this too being aged in French *barriques* of first and second passage. In American oak, instead, is matured the recently developed Shardana, an IGT Valli di Porto Pino, supposedly aimed directly at the gringo taste-bud as envisaged by their agent for the USA, Neil Empson; I am sure plenty of other nations would equally enjoy its smooth, fine-boned, fleshily fruited allure.

The mainstay of the *cantina*'s production is Rocca Rubia, a Carignano del Sulcis Riserva, also *barrique*-aged (first and second passage), a wine as previously remarked of amazing quality and consistency considering the volume of production and the relatively modest price – Rocca Rubia is surely a candidate for any list of the best value-for-money wines in Italy. Completing the list are Arajà, an IGT blend of Carignano and Sangiovese (15%) which receives a bit of *barrique*ing (at Santadi, as you will have gathered, and perhaps not surprisingly considering the Tachis influence, *barrique* is the only kind of oak they've got); and the basic DOC Grotta Rossa (production over 200,000 bottles), a great little quaffer with friendly, fruity aromas and plenty of fruit at a frankly low price for the quality. Oh, and the really rather tasty, perfect-on-a-hot-summer's-day Rosato called Tre Torri.

Santadi make a number of other wines, the most memorable of which are a newly developed sweet IGT called Latinia made from late-picked Nasco grapes, *barrique*-aged, of course; and a couple of dry whites called Cala Silente, a Vermentino di Sardegna DOC, though it's got a touch of Chardonnay and Sauvignon too; and the IGT Villa di Chiesa, a blend of Vermentino and Chardonnay (40%). The former is 10% oak-fermented, fresh but with a certain juicy richness; the latter, fully oak-fermented, separately according to variety, then aged seven months in oak after *assemblaggio*, having greater wealth of extract and more complexity of flavour. On the lighter, quaffing side are the whites Villa Solais (Vermentino plus 30% Nuragus) and Pedraia (100% Nuragus).

A good Carignano del Sulcis is also made by Argiolas under the name Costera.

MONICA

This is Sardinia's second most diffused black grape, being planted in most parts of the island though principally in the Campidano di

Cagliari. Nothing is known of its provenance, so conjectures have been rife. Because it is sometimes known as Mora (moor in the feminine) or Niedda Mora (black moor) some have claimed it arrived with Moorish invaders, probably in the Alghero area. Others, rejecting this thesis on the basis that, in times of invasion, no one has a lot of time to sit around developing new strains of the vine, claim that it is Spanish in origin and cite the synonym Monica di Spagna in evidence. The original Spanish name, these maintain, would perhaps have been Morilla, and Monica would be a corruption of that name. The synonym Monaca has, on the other hand, been said by some to indicate that it either arrived with, or was cultivated and spread by, monks (*monaci*), specifically of the Camaldolese order.

So we know nothing, except that Monica has been around for a few centuries, probably about ten, making good but rarely exceptional quaffing wine then as now. An abundant and reliable producer, with good resistance to fungal complaints and a predilection for warm non-fertile, non-humid soils, of the kind that abound in the Campidano, the principal reason for Monica's continued survival has no doubt been its popularity with growers.

The best wines under the Monica di Sardegna or Monica di Cagliari DOCs, generally pleasant if hardly exciting, are Perdera from Argiolas and Antigua from Santadi. Dolianova, Meloni Vini and C.S. Trexenta (Duca di Mandas) also make versions.

BOVALE

Since being introduced by the Spaniards during the occupation, Bovale has split into two clones, Bovale Grande and Bovale Sardo. Among the synonyms of the first is Bovale di Spagna, while the second is aka Muristellu, Muristeddu or Bovaleddu, and resembles, according to Argiolas's oenologist Mariano Murru, southern France's Mourvèdre. Both are diffused throughout the island, both are used mainly in blends, rather than varietally, to enhance body and colour, both have been losing ground to more popular varieties, though there is a movement to revive Bovale Sardo, considered the superior of the two. The main varietal, or near varietal wine, is the DOC called Campidano di Terralba, or just plain Terralba, of which the two Bovales together must form at least 80%. A producer is the C.S. **Marrubiù** at the town of that name in the province of Oristano;

also the C.S. Terralba at Terralba, whose wine reminded me more of rhubarb than any I have previously tasted, not that I am particularly keen to be reminded of rhubarb, particularly in vinous form. Bovale Sardo is also a main ingredient of Mandrolisai DOC, the main producer of which being C.S. del Mandrolisai at Sòrgono.

Probably the finest example of a Bovale-based wine is the IGT Isola dei Nuraghi called Kore from Argiolas. This was developed towards the end of the 1990s to bridge the gap between Turriga and their other reds, according to commercial director Giuliano Pau, who also states that their intention is to produce the not inconsequential volume of 100,000 bottles per annum. While Bovale Grande, with Bovale Sardo dominates, other grapes in the blend include Carignano, Cannonau, Syrah and Merlot – all *barrique*-aged for up to 12 months (sounds very Tachis). I found Kore to be of deep colour, subtly blending aromas of fruits, fresh vegetables (in a positive sense) and oak, the latter being perhaps a touch excessive although this is recognised by winemaker Murru who is working on intensifying the fruit.

CAGNULARI

This is another clonal differentiation of a grape of Spanish origin, possibly having the same forebear as the Bovale pair, like which it is used primarily in blends and like which it is said to bear some resemblance to France's Mourvèdre as well as to Spain's Morastell. Cagnulari rejoices in the synonym 'Bastardo Nero'. A producer of varietal Cagnulari is Giovanni **Cherchi** of Usini in the province of Sassari.

PASCALE DI CAGLIARI

Said to be of Tuscan origin (though I've never heard of it or knowingly seen it in a Tuscan context); aka Barberone – which would indicate rather a Piemontese origin, no? Pascale is one of the most diffused grapes of the island, although it forms the basis of no DOC wine. It is mainly used in blends or for homemade *casalingo* wines.

NIEDDERA, NIEDDUMANNU

Nieddu means black in Sardinian, and while both of these grapes are said to be indigenous, I find no evidence of any other similarity.

Nieddera is made varietally in the area of Oristano (Valle del Tirso IGT), both in Rosso and Rosato form. I noted the Nieddera of Attilio Contini – see under Vernaccia di Oristano – as being deep of colour, having something vegetal on the nose, soft tannins, a bit jammy, with this vegetal follow-through. Not a world-beater in the wings, I suspect. It may be related to, or the same as, Sicily's Perricone.

I am not aware of any varietal use of Nieddumannu, which is also mainly to be found mainly in the province of Nuoro. It is said to bear some resemblance to Pascale di Cagliari.

GIRÒ

Girò, of Spanish origin, makes sweet red wine traditionally of a fortified style from grapes grown prevalently in the low-lying plains of Cagliari – the DOC being Girò di Cagliari. Fairly widespread in the past, popular with those who fancied a sweet port-like red after dinner, it was largely abandoned by growers after phylloxera because of a tendency to low production and poor resistance to cryptogamic attacks. Today it represents less than 1% of total planted area.

The wine is usually sweet and unfortified, but may also be dry and/or fortified. A producer is Meloni Vini (Donna Jolanda) of Selargius.

NEBBIOLO

A wine produced in Gallura as 'Nebbiolo IGT Colli del Limbara' turns out to be of Piemontese origin all right, from the time when Sardinia was under Piemontese rule, around 1800, but not Nebbiolo – rather it is, according to the principal producer, C.S. Gallura (see below), probably Dolcetto of the Ovada clone. An example is Gallura's Karana. The give-away, in case one hadn't already been tipped off, is the softness of the tannins, something one would not expect from Nebbiolo anywhere. There is, apparently, 'real' Nebbiolo also to be found in the northwest, but it is difficult to say to what extent any given wine is purely varietal. The nearest thing to it would be Gallura's Dolmen, a wine of considerably greater seriousness than Karana, aged 15 months in new and second passage French *barriques*. The tannins do seem somewhat soft for a

'Nebbiolo', but the acidity is firm and the aromas have a distinct Piemontese note about them plus a hint of liquorice. Like many a maker of Piemontese Nebbiolo the producer has problems fixing the colour, so there is a 5% inclusion of Cabernet, which shows through in a slight vegetal whiff.

SANGIOVESE

There is a certain presence of the Tuscan star in the centre-west, around Oristano. The DOC is called Arborea, and may be Rosso or Rosato. Some producers are now planting Sangiovese, which they like to call 'Brunello', for use in blend.

A producer is C.S. **Marrubiù** at Marrubiù.

GRAPES, WINES AND PRODUCERS – WHITE

VERMENTINO

(For general notes see under Tuscany.)

It was noted previously that Vermentino only arrived in Sardinia, from Corsica, towards the end of the nineteenth century. Or did it come from Liguria? Or was it directly from Spain where, according to one authority, it is known as Listan d'Andalusia? At any rate, until the early twentieth century it was never mentioned in Sardinian ampelographical lists, and it was only after replanting commenced following the phylloxera scourge that what had previously been an *aficionado* of coastal areas was found to thrive also in the dry, stony interior of <u>Gallura</u> in Sardinia's northeast.

From the northeast it spread to most parts of the island with the denomination <u>Vermentino di Sardegna</u> DOC. Gallura, however, remains the classic zone as has been recognised by the granting, in 1996, of DOCG status. Within the DOCG it is important to differentiate between Vermentino di Gallura DOCG and Vermentino di Gallura <u>Superiore</u> DOCG, the latter requiring a minimum alcohol level of 13% which it often exceeds, this being achievable only in conditions of low cropping, preferably on *alberello* or at least low *spalliera*, perhaps with the help of a week or 10 days surmaturation on the vine. It seems that Vermentino needs this kind of alcohol level to reach its epitome of body and concentration. The light style of Vermentino often, but not always, seems a pale shadow beside the Superiore DOCG. Whatever the style, Vermentino today has the image of being Sardinia's most representative white wine, despite being far less planted than Nuragus, while Vermentino di Gallura is her only DOCG.

Production in Gallura is dominated volume-wise, and to a certain extent also quality-wise, by cooperatives, all established during the 1950s. The biggest of these is the aptly named Cantina del **Vermentino**, at Monti, today boasting 250 members and 370 hectares of vineyard, producing nearly 2 million bottles of wine per annum. Monti (as it's generally called) make various levels of Vermentino di Gallura, starting at the top with a Superiore called Aghiloia, at 14% alcohol (its grapes are harvested about 10 days later than the norm, only from *alberello*-trained vineyards) a hefty, sometimes overweight wine – i.e. too much alcohol for the amount of fruit. Less alcoholic and better balanced is Funtanaliras, from selected vineyards of relatively high altitude (300–350 metres). S'Eleme is the one most produced – some 800,000 bottles p.a. of this one – and while its character is somewhat attenuated, it is good value. Perhaps the most interesting and individual of their Vermentinos is Soliana, made by carbonic maceration and partially *barrique*-aged. Other variations on the Vermentino theme include a *frizzante* (Bàlari), a couple of *spumanti* (Vigne del Portale, Brut and Demi-sec) and a *passito* (Aldiola).

Monti is also the centre for an export project in which they collaborate with the two other principal *cantine sociali* of the zone referred to immediately below. The chief product here is called Kàlike – light, salt-biscuity, a touch of tropical fruit; a wine which, for Monti's oenologist Alberto Raccanelli, typifies Vermentino di Gallura.

Perhaps the cooperative with the highest profile in quality terms today is C.S. **Gallura** at Tempio Pausania, which is also the cork-producing centre of the island. Run by agronomist/technical director/sales director Dino Addis, Tempio – as it's known – has some 325 hectares farmed by around 160 *soci*, most of the vineyards being between 250 and 600 metres altitude on poorish, stony, decomposed granite soil, trained to single guyot. Therefore, low production per plant, especially in the recent vineyards planted, in the Vallata di San Leonardo, at 5,000 vines/hectare – and you can taste it in the wines. Best wine, in my view, is the recently developed Canayli (pron. kan-a-ee-lee), a slightly late-picked wine – 10–15 days later than the norm, i.e. during the last week of September – of 13% alcohol which earned a rave from the *Gambero Rosso/Slow Food Annual Wine Guide* as 'one of Italy's best white wines from authochthonous grapes', having 'rich fruity/appley aromas with exotic notes, being on the palate potent and harmonious, intense and persistent'; a comment I poach because I agree. The normally picked Piras, from the San Leonardo vineyards, is also impressive with full, sweet fruit and a palate combining the biscuity and the tropical; not bad considering production is a quarter of a million bottles. Even the basic Vermentino di Gallura, Mavriana, with its balanced, biscuity and reasonably penetrating palate, is surprisingly good at a modest price. The wine they consider to be their top of the range is a *barrique*-fermented job called Balajana, which to my mind has suffered, to date, from too much oak with consequent loss of the all-important fruit aromas.

The third big cooperative of the area is C.S. **Giogantinu** at Berchidda, whose Vermentino range includes an excellent Superiore from old vines on *alberello* called Vigne Storiche – powerful, spicy, concentrated, a certain viscosity and a quasi-liqueur-like tropical fruit tone reminiscent of candied pineapple. Their other Superiore – not Vigne Storiche – is no less delicious, having perhaps better balance.

In the private sector one name stands out – that of Tenute **Capichera** at Arzachena, in the extreme northeast corner of the island near the Costa Smeralda, which proximity no doubt has helped them to succeed with prices three or four times higher than anyone else. I have to say, in vindication, that the Ragnedda brothers' Vermentinos – Vigna 'Ngena, Capichera and Vendemmia Tardiva – are the best I've tasted, if only marginally and certainly not by a factor of three to four times. Still, working on the Gaja principle that people will pay up for the best, not only do the Ragneddas sell everything they produce – not that that's a great deal – but also there's a line forming at the rear, begging for more.

Another good private producer of Vermentino di Gallura DOCG is Piero **Mancini** of Olbia, whose Cucaione, of which I briefly noted: 'lemony, touch of fruit, forgettable', is produced at the impressive rate of half a million bottles per annum. They are working on their *cru* Vignalta to differentiate it more from Cucaione; in future it will be slightly late-harvested to achieve greater depth and concentration.

These are the principal authors of Vermentino di Gallura DOCG, which must be produced within the delimited zone. There are also numerous examples of Vermentino di Sardegna DOC, some from within the Gallura zone – where they don't reach the minimum 12% alcohol; e.g. Berchidda's S'Aldia – most from other parts of the island. The majority of the latter are aiming for a very different wine – light and easy-to-quaff as distinct from Gallura's rich, full style – the archetype of this type being Sella & Mosca's La Cala, at 11.5% a pleasantly perfumed, hay and floral-bouqueted wine with reasonable flavour and balancing acidity, but ultimately fairly forgettable.

In a similar mould are also C.S. **Santa Maria La Palma** of Alghero's well-known Aragosta; Giovanni Cherchi's equally famous Tuvaoes; and others too numerous and too anonymous to mention. In a fuller, fruitier, more serious style are the well-made Costamolino of Argiolas and their even better Argiolas Bianco IGT, which includes 6% Malvasia di Sardegna. Santadi's Cala Silente is another impressive example, although their star white, the *barrique*-fermented Villa di Chiesa, blends Vermentino with Chardonnay.

NURAGUS

This is Sardinia's most planted variety. Its main area of concentration is the centre–south, as is reflected in its sole DOC, Nuragus di Cagliari, though it is found more or less everywhere. Its very name, associated with the prehistoric constructions that still dot the island, is an indication of its antiquity, although it has not been definitively decided by ampelographers whether it is indigenous or was brought to Sardinia by the Phoenicians. Perhaps it was used to decorate the *nuraghi* while providing fruit and wine for the inhabitants. Certain it is that it has forever been the people's favourite, as indicated by synonyms like Abbondosa and Axina de Popurus (grape of the poor). This was and always has been Sardinia's 'Pagadepidu', the banker, though another alias, Burdu (bastard), shows what Sardinians think of bankers, the cads. Being 'abundant', as the synonym suggests, it was particularly popular in the days, now slightly past, or at least passing, when quantity not quality was the prime criterion for planting. Nuragus probably has little or nothing to do with Trebbiano Toscano, as the ampelographer Cettolini would have us believe, but it does share an inability to rise above a certain fairly basic level of mediocrity winewise, although, also like Trebbiano, in the hands of an expert its wine can be quite sappy and juicy with good acidity. Such a result, obviously, does not arise where producers take full advantage of the 20 tonnes per hectare production to which the Nuragus di Cagliari *disciplinare* entitles them.

Acceptable to good examples of Nuragus di Cagliari come from the following: Argiolas (S'elegas); Dolianova; Santadi (Pedraia); C.S. Trexenta.

VERNACCIA DI ORISTANO

As previously stated, the name Vernaccia derives from the late-Latin *vernaculus* (home-grown) and denotes no relationship with any other grape of similar name. Indeed, as a side-shot, my view is that it, or at least the wine, should drop the Vernaccia part, which creates confusion in the mind of the consumer, and just call itself 'Oristano', preferably Oristano DOCG since the wine, unlike some, undoubtedly has the uniqueness and the quality to merit such a classification.

Vernaccia di Oristano – the grape – is an ancient variety, either introduced by the Phoenicians in the millennium before Christ or indigenous to the zone where it still principally thrives, i.e. the valley of the Tirso around the town of Oristano in mid-west–central Sardinia. The wine it produces in this zone is often compared with sherry, being made in a similar way complete with space at the top of the barrels for ageing to allow the development of *flor*, as well as a type of *solera* system. The comparison, however, is somewhat unfair, partly because it has a different aromatic character, smelling as it does of dried apricots, but mainly because it is not, in the best versions, fortified. Nonetheless, the similarities must have been sufficient to render it popular with occupying Spaniards during the four centuries of their rule – it may well be that the style and method were influenced by them.

It is interesting to note that Vernaccia di Oristano, produced in any other part of the island, is not able to develop these 'sherry-like' characteristics and becomes what a major producer referred to as 'just another white wine'.

Given the international market's current rejection of the oxidised style of wine, there are few producers and only one that makes outstanding wine, namely:

Attilio **Contini** (pron. kon-tee-nee), Cabras. This firm, run by Attilio's sons Paolo and Antonio Contini, celebrated its centenary in 1998. In their time they have been awarded many medals but should in my view receive a special one for courage in the face of adversity, since they carry on making their special wine in the same time-consuming, cost-ineffective way as ever despite massive rejection by markets of our age. To cope with this situation Contini have diversified into other wines – Nieddera, Cannonau, Vermentino and Moscato – but a sizeable minority of their annual production of around 500,000 bottles is still to Vernaccia. Their 35–40 hectares of vineyard, whether owned by them or under contract, are mostly planted to Vernaccia on *alberello*, producing rarely more than 3 or 4 tonnes per hectare which is much reduced after ageing.

The method? The Vernaccia grapes are picked around the end of September/beginning of October when their sugar rating is near 15%. Fermentation takes place in stainless steel or large *botti*; after 12 months the wine of a given year is racked into medium-sized barrels, never filled so as to allow the formation of *flor*, then after three years, following *assemblaggio*, it goes into smaller barrels in a variation of Jerez's *solera* system. The barrels filled contain a *madre* of the previous wine, so that every vintage wine mingles with traces of older wine going back up to 100 years or more. The wine is then left for varying periods in barrel as it ages, concentrating its alcohol so that in time it may go from 15 to as high as 19 degrees alcohol *naturale*, that is without fortification.

'Another wine made like this would become vinegar', said Paolo Contini, and indeed where it is attempted elsewhere that's exactly what happens – one of wine's little mysteries. The wine, he said, has 'great longevity; the weakness is the cork, which has to be changed periodically'.

Vernaccia di Oristano is traditionally dry, and comes in various forms. The wines that do not develop *flor* (another mystery: why do some get *flor* while others don't?) are made into a relatively early drinking table wine. Those that do may remain many years in

barrel, finally being bottled as vintage wines. Or there may be a blending of vintages, as in Jerez, to produce a special *cuvée*.

The basic version, a non-*flor* wine called Karmis, IGT Valle del Tirso, is bottled after a year at around 12.5% alcohol. Dry almost to the point of austerity, not particularly complex on the palate, it needs time in bottle to go past the stage of being slightly hard work. It is only when the wine takes on an unambiguous aperitif style that it becomes really interesting. A 1990 bottled in 1998 was displaying a light golden colour, aromas of apricots and dried fruits, and considerable penetration on the palate; it didn't seem at all oxidised in the negative sense, indeed aromatically displayed little resemblance to sherry, and despite its declared 15% alcohol it seemed quite light. An excellent accompaniment, I later discovered, with the local Bottarga, or dried mullet roe, eaten here in slices or grated onto spaghetti.

Things really began hotting up with the 1980 Riserva, also bottled in 1998. Here notes of vanilla fudge entered into the equation, and while there were hints of sherry-style oxidation the 1978, bottled in 1997, showed that the dried fruit character could be maintained over the years – a wine of great power and character. The 1970, bottled 1989, was still going strong with beautifully complex aromas of dried apricot and vanilla fudge – 'fantastic', I noted, 'real meditation wines'.

The *coup de grâce* was delivered by the blend of vintages, called Antico Gregori, a wine of which the youngest component was from the early 1970s and the oldest from the 1950s. My note: 'Deep colour, nuts, dried fruits and spices on nose and palate, terrific concentration and length, stunning personality'. Interesting to note that from a barrel of 600 litres capacity, filled to 500 litres 10 years ago, they got a mere 200 litres of wine.

The only other producer of this wine in any sort of volume is the C.S. della Vernaccia at Oristano.

MALVASIA DI SARDEGNA

(For general remarks on Malvasia see under centre west.)

Presumably of Greek origin, probably arriving in the early Middle Ages, this is a member of the aromatic branch of the Malvasia family and, as said previously, 'is used mainly for making sweet wines, which is probably what it does best and what it was doing originally back in the hot, dry stony Peloponnese'. Although Malvasia is found in several parts of Sardinia, its main growing area is in the central–west, north of Oristano and south of Alghero, around the town of Bosa which gives it one of its DOC names – Malvasia di Bosa – the other being Malvasia di Sardegna. Both DOCs provide for Secco and Liquoroso versions, Bosa having also a Dolce Naturale style made from surmatured or partially dried grapes.

There is now a movement away from the Bosa DOC, which requires the wine to be aged at least two years before going on the market. Certain young producers are looking for a fresher, more aromatic, less oxidised style and are consequently downgrading their wines to Planargia IGT without mention of the grape variety, such mention being forbidden to an IGT where there is a DOC mentioning the grape in the same zone – another example of the restrictiveness of a system which does not allow a serious producer creative expression. The best-known quality producer is Gianvittorio **Naitana** of Magomadas, who makes only the one wine with a quiet passion, setting quality as his goal in vineyard and *cantina*, and not conformity to the law.

MOSCATO BIANCO

(For general remarks on Moscato, and specifically Moscato Bianco, see *Barolo to Valpolicella*, p. 122.)

This is the Moscato di Canelli of Piemonte, not the Moscato di Alessandria of Pantelleria or the Moscato Giallo of northeast Italy. When, and from where, it arrived in Sardinia is not recorded.

Moscato is used in Sardinia for the making of sweet wines of various sorts. There are a number of versions of Moscato Spumante, similar to Asti, indeed there is a DOC Moscato di Sardegna Spumante. The principal production zone is in Gallura, specifically at Tempio Pausania, both of which have their sub-zones recognised in the *disciplinare*.

There is also Moscato di Cagliari DOC, a still wine which may be *naturale* or *liquoroso*. Then there is the rather obscure Moscato di Sorso Sennori, from the province of Sassari.

Grapes may be concentrated by various methods: late harvest, brief *appassimento* in the sun, or a somewhat longer *appassimento* in the winery.

NASCO

This one seems to be a native Sardinian, at any rate it appears to have been grown here since time immemorial. The name probably derives from the Sardinian *nuscu*, modern Italian *muschio* (= musk), for the lightly musky aroma given off by the slightly dried grapes.

The growing zone is almost entirely restricted to the Campidano di Cagliari and indeed the only DOC is Nasco di Cagliari. The wine may be dry but is more often sweet, the DOC providing for versions both *naturale* and fortified.

As for Cannonau, so for Nasco the pre-eminent producer in terms of quality is Argiolas, whose dessert-wine Angialis is made predominantly from Nasco (they call it Nasca) with a small addition of Malvasia di Cagliari. Made from late-harvested grapes, Angialis is fermented to about 13.5% alcohol, then stopped with some 8% natural sugar remaining. The wine is aged in French *barrique* for a number of months, giving a vanilla, almost a butter-scotch twist to the ripe tropical fruit flavours which include banana and pineapple.

A few words, in this place about **Argiolas** in general, given that they are probably the best producer on the island in overall terms. The firm is currently run by brothers Franco and Giuseppe Argiolas, whose father Antonio established it as far back as the 1930s. The property consists of 220 hectares of vineyard in four different sub-zones to the north of Cagliari. Considering the renown they have achieved it is surprising to learn that they have only been selling under their own label since 1991 – prior to which they bottled for others or sold in bulk to people like Antinori in Italy (Giacomo Tachis remains their consultant, possibly one reason for their meteoric success) and to various customers in France and England.

Virtually every wine of Argiolas is mentioned at some point or other in these pages, for the simple reason that every wine they put out is at least a good, sometimes an outstanding, example of its type. The fact that Argiolas can do it means that others can, and it is to be hoped, though alas! not expected, that more like them will spring up in Sardinia.

TORBATO

Uniquely grown in the Alghero zone, to which it came probably during the fourteenth century from Catalonia where it is known as Trubat, Torbato may be a member of the extremely diverse Malvasia family. (Its name in France is Malvoisie de Roussillon.) It was fading from existence when it was revived by Sella & Mosca in the 1970s. It makes a pleasant but not particularly complex dry white wine of some character. The DOC is, not surprisingly, Torbato di Alghero.

As Torbato is virtually an exclusivity of **Sella & Mosca** it seems appropriate to profile that most important producer in this place, even though they make wines from a number of other grapes. In fact nearly a third of their 500+ hectares of vineyard – all in a single block, all on flat land near sea-level on a form of *tendone* they call *pergola sarda*, all irrigated – are planted to Torbato, another near-third going to Vermentino while Chardonnay, Sauvignon, Malvasia, Trebbiano and Nasco among whites, Cannonau, Cabernet Sauvignon, Cabernet Franc, Merlot, Sangiovese and Carignano among reds make up the rest. The mixture of grape varieties seems appropriate for a firm that began life in 1899 primarily as a vine nursery, set up by Messrs Sella and Mosca of Piemonte following the disaster of phylloxera. The owners today are the Bonomi family of Milan, but the real power since the early 1960s has been the general manager from Veneto, Mario Consorte, backed, since the late 1960s, by oenologist Gavino Ninniri.

It was Consorte who, following what he believed to be future market trends, introduced high-training to achieve better balanced fruit, compared with the Sardinian norm of high alcohol, low acid, and lighter wines. He also completely re-equipped and computerised the winery so that the facilities at Sella & Mosca can stand comparison with the most technologically advanced in the world today. Consorte's continuing faith in high-trained vineyards and relatively high-volume production – they maintain they can't achieve the desired balance at below 15 tonnes per hectare – despite being against the trend for quality viticulture in Italy, is demonstrated by the fact that new plantings now underway continue the *pergola* style.

Sella & Mosca make two Torbatos, one simply named Alghero Torbato and the other called Terre Bianche after the chalk-rich white soil of marine origin of the relevant vineyards. No fewer than 200,000 bottles of this latter are produced annually, the wine being deliberately on the light side for Sardinia with good acid-fruit balance, a touch of viscosity, somewhat nutty (pistachio?) of aroma.

Terre Bianche is not Sella & Mosca's most impressive product, to be sure, just one of their most unusual. Other more prestigious wines have been considered above and will be looked at subsequently, under Nasco, International Varieties and Blends. Suffice it to say that Sella & Mosca, with their wide range of wines from

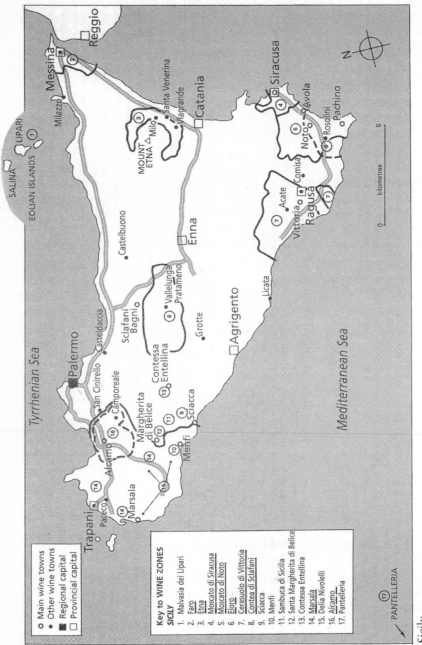

Sicily

Key to WINE ZONES
SICILY
1. Malvasia dei Lipari
2. Faro
3. Etna
4. Moscato di Siracusa
5. Moscato di Noto
6. Eloro
7. Cerasuolo di Vittoria
8. Contea di Sclafani
9. Sciacca
10. Menfi
11. Sambuca di Sicilia
12. Santa Margherita di Belice
13. Contessa Entellina
14. Marsala
15. Delia Nivolelli
16. Alcamo
17. Pantelleria

o Main wine towns
○ Other wine towns
■ Regional capital
□ Provincial capital

Tyrrhenian Sea

Mediterranean Sea

EOLIAN ISLANDS
SALINA
LIPARI

Reggio
Messina
Milazzo
Santa Venerina
Milo
MOUNT ETNA
Magrande
Catania
Castelbuono
Castellaccia
Palermo
San Ciorello
Camporeale
Margherita di Belice
Menfi
Sclafani Bagni
Vallelunga
Pratameno
Contessa Entellina
Sciacca
Grotte
Enna
Agrigento
Licata
Acate
Vittoria
Comisa
Ragusa
Siracusa
Avola
Rosolini
Pachino
Noto
Alcamo
Marsala
Paceco
Trapani
PANTELLERIA

N

kilometres
0   5

one of Europe's most important integral estates, continue to maintain into the twenty-first century a position of primacy in Sardinian viniculture.

SEMIDANO

A grape of unknown origin, possibly indigenous, once much grown in the Campidano di Cagliari zone, where, however, it yielded substantial ground post-phylloxera to Nuragus and Vermentino which are considerably more productive and resistant to disease, i.e. grower-friendly. The only DOC is Sardegna Semidano, and the sub-zone Mogoro is mentioned in the *disciplinare* as being, as it were, the 'classic' area. The wine tends to be light and dry, though a sparkling as well as a Passito version are provided for. Today Semidano is found more often in small amounts in blend with Nuragus and the like rather than *in purezza*.

Cantine **Il Nuraghe**, at Mogoro, produce a Sardegna Semidano as well as a Semidano di Mogoro.

TREBBIANO

Some Trebbiano, mainly Toscano, is produced in the central–western zone of Arborea. The wine here is as dull as it is in most other places.

SICILY

'Nunustentimimarustainamiemitomestiduromnaniposduromiemit-omestiveliomnedemponitantomeredes**viino**brtom.'

No, not an elaborate version of abracadabra but the first known use of the word *vino*, albeit spelled *viino*, anywhere in Italy. It is to be found inscribed on the lid of a terracotta vase of the fifth century BC, found at Centorbi in the Province of Enna.

Wine, mainly imported, was being consumed and perhaps produced in Sicily centuries before the Greeks began their 500-year colonisation of the Mediterranean's largest island around 750 BC. But it was the Greeks who brought systematic viticulture and wine-making techniques, as well as various still-existent grape-varieties. They were followed by a motley collection of invaders/occupiers: Romans, Arabs, Byzantines, Christian monks, Normans (Lionheart

= Corleone et al.), Swabians (Frederick II), Angevins, Aragonese, Spaniards, Piemontese and Austrians, Bourbons, Britons, Garibaldi's thousand and the Italian one-nationists, Germans, Americans and finally, the most terrible of all, the faceless ones, the unspeakable monsters that have held the land to ransom for decades now until the very present, crippling with their cruel indifference and bare-fanged corruption every attempt to bring sound sense into a chaotic situation, that's right, the Bureaucrats. Oh yes, and I almost forgot, the Mafia.

One, two, skip a few, 99, 100. Well, it may seem like that, but this is not the place to expound at length on the story of wine in Sicily, of which there is a great deal (story, I mean: see Bruno Pastena, *La Civiltà della Vite in Sicilia*). Suffice it to say that throughout her chequered history grapes, together with olives and wheat, have always, even under Islamic rule, played a central role in Sicilian agriculture, although Sicilians are statistically less avid drinkers than most Italians – something to do with the heat?

There's a great deal of wine, too, about two-thirds of it still white despite the present-day domination of reds in the marketplace. Sicily generally vies with Puglia or Veneto for top-dog status among Italian wine-producing regions, and certainly she has the most hectares under vine – something like 150,000 at last count (in 1960 it was over 230,000, and still in 1987 it was in excess of 200,000). Until quite recently Sicily was churning out over 10 million hecto-litres of wine annually, a large part of it ultimately destined for distillation, and although production is steadily reducing it remains very high – until recently around double that of Australia, for example, which sells a hell of a lot more in bottle (Sicily's bottled sales amount to less than 10% of total production).

The EU's inspired response was to fund the extirpation of thousands of low-yielding, difficult to work but highly qualified vineyards, these being replaced with kilometres of hideous plastic tunnels for the growing of countless tons of tasteless melons and other forced fruits and vegetables. A notable example comes from the southeast of the region, south of Noto, where between 1985 and 1995 the production of the Cantina Sociale La Elorina, which deals almost exclusively with Nero d'Avola from *alberello* and *spalliera* vineyards, descended to virtually one-tenth of its previous figure. Today, melons grown under plastic rule.

But why dwell upon the negative? Perhaps because it is so

infuriating to see a land with such a vocation for quality viticulture being so exploited by fools or devils with their high-yielding, disease-free, character-free grape varieties, their high trellis systems and their 'modern' techniques and technology guaranteed to squeeze every remaining trace of interest out of the 'product'. Because in a situation where thousands of livelihoods depend on wine you'd think there would be more urgency about turning the amazing potential – based as has been said on plentiful sun and luminosity, good soil conditions, low rainfall (in 2000 it did not rain during the entire growing season) and a wide choice of micro-climates due to the many altitudes available in the mountainous terrain, not to mention an excellent selection of native and imported grape varieties to choose from – into commercial reality.

Sicily could be not just California (see introduction to the South) but Australia, Chile, southern France, Jerez and middle Italy all rolled in one. An eminent Antipodean viticulturist actually joked that he would have believed Australian spies were working under cover to maintain the *status quo* if he had not realised that Sicilians have no need of outside enemies for purposes of sabotage.

But there is today, at the start of the twenty-first century, a growing enthusiasm which, when all the hype is discounted, still amounts to a substantial basis on which to found an exciting future for Sicilian wine. The enthusiasm is based not entirely on hot air but also on a considerable amount of effort put into both the viticultural and the oenological aspects of production by people like the *Cantina Sperimentale* of the *Istituto Regionale della Vite e del Vino*. Their excellent work on clones and planting systems, backed by micro-vinifications and interesting new blends overseen by Dr Giacomo Tachis, clearly indicates some of the splendid results possible from native and international varieties, experiments which are beginning now to find splendid expression in commercial wines.

'Time is the crisis of wine', as Tachis has said, with specific reference to Sicily. But he adds: 'There are those who have begun to realise, and they are going through a difficult period now, but will emerge strong. The rest will be forced to realise what they must do by circumstances. There will be no choice.'

If it is true, then, that Sicily is undergoing something of a 'revolution' in its vinicultural fortunes, the reality of that process has affected to date only a tiny minority at the tip of the mountain.

The real test of the twenty-first century will be whether this positive attitude and endeavour can have the effect of bringing the entire mountain out of the depths of the Mediterranean, or whether this vast potential will remain 95% submerged.

Nowhere does it make less sense to concentrate on DOC in describing wine-zones than in Sicily. VQPRD wines represent a tiny percentage of total production, practically all of it being Marsala, followed a long way behind by Bianco d'Alcamo. Several new DOCs have sprung up in the past decade, often only to be ignored by producers who either distrust the integrity or competence of the tasting commissions or who dismiss names like Santa Margherita di Belice and Delia Nivolelli as being meaningless to the consumer. Such producers preferring to stick to IGT Sicilia, the proposal for DOC Sicilia having been defeated (see Marco de Bartoli under Zibibbo).

Nevertheless, following the DOCs may offer some geographical cohesion to any prospective wine tour of Sicily.

Such a tour of Sicily, at least for the motorist, will begin in Messina, the town one takes the car ferry to from mainland Reggio Calabria. From the very dawn of wine's history until the onset of phylloxera, it was the east that led the way both in terms of prestige and of volume. Mamertino, which Roman authors such as Pliny and Martial cited as being among Italy's finest, came from the environs of Messina, which even as recently as this century was a major producing area and which now is reduced to virtually nothing. There is a smidgin of Faro, made mainly from the Nerello varieties, today brilliantly being revived in the form of the wines of the producer Palari. And, if you include the offshore islands, there is slightly more than a smidgin of that extraordinary apricots-and-honey *passito* wine, Malvasia delle Lipari, represented with some glory in the latter half of the twentieth century by the wines of the late Carlo Hauner.

These apart, vinous eastern Sicily, today, may be considered in three sections. First, Etna, in the province of Catania, where on the terraces of the still terrible volcano, at between 400 and 1,000 metres, the Nerello varieties, Mascalese and Cappuccio, rule among reds and Carricante among whites. Catania was a major long-term victim of phylloxera, going from number one position among provinces for hectares planted in 1888 to a mere fraction of that today (around 7,000 hectolitres of Etna Rosso and Bianco per annum on average), most of it produced by smallholders uninterested in making quality wine. A producer returning this zone to some eminence is Benanti of Viagrande.

Second, the extreme southeast corner (province of Siracusa), where Nero d'Avola hails from, informing today's Eloro Rosso, named after the ancient, long defunct Greek port of Eloros (mentioned in Homer's *Odyssey*), and mainly produced by the Cantina Sociale La Elorina. Once famous Moscato di Siracusa came from here, too – though now it's more of a memory than a presence. On the other hand, Moscato di Noto continues to maintain a precarious existence in both Naturale and Liquoroso forms.

Third, the province of Ragusa, where Frappato joins Nero d'Avola in Cerasuolo di Vittoria. The producer that has done most to revive the fortunes of Vittoria is COS.

In the central Sicilian provinces of Enna and Caltanissetta a certain amount of wine is produced, but anonymously, ending up as likely as not in the giant Corvo's mixing pot. Farther west and south, in the province of Agrigento, production is a lot greater, the most important of it under IGT Sicilia (C.S. Settesoli, Planeta), much of the rest anonymous but some under recently cobbled DOC names like Menfi, Sambuca di Sicilia, Sciacca and Santa Margherita di Belice. These are all multi-DOCs using a multitude of grape varieties, native and imported, either varietally or in blend.

In the province of Palermo, again, there is much anonymous production, but a couple of new multi-DOCs have gathered together various communes using quite a wide diversity of grape varieties. The more important one, overlapping the borders of Palermo and spreading into those of Caltanissetta and Agrigento as well, is Contea di Sclafani, where there is a sub-DOC for just about any grape variety you can think of in the Sicilian context plus a couple you might never have guessed: Syrah, for example, and Sauvignon. The name may sound ugly, but there was no way the Counts Tasca d'Almerita Vallelunga Pratameno of Regaleali, the most important producer of the zone if not, in recent history, of Sicily generally, were going to allow surrounding peasants to use as a DOC, and thereby degrade, the name they had fought so long and hard to build up.

The Tascas are among those not entirely convinced about the merits of the DOC, saying that they will use it for their top wines but not for those other wines of the range which are less well-known by their own names. For these they will continue to use the more recognisable IGT Sicilia.

Contessa Entellina, the other new multi-DOC of Palermo, though it is almost exclusively the fiefdom of Donnafugata of Marsala in the province of Trapani, has a similar if somewhat more restricted range of sub-titles. It too springs the odd surprise in the form of Pinot Nero and Sauvignon, neither of which could be expected to thrive in this climate.

In the western section of Palermo province and the eastern part of Trapani we arrive at what used to be the European wine lake's central reservoir. It's called Alcamo and it's alchemical alright if turning wine into water qualifies for that description. The production here, mostly of Catarratto but with quite a lot too of Trebbiano Toscano on *tendone*-trained vines stretching as far as the eye can see in every direction, is vast, only a tiny percentage of it, 20,000+ hectolitres, having pretensions to DOC. Recent modifications to the *disciplinare* have specifically allowed a number of grape varieties which can only improve matters, even though half of them are international – Chardonnay, Müller Thurgau, Sauvignon, Cabernet etc. – and most of them were being used before by the best producers.

Officially in Trapani province but actually nearer to Tunisia, is a small, dark-soiled volcanic island which has been the scene, in the mid-1990s, of some extraordinary feuds among wine-producers and authorities, as well as being the production centre of the one 'Sicilian' wine which everyone agrees is delicious: Moscato Passito di Pantelleria. More under Zibibbo.

However, Trapani's best-known place name is the town of Marsala, famous for its association with Woodhouse, Garibaldi, egg-nog, veal escalope, *zabaglione* and that other virgin of Italian gastronomy, Marsala Vergine. Actually the Marsala DOC territory extends to practically every part of the sun-baked, mainly flat province of Trapani, apart from Alcamo.

GRAPES, WINES AND PRODUCERS – RED

NERO D'AVOLA

The name obviously comes from the Sicilian town of Avola near Siracusa, its much-used alternative appellation, Calabrese, being a corruption of the Greek-based Siracusan dialect name *kalavrisi*, meaning, I am informed, good grape, rather than having anything to do with Calabria where its presence is not now and never has been significant. The baking-hot, flat or scarcely rolling calcareous lands of the southeast corner of Sicily, around Rosolini and Pachino, is where its heaviest concentration is to be found, now and in the past, the length of that past being unknown although probably quite ancient.

In its home zone Nero d'Avola lost a phenomenal amount of land-space to plastic-tunnelled fruits and vegetables in recent years as a result of EU extirpation policy, as earlier explained. On the other hand, being increasingly seen as Sicily's highest quality grape variety in absolute, it is today, with red wine in the ascendant generally, finding homes all over the island, and is by far and away Sicily's most-planted black grape. It is unusual for a Sicilian producer plotting new plantings these days not to include Nero d'Avola in his calculations.

As a blender, Nero d'Avola is ideal, since it combines tremendous colour – a mere 36 hours maceration will yield wine as 'black' as the ace of spades – with high sugar levels and very firm acidity even in conditions of great heat. In fact it is this acidity, almost all of which is tartaric and therefore not easily reducible by malo-lactic fermentation, which in certain soil conditions constitutes the big problem for Nero d'Avola as a varietal. This is why it is so often blended with lower-acid varieties such as Nerello Mascalese, Frappato or even the white Inzolia; or, more recently, with Cabernet, Merlot or Syrah. Even leaving the grapes on the vine past their mid-September due-date doesn't solve the high-acid problem, as they begin to raisin and ascend to unacceptably high sugar-levels.

There are those who claim a close connection with Syrah, basing their theory on similarities of leaf and berry shape, and depth of colour, even going so far as to offer the first two syllables of the ancient port of Sira-cusa as etymological evidence. Connoisseurs of Syrah/Shiraz reject the claim, saying that, while Syrah's branches tend upwards, those of Nero d'Avola grow downwards; and that the perfumes are not at all similar, those of Nero d'Avola being akin to black soft-fruits while those of Syrah are nearer to the red type.

Of course we are talking about vines which would have had one or two thousand years or so to develop different characteristics under diverse conditions. In fact, there seems to be an increasing acceptance of the relationship between Nero d'Avola and Syrah, and many are willing to think of them as descendants from a common ancestor.

Not surprisingly, Nero d'Avola stars in the DOC of its home territory, the not-exactly-world-famous Eloro Rosso, with its superior *cru*, Pachino. It is co-principal in Cerasuolo di Vittoria from neighbouring Ragusa province. And it figures prominently in Contea di Sclafani Rosso, under which multi-DOC it also enjoys varietal status; in Contessa Entellina in which it may be blended with Syrah; in the Bonera of Menfi, province of Agrigento; and in the Rossos of Menfi, Sambuca di Sicilia and Santa Margherita di Belice.

But all this is somewhat irrelevant in a situation where most producers ignore the various obscure DOCs, which no one has heard of and resort instead to IGT Sicilia. The fact is that Nero d'Avola, while producers acknowledge its supreme situation to be the southeast, is as has been noted being increasingly planted in all parts of the island, almost invariably, in the case of the trendy wines, for purposes of blending with French grapes – with Merlot, with Syrah, with Cabernet – making wines capable of combining great substance and weight with elegance and subtlety of perfume.

The producers

Regaleali/Tasca d'Almerita. When speaking about the 'revolution' in Sicilian wines from around the mid-1990s one should give tribute to the few estates which kept the flag of quality flying in the preceding decades during which mediocrity or worse was in the ascendent. Of these, without a doubt, Regaleali is the leader. The story of the estate itself goes back at least to the sixteenth century, but it was in 1830 that it came into the hands of the present owners, the Tasca family, currently led by Count Lucio Tasca d'Almerita assisted by his sons Giuseppe and Alberto as well as by the recently appointed general manager, Gaetano Zangara, ex of Corvo and, of course, by the long-standing though still young resident winemaker, Luigi Guzzo.

Regaleali finds itself in an inland enclave about an hour and a half's drive south and east of Palermo, between Vallelunga in the province of Caltanissetta and Valledolmo in the province of Palermo. It is an area of extremely limited rainfall, traditionally for thousands of years the 'granary' of Italy. The estate, which until the government's enforced redistribution of land in the 1950s boasted 1,200 hectares, now has something over 500, some 350 of which are planted to vineyard, mostly on *spalliera* – an innovation of Lucio's father Conte Giuseppe – at between 450 and 700 metres altitude. It was Conte Giuseppe who set the estate on the road to quality, back in the late 1960s, and his son since the early 1980s has built upon those foundations to make Regaleali the pride of Sicily and one of the finest estates in all Italy.

Although Nero d'Avola is only one of 16 grapes grown commercially here, and although it is not even the one most planted, being second after Grecanico, it is the core variety of all but one of their red wines: Regaleali Rosso – the spicey, peppery, Rhône-like house red, easy-drinking and amazingly characterful for a wine

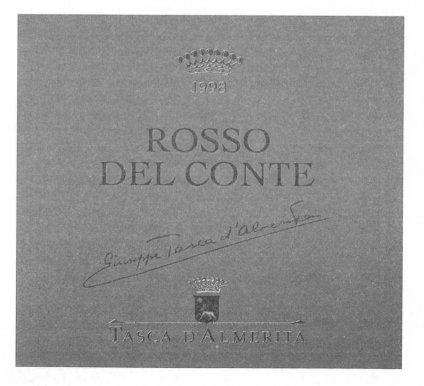

produced in such numbers (700,000 bottles). The star (for me) is Rosso del Conte – including 10% Perricone, a wine of grandiose personality, balance and depth in good years (90,000+ bottles produced); Then there is Novantasei (with 25% Merlot), thus named because it was introduced in 1996 although perhaps the suggestion is that it should have 96 points, which it doesn't quite deserve yet – perhaps 90. The more recently introduced Cygnus (with 25% Cabernet Sauvignon) is so named because Nero d'Avola, which used to be the 'ugly duckling', has in this wine, according to the blurb, become a beautiful swan (I would prefer the Rosso del Conte in that role rather than this somewhat over-oaked and less typical example). And, in future, there will be a Nero d'Avola/Syrah which should be the best of the three international blends since the two grapes are more likely to marry well. The only major red which contains no Nero d'Avola is the famous Cabernet Sauvignon, which has thankfully moved back from the blockbuster proportions it displayed in the vintages of the early 1990s to a more restrained, and very fine and elegant, level.

As for the whites, which represent over half of the production, we find the same mix of native and international grapes, with Grecanico constituting the main variety followed by Ansonica (Inzolia) and Chardonnay. The first two form the basis of the easy-drinking Villa Tasca – with a touch of Chardonnay – and the slightly more demanding Regaleali Bianco (with Catarratto; 1,200,000 bottles produced!), as well as the discreet but mouth-filling Nozze d'Oro. Chardonnay comes into play more with Leone d'Almerita and of course with the international-style Regaleali Chardonnay, another wine that has moved back from the brink of excess to a more moderate and refined level.

The key to success has always been the Tasca d'Almeritas' willingness to invest and move with the times. Hence their planting of international grapes in the 1980s, their continued research, in tandem with the University of Milan, into improved clones and different varieties – they are currently experimenting with some 60 varieties of various provenances, Italian and generally Mediterranean – their digging of lakes and establishing of irrigation plant in order to come to the rescue of vines in extreme stress. The new and costly *cantina*, completed in 1999, contains, apart from the latest equipment for the main wines, a number of 50 hectolitre fermentors for the vinification of the experimental parcels – so the whole operation can take place in-house. Conte Lucio's comment: 'I maintain that research is fundamental – I am a big pain in the arse in that respect.'

But without such pains in the arse where would Sicily be today?

Duca di Salaparuta, Casteldaccia. This vast enterprise, turning out over 10 million bottles per annum, was founded in 1824 by Giuseppe Alliata, Duke of Salaparuta. The brand Corvo dates from not long after that time, although it was not registered until 1874. When, in the late-middle nineteenth century all of Europe was suffering a wine-drought due to phylloxera the Dukes had the wisdom to graft early and were thus able to carry on in business, achieving the notable feat of having their wines, lighter and more refined than the blockbusters of which Sicily is capable, served in various royal courts of Europe.

After World War II business in general and wines in particular fell on hard times, and the last private owners, the heirs of Duke Enrico di Salaparuta, were in 1961 forced after heavy but unsuccessful investments to sell the operation to the Sicilian regional government, who needed the producer to keep going for purposes of employment, not just at the winery, but on farms throughout Italy, since it has long been the winery's method to purchase grapes from various parts of the island. The brand grew bigger in Europe and in the world so that, in the 1990s, the *cantina* was able to completely re-equip to the highest modern standards.

At the time of writing the *cantina* has just been sold for 141.5 billion lire (about US$70 million) to Ilva of Saronno, makers of the world-famous Amaretto di Saronno. Meanwhile, having lost its highly respected winemaker, Franco Giacosa, to Zonin and its chief executive, Gaetano Zangara, to Regaleali, the *cantina* finds itself in difficult times, although the arrival of Giacomo Tachis as consultant should go some way towards righting the balance. At any rate, the winery has the brands and the reputation to be able to ride the storm, and meanwhile its wines continue to sell without problem.

Nero d'Avola is, unsurprisingly, the principal red grape, and they use it exclusively for the making of their much lauded and awarded top wine, Duca Enrico, the grapes being sourced in vineyards of at least 20 years age, of low production and trained to *alberello*.

The basic Corvo Rosso is also based on Nero d'Avola, with some Perricone and Frappato, similar to the one in between, Terre d'Agala, which latter must come from high density, low yielding vineyards and contains significant amounts of Perricone and Frappato.

Corvo is equipped for multiple micro-vinifications for purposes of controlling the product of the various experimental vineyards in which they are researching, together with the universities of Turin and Palermo, clones and other viticultural aspects of the native varieties: Nero d'Avola, Perricone, Frappato (reds), Inzolia, Catarratto and Grecanico (whites). Even the giants who don't know quite where they are going need these days to progress if only in order not to lose their place in the world rankings.

Azienda Agricola **Melia Antonino**, Alcamo. The name 'Alcamo' conjures up images, in the mind of anyone who has followed Sicilian wines over a period, of oceans of white plonk good at best for vermouth and at worst for distillation. The last thing one might think of is quality red – or red wine at all, for that matter, even though the revised *disciplinare* for Alcamo DOC of 1999 has officialised the concept. Yet red, and at a very high quality level, is what is beginning to give Alcamo – the zone, if not the DOC – a new image and a new mission in life. And the movement is being led by the three brothers Melia (pronounced me-lee-a) – Antonino, who looks after the vineyards, Vincenzo and Giuseppe, oenologists, at their winery Baglio Ceuso near the town of Alcamo itself.

It's a small estate – 22 hectares – but the Vigna Custera from which the grapes for the one wine they bottle, Ceuso Custera, is only 8.5 hectares, planted to Nero d'Avola (about 50%), Cabernet Sauvignon (about 30%) and Merlot (20%). The idea for the project probably came through Vincenzo's work with the Cantina Sperimentale of the Istituto Vite e Vino of Sicily, to whom the great Giacomo Tachis has been consultant for several years. Tachis's thesis is that Sicily, despite its reputation for whites, is potentially an outstanding red wine-producing region, and of course it was Tachis who through the Cantina Sperimentale introduced strange ideas like blending the native grapes with internationals like Cabernet and Merlot.

First plantings of the red interlopers were made in 1990, but it wasn't until the 1995 vintage, which came out in 1997, that they were sufficiently happy with the wine to unveil it. Since then it has had nothing but success, both in the press and with consumers, and has been hailed internationally for its 'lush, rich and dense, concentrated, very smooth berry and tobacco flavors' (to quote the American taster Steve Tanzer), for its finesse, for its drinkability. True to the Tachis style – though the *maestro* doesn't consult to them, just gives friendly advice – the wine is aged in *barrique* but subtly, because they 'don't want too much wood', the tannins are ripe yet firm and the mouth-feel, perhaps partly because it has received no filtration, is complete and voluptuous.

With reds like these, Sicily does indeed have a bright future. It only remains for a few more producers to jump on the bandwagon.

Abbazia **Santa Anastasia**, Castelbuono. This fabulous property, reached by a winding uphill road in a relatively little populated sector of the north coast of the island, commands a magnificent view from the ancient converted monastery at 400 metres past vineyards and olive groves down to the sea. Builder Francesco Lena of Palermo bought the estate in the late 1970s with the idea of turning it into a holiday resort, but along the way he got bitten by the wine bug. 'Wine takes hold of you', he said, 'because you are never sure you've arrived at the maximum'. He started experimenting with various grape varieties, improving the *cantina*, calling in assistance from no less oenological luminaries than Giacomo Tachis (first) and Riccardo Cotarella.

In the last three or four years, with grapes from their 65 hectares plus a further 100 hectares in three other properties they control in various parts of the island Santa Anastasia have started making some of the finest modern-style wines in Sicily. The principal grape for the reds, which untypically for Sicily make up two-thirds of their production, is Nero d'Avola, though they also use Cabernet and Merlot in some wines and have planted Syrah and Petit Verdot. The reds rise in a crescendo from Santa Anastasia – Nero d'Avola *in purezza*, through Passomaggio – Nero d'Avola and Merlot, Montenero – Nero d'Avola + Merlot and Syrah, to the summit, Litra – Nero d'Avola + Cabernet Sauvignon; there is a perceptible quality leap from wine to wine, in terms of concentration and of wood-ageing, but all are great value at their level, with Litra set to become one of the island's cult wines of the future.

Cantina **La Elorina**, Rosolini. This *cantina sociale* was founded in 1978 for the purpose of serving the numerous small and part-time growers in this generally flat or slightly rolling extreme southeast corner of Sicily, the land of origin for Nero d'Avola, not far from the town of Avola, and still regarded – especially the sub-zone Pachino – as the classic zone for the grape. The *cantina* was built to handle a capacity of 15,000 tonnes of grapes, yet such were the depredations of the insane EU extirpation policy of the late 1980s/early 1990s, paying growers to extirpate high quality (though low yielding) vineyards planted to *alberello* and *spalliera*, that well under a tenth of that capacity is realised today. Noting that the trend was moving away from volume towards quality, Elorina under its long-standing president Rosario Ciccazzo decided to redirect their production and equip themselves with the necessary technology as well as with a switched-on winemaker. Today they turn out Nero d'Avola wines of varying levels of quality from good to excellent, depending mainly on grape selection. The good is represented by Villadorata Eloro Rosso DOC, coming from selected grapes from all zones except for sub-zone Pachino, which is where producers like Duca di Salaparuta have always sourced the finest, fullest Nero d'Avola fruit for their top wines. Needless to say, the *cru* Pachino, also an Eloro Rosso DOC, represents the 'excellent'. In between is the Riserva, made only in the better years, and subject to two years *invecchiamento* from the October of the vintage.

Another tradition the *cantina* is bravely trying to follow is that of Moscato di Noto, an endeavour in which to date they have been conspicuously less successful.

Other good to excellent producers of Nero d'Avola varietal or based wines include: **Avide** (Herea Rosso), Comiso; **Barone la Lumia** (Don Totò), Licata; **Donnafugata** (Milleunanotte), Marsala; **Grasso** (Caporosso – + Nerello Mascalese), Milazzo; **Morgante** (Don Antonio; Nero d'Avola), Grotte; **Pellegrino** (Cent'Are), Marsala; Cantine **Torrevecchia** (Casale dei Biscari), Acate; C.S. **Trapani** (Forti Terre di Sicilia), Trapani.

NERELLO MASCALESE AND NERELLO CAPPUCCIO

The only other red variety to come anywhere near Nero d'Avola's vineyard coverage in Sicily is Nerello Mascalese. The variety, which takes its name from the plain of Mascali at Etna's foot, and which is known in local dialect as *niureddu mascalisi*, has been grown on the slopes of the volcano, at up to 1,000 metres – which, needless to say, is extremely high for black grapes – for at least 200 years, probably much longer; there is evidence to indicate that viticulture has been practised on Etna since antiquity. The soil here is black, volcanic, of course, rich in minerals, poor in humus, and the best old vineyards, often on terraces, are planted at high density (6–9,000 plants per hectare) to *alberello* and may be up to 100 years old.

Nerello Mascalese is usually blended with other grapes, more often than not with Nerello Cappuccio, the one compensating for what the other lacks in anthocyanins (colouring matter) and vice versa in respect of tannins. Both are late varieties, ripening around the end of October and into November for the higher vineyards, although clonal selection should bring those times forward.

Insofar as the Nerellos are high quality grapes, which is debatable, it is the Mascalese which is superior, for which reason it has spread from its northeastern base right round the island, being favoured for the making of lighter reds and *rosato*s, often used in blends for purposes of lightening colour and adding perfume. The 'debatable' factor, quality-wise, derives less from Nerello Mascalese's intrinsic character than from abusive treatment – it is capable of high production on *tendone* and has been used in the recent past for purposes of volume, in which case it can be quite weedy. A fair assessment of Nerello Mascalese needs to be based on a limited production from *alberello*-trained vines at high density in a stressful environment like the terraces above Messina (DOC Faro) or the heights of Etna.

THE PRODUCERS

Azienda Agricola **Palari**, Messina. The first chapter of the wine Faro goes back to the fourteenth century BC, an age when, according to archeological evidence, wine was already being produced from grapes grown on the steep volcanic slopes behind the town of Messina across the straits from Calabria. This chapter continues with the arrival and dominance of numerous invaders, including Arabs who put an end to wine production altogether, and, much later, phylloxera, which had a similar effect.

The second chapter begins with the granting of the DOC to the ancient wine in 1976, despite the quasi non-existence of anyone willing to make the effort to produce it for a mere pittance in back-breaking conditions on steep terraces at 400–450 metres altitude overlooking the sea, and ends with its near extinction around 15 years later.

In the beginning of the third chapter Luigi Veronelli, grand guru of the Italian quality wine revival, comes to architect Salvatore Geraci, owner of the eighteenth-century Villa Geraci in the Faro zone, and tells him that if no one produces Faro DOC within the next three years the DOC will be revoked.

The story continues with Geraci accepting the challenge and persuading, with Veronelli's help, the outstanding Piemontese wine-maker, Donato Lanati, to help him. Both agree that the wine has to be outstanding, or nothing. They also agree that it should be made from traditional grapes using the best modern techniques.

And the ending is a happy one! Lo and behold, in conditions that few would brave in the wine world today, Salvatore and agronomist brother Giampiero Geraci have brought forth a wine of transcendent individuality and elegance from the unlikeliest of material – Nerello Mascalese for the most part, with Nerello Cappuccio, plus other obscure natives such as Nocera, Tignolino, Cor'e Palumba, Acitana, Galatena. The first vintage to appear, in 1996, is the 1994, and it takes the wine world by storm with its entrancing strawberry/raspberry fruit, its creamy texture married to ripe but unobtrusive tannins, its lilting, elegant finish with just a hint of quality oak to round it out.

And the success has continued uninterrupted, the Palari DOC being joined by a second wine of the same grapes, Rosso del Soprano, an IGT Sicilia despite qualifying on paper for the DOC because, despite being the saviour of the DOC, Geraci calls it 'out of date', for example allowing a yield of 10 tonnes of grapes per hectare when he knows that it's next to impossible to produce half of that for the real thing.

Worse still would be the allowing of international grapes. This wine is so full of personality that it would be a crying shame to sacrifice that attribute on the altar of the universal Bordeaux.

Azienda Vinicola **Benanti** (ex Tenuta di Castiglione), Viagrande. Mount Etna, Europe's highest volcano, has a long, indeed millennial, history of grape-growing for wine production. The breast-shaped mountain offers various advantages to the viticulturist: a unique soil, obviously richly volcanic; a variety of exposures from due north right round in a backwards C shape to southwest; a choice of altitudes from 350 to 1,000 metres; and dramatic night–day temperature shifts which favour aromas and discourage pests and fungi.

Dr Giuseppe Benanti, proprietor of a prosperous pharmaceutical firm on the outskirts of Catania, belongs to a family long associated with Etnean viticulture. In 1988, wishing to revive a tradition which had fallen on hard times, he decided to undertake various studies aimed at determining under what conditions vines might be cultivated to obtain best results. He started with the local vines – Nerello Mascalese, Nerello Cappuccio and Carricante, renting and purchasing vineyards in various parts of the mountain, preferably vineyards planted to *alberello*, some old enough to be pre-phylloxera, to produce wines typical of the zone. In the early stages the best of these were Pietramarina, Etna Bianco Superiore DOC, from 80-year-old vines in an east-facing vineyard at 950 metres planted solely to Carricante – a wine of neutral aroma but lively, lemon-acid-drop style, very clean and pure and hardly 'southern'; and Rovittello, from similarly aged Nerello Mascalese (80%) and Nerello Cappuccio vines planted at 750 metres on the north side of the volcano at Castiglione – a wine of intense cherry-berry fruit, some teeth-coating tannins but with fruit equal to the challenge; aged one year in *barriques*.

Meanwhile, he hired ex Donnafugata winemaker Salvatore Foti, a native of Etna and expert in her vines and wines, and together with the agronomy department at the University of Catania and the Istituto Sperimentale di Enologia at Asti in Piemonte they began developing clones from cuttings taken from various sites on the mountain and carrying out micro-vinifications in support. At the same time he increased his vine-yard holdings, which at the time of writing stands at 20 hectares in six different sites on the mountain from north round the east to the southwest. And he decided, too, to plant a couple of inter-national varieties, Chardonnay, for blending with Carricante in the recently developed IGT Sicilia Bianco 'Edèlmio' (means 'it is mine'); and Cabernet Sauvignon, for blending with Nerello Mascalese and Nero d'Avola, which latter grapes are bought in from the southeast, in the IGT Sicilia Rosso Lamorèmio (means 'my love').

Dr Benanti's most recent and perhaps most fascinating experiment involves the development of a flight of 100% varietals: four reds – Nerello Mascalese, Nerello Cappuccio, Nero d'Avola and Cabernet Sauvignon; and two whites, Carricante and Chardonnay. All of these, when I tasted them, showed good standards of wine-craftsmanship, the stand-out being the pure Nerello Mascalese, with well-defined, very pure fruit-flavours, mainly ripe cherry. The Nerello Cappuccio – possibly the only one of its kind – was interesting as an experiment but less convincing as a wine, having a tannic edge which the fruit was unable to overcome.

Did I say 'most recent'? Actually, the newest arrival in the Benanti portfolio is a wine called Serra Della Contessa, Etna Rosso DOC, a blend of the two Nerellos from a vineyard on the south side of the mountain, fermented in 55-hectolitre oak *tini*. This is an upmarket version of Rovittello with riper, richer fruit, softer tannins, a voluptuously smooth palate and a long, fruit-dominated finish. After tasting it, one begins to be convinced of the Benanti thesis that, on Etna, it is possible to make wines of great quality and personality.

Other producers capable of good Nerello Mascalese and N. Cappuccio include: **Barone Scammacca del Murgo** (Etna Rosso), Santa Venerina; **Barone di Villagrande** (Etna Rosso), Milo; **Firriato** (Etna Rosso), Paceco.

FRAPPATO DI VITTORIA

Its homeland is in the Province of Ragusa in the southeast, where it is a mainstay of the characterful Cerasuolo di Vittoria. Its role is to add perfume, of which it's got plenty, of a quite particular type – between floral and cherry-fruit. It lacks backbone, however, so needs to be blended with the more sturdy Nero d'Avola, but judiciously, since its delicacy is in danger of being overshadowed.

Frappato's origins are unknown to ampelographers. It may be a native of the area of Vittoria, from which obviously it derived the name, and where it has been known since the seventeenth century – it is still little grown outside of this area; or it may have been imported during one of the many periods of occupation which have been Sicily's lot through the ages, perhaps that of Spain (1282–1713). It may even have come from Calabria – there is said to be a link between Frappato and Gaglioppo.

The producers

COS, Vittoria (prov. of Ragusa). Students Giambatista Cilia (C), Giusto Occhipinti (O) and Giuseppina Strano (S) started this acronymically titled winery in 1979 on a shoestring, crushing the first two tonnes of grapes by foot, fermenting it in old concrete vats and selling the resulting bottles in the wine-shops of Palermo. As such they established themselves as perhaps the first of the pioneers of new Sicily, years before other young enthusiasts started clambering onto the bandwagon.

Year by year Cilia and Occhipinti improved methods and upgraded equipment, taking advice from winemakers like Giacomo Tachis, from agronomists and journalists (e.g. Luigi Veronelli) alike, absorbing it and turning it into wines which shone ever more brightly in what was after all, until around the mid-1990s, a drab oenological scene.

They were certainly among the first to introduce what Sicilians are fond of calling 'allochthonous' (of different origin, i.e. international) varieties: Chardonnay for Le Vigne di COS Bianco, Cabernet Sauvignon and Merlot for Le Vigne di COS Rosso, wines of consistently fine conception and execution. And Occhipinti remains an enthusiastic fan of these grapes, which give growers so little trouble compared with their natives (it shouldn't be that way, one would think; but one hears the same lament all over Italy), ripening early, all at the same time, requiring relatively little attention both in vineyard and in *cantina*.

Nevertheless it is for the wines of 'autochthonous' (of local origin) grapes of their southeastern corner of Sicily that they have become best known. Today, apart from a characterful white, called Ramingallo, made from the indigenous Ansonica or Inzolia, they make a range of reds under the Cerasuolo di Vittoria DOC, this being by law a blend of at least 40% Frappato and not more than 60% Nero d'Avola (in other words, it can theoretically be 100% Frappato, though it rarely is). Despite Giusto's complaints that Frappato is a nuisance-grape, with different ripening times within a single vineyard, indeed within a single bush – the nearer the grapes are to the trunk the less ripe they tend to be – they have elicited from critics a growing crescendo of praise for Cerasuolos of charming aroma and sweet fruit, not big wines – indeed, the more Frappato there is, the less 'big' the wine will be – but graceful and certainly moreish.

Recently they have turned their interest more towards Nero d'Avola *in purezza* and are working on a range of *crus* from different soils and microclimates, still within the southeastern corner of the island: Vittoria, Riesi and Pachino. Early indications are that these, especially the *selvatico* Pachino, will be serious contenders for honours among Nero d'Avola wines in the near future.

Other good to very good producers of Frappato include: Avide (Cerasuolo di Vittoria Barocco; C. di V. Etichetta Nera); Cantine Torrevecchia (Frappato); Cantine **Valle dell'Acate** (Frappato), Acate.

PERRICONE OR PIGNATELLO

This grape has been known in Sicily for a long time, though nobody seems to know how long. Perhaps it is of Sicilian origin, although it might also have come from Spain. Until about 100 years ago it was much more widespread on the island than it is today, prized mainly for its depth of colour, fullness of body and tannicity and used for the production of concentrated grape must. These are the qualities that make it a good blending grape with lighter wines, and the fact that it is slipping today is probably due to the fact that Nero d'Avola has similar qualities and is better. Nonetheless it is with Nero d'Avola that it is often blended, as for example by Tasca d'Almerita in Regaleali Rosso and Rosso del Conte, and by Duca di Salaparuta in Corvo Rosso and Terre d'Agala.

It has its own sub-DOC, as Pignatello, under the Eloro banner, and as Perricone under that of Contea di Sclafani. In either place, however, you will have your work cut out to find a bottle under the varietal label.

OTHER RED VARIETIES

Sangiovese and Barbera have a certain presence in Sicily, the former having its own sub-DOC under Contea di Sclafani and Santa

Margherita di Belice, the latter being mainly used for blending which, as we know, it is good at. There are also various vineyard experiments going on with Italian as well as international varieties.

GRAPES, WINES AND PRODUCERS – WHITE

CATARRATTO

As far as we know Catarratto Bianco originated in Sicily and has existed there *da sempre*; which means that no one knows since when. Over the ages it has had time to develop various sub-varieties, of which the two most diffuse are Catarratto Bianco Comune and Catarratto Bianco Lucido. Both are very productive – the very name suggests a veritable cataract of wine – but Bianco Comune is considerably more so, and was the growers' favourite when volume was the name of the game, though the finer Bianco Lucido is much more frequently planted now that sales of cheap wines have slumped. Even after the EU's massive cull of superfluous vineyards in the 1980s and early 1990s – and apart from Trebbiano more superfluous than Catarratto doesn't exist – there remain well in excess of 50,000 hectares planted to Catarratto, still mainly Comune. Practically all of these are in the western Sicilian provinces of Trapani, Palermo and Agrigento; although the variety does have limited diffusion in other parts of the island as a blender, including in Etna Bianco. And in fact, as a blender, it (Bianco Lucido) does have some positive characteristics, being quite full of body and well structured if rather lacking in aroma.

One of Catarratto's main functions in life over the past century or so has been for the making of Marsala, and indeed it has a ready tendency to *marsaleggiare* (Sicilian for 'maderise'). More recently it has been used also as a base for Vermouth. And when the EU generously offered money to producers who couldn't sell their wine wholesale, distillation became its fate. Since 1972 it has had its own DOC, Alcamo – changed and substantially altered in 1999 to include red wines as well as various new international grapes for the white – the number of bottles of which, however, represent but a tiny fraction of total Catarratto production in the zone. On rare occasions Bianco d'Alcamo can display a glimmer of real quality, although the best varietal Catarratto I have tasted didn't come from Alcamo at all, but from a producer whose vineyards are at a considerably higher altitude (see below).

The producers

Calatrasi/Terre di Ginestra, San Cipirello (province of Palermo). 'Where the Focus is on your Dream', runs the blurb on the cover of this supernova of a company whose universe seems to be expanding almost as fast as the speed of light. But the dream, dear reader, is not ours, is it, but that of the owner and guiding genius of the firm, medical doctor Maurizio Miccichè, with his lawyer brother Giuseppe.

The Miccichè brothers started their business in 1980, continuing the activities of their father, another medical doctor with a penchant for wine. The first wine to come to international attention from the Terre di Ginestra family vineyards – at between 600 and 1,200 metres above sea-level – was the Bianco, made from grapes grown at various altitudes and picked at different times. It was so clean and fresh, herbaceous and spicy and racy that people at the time could not believe (a) that it came from Sicily or (b) that it didn't contain some other grape like Sauvignon Blanc.

To me, this remains their most interesting product, though as I say there has been an explosive growth since then. Today, their three family estates are joined to those of their partner, the cooperative Castel di Maranfusa, totalling 2,000 hectares of vineyard, not including those from whom they buy in grapes. With a wide range of grape varieties, Sicilian and international, to choose from, not to mention an ambitious replanting programme; with their various viticultural experiments with different varieties and clones in conjunction with the viticulture department of the University of Milan; with their policy of paying growers not according to sugar alone but rather sugar-acidity ratio; with their Australian wine-maker Brian Fletcher, from the formidable western Australian producers Evans & Tate; with their *cantina* at San Cipirello under-going US$7.5 million worth of expansion and upgrading over a five-year period; with their 50–50 partnership with the Australian giant Hardys to produce southern wines under the D'Istinto label; with their 230-hectare project in Puglia overseen by another Australian, Lisa Gilbery; and with their two recently leased estates in Tunisia, from whose 400+ hectares of vineyard they are already making excellent red wines under the Selian label from Carignan and Carignan/Mourvèdre (other grapes at their disposal include Grenache, Cinsault, Alicante Bouchet, Sangiovese, Syrah, Pedro Ximènez and Muscat, and they are investing a further US$8 million here); with their 'Accademia del Sole' project to include a cooking school, a wine museum and the marketing of typical southern Italian products such as honey, oil, cheese, ceramics, embroidery – there will also be a sumptuous hospitality centre; with all this, Calatrasi must be the most dynamic outfit in Sicily today, perhaps in the whole of the south – as is, by their own admission, the 'dream'.

And that's not all: the dream includes the encouragement of honest government and constructive investment in Sicily and the south in defiance of the Mafia and institutional incompetence and corruption (it sounds great; one is tempted to say: Dream on!, but the most unlikely results have been achieved by dreamers); and, specifically business-wise, a plan 'to develop a new Meditterranean brand, fully recognised in the international markets' and to 'deliver and maintain unparallel (sic) quality for all our Mediterranean, multi-regional products, sold under the Calatrasi corporate banner.'

With all this one would expect a plethora of wines and labels, and one would not be mistaken. My advice to lovers of wines of real *terroir* is to keep the eye on the Terre di Ginestra wines and on the Tunisians. For the rest the wines will be well made, certainly, and probably good value, but with perhaps a touch too much concession to internationalism and winemaking-to-price-points.

The only other producer of good Catarratto I know of is **Rapitalà** (Alcamo and Alcamo Riserva DOC), Camporeale, owned by Comte Hugues de la Gatinais in conjunction, now, with the giant GIV (see Melini under Poggibonsi, Chapter 2).

INZOLIA/ANSONICA

Much less intensively planted than Catarratto, but more diffuse, and considerably more interesting as a wine-grape, is Inzolia, sometimes spelt Insolia, also known as Ansonica, originally Ansoria, meaning 'type of grape'. Presumed to be a native Sicilian, it has been planted widely throughout the island over hundreds of years at least, developing different characteristics under varying pedo-climatic conditions. The sub-variety most used today is called Verde-Cappuccia, a medium-early ripener – first half of September – whose main purpose has been to add softness and flavour to white table wines such as Corvo Bianco and Regaleali Bianco, and although it once figured strongly among the recommended varieties for Marsala it is little used for that purpose today.

Just as Catarratto's star is in the descendant, Inzolia's is in the ascendant, and it has been chosen to play the lead role in a number of recently created DOCs with Catarratto and/or Grecanico at second fiddle, among which: Contea di Sclafani Bianco, under which multi-DOC it can also be made as a varietal; Contessa Entellina Bianco, same comment (here there is provision for a sweet or semi-sweet Vendemmia Tardiva if the grapes are picked after 1 October); Menfi Bianco, where again there is provision for a varietal as well as an Inzolia/Chardonnay blend called Feudo dei Fiori; Santa Margherita di Belice Bianco, also including a varietal; and Sambuca di Sicilia Bianco.

As Ansonica, the variety has a limited presence along the Tuscan coast, especially on the islands of Elba and Giglio – indeed, one of its synonyms is *Uva del Giglio* – where it may be made dry or sweet (*passito*). It has its own Tuscan DOC as Ansonica Costa dell'Argentario.

The producers

Tenuta di **Donnafugata**, Marsala. There is potential for confusion here, since this estate is owned by the Rallo family which made its name as producers of Marsala from the mid-nineteenth century. However, fourth-generation Giacomo Rallo, seeing the writing on the wall for oxidised wines in today's market, sold his entire interest in Rallo Marsala in the early 1990s, having initiated the production of table wines in 1983 under the Donnafugata name, and today has nothing further to do with the Marsala firm which continues to fly under the name Rallo (see under Grillo).

Around 100 of the hectares of vineyard owned by the firm were in fact inherited in the 1970s by Giacomo Rallo's wife, Gabriella Anca. They are situated in the Contessa Entellina DOC zone of western Sicily, inland at altitudes ranging from 300 to 600 metres, where the firm controls a further 70 hectares under long-term contracts. The grapes are a mix of the 'autochthonous' and the 'allochthonous', as they like to call them, but the most important is Inzolia/Ansonica (they use the latter name) which informs several of their wines in both the 'Linea Classica' and the 'Top Line' (almost half of their 1.5 million bottles are entirely or partly Ansonica).

The most basic, and biggest-selling (600,000 bottles), of their products is Anthilia, Ansonica with a bit of Catarratto, this being a thoroughly modern, clean, fresh wine which could come from much farther north. The most notable Ansonica, virtually 100% varietal, is Vigna di Gabri, with the same restrained – for Sicily – alcoholic degree of 12.5% but with considerably more weight and personality. Chiarandà is a 50–50 blend with Chardonnay, a *barrique*-fermented wine which spends six months in cask before release – 13.5%, it is rich and unashamedly oaky, almost a new world style; but it works. Lighea is another blend, 50% Ansonica with 25% each of Sauvignon Blanc and, surprisingly, Müller Thurgau.

In the red department the most important grape is Nero d'Avola, informing in whole or in part the wines for which, probably, the firm is best known. Among these are Tancredi, 70% Nero d'Avola/30% Cabernet Sauvignon, *barrique*-aged 15 months – a wine of warm, rich berry fruit mingling with the toast and vanilla of oak; Angheli – 50–50 Nero d'Avola and Merlot. And two *in purezza* (or nearly) – Sedara, the basic red (200,000 bottles produced), soft and jammy, highly drinkable and good value; and the one released in 1999 in a flurry of publicity, Mille e Una Notte, a wine, aged two years in new French *barriques*, of complex aromas and several dimensions – classy, lead-pencil and blackberry nose, with ripe berry fruit, spices and herbs on the nose, plenty of fine tannins and a sumptuous mouth-feel; to be noted that neither this nor Tancredi are filtered or cold-stabilised.

The Rallo family – son Antonio and daughter Josè work alongside their parents – also have 11 hectares of vineyard in Pantelleria, of the wines from which they are particularly proud.

Other good producers of Inzolia or Inzolia-based wines include: Avide (Vigne d'Oro; Herea Bianco); Barone la Lumia (Sogno di Dama); Duca di Salaparuta (Bianco di Valguarnera); **Grasso** (Sulleria Bianco Feudo Solaria – + Catarratto), Milazzo.

GRILLO

Opinions seem to be divided as to whether Grillo has been in Sicily, especially in the Marsala-producing zone in the west, for ever, since the Phoenicians brought it, for a few centuries, or only since phylloxera. The latter view is expressed in no less an authoritative opus than the *Principali Vitigni* of the Ministry of Agriculture (Mazzei and Zappalà), who also seem to think it is a native of Puglia. This thesis is weakened by the apparent absence of any such variety – by name or by behaviour – in Puglia today. The Phoenician theory sounds best, so let's go with that.

In the early part of the twentieth century Grillo was the main grape for the making of Marsala, but it was overtaken by Catarratto in the race for quantity over quality. Now that quality is 'in' again, so is Grillo, able as it is to climb to impressive sugar-levels if left to 'grill' to over-ripeness in the sun on low-yielding *alberello* vines. Producers like de Bartoli swear by it, saying that it is the **only** grape for quality Marsala.

If required for this purpose Grillo may be left on the vine until the end of September, by which time in a normal year the grapes will be very rich in sugar – up to 16 or 17% – if rather low in acidity. On the other hand, cropped around the end of August, Grillo can make a very characterful, quite aromatic, dry white table wine. Exponents are the firm of Rallo, with their Grillo Bianco di Sicilia and Marco de Bartoli with his excellent Grappolo del Grillo. Indeed, Grillo now has its own varietal section in the Contea di Sclafani multi-DOC as well as honourable mention in the complex grape-mix for Contessa Entellina Bianco.

MARSALA

Marsala is a complex wine, from both the viticultural and oeno-logical points of view. It may be made from a diversity of grapes – Grillo, Catarratto, Inzolia and Damaschino on the white side; Pignatello, Calabrese/Nero d'Avola and Nerello Mascalese on the red – so that it is difficult in a book organised according to grape varieties to categorise under a single one. Grillo being, according to the experts, the one that produces the best wine, I have elected to describe it under that category.

Briefly, from an historical point of view: strong wine, consisting of table wine laced with *mosto cotto* (cooked must) or other reduced musts, seems to have been produced in western Sicily since at least Roman times, and we know from various documents that such wines were being commercialised at least four centuries ago; apparently the painter Rubens took away with him to Holland a substantial quantity.

Nevertheless, just as Columbus 'discovered' what was already there, John Woodhouse, an Englishman with a palate for Sherry and Madeira, is said to have 'invented' Marsala in the late eighteenth century, his particular contribution – from today's perspective one of dubious merit – being essentially to add alcohol to the existing wine so that it might survive lengthy sea journeys, thus recommending itself to the British Royal Navy, including one Horatio Nelson, and subsequently to the English people, already inured to the delights of Sherry, Port and Madeira – the latter being the nearest in style. Several Inghams, Whitakers, Paynes, Hoppses, Goods, and subsequently Florios, Pellegrinos and Rallos later, the fortified Marsala found itself a hot seller on the world market, and increasingly prized not just as a drink but also as a culinary aid. At its peak, around the turn of the nineteenth and twentieth centuries, there were in excess of 100 *bagli* (equivalent of *bodega*; singular – *baglio*), today reduced to around a dozen.

The transformation of Marsala into a cooking wine – and worse, into a flavoured wine (with eggs, almond and banana essence, etc.), proved, among other factors (lack of investment, lack of promotion) to be its Trojan horse because the more Marsala got the reputation of being a 'must stock' in the kitchen, the less it was taken seriously as a wine. Meanwhile, a lot of investment was poured into the Marsala 'industry', making it financially impossible to backtrack to quality with the attendant loss of turnover.

The decline of Marsala is written in the figures. Towards the end of the last century production was averaging about 250,000 hectolitres per annum. The all-time peak was reached in 1960 with over 450,000 hectolitres per annum. By 1978 it was under 200,000, and in 1997 it was around 125,000. At the same time, production at the quality end of the market was heading for extinction, with Marsala Superiore at around 15,000 hectolitres in the early 1990s and the only truly 'superior' Marsala, the *solera* 'Vergine', at a mere 500 hectolitres or less.

Some of this, admittedly, is due to a worldwide movement away from wines of the oxidised, fortified style. For all too much of it, however, the producers or their lawmakers have only themselves to blame, not just for having gone too far in exploiting a quality name to sell industrial products but for wrapping it up, in their *disciplinare*, in such a complicated mass of terminology that not even a Marsalese could understand it let alone a hapless customer in a wine store in Kansas, USA or Osaka, Japan. There are references to various styles – Fine, Superiore, Superiore Riserva, Vergine, Solera and Stravecchio; to a number of variations on the theme of Superiore – Vecchio, I.P. (Italia Particolare), S.O.M. (Superiore Old Marsala), G.D. (Garibaldi Dolce) and L.P. (London Particular); to different colours – Oro, Ambra and Rubino; to varying levels of residual sugar – Secco, Semisecco and Dolce, the Secco being allowed up to 40 grammes per litre of residual sugar with is frankly a lot nearer to sweet than dry; not to mention *mistella*, *sifone*, *mosto cotto* and pure *alcool* – additives for achieving different results; until the head is fairly spinning.

None of which is of much interest in the context of quality wine, especially when you realise that in all this mass of verbiage they have legislated out, by virtue of the insistence on a minimum alcohol level of 18%, the one wine-style which could return the Marsala name to glory, namely the unfortified Vergine/Solera such as Marco de Bartoli produces under the name of Vecchio Samperi. As a matter of fact, despite all the opprobrium that de Bartoli has had to put up with as a renegade scion of two established Marsala industrialist families, it is this officially unrecognised wine which has done more in the latter half of the twentieth century to bring Marsala back, by association, to some kind of public perception of quality than any other.

About time they recognised in the *disciplinare* that neither excellence nor style are inextricably linked to alcoholic degree.

Note: the process of making Marsala is detailed under the producer Rallo, below.

The producers

Marco **de Bartoli**, Marsala. I have referred above, and elsewhere (see profile in *Life Beyond Lambrusco*, p. 260), to the 'renegade' characteristics of this exceptional producer, and to the fact that he, more than any other individual, has made Marsala respectable again after it had fallen to the bottom of the image pit – and this with a wine that is not even allowed to call itself Marsala; another example of the law as an ass. For this service he has been hounded and persecuted relentlessly by the petty-minded and the jealous and others with a variety of hidden agendas. All that, too, is another story (recounted in an article for the website www.winepros.com, dated February 2001). Our business here is to talk about the wines.

One of the most awesome – to use that trendy American word – tasting experiences of my life came in the cellars at Samperi in the autumn of 2000. Pursuing his mission to return Marsala to the greatness of old, that greatness that he himself recalled tasting in liquid form in the cellars of his extended family during childhood, both his parents being of old Marsala families, Marco over the years since he started his independent business in 1980 had acquired a formidable stock of barrels of old single-vintage wines going back to the earliest years of the twentieth century and beyond, wines which, being oxidised, were more likely to improve and concentrate in wood than to deteriorate – both directions being possible.

In 1995, however, over a trumped-up charge relating to his production, not of Marsala, but of Moscato di Pantelleria, his premises were raided by the Carabinieri and effectively closed by the Repressione dei Frodi (Fraud Squad, whose job it is to control *sofisticazione* or cheating in wine production) who sealed up his barrels so that he could not get at them to make his normal blend for five years.

In the spring of 2000, after five years during which, had it not been for his mother bailing him out, he would have gone bankrupt, as his enemies had hoped, he was entirely absolved of the spurious charges against him and given access once again to his wines. Happening to visit a few months later, I was taken into the cellars by Marco's oenologist son Renato and given a comprehensive tasting, the first anyone had had for five years since Marco himself had not been able to bring himself to face his neglected babies – if you can call these ancient brews 'babies'. I can only say that I was stupefied by the range of flavours and aromas on offer from these extraordinary wines, from mineral and medicinal (iodine) to caramel and toffee, from spices and herbs to nuts and dried fruits, and around and back again in a cyclical swirl of tastes, smells and sensations.

It was only then, I think, that I fully understood the thesis that

Marco has spent his life trying to demonstrate, i.e. that 'Marsala' – but remember, these are not technically Marsala because they are unfortified and therefore below the legal threshhold of 18% alcohol – is indeed capable of being, not just good wine, but truly great wine, far greater than some of the alcoholic fruit juices that are held up as representing excellence in our superficial time; these for me, indeed, put wine in general alongside great painting and music as one of the divine miracles of our existence. Much is spoken about wine as an art form, but there is very little on the level of Turner or Mozart. These wines had that kind of power.

Of course, these wines are not intended for bottling as such, but for use in the blending of the wines Marco sells commercially. De Bartoli's commercial 'Marsalas' have gone through various stages, some of them forced upon him, but at present there are three, all derived from the same process but bottled at different stages. First stage: the ripest Grillo grapes are picked in the 20-hectare vineyard at Samperi; these will have a degree Babo of up to 25, meaning a potential alcohol of around 16.5%. The resultant wine is blended with *mistella* (see glossary) and this is 'Marsala' number one: Vigna la Miccia, the freshest and juciest of his wines, officially a Marsala Superiore 'Oro'.

If it isn't bottled as Vigna la Miccia it goes on to age for 10 years or so in a sort of *solera* (see glossary) system, as the Spanish call it, and this, sweetened and fortified up to 18% with *mistella* – and it should be noted that even *mistella* in de Bartoli's *cantina* may be aged 8 to 10 years in barrel – becomes the second wine, his lead 'official' wine, Marsala Superiore. Wine that does not become Marsala Superiore then goes into an older *solera*, at the end of which process it is blended with a splash of those old wines from the lower *cantina* and becomes Vecchio Samperi Ventennale, a wine whose average age is at least 20 years, though it is a mix of many different vintages. This, unfortified and unsweetened, is the nearest the consumer will get to those old wines I was raving about above, short of visiting the *cantina* itself.

Sometimes Marco also makes a wine called Josephine Doré which he refers to as being from the *inizio di solera*, the beginning of the *solera* – a dry, less complicated aperitif-style wine like the Ventennale but aged only four years.

Today Marco de Bartoli, the only one of three heads of company accused of malpractice in 1995 to have survived the years of persecution, Ignazio Miceli of MID Distribution and Marco's uncle, Benedetto Tumbarello of Pellegrino, both having died under the pressure, is not so much bitter as resigned, philosophical. 'I have continued to live, and to believe in Grillo and Zibibbo. But I recognise that I have to be more flexible today', he adds with a wry smile. 'No more thinking I can mould the world to what I think it ought to be; you stir up too much hatred.' Nevertheless, he peppers his description of those times with snide remarks about those whom he believes to be his attackers, just as he heaps opprobrium on certain journalists he considers to be unworthy of the power they wield. As a past president of the Istituto della Vite e del Vino, Sicily's wine regulatory body (this being a major factor in his troubles, he believes, since he was trying to push through a DOC Sicilia which certain very powerful interests didn't want; bankrupted, he would have had to stand down) he is an acute observer of the regional wine scene, and he feels that the current 'bubble' might burst, that talk of Sicilian wine rising to great heights is, at least for now, just a 'bluff'.

But Marco de Bartoli is back. And you can bet he will be getting his revenge in vinous form.

Cantine **Rallo**, Marsala. This was one of Marsala's original Italian-owned – as distinct from British-owned – wineries, dating back to 1860. In the early 1990s the brand and one *baglio* of Spanish design were sold by the heirs of the founder, Diego Rallo, to the firm of Alvis, owned by the Vesco family, who apparently had greater faith in the future of Marsala than Giacomo Rallo and family (see Donnafugata).

The Vescos were already producers of table wines in Trapani, the purpose of the purchase of the Rallo name and premises being to diversify their production; they have since further diversified into the wines of Pantelleria. The table wine range includes a dry *barrique*d Grillo, as mentioned earlier, as well as a Nero d'Avola/Cabernet blend and an Inzolia/Chardonnay blend under the Vesco brand which are remarkably inexpensive for the quality they deliver.

Our chief interest here, however, lies in Marsala production. The chief oenologist, Gasparo Vinci, a man I found very switched on in all matters of wine production and tasting, took me through the processes involved in making good quality commercial Marsala. Of the grapes that come in at vintage time – Grillo for the highest grades, aged Marsala Superiore and Marsala Vergine, Grillo blended with Inzolia for the lesser-aged Marsala Superiore wines, Catarratto for Marsala Fine and the cooking range – some are converted to *mistella* (grape-must stunned by alcohol up to 18%), some are made into *vino* for use in the blends and some are used for the making of concentrate and *mosto cotto* or a sort of caramelised cooked must (48 hours at 60–70 degrees Celsius).

The next stage is the *miscela*, or mix: for Marsala Superiore Dolce the formula is 60% *mistella*, 30% *vino*, 2% *mosto cotto* and 8% alcohol. For Marsala Fine it will be 60% *vino*, 30% *mistella*, 2% *mosto cotto* and 8% alcohol. Marsala Vergine is simply 80% *vino* and 20% alcohol.

Marsala Fine must age – in oak and chestnut barrels of between 15 and 80 hectolitres – a minimum of one year, Marsala Superiore two years, Marsala Vergine five years and Marsala Vergine Stravecchio Riserva 10 years. These are the legal criteria – in effect Rallo will often age their wines longer than the minimum.

Under Vinci's guidance Rallo have introduced various non-traditional techniques aimed at raising the quality of their products – apart from the obvious ones of stainless steel and temperature control. These include crio-maceration for the *vino*, ageing of the *vino* one year before using it in the *miscela* – as distinct from using new wine – micro-oxygenation of the wines at the *miscela* stage and a type of *bâtonnage* on the longer-aged Marsala Vergine.

Being a quality Marsala producer represents a large investment in old wines, at any one time Rallo's stock will be around one million litres. In current market conditions it is amazing that they are willing to do it at all.

I found their range of Marsalas remarkably good considering the very modest prices asked. Anima Mediterranea, a two-year-aged Marsala Superiore Ambra Semisecco of Grillo and Inzolia, was rich with an attractive but not excessive sweetness and a hint of herbs and spices, nuts and fudge. The Vergine had a fine bouquet with notes of sesame and an intense, dry but full palate; an excellent aperitif wine. By contrast I did not find that the Marsala Superiore Secco worked particularly well, but the Dolce of the same style was very tasty, rich and opulent with notes of candied fruits, caramel, sesame, nuts; a very tasty dessert wine and one, I suppose one can say today, with Marsala thoroughly out of fashion, with a difference.

GRECANICO DORATO

I have already referred to the similarity between this variety and the Garganega of Verona, to support which I now translate from the General Catalogue of the Vivai Cooperativi Rauscedo:

> Apparently belonging to the group of grape varieties of Greek provenance, it initially diffused itself in Sicily and then in other areas and in particular in the Veneto where a practically identical variety is cultivated called Garganega.

Grecanico's diffusion in Sicily, in fact, is fairly modest compared with Catarratto, Trebbiano and Inzolia; but its proponents are enthusiastic about its ability to give freshness and ageing potential to a blend. It is a well-established component of the Regaleali Bianco blend and of Contea di Sclafani Bianco, under which multi-DOC it may also be made varietally, the same being true of Contessa Entellina, Menfi and Santa Margherita di Belice DOCs.

CARRICANTE

A native variety of Etna, Carricante is so named because of its impressive productivity (*carico* = loaded). Though it was quite popular among growers of the province of Catania in the 1950s, its career in recent years has been pretty undistinguished, slipping in hectarage because of loss of market and losing markets because of inadequate quality. Not a great deal of it remains today – about 50 hectares – and there are few new plantings, but it is hoped that with intelligent clonal selection and planting in the right places, plus intelligent vinification, it can stage a modest comeback. When care is taken to limit yields and it comes from *alberello*-trained vines at uppish altitude (on Etna) it can produce a wine of crisp, concentrated, lemony zip. Carricante wine can be excessively sharp, however, in both tartaric and malic acids, and it is felt necessary to carry out the malo-lactic fermentation, this having been achieved traditionally by leaving the wine on the fine lees until temperatures rose in the spring, rather like Muscadet *sur lie*.

There was some effort earlier in the twentieth century to interest growers in western Sicily in Carricante, but it didn't take to their conditions, or they didn't take to it.

Good Carricante can be obtained from Benanti (Pietramarina, Bianco di Caselle or Monovitigno; or Edèlmio, blended with Chardonnay) or Barone Villagrande (Etna Bianco Superiore).

DAMASCHINO

A minor grape of the Marsala mix, also of Alcamo, it is occasionally produced varietally but not under any of the DOCs. That it may have been brought be Arabs from Damascus is purely conjectural. Donnafugata make a wine called Damaskino, which is blended with Catarratto.

TREBBIANO TOSCANO

(For general comments see the section on Tuscany.)

Trebbiano is the second most planted white variety in Sicily, having a hectarage, almost entirely in the prolific west, equal to about one-third that of Catarratto, though its yield in total weight of grapes is almost identical. You have rightly concluded that it was brought in for purposes of volume production, that it adds nothing to the glory of Sicilian viticulture but rather detracts both from the image and from the need to concentrate on higher quality from native grapes and imported ones of proven character.

MALVASIA

(For general comments see section on Malvasia under central Italy.)

Malvasia has been cultivated on the Eolian Islands, north of Sicily, and especially on the island of Salina, since time immemorial. The wines come in two styles: sweet and sweeter. The former is called Naturale, around 13% alcohol with a further 8–9 degrees residual sugar, where the slightly late-picked grapes undergo a certain drying on the plant. The latter is the traditional Passito, slightly lighter in alcohol at around 12%, but having a much higher residual sugar content (12–14%), where the grapes are dried both on the plant and, after picking, on mats under the sun.

There is not a lot of Malvasia delle Lipari – perhaps 50 or 60 hectares under vine – and what there is is divided into very small parcels, most of which are well under one hectare. The smaller growers tend to sell their grapes to larger ones, or if they do make a bit of wine they sell it to tourists. This kind of production tends to be very artisanal, and of professional producers whose wines may be found internationally there are principally two, Hauner and Colosi.

Carlo **Hauner**, of Salina, is the name of the winery that has attracted the most attention in recent decades. Carlo himself died in the mid-1990s, but the business has been taken in hand by his three children, who have continued to produce the unique sweet wine with the taste of dried apricots and orange marmelade and a hint of resin.

Half-owner of the Hauner winery is Pietro **Colosi,** whose son Piero runs the winery at Messina. Pietro and subsequently Piero have been making Malvasia delle Lipari from the ancient Malvasia grape for 30 years, but they only started bottling in 1987. They make both styles and I have to say that of the two I prefer the Naturale which displays a wonderful peachy, flowery perfume and a good fruit-acid balance giving the wine freshness, avoiding excessive heaviness or stickiness. The Passito is impressive, to be sure: more dried apricot than peach, richer, heavier, more perfumed and indeed more traditional; but a sipper, rather than a drinker.

MOSCATO BIANCO

(For general comments see section on Moscato in *Barolo to Valpolicella*, northwest.)

This is the grape behind the antique Moscato of Siracusa, according to some the first wine in Italy, called Pollio after 'the Argive Pollis, who reigned in Syracuse' (Pastena, p. 203). In the nineteenth century it was 'famed throughout the world, although most of the wine sold under that name certainly had never, not even from afar, seen the cellars of Sicily' (Pastena, p. 203). Such *sofisticazione*, as the Italians call fiddling, apparently brought the wine's reputation so low that today there is a law covering the production of Moscato di Siracusa, specifying that it must be made by the *passito* method; but there is very little actual wine.

In nearby Noto, however, there has been a very modest return to the production of Moscato Bianco in the form of Naturale – neither from semi-dried grapes nor fortified, but a sort of perfumed cross between table wine and aperitif – and Liquoroso, which consists of the stunning of fresh Moscato grape-must by addition of alcohol. Neither has yet reached a particularly lofty level, nor are they likely to unless they can get the right to *appassire* that Siracusa has but doesn't use.

The main significant producer of the two styles of Moscato di Noto – which also, incidentally, claims descendance from the famed 'Pollio' of antiquity – is the Cantina (Sociale) la Elorina.

ZIBIBBO

Zibibbo is the sub-variety of Moscato known as Moscato d'Alessandria, or Muscat of Alexandria, sometimes Moscatellone, sometimes Malaga (cf. the grape and thick, black, supersweet wine of southern Spain), once much demanded as a table-grape or raisin until the market switched to seedless varieties. It is a grape whose berries would normally be considered too large to produce good wine, and in fact its best and most traditional product, Moscato Passito di Pantelleria, comes from grapes which have been reduced in size by drying on the plant or, more drastically and more traditionally, by drying on mats in the sun.

The Arab-sounding name is not a coincidence. According to Bruno Pastena, it was introduced to the island of Pantelleria during the years of Arab occupation, between 827 and 1061, from Capo Zebib, that promontory of present-day Tunisia which is opposite Pantelleria (I am informed, I don't know how accurately, that Zebib or Zibibb actually means 'raisin'). Whether the Arabs' purpose was to make wine, as forbidden by the Koran, or raisins, is not known, but raisins would certainly be the official version.

Pantelleria is an island of contrasting colours – the black of the ubiquitous stones (one person claimed that there are 4,000 kilometres of dry stone wall on the island, most of them used for terracing on the steep slopes) against the white or pastel pink of the *dammusi* or Arab-style hump-roofed – for rain collection – houses and the lush green of the vegetation, part tropical, part temperate, this greenness being due, despite long months without precipitation, to the copious morning dews caused by sharp differences in day–night temperatures; by contrast there is the emerald and azure of the sea, visible from most parts of the island.

Viticulture in the black volcanic soil of Pantelleria is of an unusual nature, the low, free-standing vines being dug into individual hollows to protect them from the sand-blasting Sirocco winds that whip across from the Sahara – not for nothing is this called the *'Isola del Vento'* – causing havoc especially at the times of flowering and fruit-set. The grapes of the main shoots, cooked in a mighty heat, irrigated by morning dew and dried by the constant breeze, are generally ripe by mid-August, and these are raisined in the sun – supposedly; see below – for use in the sweetest *passito* wines for which the island is traditionally renowned. Grapes of the main shoots may be left on the vine somewhat longer for use as base wine in which to macerate the *uva passita*, since the dried raisins will have too little liquid to enable fermentation to take place. Sometimes, too, the wine called Moscato di Pantelleria is made from late-picked grapes, though this style may also simply be the product of a lesser/lighter year.

Zibibbo is an unusual vine in that it also fruits from secondary shoots (*racemi*), these being cropped as late as October or even November and used either to make base wine or, increasingly, dry table wine.

It is over the drying process that an unholy rumpus broke out in the mid-1990s, certain producers claiming that others, based not on the island but in Sicily – 'industrialists', that is – were using artificial wind machines (*essicatori*) to make *passito* 'unnaturally', bypassing the difficult and labour-intensive stage of *appassimento* in the sun. Well, it's not quite like that, because the *essicatore*, which was being used also by quality producers, is designed not to complete the drying process but only to hurry the first, risky part of it during which environmental humidity may bring the whole operation to naught by introducing negative moulds. Those who defend such a process, now no longer openly used by anyone for fear of the purists' wrath, claim that plastic tunnels, as used by some of their accusers to 'protect' the grapes from humidity, are distorting the wine into a kind of *'marmellata'*, brought about by intense and suffocating conditions in the long plastic semi-tubes, and are therefore much more 'unnatural' than their product which would undergo nine-tenths of its drying process in the open sunlight.

However that may be, the *essicatore* row was, according to some, only a cover-up for much more sinister goings on including a deadly rivalry between two of the major merchants of Marsala, as well as a disguised way of attacking enemies for other quite unrelated perceived crimes. In other words it all got very Sicilian if not quite Byzantine. Some small producers got into the back-stabbing by claiming that the industrialists were committing a systematic 'leadening' of the island's 'gold' with bureaucratic connivance. They complained that the decimation of the production of Zibibbo grapes from a high of 38,000 tonnes in 1960 was due to the off-loading at ridiculously low prices of Zibibbo must to the *sofisticatori* of Asti by these same Marsala industrialists who 'traditionally and currently have used the denomination "Moscato Passito Liquoroso" . . . without having ever used a single Moscato grape, still less a dried Moscato grape.' To some extent this is true, but a much bigger reason for the decline is the collapse of the market for raisins with pips in.

The row has recently taken an interesting twist with the publication of a new *disciplinare*, supported by one of the two consortia (with only four members, including the island's three biggest; its critics call the president of this consortium a stooge of the industrialists, though he is probably the most internationally recognised 'small' producer of top Pantelleria wines) and bitterly but unsuccessfully opposed by another. These new rules allow for a production of 10 tonnes per hectare, up from seven – one of the few revised DOCs in Italy actually to allow increased production – which obviously, critics claim, favours industrialists, while doing nothing to enforce bottling on the island which would help to ensure the authenticity of a product which they declare, with considerable evidence, is being shamefully falsified.

Leaving aside these hopelessly complex plots and counterplots, genuine Passito di Pantelleria, for the intensity and complexity of sheer grape, floral and female-scent aromas that it is capable of releasing, is surely one of the world's great sweet wines. This, as indicated, is the traditional product, having a minimum alcohol level of 14% with 140 g/l of residual sugar. The relatively recently introduced Moscato di Pantelleria – without the word 'Passito' – is required to have only 13% alcohol and 120 g/l residual sugar. For both wines these values may be considerably higher. Prospective buyers should watch out for wines which are labelled (perhaps only on the back-label) *'liquoroso'*, meaning fortified with alcohol. Such wines are not likely to have the quality, and certainly lack the purity, of the natural product.

The producers

Salvatore **Murana**, Khamma in Pantelleria. Murana, by trade a fireman, is perceived in the outside world as the best producer, regularly being awarded *tre bicchieri* and all the rest of it, although opinions on the island itself are sharply divided as to the authenticity of his credentials. He was placed under investigation during the mini-inquisition referred to above and spent four years under suspicion with his wines sequestrated, only being let off on payment of an extremely hefty fine.

Certainly he is a very odd character indeed, and my visit to his *cantina* was one of the strangest in an extended history of winery visits. To cut a medium-long story short, I have never previously, for example, been invited to climb a ladder and put my hand into a tank (fibreglass) of fermenting wine – which inevitably must smell mainly of unpleasant fermentation odours – to *sentire i profumi*, as he put it. Nor have I ever seen a producer, opening a container (plastic) of his precious finished wine of the vintage before last, one which customers must pay dearly for, recoil in horror at the smell, saying that he can no longer stand the stuff: '*non lo sopporto più*'). Perhaps I was being *preso in giro* (having the mickey taken) but his behaviour struck me as paranoid from the beginning, as if he was convinced I was there to spy on him, and he made no move to open any bottles of his Moscato or Passito. The next day when we met at the winery where his products are bottled he gave no sign of recognition. Oh well, strange things do happen in life.

But enough of that. I have tasted his sweet wines on other occasions and have always found them delicious and, as far as I can make out, perfectly genuine. Murana owns 14 hectares of vineyard in various parts of an island where, as another producer put it, 5 hectares is like 50 elsewhere. His best-known Moscatos and Passitos carry the name of the sub-zone: Mueggen for Moscato, Martingana and Khamma for Passito; the difference, winewise, being merely the length of drying time – about 12 days for Moscato, 18 for Passito.

He also has a vineyard at Gadir where he grows grapes for his dry Zibibbo, called Gadì, a wine – of which he did vouchsafe me a taste – of light muscatty aroma and excellent equilibrium between concentration of fruit and acidity. 'This', he says, 'should be the ambassador of the island.'

Poor Salvatore, condemned to produce unbearable wines that the world is on its knees for.

Nuova Agricoltura. This winery, owned by the d'Amico family – father Salvatore, son Luca – began life as a private cooperative in the mid-1980s, when it became clear that the island's main cooperative was going bankrupt – which indeed it subsequently did, though it still survives under receivership using the name Enopolio (curiously, 80% of the island's growers remain members even in this suspended state). It wasn't, however, until 1992 that the d'Amicos were able to raise enough funds from a slow-moving government to start production. Today they number 19 members having between them 37 hectares of vineyard, plus almost as much again recently planted or to be planted, and turn out substantial numbers of the typical wines of the island under the Koussiros label – Passito, Moscato and dry Zibibbo of a reasonable but not yet exciting standard.

Why then are they being featured? Because as a parallel business Nuova Agricoltura carry out bottling for a number of the island's best independent growers, a crucial service for those who believe, sometimes quite vociferously, that bottling on the island should be made compulsory, despite the paucity of bottling facilities available. Nuova Agricoltura's clients include the fire-breathing Roberto Casani, Misette Casano, Abraxas, Dezzani, Murana himself, as well as Nuova Agricoltura's own oenologist, Giacomo **d'Ancona.** This latter, from his own small vineyard plus a few hectares rented, makes wines under the brand name Solidea – Passito, Moscato and a dry Zibibbo – of a high standard, as has been recognised by his receiving *tre bicchieri* on more than one occasion.

A few words on Misette **Casano's** production, since she represents one of the most important producing families on the island. Misette is a young and strikingly beautiful lady who happens to be the sister of the aforementioned Roberto Casano, whose Bonsulton is considered one of the benchmark Passitos, and, more importantly, the daughter of Salvatore Casano, the doyen of Pantelleria's winemakers. It was from Salvatore that Marco de Bartoli sought advice when he decided to get involved in Pantelleria wines, and many similarly minded aspirants have beaten a trail to Salvatore's door in the zone of Bukkuram. Misette, having a small, well-aged vineyard producing excellent quality grapes and the wisest winemaker on the island for a consultant, decided in 1999 to produce her own wine independently of older brother. She chose the brand Cossyra partly because it was the Roman name for the island, partly because her grandfather had made wine under that name. Misette belongs to the school of thought that, in a given year, you should make either Moscato or Passito, depending on the quality of the harvest. A Moscato that I tasted was beautifully balanced, light in colour, fruity and perfumed with a hint of something mineral (iodine), its sweetness considerable (130 g/l residual) but attenuated by a fine line of acidity cleaning the mouth on the finish.

Bukkuram/de Bartoli. Marco de Bartoli has two *cantine* reflecting the two quite distinct sides of his business: at Marsala and at Pantelleria. At Pantelleria the *cantina* is named after the commune, Bukkuram, meaning (in Arabic) father of the vine, which Marco purchased in the mid-1990s from the man from whom he had previously been buying grapes, and who gleefully joined in the persecution of de Bartoli when it became apparent that he might go under, which would have meant that the land would have reverted back to its previous owner.

But enough of the seamy side of Pantelleria production; let's get on to the glory side. De Bartoli makes four Pantesco wines: Bukkuram Passito and Bukkuram Moscato – i.e. the two sweet wines from dried grapes; these both produced and bottled in Pantelleria; plus Pietra Nera, a dry Zibibbo *in purezza*; and Sole & Vento, a blend of Zibibbo and Catarratto – these two made and bottled in Marsala from Pantelleria fruit. The two dry wines are good without being exceptional – though the Pietra Nera can have a quite alluring aroma of orange peel and flowers, which makes the dry palate come as quite a surprise.

But the sweet wines can be stunning. The Moscato, at around 14.5% alcohol and over 100 g/l residual sugar, sports a rich, peachy/apricotty nose, together with perfumed grapes and herbal notes. On the palate the wine's viscosity is wonderfully voluptuous; peach, apricot, grape and tropical fruits mingle deliciously. The wine has good balancing acidity and closes on a non-cloying note.

A typical Passito today, having spent 15 months in used *barriques*, emerges with a rich golden hue and a huge bouquet with great waftings of musky, spicey scent, plus pineapple, peach, pear – a fruit salad composed of temperate climate and tropical fruits. The mouth is filled with volumes of aromas and fruits, flowers and spices of all sorts, there is a good acidity to offset the 135 g/l residual sugar (14% + alcohol) and a long, perfumed finish. One of the world's great sweet wines, surely; completely unmistakable.

These wines represent the essence, indeed the quintessence of Pantelleria. I know of no producer equalling de Bartoli for quality at this level – and yet he rarely does well in guides, doubtless because of his volatility and confrontational style with lesser mortals who presume to judge him. But if there is one thing I would recommend readers to do it is to take guides and the pronounce-

ments of pundits with very large pinches of salt. Ultimately the only valid judge is yourself.

Other good to excellent producers of Moscato Passito di Pantelleria are: **Abraxas**, Pantelleria; Colosi; Donnafugata (Ben Ryé); Grasso (Ergo); Miceli (Nun); Pellegrino (Nes); Rallo (Mare d'Ambra).

5

International varieties in Central and Southern Italy

In *Barolo to Valpolicella* I defined an 'international variety', in an Italian context, as one which is both non-native to Italy and cultivated in a number of countries round the world. Thus Cabernet Sauvignon, Merlot, Syrah, Chardonnay, Sauvignon Blanc and Rhine Riesling are clearly internationals; Nebbiolo, Sangiovese and Barbera equally clearly not, because, while cultivated in various countries, they are of Italian origin. Borderline vines like Moscato or Malvasia are not considered international for our purposes, having been present in Italy for so many centuries as to have become honorary natives.

In the same book I explained that my reasons for separating international varieties from indigenous ones, or naturalised ones, were twofold: to put the emphasis on what makes Italy unique among wine-producing nations, i.e. her treasure-trove of original vine varieties; and because the internationals, being imported, are not historically or geographically associated with any given region or zone in Italy.

The internationals have been present in Italy since the early years of the nineteenth century, as I have described at length in the earlier volume, but until recently practically all the development has been in the north, and in particular the north-east of the country. That development may be divided into three phases: the first would be from introduction in the 1820s until towards the end of the nineteenth century; a tentative period of experimentation, of 'getting to know you'. The second began in the latter part of the nineteenth century with the scourge of phylloxera forcing all growers to rethink their planting policy, and lasted until after World War II. This was a time during which the Bordeaux grapes' relatively low acidity, good colour and abundant fruit was winning them increasing favour among northern Italian growers, especially where native varieties tended to display an aggressivity of acids and tannins which consumers found increasingly difficult to accept.

The third phase, which has seen the Italianised Bordeaux and Burgundy grapes rise to absolute prominence in some parts of northern Italy and to quasi-parity in others, began after World War II and still continues. Today, Cabernet, if you combine C. Sauvignon and C. Franc, or Carmenère as the latter often is in reality, is in the top 30 grapes grown in Italy with some 6,000 hectares under vine – more than Nebbiolo, to put it in context.

There is a fourth phase, and it is the first to have had a major impetus from and effect upon Italy south of the Po. It consists in a rejection of the 'Italianised' clones or sub-varieties developed in the north, which is also where the major commercial vine-nurseries are found, and a turning back to France for propagational material. This grew out of the quality *rinascimento* that has been taking place in Italian wines during approximately the final third of the twentieth century and into the twenty-first. Since the early years of the nineteenth century there has been a certain presence in and experimentation with foreign grapes in Tuscany especially, but it was not until the success of Sassicaia and the early SuperTuscans that Cabernet & Co. began to become 'big' – in importance; they are still fairly minuscule in terms of volume.

The driving principle behind this movement being quality, growers – and especially those who, from the 1970s on, made a regular point of visiting French wine zones – decided that they could not be sure of getting the vinestock they needed in Italy, especially following the fiasco of the mass supply of inferior Sangiovese clones perpetrated from the north in the 1960s and 1970s. This has led to producers of both north and south sourcing their material either directly from France or, once the *vivaisti* of the north had got the message, from imported French stock propagated in Italy.

Looking at Italy south of the Po as a whole, by far the most important developments in respect of international varieties have been in Tuscany, so that region will be the primary focus of our attention. Other areas of central Italy, notably Romagna and Umbria, have been increasingly active in the past few years. So far, the influence of France in the south and islands has been relatively slight, with the exception of Sicily where Chardonnay, Cabernet,

Merlot and especially Syrah have made significant inroads over the past few years.

I propose to consider the internationals as they have imposed themselves in these three areas – Tuscany, the rest of the centre, and the south and islands – dividing them into groups according to provenance – Bordeaux, Burgundy, Rhône etc., beginning with reds.

BORDEAUX GRAPES – RED

During the past few decades, the Bordeaux grapes in particular have been increasingly prized in Tuscany and to a lesser extent the rest of central and southern Italy for three reasons. First, following the success of Sassicaia, they have been seen as capable in certain zones and under certain circumstances of producing wines every bit as fine as their counterparts from the Gironde – unlike the Burgundian red varieties, Pinot Noir and Gamay, which find central Italian conditions rather less to their liking. There has, indeed, been in recent years a veritable explosion of Bordeaux-style wines – Cabernet Sauvignon varietals, Merlot varietals, the occasional Cabernet Franc or even Petit Verdot varietal, or blends of two, three or all four of them. A few of the pure Cabernets and some of the blends go back now up to a quarter of a century, while pure Merlot is a relatively recent phenomenon.

Second, the Bordeaux grapes have been increasingly used as blenders with local Italian varieties for purposes of adding colour and body, as well as for suggesting a style of fruit familiar to the international wine-bibbing community. Where Sangiovese is in the ascendant I have tended to discuss the wines in the section on Sangiovese. Where Cabernet is dominant and the wine in question is distinctly 'Bordelais' in style – and it must be remembered that Cabernet Sauvignon and to a slightly lesser extent Cabernet Franc are intrinsically aggressive varieties compared with Sangiovese – the wines are dealt with below.

And third, the Bordeaux grapes are seen as easy to deal with, giving a quality product with maximum regularity and predictability, and minimum heartache. How many growers have I heard in how many parts of Italy groaning about the difficulty of controlling vegetation and productivity in their local variety, of obtaining an even ripening of berries within a cluster, of bunches within a plant, of plants within a vineyard. 'Cabernet and Merlot don't give any of those problem', said one producer; 'you always know where you are. Sangiovese on the other hand', he continued; he might have said Aglianico or Montepulciano or Primitivo or Nero d'Avola 'sometimes makes me want to tear my hair out'.

My answer is usually along the lines that the French have been cloning their grapes for several decades, if not, if you include massal selection, centuries. The Italians have only come to this recently, even the avant-garde having started in earnest within the last decade or two of the twentieth century. Once Italy gets its clones sorted out many problems will fall away. Alas, some of the interest and personality may fall away too, but you can't have it all ways.

The wines in Tuscany

The area to which the Cabernets and Merlot have adapted most impressively as a group is that sometimes called the Alta Maremma, or the Costa degli Etruschi, as it is now being marketed. This, as previously explained, is the stretch of Tuscan coast from Livorno south to Piombino, taking in a slice of southern Pisa province and including the now famous DOC of Bolgheri and that, rapidly gaining, of Val di Cornia–Suvereto, together with Montescudaio, Elba and a smattering of wines which are outside of DOC areas – as distinct from being outside of DOC controls, which many have elected to be. It would make geographical sense to approach these in a north–south direction, but precedence must go, I think, to the commune and the producer from which all this amazing activity has flowed.

Bolgheri

Tenuta San Guido. The story of Sassicaia has been told innumerable times, but for those who don't know it I think a sketch is called for.

The wine originated with Marchese Mario Incisa della Rocchetta, a Piemontese nobleman who married a Tuscan noblewoman of the Della Gherardesca family whose property then extended over many thousands of hectares of coastland, land traditionally considered good for cows and horses but not, until the draining, particularly good for humans nor for vines. Marchese Mario was a lover of claret and decided in the 1940s that meteorological and geological

conditions in the area of the picturesquely arty village of Bolgheri near which his wife's lands were situated were sufficiently similar to those of Bordeaux – mild winters, hot summers, tempering effect of the nearby sea, plenty of gravel for drainage[1] – to warrant an attempt at producing a claret-like wine.

1 The name 'Sassicaia' indicates a stony field, from Italian *sasso* (stone).

For years the wine was used only for family consumption, but in the 1960s Marchese Mario, finding the now mature wines a great deal more palatable than they had been at first – as one would expect, indeed, from a Bordeaux *cru classé* – looked for help to Piero Antinori, whose Della Gherardesca mother was sister to Mario's wife. From the 1968 vintage onward Piero brought invaluable assistance both in the area of production – the great Giacomo Tachis, himself consulting initially with Bordeaux' famous Professor Emile Peynaud, continues to this day to oversee oenology at San Guido – and in that of distribution, Sassicaia subsequently for a number of years being part of the Antinori portfolio.

In the late 1970s a tasting of the great claret-style wines of the world, organised by Hugh Johnson, was held by *Decanter* from which the 1972 Sassicaia emerged victorious. Since that time Sassicaia has been considered by many to be Italy's number one fine wine, rightly or wrongly (there are those who dislike the idea that a wine made from foreign grapes should carry that reputation). Little has changed in respect of the production of the wine whose style Marchese Mario's son Marchese Niccolò maintains along rigorously Bordelais lines. The blend remains 85% Cabernet Sauvignon, 15% Cabernet Franc. The yields, both from the stony vineyards on the slopes beneath Bolgheri's landmark Castiglion-cello, perched high on a peak overlooking the entire area, and on the flatter, pebbly fields below, average around 30 hectolitres per hectare (Grand Cru level). Ageing still takes place over 24 months in French *barriques* of which around one-third are new every year. Production from the 60 hectares of vineyard still averages around 100,000 bottles per annum. Demand continues to outstrip supply by a comfortable margin – a wander in the Tenuta's stock-room is like walking through the United Nations General Assembly.

And the wine? What can one write that hasn't been said a hundred times? So far there is no 'second wine', so all the grapes considered fit for Sassicaia go into the top *cru*. In this age when highest marks tend to go to the jammy, the dense, the super-concentrated rather than to the elegant and non-obvious, Sassicaia, in its youthful phase, sometimes does not get the highest ratings in guides or from pundits. But from a good year Sassicaia, after 10 years or so, can stand with the best of them, worldwide. It is truly an aristocratic wine and fully deserves its high reputation.

The only novelty is a new Bolgheri wine from the property of Incisa's cousins, the Zileri, also De Gherardesca descendants, who have 10 hectares – going on 20 – planted to Cabernet Sauvignon and Franc (60%) and Merlot (40%). This wine, a Merlot-Cabernet-Sangiovese blend called Guidalberto, first saw the light of commercial day in 2002. It is made in a different *cantina*, and does not affect Sassicaia at all.

Tenuta Dell'**Ornellaia**. Lodovico Antinori, younger brother of Piero Antinori, having acquired as did his more famous sibling a piece of prize Bolgheri real estate from his Della Gherardesca mother, decided in the early 1980s to turn it into an outstanding vineyard. The factors affecting his decision included an appreciation of what his uncle by marriage, Mario Incisa, had achieved with Tenuta San Guido, together with a recognition that high quality and good profit could be derived from Bordeaux-style wines in this territory. He also had a fairly extensive knowledge of the wine scene in California, in part working for the family firm, during which he came to focus on a style of wine which he felt he might eventually like to produce and made certain acquaintances, notably that of André Tchelistchev, one of the pioneers of quality California Cabernet, who was destined to help him make it.

Seventy hectares, no small investment considering the quasi-virgin territory in which he found himself (one gets the impression that Lodovico has found himself in quite a lot of virgin territory in his time), were planted in the early 1980s to Cabernet Sauvignon, Cabernet Franc, Merlot, Sauvignon Blanc and a couple of others. In the latter part of the decade a space-age winery, California-style, was purpose-built to accommodate with efficiency and taste everything necessary for the making of top quality wine.

The first of these to emerge was the 1985 Ornellaia, the property's flagship wine, a blend of the two Cabernets and Merlot which, by comparison with the strongly structured Sassicaia, has pleased its *aficionados* by being relatively soft and seductive. But much as Ornellaia (the wine) has won hearts, the real queen here is the varietal Merlot called Masseto, which as a prototype of the now rapidly expanding school of outstanding Pomerol-like Merlots of central Italy, from its first release in 1986, became an icon in Italian and indeed international wine circles. There are rumours of people being prepared to kill for a case of Masseto.

Another bull's eye scored by Ornellaia, somewhat surprisingly for central Italy where the summer heat is a good deal more intense than in the Loire, is its crisp, herbaceous Sauvignon Blanc, Poggio alle Gazze (Magpie Hill). A relatively recent introduction is Le Serre Nuove, a blend of Cabernet Sauvignon (75%) and Merlot (25%), described as the 'second wine' of the estate, arising as it did out of a particularly rigorous selection of grapes for the 1997 vintage Ornellaia. More recent still is the sale of the property to the Mondavi-Frescobaldi consortium, though this as yet has had little impact on the wines.

Le Macchiole. The late Eugenio Campolmi who died in his prime of cancer in 2002, took over Le Macchiole from his father and grandfather in 1981 and wasted no time changing everything. He wanted to make top quality wine, but he realised that the grapes were wrong, even the site was wrong, so he transferred the entire operation to a position which was more suitable than the original one – the position being, in fact, adjacent to Lodovico Antinori's Ornellaia. Then he spent some years experimenting with varieties, clones, rootstocks and planting systems until he came up with the present mix of Cabernet Sauvignon, Cabernet Franc, Sangiovese, Merlot and Syrah, Chardonnay and Sauvignon, at 10,000 plants per hectare, drastically reducing the weight of grapes per plant to less than a kilo.

Today Eugenio's widow Cinzia, with the help of star consultant Luca d'Attoma who was a great buddy of Campolmi, is making wines from 17 hectares of vineyard, plus a few *in affitto*, which continue to win raves from every quarter of the globe. In a way the experience has been similar to that of Ornellaia – the flagship wine, Paleo Rosso, from the 2001 vintage a pure Cabernet Franc, while recognised as a worthy rival to Sassicaia, has been thrown slightly in the shade by the stunning varietal Merlot Messorio, produced in increasing if still very small quantities. Not quite as much fuss has been made about the varietal Syrah, Scrio, but it is the first of its type in this zone and looking good. Paleo Bianco, meanwhile – a *barriqued* white based on Sauvignon with some Chardonnay and a touch of Vermentino – is quite simply the most serious white of the zone, a wine of positively Californian richness and wealth of fruit.

The most recent addition to the portfolio is Macchiole, a

Sangiovese-based red blended with the Cabernet, Merlot and Syrah not used in the crus.

For a small zone Bolgheri boasts more than its fair share of famous names among its producers, including probably the two biggest in Italian wines: Antinori and Gaja. Piero Antinori's vineyards form part of the 850+ hectare estate, Tenuta **Guado al Tasso** (ex-Tenuta Belvedere), which stretches from the coast inland for several kilometres. Vine-plantings are a mix of the indigenous and the international: Sangiovese and Canaiolo blend with Cabernet Sauvignon to make Scalabrone, a *rosato* representing the best of tradition here in Bolgheri where *rosato* was the standard style before the advent of the claret syndrome. Vermentino at 85%, with touches of Chardonnay and Sauvignon, goes to make up the estate's top white. But the star performer these days, not surprisingly, is the Cabernet (70%)/Merlot (30%) blend Guado al Tasso, from vineyards on a gentle slope rising towards the range of hills which runs parallel with the coast some eight kilometres inland called the Colline Metallifere. Guado al Tasso, introduced with the 1990 vintage, is effectively Piero's answer to his cousin's Sassicaia and his brother's Ornellaia. The consensus is that Guado has not quite caught up with the rivals, and as yet it has not achieved the cult status of Sassicaia, Masseto or even Messorio. But with every vintage the wine gets a little more convincing and stylised – somewhere between Sassicaia's St Estephe-like structure and Ornellaia's Margaux-esque fleshiness.

Angelo Gaja bought his property, **Cà Marcanda**, in the mid-1990s and immediately set to work, as one would expect from such a dynamic person, to build the finest winery and make the best wine of Bolgheri. This, he says, is where he means to 'divert himself' making wines solely from red French grapes, having pitted his will against the Nebbiolo in Piemonte most of his life and against Sangiovese in Montalcino for a decade. His ideas are quite clear. He means to arrive at 60 hectares of vineyard – though the winery will accommodate the production of twice that area – and he will do it with a precise blend of Cabernet Sauvignon (48%), Merlot (44%), Cabernet Franc (5%) and Syrah (3%). There will be two wines of the same grape make-up, one, called Cà Marcanda, made for the top of the market, which will not appear until the vines are sufficiently mature; and one, called Magari, aimed at the 'premium wine' market – not a boutique wine of low production but 30,000 to 50,000 cases of something which can be 'easily afforded'. It may not sound like the Gaja we know, but those are his words. Angelo believes that the premium wine market will become a great deal more competitive in the next 10 to 15 years, and he wants to be in there competing. 'After all,' he points out, 'people like Ruffino have invaded my market; why shouldn't I invade theirs?'

Watch out, there's a Gaja about.

Other producers of Bordeaux-style wine in Bolgheri include especially Piermario Meletti Cavalleri of Podere **Grattamacco**, a refugee from the industrial north who first ensconced himself in this zone in the early 1980s and has been experimenting with various vines and clones ever since in an effort to find the best formula. His red Grattamacco, currently 50% Cabernet Sauvignon, 25% Merlot and 25% Sangiovese, is hailed among the best of Bolgheri. And Michele **Satta**, better known for his excellent Sangioveses Cavaliere and Vigna al Cavaliere, but whose Cabernet–Merlot–Syrah–Sangiovese blend, Piastraia, is increasingly highly considered.

Suvereto–Val di Cornia

Tua Rita. Suvereto, a town some 20 kilometres south of Bolgheri with a very similar profile in terms of climate and soil, has not achieved the international fame of its neighbour but it is gaining. As at Bolgheri, after the success of a handful of producers, a few big names have been attracted here – not as big as at Bolgheri, but the Moretti of Franciacorta's Bellavista, for example, are big enough.

Of that 'handful of producers', perhaps none has had quite the success of Tua Rita, a small but jewel-like property run by Rita Tua (the Italians have a curious habit of inverting their names) and her husband Virgilio Bisti, more latterly joined by their son-in-law Stefano Frascolla. The couple began in the 1980s with Sangiovese and other grapes, but had the foresight in 1988 to plant Cabernet Sauvignon and Merlot. The first breakthrough came when the 1992, 1993 and 1994 vintages of their blend of the two, Giusto di Notri (60% Cabernet Sauvignon/40% Merlot), were hailed as going from excellent to outstanding, with their deep fruit and coffee, chocolate and tar notes. Luca d'Attoma, their oenologist for most of the 1990s, then turned his hand to varietal Merlot, and the stunning Redigaffi was the result – a wine of enormous concen-

tration and ripe, succulent, tobacco-scented fruit, made in tiny if mercifully somewhat increasing quantities thanks to some new plantings. D'Attoma has now passed the baton to the equally worthy Stefano Chioccioli and it seems likely that the success of the early years will continue apace.

A wine which looks set to become one of the classics of this area is Gabbro, a rich-flavoured and firm-structured Cabernet Sauvignon *in purezza, barrique*-aged of course, from **Montepeloso,** just up the hill and round the corner from Tua Rita. The recently installed proprietor, Swiss–Italian historian Fabio Chiarelotto, is determined to produce top quality with Gabbro, the Sangiovese–Cabernet blend Nardo, and perhaps, in future, Syrah. He has every reason to be optimistic, given that his vineyards are in a perfect situation on gentle slopes facing southwest towards the sea and his winemaker-consultant is, and remains, the talented Luca d'Attoma.

Another Cabernet-dominated wine – with Merlot – which has impressed is Federico Primo from Az. Ag. **Gualdo del Re.** The most recent arrival on the scene is **Petra,** a Cabernet–Merlot blend from the *azienda* of the same name, owned by the Moretti family of Franciacorta as mentioned above.

Still in the Costa degli Etruschi, north this time of Bolgheri on the border between the provinces of Pisa and Livorno, is an estate vying with Sassicaia itself for pre-eminence in the claret-style stakes in Alta Maremma. This is Tenuta del **Terriccio,** in the commune of Castellina Marittima, owned by a man with no less a moniker than Gian Annibale Rossi di Medelana Serrafini Ferri, known to his numerous attractive female employees as Pucci. This is a vast estate – 1,700 hectares in total – in an area previously unrecognised for fine wine production, known rather for the growing of grain and the training of horses. Technically, the land is in the DOC zone of Montescudaio, but geographically and spiritually it is nearer to Bolgheri. Dr Rossi seems to take the view that if he can't be in the Bolgheri DOC, where he feels he belongs, he'd rather go IGT – at least for his top wines. The lesser products – and the estate always did make everyday plonk – ever were and to some extent still are sold in bulk as Montescudaio DOC. It's an excellent example of how Italian wine law has got itself in such a mess, where top producers in a given zone deliberately avoid the quality designation because it is seen as irremediably down-market.

Dr Rossi is, indeed, a very determined man, not to mention a very wealthy man, and when he made his mind up, after a horse-riding accident in the 1980s which left him wheelchair-bound, to make great wine, he meant business. Although horse breeding – mainly for show-jumpers – remains an important aspect of the estate's activities the success of his wine has demanded an ever-greater share of his energies. Dr Rossi himself made the trip to France to source the best clones in the 1980s, and since that time he has systematically overseen the replanting and grafting out of the existing Trebbiano and Sangiovese vines, replacing them with Cabernet Sauvignon, Merlot, Cabernet Franc, Petit Verdot, some Pinot Nero, plus Chardonnay, Sauvignon and a bit of Pinot Bianco and Gewürztraminer.

As his consultant oenologist he hired one of Italy's finest, Carlo Ferrini, in 1992. The red wines they put together were mainly Bordelais in conception, in terms of grape varieties, viticultural and vinification methods; but with an extra ripeness of the warmer Tyrrhenian, plus a dash of Mediterranean spice and a hint of eucalyptus from the numerous trees of that type on the property.

The star wine – one whose price *franco cantina* has risen appreciably higher than that of Sassicaia – is Lupicaia, a blend of Cabernet Sauvignon and Merlot, aged for 18 months in new French *barriques*. Lupicaia, which became in a very short time a must-buy for all those seeking the best from Italy, is made from grapes planted low-trained in vineyards with a southern exposure. It achieves the classic blackcurrant aromas but mixed with these are hints of toast, coffee and dark chocolate (from the finest oak) – an irresistible combination for lovers of the international style. Tassinaia, Cabernet Sauvignon, Merlot and a bit of Sangiovese from higher-trained, more north-facing vineyards, aged 12 months in second-passage *barriques*, is not dissimilar but less lush, less intense.

Dr Rossi is almost as proud of his whites as he is of his extremely successful reds – after all, it is much more difficult or at least more unusual in Tuscany to produce a great white wine than a great red. He has come nearest with Saluccio, a *barrique*-fermented and aged Chardonnay, a wine, though recently introduced, showing promise, with its rich, mellow and complex palate, of real excellence, provided they can get the acidity up somewhere near Burgundy levels and tone down the toast and oak aromas. The slightly late-picked Chardonnay–Sauvignon blend Rondinaia has better acidity thanks to the Sauvignon Blanc, but lacks the complexity necessary for greatness, while the pure-Sauvignon Con Vento has so far proved somewhat deficient in varietal definition.

An amusing irony of this estate, Bolgheri in soul but not on paper, is that one of the vineyards is called Sassicaia. Dr Rossi is too discreet to wish to print that name on his label, but he does like to have a laugh about it.

On the southern side of the Costa degli Etruschi, in the Maremma proper, the biggest name in Bordeaux-style wine is unquestionably **Le Pupille** of Magliano in Toscana, mentioned in the chapter on Sangiovese. Its Saffredi, a blend of Cabernet Sauvignon and Merlot, with a bit of Alicante, has for years been recognized as one of the stars of the genre in Tuscany, manifesting as it does the lusher fruit of the south combined with a sufficiently firm structure (the hills of this area make for a climate appreciably cooler than that of the coastal lowlands) to allow the wine to age well over a number of years. Another major point in its favour is that the vineyards, having been planted long before the mid-1990s' gold rush to this area on the part of producers of central Tuscany, are mature.

Combine this with the fact that, with Tachis, then Riccardo Cotarella, and now Luca d'Attoma it enjoys or has enjoyed some of the finest *consulenza* in central Italy and one understands that its pre-eminence in the southern Maremma is not likely to be challenged for some time to come.

A relative newcomer to the claret-style scene in Tuscany is Andrea Franchetti's Tenuta di **Trinoro** at Sarteano in the province of Siena just south of Montepulciano. Franchetti, a wine broker with a passion for the wines of Bordeaux, and specifically St Emilion (he is a great friend of Jean-Luc Thunevin of Château de Valandraud), began this operation from scratch in the early 1990s, planting Cabernet Franc and Cabernet Sauvignon, plus Merlot and Petit Verdot, on a clay–gravel soil at high density. Yields are extremely low, thanks to rigorous bunch and even berry thinning, and vinification methods are largely Bordelais, with ageing, of course, in new French *barriques*. Franchetti's two wines, produced in very limited quantities from his 8 hectares of '*graves*' and 8 of '*côtes*' are Tenuta di Trinoro (Cabernet Franc with Cabernet Sauvignon and a bit of Petit Verdot); and Le Cupole di Trinoro, mainly Cabernet Franc with Merlot, Cesanese and Uva di Troia. Both have attracted enthusiastic praise from pundits like Parker and the *Wine Spectator* and it may be safely predicted that they will soon be up there with the likes of Sassicaia and Masseto in the eyes of the world. Certainly Franchetti's avowed intention is to make 'the best Italian wine', and while it is difficult to imagine that the best Italian wine could ever be a Bordeaux look-alike there is hope for his wine, yet to come, from the Cesanese d'Affile grape, which he himself thinks may one day prove his masterpiece.

Space does not permit an in-depth consideration of all the Bordeaux-style wines of Tuscany, of which there are, at the time of writing, well in excess of 50 of a good to excellent standard – and many more of a mediocre standard. At any rate they are virtually all made to a formula which would not be out of place in Bordeaux itself, except where small portions of Sangiovese or other local grapes are included, a major difference being that production of this type of wine per estate is in all but one or two cases relatively tiny compared with the Gironde, a restriction which should make high quality more easily achievable. As for variations in quality within Tuscany the principal differential, apart from that deriving from the grape make-up, comes – as in Bordeaux – from the amount of money the producer is prepared to invest in terms of low yield, expensive equipment, even more expensive oenological consultation and new oak. But that perhaps is excessively cynical: there is also the factor of the *territorio* not to mention that of skill, occasionally genius, on the part of the producer and/or his consultant. As I have said elsewhere: the limit of quality in wine – other factors being equal – is the limit of the winemaker's palate. And while this dictum is perhaps over-simplified, it contains an essential truth.

Claret-type wines are spread throughout the region of Tuscany, with a strong preponderance in the Chianti Classico zone where political–bureaucratic problems have encouraged the growth of alternative wines. Here there is the investment on the one hand and the market on the other to permit the sort of trials that need to be carried out over a period of years in order to finish up with a first-class product. Such trials involve the sourcing and propagation of clones, the matching of rootstocks, planting densities, picking times, wood-ageing and bottling times, to name a few.

There is one producer in the Chianti Classico zone who has particularly championed Cabernet (and Petit Verdot) while partially turning its back on Sangiovese: Castello dei **Rampolla** at Panzano. That this has remained one of the leading estates of Italy for at least two decades would be disputed by few, a fitting tribute to which fact being that the top wine, La Vigna di Alceo, was voted, by the *Gambero Rosso/Slow Food Wines of Italy Guide*, Red Wine of the Year for the 1996 vintage, its first year of production. A demonstration, this, that in a not-so-good year for Sangiovese in Chianti Classico the Bordeaux grapes can thrive, which thesis was dear to the heart of the Alceo in question whom I vividly remember literally kicking an unripe Sangiovese vine in September 1984 while lovingly caressing the nearby Cabernets. The Alceo in question was Alceo de Napoli, an eccentric nobleman – a prince, no less, of Sicilian extraction, though these things are fairly meaningless in Italy and the real aristocrats keep quiet about their titles, as he did – who, having befriended the great Giacomo Tachis in the early days of the Tuscan wine *rinascimento*, was turning out first-class Sangiovese–Cabernet blends when some of the present young bloods were in another world. After Alceo himself went to another world in 1991 the estate sank into a period of confusion from which it has now fully emerged under the aegis of Alceo's son Luca, still advised

discreetly by Tachis. Indeed the wines today are better than ever, perhaps due in part to Luca's new plantings and biodynamic approach in the vineyard.

Alceo's passion for the grapes of Bordeaux is reflected in the continuing predominance of Cabernet Sauvignon over Sangiovese in the vineyard – 22 hectares against 16, in a bastion of the Sangiovese grape. There is also a bit of Petit Verdot and some newly planted Merlot, with new vineyards being planted, as is the trend in Tuscany today, at densities of 8,000–10,000 plants per hectare (5,000–6,000 for Sangiovese). True, Bordeaux-mania has not suppressed the traditional wines of the zone, even if the best are distinctly Girondesque. The Chianti Classico, admittedly the humblest of the reds, is almost entirely Sangiovese, a full-bodied version with something of a coffee-grounds texture supporting fine fruit. The Chianti Classico Riserva is 80% Sangiovese backed by 20% Cabernet, deep and full yet with typical Sangiovese acidity and a firm tannic structure promising good life ahead. However, it's being phased out so that the Cabernet can be put to better use elsewhere, and Chianti Classico *normale* will remain the estate's only Sangiovese. The SuperTuscan Sammarco, 85–90% Cabernet plus Sangiovese, has the perfumes and concentration of grapes grown with loving care and the elegant tannins typical of a Tachis special; a wine that needs time to come round.

La Vigna di Alceo, approximately 80% Cabernet Sauvignon with 20% Petit Verdot, is the *pièce de résistance*, an inky brew with raspberry/blackberry/blackcurrant aromas and that typical Bordelais 'lead-pencil' on the nose. This is a wine of tremendous power, concentration and length in the mouth yet having such poise and balance that, even young, it is a joy to drink. Alceo would have been proud of it.

The outlying 'Chianti' zones have proved a fertile breeding ground for alternative wines, as in the case of Trinoro, largely because the local DOCs, especially 'Chiantis', have failed to inspire enthusiasm, and therefore the desire to go out and empty wallets, in the drinking public. It is noticeable that there has been less of a rush to do something different where the local wine has a strong identity – i.e. in Montalcino, Montepulciano and Carmignano, which latter has in itself been somewhat 'alternative' for the past 30 years or so.

What I rather arbitrarily propose to do is rate the claret-style wines of Tuscany, dividing them into four categories: pure Cabernet (including Cabernet Franc); pure Merlot; blends of a purely Bordelais type; and blends which include a small and generally insignificant amount of Sangiovese, then identify the wines in each category which seem to me the best. However, all the wines included in these lists are capable of being at least good if not excellent on their day. Often, particularly in respect of the top wines, the producers will already have been profiled either in this chapter or under Sangiovese, so little more needs to be said about them.

The order in which wines below are listed is alphabetical according to estate name and does not reflect preference.

Pure Cabernet – the top five

Fattoria di **Felsina**, Castelnuovo
  Berardenga
Isole e Olena, Barberino Val d'Elsa
Le **Macchiole**, Bolgheri

Maestro Raro
Collezione De Marchi
Paleo Rosso

Castello dei **Rampolla**, Panzano   La Vigna di Alceo
Tenuta **San Guido**, Bolgheri   Sassicaia

Others not mentioned include:

From *Chianti Classico*: **Carobbio** (Pietraforte del Carobbio), Panzano; **Carpineto** (Farnito), Greve; **Casina di Cornia** (L'Amaranto), Castellina; **Castellare** (Coniale), Castellina; Cennatoio (Rosso Fiorentino), Panzano; **Cecchi** (Vigneto la Gavina), Castellina; **Macchiavelli** (Ser Niccolò Solatio del Tani), San Casciano; Montepeloso (Gabbro); **Monsanto** (Nemo), Barberino Val d'Elsa; Fattoria di **Nozzole** (Il Pareto), Greve; **Rocca di Castagnoli** (Buriano), Gaiole; San Cresci (San Cresci–Cabernet Franc), Greve; **Vignamaggio** (Vignamaggio–Cabernet Franc), Greve.

From elsewhere in *Tuscany*: **Altesino** (Borgo d'Altesi), Montalcino; **Banfi** (Tavarnelle), Montalcino; **Col d'Orcia** (Olmaia), Montalcino; **Fossi** (Sassoforte), Signa; **Frescobaldi** (Mormoreto), Rufina; **Il Corno** (I Gibbioni), San Casciano Val di Pesa; **Il Palagio** (Curtifreda), Mercatale Val di Pesa; **Le Calvane** (Borro del Boscone), Montespertoli; **Montechiari** (Montechiari Cabernet), Montecarlo.

Merlot – the top five

Castello di **Ama**, Gaiole in Chianti   Vigna l'Apparita
Le Macchiole   Messorio
Tenuta dell'**Ornellaia**, Bolgheri   Masseto
Fattoria **Petrolo**, Mercatale Valdarno   Galatrona
Tua Rita, Suvereto   Redigaffi

Others include:

Altesino (Quarto d'Altesi); **Avignonesi** (Toro Desiderio), Montepulciano; Banfi (Mandrielle); **Casa Emma** (Soloio), Barberino Val d'Elsa; Fattoria del **Cerro** (Poggio Golo), Montepulciano; **Cima** (Montervo), Massa Carrara; Fossi (Portico); **Castelgiocondo** (Lamaione), Montalcino; **Ghizzano** (Nambrot), Peccioli; **Guicciardini Strozzi** (Selvascura), San Gimignano; Il Palagio (Montefolchi); **La Braccesca** (Merlot), Montepulciano; **La Rampa di Fugnano** (Gisèle), San Gimignano; **La Rendola** (Merlot di Toscana), Mercatale Valdarno; **Lilliano** (Vignacatena), Castellina; **Meleta**

(Massaio), Roccatederighi/Maremma; **Poggio Salvi** (Lavischio), Montalcino; **Rietine** (Tiziano), Gaiole; **Rodano** (Lazzicante), Castellina in Chianti; **San Giusto a Rentennano** (La Ricolma), Gaiole.

Bordeaux blends – the top five

Capezzana, Carmignano	Ghiaie della Furba
Il Terriccio, Castellina Marittima	Lupicaia
Poliziano, Montepulciano	Le Stanze
Tenuta di **Trinoro**, Sarteano	Trinoro
Tua Rita, Suvereto	Giusto di Notri

Others include:

Banfi (Excelsus); **Il Carnasciale** (Caberlot – from a vine said to be a genetic mutation of Cabernet displaying some characteristics of Merlot), Mercatale Valdarno; Tenuta **Guado al** Tasso (Guado al Tasso), Bolgheri; **Il Paradiso** (Saxa Calida), San Gimignano; **La Badiola** (Vigna Flora), Marlia; **Le Sorgenti** (Scirus), Bagno a Ripoli; **Il Paradiso** (Saxa Calida), San Gimignano; **Montellori** (Salmartano), Fucecchio; (Seraselva), Tavarnelle Val di Pesa; Tenuta dell'Ornellaia (Ornellaia); **Querceto** (Cignale), Greve; **Vignamaggio** (Obsession), Greve; Tenuta di Trinoro (Palazzi).

Cabernet or Cabernet/Merlot dominated blends with local grapes – the top five

Antinori, Florence	Solaia
Grattamacco, Castagneto Carducci	Grattamacco Rosso
Le Pupille, Magliano in Toscana	Saffredi
Castello dei **Rampolla**, Panzano	Sammarco
Vecchie Terre di Montefili, Panzano	Bruno di Rocca

Others capable of a good-to-excellent standard include:

Agricoltori del Chianti Geografico (Vigneti del Geografico), Gaiole; Tenuta di **Bossi** (Mazzaferrata), Pontassieve; Villa Cafaggio (Cortaccio); **Casale-Falchini** (Campora), San Gimignano; **Casa Sola** (Montarsiccio), Barberino Val d'Elsa; Azienda **Elisabetta** (Le Marze), San Pietro in Palazzi, **Il Poggione** (San Leopoldo), Montalcino; **Il Vivaio** (Semifonte), Barberino Val d'Elsa; Villa **la**

Selva (Selvamaggio), Bucine; **Meleta** (Rosso della Rocca), Roccatederighi; Podere **San Luigi** (Vigna Casanova), Colle Val d'Elsa;
Michele **Satta** (Piastraia), Castagneto Carducci; **Valdipiatta** (Trefonti), Montepulciano; **Viticcio** (Monile), Greve.

The wines in central Italy excluding Tuscany

While Tuscany has been the focal point for activity relating to
international varieties in central and southern Italy, others have not
been idle. Not surprisingly, perhaps, Umbria – sometimes not
entirely fairly, indeed in some ways very unfairly, seen as a clone of
Tuscany – is the non-Tuscan region where the most experimentation
is going on. Umbria, indeed, with northern Latium, is the main
stamping ground of consultant Riccardo Cotarella, cited earlier as
'Robert Parker's favourite Italian winemaker'. Most of the many
rave reviews that he has received have centred on wines made
partially or wholly from Bordeaux grapes.

On the east side of the Apennines, as on the west, interest in and
plantings of the Bordeaux grapes get thinner as you go south. It
would seem to be a fact that where Sangiovese thrives there too will
the Bordeaux grapes – a proposition whose inverse implication
might interest Cabernet and Merlot growers in other parts of the
world.

In the list of good-to-excellent Bordeaux-style wines given below,
since I have lumped the whole of the 'rest' of central Italy together,
I will specify the region as well as the commune, unless – as usual –
the producer has been mentioned earlier in this chapter. To be noted
that I have included a few producers in the Colli Bolognesi area –
which, for the purposes of this book, is where north meets centre –
who may have appeared in the earlier volume. On reflection I think
they more properly belong here.

Pure Cabernet

Boccadigabbia (Akronte), Civitanova/Marche; **Bonzara** (Bon-
zarone), Monte S. Pietro/Romagna; **Drei Donà** (Magnificat), Forlì/
Romagna; **Palazzone** (Armaleo), Orvieto/Umbria; **Orlandi Contucci
Ponno** (Liburnio; Colle Funaro), Roseto degli Abruzzi/Abruzzo;
Pandolfa (Pezzolo), Predappio/Romagna; **Terre Rosse** (Il Rosso di
Enrico Vallania), Zola Predosa/Bologna; **Tre Monti** (Turico),

Imola/Romagna; **Vallona** (Colli Bolognesi Cab. Sauvignon Selezione), Castello Serravalle/Romagna; Villa **Pigna** (Cabernasco), Offida/Marche.

Pure Merlot

Bonzara (Rocca di Bonacciara); C.S. **Colli Amerini** (Carbio; Olmeto), Amelia/Umbria; Falesco (Montiano), Montefiascone/Latium; **La Palazzola** (Merlot), Stroncone/Umbria.

Bordeaux blends

Casale del Giglio (Madreselva), Le Ferriere/Latium; Paola **di Mauro** (Vigna del Vassallo; Le Vignole Rosso), Marino/Latium; **La Carraia** (Fobiano); **La Palazzola** (Rubino); **Palombo** (Colle della Torre), Atina/Latium; **Rio Grande** (Casa Pastore), Penna in Teverina/Umbria; **Santa Barbara** (Stefano Antonucci), Barbara/Marche.

Cabernet-dominated blends

Colacicchi (Torre Ercolana – + Merlot and Cesanese), Anagni (Latium); Falesco (Vitiano – + Merlot and Sangiovese); **Lungarotti** (San Giorgio – + Sangiovese and Canaiolo), Torgiano/Umbria.

The South and Islands

So far the influence of the internationals in this part of the world has been limited largely to white wines and blends – the latter to be considered in the following chapter, the former later in this chapter. The growers of the south have a wealth of indigenous red varieties of quality and character at their disposal so that they do not need the invaders so much as some of their northern colleagues, nor does the meridional climate lend itself in most areas to the cultivation of grapes which hail from parts much farther north.

With specific regard to the Bordeaux grapes, one could count the high quality, pure claret-style wines of the south on the fingers of one hand – indeed the total number of wines of even reasonable quality would not require two. And they are almost all from the islands, mostly from Sicily, with the exception of a couple from Campania. Interesting that, in such a high volume wine country as the southern mainland – comprising Campania, Basilicata, Calabria and especially Puglia – there is scarcely any pure top quality Bordeaux-style wine on the market at the beginning of the millennium.

Sicily's challenge is led by Conte **Tasca d'Almerita** at Vallelunga Pratameno (see profile under Nero d'Avola). Their Cabernet di Sicilia, which when it first came out in the early 1990s was a mighty, purple-black, super-concentrated brew with layers of ripe berry fruit intermingled with coffee, dark chocolate and vanilla, has from later vintages been toned down and is now becoming more of a table wine and less of a *vino da meditazione*, having gained in elegance and breeding what it has sacrificed in power. On the other hand, a relative newcomer, **Planeta** of Sambuca di Sicilia, is maintaining the blockbuster approach with lashings of fruit, oak and alcohol in their varietal Merlot and Cabernet Sauvignon Burdese – impressive wines indeed but not for everyday drinking.

Other good to very good Sicilians include: **Barone Scammacca del Murgo** (Tenuta San Michele), Santa Venerina; **Benanti** (Cabernet Sauvignon Monovitigni), Viagrande; **COS** (Le Vigne di COS Rosso – Cabernet Sauvignon + Merlot), Vittoria; **Fazio Wines** (Cabernet Sauvignon), Erice; **Firriato** (Camelot – Cabernet Sauvignon + Merlot), Paceco; **Pollara** (Principe di Corleone), Monreale; **Settesoli** (Cabernet Sauvignon Mandrarossa), Menfi; **Spadafora** (Schietto), Monreale; C.S. **Trapani** (Forti Terre di Sicilia Cabernet Sauvignon).

In Sardinia virtually the only serious challenge comes from **Sella & Mosca** of Alghero, the dominant private estate in a land of co-operatives, whose most celebrated creation, the 100% Cabernet Marchese di Villamarina, is a wine of classic, quasi Bordeaux style having mint and cedar tones on the nose and a restrained, elegant and balanced style rather than the power and richness one might expect from such a latitude (the explanation lies in S&M's vineyards, which, as we have seen, are trained on high trellises they call Sardinian pergola). **Meloni Vini** of Selargius also does a good Cabernet Sauvignon di Sardegna.

When it comes to blends which are not entirely of a Bordeaux nature but which are Bordeaux dominated, there is, certainly, one which stands out, notably the now world-famous **Montevetrano** from the estate of that name at San Cipriano Picentino in Campania. Made by the Latian/Umbrian wizard Ricardo Cotarella, this

Cabernet Sauvignon-dominated blend, which also includes Merlot and a small percentage of Aglianico, has shot to fame on the back of some highly enthusiastic reviews from Robert Parker, guaranteeing a heavy demand among the collectors of the world of wine, especially as the estate is very small – a mere four hectares under vine.

BURGUNDY GRAPES – RED

For Burgundy in this connection read Pinot Nero (Italian for Pinot Noir), although there is just a smidgin of Gamay also in central Italy.

Pinot Noir is, of course, essentially a cool climate grape. It is delicate and complex in its aromas, which in a good example, from Burgundy itself or southern New Zealand, can evolve in an amazing way. As with Nebbiolo, these aromas are easily subdued by oak-related smells, and while oak subtly employed can enhance

Pinot Noir, too often subtlety plays second fiddle to the desire to impress on first impact (and thus please pundits struggling to assess 50 wines an hour). Pinot Noir is generally on the light side colourwise, although some producers these days seem to manage some surprising depth of hue, one is never quite sure how.

It is somewhat difficult to believe that a climate where Sangiovese and Cabernet & Co. thrive would be right for Pinot Nero, and on the whole the scattered efforts of central Italians tend to bear this thesis out. There are, however, a few good results, though one would not be tempted to pay Burgundy prices for them.

No doubt the most bizarre entry of Pinot Nero into the central Italian ampelographical scene is that which took place at the Tenuta di Bagnolo of Marchesi **Pancrazi** of Montemurlo in the province of Prato. As it happens, this is one of the coolest grape-growing areas of Tuscany, too cool for the successful ripening every year of Sangiovese. It was, however, not by design that the estate's few hectares of vineyard were converted to Pinot Nero – given the precariousness of traditional viticulture here, other crops have always majored at Villa di Bagnolo – but by a mistake which turned out to be incredibly fortuitous. Briefly, when, in the 1970s, new vinestock was ordered in order to plant new specialised Sangiovese vineyards, the nursery erroneously sent Pinot Nero instead. This wasn't discovered for over a decade when the newly hired consultant, Niccolò d'Afflitto, came to inspect the vineyards for the first time.

Since then, the grapes which had been making a distinctly strange Sangiovese have been found to be capable of making rather good Pinot Nero. Thus Marchesi Pancrazi have concentrated on that speciality, invested in it and improved it steadily. Today Villa di Bagnolo stands as central Italy's finest Burgundy-style red, though I would take issue with those who proclaim it the best in Italy – in Alto Adige (assuming that province to be Italian, which is arguable) Hofstätter, Haderburg and Haas, to name just the 'h's, are more convincingly Burgundian in their approach.

Others in Tuscany who do a reasonably good job with Pinot Nero in adverse conditions include, within Chianti Classico: Castello di Ama (Il Chiuso); Avignonesi (Valdicapraia); Fontodi of Panzano, with their Case Via; Macchiavelli (Il Principe); and Ruffino (Nero del Tondo).

Outside Chianti Classico good producers include: **Farnetella** (Nero di Nubi), Sinalunga; Fossi (Piné); and Fattoria di Montechiari (Montechiari Pinot Nero).

And from elsewhere in central Italy: Castello della **Sala**/Antinori (Pinot Nero), Ficulle/Umbria; and Boccadigabbia (Il Girone). Not much, in other words, as is sensible in the circumstances. From the south and islands, indeed, there is virtually nothing in the Pinot Nero department, as is even more sensible.

I have not tasted all the above, but of those that have passed my lips – the majority, at one time or another – the one that I have found most satisfying is the Macchiavelli Il Principe.

As for the only other Burgundian red grape of significance, Gamay, there has been very little experimentation with it in central Italy or southern Italy. Two producers are Luigi d'**Alessandro** with his Il Vescovo di Manzano, at Cortona in Tuscany; and **Duca della Corgna** (Gamay dell'Umbria) at Castiglione del Lago in Umbria; a little Cabernet is blended with this latter. Marchesi Pancrazi use a bit of Gamay together with Pinot Nero and Sangiovese in their San Donato Rosso, made at their San Donato estate at Calenzano.

RHÔNE GRAPES – RED

This effectively means Syrah, since the only other candidate, Grenache, is virtually non-existent in central and southern Italy, Sardinia's Cannonau aside.

It would be logical to suppose that in the climatic conditions of central and southern Italy Syrah would have a better chance of success on a regular basis than would Pinot Nero – and Euclid would be glad to note that here logic applies. One reason for Syrah's warm reception by growers, particularly in the centre-west, is that, unlike Pinot Nero, it makes a useful blender for those who, while seeking extra colour and richness to boost their Sangiovese, do not want the herbaceousness that may accompany the Bordeaux grapes but rather something spicy and more earthy.

That said, the amount of Syrah in central Italy remains at a modest level compared with the Bordeaux grapes in terms both of quantity and of quality, although one senses that, unlike Pinot Nero, it could explode to become the next big fad after Merlot, which followed Cabernet Sauvignon. There are a few mature vineyards, and many more recently planted ones. And there are some good varietal wines, though there is work to do before these develop into anything more than just good.

One producer to put his money on Syrah in relatively early days was Paolo de Marchi of Isole e Olena (see profile under Chianti Classico, Barberino Val d'Elsa). Paolo, who had worked in the California wine industry prior to settling in Tuscany from his native Piemonte, had an instinctive feeling that Syrah's blending possibilities were superior to those of Cabernet Sauvignon because, being less aggressive of perfume, it would impinge less on the character of the native variety – which in those days, the early 1980s, still needed all the help it could get. To this day, however, Paolo uses Syrah sparingly and only in the measure – if at all – needed to make his straight Chianti Classico a complete wine. There is no formula, and no regular dosage: the wine's the thing, not the idea.

He has, however, developed over the years a varietal Syrah in the De Marchi Collezione series called l'Eremo (= hermit, cf. Hermitage, the famous Syrah *cru* from the northern Rhône). While agreeing that this is one of the best varietal Syrahs from Italy, one would not yet place it on a level with the best of the Rhône as one would, for example, the Cabernet De Marchi Collezione in comparison with Bordeaux. Perhaps l'Eremo's greatest quality is that it does not attempt to emulate the power of the top Australian Shiraz wines but seeks rather the restraint of the European style.

Other Tuscan varietal Syrah wines include a good one from Fontodi under the Case Via label; one from Banfi called Colvecchio; from Fattoria del **Buonamico** called Il Fortino; from Luigi d'Alessandro called Podere il Bosco; from Fossi called, simply, Syrah; and from Poggio al Sole also called Syrah.

As for the rest of central Italy Syrah so far has caught on only to the west of the Apennines, and there mainly in Latium, and there mainly for blending purposes. Some of the blends, while combining French grapes, do it in a way which would be unthinkable in France. These have been included in the Chapter 6. Latium can boast at least one varietal Syrah, called Shiraz, made by Casale del Giglio.

In the whole of southern Italy I am slightly surprised to be able to unearth only two varietal Syrahs: the D'Istinto of **Terre di Ginestra**, of San Cipirello in the province of Trapani; and the Syrah of Cantine **Torrevecchia** in Acate, province of Ragusa (Torrevecchia also do a Syrah/Cabernet Sauvignon/Merlot blend called Fontana-bianca, which is better). There is, however, in the air of that island, a mini-Syrah fever, not least (as we have seen) because the Sicilians maintain that Syrah originated from their south-east corner around the town of Sira-cusa (hyphenation intentional), and not as mythology would have it from Shiraz in Persia; and that their native Nero d'Avola is an ancient offshoot from a single parent. Certainly there are distinct resemblances between the two, as well as distinct differences. Regaleali, among others, have reserved considerable vineyard space for Syrah and my betting is that we will see a lot more of this grape in years to come, this being a land capable of challenging the Australian version of 'Shiraz'. Meanwhile, the variety is being used increasingly as a blender, especially with Nero d'Avola.

BURGUNDY GRAPES – WHITE

As can be seen by a glance at the booming red wine scene, central Italy is not really white wine country. In Tuscany, for example, red wine production outstrips that of white by a wide margin, especially in the quality sector. No doubt there are other reasons for this state of affairs, but the main one is the paucity of interesting native white varieties, with the major exception of the Marche's Verdicchio and the lesser exceptions of Tuscany's Vernaccia di San Gimignano and Vermentino, Umbria's Grechetto, Latium's Malvasia Puntinata, Romagna's Albana and Abruzzo's Trebbiano d'Abruzzo.

Into this gap have been moved, over the last 30 years, a group of French varieties led inevitably by the world's most ubiquitous and accommodating quality white grape. Chardonnay, and to a much lesser extent Pinot Bianco and Pinot Grigio, have made inroads in every part of Tuscany and the centre generally raising the standard of white wine, both varietal and blended, quite noticeably. It is equally noticeable that, with the odd exception and with the greatest will in the world on the part of some producers, even these have not been able to achieve the heights of their imported counterparts in the red department, as discussed above. The best one can say of them in world terms as a group is that they are 'good second rate'. Which is a lot more than you could say of the native central Italian whites 30 or even 20 years ago.

Not all of the exceptions are based on Chardonnay and its

Burgundian colleagues, but the main ones are. If one had to single out perhaps the greatest of the group in the whole of the extended area it would probably be Cervaro della Sala, from Antinori's Castello della Sala near Orvieto, Umbria. Interestingly enough, this is a wine from a zone, rare in a central Italian context, noted more for whites than reds, the soil being tufaceous as in the Loire's Vouvray. Cervaro is not 100% Chardonnay but contains a small percentage of Grechetto. On the palate, however, it might just as well be pure Chardonnay – only a genius would guess at the inclusion of Grechetto tasting blind.

Among other top whites from imported grapes perhaps the most interesting is the Batàr of **Querciabella** of Greve in Chianti (see

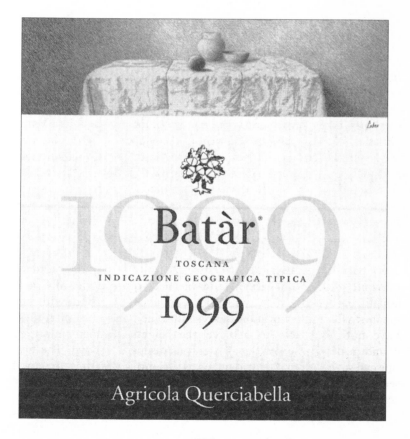

profile in section on Sangiovese). The style sought by the wine-maker, Guido de Santi, is pretty obvious from the name – in fact, it used to be spelt Bâtard until, presumably, someone in Burgundy complained. This wine, which started out as a blend of Pinot Bianco and Chardonnay but which has been going inexorably more towards the latter, is a rich, almost dense, unashamedly oak-fermented and matured white with a concentration more reminiscent of red wine than white. While having adequate acidity it does not really have the structure of classic Burgundy and is more Californian in style. It is one of the few whites of central Italy that could be placed in a line up of the best Burgundy-type whites in the world and expect to do well.

Another Chardonnay which scores consistently high marks is Isole e Olena's contribution in the De Marchi Collezione range. I once persuaded Paolo de Marchi to bottle this unfiltered and the result was the nearest thing to top white Burgundy I have tasted from Italy, with the exception of Gaja's Gaia & Rey. But it threw a deposit which had no effect on quality but gave the producer problems on the international market, so he went back to light filtration which, to my taste, takes it down just one, but one crucial, peg.

Cabreo la Pietra from Tenute **A&A Folonari** is often mentioned in the top flight of Tuscan Chardonnays, which is fair. Alongside its undeniable concentration, however, I find it is inclined to lack complexity and would rank it slightly below Cervaro or De Marchi.

Apart from the above there is a small group of Chardonnays, mainly from Tuscany, which I have found to be of consistently fine quality. These would include Avignonesi's Il Marzocco; the Chardonnay of **Capannelle** in Gaiole; Frescobaldi's Pomino Il Benefizio; Piano della Cappella from **Terrabianca** of Radda; and Saluccio from Il Terriccio.

From outside Tuscany, apart from Cervaro the main contenders would probably be Boccadigabbia of the Marche with their Montalperti; Drei Donà of Romagna with Il Tornese; and **Masciarelli** of San Martino sulla Marruccina/Abruzzo with Marina Cvetic.

Other Tuscans with a good reputation include: Castello **d'Albola** (Le Fagge), Radda; Castello di Ama (Al Poggio); **Badia a Coltibuono** (Sella del Boscone), Gaiole; Banfi (Fontanelle); Brolio (Torricella), Gaiole; Carpineto (Farnito); Castellare (Canonico); Col d'Orcia (Ghiaie Bianche); **Corzano & Paterno** (Aglaia), San

Casciano; Felsina (I Sistri); Fossi (Primopeso); Il Paradiso (Lo Cha); La Badiola (Stoppielle); Le Murelle (Le Murelle Chardonnay), Ponte del Giglio; Meleta (Bianco della Rocca); Monsanto (Fabrizio Bianchi); Montechiari (Montechiari Chardonnay); Montellori (Castelrapiti); Nozzole (Le Bruniche); Fattoria Uccelliera (Castellaccio Bianco), Fauglia; Wandanna (Labirinto), Montecarlo.

And from elsewhere in central Italy: Cesari (Morandi), Castel San Pietro Terme/Romagna; C.S. Colli Amerini (Rocca Nerina), Amelia/Umbria; La Monacesca (Ecclesia), Matelica/Marche; Orlandi Contucci Ponno (Roccesco), Abruzzo; Tre Monti (Ciardo) Romagna; Vallona (Colli Bolognesi Chardonnay), Romagna; Velenosi (Linagre; Il Barricato di Villa Angela), Ascoli Piceno/Marche.

Chardonnay has also caught on to a limited extent in the south, especially in Puglia, which has no indigenous white variety of quality and where outsiders have been drafted in *faute de mieux*, as it were; and Sicily, which does a couple of good ones but evidently feels it needs something more. Acceptable manifestations in Puglia to date include offerings from Candido (Casina Cucci), San Donaci; C.S. Copertino (Cigliano), Copertino; Rivera (Preludio), Andria; Taurino (Chardonnay del Salento), Guagnano. Perhaps one can hope for greater things from Tormaresca/Vigneti del Sud, the property recently acquired by Antinori in Puglia.

Sicily on the other hand has thrown up a couple of blockbusters from the same people who were noted busting blocks with the Bordeaux reds, namely Planeta and Tasca d'Almerita, although the latter, like the Cabernet from the same stable, has mercifully toned down the power in more recent vintages. Other producers which have attracted positive attention with their Chardonnay include: COS (Le Vigne di COS Bianco); Donnafugata (Chiarandà del Merlo), Marsala; Pollara (Vigna di Corte), Monreale; Santa Anastasia (Baccante), Castelbuono; Settesoli (Mandrarossa Chardonnay).

In central and southern Italy the overwhelming majority of white wine from grapes originating in Burgundy is Chardonnay. Pinot Bianco's only noteworthy appearance in Tuscany is as part of the Batàr blend, although Fossi make a good varietal named Terra Antica.

Rivera, at Andriano in Puglia, make a reasonable Pinot Bianco Terre al Monte.

As for Pinot Grigio, Banfi's uninspired Sant'Angelo is the only notable example in Tuscany, though Ruffino are threatening to bring out a new one soon. So far, La Castelletta from Boccadigabbia in the Marche is the best Pinot Grigio I have come across from anywhere in the centre or south.

BORDEAUX GRAPES – WHITE

Compared with Chardonnay, Sauvignon Blanc has had much less impact in central and southern Italy, though it has its following for production both as a varietal and as a blender, being prized especially for its good natural acidity. One might expect Sauvignon to be somewhat uncomfortable in this warm climate, but there are cool patches here and there – at uppish altitudes, and/or on north-facing slopes – where the grape is able to do reasonably well. Even so, Sauvignon generally has to be picked very early – even earlier than Chardonnay, usually before *Ferragosto*, the sacred Italian summer holiday of 15 August (Assumption Day). This does not give much opportunity to develop complex aromas in a grape already somewhat lacking in complexity as distinct from intensity of aroma.

There are few really good examples, but the number is sufficient to indicate that further experiments may be justified. The one that has impressed me most is Jacopo **Biondi-Santi**'s Rívolo, a wine, made without oak-ageing, which specialises in purity and definition of fruity/herbaceous aromas despite being aged for three years or more prior to release. Biondi-Santi reckons the wine can age well up to 20 years, and a seven-year-old bottle tasted recently, still fresh and lively, tends to support the claim. However, Biondi-Santi only brings the wine out in good years, and good years for Sauvignon appear to be few and far between in Tuscany.

A more regular example of the unoaked school is Ornellaia's Poggio alle Gazze, though compared with Rívolo it is inclined to be a bit simple.

Outside Tuscany, again the best comes from Antinori's Castello della Sala – not the straight Sauvignon but the *cru* developed in conjunction with Ladoucette of Pouilly Fumé fame.

Of the barrel-fermented '*fumé*' style a good example from Tuscany is Avignonesi's Il Vignola. Probably the best known from the rest of central Italy is Ronco del Re from **Castelluccio** at Modigliana in Romagna; I personally find the wine a little too heavy and lacking in the grace which I tend to look for in Sauvignon. Castelluccio also produce a pleasant non-oaked version called Lunaria.

Other reasonably good Sauvignons from Tuscany include: Banfi (Serena); Farnetella (Sauvignon); Il Terriccio (Rondinaia); Le Murelle (Colline Lucchesi Sauvignon); **Massa Vecchia** (Patrizia Bartolini), Massa Marittima. Versions featuring Sauvignon at the head of an unconventional grape-mix will be considered in Chapter 6.

From the rest of central Italy there is a scattering of Sauvignons but it's hard to get excited about any of them. Perhaps the best of the rest is Ghiaiolo from Orlandi Contucci Ponno in Abruzzo.

The same may be said regarding the Sauvignons of the south. Acceptable examples come from Candido (Vigna Vinera), Rivera (Terre al Monte Sauvignon) and **Vallone** (Corte Valesio) of Lecce in Puglia. The trouble with these wines is that, while they may satisfy as wine, they tend to lack the varietal characteristics one associates with Sauvignon, and so risk disappointing the customer thinking he's buying a typical example.

The other white grape associated with Bordeaux, Semillon, is hard find in central and southern Italian vineyards; but not impossible.

No doubt the most impressive instance is the 'Pourriture Noble' (sic) of **Petreto** in Bagno a Ripoli – on Florence's doorstep. Semillon here is minority partner in a blend with Sauvignon, the wine being, as the name indicates, a noble rot job remarkably similar to the sort of thing one might find in Sauternes – not at the highest, but at a good secondary level.

The Muffa Nobile of **Castel de Paolis** is an example from Latium of the same style, although on this occasion Semillon predominates (80% of blend, 20% Sauvignon).

RHÔNE AND THE REST – WHITE

Some of the best results from any imported white grape in central Italy are being derived from the Rhône's Viognier, even though the plantings of that grape to date have been extremely limited. Growers are still a little reluctant to commit themselves to this grape of small berries and little bunches, and consequently very low yields. The more so as it is virtually nowhere recognised among the varieties which political entities categorise as 'recommended' or 'authorised', without which recognition it is not supposed to be included in DOC wines. Where Viognier has been tried, however, the reward has been wines of highly attractive peach/apricot perfumes and an unctuous mouthfeel – wines of real character and interest.

The producer who pioneered the trend and who has had the most high-profile results to date is Castel de Paolis at Grottaferrata in Latium, on the outskirts of Rome (mentioned earlier under Frascati). The Santarellis first planted Viognier – along with numerous other indigenous and imported varieties such as Malvasia Puntinata, Bonvino and Bellone, which succeeded, and Roussanne, Marsanne and Semillon, which did not – in the mid-1980s under the supervision of viticultural guru Professor Attilio Scienza, and today have two hectares of it, which may not sound like much but is more than practically anyone else in Italy has. The *cru* that gets the lion's share of the Viognier is Vigna Adriana, which may not be entirely varietal but may be a lot closer to it than it's supposed to be.

I am not aware of any other significant producer of Viognier in central or southern Italy outside of Tuscany, but inside Tuscany there are a few that are producing good to very good wine, including: **I Campetti** at Ribolla in the Maremma (Almabruna); Montellori at Fucecchio, west of Florence (Bonfiglio); **San Michele** at San Vincenzo in the Val di Cornia/Coste degli Etruschi (Allodio Bianco); and **Trerose** at Montepulciano (Busillis).

Roussanne and Marsanne have been tried occasionally in central Italy; indeed Roussanne is included in the grape-mix for the *disciplinare* of Montecarlo Bianco. However, if they are anywhere produced varietally, or even in blend with one another, I am not aware of it. Perhaps growers found, like Castel de Paolis, that they were not suitable for central Italian conditions.

A couple of Germanic varieties have achieved minimal presence on the wine scene of central and southern Italy. Examples of Riesling Renano (Rhine Riesling) are available from Fossi (Renano) and **Cantagallo** (Carleto) of Capraia e Limite, in Tuscany; and from **Ciccio Zaccagnini** (Abbazia San Clemente) at Bolognano in Abruzzo. I cannot say I know any of these wines, but I shouldn't think I'm missing a whole lot. I have difficulty in imagining the great white grape of the semi-frozen north being able to express the steely, delicately perfumed elegance for which it is renowned in this Mediterranean clime of sweltering summers and mild winters.

Müller-Thurgau has been experimented with in a desultory sort of way by the odd grower here and there in the south, especially in Sicily, but it's making little headway and the future is not bright. **Fazio Wines** of Erice in Sicily produce an acceptable version.

6

Blends

From one perspective, wines fall into two categories: varietals and blends. The convention in Italy is to consider any wine that has 85% of a single variety as a 'varietal'. For our present purposes, however, I propose to go slightly farther and define a blend as 'one in which no single variety is predominant, either percentage-wise or in organoleptic terms'.[1] The purpose of the maker, in these cases, is 'to create a wine of disparate parts, bringing them together in a harmonic synthesis in such a way as to place the emphasis on the sum of the parts rather than on any particular constituent'.

In *Barolo to Valpolicella* I drew an analogy with music, and likened the blend to a symphony, the mix of instruments symbolising 'the blend of grapes of mixed, generally unrelated aromatic or structural styles. Although the creative blend is by no means new on the scene, this is an increasingly interesting feature of modern Italian oenology, one which Italians are, indeed, uniquely positioned to explore and exploit; and not only thanks to the enormous range of varieties available to them, originating from places as diverse as their own back yard to other parts of Italy to ancient Greece, imperial Spain, or 19th/20th century France, Germany, Austria and Eastern Europe; but also, if not principally, because their artistic and anarchic temperament allows them to go down roads which would be closed to that relatively ordered and traditionally hidebound Gallic mentality which still leads world wine opinion.'

What was said of the north is equally true of the centre and south, although in both there is a lot more experimentation going on in

---

1 All quotes on the page are from *Barolo to Valpolicella*, pp. 293–294.

some areas than in others. The region south of the Po where there is the most happening in terms of trying out new varieties and blends is, not surprisingly, Tuscany. In that context, by far the most frequent blend of this sort, with something like 30 years of history now behind it, is Sangiovese with Cabernet, occasionally with a bit of Merlot and/or Cabernet Franc, or Canaiolo or Colorino, thrown in.

It is undoubtedly true to say that Sangiovese and Cabernet are of 'unrelated aromatic or structural styles', and therefore in a sense these blends – which range from 90%–10% in one direction to 90%–10% in the other, with all the possible permutations in between – belong in this chapter. For practical purposes, however, I have taken the view that Sangiovese-cum-Cabernet is now almost a 'normal' marriage, so common has it become; and anyway when there are just the two of them, one almost always prevails. So I have included such wines under the heading of the dominant variety – Sangiovese-cum-Cabernet in the chapter on Central Italy West, Cabernet-cum-Sangiovese with International Varieties.

That still leaves, however, a goodish number of wines whose blend-structure is unusual, idiosyncratic, in some cases plain off the wall. Usually, but not invariably, these will involve one or more local grapes with one or more internationals. In the red department Merlot and/or Syrah, for example, seem to be creeping more and more into producers' calculations. Other French grapes, like Pinot Nero, are making significantly less progress.

RED BLENDS

Tuscany

The DOC regulations for Sant'Antimo, a DOC introduced in 1996 for the benefit of the innovative members of the Montalcino community, give an excellent insight into what Tuscan wine is coming from and where it's going to.

What it is coming from is a period of legal restrictiveness and constraint, which attempted to force producers of a given zone to plant only vine x, or vines x and y, on the basis of 'tradition', thus forcing people to downgrade to *vino da tavola* or go outside the law if they wanted to do anything different. This is not necessarily an unwise policy in principle: the French classic zones are all conceived along these lines. What would happen to Claret and Burgundy if an ampelographic free-for-all were declared?

The direction in which Tuscan wine is headed, on the other hand, is one where the law allows a much greater openness and choice on the part of the winemaker while remaining within the system. It's like telling growers in Saint Emilion that, if they like, they may also plant Pinot Noir and Syrah, and Sangiovese for that matter, provided they don't call the resultant wine St Emilion.

The *disciplinare* for Sant'Antimo, parallelling the restrictive Brunello di Montalcino code, simply reads: 'The controlled denomination of origin "Sant'Antimo" Rosso is reserved for wine obtained from grapes of red-skinned vine varieties recommended and/or authorised for the province of Siena'.[2] And the commandment for Sant'Antimo Bianco is like unto it.

In other words, provided a grape variety is mentioned in the list of recommendeds or authoriseds, which is pretty inclusive, the producer may proceed to grow it and make wine from it without let or hindrance, using it in any proportion he may desire within his blend. This does not mean that the classic DOCG Brunello di Montalcino is in any way compromised or reduced – indeed, it remains very much the major denomination not just of Montalcino but of Tuscany. The new regulations simply allow producers to add more strings to their bow.

In practice the blends that have arisen are not too weird (yet) because, after all, the producer still has to sell his wine, and if he's from Montalcino – or Montepulciano, or Chianti Classico, or Bolgheri – and has a lot of expensive cellar equipment to amortise and small French barrels to pay for he'll want to be fetching a pretty fair price, which he knows he can achieve more easily with a classic than with something cooked up yesterday.

One of the most successful of the trailblazers has been Solengo from Tenuta di **Argiano** in Montalcino. This much-lauded wine brings together Tuscany, Bordeaux and the Rhône in a controversial but highly convincing blend of Sangiovese, Cabernet Sauvignon, Merlot and Syrah. Deep-flavoured and complex, with tannins

2 *Codice Denominazioni di Origine dei Vini*, p. 1066.

beautifully managed, as ever with the wines of Giacomo Tachis, Solengo's success, I have no doubt, has started a trend that will flower throughout Tuscany and beyond, not necessarily involving exactly the same grapes in the same proportions but taking inspiration from its originality and daring.

A similar project from Montalcino, having no less commercial success than Solengo, is Summus from **Banfi**, a blend of Sangiovese, Cabernet Sauvignon and Syrah. As I have said earlier, this is probably the giant firm's most successful wine to date in terms of sheer quality.

A blender who works out of Montalcino, but not exclusively with Montalcino grapes, is Roberto Cipresso, one of the new stars in the firmament of peripatetic oenological consultants. At his own property of **La Fiorita** Roberto has for the past few years been working on a project aptly named La Quadratura del Cerchio ('the squaring of the circle'), also the name of his wine which generally derives from Sangiovese and Primitivo, the latter sourced from Accademia dei Racemi in Puglia, but which may also, depending on the year, contain some Montepulciano (from Abruzzo) and others from elsewhere. The circle has not been completely squared yet, but the enthusiasm to succeed is in place.

Others in Tuscany putting out interesting blends include:

Dei (Sancta Catharina – Sangiovese, Syrah, Cabernet Sauvignon, Petit Verdot), Montepulciano; **Farnetella** (Poggio Granoni – Sangiovese, Cabernet Sauvignon, Syrah), Sinalunga; **Faltognano** (Merizzo – Cabernet Sauvignon, Merlot, Pinot Nero, Malvasia Nera), Vinci; **Il Lebbio** (I Grottoni – Cabernet Sauvignon, Montepulciano), San Gimignano; **La Lastra** (Cabernet Sauvignon, Sangiovese, Merlot), San Gimignano; **Poggio Romita** (La Sassaia – Sangiovese, Cabernet Sauvignon, Pinot Nero), Tavarnelle Val di Pesa; **Varràmista** (Varràmista – Syrah, Sangiovese, Merlot), Montopoli Val d'Arno; **Wandanna** (Virente – Syrah, Merlot, Ciliegiolo), Montecarlo.

To these, I suppose, should be added the 50–50 blends of which the most famous are the joint venture between **Avignonesi,** suppliers of Merlot at 50%, and **Capannelle,** suppliers of the remainder, Sangiovese (see profiles under Sangiovese), the wine being called, in fact, '50 & 50'; and that between **Frescobaldi** and **Mondavi** called Luce (see profile on Frescobaldi under Sangiovese).

Central Italy excluding Tuscany

In the ampelographically diverse conditions of central and southern Italy there exists a diversity of blends bringing local varieties together with internationals, but it is far from a plethora, and only rarely are the wines of unusual interest.

One experiment that started off modestly but which seems to be gathering steam year by year is the Quattro Mori of **Castel de Paolis** of Grottaferrata in Latium. Originally conceived as a blend of four black grapes (the name means 'four moors', after a statue near the winery celebrating the naval victory over the Moors at Lepanto in 1571), it began in 1993 as a blend of Syrah (75%) and Merlot, simply because the vines of the other grapes were not yet mature. Today the original grapes have been joined by small percentages of Cabernet Sauvignon and Petit Verdot, so the four moors are in place. The wine is not a blockbuster, but displays the elegance and intensity characteristic of a wine made by Franco Bernabei. Without doubt it is exceptional for a red wine in a zone not noted for its reds.

Another red blend of central Italy, this time bringing Merlot and Syrah together with the local Montepulciano, is Chaos from Fattoria **Le Terrazze** of Numana in the Marche. Made by Attilio Pagli, this is a wine of admirable depth and concentration, oaky but rich in cherry/berry fruit with a full complement of fine tannins.

Other blends of central Italy capable of being interesting come from: **Adanti** (Rosso dell'Umbria – Cabernet/Barbera/Merlot), Bevagna/Umbria; **Casale del Giglio** (Mater Matuta – Sangiovese/Petit Verdot), Le Ferriere/Latium; Enzo **Mecella** (Braccano – Ciliegiolo/Merlot), Fabriano/Marche; **Monrubio** (Monrubio – Syrah/Ciliegiolo/Montepulciano/Merlot/Pinot Nero), Castel Viscardo/Umbria; **Nespoli** (Borgo dei Guidi – Sangiovese/Cabernet Sauvignon/Raboso), Civitella di Romagna; **Pieve del Vescovo** (Lucciaio – Merlot/Sangiovese/Canaiolo/Gamay), Corciano/Umbria; **Santa Barbara** (Vigna San Bartolo – Montepulciano/Cabernet Sauvignon), Barbara/Marche; **Zaccagnini** (Vigna Vescovi – Cabernet Sauvignon/Pinot Nero), Staffolo/Marche.

Southern Italy

As has been said, the south of Italy is a very heterogeneous area, each region, with the possible exception of Basilicata, having its own peculiar selection of indigenous, or at least historic, grape varieties. When it comes to blending these with imported varieties, be they from abroad or from other parts of Italy, certain zones have been more adventurous than others.

The Sicilians, in particular, have found that their Nero d'Avola, with its high fixed (tartaric) acidity, blends well with the French stars Cabernet, Merlot and Syrah, which in these hot climes have more of a tendency to lowish acidity, but which otherwise give an abundance of ripe fruit – the challenge here being to avoid over-ripeness, jamminess, cooked flavours.

Among the wines successfully blending Nero d'Avola with Bordeaux varieties (Cabernet Sauvignon and/or Merlot) are: **Donnafugata** (Tancredi), Marsala; Antonino **Melia** (Ceuso Rosso Custera), Alcamo; **Monte Olimpo** (Monte Olimpo Rosso), Sambuca di Sicilia; **Planeta** (La Segreta Rosso), Sambuca di Sicilia; **Rallo** (Vesco Rosso), Marsala; **Sant'Anastasia** (Litra; Passomaggio), Castelbuono; **Spadafora** (Don Pietro Rosso), Monreale.

A couple of good examples of Nero d'Avola with Syrah are: Planeta (Santa Cecilia); Spadafora (Vigna Virzi Rosso).

Terre di Ginestra, of San Cipirello, go one step further and add to the Nero d'Avola/Syrah mix some Merlot (Pelavet di Ginestra Rosso I) or some Cabernet Sauvignon (Pelavet di Ginestra Rosso II).

In Campania the French varieties have yet to achieve lift-off, even though the region's most praised wine in international circles in recent years has been a Cabernet/Merlot/Aglianico blend, Monte-vetrano (mentioned under Cabernet as it is really dominated by that grape).

The same may be said of Puglia. Perhaps not surprisingly, it fell to the Tuscan internationalists **Antinori** to introduce the first serious crossbreed with their Tormaresca Rosso, a rather un-Puglian blend of Aglianico – more associated with Campania or Basilicata – with Cabernet Sauvignon and Merlot.

One of the most successful international/autochthonous blends in the south to date has been Gravello from **Librandi** at Cirò Marina. With ex-consultant Severino Garofano, now replaced by Donato Lanati, the Librandi brothers spent years experimenting with this blend which today hovers around 60% Gaglioppo and 40% Cabernet Sauvignon, aged for a year in new Allier oak casks. While dominated perfume-wise and structure-wise by the French grape, Gaglioppo gives the wine a tautness and a balance –

a uniqueness if you like – without which it could easily lapse into jamminess.

Another producer mixing Gaglioppo with Cabernet in Calabria is **Statti** at Lamezia Terme with their Arvino. **San Francesco**, of Cirò Marina, make a good blend of Gaglioppo and Merlot called Martà, while **Odoardi**, of Nocera Terinese, put Aglianico together with Merlot, Cabernet Sauvignon and Cabernet Franc in their Scavigna Vigna Garrone.

In Sardinia there are a couple of examples of Cannonau – the local version of Grenache, as has been said – with Cabernet Sauvignon, notably in the shape of **Sella e Mosca's** Tanca Farrà. **Gabbas**, of Nuoro, go one, or indeed two, further by adding Sangiovese and Montepulciano to the above.

WHITE BLENDS

Tuscany and the centre

Italy is a land of reds – how many times have we heard it? – and the more so as you travel south. Nonetheless, despite what is being described in some quarters as a 'white wine crisis', there remains a demand for quality white wines and many producers feel they need one to complete their portfolio.

Just as enterprising and imaginative Italian producers have come up, in the red department, with blends that no Frenchman would contemplate in his nightmares, so have they with whites, though to a considerably lesser extent. The commonest blending grape from outside Italy is, predictably, Chardonnay, closely followed, equally predictably, by Sauvignon Blanc. Indeed the two are more and more often to be found together, as also frequently happens in the north, so that a marriage which might be seen in France as made in hell is becoming, in Italy, if not heavenly, almost commonplace. The fact that I have included such blends here and not under the respective varieties, as in the case of Cabernet, has something to do with the fact that the two are often accompanied by a third party, such as Gewürztraminer or Trebbiano; but it also doubtless indicates that I myself am not yet fully able to wrap my mind around the idea of Bordeaux and Burgundy in the same barrel.

Not surprisingly, it is Tuscany which takes the lead in experimentation. It is difficult to single out one wine as representative of a general movement, partly because there is no wine of complex blend – as distinct from simple blends where one grape is totally dominant, like Cervaro or Batàr, discussed above – from the centre or south which stands out as exceptional. One with a long pedigree, prototype – as far as I am aware – of a style which others have followed, is Le Grance, a Sant'Antimo Bianco from **Caparzo** in Montalcino. This consists of Chardonnay (75%), Sauvignon Blanc and Gewürztraminer – the equivalent of a mix of Bordeaux, Burgundy and Alsace, *quelle horreur!* – aged but not fermented in *barrique*. Vittorio Fiore, consultant oenologist at Caparzo, has been working on Le Grance since the early 1980s, and has fine-tuned it so that it achieves just the right balance of acidity and fatness, fruit and oak.

Others of this ilk are Collecimoli from **Le Calvane** at Montespertoli; Anima from **Livernano** of Radda in Chianti; Vigna Regis from **Vecchie Terre di Montefili** in Panzano. Collecimoli and Vigna Regis are also made by Fiore.

Chardonnay and Sauvignon Blanc come together too in one of Tuscany's most complex and interesting whites, Paleo Bianco from **Le Macchiole** in Bolgheri; there is a splash of Vermentino also in the mix. A similar blend, in different proportions, is that of Marna from **Sangervasio** in Palaia, province of Pisa. Both **Villa Cilnia** of Pieve al Bagnoro (province of Arezzo) and **Villa Patrizia** of Roccalbenga in the Maremma blend Chardonnay and Sauvignon Blanc without any third party. The oenologist at Le Macchiole, at Sangervasio and (previously) at Villa Patrizia is Luca d'Attoma.

Chardonnay teams up with Trebbiano in two interesting whites – Brania del Cancello from **Colle Verde** at Capannori in the province of Lucca; and Ficaia from **Uccelliera** of Empoli, province of Florence. Luigi **d'Alessandro** of Cortona, province of Arezzo, has put Chardonnay together with Viognier (Podere Fontarca) in what has proved a winning combination. **Panizzi**, of San Gimignano, have created a tasty blend of Vernaccia and Chardonnay with their Il Bianco di Gianni, although the difference between this and some Vernaccia di San Gimignano DOCGs is merely a matter of proportion since Chardonnay, nowadays, is permitted in the blend at 10%.

Occasionally one finds Pinot Bianco taking the role of Chardonnay in a complex blend. This is true for the Meriggio of **Fontodi** at Panzano as well as with the Borro Lastricato of **Selvapiana**

at Rufina – both properties followed by oenologist Franco Bernabei.

Pinot Bianco is also often a significant ingredient in Montecarlo Bianco DOC, an officially recognised blend whose *disciplinare* calls for a minimum of 40% Trebbiano and at least 10% of three other grapes among which, apart from Pinot Bianco, figure Pinot 'Gris' (sic), Semillon, Sauvignon, Roussanne and Vermentino. Given the possibilities one would expect to be able to find some fascinating Montecarlo DOC whites, but in reality it is hard to get enthusiastic. Good producers have been mentioned in the section on Trebbiano.

The rest of central Italy west, with the major exception of Umbria's Orvieto, discussed earlier under Trebbiano, is hardly a mecca for white blends, unless you include sweet wines, which I'm not, yet. No doubt the best is the so-called 'Frascati' Vigna Adriana from Castel de Paolis, mentioned previously, where Viognier combines gloriously with Malvasia Puntinata; Castel de Paolis also make a Chardonnay/Sauvignon called Selve Vecchie which can be almost as good.

From the eastern side of the Apennines probably the top candidate would be Mirum from **La Monacesca** of Matelica in the Marche – this being an intriguing mix of Verdicchio, Chardonnay and Sauvignon Blanc. **Umani Ronchi** of Osimo/Marche also make a good Verdicchio/Chardonnay blend called Le Busche.

The South and Islands

The picture in the southland is similar – a little going on by way of experimentation, but not a lot; yet. In Campania, a land endowed with various characterful white wine grapes, **Feudi di San Gregorio** of Sorbo Serpico turn out a rare work of excellence called Idem, blending Fiano, Greco, Falanghina, Coda di Volpe, all locals, with a touch of Moscato Bianco. Feudi's Campanaro, Fiano + Greco, is pretty good too. **Caggiano**, of Taurasi, also make a couple of Fiano/Greco blends, FiaGré and Mel, the latter being intended as the special cru of limited production.

Serious efforts at white wine blending in the rest of the southern mainland are few and far between. **D'Angelo**, of Rionero in Basilicata, has put together a decent Chardonnay/Pinot Bianco/Incrocio Manzoni blend called Vigna dei Pini. In Puglia, Gravina DOC is supposed to be a blend of Malvasia and Bianco d'Alessano with Greco di Tufo, the last named – qualitatively easily the best – up to a maximum of 60%; Cantina **Botromagno**'s Gravina, blending Malvasia del Chianti with Greco, is undoubtedly one of the south's most characterful and best value-for-money white wines.

Calabria's challenge is headed by Critone, a surprisingly crisp, flavoury Chardonnay/Sauvignon blend from Librandi of Cirò Marina. **Odoardi**, of Nocera Terinese, make an interesting wine called Pian della Corte Blu from Chardonnay, Riesling Italico and Pinot Bianco.

Like Campania, Sicily boasts a number of characterful white wine varieties, the difference being that Sicilians seem to be somewhat more experimentally minded than Campanians. Several producers are putting the local Inzolia together with Chardonnay, including: Santa Anastasia (Zurrica); Spadafora (Don Pietro Bianco); and **Tasca d'Almerita** (Leone d'Almerita). Inzolia also figures strongly, with Grecanico and others, in one of the best of the island's white blends, Tasca d'Almerita's Nozze d'Oro; and with Grillo in Spadafora's DiVino.

One of the shooting stars of recent years in the Sicilian firmament is Planeta – to mix celestial metaphors – of Sambuca di Sicilia. They make two blends featuring Grecanico with Catarratto and Chardonnay, La Segreta Bianco and Alastro, the latter being the more recent and supposedly superior, being subject to *barrique* treatment.

A bit of Catarratto also figures, together with Chardonnay and Viognier, in Terre di Ginestra's Pelavet di Ginestra Bianco.

French white grapes have not achieved much penetration in Sardinia to date, though no doubt it will come. For the moment there is little to report on barring Isola dei Nuraghi, one of the weaker wines of the generally excellent **Argiolas** of Serdiana, combining Vermentino with Chardonnay and Sauvignon Blanc; and Le Vigne del Sole, from C.S. **Trexenta**, featuring Nuragus and Vermentino with a splash of Chardonnay.

SWEET WHITE BLENDS

There exists a small but significant number of sweet white wines in the centre and south, most of them from indigenous or semi-indigenous varieties like Trebbiano, the chief variety for Tuscany's Vin Santo, Moscato, Malvasia, Nasco and the like; these are dealt with under their respective dominant variety.

In the past few years a few sweet wines have developed from blends of international, or international/indigenous, varieties. An increasing number of these have followed the French late-harvest/noble rot pattern of vinification, although the traditional Italian dried-grape or *passito* method remains the major force.

The wine to have had the most impact, partly because it comes from the Antinori stable and is by that fact liable to attract more media attention than most, and partly because it is a genuinely excellent product, is Muffato della Sala from **Castello della Sala** in the Orvieto zone in Umbria. This is a complex blend based on Sauvignon Blanc at 60%, the remainder made up of Grechetto, Traminer and Rhine Riesling. The French grapes are picked around mid-October, Grechetto's harvest coming almost a month later, all, in a good year, containing high levels of sugar and displaying advanced botrytis. The wine is then aged for a modest six months in French oak *barriques* before blending and bottling.

Other excellent *muffa nobile* wines from the Orvieto zone tend to follow the classic recipe for Orvieto, as has been mentioned under Trebbiano in the chapter on Central Italy West.

As far as Tuscany is concerned, apart from Vin Santo there is surprisingly little in the way of sweet white wine. Mention has been made in the chapter on International Varieties of another wine called 'Pourriture Noble', from Petreto of Bagno a Ripoli, but it is a one-off – either for reasons of marketing or by force of nature producers have shied away from taking the late-harvest, noble rot route. One trend that does seem likely to catch on is the inclusion of French or German grapes in the Vin Santo blend. Examples include the Vin Santo of **Meleta** of Roccatederighi in the Maremma, which includes Rhine Riesling and Traminer in addition to Trebbiano and Sangiovese; and the Zipolo d'Oro Vin Santo of Le Calvane, which combines Trebbiano and Chardonnay.

In the south, insofar as international/indigenous blends are employed, there seems to be a preference for the *passito* method, traditional in Italy if not so much in these parts. In Puglia, **Vallone** of Lecce blend Sauvignon Blanc and Malvasia Bianca to produce their delicious, creamy-custardy Passo delle Viscarde, the grapes being dried on the roof of their castle-like farm-complex, fortified in the Middle Ages against Saracen raids, near the sea. Another producer, similarly followed by oenologist Severino Garofano, is **Candido** of Sandonaci, who put Chardonnay together with Malvasia in a blend called Paule Calle.

7

Italian Wine Law

(The early part of the following is partly based on an article which first appeared in the December, 2000, Italian supplement to *Decanter*.)

The time has come to recognise the fact that the system regulating the naming or *denominazione* of wines in Italy is in difficulty. The problems relate partly to the general and particular regulations governing the production of wines in Italy (see *Barolo to Zibibbo* for an overview of how the system works; or 'the Italian wine label'), but more so to the sheer number of DOCs and IGTs, which seems to grow monthly. This chapter aims at presenting an independent (i.e. non-Italian) assessment of the situation as well as some fairly drastic suggestions for streamlining the system.

I am well aware that these suggestions risk being cursed and reviled by those within the system who take them seriously, who will be few, however, for scorn is a convenient means of defence against what we do not like. Nor is there much chance that they or any part of them will be adopted, for Italian wine legislation is an inferno of large and petty interests all mingling together like writhing snakes in a pit, making it extremely difficult for anything positive ever to happen on a macro level. Which is why so many of the finest individuals on the Italian wine scene have turned their back on the system and just got on with their own thing. Which only adds to the difficulty, in that more and more names are added to the list of those to remember, and it all becomes more and more of a meaningless jumble in the mind of the ultimate target of the exercise, the consumer.

The essence of the problem, then, is this: the drinking public is confused. The press and the trade are confused. I confess that, after

25 years studying the Italian wine scene, I am confused. The law may or may not be friendly to the producer – many would dispute this from their particular angle – but it is decidedly unfriendly to the consumer. And ultimately this must reflect in sales. Could we not find a simpler system that nonetheless takes account of the necessity for typicity and tradition?

Let me state parenthetically that I personally am all for tradition and local typicity. I abhor the move in this world of ours towards standardisation and internationalisation and I rejoice whenever I find genuine soul in a product, or a work of art, or a stretch of countryside, or a person. I love real Brie and Cheddar and Parmigiano and hate poor imitations. Now, one of the Italian wine law's fundamental aims is to protect tradition, and this as a principle is entirely laudable. But one can carry tradition too far, try and drag it back to life when it scarcely exists any more, impose it when it only came into existence yesterday. Italians have a definite talent for such manoeuvres.

Somehow, we need to find a *via media* between typicity and simplicity, between proliferation and clarity. Here I will put forward a few general suggestions, and in separate appendices I will consider specific generic wines of the various categories. The main idea is to reduce the number of names the public has to deal with, as well, in some cases, as introducing familiar names where unknown ones are presently employed.

IGT (INDICAZIONE GEOGRAFICA TIPICA)

Principle: **An IGT is valid when it identifies a general, preferably recognisable, geographical production area.**

The concept of IGT, a superior Vino da Tavola roughly equivalent to the French Vin de Pays, came in by virtue of presidential decree 164 of 1992 which superseded decree 930 of 1963. Ostensibly it was created in order to offer a less rigid alternative to DOC, while at the same time increasing the level of control over the kind of wildcat wines that have proliferated since the 1970s. A subtle motive for this category is also to force producers out of the humiliating (for the government) category of simple Vino da Tavola for top wines such as SuperTuscans. An IGT is not obliged to use those demeaning words ('Vino da Tavola') on the label, although technically it is one. The device used by the new regulations is the stipulation that a wine without geographic indication – and which therefore is not obliged to account for the provenance of the grapes or the method of making the wine – may not display a place name, grape name or, most inconvenient of all, date on the label. It would obviously be unthinkable to propose, say, Tignanello as a non-vintage product.

Unfortunately, the IGT category opened a can of worms out of which all manner of obscurities have wriggled and continue to wriggle, adding enormously to the overload of names; at the time of writing there are something over 120 of them. The simple solution to this, I submit, is to limit the regions, or in a couple of cases parts of regions, to a single IGT, or perhaps where the more important wine-producing regions are concerned to two or three – but recognisable. Usually the single name will be that of the region itself, although in a couple of instances, where the name of the region is used in the DOC, this may be difficult, for example Abruzzo and Piemonte. This gives the consumer in Kyoto or Melbourne a fighting chance of recognising the name on the label and of thereby forming some kind of idea of what might be expected from the liquid in the bottle.

It will be objected that different IGTs exist because they reflect different zonal and sub-zonal realities, specifying the use of this variety (or varieties) and excluding the use of that (those). And it is true that under the suggested system the list of permitted varieties would have in some examples to be somewhat broadened to include most or all of what people are likely to want to plant.

'But then it won't be typical', I hear people object. Come on, it wasn't typical anyway, virtually all of these IGTs admit varieties, international and extra-regional, that are not traditional in the zone in question. And they are all inventions of the past few years. There is plenty of scope to be 'typical' within the DOC system, and if the DOC system doesn't give you what you want, be content with a broad IGT which allows you to be as creative (if not typical) as you want, within reason. That's what the Tuscans do, and if it's good enough for Tuscans, who are doing very nicely out of it, why wouldn't it be good enough for others?

And if you want to be strictly honest – and why not, for a change? – you could alter the name of IGT to IG, removing the 'Tipico'.

It will further be objected that a lot of work has gone into creating these IGTs and 'we're not about to destroy the fruits of all that effort'. Frankly, the effort was 95% bureaucratic, which has little or nothing to do with wine, tradition or typicity.

Returning to the question of names, let us take the example of Latium, where five IGTs exist at the time of writing: Civitella d'Agliano, Colli Cimini, Frusinate, Nettuno and Lazio. Let's face it, nobody outside of the immediate area has ever heard of any of these apart from Lazio, which they may recognise as the name of a Rome football team. Do these places really have such a precious tradition to protect? If so, why are they not DOCs, and why have we never heard of them?

Indeed, on inspection, we find the *disciplinari* for these IGTS to be very similar to one another. To bring them all together under one name would be a matter of mere tweaking.

Or take Abruzzo, where no fewer than nine IGTs exist, each more obscure than the previous (examples include Colline Teatine and Valle Peligna). Assuming that one cannot use the name 'Abruzzo', already used in Montepulciano d'Abruzzo and Trebbiano d'Abruzzo DOC (although I do not see the overwhelming logic of this prohibition) one could resort to something like Colli Abruzzesi IGT. Sophists will say that such a name is too close to Abruzzo itself, but the purpose here is to satisfy consumers, not sophists.

A full list of suggested IGTs by region follows in Appendix A. It will be noted that it would be possible to reduce the number of IGTs from over 120 to just over 20, all of them more or less recognisable to the public at large. This would greatly relieve the congestion on bureaucrats' desks and in consumers' minds.

Before leaving the subject of IGTs, it might be instructive to consider in detail one example, that of the most often seen: Toscana/Toscano.

'The *indicazione geografica tipica* "Toscano" or "Toscana" ... is reserved for the following wines: whites, including *frizzante* and *abboccato* styles; reds, including *novello* and *abboccato* styles; *rosato*s, including *abboccato* styles' (*Codice Denominazioni di Origine dei Vini*, p. 1475). Doesn't leave a lot out, does it?

These wines 'must be obtained from grapes originating from vineyards composed of one or more varieties recommended and/or authorised in the provinces specified below (in fact, all the provinces of Tuscany).'

It would be difficult to think of a variety that growers might be interested in which is not included, except perhaps for Viognier, which will probably be included at the next revision.

There follows an extensive list of the grapes that may be used varietally at a minimum of 85% of a given wine. The list includes almost all of the principal native Tuscan grapes and most of the principal international grapes.

Volume-wise, a production of between 13.5 (reds, *rosatos*) and 14.4 (whites) tonnes per hectare is permitted. In other words, high.

And this is 'typical' of the sort of *disciplinare* one finds for *vini tipici*. I must point out that I am not faulting this category – it is perfectly adequate to meet the needs of our principle, stated above, not to mention for the unstated but underlying aim of bringing renegade top wines into line with the law. The point is that the *disciplinare* is very broad and can hardly be described as 'typical' in a traditional sense, since wines can come from any part of the region using just about any grape variety or varieties at, if one wishes, a pretty high yield per hectare. Nor would it matter if the area described were smaller, the parameters regarding grape varieties and production maxima being sufficient to undermine any guarantee of 'typicity'.

In short, I see no point in dividing IGT into multiple parts with multiple names which serve little purpose other than to confuse the consumer.

DOC (DENOMINAZIONE DI ORIGINE CONTROLLATA)

Principle: A DOC is valid if its wines are at least potentially truly distinctive.

This is an altogether more difficult area to revise. We must remember that DOC's sacred role is to protect tradition and typicity, and that must remain the paramount consideration. IGT, as we have seen, cannot be viewed as a valid guarantee of typicity because permitted yields are excessive and permitted varieties too numerous and heterogeneous. If high quality does come under the IGT banner – and it does, some of the highest in the land – that has everything to do with a personal decision on the part of the producer and nothing to do with the law.

All the same, there are considerable areas of DOC country that could do with a bit of rationalising. Take, for example, the DOCs of southern Puglia: Alezio, Brindisi, Copertino, Leverano, Lizzano, Matino, Nardò, Salice Salentino, Squinzano. These are all named after villages in fairly close proximity to one another on almost identical terrain, flat and near sea-level, with very similar methods of training: old vines, and some new, planted on the *alberello* or bush system, vines planted in the period 10–30 years ago to the *tendone* system, vines planted more recently to the *spalliera* system, and very similar varieties. All of them save one legislate for Negroamaro at up to 100% (Lizzano up to 80%) with a minimum of between 50% and 80%. Complementary grapes invariably feature Malvasia Nera (di Lecce or di Brindisi, little difference) plus, in most cases, Montepulciano and Sangiovese (in only one instance, that of Leverano, could international varieties sneak in – legally).

This situation, it seems to me, cries out for simplification. The name that is common to them all is Salentino, since they all hail from the Salento peninsula. By a happy coincidence, by far the best known of them internationally is Salice Salentino, so the name Salentino is not only common but also recognised. Why not, then, bring them all together under the banner of a single multi-DOC, 'Salentino' – already an IGT, but so what – tweaking the *disciplinari* as necessary and even, to save local feelings, adding the name of the sub-zone? So: Salentino Alezio, Salentino Brindisi, Salentino Copertino etc. This approach has been adopted in Friuli (Friuli Aquileia, Friuli Grave etc.) with largely positive reactions from producers and undoubted benefit for the consumer. Many will have a reasonable idea of where Friuli is, or Salentino. Few will have any idea where on the map to find Annia or Nardò, or, consequently, what to expect from a bottle so named.

And there are plenty more areas where a confused or over-crowded nomenclature could be simplified without loss of real identity or compromise of principle. A list of suggestions is given in Appendix B.

DOCG (DENOMINAZIONE DI ORIGINE CONTROLLATA E GARANTITA)

Principle: **DOCG is only valid if the wines are not only distinctive but also at least capable of excellence and never less than good.**

One might perhaps have thought that a category like DOCG, a club difficult to enter precisely because it represents the top, would not need revising. Indeed, it does not need a great deal, although there are two or three areas which could do with reconsideration, possibly even demotion to DOC, and one at least which cries out for attention, not only in itself but because it undermines the credibility of the category as a whole.

That area is Chianti and we will come to it last.

Let us begin by remembering that a DOCG wine is by definition '*garantita*' and that the guarantee in question refers to quality as determined by a tasting commission. As a general statement, I think many will agree that they have come across DOCG wines which it is hard to believe have ever been anywhere near the nostrils and palate of a qualified taster. Certain cheap so-called DOCGs are nothing less than a disgrace, and one can only suspect corruption or gross incompetence, or producers' fear at failing their own wine, in their having passed the supposed taste test. How is one to give credence to any part of a system that allows such persistent violation of its own principles? It is apparent that something must be done to ensure that tasting commissions carry out their function honestly and correctly, to guarantee the guarantee, as it were.

There is also the aspect of certain DOCGs trading on past glory, or on a glory which owes as much to other factors – tourism, politics – as it does to wine. Wines in the first category might include Gattinara, Ghemme and Torgiano Rosso Riserva; in the latter category, Albana di Romagna, Gavi and Vernaccia di San Gimignano.

But the biggest problem child of DOCG is undoubtedly Chianti. To begin with, most 'Chianti' (as suggested under 'Sangiovese' in Chapter 2) does not have a historic right to that name. The only area that can claim such a right is Chianti Classico, so named because it is situated in the Chianti Hills between Florence and Siena. Specific suggestions for dealing with this situation are given in Appendix C.

Cheap 'Chianti' is also by far the worst offender where the quality guarantee is concerned, followed at a distance by dull Vernaccia di San Gimignano and characterless Gavi, not to mention mediocre Chianti Classico. I am talking about the bottom end of these denominations, it should be understood.

On the whole, however, it should be recognised that DOCG

fulfils a valuable role and one only wishes it were better at living up to its own high ideals.

Before concluding, let us listen to a sympathetic voice from a somewhat unexpected quarter, a voice that carries great weight in matters of DOC legislation. Senator Riccardo Margheriti, President of the National DOC Committee, also believes that the race to create evermore DOCs is folly. Senator Margheriti is coming from the direction of the producer and the system rather than from that of the consumer and the market. Nonetheless, his bottom line is uncannily similar.

'DOC', he says, 'cannot be considered as an instrument of promotion. It cannot be conceded wherever and however, otherwise it would lose its function. A DOC is the fruit of hard work and bears witness to the commitment of a group of producers towards quality. Only after having acquired merit in the field can one begin thinking about DOC and not vice versa. Otherwise the denomination of origin would have no meaning.

'I believe that 312 DOCs (the number in existence at the time he spoke; note that a number of these are umbrella names for multiple sub-DOCs, so the real figure is much higher) are already plenty for the moment. One must be careful: I do not believe that it is in the interests of Italian viticulture to promote the birth of new DOCs which, for example, involve almost exclusively international varieties because, in my view, it would distort the very meaning of the denomination.'

Margheriti notes that there already exist within the existing system DOCs and IGTs of vast scope, under whose banner producers are able to propose a great diversity of wines. 'The risk, however, is that this can lead to an excess of individualism which suits no one, both because it undermines the principle of competition, and because deregulation in this area would, in my view, be harmful.

'It would be far better', Margheriti concludes, 'to increase quality in respect of existing DOCs, conceding, when the requirements are met, passage to DOCG. This is an important choice, because it signifies an advance in quality by diminution of production and increase of controls. Not for nothing are there only 22 DOCGs' (at the time of speaking).

Senator Margheriti does not voice support of a move actually to **reduce** the number of DOCs and IGTs – nor could he, in his position, though he might believe in it in his heart. But he clearly considers that the tendency of the existing system to run away with itself in a rather typically Italian anarchic manner has gone too far.

Who knows? With support like this perhaps a move to rationalise the system might actually get going.

If so, it will be necessary to appoint a presiding authority capable of overriding objections from all sorts of directions – a 'DOC Reform Tsar', as the British press might put it. Such a person would have to be incredibly tenacious not to say courageous, as he (or she) could be risking a lot in crossing the desires of the various pressure groups. He would need to be able to take decisions in the interest of the whole, in the name of principle, not be swayed by local politics and industrial considerations. In Italy, such an undertaking could be not just difficult, but dangerous.

APPENDIX A

Suggested revision of IGT system, by region, in geographical order

---

PIEMONTE

The Piemonte region has opted for 100% DOC status, hence the existence of Piemonte DOC and the unlikelihood of calling an eventual IGT 'Piemonte'. IGT 'Colli Piemontesi', however, would broaden the scope so as to allow the production of geographically denominated wines in areas not covered by the DOC, and would bring Piemonte into line with other regions.

VALLE D'AOSTA

No IGT exists and none is needed as the minuscule production is covered by Valle d'Aosta DOC.

LOMBARDY

Twelve IGTs exist, not including 'Lombardia', under which all those existing could be subsumed.

VENETO

Nine IGTs exist, including 'Veneto', 'delle Venezie' and 'Verona'. 'Verona' is a rare example of a high-profile provincial IGT under which millions of bottles are currently sold, and could accordingly be kept. 'Delle Venezie' covers wines from anywhere in northeastern Italy except Alto Adige, i.e. Veneto, Friuli or Trentino. 'Veneto' could take care of the rest.

FRIULI-VENEZIA GIULIA

Apart from 'Delle Venezie' (see above), 'Venezia Giulia' should suffice. Any others, like 'Alto Livenza', are superfluous.

TRENTINO-ALTO ADIGE

Alto Adige, an existing DOC, could restrict itself to 'Mitterberg'. Trentino, also an existing DOC, could choose between 'Atesino' or 'Vigneti delle Dolomiti' as its exclusive IGT; apart, again, from the inter-regional 'Delle Venezie'. One is enough.

EMILIA-ROMAGNA

Ten IGTs exist, only two needed. Suggest retaining 'Dell'Emilia' ('Emilia' on its own to move up to DOC; see Appendix B) and, since Romagna is an existing DOC, inventing something like 'Colli Romagnoli'.

TUSCANY

Five IGTs exist, including 'Toscana'/'Toscano', 'Colli della Toscana Centrale' and 'Maremma Toscana'. In view of the high profile of the latter two there might be a case for keeping them both (perhaps reducing 'Colli della Toscana Centrale' to plain 'Toscana Centrale') to distinguish between wines of inland zones and coastal zones respectively. 'Toscana'/'Toscano' could perhaps be retained as a catch-all where in doubt.

UMBRIA

Six IGTs exist, all very obscure apart from 'Umbria'. Suggest subsuming them all under this latter.

LATIUM

Suggest retaining only 'Lazio' of the existing five.

MARCHE

A model for our system: only 'Marche' exists or need exist.

ABRUZZO

Nine IGTs exist, all virtually unknown outside their immediate areas, and probably within them too. Since 'Abruzzo' is the basis of the regional DOC, suggest replacing them all with something like 'Colli Abruzzesi'.

MOLISE

Two IGTs of stunning nonentity exist: 'Osco' and 'Rotae'. As in the case of Abruzzo, suggest replacing them both with 'Colli Molisani', 'Molise' being a useful regional DOC.

CAMPANIA

Eight IGTs exist, not including 'Campania', which I would suggest in replacement for all of them save perhaps 'Irpinia', already fairly well known, in widespread use and, significantly, restricted to local varieties.

BASILICATA

Another model for our system. Only one IGT exists – 'Basilicata'.

PUGLIA

Six IGTs exist, among which two or three which, unusually, are quite well known, like 'Salento', 'Tarantino' and 'Murgia'. These, however, could be translated into DOCs and the rest subsumed under the already existing 'Puglia'.

SARDINIA

No fewer than 15 IGTs exist, all of them utterly unknown to the world without and having very similar regulations. The name 'Sardegna' is used for DOC purposes, but one could either subsume all of them under the existing 'Isola dei Nuraghi' or invent something like 'Colline Sarde'.

SICILY

Six extremely unrecognisable IGTs exist, plus 'Sicilia', which could subsume the lot. Many producers actually prefer IGT 'Sicilia' to their local DOC.

SUMMARY OF SUGGESTED IGTS IN GEOGRAPHICAL ORDER

Colli Piemontesi; Lombardia; Delle Venezie; Veneto; Verona; Venezia Giulia; Atesino (or Vigneti delle Dolomiti); Mitterberg; Emilia; Colli Romagnoli; Toscana; Toscana Centrale; Maremma Toscana; Umbria; Lazio; Marche; Colli Abruzzesi; Colli Molisani; Campania; Irpinia; Basilicata; Puglia; Calabria; Isole dei Nuraghi (or Colline Sarde); Sicilia.

Total: 25 (from existing 122).

APPENDIX B

Suggested revision of DOCs

The following lists do not pretend to be exhaustive, but merely indicative of the kind of changes that would gather the confusion of DOCs into a relatively coherent whole. Numerous names, not mentioned, could be subsumed under existing or new DOC names or downgraded to the relevant IGT.

Readers will of course be aware that some of the best-known names are not included here, being DOCGs. These will be treated subsequently.

PIEMONTE

This region suffers from an excess of DOC names (43 at the time of writing), a number of which are overlapping, or superfluous, or too obscure to warrant DOC status. These could be reduced to around 10, as the following list, which includes those which seem necessary, sometimes in amalgamated form, suggests. The rest, as I say, could be dealt with in various ways, for example by recasting as Piemonte DOC, perhaps with the sub-zone attached; or by downgrading to Colli Piemontesi IGT.

1. Alba Barbera/Dolcetto/Nebbiolo. Alba Dolcetto to include Dogliani, Diano d'Alba and Langhe Monregalesi, if necessary with mention of sub-zone, e.g. Alba Dolcetto di Dogliani. A new DOC Alba is in fact being prepared at the time of writing. There is no reason why it should not subsume the above.
2. Asti Barbera/Dolcetto/Freisa/Grignolino/Rosso.
3. Caluso
4. Carema: possible upgrade to DOCG.
5. Coste della Sesia: to include, with sub-zones, Boca, Bramaterra, Fara, Lessona and Sizzano; also Colline Novaresi.
6. Langhe: this could possibly be subsumed by Alba and/or Roero.
7. Monferrato Barbera/Cortese/Ruchæ, as well as Bianco and Rosso.

8. <u>Ovada</u>: Dolcetto and other wines from the zone.
9. <u>Piemonte</u>: A catch-all which would probably be better as an IGT; either way, soaking up a lot of unnecessary baggage. Various existing DOCs could be reduced to sub-zones of Piemonte DOC.
10. <u>Roero</u>.

VALLE D'AOSTA

No problem with regional DOC plus sub-denominations.

LIGURIA

Considering the very limited production of the region I would have thought the existing seven DOCs could be reduced to one regional one, or possibly two: Liguria Levante and Liguria Ponente, with sub-zones.

LOMBARDY

The current list of 14 DOCs could be reduced by half, as follows:

1. <u>Brescia</u>: could include obscure or archaic wines of the province of Brescia such as Botticino, Capriano del Colle and Cellatica, with sub-zones if need be.
2. <u>Garda</u>: to include, as at present, a broad sweep of wines of the west and east shores of the lake, and beyond; could absorb Garda Bresciano and Garda Colli Mantovani, as well as San Martino della Battaglia.
3. <u>Lugana</u>.
4. <u>Oltrepò Pavese</u>: could absorb San Colombano.
5. <u>Terre di Franciacorta</u>
6. <u>Valcalepio</u>
7. <u>Valtellina</u>.

Anything else could be subsumed under IGT Lombardia.

VENETO

Several of the existing DOCs of the Veneto region have established an identity of sorts. I would leave as they are Bagnoli, Bardolino, Breganze, Colli Berici, Colli Euganei, Lison-Pramaggiore, Montello e Colli Asolani (but reduce the name to simply Montello), Soave, Valpolicella – the last two to be re-invented as DOCG – and Piave. Others could be absorbed, probably with sub-zones: e.g. Bianco di Custoza, or Custoza, into Garda, Prosecco di Conegliano-Valdobbiadene into Conegliano, Gambellara into Soave, Lessini Durello into Garda. Others, inter-regional, have already been mentioned. Valdadige should perhaps be restricted to Trentino-Alto Adige, or downgraded to IGT.

FRIULI-VENEZIA GIULIA

This region seems to have got it just about right, subsuming the five relatively obscure areas, Annia, Aquileia, Grave, Isonzo and Latisana, under a Friuli DOC, although this could be one DOC with various sub-zones instead of five separate DOCs, while leaving the famous ones, Collio and Colli Orientali del Friuli, as they historically have been. To be consistent, Carso should probably also be Friuli Carso.

TRENTINO

No argument with Teroldego Rotaliano, though it should probably be upgraded to DOCG, Trentino – with multiple sub-denominations – and Trento. Casteller and Valdadige, as suggested above, could perhaps be downgraded to IGT.

ALTO ADIGE

Alto Adige/Sudtiroler plus sub-denominations seems as clear as needs be. Trust the Germans.

EMILIA-ROMAGNA

I would have thought that three DOCs, with sub-zones/denominations, would suffice: Emilia – e.g. Emilia Colli di Parma, Romagna – Sangiovese di Romagna; Romagna Colli d'Imola, and Lambrusco. At the moment there are no fewer than 19 DOCs for the hapless consumer to try and sort through.

TUSCANY

Most of the big names of Tuscany have been elevated to DOCG status and the remaining 34 DOCs contain some wondrously obscure wines; there is much scope for amalgamating, downgrading or eliminating here. For example, it would be helpful if all the white, mainly – but not exclusively – Trebbiano-based wines were to be reduced to one name with sub-denominations, for example Bianco Toscano Pitigliano, or Bianco Toscano Elba; i.e. this category could include also the whites which presently form part of a red–white DOC. This tells the consumer all he needs to know at a glance, and if he wants more he can always read the back label, or decipher the purport of the sub-denomination.

A similar job could be performed upon all the Sangiovese-based Rossos of the region, although I would keep certain high-profile ones, like Rosso di Montalcino, as they are. There is no reason why, for example, Montecucco, of which recently concocted DOC virtually no one, even in Tuscany, has ever heard, shouldn't be Toscana Montecucco Rosso or Toscana Montecucco Sangiovese.

No doubt historic or otherwise famous names like Barco Reale, Bolgheri – another candidate for DOCG, one would have thought, Montecarlo, Pomino and Morellino di Scansano should stand. But, as I say, the opportunities for rationalising the DOC situation in Tuscany are several.

UMBRIA

A similar operation could be performed here, with the 11 existing DOCs being reduced by about half by retention of the established names – Montefalco, Orvieto, Torgiano, perhaps Assisi, since everyone knows where it is – standing and the others being absorbed into names of regional recognisability, in which event an accommodation with IGT would need to be found.

LATIUM

There are 25 DOCs, no less, in a region known internationally for one wine only, at most two – Frascati and Est! Est!! Est!!!. Much scope for rational-ising here, but I won't go into detail except to suggest that it might not be a bad marketing decision for all the Frascati-style wines to adopt that famous name, rather than have to struggle on the markets with nonentity names like Montecompatri or Zagarolo. A full-scale re-arrangement of the Trebbiano–Malvasia whites and the Sangiovese–Cesanese reds would seem to make sense too, the regional name fronting the presentation followed by that of the varietal(s) or the sub-zone as a sop to *campanilismo*.

Again, if this were to happen an accommodation would have to be sought with IGT.

MARCHE

Most of the existing 11 DOCs would need to stand, either because they are reasonably well known or because they are quite idiosyncratic. Colli Maceratesi, Colli Pesaresi and Esino would seem to be candidates for amalgamation, one way or another; but Bianchello del Metauro, Falerio dei Colli Ascolani, Lacrima di Morro d'Alba, Rosso Conero, Rosso Piceno, Verdicchio dei Castelli di Iesi, Verdicchio di Matelica and Vernaccia di Serrapetrona are either well established in their own right or would have nowhere else to go.

ABRUZZO

The historic policy of dispensing official blessings upon two grape varieties only, Montepulciano and Trebbiano, has kept things simple here, denomination-wise, but the authorities are going to have to find a way of including in the system the other grapes which are beginning to burst upon the scene. Controguerra DOC is a first step in this direction, but it would be advisable to find a regional identity for this and other such little-known sub-zonal denominations.

MOLISE

The recently fashioned Molise DOC, with its diverse modifications and varietal sub-DOCs, seems to have been a smart move. Perhaps now they will consider getting rid of the apparently non-existent Pentro DOC.

CAMPANIA

There are 18 DOCs here, some of them helped by the world's vague knowledge of ancient history or modern tourism, e.g. Falerno del Massico, Vesuvio, Ischia, Penisola Sorrentina, Costa d'Amalfi, Campi Flegrei. Others are well established in their own vinous right – Fiano di Avellino, Greco di Tufo, probably both eventual candidates for DOCG. Still others can reasonably justify their separate existence by the diversity and interest of their production and the uniqueness of their territory – e.g. Aversa, Taburno. The rest could be considered as candidates for repositioning, a prime example being Galluccio in the province of Castera, the production of which is neither original, for Campania, nor particularly distinguished, nor indeed at all voluminous.

BASILICATA

With but one well-established and historic DOC, and one regional IGT, Basilicata would seem to have understood the beauty of simplicity.

PUGLIA

The same cannot be said of Puglia, an example of whose profligacy in the matter of dispensing DOCs has been given above. No doubt other opportunities for simplification could be found without excessive effort.

CALABRIA

Since this region produces almost nothing in the way of fine wine, with a few honourable exceptions, it is amazing that it should have 12 DOCs. A few deserve their status on recent track-record, notably Cirò, perhaps a future candidate for DOCG, Greco di Bianco, Savuto and Scavigna; others can perhaps, at a stretch, claim historic connections – Donnici, Lamezia, Melissa, Pollino. The rest – Bivongi, S. Anna di Isola Capo Rizzuto, San Vito di Luzzi, Verbicaro – probably owe their status more to Mafioso politicians than to oenological accomplishment.

SARDINIA

Of the 19 existing DOCs, four – Cannonau, Monica, Vermentino and Semidano – have Sardegna in their title and could be gathered together under a regional multi-DOC. Another five could be brought together under their common zonal name Cagliari: Girò, Malvasia, Moscato, Nasco and Nuragus. Most of the remaining nine could probably justify their separate existence, if in certain cases rather tenuously.

SICILY

Considering that the vast majority of Sicilian wine, including most of Sicilian quality wine, especially if you exclude Marsala and Alcamo, exists outside of the DOC system, it is tempting to wonder why Sicilians require 18 separate denominations. Included among these is at least one DOC, Menfi, where the major, indeed the sole significant producer, C.S. Settesoli, refuses to use the DOC name, preferring IGT Sicilia which they wisely judge to be more recognisable; plus at least one, Moscato di Siracusa, of which production hovers around the zero mark.

There would appear to be some sorting out to do in Sicily.

A critique of the DOCGs
– in alphabetical order

ALBANA DI ROMAGNA

Whether Albana did or did not deserve the kudos of being the first white DOCG in 1987 (the consensus is that it did not), it is difficult to argue that it did so for any style other than the *passito*. Certainly on grounds of relative quality, if Albana in all its styles can justify this rank, so can other Italian whites like Soave – which at the time of writing is DOCG for Recioto only though Soave Superiore DOCG is on its way – Verdicchio, Orvieto to name a few.

ASTI

This word on its own denotes what used to be called Asti Spumante, but also includes Moscato d'Asti. On the basis of its uniqueness and the quality, at least, of certain products – some *spumanti* are pretty industrialised, not to say cheap and vulgar, which doesn't somehow sit well with DOCG – it just about deserves the DOCG, although personally I would prefer to see those initials reserved for Moscato d'Asti only.

BARBARESCO

This wine unquestionably merits the DOCG as long as it sticks to its present formula (100% Nebbiolo) and makes more effort to weed out those who are cheating by adding Cabernet etc.

BAROLO

As Barbaresco, only more so.

BRACHETTO D'ACQUI

All right, it's unusual, and can be very pleasant, but have not politics played a major part in this wine's elevation?

BRUNELLO DI MONTALCINO

Brunello is a good advertisement for DOCG in that its general standard, and image, is high. Perhaps another rethink on ageing requirements is due – three years instead of four? And the dangers of Frenchification by blending or excessive oaking might be looked at.

CARMIGNANO

No quarrels with this one. For one thing, Bordeaux grapes are and have been since inception as a DOC a specific aspect of the profile. For another, Sangiovese from these parts needs the boost of Bordeaux varieties, and marries well with them.

CHIANTI

This is what Ted Heath might call the unacceptable face of DOCG. Not only did the wines that fly under this name effectively steal it from Chianti Classico, too many of them are among the lowliest of their respective zones (in Montalcino, for example, a grower will only resort to the denomination Chianti Colli Senesi after he has exhausted the possibilities of Brunello di Montalcino, Rosso di Montalcino, Sant'Antimo Rosso and even IGT Toscana). That a DOCG should be so despised is clearly an insult to other DOCGs and a fatal flaw in the system itself.

In my opinion the wines of the outlying Chianti sub-zones would do themselves and the DOCG system in general a big favour by dropping the name Chianti from their respective titles. One or two of them – Rufina, Colli Fiorentini – might then justifiably aspire to DOCG status on their own merits. The others could drop back to DOC or IGT status, this latter being where most wine currently labelled plain 'Chianti', with no sub-zone, belongs.

CHIANTI CLASSICO

This clearly deserves the DOCG status, but producers are going to have to resolve the blending problem. In what ought to be the most prestigious zone in the world for Sangiovese and the satellite Tuscan red grapes (Colorino, Canaiolo), should Cabernet & Co. really be allowed in at 20%? Should not these 'SuperTuscans', valid and extraordinary as they may be, be classified in some other way?

FRANCIACORTA

No argument with this one as it stands (for high class *metodo classico* sparkling wines only), although perhaps more effort could be made to educate the public regarding the potential confusion with Terre di Franciacorta DOC (table wines).

GATTINARA

It is difficult, on the basis of the wines coming out of this small zone, not to escape the conclusion that this one owes its DOCG more to the past than to the present, unless in 'the present' we include political pull.

GAVI

I am not a great fan of this wine but I will defend to the death – well, not quite – its right to the DOCG.

GHEMME

Comments as for Gattinara.

MONTEFALCO SAGRANTINO

This small, high quality producing zone unquestionably deserves DOCG status, not only for Sagrantino but also for Montefalco Rosso Riserva.

SOAVE RECIOTO

No problem re Recioto di Soave, although a lot of hoo-ha has accompanied the effort to extend DOCG to Soave (Classico) Superiore – a good idea undermined by bureaucrats.

TAURASI

A classic of the south which undoubtedly merits DOCG status.

TORGIANO RISERVA

Let us not quibble about the right of the sole producer of this wine, Lungarotti, with their considerable political sway, to the DOCG for this wine which was in a way a classic of the twentieth century.

VALTELLINA SUPERIORE

The concept of separating a 'Superiore' style as DOCG from the common DOC seems to me a good one, representing a lead which others might follow, e.g. Soave, Verdicchio, Valpolicella. Fully deserved.

VERMENTINO DI GALLURA

The producers of Gallura in northern Sardinia, who make one of Italy's most characterful native whites, were quite right to want to distance themselves from producers of the rather monotonous Vermentino di Sardegna DOC.

VERNACCIA DI SAN GIMIGNANO

The red wines from this zone are, potentially at least, considerably more interesting than the whites, but politics have prevailed.

VINO NOBILE DI MONTEPULCIANO

I am not convinced by the recent change to allow up to 20% international grapes, but I suppose Vino Nobile has got to distance itself from Brunello di Montalcino in some way.

Glossary

affinamento – the process of ageing or refining in cask and/or bottle.
affinato – aged or refined in cask and/or bottle.
agronomo – agriculturist.
albarese – calcium-rich soil typical of the Chianti Classico and certain other Chianti zones.
alberata – an Etruscan system of training vines up trees, once fairly widespread, now virtually confined to the Aversa zone of Campania.
alberello – bush or free-standing method of training, probably imported by ancient Greeks.
amabile – medium sweet.
Amarone – powerful wine made in Valpolicella area from dried grapes (from *amaro* = bitter + suffix *-one* = big).
ampelography – (the study) of vines.
anthocyanins – colouring matter in the skins of grapes.
appassimento – the process of drying grapes, usually – in Tuscany, for Vin Santo – under a non-insulated roof with plenty of windows which can be opened to allow for dry air circulation or closed to keep out moisture; or – in the South – under the sun for a brief period. The grapes are either lain on cane or bamboo racks or hung from wires. See also *passito*.
aromas (primary, secondary, tertiary) – referring to the aromatic substances in grapes (primary), finished wines (secondary), aged wines (tertiary).
assemblaggio – the putting together of different parts of a blend.
autochthonous – indigenous.
autoclave – pressurized, thermo-controllable stainless steel container for purposes of fermenting or storing wine, especially sparkling.
azienda – estate; *azienda agricola/agraria* – estate whose wines are made entirely or mostly from grapes grown at the property; *azienda leader* (sic) – an Italian phrase for 'leading producer' (of a given zone).
Babo – a method of measuring potential alcohol in grape must; divide by approximately 2/3 to obtain potential degrees alcohol.

baglio – in Sicily, especially Marsala, a winery or '*bodega*'.

barrique – French term for a small barrel of 225 to 350 litres' capacity; *barricato* – fermented and/or stored in *barrique*.

bâtonnage – French term, widely used in Italy, for the stirring up of the lees in barrel, with a more or less sophisticated form of *baton* (stick).

bianco – white; *in bianco* – of red grapes vinified off the skins, as if they were white (what the French call *blanc de noirs*).

bicchiere(i) – *glass(es)*.

blocked fermentation – fermentation which stops before completion when yeasts are no longer able to transform sugars into alcohol.

borgo – a group of houses (cf. English '-burg').

botte – wooden barrel of wide-ranging capacity – anything from around 10 to 100 hectolitres or more; traditionally of chestnut or, more recently, of oak from Slavonia, more recently still of oak from France.

botrytis (cinerea) – a grey mould that forms on ripe grapes at harvest-time; negative in cases where skins are split, it can be positive for the making of sweet wines where skins are only punctured by tiny holes, in which case it is called 'noble rot' (Italian '*muffa nobilé*').

caffè – bar, similar to French café.

campanilismo – an attitude of mind which concerns itself only with events happening within sight or sound of the village bell-tower (*campanile*).

canneto – bamboo-supported teepee-shape training method peculiar to Rionero in Basilicata.

cantina – winery.

cantina sociale – cooperative winery; *c.s. di secondo grado* – cooperative which bottles wines vinified by producing cooperatives.

cantiniere – cellar-master.

capovolto toscano – traditional Tuscan training method whereby canes are arched over wires in one or two '*archetti*'.

caratelli – small barrels, usually of 50 litres capacity, used in the vinification and maturation of Vin Santo.

casalingo – homemade, as in *cucina casalinga*, home cooking.

cascade – when a wine which might qualify for a higher DOC is downgraded, for reasons of quality, image or commerce, to one of less stringent requirements, the process is called 'cascade'.

case coloniche – houses once belonging to a large estate, often sold off for increasingly high prices following the termination of *mezzadria* (q.v.).

chaptalisation – the adding of cane or beet sugar to wine-musts pre-fermentation in order to increase alcohol; illegal in Italy, widely practised in France and Germany.

charmat – a method, named after its French originator, of inducing secondary fermentation in sparkling wines in large volumes (see *autoclave*).

classico – the historic section of a long-established wine-zone, as distinct from the part tacked on generally in the 20th century. Also means 'classic' in the normal sense.

clone – a vine identical in terms of DNA to its source vine.

colle/colli – hill/hills.

collina/colline – smaller hill/hills.

commerciante – dealer in bought-in grapes or wines; French equivalent is *négociant*.

commune – Italian *comune,* the smallest administrative unit, comprising one or several towns or villages (see *frazione*).

conca – literally 'shell'; refers to hills in the shape of a shell, concave and heat-retaining.

cordone speronato – (English 'cordon spur'); a vine-shaping method whereby a mature branch, as distinct from a new cane (*guyot*), is trained horizontally along a wire; with *guyot* one of the two methods referred to by the term *spalliera* (q.v.).

crio maceration – refers to the retention of juice on skins at low temperature for purposes of extracting aromatic substances (in respect of whites), or colour (in respect of reds) with minimum leeching of tannins.

cru – French term for a particular plot, or its wine. Italians have borrowed the term but interpreted it more broadly to indicate anything from a growth (in the French sense) to a marketing name.

cutting-wine – cheap wine, generally of deep colour or high alcohol, or both (and therefore usually from the deep South), used to improve wines which are deficient.

damigiana – large, often raffia-wrapped bottle containing around fifty litres, used for selling wine in bulk to individuals or for storage of excess or topping-up wines.

dégorgement – French term, often preferred by Italians to their own '*sboccatura*', referring to that process in the making of bottle-fermented sparkling wines when the inverted bottle is opened and the sediment trapped in the neck ejected.

dialetto – dialect.

diradamento – the cutting away of already formed bunches in order to increase concentration of extract in those remaining.

disciplinare – rules governing a particular DOC.

DOC(G) – **Denominazione di Origine Controllata** (e Garantita); the Italian quality designation. DOC guarantees origin, grape type(s), aspects of production, but not necessarily quality. DOCG is supposed also to guarantee a minimum level of quality. See also multi-DOC.

enologo – winemaker or wine expert; *enotecnico* – qualified wine technician.

enoteca/enoteche – wine-shop(s); can be a wine-bar, even a restaurant.

esca (Italian 'mal dell'esca') – a fungal disease which attacks the trunk of older vines, usually with fatal results; spreading alarmingly in Italy.

essicatore – an artificial wind-tunnel whose purpose is to dry grapes without risk of rot forming in the early stages of *appassimento* (q.v.).

fattore – estate manager.

fattoria – largish farm, not to be confused with English 'factory'.

filtrato dolce – sweet grape must, obtained by filtration, for boosting other wines.

flor – as in Jerez, a yeast-film forming on the top of a wine in barrel, protecting it from oxygen and imparting a particular aroma.

franco cantina – in the parlance of wine-shipping, the price of a wine at the cellar door. English equivalent: 'ex cellars'.

frazione – part of a *comune*.

frizzante – semi-sparkling.

fusto – barrel of 5 to 7.5 hectolitres' capacity; French equivalent is *tonneau*.

governo all'uso toscano – a slight refermentation caused by pouring a finished wine over partially dried grapes.

graticci – cane or bamboo mats on which bunches intended for *passito* wines are laid to dry.

grigio – gray; in grape terms, between black and white.

guyot – see *cordone speronato*.

IGT – *Indicazione Geografica Tipica*; the higher form of *Vino da Tavola* (q.v.), equivalent to French Vin de Pays.

imbottigliato (a) – bottled (at).

impegnativo – demanding of the attention, as of a complex, firm-structured wine.

in purezza – at 100%.

invecchiamento – ageing.

layering – the propagation of new vines by working branches of existing vines into the soil; no longer practised because the danger of phylloxera forces planting on American rootstock.

liqueur d'expédition – referring to bottle fermented sparkling wines, after *dégorgement* (French) or *sboccatura* (Italian), when the deposit is removed, a liquid usually of sugar dissolved in brandy is added by way of replacement.

liquoroso – wine of high alcoholic degree, generally over 15%, generally fortified.

lotta guidata ed integrata – an ecological approach to viticulture, not always synonymous with organic viticulture.

lyre – a vine-training method whose shape resembles that of the musical instrument.

madre – literally 'mother', the part that remains in a barrel after the wine is racked, and which subsequently mixes with the young wine.

malo-lactic fermentation – the transformation, these days induced in most red wines immediately following the alcoholic fermentation, of the grape's natural malic, or appley, acid into the much milder lactic, or milky, acid.

massal selection – where vines for re-planting are propagated from the best vines of a given property, as distinct from being bought in from a nursery in the form of clones (q.v.).

meno male – common Italian phrase meaning 'just as well'.

metodo classico – refers to the method, used in Champagne, of inducing an alcoholic refermentation in bottle (as distinct from in tank) by adding yeasts and sugars to the made wine prior to bottling; the process is completed by *remuage* (see *pupitre*) and *dégorgement* (q.v.).

mezzadria – the traditional system of share-cropping whereby a tenant-farmer would pay for the use of his land by giving roughly half his produce to the landlord.

millesimato – vintage, as in 'vintage Champagne'.

miscela – blending of various components of wine, especially in Marsala.

mistella – wine for use in the *miscela* obtained by stunning grape must with alcohol.

mosto – must, unfermented grape juice.

mosto cotto – grape must rendered down by heating, resulting in a thick, dark, very sweet syrup.

mosto concentrato rettificato (mcr) – rectified concentrated must, a neutral sugary liquid made from generally excess production southern Italian grape juice, used for increasing sugar levels in a must, and consequently alcohol levels in a wine, in a situation where the use of cane sugar is forbidden, as it is throughout Italy for still wines.

muffa nobile – noble rot.

multi-DOC – neologism (invented by myself) for an 'umbrella' DOC, such as Sant'Antimo, which has many sub-DOCs (e.g. Sant'Antimo Rosso, Sant'Antimo Bianco, Sant'Antimo Chardonnay, Sant'Antimo Merlot, etc. etc.).

normale – a non-official term widely used to designate the basic wine of a given type, e.g. Chianti Classico *normale* as distinct from Chianti Classico Riserva or SuperTuscan (q.v.).

oenology – the study or science of wine; oenologist – winemaker.

oidium – powdery mildew, which attacks leaves, stalks and grapes, capable of ruining wine and, ultimately, destroying the vine; dealt with by sulphur, generally mixed in powder form with the copper sulphate spray used against peronospera (q.v.).

paese – means both country, as in nation, and village.

pantesco – native to Pantelleria.

passito – a wine made by the process of *appassimento* (q.v.).

patrimonio – the inheritance handed down by previous generations.

pergola – high-training method enabling a single plant to produce multiple bunches, gradually being replaced as quality becomes increasingly an imperative. Tendone (q.v.) is a form of *pergola*.

peronospera – commonly known as mildew; controlled by copper sulphate sprays.

pezzi – bottles, literally 'pieces'.

phylloxera – aphid of American origin which destroys European *vitis vinifera* vines by gnawing at their roots, the solution being to graft the Europeans plant onto American rootstock.

pianura – the plain.

podere – a small farm.

poggio – hill, mainly in Central Italy.

polyphenols – substances present in grape-skins, including anthocyanins (q.v.) and tannins.

privati – private individuals.

profumato – scented.

province – see region.

quintal, *quintale* – still widely-used term for 100 kg of grapes or 100 litres of wine; now replaced in official parlance by *tonnellata*, English 'tonne' (1000 kg).

raceme – stalk supporting secondary bunches.

raggiera – Etruscan-style four-branched high-training method employed in Benevento.

razza – race, breeding, as for race-horses.

region – specifically, a region in Italy is like a state in the USA. There are twenty of them, and they are divided into provinces, named after their principal city. In this book the word 'region' is also sometimes used in the normal sense.

Rinascimento – Italian for *renaissance* or rebirth. As I have said elsewhere, I fail to understand why English speaking people have to use a French word for an Italian phenomenon.

riserva – principally used in an official capacity to indicate a wine which has been aged longer than the equivalent *normale* (q.v.).

rosato – pink, rosé.

rosso – red.

roto-fermentor – a fermentation vessel which rotates to facilitate maceration, particularly to extract maximum colour from red skins in minimum time.

salasso – the process of bleeding, or drawing off a small percentage of wine from a recently crushed *cuvée* of red wine to make a rosé or concetrate a red wine, or both.

selvatico – wild.

serbatoio – large wine-container, tank.

sfuso – in bulk.

sifone – alternative term for *mistella* (q.v.).

socio/soci – member(s), usually of a *cantina sociale* (q.v.).

sofisticazione – fraud.

solera – a system, imported from Spain to Sicily by Benjamin Ingham in the nineteenth century, whereby wines like Sherry or Marsala are aged in a series of stages from younger to more mature so as to arrive at a consistent product.

sottozona – with particular reference to wine-law 164 of 1992, an officially recognized sub-zone or 'geographical sub-denomination' of a DOC; e.g. Bolgheri <u>Sassicaia</u>.

spalliera – a vine-training formation whereby a cane or cordon is run along a wire horizontally at right angles to the vertical trunk.

spargolo – referring to a bunch whose grapes are loose as distinct from tightly packed.

spessore – literally 'thickness', in wine appreciation terms used to indicate concentration.

specializzazione – the practice of planting vines as an exclusive crop in a given terrain.

spumante – sparkling; *spumantista* – sparkling wine producer.

sub-DOC – see multi-DOC.

sub-zone – used in this book in two ways: (1) loosely, to indicate a geographical area within one of the four 'zones' of Italy; (2) precisely, as translation of the official term '*sottozona*' (q.v.).

superiore – an official term indicating a wine with a little more alcohol, perhaps a little extra age, compared with the *normale* of the same.

SuperTuscan – neologism meaning a Tuscan wine of high quality which does not conform to local or traditional norms.

t-bud – method by which an alternative vine variety may be field-grafted onto existing stock.

tendone – literally 'big tent'; high-producing, high training system adopted in hot areas, using leaf canopy to shade the grapes.

terra bianca – terrain which is white due to a high chalk content.

terroir – a combination of factors involved in grape and therefore wine quality, relating particularly to soil and climate but also sometimes to viticultural practices and tradition generally.

tino/tini – vat(s); specifically often used to refer to the sort of upright oaken container making an increasing comeback as a fermentation vessel for red wines.

tipicità – sometimes (inadequately) translated as 'typicity', this refers to a given wine's level of conformity to a norm or type.

titolare – the person after whom an estate, e.g., is named.

tonneau – French for barrel of (usually) 5 hectolitres.

tre bicchieri – top award in the annual Gambero Rosso/Slow Food guide to Italian wines, 'Vini d'Italia'.

trulli – curious inverted-cone shaped houses found in the area of mid-Puglia around Locorotondo and Martina Franca.

tufo – calcareous, siliceous rock which, broken down, forms good soil for white grapes; relatively easily excavatable, can form useful tunnels for wine-storage.

tunnel – a recent invention designed to achieve the first 10% or so of the *appassimento* (q.v.) process under synthetic conditions, thus practically eliminating any subsequent risk of rot.

umbrella-DOC – see multi-DOC.

uvaggio – mix of grapes in a given blend; *uvaggio di vigneto* – where the said mix of grapes exists in the vineyard itself.

VA – see volatile acidity.

Vin Santo – sweet wine made mainly in Tuscany from semi-dried Trebbiano, Malvasia and/or Sangiovese grapes.

vasca – vat.

vendemmia – vintage, harvest; *vendemmia tardiva* – late harvest.

vigna, vigneto – vineyard.

vignai(u)olo – grape-grower.

viniculture – the culture of wine.

vino da meditazione – meditation wine; a wine of such concentration and richness that it lends itself to being sipped on its own; a meditation wine would qualify as *impegnativo* (q.v.).

vino da tavola – table wine, in ordinary sense.

Vino da Tavola – in the legal sense, refers to what is supposedly the lower grade of wine (but which in Italy has often been the highest); V. da T. con indicazione geografica – pre-mid-1990s way of describing on labels a table wine of a particular provenance.

viticoltore – grape-grower; alternative name, *vignaiolo*.

viticulture – the growing of grapes.

volatile acidity – acetic or vinagrey acid, present in tiny doses in all wines but negative in larger doses; 'volatile' because it comes out on the nose. Abbreviated as VA.

VQPRD – Quality wine produced in delimited regions; the basic EU quality wine designation.

Key to Italian Pronunciation

Italian is almost entirely phonetic and follows simple rules of pronunciation, unlike French and especially English. A few minutes studying those rules will be found to be deeply rewarding in respect of the study of Italian wines and is strongly recommended.

a – as in 'pat'

b – as English

c – **always** pronounced 'k' except before 'e' or 'i' when it is like English 'ch' ('chop'); conversely 'h' hardens 'c' before 'e' or 'i'. so *Ciampi* = **champ**-ee, *Chianti* = **kyan**-tee

d – as English

e – as in 'pet'

f – as English

g – **always** pronounced 'g' ('got') except before 'e' or 'i' when it is like English 'j' ('jot'); 'h' hardens 'g' before 'e' or 'i'. Consider *Giotto* (= **jot**-to), *spaghetti*. Also see *gl*, *gn*, below

h – silent as in cockney; but see 'c' and 'g'

i – as 'ee' ('feet') when dominant in a syllable, e.g. *trattoria* (= trat-to-**ree**-a); as 'y' when subordinate to a following vowel, e.g. **kyan**-tee; or just as a softener (*Ciampi*, *Giotto*)

j – as 'y' ('yet'), rarely occurs

k – as English, rarely occurs

l – as English; but see *gl* below

m – as English

n – as English; but see *gn* below

o – as in 'pot'

p – as English

qu – always pronounced 'kw' (e.g. *questo* = **kwes**-to)

r – pronounced using tip of tongue, as in Scottish

s – as English, though sometimes pronounced as 'z' alone in middle of word. Compare *spesso* (= **spes**-so; often), and *speso* (= **spe**-zo, spent).

t – as English
u – as 'oo' ('boot')
v – as English
w – as 'v', rarely occurs
x – as English, rarely occurs
y – occurs extremely rarely
z – 'ts' or 'dz'

ANOMALIES

gl – as 'ly', e.g. *Aglianico* = a-**lya**-nee-ko
gn – as 'ny', e.g. *agnello* = a-**nyel**-lo
sc – before 'e' or 'i', pronounced as English 'sh' as in 'show'. Thus *scelto*
   (= **shel**-to; selected)
double consonants: both are pronounced. Compare *cane* (= **ka**-ne; dog)
and *canne* (= **kan**-ne; canes); *latte* (= **lat**-te; milk) and *lato* (= **la**-to; side)

STRESS

Usually falls on penultimate syllable, e.g. *Barolo* (= ba-**ro**-lo), *Barbaresco*
(= bar-bar-**es**-co). If on final syllable, it is written with a grave accent, e.g.
Cirò (= chee-**ro**), *Prapò* (= pra-**po**). Sometimes occurs on third syllable
from last, in which case there is no orthographic clue, e.g. *Garganega*
(= gar-**ga**-ne-ga), *Aglianico* (= a-**lya**-nee-ko); you just have to know.

Bibliography

Anderson, Burton, *Wine Atlas of Italy*, Mitchell Beazley, London 1990.

Belfrage, Nicolas, *Life Beyond Lambrusco*, Sidgwick & Jackson, London 1995.

Belfrage, Nicolas, *Barolo to Valpolicella* – *The Wines of Northern Italy*, Faber & Faber, London 1999.

Calò Antonio, Scienza, Attilio, and Costacurta, Angelo, *Vitigni d'Italia*, Calderini Edagricole, Bologna 2001.

Consorzio Vino Chianti Classico, *Chianti Classico 2000*, Vols 1–5.

Contini Bonacossi, Ugo et al., *Carmignano, l'arte del vino*, Il Fiore, Firenze 1992.

De' Crescenti, Piero, *Ruralium Commodorum*, 1303.

Di Lello, Luciano, *Viaggio nel nuovo vino italiano*, Lithos, Roma 1997.

Di Rovasenda, Giuseppe dei Conti, *Saggio di una ampelografia universale*, Torino 1877.

Enoteca Italiana: *Il paese del vino/The Wine Country* – *Guide to the DOC and DOCG wines* (in English and Italian), compiled and regularly updated by the Enoteca Italiana, Siena.

Fini, Marco, *Sassicaia* – *The Original Super Tuscan*, Centro Di, Florence 2000.

Fregoni and Schiavi, *I Primi Cento Nostri Vitigni*, Civiltà del Bere, February 1996.

Gambero Rosso/Slow Food, *Vini d'Italia* or *Italian Wines* (highly useful annual guide to the wines of Italy, with evaluations of wines and brief discussion on developments in featured wineries over the past 12 months; also useful for locating wineries in communes and for telephone numbers).

Mannini, Schneider, Gerbi and Credi, *Cloni selezionati dal Centro di Studio per il miglioramento genetico della vite*, Consiglio Nazional delle Ricerche, Torino 1989.

Masneghetti, Alessandro, *Enogea* (bimonthly review of, mainly, Italian wines, very useful for keeping up to date and getting unbiased, intelligent views); by subscription only, available from fax (0039) 039 2302601.

Ministero delle Risorse Agricole, Alimentari e Forestali, *Riepilogo delle produzioni provinciali di vini DOC e DOCG* (updated annually).

Ministero dell'Agricoltura e delle Foreste, *Principali vitigni ad uve da vino coltivati in Italia* (4 vols), Roma 1952–1965.

Molon, G., *Ampelografia*, Milano 1906.

Mondini, Salvatore, *I vitigni stranieri da vino coltivati in Italia*, Firenze 1903.

Panicola, Nino, *Viino – Dizionario Vinicolo Siciliano*, Gruppo Italia, Palermo 1998.

Paolini, Davide, *Guida alle città del vino d'Italia*, Sterling & Kupfer, Milano 1996.

Pastena, Bruno, *La Civiltà della Vite in Sicilia*, Palermo 1989.

Pellucci Emanuele, *Vino Nobile di Montepulciano*, Vipsul, Fiesole 1998.

Phillips, Kyle, *Kyle Phillips's Italian Wine Review*, English-language periodical specialising in Italian wines, informed, informative and impartial. Contact through www.italianwinereview.com.

Soderini, Giovanvettorio, *Trattato della coltivazione delle viti*, Firenze 1600.

Supp, Eckhard, *Enciclopedia del vino italiano/Enzyklopädie des Italienishen Weins*, Enotria News, Offenbach 1995.

Tachis, Giacomo, *Il Libro del Vin Santo*, Bonechi, Firenze 1988.

Unione Italiana Vini, *Codice Denominazioni di Origine dei Vini*, 2000 edition, UIV, Milano 2000.

Veronelli, Luigi et al., *I vini di Veronelli* (useful for evaluating wines of Italy and for determining grape mix of wines if not official; also for locating wineries in communes and for telephone and fax numbers), Veronelli Editore, Bergamo (annual).

Volpi, Aldo, *Pantelleria*, La Medusa, Marsala 1999.

Index

25 Anni Sagrantino di Montefalco, wine, 172
50 & 50, wine, 427

A Sirio, wine, 108
A&A Folonari, producer, 101, 418
Abbazia San Clemente, wine, 423
Abbazia, Santa Anastasia, 357
Abbona, Rossano, consultant, 262–3
Abraxas, producer, 387
Abruzzese, Vincenzo, 133
Abruzzo, 213, 215–24, 416, 422, 439
  wines in, 191–3, 219–24
Acate, 349–50
Accademia dei Racemi, producer, 281–2, 293–5
Acquabona, producer, 159, 180, 208
Acuti, Roccaldo, 81
Adanti, producer, 173, 428
Affile, production area, 38
Aghiloia, wine, 334
Aglaia, wine, 418–19
Aglianico del Vulture
  zone, 251–2, 259–63
  grape, 321–2, 248–9, 252–2, 300–1
Aglianico grape, 230–1, 248–9, 252–4, 300–1
Agricoltori del Chianti Geografico, producer, 77, 408
Aguilaia, wine, 159
Aivaliotis, Stak, 87–8
Akronte, wine, 409
Al Poggio, wine, 418
Albana di Romagna, 238
Albana grape, 237–8
Albanese, Massimo, 131
albarese soil, Tuscany, 25–8

alberello, 13–14, 241, 282, 287, 311, 315, 357, 361
Alberello/Felline blend, 282
Alberto Loi, wine, 323
Alcamo, 350–1, 356, 366
Aldiola, wine, 335
Aleatico di Puglia, 277–8
Aleatico grape, 180, 302–3
Alezio, 278, 441
Alghero Torbato, 344
Alghero, 321–2
Allodio Bianco, wine, 422
Almabruna, wine, 157
Alta Maremma, 392
Alte d'Altesi, wine, 114
Altero, wine, 131
Altesino, producer, 114–15, 407
altitude, influence, 25, 113–14, 247
Ama, producer, 67
Ambra, producer, 151
Ambrosini Lorella, producer, 155, 228
Aminea Gemella grape, 269–70
Anagni, producer, 410
Anfiteatro Chianti Classico Riserva, wine, 81
Angelini family, 133–5
Angheli, wine, 370
Anghelu Ruju, wine, 319, 325
Angialis, wine, 319
Anima, wine, 431
Ansonica grape, 207–8, 368–9
Anthilia, wine, 370
Antica Masseria del Sigillo, producer, 297
Antica Masseria Torre Mozza, producer, 297
Antico Gregori, wine, 340–1
Antigua, wine, 330

Antinori, Lodovico, 395, 396
Antinori, Piero, 51, 53, 55, 394
Antinori, producer, 13, 51–5, 301, 408,
    429
Antonelli, producer, 174
Antonini, Alberto, consultant, 30, 147,
    150–1
Apennines, influence, 24–5, 96, 211
Aprilia
    production area, 38
    Sangiovese, 163
    Trebbiano, 191
Arajà, wine, 329
Arborea zone, 321
Ardingo, wine, 126
Arezzo province, 107–8
Argiano, producer, 115, 426–7
Argiolas, producer, 324, 337, 342–3,
    434
Armaleo, wine, 409
Armécolo/Castel di Salve blend, 282
Arquata wines, 173–4
Artimino, producer, 151
Arvino grape, 310
Ashley, Maureen, 123
Asinone Vino Nobile di
    Montepulciano, wine, 143–4
Asprinio grape, 273–4
Assisi Bianco, 190
Assisi, production area, 37
Ateo, wine, 124–5
Aurico, wine, 207
Avellino, 248
Aversa, 250
Avide, producer, 358, 365, 370
Avignonesi, producer, 13, 137–9, 160,
    194, 407, 413, 418, 421, 427
Avvoltore, wine, 156

Baccante, wine, 420
Baccio, wine, 157
Badia a Coltibuono, producer, 69–71,
    418
Badia a Passignano, 53–4
Badia di Morrone, producer, 108
Baggiolino, producer, 107
Baie Rosso, wine, 328
Balajana, wine, 335
Bàlari, wine, 335
Balifico, wine, 92–3
Banfi, producer, 115–17, 207, 407,
    408, 415, 418, 420, 421, 427
Banti, producer, 155, 159

Barbarossa grape, 228–9
Barbera grape, 265
Barberani-Vallesanta, producer, 188
Barberino Val d'Elsa, 55–8, 406
Barberone grape, 332
Barbi, 189–90
Barbi, producer in Montalcino, 117–18
Barco Reale, 95, 147, 149
Bardi, Francesco, 189
Baricci, producer, 135
Barioffi, Guido, 141–2
Barletta, 277
Barolo to Valpolicella, see Belfrage,
    Nicolas
Baroncini, producer, 195, 205
Barone Cornacchia, producer, 223–4
Barone di Villagrande, producer, 363
Barone la Lumia, producer, 358, 370
Barone Scammacca del Murgo,
    producer, 363, 411
Barone Villagrande, producer, 378
barriques, 19–20, 45
Bartoli family, 93–4
    see also Marco de Bartoli
Basciano/Masi, producer, 97–8
Basilicata, 247–74
    wines in, 259–63
Basilisco, producer, 262–3
Basilium, producer, 263
Basla, Claudio, 114
Batàr, wine, 80–1, 417–18
Bea Paolo, producer, 174
Belfrage, Nicolas:
    Barolo to Valpolicella, 89, 180, 207,
        265, 305, 341, 380, 389, 424, 436
    Life Beyond Lambrusco, 118, 211,
        235, 266, 373
Bellacini, Leonardo, 66
Bellavista Chianti Classico Riserva,
    wine, 67,179
Bellini, Roberto, 130
Bellone grape, 210
Benanti, producer, 349, 361–3, 378,
    411
Bentivoglio, wine, 109
Bernabei, Franco, consultant, 30, 84,
    104, 159, 166–7, 202, 224–5, 324,
    428, 431–2
Biancame grape, 239
Bianchello del Metauro, 215
Bianchello grape, 239
Bianchi, Albino, 109
Bianco d'Alcamo, 348

Bianco d'Alessano, grape, 304
Bianco della Rocca, wine, 419
Bianco della Valdinievole, 185, 195
Bianco dell'Empolese, 185, 195
Bianco di Pitigliano, 186
Bianco Pisano di San Torpè, 186, 195
Bianco Vergine Valdichiana, 186
Bianco (village), 308
Biancolella grape, 248, 272–3
Biferno, 216
Bigi, producer, 188–9
Bindella, producer, 145
Bindocci, Fabrizio, 127
Bini, producer, 107
Biondi-Santi family, 5, 112, 118–20,
    421
  Ferrucio Biondi-Santi, 112, 118–20
  Franco Biondi-Santi,, 112, 118–20,
    158
  Jacopo Biondi-Santi, 112, 118–20,
    157–8, 420
  Tancredi Biondi-Santi, 112
Bivongi, 308
Bizantino Rosso/Pervini blend, 282
blending, Chianti Classico, 18–19
Boccadigabbia, producer, 226, 240,
    409, 414, 418, 420
Bolgheri Bianco, 186
Bolgheri, production area, 25, 34, 152,
    154–5, 392–8
Bolgheri Rosato, 154–5
Bombino Bianco grape, 192, 193,
    238–9, 304
Bombino Nero grape, 301–2
Bongoverno, wine, 109
Bonzara, producer, 409, 410
Bonzarone, wine, 409
Bordeaux blends, 410
  top five, 408
Bordeaux grapes, red, 391–412
Bordeaux grapes, white, 421–2
Borgo Canale, producer, 299
Borgo d'Altesi, wine, 114, 407
Borgo dei Guidi, wine, 428
Borgo di Colloredo, producer, 227–8
Borgo Salcetino, producer, 93
Borgo Scopeto, producer, 62
Borro del Boscone, wine, 407
Borro Lastricato, wine, 432
Bosa, 341
Boscarelli, producer/wine, 139
Bosco Eliceo zone, 214
Bossi/Marchesi Gondi, producer, 106

Bossi, producer, 195, 408
Botromagno, producer, 263, 300, 433
Bovale grape, 330–1
Bovaleddu grape, 330
Braccano, wine, 428
Brania del Cancello, wine, 431
Bremer, producer, 156–7
Brigante dei Barbi, wine, 118
Brindisi, 278
Brisighellese, producer, 168
Brolio, Castello di/Ricasoli, Barone,
    producer, 71–3, 418
Brunelli, Gianni, 127–8
Brunello di Montalcino, 95, 111–35
Bruno di Rocca, wine, 81, 408
Brunori, producer, 230, 234
Brusco dei Barbi, wine, 118
Bucci, producer, 233
Bucerchiale Chianti Rufina Riserva ,
    wine, 104
Bukkuram/de Bartoli, producer, 386–7
Buonamico, producer, 151, 415
bureaucracy, 245, 345
Burgundy grapes, red, 412–14
Burgundy grapes, white, 416–20
Buriano, wine, 407
Busillis, wine, 135, 423

Cà Marcanda, producer, 397–8
Caberlot, wine, 408
Cabernasco, wine, 410
Cabernet blends, top five, 408
Cabernet Marchese di Villamarina,
    wine, 411
Cabernet Olmaia, wine, 125
Cabernet wine, top five, 406–7
Cabreo Il Borgo, wine, 102
Cabreo La Pietra, wine, 102, 418
Cacc'e Mmitte di Lucera, 277
Cacchiano, producer, 73
Cafaggio, producer, 407
Caggiano, producer, 258, 269, 433
Cagliari, 320–1
Cagnina, grape, 228
Cagnina di Romagna, 214, 228
Cagnulari grape, 331–2
Cala Silente, wine, 329
Calabria, 306–17
Calatrasi/Terre di Ginestra, producer,
    367, 368,415, 429, 434
Calbello, wine, 126–7
Calò, Michele, producer, 282–3
Calzolari, Mario, 134

Camartina, wine, 80
Camelot, wine, 411
Camigliano, producer, 121
Campaccio, wine
Campanaro, wine, 268
Campania, 247–74
   wines in, 254–9
Campi Flegrei, 250
Campi Flegrei, 264, 265, 271
Campidano di Terralba, 321, 330
Campiglia Marittima, 155
Campo ai Sassi, wine, 100
Campo al Sorbo, wine, 106
Campoleone, wine, 162
Campolmi, Eugenio, 396–7
Campora, wine, 408
Canaiolo Bianco grape, 209–10
Canaiolo grape, 131–2, 135, 136, 147,
   175–6
Canalicchio di Sotto/Lambardi,
   producer, 135
Canayli, wine, 335
Candido, producer, 180, 283–4, 303,
   420, 422, 435
Canina grape, 229
Canneto, producer, 145
Cannonau grape, 322–5
Cannonau, 320–1
Canonico, wine, 418
Canosa, wine, 277
Cantagallo, producer, 423
Cantele, producer, 291
Cantina dei Colli Ripani, producer, 226
Cantina del Notaio, producer, 263
Cantina Sociale di Gradoli, producer,
   180
Capaccia, producer, 93
Capannelle, producer, 74–5, 418, 427
Capara & Siciliani, producer, 315
Caparzo, producer, 121–2, 431
Capezzana, producer, 148–50, 195,
   408
Capichera, producer, 320, 336
Capo Ferrato, 320
Caporali, Giulio, 145
Cappello di Prete, wine, 284
Cappellaccio, wine, 299, 301
Caprai, Arnaldo, producer, 171–3, 209
Caprai, Marco, 13–14, 171–3
Capri, 250
Capri Rosso, 264
Caprili, producer, 135
Capurso, Nunzio, oenologist, 88

Caputo, producer, 274
Carbio, wine, 410
Cardedu, wine, 323
Carignano grape, 325–9
Carignano, 321
Carleto, wine, 423
Carletti family, 142–4
Carmen, wine, 204
Carmignani, producer, 195
Carmignano, 107, 146–51, 195
   production area, 33
   wine, 95, 149
Carobbio, producer, 88, 407
Carpineto, producer, 77–8, 145, 407,
   418
Carricante grape, 378
Casa alle Vacche, producer, 111, 205
Casa Chiara, producer, 168
Casa Emma, producer, 55–6, 407
Casa Pastore, wine, 410
Casa Sola, producer, 56, 408
Casal Pilozzo, producer, 200–1
Casale Bevagna, producer, 297
Casale del Giglio, producer, 410, 415,
   428
Casale dello Sparviere, producer, 62
Casale-Falchini, producer, 111, 205,
   408
Casale Marchese, producer, 202
Casalfarneto, producer, 234
Casalferro, wine, 72
Casaloste, producer, 88
Casano, producer, 385
Casanova di Neri, producer, 122
Casato, producer, 122–3
Casavecchia, producer, 58–9
Case Basse, producer, 123–4
Case Via, wine, 413, 415
Casetto dei Mandorli, producer, 168
Casina Cucci, wine, 420
Casina di Cornia, producer, 407
Castagneto Carducci, 154
Castagnolo, wine, 188
Castel de Paolis, producer, 201, 422,
   423, 428, 432–3
Castel del Monte, 277
Castel di Maranfusa, producer, 367
Castel di Salve, producer, 297
Castel Giocondo, producer, 100
Castel Ruggero, producer, 83
Castel San Lorenzo, 251, 265
Castelgiocondo, 100, 135, 407
Castellaccio Bianco, wine, 419

Castellare, producer, 59–60, 407, 418
Castelli del Grevepesa, producer, 94
Castelli, Maurizio, consultant, 30, 59,
    71, 92, 125, 128, 139, 188
Castelli Romani, production area, 37
Castell'in Villa, producer, 67
Castellina, 58
Castello d'Albola, producer, 93, 418
Castello di Poppiano, producer, 107
Castello dei Rampolla, producer,
    404–6, 407, 408
Castello della Paneretta, producer, 58,
    176
Castello della Sala, producer, 414, 421,
    434–5
Castello di Ama, producer, 67–9, 407,
    413, 418
Castello di Argiano, producer, 115
Castello di Bossi, producer, 67
Castello di Brolio/Barone Ricasoli,
    producer, 71–3, 418
Castello di Cacchiano, producer, 73–4,
    194
Castello di Farnetella, producer, 109
Castello di Fonterutoli, producer/wine,
    60–1
Castello di Meleto, producer, 77
Castello di Modanella, producer, 176
Castello di Nipozzano, wine, 98–9
Castello di Pomino, producer, 32, 96–7,
    99–100
Castello di Querceto, producer, 82–3
Castello di San Polo in Rosso,
    producer, 77
Castello di Trebbio, producer, 106
Castello di Verrazzano, producer, 83
Castello di Volpaia, producer, 92–3
Castello Il Corno, producer, 107, 178
Castello Vicchiomaggio, producer, 81–2
Castello di Brolio Chianti Classico,
    wine,
Castello di Fonterutoli Chianti
    Classico, wine,
Castellucio, producer, 164–5, 421
Castelnuovo Berardenga, 63–7, 406
Castelrapiti, wine, 419
Castiglion del Bosco, producer, 135
Castruccio, wine, 157
Casuccia Chianti Classico Riserva,
    wine, 67
Cataldi Madonna, producer, 224
Catarratto grape, 366–8
Cavalleri, Piermario Meletti, 398

CC2000, see Chianti Classico 2000
    project
Cecchi, producer, 62, 407
Cella, Piero, oenologist, 328
Celli, producer, 168, 196, 238
Cennatoio, producer, 88, 407
Central Italy East, 211–40
    map, 212
    production areas, 214–16
    red (grapes, wines, producers),
        216–32
    white (grapes, wines, producers),
        231–40
Central Italy West, 24–210
    black grape varieties, other, 175–81
    map, 26–7
    production areas, 30–8
    red (grapes, wines, producers),
        38–181
    white (grapes, wines, producers),
        181–210
Cepparello, wine, 57
Cerasuolo di Vittoria, 349–50, 364–5
Cerbaiona, producer, 135
Ceregio, wine, 165–6
Cero del Masso, producer, 107
Cerretalto Brunellodi Montalcino, 122
Cerro Bianco, wine, 140
Cerro, producer, 139–41, 407
Cervaro della Sala, wine, 51, 53,
    416–17
Cerveteri Bianco, 191
Cerveteri, producer, 163, 228
Cerveteri, production area, 38
Cerveteri Rosso, 163
Cerviolo Rosso, wine, 63
Cesanese del Piglio, producer, 177
Cesanese grape, 176–7
Cesani, 111
    producer, 205
Cesari, producer, 168, 238, 420
Ceuso Rosso Custera, wine, 356, 429
Chaos, wine, 226, 428
Chardonnay grape, 420
Cherchi, producer, 332, 336
Chianti
    DOCG anomalies, 442–4
    production area, 30–1
    sub-zones, 94–111
Chianti Classico, 407
    barriques, 45
    blending, 41–5
    communes, 51–94

Consorzio Chianti Classico, 48–9, 50
defining, 41–8
DOCG anomalies, 442–4
image issues, 49–50
maceration, 45–6
map, 42–3
producers, 50–94
production area, 31
Riserva, 46–7, 61–2, 63–4, 92–3
variation, commune, 47–8
wine, 41–94
Chianti Classico 2000 project
(CC2000), 5–15, 49
Chianti Colli Senesi, 109
Chianti Superiore, 109
Chiarandà del Merlo, wine, 420
Chiarelotto, Fabio, 155
Chigi Saracini, producer, 109
Chioccioli, Stefano, consultant, 30, 83,
119, 147, 149, 150, 151, 155,
314, 399
Chuerra, wine, 324
Ciabrelli, producer, 265
Ciacci Piccolomini, producer, 124–5
Ciardo, wine, 420
Ciccazzo, Rosario, 358
Ciccio Zaccagnini, producer, 423
Cigliano, wine, 420
Cignale, wine, 408
Cilento, 251
Cilento Bianco, 266
Cilento Rosso, 264, 265
Ciliegiolo grape, 177
Cima, producer, 407
Cinzano, 115
Cinzano Francesco, 125
Cipresso, Roberto, consultant, 30, 124,
126, 294, 427
Circeo Bianco, 191
Circeo Trebbiano, 191
Circeo, 163
Cirò, 306–13, 307–8
Ciufoli, Fabrizio, consultant, 134
classification, anomalies, 94–6
clones
CC2000, existing, 9–10
CC2000, newly developed, 10–11
cloning, 391–2
Cocci Grifoni, producer, 192, 226, 239,
240
Coda di Volpe grape, 248–9, 272
Col d'Orcia, producer, 125–6, 207,
407, 418

Colacicchi, producer, 410
Coletti Conti, producer, 177, 239
Colle Bereto, producer, 93
Colle della Torre, wine, 410
Colle Funaro, wine, 409
Colle Gaio, wine, 200
Colle Picchioni, producer, 202
Colle Santa Mustiola, producer, 109
Colle Verde, producer, 431
Collecimoli, wine, 431
Collelungo, producer, 62
Collezione de Marchi, wine, 406
Colli Albani, production area, 37
Colli Altotiberini Bianco, 190
Colli Altotiberini, production area, 37
Colli Amerini Bianco, 190
Colli Amerini, producer, 162, 190, 209,
410, 420
Colli Amerini, production area, 37
Colli Aretini, production area, 32,
107–8
Colli Bolognesi, 410, 420
Colli del Trasimeno, production area,
37
Colli della Sabina Rosso, 163
Colli dell'Etruria Centrale Bianco, 186
Colli dell'Etruria Centrale, production
area, 35
Colli di Catone, producer, 199–200
Colli di Faenza, production area, 214
Colli di Luni Bianco, 186
Colli di Rimini, production area, 214
Colli d'Imola, production area, 214
Colli Etruschi Viterbesi Bianco, 191,
209
Colli Etruschi Viterbesi Rosso, 163
Colli Fiorentini, production area, 32,
107
Colli Maceratesi, 215, 239–40
Colli Martani, production area, 37
Colli Martani Trebbiano, 190
Colli Perugini Bianco, 190
Colli Perugini, production area, 37
Colli Pesaresi, 192, 215
Colli Senesi
production area, 32, 109–11
wine, 95
Colli Spoletini, producer, 174
Colline Lucchesi Bianco, 186
Colline Lucchesi, production area, 34,
151–2
Colline Pisane, production area, 32,
108

Colline Teramane, *sottozona*
   Montepulciano d'Abruzzo,
   218
Colognole/Contessa Spalletti, producer,
   106
Colombaio di Cencio, producer, 77
Colombini family, 117–18, 122–3
Colonna Giovanni, producer, 168
Colonnara, producer, 233, 234
Colorino grape, 131–2, 140, 177–8
Colosi, producer, 380, 387
Colpetrone, producer, 174
Coltassala, wine, 92–3, 179
Colvecchio, wine, 415
Concadoro, producer, 62–3
Coniale, wine, 407
Consonno, Giulio, 114–15
Consorte, Mario, 343–4
consortia
   Chianti Classico, 48–9, 50
   Montalcino, 113
consultants, oenological, 20–1, 29–30
Conte della Vipera, wine, 53
Conte Zandotti, producer, 202
Contea di Sclafani, 350, 365, 369
Contessa Entellina, 350, 369
Conti, producer, 168, 238
Contini Bonacossi, Conte Ugo, 146,
   147, 148–9
Contini, producer, 338–41
Controguerra, 216
Contucci, producer, 141
Copertino, 278
   producers, 284, 420
Corino, Carlo, oenologist, 106
Coroncino, producer, 233–4
Corradi family, 139
Cortaccio, wine, 83–4, 407, 408
Corte Normanna, producer, 258
Corte Valesio, wine, 422
Corti-Corsini, producer, 94
Corvo, wines, 365
Corzano e Paterno, producer, 107,
   418–19
COS, producer, 364–5, 411, 420
Cossyra, wine, 385
Costa d'Amalfi, wines, 251, 265
Costa degli Etruschi, 152, 392
Costamolino, wine, 336
Costanti/Colle al Matrichese, producer,
   126
Costera, wine, 329
Cotarella, Renzo, 190–1

Cotarella, Riccardo, consultant, 30,
   142, 158, 160, 162–3, 163, 168,
   190–1, 227, 258, 267, 287, 357
Critone, wine, 312, 433
Cucaione, wine, 336
Cuomo, producer, 264
Curtifreda, wine, 407
Cutizzi, wine, 268
Cutolo, Michele, 262–3
cuvée du journaliste, 22
Cygnus, wine, 354

d'Afflitto, Nicolò, consultant, 30, 55,
   99, 100, 413
d'Alessandro, producer, 108, 414, 415,
   431
d'Alfonso del Sordo, producer, 228,
   299
Damaschino grape, 379
d'Ambra, producer, 264, 273
d'Amico family, 384–6
d'Ancona, producer, 385
d'Angelo, producer, 259–61, 433
d'Attoma, Luca, consultant, 30, 71, 94,
   108, 151, 154, 155, 157, 158,
   396, 398–9, 400, 431
de Angelis, producer, 226
de Bartoli, *see* Marco de Bartoli
de Castris, producer, 284
de Conciliis, producer, 259
de Lucia, producer, 258, 272
de Marchi, Paolo, 56–8
de Santi, Guido, oenologist, 80
Decugnano dei Barbi, producer,
   189–90
Dedo, wine, 201
Dei, producer, 145, 427
density, CC2000, 11
Desiderio, wine, 138
Dezi, producer, 226
di Majo Norante, producer, 193, 227,
   263, 266, 272
di Mauro, producer, 410
di Meo, producer, 258
Dievole, producer, 67
D'Istinto, wines, 367
Dittajuti, producer, 226
DiVino, wine, 434
DOC (Denominazione di Origine
   Controllata)
   principle, 440
   revision, suggested system,
   449–55

DOCG (Denominazione di Origine
  Controllata e Garantita)
  critique, 456–9
DOCG/IGT anomalies, 94–6, 112
  principle, 441
Dogajolo, wine, 78
Dolianova, producer, 325, 337
Dolmen, wine, 333
Don Pietro Bianco, wine, 433
Don Pietro Rosso, wine, 429
Don Vincenzo Chianti Classico Riserva,
  wine, 88
Donna Lisa, wine, 281, 285
Donna Marzia Rosso del Salento, wine,
  291
Donnafugata, producer, 358, 369–70,
  387, 420, 429
Donnici, wines, 308
Dorgali, producer, 325
Dorico Rosso Conero, wine, 225
Drei Donà, producer, 166–7, 409,
  418
Drupeggio grape, 209–10
Duca d'Aragona, wine, 228, 281,
  283–4
Duca della Corgna, producer, 414
Duca Enrico, wine, 354–5
Duca di Salaparuta, producer, 355–6,
  365, 370
Duca San Felice, wine, 313

Ecclesia, wine, 420
Edèlmio, wine, 362
Elba, 152, 159, 195, 208
Elba Bianco, 186
Elisabetta, producer, 408
Eloquenzia, wine, 286
Eloro Rosso, 349, 352
Emilia, 211
Ercole Velenosi, producer, 192
Ercolino brothers, 266–9
Eredi Danei, producer, 208
Erta e China, wine, 97–8
Esino, wine, 215
Est!Est!Est! di Montefiascone, 190–1
Etna, 349
Etna Bianco Superiore, 362
Excelsus, wine, 117, 408

Fabrizio Bianchi, wine, 419
Falanghina grape, 248–9, 270–2
Falerio dei Colli Ascolani, 192, 215
Falerno del Massico, 249

Falerno del Massico, wine, 258, 264,
  265, 271
Falerno Rosso, wine, 265
Falesco, producer, 190–1, 410
Faltognano, producer, 427
Fanti, producer, 135
Farkas, Stefano, 83–4
Farneta, producer, 109
Farnetella, producer, 414, 421, 427
Farnito, wine, 78, 407, 418
Faro, 349
Fassati, producer, 145
Fattoria Aldobrandesca, 54
Fazi Battaglia, producer, 226, 233,
  234–5
Fazio Wines, producer, 411, 423
Felline Primitivo, wine, 294, 296
Felline, producer, 296
Felsina, producer, 63–5, 406, 419
Ferrara, producer, 270
Ferrini, Carlo, consultant, 7, 30, 60,
  72, 108, 118, 122, 131, 131–2,
  142, 401
Ferrucci, producer, 168, 238
Feudi di San Gregorio, producer, 258,
  266–9, 272, 433
Feudo dei Fiori blend, 369
FiaGre, wine, 433
Fiano di Avellino, 267, 268
Fiano grape, 248, 265–6
Ficaia, wine, 431
Ficomontanino, producer, 109
Filomusi Guelfi, producer, 224
Fiore, Claudio, 164–5
Fiore, Vittorio, consultant, 30, 40–1,
  78–9, 79–80, 81, 91, 119, 121,
  164–5, 165, 431
Firriato, producer, 363, 411
Flaccianello, wine, 84–6
Flauto, wine, 135
Flegrei Rosso, 264
flor, 340
Florence province, 107
Fobiano, wine, 410
Folonari, family, 101–2
Fontana Morella, wine, 163
Fontalloro, wine, 49, 65
Fontana Candida, producer, 199
Fontanabianca, producer, 415–16
Fontanelle, wine, 418
Fonterutoli, producer, 60
Fonterutoli, versus Castello di
  Fonterutoli, 60–1

Fontodi, producer, 84–6, 413, 415, 431–2
For Duke, wine, 151
Forano, producer, 240
Forastera grape, 272–3
Foresco, wine, 163, 188
Forestera grape, 248
Fornace Chianti Rufina Riserva, wine, 104
Forti Terre di Sicilia Cabernet Sauvignon, wine, 411
Fossi, producer, 407, 414, 415, 419, 420, 423
Foti, Salvatore, 362
Francavilla grape, 305
Franceschi family, 131
Franchetti, Andrea, 403
Frappato di Vittoria grape, 363–5
Frappato grape, 309–10, 363–5
Frascati, 198–9, 199–205
    production area, 37
    tufa soil, 28
    wine, 191
Frescobaldi
    family, 99
    producer, 98–100, 407, 418, 427
Fucecchio, producer, 408
Fuligni, producer, 135
fumé style, 421
Funtanaliras, wine, 334
Furore, 251
Fuso Carmignani, producer, 151

Gabbas, producer, 325, 430
Gabbro, wine, 155, 399–400, 407
Gadì, wine, 384
Gaglioppo grape, 309–15
Gaia & Rey, wine, 418
Gaiole, 67–77
Gaiospino, wine, 234
Gaja, Angelo, 130–1, 397–8, 418
Galardi, producer, 258
Galatrona, wine, 407
galestro soil, 96
    Tuscany, 25
Galestro, wine, 187
Gallico Rosso, wine, 287
Gallucio, 249
Gallura, producer, 335
Gallura zone, 319–20, 334
Gamay dell'Umbria, 414
Gamay grape, 135, 414

Gambelli, Giulio, consultant, 30, 90, 107–8, 141–2
Garofano, Severino, consultant, 283, 285–6, 288, 290, 300, 310, 311–13
Garofoli, producer, 226, 233, 235
Geminiani, Cristina, 165–6
Genazzano Rosso, 163
Geppetti, Elisabetta, 158
Geraci, Salvatore, 361
Ghiaie Bianche, wine, 125–6, 418
Ghiaie della Furba, wine, 95, 408
Ghiaiolo, wine, 422
Ghizzano, producer, 108, 407
Giogantinu, producer, 335–6
Gioia del Colle, 293, 302–3
Giomarelli, Giuliano, 142
Giorgio Primo Chianti Classico, wine, 86
Girò grape, 332–3
Gisèle, wine, 407
Giuntini, Francesco, 103–4
Giuratrabocchetti, Gerardo, 263
Giusto di Notri, wine, 398–9, 408
GIV, *see* Gruppo Italiano Vini
Gloder, Paola, 131
glossary, 460–7
glycerine, 46
Gomieri, Lucio, 126
Goretti, producer, 162
Gotto d'Oro, producer, 202
Gran Furor, producer, 272
Granaio, wine, 89
Grandi Annate, wine, 138
Grasso, producer, 358, 370, 387
Grati family, 105–6
Graticciaia, wine, 281, 290
Grato Grati, wine, 106
Grattamacco, producer/wine, 207, 398, 408
Gravello, wine, 312, 313, 429–30
Gravina, wine, 277, 433
Graziani, producer, 155
Grecanico Dorato grape, 377–8
Grecanico grape, 354
Grecante, wine, 173
Grechetto grape, 208–9
Grechetto, wine, 188, 209
Greco de Cirò grape, 315–17
Greco di Bianco grape, 315–17
Greco di Tufo grape, 248, 248–9, 269–70, 304–5
Greco di Tufo, wine, 257, 268

Greco Nero grape, 310
Greve, 7–8, 77–83, 406
Grifi, wine, 138
Grillo grape, 370–1
Grosso Sanese, wine, 75
Grotta del Sole, producer, 264
Grotta Rossa, wine, 329
Gruppo Italiano Vini (GIV), 88–90
Guadipiani, wine, 154
Guado al Tasso, producer, 206, 397, 408
Gualdo del Re, producer, 155, 400
Guardia Sanframondi, 249
Guardiolo, 249, 264, 271
Guarnaccia grape, 265
Guicciardini Strozzi, producer, 107, 111, 205, 407
Guldener, Roberto, 91–2
Guzzo, Luigi, 353

Harri, Pablo, 125
Hauner, producer, 380

I Botri, producer, 159
I Campetti, producer, 157, 423
I Gibbioni, wine, 407
I Grottoni, wine, 427
I Monili, wine, 294–5
I Pini, wine, 97
I Sassi, wine, 89
I Sistri, wine, 419
I Sodi di San Niccolò, wine, 179
I Tamerici Rosso, wine, 287
Idem, wine, 433
IGT (Indicazione Geografica Tipica)
    IGT/DOCG anomalies, 94–6, 112
    IGT Toscana, 49–50, 439
    principle, 437
    revision, suggested system, 445–8
Il Barricato di Villa Angela, wine, 420
Il Benefizio, wine, 418
Il Bianco di Gianni, wine, 431
Il Carbonaione, wine, 80
Il Carnasciale, producer, 408
Il Chiuso, wine, 413
Il Colle, producer, 109
Il Corno, producer, 407
Il Falcone, wine, 228, 277, 298–9
Il Fortino, wine, 415
Il Girone, wine, 414
Il Lebbio, producer, 178, 427
Il Marzocco, wine, 418
Il Nuraghe, producer, 345

Il Palagio, producer, 407
Il Palazzino, producer, 75
Il Paradiso, producer, 111, 408, 419
Il Pareto, wine, 102, 406
Il Podere San Luigi, producer, 109
Il Poggiolo, producer, 135, 151
Il Poggione, producer, 127, 409
Il Principe, wine, 89, 413, 414
Il Rosso di Enrico Vallania, wine, 410
Il Sodaccio, wine, 91
Il Terriccio, producer, 400–2, 408, 418, 421
Il Tornese, wine, 418
Il Trincerone, wine, 145
Il Vescovino, producer, 88
Il Vescovo di Manzano, wine, 414
Il Vignola, wine, 138, 421
Il Vivaio, producer, 409
Il Volo di Alessandro, blend, 301
IL, wine, 189
Illuminati, producer, 193, 221–2
Ilva, producer, 355
Impigno grape, 305
Impruneta, 83
Incisa dell Rocchetta
    Marchese Mario, 392–5
    Marchese Niccolò, 394
Incontri, wine, 155
international varieties, central and
    southern Italy, 389–423
internationalism, versus typicity, 15–23
Inzolia grape, 207–8, 368–9
Ischia, 250, 264
Isola dei Nuraghi, wines, 330–1
Isole e Olena, producer, 56–8, 406, 415, 418

Jerzu, 320
    producer, 323–4
Josephine Doré, wine, 375
journalists, influence, 21–3

Kàlike, wine, 335
Karana, wine, 333
Karmis, wine, 340
Kore, wine, 330–1

La Badiola, producer, 152, 408, 419
La Berta, producer, 168
La Braccesca, Montepulciano, 54
La Braccesca/Antinori, producer, 407
La Brancaia, producer, 63
La Cala, wine, 336

La Calonica, producer, 145
La Cappella, producer, 94
La Carletta, producer, 159
La Carraia, producer, 189, 410
La Casa Brunello di Montalcino, wine,
    121–2
La Casetta, producer, 107
La Castelletta, wine, 420
La Cerbaiola/Salvioni, producer, 135
La Chiusa, producer, 159, 208
La Elorina, producer, 358
La Fiorita, producer, 126, 427
La Fortuna, producer, 135
La Gerla, producer, 135
La Gioia, wine, 76
La Lastra, producer, 427
La Leccia, producer, 63
La Madonnina, producer, 78–9
La Massa, producer, 86–7
La Mea/Maci, producer, 291
La Monacesca, producer, 420, 433
La Palaia, wine, 79
La Palazza, producer, 168, 196
La Palazzola, producer, 210, 410
La Parrina, producer, 159
La Poderina/Saiagricola, producer,
    140–1
La Prima Chianti Classico Riserva,
    wine, 82
La Quadratura del Cerchio, wine, 427
La Querce, producer, 107
La Rampa di Fugnano, producer, 111,
    407
La Rendola, producer, 407
La Ricolma, wine, 77, 408
La Sala, producer, 94
La Sassaia, wine, 427
La Segreta Bianco, wine, 434
La Segreta Rosso, wine, 429
La Selva, producer, 239, 409
La Selvanella Chianti Classico Riserva,
    wine, 89
La Solatia, wine, 103
La Stellata, producer, 186
La Torre, producer, 151–2
La Valentina, producer, 224
La Vigna di Alceo, wine, 404–6, 407
La Villa Vino Nobile di
    Montepulciano, wine, 135
La Vite/Monte Schiavo, producer, 226,
    235
Labirinto, wine, 419
Laborel, wine, 89

L'Accesa, wine, 157, 202
Lacrima di Morro d'Alba
Lacryma Christi del Vesuvio, 250, 258
Lamaione, wine, 407
L'Amaranto, wine, 407
Lamborghini, producer, 162
Lamezia, wines, 308
Lamole e Vistarenni, producer, 77
Lamorèmio, wine, 362
Lanari, producer, 226
Lanati, Donato, consultant, 14–15, 30,
    312, 361, 429
Lanciola II, producer, 83
Landi, Lorenzo, 139
Landi, Luciano, producer, 230
Latinia, wine, 329
Latium
    Frascati et al., 199–205
    wines in, 163, 190–1, 199–205
Laurus, wine, 126
Lavacchio, producer, 106
Lavischio, wine, 408
law, Italian wine, 436–44
Lazio, production area, 37
Lazzari, Donato, 290
Lazzicante, wine, 408
Le Boncie, producer, 66–7
Le Bruniche, wine, 419
Le Busche, wine, 433
Le Calbane, producer, 168
Le Calvane, producer, 407, 431, 435
Le Caniette, producer, 192, 226
Le Casalte, producer, 141–2
Le Chiuse di Sotto/Brunelli, producer,
    127–8
Le Cinciole, producer, 88
Le Colline, wine, 154
Le Colonne, producer, 205
Le Fagge, wine, 418
Le Farnete, producer, 151
Le Filigare, producer, 58
Le Fonti, producer, 88
Le Grance, wine, 122, 431
Le Macchiole, producer, 154, 396–7,
    407, 408, 431
Le Maestrelle, Montepulciano/Cortona,
    54
Le Marche, see Marche
Le Marze, wine, 408
Le More, wine, 165
Le Murelle, producer, 419, 421
Le Passule, wine, 312
Le Pergole Torte, wine, 90–1

Le Pozzelle, wine, 284
Le Pupille, producer, 158, 402–3, 408
Le Querce, producer, 238
Le Quinte, producer, 202
Le Serre Nuove, wine, 396
le Sommer, Christian, consultant, 156,
    158
Le Sorgenti, producer, 408
Le Stanze, wine, 144, 408
Le Stoppie, wine, 108
Le Terrazze, producer, 225, 428
Le Velette, producer, 163, 190
Le Vigne del Sole, wine, 434
Le Vignole Rosso, wine, 410
Le Volte, wine, 396
Legno Duro grape, 325–9
Lentisco, wine, 157
Lento, producer, 315
Leone d'Almerita, wine, 433
Leone de Castris, producer, 284–5,
    303, 304
Leone Rosso, wine, 123
l'Eremo, wines, 415
Leverano, 278, 291
Libra, producer, 291
Librandi, 14–15, 306
    producer, 311–13, 429–30, 433
Liburnio, wine, 409
Life Beyond Lambrusco, see Nicolas
    Belfrage
Lighea, wine, 370
Lilliano, producer, 63, 407
Linagre, wine, 420
Lipari, 349
Lisini, producer, 135
Litra, wine, 429
Livernano, producer, 93, 431
Lizzano, 278
Lo Cha, wine, 419
Lo Locco, producer, 151
Locorotondo, 278
    producer, 297, 303–4, 305
Lodola Nuova/Ruffino, producer, 145
Loggia della Serra, wine, 270
Loi, producer, 323
Lomazzi & Sarli, producer, 291
L'Oro di Moroder, wine, 225
Lucciaio, wine, 428
Luce, wine, 100, 427
Lucente, wine, 100
Luchetti, producer, 230
Lucilla, wine, 109
Luenzo, wine, 1110

Lugana, wine, 232–3
Lunaria, wine, 165
Lumen, wine, 221
Lungarotti, producer, 161, 190, 410
Lupicaia, wine, 401–2, 408

Macchiavelli, producer, 407, 413, 414
Macchiole, wine, 154, 396–7
Maceratino grape, 239–40
Macereto, producer, 159
Macrina, wine, 235
Madonia Giovanna, producer, 168
Madonna del Piano, wine, 132
Madreselva, wine, 410
Maestro Raro, wine, 406
Maffini, producer, 259, 269
Mafia, 245–6
Magari, wine, 397
Magliocco grape, 310
Maglioccone grape, 310
Magnificat, wine, 167, 409
Magno Magonio, wine, 311, 312–13
Malacari, producer, 226
Malfatti, Costanza, 159
Malvasia
    Bianca, 135, 157, 191, 200, 196–9,
        305, 317, 32, 1341, 349, 379–80
    Nera, 178–9, 300
Mammolo grape, 135, 136, 179
Mancinelli, producer, 230, 234
Mancini, producer, 192, 325, 336
Mandarossa Cabernet Sauvignon, wine,
    411
Mandrarossa Chardonnay, wine, 420
Mandrielle, wine, 407
Mandrolisai, 322
Manduria, 278, 293
Manero, wine, 140
Manetti, Giovanni, 84
Manetti, Sergio/family, 90–1
Mantellassi, producer, 159
Mantonico grape, 317
Marche, 213
    wines in, 168–75, 177, 191–3, 218,
        224–9
Marchetti, producer, 225
Marco de Bartoli, producer, 371,
    373–6, 386–7
Marconi, producer, 230
Maremma
    map, 153
    production area, 34–5, 152–9
Marghia, wine, 324

Mariani brothers, 116
Marina Cvetic, wines, 222
Marino Oro, wine, 202
Marino, production area, 37
Marna, wine, 431
Marone, Giorgio, consultant, 30, 62,
    81–2, 87, 221, 290–1
Marramiero, producer, 193, 224
Marrano, wine, 209
Marrubiù, producer, 330, 333
Marsala town, 351
Marsala, wine, 348, 366, 371–7
Marsanne grape, 423
Marsigliana grape, 310
Martà, wine, 430
Martelli e Busdraghi, producer, 155
Martina Franca, 278
Martini di Cigala, family, 76–7
Martino, producer, 263
Marzieno, wine, 166
Masciarelli, producer, 193, 222, 418
Masi, Paolo, 97
Massa Marittima, 25
    production area, 35, 156–7
Massa Vecchia, producer, 421–2
Massaio, wine, 408
Masseria Monaci, producer, 285–6
Masseria Pepe, producer, 296
Masseti, Federico, 104
Masseto, wine, 395, 407
Massimi Berucci, producer, 177, 239
Mastroberardino, producer, 254–8,
    266, 269, 270, 272
Mastrojanni, producer, 128–9
Mater Matuta, wine, 428
Matino, 278
Matta, John, 81–2
Mavriana, wine, 335
Mazzaferrata, wine, 408
Mazzei, family, 60–1
Mazzei, Filippo, 72
Mazzini, producer, 186
Mazziotti, producer, 191
Mazzocolin, Giuseppe, 63–5, 109, 180
Mazzoni, Andrea, consultant, 74
Mecella, producer, 177, 226, 428
Mel, wine, 433
Meleta, producer, 160, 407–8, 409,
    419, 435
Meleto, Castello di, producer, 77
Melia, producer, 356–7, 429
Melini/GIV, producer, 88–9, 205
Melissa, 308

Meloni Vini, producer, 325, 333, 411
Menfi, 350, 369
Meriggio, wine, 431–2
Merizzo, wine, 427
Merlini, producer, 154
Merlot, 389, 391, 392, and see
    Bordeaux grapes
Merlot wine, top five in Tuscany,
    407
Merletto, wine, 88
Messapia, wine, 304
Messorio, wine, 407
mezzadria, 4–5
Miccichè brothers, 367
Miceli, producer, 387
Michi, producer, 186
Miglianico, producer, 224
Millanni, wine, 111
Mille e Una Notte, wine, 370
Millennio Chianti Classico, 73–4
Milziade Antano, producer, 174
Mirum, wine, 433
mistella, 375, 376, 377
Mjere wines, 282–3, 304
Modus, wine, 102
Moio, Luigi, consultant, 271
Moio, producer, 265, 272
Molettieri, producer, 258
Molì Bianco, 193
Molise, 216
Monaci, Francesco, 129
Moncaro/Terre Cortesi, producer, 226,
    233, 237
Monciatti, Simone, oenologist, 74
Mondavi, producer, 427
Monica
    grape, 329–30
    wines, 330
Monicchi, Mauro, oenologist, 173
Monile, wine, 409
Monna Claudia, wine, 62
Monrubio, producer, 189, 428
Monsanto, producer, 58, 407, 419
Monsenese, wine, 134
Montalbano
    production area, 32, 107
    wine, 95, 149
Montalcino, production area, 32, 110,
    111–35
Montalperti, wine, 418
Montarsiccio, wine, 408
Monte Bernardi, producer, 87–8, 408
Monte Olimpo, producer, 429

Monte Schiavo, *see* La Vite/Monte Schiavo
Montecalvi, producer, 82
Montecarlo Bianco, 186, 195
Montecarlo, production area, 34, 151–2
Montecchio, producer, 94
Montechiari, producer, 151, 407, 414, 419
Montecucco, production area, 35
Montefalco production area, 36 wine, 162
Montefalco Sagrantino, wine, 170–1
Montefiascone, production area, 37–8
Montefolchi, wine, 407
Montellori, producer, 107, 408, 419, 423
Monteloro, 54
Montenidoli, producer, 111, 176, 205
Montepeloso, producer, 155, 399–400, 407
Montepò, Castello di, 157–8
Montepulciano, Tuscany, production area, 32–3, 135–45
Montepulciano grape, 169, 216–19, 299
Montepulciano d'Abruzzo *sottozona* Colline Teramane, 218
Montepulciano d'Abruzzo, wine, 215–24
Monteregio di Massa Marittima, 25, 35, 156–7
Monteregio di Massa Marittima Bianca, 186, 195
Montervo, wine, 407
Montescudaio Bianco, 186, 195
Montescudaio, production area, 34, 152–4
Montesodi Chianti Rufina, wine, 98, 99
Montevertine, producer, 90–1
Montevetrano, producer/wine, 251, 411–12
Montiano, wine, 191, 410
Montiverdi, producer, 77
Montori, producer, 193, 224
Montosoli, wine, 114–15
Moos, producer, 108
Morandi, wine, 420
More Maiorum, wine, 257, 266
Morelli, producer, 239
Morellino di Scansano, wine, 25, 156

Morgante, producer, 358
Morganti, Enzo, 13, 65–6
Morganti, Giovanna, 13, 66–7
Moris Farms, producer, 156
Mormoraia, producer, 111, 205
Mormoreto, wine, 99, 407
Moroder, producer, 224–5
Morrellino di Scansano, Cantian Sociale, producer, 159
Moscadello grape, 207
Moscato Bianco grape/wines, 305
Moscato di Noto, 349
Moscato di Siracusa, 349
Moscato di Sorso-Sennori, 322
Moscato Passito di Pantelleria, 351, 382, 383, 386–7
Moscato Rosa, 30
Moscato Rosa grape, 180–1
mosto cotto, 371, 377
Motta, Giampaolo, 86–7
Muccioli, Andrea, 167–8
Muffa Nobile, wine, 202, 422
Muffato della Sala, wine, 53, 434–5
Mulinvecchio, wine, 141
Müller-Thurgau grape, 423
Murana, producer, 383–4
Murge, 274, 292, 296, 300
Muristeddu grape, 330
Muristellu grape, 330
Murru, Mariano, oenologist, 330
Mustilli, producer, 258

Naitana, producer, 341
Nambrot, wine, 108, 407
Nardi, Silvio, producer, 135
Nardò, 278
Nardo, 155
Nasco grape, 342–3
Naturalis Historia, wine, 257–8
Nebbiolo grape, 333
Negroamaro grape, 278, 279–91
Nemo, wine, 407
Nerello Cappucio grape, 310, 359
Nerello Mascalese grape, 310, 359
Neri, Giacomo, 122
Nero d'Avola grape, 310, 351–3 wine, 347, 349
Nero del Tondo, wine, 413
Nero di Nubi, wine, 414
Nero Outsider, wine, 173
Nero, wine, 291
Nespoli, producer, 168, 428

Nicodemi, producer, 193, 224
Nieddera grape, 332
Nieddumannu grape, 332
Ninniri, Gavino, 343–4
Nipozzano Chianti Rufina Riserva,
    wine, 99
Nittardi, producer, 63
Nocera grape, 310
Notarpanaro, wine, 288
Noto, 349
Nottola, producer, 142
Notturno, wine, 167
Nova Serra, wine, 257
Novantasei, wine, 354
Nozze d'Oro, wine, 434
Nozzole, producer, 406, 419
Nuova Agricoltura, producer, 384–6
Nuragus grape, 337

oak barrels, versus stainless steel,
    19–20
Oasi degli Angeli, producer, 192, 227
Obsession, wine, 408
Occhio di Pernice, 138, 160, 194
Ocone, producer, 258
Odoardi, producer, 308, 313–15, 430,
    433
Olevano Romano, production area, 38
Oliena, 320
olive oil, 106
Olivella grape, 265
Oliveto, producer, 135
Olmaia, wine, 407
Olmeto, wine, 410
Opinioni, wine, 189
Orazio Rillo, producer, 272
Orlandi Contucci Ponno, producer,
    224, 409, 420, 422
Ormanni, producer, 90
Ornellaia, producer/wine, 395, 407,
    408, 421
Orto di Boccio, wine, 159
Orvieto
    late-harvest sweet whites, 30
    production area, 36–7
    tufa soil, 28, 36–7
    wine, 187–90
Osteria Le Logge restaurant, 127
Ostuni, 278, 305
Ottavianello grape, 302

Pacenti Siro, producer, 135
Pachino, wine, 352, 358, 365

Pagadebit/Bombino Bianco grape,
    238–9
Pagli, Attilio, consultant, 13–14, 30,
    76, 132, 155, 156, 172, 225, 428
Palagetto, producer, 111
Palari, producer/wine, 359–61
Palazzi, wine, 403, 408
Palazzo Altesi, wine, 115
Palazzo Vecchio, producer, 145
Palazzone, producer, 190, 409
Paleo Bianco, wine, 396, 431, 432
Paleo Rosso, wine, 396, 408
Palini, Alvaro, 173
Pallio di San Floriano Verdicchio dei
    Castelli di Iesi, wine, 236
Palombo, producer, 410
Pambuffetti, producer, 174
Pampanuto grape, 304
Pancrazi, producer, 413, 414
Pandolfa, producer, 168, 410
Panerai, Paolo, 59
Panizzi, producer, 111, 205, 431
Pantelleria
    island, 381–3
    wines, 351, 370, 381–3, 386–7
Panzano, 83–8
Paoletti, Andrea, 132
Paradiso, producer, 111, 168, 205, 229,
    238
Paris Chianti Classico, wine, 87
Parker, Robert, 162, 191, 251, 412
Parrina Bianco, wine, 186
Parrina, production area, 35, 159
Pascale di Cagliari grape, 332
Pascena Moscadello di Montalcino,
    wine, 125, 126, 140
Pasetti, producer, 224
Pasetti, Rocco, oenologist, 223
Passerina grape, 239
Passione, wine, 201
Passito di Pantelleria, 383, 386–7
passito wines, 30, 241, 249, 434, 435
Passo delle Viscarde, wine, 290, 435
Passomaggio, wine, 429
Paternoster, producer, 262
Patriglione, wine, 281, 288
Patrizia Bartolini, wine, 421–2
Paule Calle, wine, 435
Pecorino grape, 240
Pedraia, wine, 337
Pelavet di Ginestra Bianco, wine, 434
Pelavet di Ginestra Rosso I and II,
    wine, 429

Pellegrino, producer, 358, 387
Penisola Sorrentina, 250
Penisola Sorrentina
    Bianco, 271
    Rosso, 264, 265
Pentro, 193, 216
Peppoli, 53
Percarlo, wine, 77
Perdera, wine, 330
Perlato Rosso, wine, 155
Perricone grape, 365
Perrucci family, 293–5
Pertimali, producer, 129
Pervini, producer, 296
Petra, producer, 400
Petreto, producer, 107, 422
Petrognano, Pomino Rosso, wine, 104
Petroio, producer, 67
Petrolo, producer, 107–8, 407
Peucezia, 275
Peynaud, Emile, 394
Pezzi, Mario, 228
Pezzolo, wine, 410
Piaggia, producer, 150–1
Pian della Corte, wine, 314, 433
Pian delle Vigne/Antinori, producer, 135
Piana del Sole, see Rubino
Piancornello, producer, 135
Piano del Cipresso, wine, 92
Piano della Cappella, wine, 91–2, 418
Piastraia, wine, 409
Piedirosso grape, 248–9, 263–4
Piemonte, 24
Pier delle Vigne, wine, 228
Pieri Agostina, producer, 129
Pietra Nera, wine, 387
Pietracalda, wine, 267, 268
Pietraforte del Carobbio, wine, 407
Pietramarina, wine, 362
Pietramora, wine, 166
Pietramora Sangiovese di Romagna, wine, 195
Pietraserena, producer, 205
Pietrello d'Oro, wine, 160
Pieve del Vescovo, producer, 162, 209, 428
Pieve Santa Restituta, producer, 130–1
Piglio, production area, 38
Pigna, producer, 192, 227, 410
Pignatello grape, 365
Pinchiorri restaurant, 126
Piné, wine, 414

Pinot Nero grape, 412–14
Piras, wine, 335
Pisa province, 108
Planargia, 341
Planeta, producer, 411, 420, 429, 434
Podere Colle Vecchio, wine, 240
Podere Fontarca, wine, 431
Podere il Bosco, wine, 415
Poderuccio, wine, 121
Podium, wine, 235
Poggerino, producer, 93
Poggiassai, wine, 109
Poggibonsi, 88–90
Poggio al Sole, producer, 94
Poggio alle Gazze, wine, 396, 421
Poggio Antico, producer, 131
Poggio Argentiera, producer, 159
Poggio Belvedere, wine, 173
Poggio Bonelli, producer, 67
Poggio di Sotto/Palmucci, producer, 135
Poggio Gagliardo, producer, 154
Poggio Golo, wine, 140, 407
Poggio Granoni, wine, 109, 427
Poggio Mentali, producer, 226
Poggio Romita, producer, 427
Poggio Rosso, wine, 65–6
Poggio Salvi, producer, 109, 135, 207, 408
Poggio San Polo, producer, 135
Poggio Scalette, producer, 79–80
Poggio Valente, wine, 158–9
Poggiopiano, producer, 93–4
Poliziano, producer, 142–4, 408
Pollara, producer, 411, 420
Pollino, 308
Pomino
    production area, 32, 96–7, 99–100
    Pomino Bianco, 100, 195
    Pomino Rosso, 100
Ponte a Rondolino, producer, 111, 204
Portico, wine, 407
Pourriture Noble, wine, 189, 422, 435
Pozzesi, Enrico, 62
Pozzesi, Vittorio, 62
Preludio, wine, 420
Primitivo di Manduria, 278
Primitivo grape, 265, 291–7
Primo Amore, wine, 295
Primopeso, wine, 419
Principe di Corleone, wine, 411
Privilegio, wine, 268
Procanico, 191

Promis, wine, 130
Provveditore-Bargagli, producer, 159, 186
Prugnolo Gentile, 32–3, 135, 136
Pruneto, producer, 93
Pruno, wine, 167
Puglia, 274–305
  wines in, 218–19
Pugnitello grape, 140
Puiatti, Vittorio, 58
Pulcinculo (Grechetto Bianco), 135
Pulcini, Antonio, 199–201
Pulicchio, wine, 188

Quacquarini, producer, 230
Quarto d'Altesi, wine, 407
Quattro Morì, wine, 202, 428
Querceto, producer, 408
Querciabella, producer, 80–1, 417–18
Quindici Anni, wine, 106

Raccanelli, Alberto, oenologist, 335
Radda, 90–3
Radici, wine, 256, 257
Ragnedda brothers, 336
Ragusa province, 349–50
Rallo family, 369–70
Rallo, producer, 371, 376–7, 387, 429
Ramingallo, wine, 364
Rampolla, producer, 404–6, 407, 408
Rancia Chianti Classico, 63–5
Rapitalà, producer, 368
Rascioni & Cecconello, producer, 177
Ravello, 251
Redi, producer, 145
Redigaffi, wine, 398–9, 407
Refosco grape, 264
Regaleali/Tasca d'Almerita, producer, 353–6, 416
  Regaleali Bianco, 354
  Regaleali Rosso, 365
Regina Vitae, wine, 201
Remole, wine, 100
Rennina, wine, 130
Reno, production area, 214
Renzo Masi, producer, see Basciano/Masi
Rhône grapes, red, 414–16
Rhône grapes, white, 422–3
Ricasoli family, 71–3
Ricasoli, Francesco, 71–3
Ricasoli, Giovanni, 73
Ricasoli, Marco, 76, 176

Riecine, producer, 75–6
Riesi, wine, 365
Riesling Renano grape, 423
Rietine, producer, 408
Riflesso Antico, wine, 228
Rillo/Fontanavecchia, producer, 258
Rio Grande, producer, 410
Rionero, 251
Ripa delle More, wine, 82
Ripanera, producer, 94
Riparosso Montepulciano d'Abruzzo, wine, 221
Riseccoli, producer, 83
Riserva Ducale, wine, 101
Rivella, Ezio, consultant, 116, 156
Rivella, Pietro, consultant, 30, 114, 121
Rivera, producer, 298, 304, 305, 420, 422
Rívolo, wine, 119, 157, 421
Rocca delle Macìe, producer, 61–2
Rocca di Bonacciara, wine, 410
Rocca di Castagnoli, producer, 77, 407
Rocca di Fabbri, producer, 174, 209
Rocca di Montegrossi, producer, 76
Rocca Nerina, wine, 420
Rocca Rubia, wine, 328–9
Roccesco, wine, 420
Rodano, producer, 62, 408
Romagna, 213, 214
  wines in, 164–8
Romano, Antonio, 290–1
Romeo, producer, 145
Romitorio di Santedame, wine, 101–2, 179
Ronco dei Ciliegi, wine, 165
Ronco del Re, wine, 165, 421
Ronco della Simia, wine, 165
Ronco delle Ginestre, wine, 165
Rondinaia, wine, 421
rootstocks, CC2000, experimentation, 9, 11
Rosa del Golfo, producer, 286–7
Rosa di Montacuto, wine, 225
Rosathea, wine, 202
Roscetto, Rosciola Rossetto, 191
Rossi di Medelana Serrafini Ferri, Dr Gian Annibale, 400–2
Rosso Conero
  production area, 224–5, 226
  wine, 169, 215, 226
Rosso degli Spezieri, wine, 125
Rosso del Conte, wine, 353, 354, 365

Rosso della Rocca, wine, 409
Rosso delle Miniere, wine, 154
Rosso dell'Umbria, 428
Rosso di Cercatoia, wine, 151
Rosso di Montalcino, 95, 113, 125, 129
Rosso di Montepulciano, 135, 137
Rosso di Palistorti, wine, 152
Rosso di Sera, wine, 93–4
Rosso Fiorentino, wine, 407
Rosso Piceno, 169, 215, 226
Rosso Rovo, wine, 154
Roussanne grape, 423
Roveto Chianti Classico, wine, 62
Rovittello, wine, 362
Roxan, producer, 193, 222–3
Rubino/Piana del Sole, producer, 287
Rubino, wine, 410
Rubrato, wine, 268
Ruffino, producer, 100–3, 413
Rufina
    production area, 31–2, 96–7
    wine, 97
Ruggeri, producer, 174
Rupicolo di Rivera, wine, 299

Sacchet, Giovanni, 77–8
Sa'etta, wine, 87
Saffredi, wine, 159, 402, 408
Sagrantino
    grape, 39
    wine, 162, 169–75
Saiagricola group, 139–41
Saladini Pilastri, producer, 192, 226
Salcheto, producer, 144–5
S'Aldia, wine, 336
Salentino, 275
Salice Salentino, 278
Salicutti, producer, 135
Salivolpe, wine, 134
Salmartano, wine, 408
Salterio, wine, 135
Saluccio, wine, 402, 418
Salviano, producer, 190
Salvioni, producer, 135
Sambuca di Sicilia, wines, 350, 369
Sammarco, wine, 406, 408
San Basso Falerio dei Colli Ascolani,
    wine, 240
San Casciano Val di Pesa, 93–4
San Cresci, producer, 407
San Cristiano, wine, 201
San Donato, producer, 205

San Donato Rosso, wine, 414
San Fabiano Calcinaia, producer, 63
San Felice, producer, 65–6
San Francesco, producer, 315, 430
San Gimignano, 176, 178, 195
    production area, 33, 111
    Vernaccia di, 202–5
San Giorgio, wine, 161
San Giovanni, producer, 192, 226
San Giusto a Rentennano, producer,
    76–7, 408
San Gregorio, producer, 270
San Guido, producer, 392–5, 407
San Leonino, producer, 63, 134
San Leopoldo, wine, 127, 409
San Luigi, producer, 409
San Martino, wine, 83–4
San Michele, producer, 423
San Patrignano, producer, 166, 167–8,
    196
San Pio, wine, 129
San Severo zone, 276
San Vincenti, producer, 77
San Vito di Luzzi, 308
Sancta Catharina, wine, 427
Sangervasio, producer, 108, 431
Sangiovese
    grape, 38–41
    production areas and producers,
    41–169
Sangioveto , wine, 59, 70
Sannio, 249, 264
Sansovino, wine, 141
Sant' Agata de' Goti, 249, 264
Sant' Angelo, wine, 420
Sant' Anna di Isola Capo Rizzuto, 308
Sant' Antimo
    production area, 32
    regulations, 425–6
    wine, 95, 113, 128, 195
Santa Anastasia, producer, 357–8, 358,
    420, 429, 433
Santa Barbara, producer, 234, 291,
    410, 428
Santa Cecilia, wine, 429
Santa Lucia, producer, 299
Santa Margherita di Belice, 350, 365,
    369
Santa Maria del Fiore, wine, 230
Santa Maria La Palma, producer, 336
Santadi, producer, 326–9, 337
Santarelli family, 423
Saputi, producer, 240

Sardinia, 317–45
  map, 316
Sartarelli, producer, 234
Sassetti, Livio, producer, 129, 207
Sassi Neri, wine, 225
Sassicaia, 34, 392–5, 407
Sassoalloro, wine, 119, 157, 158
Sassoforte, wine, 407
Sassolo, producer, 108
Sassotondo, producer, 186
Satta, producer, 154, 206, 398, 409
Sava, 278, 297
Savuto, 308, 314
Saxa Calida, wine, 408
Scacco Matto, wine, 166
Scaloti, wine, 288
Scansano, production area, 35, 157–9
Scassino, wine, 92
Scasso dei Cesari, wine, 152
Scavigna, 308, 314
Schidione, wine, 119, 157
Schiena d'Asino, wine, 128–9
Schietto, wine, 411
Sciacca, 350
Sciascinoso grape, 265
Scienza, Professor Attilio, consultant,
  14–15, 130, 312, 423
Scirus, wine, 408
Scopetone, producer, 135
Scrio wine, 396
Sedara, wine, 370
seeding between rows, CC2000, 12–15
S'elegas, wine, 337
S'Eleme, wine, 334
Sella & Mosca, producer, 319, 325,
  343–4, 411, 430
Sella del Boscone, wine, 418
Sellari Franceschini, producer, 159
Selvamaggio, wine, 409
Selvapiana, producer, 96, 103–5, 432
Selvascura, wine, 407
Selve Vecchie, wine, 202
Semidano, 344–5
Semifonte, wine, 409
Sensazioni del Frutto, wine, 230
Ser Niccolò Solatio del Tani, wine, 407
Seraselva, wine, 408
Serboni, producer, 230
Serena, wine, 421
Ser Gioveto, wine, 62
Serpico, wine, 268
Serra Della Contessa, wine, 363
Serra Fiorese, wine, 235

Serra delle Querce, wine, 261
Serraiola, producer, 157
Settesoli, producer, 411, 420
Shardana, wine, 328
share-cropping, 4–5
Sicily, 345–88
  map, 346
Siena province, 109–35
Siepi, wine, 61
Signano, producer, 111, 205
Simposio Vino Nobile di
  Montepulciano, wine, 135
Sinfarosa, producer, 296
Siracusa, 349
Sirica, wine, 268–9
Sodole, wine, 111
Solaia, wine, 51, 53, 408
Solatio Basilica Chianti Classico
  Riserva, wine, 84
Soldera, Gianfranco, 123–4
Sole Leone/Torre Mozza blend, 282
Solengo, wine, 426–7
Soliana, wine, 334–5
Soloio, wine, 407
Solopaca, 248
  Solopaca Bianco, 271
  Solopaca Rosso, 264, 265
Sorbaiano, producer, 154
Sorso-Sennori, 322
South and Islands, 241–387
  potential of, 241–7
Southern Mainland, map, 242–3
Spadafora, producer, 411, 429, 433,
  434
Spinola, Franca, 159
Sportoletti, producer, 163, 190
Squinzano, 278
stainless steel, versus wood, 19–20
Statti, producer, 315, 430
Stefano Antonucci, wine, 410
Stoppielle, wine, 419
Strologo, producer, 226
Struzziero, producer, 258
Stucchi, Emanuela, 70
Stucchi, Roberto, 69–71
Subertum, wine, 155
Sugarille, wine, 130
Summus, wine, 117, 427
SuperTuscans, 61, 67–9, 77, 80–1,
  83–4, 84–6, 93–4, 178, 406
Susumaniello grape, 302
Suvereto, 155, 398–409
Syrah grape, 131–2, 135, 414–16

Taburno, 249
  producer, 258, 271–2
  wine, 264, 271
Tachis, Giacomo, consultant, 30, 40,
  105–6, 109, 115, 158, 237, 324–5,
  328, 348, 355, 356, 357, 394
Talenti/Pian di Conte, producer, 131–2
Talenti, Pierluigi, 127, 131
Talenti, Riccardo, 131–2
Tallinaio, wine, 303
Tanca Farrà, wine, 430
Tancredi, wine, 370, 429
Tani, Gabriella, consultant, 30
Taraborrelli, Romeo, oenologist, 222
Tarquinia Bianco, 191
Tarquinia Rosso, 163
Tasca d'Almerita, producer, 420, 433–4
  Counts Lucio et al, 350, 353, 355,
    365, 411
Tassinaia, wine, 402
Taurasi, 248, 254–8, 268
Taurino, producer, 287–8, 420
Tavarnelle Val di Pesa, 94
Tavarnelle, wine, 407
Tavignano, producer, 234
Te Deum Laudamus/Casale Bevagna
  blend, 281
Tenuta Frassitelli, wine, 273
Tenuta San Michele, wine, 411
Terra Antica, wine, 420
Terra degli Angeli, wine, 270
Terra dei Messapi, wine, 301
Terrabianca, producer, 91–2, 418
Terralba, wine, 321, 330
Terre al Monte, wines, 300–1, 420, 422
Terre Bianche, wine, 344
Terre Brune, wine, 327, 328
Terre d'Agala, wine, 356, 365
Terre de Trinci, producer, 174
Terre dei Cascinieri, wine, 152
Terre di Ginestra, see Calatrasi
Terre di Tufi, wine, 204
Terre Dora di Paolo, producer, 258,
  270
Terre Lontane, wine, 312
Terre Rosse, producer, 410
territorio, 16–17
Teruzzi, Enrico, 204
Teruzzi & Puthod, producer, 111
Tignanello, wine, 51–3
Tili, producer, 209
tipicità, 15–23
Tiziano, wine, 408

Tollo, producer, 224
Tonveronachi, Dr., 7
Torbato
  grape, 322, 343–4
  wine, 344
Torgiano, production area, 36
Tormaresca Bianco, wine, 420
Tormaresca Rosso, wine, 301, 429
Tormaresca/Vigneti del Sud, producer,
  420
Toro Desiderio, wine, 407
Torre di Ceparano, wine, 165–6
Torre di Giano, wine, 190
Torrevecchia, producer, 358, 365,
  415–16
Torrevento, producer, 299, 305
Torricella, wine, 418
Toscana, production area, 35–6
training, CC2000, 11–12
tramontana, 24
Tramonti, 251
Tramonti, producer, 63
Trani, 277
Trapani, C.S., producer, 358, 411
Travignoli, producer, 106
Tre Monti, producer, 168, 196, 238,
  410, 420
Tre Torri, wine, 329
Trebbiano
  grapes, 147, 181–5, 305, 317, 345,
    379
  production zones and producers,
    185–196
Trebbiano d'Abruzzo, 215–16
Trebbiano di Romagna, 196
Trebbiano Romagnolo 195–9
Trebbiano Toscano grape, 317, 379
Trefonti, wine, 145, 409
Trerè, producer, 168
Trerose, producer, 423
Trexenta, producer, 325, 337, 434
Triacca, Luca, 78–9
Trinoro Tenuta di, producer, 403,
  408
Triusco, wine, 299
Tua Rita, producer, 155, 398–9, 407,
  408
Tudernum, producer, 209
tufa soil, 248
Turico, wine, 410
Turriga, wine, 324, 330–1
Tuscany
  production areas, 30

Tuvara, wine, 323
Tzingana, wine, 87, 408

Uccelliera, producer, 108, 135, 419, 431
Uccellina, producer, 168, 238
Umani Ronchi, producer, 226, 237, 433
Umbria
    production areas, 36–7
    wines in, 160–3, 187–90
Umbria Viticoltori Associati, producer, 190
Uva di Troia grape, 297–9

Vaggagini, Paolo, consultant, 30, 124–5, 128, 145
Vagnoni, producer, 205
Val d'Arbia, 186, 195
Val di Cornia-Suvereto, 25
    production area, 34, 152, 155, 398–409
    wine, 155, 186–7
Val di Suga, producer, 133–5
Valdicapraia, wine, 413
Valdicava/Abruzzese, producer, 132
Valdipiatta, producer, 145, 409
Valentini, Edoardo, producer, 193, 217–18, 219–21
Valeo, wine, 314–15
Valgiano, producer, 152
Valle del Tirso, 340
Valle del'Acate, producer, 365
Valle dell'Asso, producer, 291
Vallerosa Bonci, producer, 234
Valli di Porto Pino, 328
Vallona, producer, 410, 420
Vallone, producer, 289–90, 422, 435
Valtellina, producer, 77
Vannuci, Mauro, 150–1
Varràmista, producer, 427
Vecchie Terre di Montefili, producer, 81, 408, 431
Vecchio Samperi Ventennale, wine, 375
Velenosi, producer, 227, 420
Velletri, production area, 37
Velletri Rosso, wine, 163
Vendemmia Tardiva, wine, 336, 369
Venerosi Pesciolini family, 108
Veneroso, wine, 108
Verbicaro, wines, 308
Verdeca grape, 303–4
Verdello grape, 210

Verdicchio dei Castelli di Jesi
    production area, 214–15
    wine, 232
Verdicchio di Matelica
    production area, 215
    wine, 232
Verdicchio, grape, 231–3
Vereto Salice Salentino, wine, 289–90
Vermentino
    grape, 205–7, 333
    producer, 334–5
    wines, 319–20
Vermentino di Gallura, 334
Vermentino di Sardegna, 334
Vernaccia di Oristano
    grape, 337–41
    Superiore, 319
    production zone, 321
Vernaccia di San Gimignano, 202–5
Vernaccia di Serrapetrona
    grape, 230
    wine, 215
Veronelli, Luigi, 361
Vesco Rosso, wine, 429
Vesuvio, 249, 264, 265
Vetrice, producer, 105
Vicchiomaggio, producer, 81
Vigna Adriana, wine, 201, 423, 432
Vigna al Cavaliere, wine, 154
Vigna Camarato, wine, 258
Vigna Casanova, wine, 409
Vigna Casselle, wine, 261
Vigna dei Preti, wine, 201
Vigna del Fattore Vino Nobile di
    Montepulciano, wine, 142
Vigna del Feudo, wine, 294
Vigna del Fiore, wine, 118
Vigna del Lago Brunello di Montalcino,
    wine, 134
Vigna del Nocio, Vino Nobile di
    Montepulciano, wine, 139
Vigna del Saraceno, wine, 291
Vigna del Sorbo Chianti Classico
    Riserva, wine, 84–6
Vigna del Vasallo, wine, 410
Vigna della Croce Riserva, wine, 92
Vigna di Corte, wine, 420
Vigna di Fontalle Chianti Clasico, wine,
    89
Vigna di Gabri, wine, 370
Vigna di Pianrosso Rosso di
    Montalcino, wine, 124

Vigna Flaminio, wine, 228
Vigna Flora, wines, 408
Vigna Garrone Savigna, wine, 430
Vigna Grande, wine, 163
Vigna il Corto, wine, 97
Vigna il Pino, wine, 190
Vigna la Miccia, Marsala, 375
Vigna l'Apparita, wine, 67–8, 407
Vigna Monticchio Torgiano Riserva,
    wine, 161
Vigna 'Ngena, wine, 336
Vigna Regis, wine, 431
Vigna San Bartolo, wine, 428
Vigna Spano, wine, 283
Vigna Spuntali Brunello di Montalcino,
    wine, 133, 134
Vigna Vescovi, wine, 428
Vigna Vinera, wine, 422
Vigna Virzi Rosso, wine, 429
Vignacatena, wine, 407
Vignalta, wine, 336
Vignamaggio, producer, 83, 407,
    408
Vignanello, 163
Vignavecchia, producer, 93
Vigne del Portale, wine, 335
Vigne di Piellero, wine, 273
Vigne Storiche, wine, 335
Vigneti del Geografico, wine, 408
Vigneto Antica Chiusina, wine, 140
Vigneto Filonardo, wine, 201
Vigneto la Gavina, wine, 407
Vigneto Torricella, wine, 189
Vigni dei Pini, wine, 433
Vignole, producer, 88
Vigorello, wine, 165
Villa Cafaggio, producer, 83–4, 408
Villa Cilnia, producer, 108, 431
Villa di Bagnolo, wine, 413
Villa di Capezzana Carmignano, wine,
    148
Villa di Chiesa, wine, 329
Villa di Trefiano, wine, 149
Villa di Vetrice/Fratelli Grati, producer,
    105–6
Villa Forano, producer, 227
Villa Gemma Bianco, wine, 222

Villa Gemma Montepulciano
    d'Abruzzo, wine, 222
Villa la Selva, producer, 108
Villa Matilde, producer, 258, 272
Villa Monte Rico, producer, 155
Villa Monticelli, wine, 188, 207
Villa Patrizia, producer, 159, 431
Villa Patrizia, wine, 160
Villa Pigna, producer, 192, 227, 410
Villa S. Anna, producer, 145
Villa Simone, producer, 201
Villa Solais, wine, 329
Villa Spoiano, producer, 107
Villa Tasca, wine, 354
Villadorata Eloro Rosso, wine, 358
Vinruspo, Rosato di Carmignano, 147
Vin Santo, 30, 33, 138, 150, 194–5,
    435
Vinci, Gasparo, 376–7
Vino Nobile di Montepulciano, 78,
    112, 135, 136–45
Viognier (Almabruna), wine, 157
Viognier grape, 201, 422
Virano, Edoardo, 125
Virente, wine, 427
Visions of J, wine, 226
Vitiano, wine, 191
Viticcio, producer, 83, 409
viticulture, experimentation, 4–15
Volpaiole, producer, 155
Vulture zone, 251–2, 259–63

Wandanna, producer, 152, 419, 427
wood, versus stainless steel, 19–20

Zaccagnini, producer, 224, 234, 428
Zaccheo, Antonio, 77–8
Zangara, Gaetano, 353
Zanna, wine, 221
Zarricante, wine, 168
Zecca, producer, 290–1
Zerbina, producer, 165–6, 196, 238
Zibibbo grape, 314, 348, 376, 381–8
Zileri, producer, 395
Zinfandel grape, 292, 293
Zipolo d'Oro Vin Santo, wine, 435
Zurrica, wine, 433